Tax Planning 20...

Tax Planning 2007/08

Edited by

Mark McLaughlin CTA (Fellow) ATT TEP

With contributions by

Jennifer Adams FCIS TEP ATT
John Baldry LLB LLM (London), Partner, Kirkland & Ellis International LLP
David Brookes FCA, Tax Partner, BDO Stoy Hayward LLP
Rebecca Cave CTA FCA MBA
George Duncan Solicitor CTA TEP, Partner, Charles Russell
Toby Harris LLB CTA TEP
Robert Maas FCA FTII FIIT TEP, Tax Partner, Blackstone Franks LLP
Gavin Moffatt Senior Technical Adviser, SBJ Benefit Consultants Limited
Peter Rayney FCA FTII TEP, National Tax Technical Partner, BDO Stoy Hayward LLP
Alec Ure Associate of Alec Ure & Associates, Partner of UHD Pension Services LLP

Tottel Publishing Ltd, Maxwelton House, 41–43 Boltro Road, Haywards Heath, West Sussex, RH16 1BJ

© Tottel Publishing Ltd 2008

All rights reserved. No part of this publication may be reproduced in any material form (including photocopying or storing it in any medium by electronic means and whether or not transiently or incidentally to some other use of this publication) without the written permission of the copyright owner except in accordance with the provisions of the Copyright, Designs and Patents Act 1988 or under the terms of a licence issued by the Copyright Licensing Agency Ltd, Saffron House, 6–10 Kirby Street, London, England EC1N 8TS. Applications for the copyright owner's written permission to reproduce any part of this publication should be addressed to the publisher.

Warning: The doing of an unauthorised act in relation to a copyright work may result in both a civil claim for damages and criminal prosecution.

Crown copyright material is reproduced with the permission of the Controller of HMSO and the Queen's Printer for Scotland. Any European material in this work which has been reproduced from EUR-lex, the official European Communities legislation website, is European Communities copyright.

A CIP Catalogue record for this book is available from the British Library.

ISBN: 978 1 84766 043 5

Typeset by Kerrypress Ltd, Luton, Beds

Printed and bound in Great Britain by Athenaeum Press, Gateshead, Tyne and Wear

Preface

Welcome to the first edition of this book. Tax planning is an increasingly important part of the everyday work of many practitioners for their clients. There was a time when tax planning was additional to the core services offered by accountants, such as tax return and accounts preparation. These days, it is more or less expected that firms will offer tax planning advice, except for the smallest of clients.

The world of tax is fast moving. What is a 'hot topic' in tax planning today may be rendered obsolete or much less important tomorrow by a change in tax legislation. A recent example was the announcement in the Pre-Budget Report 2007 of the introduction of a transferable IHT nil-rate band between spouses or civil partners. Previously, discretionary will trusts were a popular means of ensuring that the nil-rate band of the first spouse or civil partner to die was used if possible. The announcement that from 9 October 2007 (subject to becoming law in Finance Act 2008) the survivor's estate can benefit from the unused proportion of the nil- rate band of the first spouse or civil partner to die means that the popularity of discretionary will trusts of the nil rate band will diminish, probably dramatically.

The subjects covered in *Tax Planning 2007/08* have been carefully chosen in terms of what may be of practical use to the majority of small- to medium-sized professional practices dealing with day-to-day tax planning issues. No doubt the subject matter will change in future editions, not only due to changes in tax law as mentioned above, but also following constructive suggestions from readers on what they would like to see covered in 2008/09 and future editions, which will no doubt be most welcomed by the publishers.

I would like to express my sincere thanks and congratulations to all the authors who have contributed material to this book. Communicating tax planning ideas in a single, short chapter can be extremely difficult to accomplish successfully. Hopefully, readers will agree that this task has been performed with both skill and expertise.

Last but not least, a big 'thank you' to everyone at Tottel Publishing, and in particular to Sarah Blair. Sarah and I first discussed the concept of a tax planning annual more than twelve months ago, and Sarah has since been instrumental in sourcing the authors and making the book happen. Her energy and enthusiasm is inspirational. My thanks as well go to Heather Saward for

Preface

her patience and understanding during the editing of the book. I hope that readers will find the book both useful and informative.

Mark McLaughlin
General Editor
Manchester, December 2007

Contents

Preface	*v*
Table of Statutes	*xix*
Table of Statutory Instruments	*xxxv*
Table of EU Legislation	*xxxvi*
Table of Cases	*xxxvii*

Chapter 1: Starting a business – choosing an appropriate trading vehicle	**1**
Introduction	1
Why the choice of trading vehicle is important	1
Issues underlying the choice	2
Number of people involved	2
Flexibility	2
Administrative costs	3
Tax costs	4
Commercial considerations	5
Privacy	6
Retention of control	6
National minimum wage	7
Share options	8
Exit strategy	8
Sole trader	8
Structure	8
Accounting date	9
Partnerships	10
Why use a partnership?	10
General partnership	11
Limited partnership	14
Limited liability partnership	16
Tax benefits of all partnerships	17
Companies	19
Type of company	19
Limited liability	21
Tax treatment	21
Tax benefits of a company	35
Company versus another medium	38
Retention of profits	46

Contents

Long-term intentions	46
Chapter 2: Incorporation	**51**
Introduction	51
Income tax	52
Cessation computation	52
Payment of tax	53
Treatment of stock and work in progress	54
Capital allowances	55
National Insurance contributions	59
Capital Gains Tax	61
Goodwill	75
Stamp duties	80
Inheritance Tax	81
Value Added Tax	84
Investment businesses	85
Disincorporation	87
Chapter 3: Company purchase of own shares	**90**
Introduction	90
Checklist	91
Company status	93
Purpose of the payment	94
Retaining an interest in the company	95
Factors to consider	97
Residence of vendor	98
Period of ownership	99
The 'substantial reduction' test	100
The 'no continuing connection' test	102
Meeting the conditions	102
Income or capital?	105
Status of the shares	106
Company status	106
Clearance applications to HMRC	112
Breaking the conditions for capital treatment	113
Appendix	116
Company law	117
Corporate vendors	120
Trustee vendors	120
Other points	122
Associated persons	122
Chapter 4: Groups	**125**
Introduction	125
Definitions	126

75% Subsidiary	126
ICTA 1988, Sch 18	127
Group relief	128
Qualifications for membership of a group	128
Residence qualifications for group relief	130
Types of loss available for group relief	130
Limits on group relief	130
Relief for overseas losses of non-resident companies	131
Administrative requirements for group relief	132
Payment for group relief	133
Chargeable gains groups	133
Qualifications for membership of a group	133
Residence qualifications	134
Transfer provisions	134
Company ceasing to be a member of a group	135
Companies leaving a group at the same time: Johnston Publishing	136
Merger exemption; TCGA 1992, s 181	137
Reallocation of s 179 gains under TCGA 1992, s 179A	138
Notional transfers prior to a sale; TCGA 1992, s 171A	138
Transfers of trades under ICTA 1988, s 343	138
Common ownership requirements	139
Effect of application	139
Anti-avoidance	140
Other issues on a transfer of trade	140
Pre-entry gains and losses	140
Pre-entry losses – TCGA 1992, Sch 7A	141
Pre-entry losses – s 184A	143
Pre-entry gains	143
Depreciatory transactions	144
TCGA 1992, ss 176 and 177	144
TCGA 1992, s 30 ff	144
Substantial shareholdings exemption	146
Basic application	146
Investing company requirements	147
Investee company requirements	147
Meaning of trading	147
The subsidiary exemptions	148
Interaction with other provisions	149
Anti-avoidance	150
Other relevant provisions for groups	150
Transfer pricing	150
Loan relationships	151
Derivative contracts	152
Intangibles	152
Group payment arrangements	153

Contents

Chapter 5: Disincorporating a business — 154
Background — 154
Planning a disincorporation — 154
Legal mechanics — 155
  Members' voluntary liquidation — 155
  Dissolution — 155
Case study – Torquay Towers Ltd and Mr Basil — 156
  Main corporation tax consequences — 157
  Capital gains on transfer of assets — 159
  Property — 159
  Goodwill — 160
  Tax liabilities arising on shareholders — 161
Potential impact of transactions in securities rules — 162

Chapter 6: Current tax planning issues for owner managed company sales — 164
Impact of Pre-Budget Report 2007 proposals — 164
Sale of company before 6 April 2008 — 165
Basic deal structuring issues — 165
Basic capital gains tax (CGT) rules on share sales — 166
  Date of disposal — 166
  Calculation of capital gain — 167
  Indexation allowance (for pre-6 April 2008 disposals) — 167
  Taper relief (for pre-6 April 2008 disposals) and the annual exemption — 167
  Proposed CGT treatment for post-6 April 2008 disposals — 168
Taper relief on share sales (before 6 April 2008) — 169
  Basic principles of taper relief — 169
  Relevant period of ownership — 170
  Business taper relief — 170
  Trading company/group test — 171
  Non-business taper relief — 172
  Potential dilution of business taper relief before 6 April 2000 — 172
  Special business taper rules for shares in listed companies — 173
Treatment of sale consideration satisfied by shares/loan notes in the acquirer — 173
  Deferral of capital gain — 173
  Consideration shares in the acquirer — 174
  Loan notes — 175
  Dealing with QCBs — 175
  Non-qualifying corporate bonds (non-QCBs) — 177
Earn-out deals — 178
  Basic tax treatment of 'cash-based' earn-outs — 178
  Earn-outs satisfied in shares/loan notes — 179
  Share/loan note-based earn-outs straddling the CGT changes — 180
Application of ITA 2007, s 684 anti-avoidance rules — 180

Chapter 7: Winding-up the family or owner-managed company	**182**
Background	182
Consequences for the company	183
Pension provision	183
Termination of CTAP and closure costs	183
Sale of plant and industrial buildings	184
Capital gains on property sale	185
Sale of trading stock	185
Trading losses	185
Setting off trading losses against post-trading receipts	186
Close investment holding company status	187
Pre-liquidation tax liabilities	187
Post-liquidation tax liabilities	188
Legal formalities	188
Dealing with surplus available to shareholders	190
Capital distributions	190
Taper relief on capital distributions made before 6 April 2008	191
Timing of capital distributions	192
Calculation of taxable gain on capital distribution	193
Multiple capital distributions	194
Small capital distributions	197
Distributions in specie	197
Pre-liquidation/dissolution dividend versus capital distribution	198
Benefits of CGT treatment	198
Post- 5 April 2008 capital distributions	198
When pre-liquidation dividends are beneficial	198
Liquidation and ITA 2007, s 684 issues	201
Phoenix company arrangements	201
Section 684 and the Joiner case	202
Relief for shareholders of insolvent companies	202
Negligible value claim	202
Income tax relief for capital losses on shares	204
Relief for shareholder loans	207
Capital loss relief for irrecoverable loans	207
Guarantee payments	208
Converting loans into new shares	209
Losses incurred on Qualifying Corporate Bonds (QCBs)	210
Loans made by companies	210
Chapter 8: Tax planning for the non-resident and non-domiciled	**212**
Introduction	212
Residence	212
Ceasing to be UK resident	214
Contract of employment	214
Leaving the UK permanently or indefinitely	216

Contents

No presence in UK during tax year	217
Deemed non-residence	217
The 91-day test	218
Available accommodation	220
Ordinary residence	220
The Gaines-Cooper case	222
Domicile	223
The tax significance of the three concepts	224
The remittance basis	225
Remittances from mixed funds	227
What to do with a mixed fund	229
Deemed remittances	230
Employment Income	231
Travelling expenses	233
Self-employment income	234
Taxation of non-UK residents	234
Investment income	234
Employment income	235
Trading income	236
Property income	236
Capital Gains Tax	237
Inheritance Tax	240
Double tax treaties	242
Residence of trusts	243
Company residence	243
Companies incorporated in the UK	248
Non-resident company trading in the UK	249
Change of residence	249
Dual resident companies	250
Companies treated as non-resident	250
Chapter 9: Tax efficient investments	**251**
Investment in unquoted trading companies	251
Capital Gains Tax (CGT)	251
Enterprise Investment Scheme (EIS) relief	254
Income tax relief	254
EIS qualifying investors	256
Venture capital trusts (VCTs)	258
Criteria for qualifying EIS and VCT companies	259
EIS funds – approved and unapproved	262
Approved EIS funds	262
Unapproved EIS funds and schemes	263
Real Estate Investment Trusts (REITS)	263
Insurance products	263
Life assurance policies	263

General treatment of non-qualifying insurance policies	265
Group life policies	268
Investment and savings products	269
Investment products and IHT planning	269
ISAs, PEPs, TESSAs and SAYE	273

Chapter 10: Pensions — **275**

Introduction	275
Membership and contributions	275
Membership	275
Investment opportunities	285
Drawing benefits	290
Death benefits	300
Pension sharing	305
The main charges, surcharges, penalties and sanctions	310
Appeals	313
Reviewing existing registered schemes	314
Reviewing existing unapproved arrangements	314
Overseas tax planning	316

Chapter 11: Business property relief — **321**

Introduction	321
Conditions	321
Caravan parks	323
The 'right' business?	324
'Wholly or mainly'	325
Period of ownership	326
BPR and interests in possession	327
Value of the business	328
Excepted assets	328
Investment 'business'?	329
'Surplus' cash	330
Investment 'business'	331
Groups of companies	332
Other points	334
Company liquidations, reorganisations etc	334
Partnerships	335
Retirement of a partner	336
Lifetime gifts and BPR	338
Avoiding a clawback of BPR	338
Replacement property	339
The order of gifts	340
Death and BPR	341
Maximising BPR	341
Avoiding the loss of BPR	341

'Doubling up' BPR	343
Protecting against future BPR changes	345
BPR and CGT	346

Chapter 12: Agricultural property relief and woodlands relief — 349

Agricultural assets: property	349
Clawback	350
Use of chargeable transfer to limit clawback	350
Investments in the context of farming	351
Farming partnership	351
Partnership farmland	352
Period of ownership or occupation	352
Minimum period of ownership	352
Spouses and civil partners: a special succession rule	352
Successions	352
Successive transfers	353
Replacements	353
Residuary estates	354
Agricultural value	354
Agricultural value	354
Special valuation issues	355
The level of relief	356
Assets qualifying for 100% relief	356
Assets qualifying for 50% relief	357
Concessionary reliefs	358
The main estate planning lessons	358
Shareholdings and partnerships	358
Use of discretionary trusts	359
APR 'recycled'	360
Creation of several lifetime trusts to achieve protection against future changes in the reliefs	362
Other ways of using agricultural property relief	363
Gifts to elderly relatives	363
Elderly relative transfers to offshore trust on death	364
Will planning	364
Other advantages of delaying such gifts until death	365
Deeds of variation (IHTA 1984, s 142)	366
Mortgaging or charging agricultural or business assets	366
Avoid mortgaging or charging a farm	366
Timing: instant relief, at minimal cost	367
Tax planning for agricultural property: agricultural cottages and the farmhouse	367
Tax planning for agricultural property: fallow land and other farming assets	372
Tenant farmers	374

Farming companies	374
Habitat schemes	375
Special types of farming	375
Farm sharing	375
Contract farming	376
Single farm payment scheme	376
'Buy and sell' agreements/arrangements	377
Woodlands – the relief	377
Nature of relief	378
Conditions of relief	379
Transfers of woodlands subject to a deferred estate duty charge	380

Chapter 13: Wills, variations and disclaimers — 382

Intestacy	382
Why make a will?	382
Executors and trustees	382
Wills	386
The correct type of will	386
The appropriate type of will for IHT purposes	390
Wills for the relevant IHT circumstances	390
Variations and disclaimers: post-death planning	393
Alternative use of deed of variation	402
Husband, wife and civil partner	404
Civil partnerships	404
Husband and wife estates: should we still use the nil-rate band on the first death?	408
The matrimonial home	413
Mortgages and other outgoings	417
Nil-rate band transfers: background	419

Chapter 14: Tax planning with trusts — 430

Introduction	430
Types of trust	432
Residence of trustees	433
Extended meaning of settlement	434
The taxation of UK resident settlements	436
Income tax	436
Charge on settlor	438
Capital Gains Tax	442
Charge on settlor	444
The taxation of non-resident trustees	447
Income tax	447
Capital Gains Tax	448
Inheritance Tax	453
The standard or discretionary trust regime	454

Contents

The entry charge	454
The ten-yearly charge	454
The exit charge	456
The interest-in-possession regime	456
Pre 22 March 2006 IIP trusts	457
Accumulation and maintenance settlement	458
Immediate post-death interests	459
Trusts for disabled persons	460
Protective trusts	461
Special trusts	461
Trusts for bereaved minors	461
Age 18 to 25 trusts	462
Charitable trusts	463
Employee trusts and newspaper trusts	463
Maintenance funds for historic buildings	464
Other points	464
IHT planning with trusts	464
Things to avoid	467

Chapter 15: Tax planning for the family home — 468

Introduction	468
Capital Gains Tax	468
Principal private residence	468
Conditions	468
What constitutes a 'residence'?	469
Whether the house is the only or main residence of the owner	470
What is the meaning of 'throughout the period of ownership'?	473
Rental and lettings	474
Non-domiciliaries and the UK family home	480
Inheritance Tax	480
Introduction	480
Lifetime planning	481
Valuation	486
The basic charge	487
Tax planning schemes	490
Elections	494
Double charges	495
Current lifetime IHT planning and the family home	495
Equity release schemes	496
IHT position	497
Planning via a will	498
Nil-rate band (NRB) scheme	498
The debt scheme	500
The charge scheme	501
Insurance schemes	502

Chapter 16: Separation and divorce	**504**
Introduction	504
An outline of the steps involved in a divorce where significant financial issues exist	504
Income tax	506
Maintenance payments	506
The settlement rules now contained in ITTOIA 2005	507
Capital Gains Tax	507
Disposals between spouses before the end of the tax year of permanent separation	508
Transfers between the end of the tax year of permanent separation and decree absolute	508
Transfers between spouses after decree absolute	508
Hold-over relief	509
The receipt of lump sums under court orders	510
Inheritance Tax	510
Stamp duty land tax and stamp duty	511
Pre-owned assets tax	512
Particular issues	513
The matrimonial home and the CGT main residence exemption	513
Extra-Statutory Concession D6	514
The position where the former matrimonial home is to be retained following separation of the couple for occupation by one spouse only and where the non-occupying spouse wishes to keep a stake in the property	515
Particular situations	518
Extracting funds from companies and settlements	518
Spouses with non-UK domicile	519
The assignment of life policies	519
Chapter 17: Anti-avoidance	**521**
Introduction	521
ICTA 1988, ss 703–707 – transactions in securities	522
ICTA 1988, ss 739–744 – transfers of assets abroad; ICTA 1988, s 13 – gains of non-resident companies; and TCGA 1992, ss 86–90 – gains of non-resident settlements	525
ITTOIA 2005, ss 619–648; TCGA 1992, ss 77–79 – settlements where the settlor retains an interest	532
ICTA 1988, s 768 – change in ownership of company-disallowance of losses	536
ITA 2007, ss 102–116 – losses of limited partnerships, etc	540
VATA 1994, Sch 1, para 2 – aggregation of activities of separate persons	541
VATA 1994, ss 43–44 – group of companies	544
ICTA 1988, s 770A – provisions not at arm's length	547
TCGA 1992, s 179 – company ceasing to be a member of a group	551

Contents

The TAARs	552
The CGT TAAR (TCGA 1992, s 16A)	553
The SDLT TAAR (FA 2003, s 75A)	554
The Ramsay principle	556
The Ministerial Statement of 2 December 2004	559
Index	*561*

Table of statutes

Administration of Estates Act 1925
s 46 .... 14.48
  47(1) 14.48
Capital Allowances Act 2001
s 46 .... 2.19
  (2) 2.17
  55 .... 2.19
  (2) 2.18
  (3) 2.18
  (4) 2.17
  61 .... 2.18
  (2) 2.21, 7.7
  65(1) 2.17
  266 .... 2.20, 5.6, 5.11
  267 .... 2.19, 5.11
  314 .... 2.26
  315 .... 2.26
  316 .... 2.26
  375 .... 2.28
  382 .... 2.28
  567 .... 2.26
  568 .... 2.26
  569 .... 2.27
  573 .... 2.26
  575 .... 2.18
Charities Act 2006 .... 1.75, 1.77
s 7 .... 1.76
  755–760 .... 1.77
Civil Partnership 2004 .... 13.57
Companies Act 1948 .... 3.66
Companies Act 1985 .. 1.6, 1.73, 1.115, 3.27, 3.65, 3.66
s 1(2)(a) 1.74
  81 .... 1.77
  159(3) 3.66
  160(1) 3.66
  (4) 3.66
  162(1) 3.66
  (2) 3.66
  (3) 3.66

Companies Act 1985 – *contd*
s 164(5) 3.66
  169 .... 3.75
  (1) 3.66
  (1A) 3.66
  (4) 3.66
  171–177 .... 3.66
  247 .... 1.10
  254 .... 1.19
  283(2) 1.6
  334 .... 1.115
  652 .... 5.5, 7.17, 7.25
  652A 7.17, 7.25
  653 .... 7.19
  654 .... 7.18
Companies Act 2006 .. 1.11, 1.73, 3.63, 3.65, 3.66, 3.67, 17.59, 17.64
s 3(2) 1.74
  4(1) 1.74
  270 .... 1.6
  382 .... 1.6
  690 .... 3.66
  691 .... 3.66
  692(1) 3.66
  (2) 3.66
  693 .... 3.66
  694(2) 3.66
  696(2) 3.66
  702 .... 3.67
  706 .... 3.66
  707 .... 3.66
  708 .... 3.66
  709–723 .... 3.66
  1136 .... 3.67
Pt 18 .... 3.63
Company Directors (Disqualification) Act 1986 ... 1.82
Family Law (Scotland) Act 1985
s 8(2) 16.26
  14(1) 16.26

Table of statutes

Finance Act 1975 .... 13.69
  Sch 8
    para 2 .... 12.20
    para 5 .... 12.20
Finance Act 1985
  s 83 .... 16.27
Finance Act 1986 .... 15.33
  s 66 .... 3.74
    102 .... 11.56, 12.36, 13.49, 13.81,
                        15.33, 15.49
      (1) 15.35
      (5)(a) 9.38
      (5A) 15.48
    102B 13.85
      (4)(b) 15.41
    102ZA 13.15, 13.19, 13.50
    103 .... 15.70
  Sch 19
    para 46 .... 12.68
  Sch 20 ... 11.56, 13.49, 13.81, 15.33
    para 6(1)(a) 13.82
    para 8 .... 11.56, 12.24
      (1A)(b) 12.24
Finance Act 1988
  s 130 .... 8.88
    132 .... 8.88
Finance Act 1989
  s 68(2) 14.22
    71(4) 14.22
Finance Act 1990
  s 25 .... 14.30
Finance Act 1993 .... 4.45
Finance (No 2) Act 1993 .... 8.20
Finance Act 1994
  s 249 .... 8.84, 8.91
    (2) 8.91
Finance Act 1995
  s 121(1) 8.50
    126 .... 8.88
    128(2) 8.50
      (3) 8.50
Finance Act 1996
  s 87 .... 4.71
    (3) 7.57
    87A 7.57
    102 .... 13.81
  Sch 9
    para 6 .... 7.56
    para 6C 7.56, 7.57
    para 12 .... 4.73

Finance Act 1996 – *contd*
  Sch 9 – *contd*
    para 12A 4.73
  Sch 20 .... 13.81
Finance Act 1998 .... 7.23, 16.7
  s 36 .... 4.75
    (3) 4.75
    66 .... 8.84
  Sch 14
    para 7 .... 9.27
  Sch 18
    para 66 .... 4.23
    para 70 .... 4.23
    para 73 .... 4.23
    para 74 .... 4.23
Finance Act 1999
  Sch 13
    para 1(1) 17.92
      (2) 17.92
Finance Act 2000 .... 4.14, 4.29
  s 98 .... 8.88
Finance Act 2002 . 2.2, 2.23, 2.45, 4.36,
                                  4.58, 7.10
  Sch 13
    para 7 .... 2.72
  Sch 26 .... 4.73
    para 28 .... 4.73
    para 30A 4.73
  Sch 29 .... 2.69, 5.15
    para 2 .... 2.69
    para 4 .... 2.69
  Pt 8 .... 4.74
  Pt 9
    para 55 .... 4.74
    para 95 .... 2.70
    para 118 .... 1.129, 2.70
      (2)(b), (c) 2.71
  Pt 12 .... 4.74
Finance Act 2003 .... 9.33, 9.38
  s 48(2)(b) 2.75
    53 .... 2.74, 2.96
    75A 17.84
      (1) 17.84
      (2) 17.88
      (3) 17.85, 17.87
      (4) 17.85
      (6) 17.85
      (7) 17.88
    75B(1), (3) 17.86
      (2) 17.87

Finance Act 2003 – *contd*

s 75B(4)	17.87
75C(1)	17.88
(2)	17.88
(3)	17.88
148(1)–(5)	8.86
150	8.88
151	8.88
152	8.88
185	9.37, 9.38
195(2)	3.53, 3.64
Sch 3	
para 1	5.14, 13.70, 13.87
para 3	16.26
para 4	13.52
Sch 4	
para 8	13.89

Finance Act 2004 ... 4.71, 10.32, 10.34, 10.89

s 140	9.29
150(1)	10.4
152	10.18
154	10.8
162	10.32
163	10.31
169	10.116
178	10.58
179	10.31
182–185	10.31
186	10.30
187	10.30
189	10.12
205	10.58
208	10.91
209	10.92
227	10.14
238	10.23
239	10.93
266	10.91
267	10.92, 10.93
268	10.92, 10.93
Sch 15	13.83
para 3(2), (3)	15.38
para 10	15.40
(1)	16.28
(2)(c)	13.86
para 11(5)(c)	13.86
para 16	13.49
Sch 22	
para 5	15.26, 15.27

Finance Act 2004 – *contd*

Sch 22 – *contd*	
para 6	15.27
Sch 29	
para 3A	10.29
Sch 29A	
para 20	10.37
Sch 30	10.32
Sch 34	10.114
Sch 36	
Pt 1, para 3	10.103
Pt 4, para 38	10.32

Finance Act 2005

s 30	14.47
31	14.47
32	14.47
33	14.47
34	14.48
35	14.48
38	14.49
48A	10.62
Sch 15	
para 10	15.61

Finance Act 2006 ...... 3.70, 4.45, 4.50, 4.71, 10.30, 10.34, 10.79, 10.87, 11.1, 12.25, 12.49, 13.15, 13.19, 13.21, 13.31, 13.41, 13.42, 13.59, 14.94, 15.40, 16.22, 16.24, 16.38

s 27	8.88
Sch 9	4.72
para 2	4.72
para 4A	4.72
para 5(3)	4.72
para 6	4.72
(6)	4.72
para 6A	4.72
para 12	4.72
para 12A	4.72
para 17	4.72
Sch 20	
para 3	14.79
(3)	14.80

Finance Act 2007 ...... 2.23, 3.70, 5.14, 9.16, 10.49, 10.72, 13.55, 15.72

s 36	2.23
53	10.62

Table of statutes

Finance Act 2007 – *contd*
s 66 .... 15.54
Sch 20
  para 2 .... 10.8
Sch 37
  para 1 .... 2.72
Finance Act 2008 ... 2.98, 10.55, 13.24, 13.53, 15.63
Gender Recognition Act 2004 ... 10.44
Income and Corporation Taxes Act 1988 .... 3.2, 3.13, 8.20
  Ch 3, Pt 7 .... 7.47
  s 11A 8.86
    12(3)(c) 5.8, 7.5
    (7) 7.15
    13A 1.93, 7.12
      (4) 7.12
    14(2) 3.70
    42A 8.53
    74(1) 1.96
      (a) 1.120
      (f) 3.76
  90 .... 7.6
  100
    (1)(a) 7.9 4.42
    (1A) 5.10
      (a) 7.9
    (1C) 5.6, 5.10
    (1F) 5.10
    (1ZA) 5.10
  103 .... 7.11
  104 .... 7.11
  105 .... 7.5, 7.11
  108 .... 7.111
  118 .... 17.52
  208 .... 3.68
  209 .... 1.117
    (1) 7.20
    (2)(b) 2.64, 3.1, 3.49
    (4) 2.64
  210(1) 3.50
  211(1) 3.1, 3.50
    (5) 3.49
  219 .... 1.117, 3.1, 3.2, 3.5, 3.37, 3.56, 3.57, 3.62, 3.70, 3.72
    (1) .. 3.5, 3.11, 3.15, 3.62, 3.70
      (a) . 3.5, 3.8, 3.9, 3.11, 3.12, 3.16, 3.19, 3.26, 3.58, 3.60, 3.62

Income and Corporation Taxes Act 1988 – *contd*
s 219(1)(b) 3.7, 3.58
    (2) 3.5, 3.8
    (3)–(9) 3.5
  220 ...... 3.2, 3.5, 3.12, 3.57, 3.62, 3.72
    (1) 3.5, 3.20, 3.61
    (2) 3.5
    (3) 3.5, 3.20, 3.23
    (4) 3.5
    (5) 3.5, 3.24, 3.48, 3.62
    (6) 3.5, 3.24
    (7) 3.5, 3.24
    (8) 3.5, 3.24
    (9) 3.5, 3.24
  221 ...... 3.2, 3.5, 3.12, 3.57, 3.62, 3.72
    (1) 3.26, 3.62
    (2) 3.62
  222 ...... 3.2, 3.5, 3.12, 3.57, 3.62, 3.72
    (3) 3.62
    (9) 3.28, 3.62
    (10) 3.30, 3.62
    (11) 3.30
    (12) 3.30, 3.62
  223 ...... 3.2, 3.5, 3.12, 3.31, 3.57, 3.62, 3.72
    (1) 3.62
    (2) 3.33, 3.62
    (3) 3.33
  224 ...... 3.2, 3.5, 3.12, 3.34, 3.57, 3.62, 3.72
  225 ..... 1.117, 3.2, 3.5, 3.41, 3.57, 3.58, 3.59, 3.62, 3.72
    (1)(a) 3.57, 3.62
      (b) 3.57
    (2) 3.59
    (5) 3.58
  226 .... 3.2, 3.57, 3.72, 3.73
    (3) 3.74
  227 .... 3.2, 3.57, 3.62, 3.72
  228 ...... 3.2, 3.5, 3.32, 3.57, 3.62, 3.72
  229 .... 3.2, 3.57
    (1) 3.9, 3.45, 3.62
  266 .... 9.21

Table of statutes

Income and Corporation Taxes Act 1988 – *contd*

s 267	9.21
274	9.21
336	8.20
337	4.38, 4.43, 8.88
(1)	5.7
343	4.12, 4.38, 4.39, 4.40, 4.42, 4.43, 4.44, 17.41
(1)(a)	4.39
(2)	4.40, 4.41
(3)	4.40, 4.41, 17.39
(8)	4.43, 17.41
344	4.39
(1)	4.39
(4)	4.39
393(1)	5.9, 7.10, 7.11, 17.40
(a)	7.10
(2)	5.9, 7.10
(2A)	5.9, 7.10
(2B)	7.10
393A(1)	5.9
Pt X	4.11
402	4.11
(2)	4.14
(2A)	4.14
403	4.15
403A	4.17
(8)	4.17
403B(1)	4.18
(2)	4.18
403F	4.21
403G	4.21
404	4.19
(6)	4.19
410	4.12, 4.13
413(3)	4.11
416	4.49
419	1.115, 2.64, 3.65
539	9.22
539A	9.33
540–548	9.22
549	9.22, 9.29
550–554	9.22
574	3.54, 7.44, 7.49, 7.54, 9.8
575	3.54
(1)	7.44
576	3.54
579(2)	7.6
628(5)	14.22

Income and Corporation Taxes Act 1988 – *contd*

s 630(2)	14.22
703	3.5, 17.6, 17.10
(1)	17.6, 17.8
704C	3.59
704D	3.59
707	3.5, 3.59, 3.62, 6.26
739	8.28, 17.12, 17.14, 17.15, 17.17, 17.27
(2)	17.12
740	16.43, 17.14, 17.15, 17.16, 17.17
(1)	17.15
741	17.17
741A	17.17
(4)–(7)	17.18
741B	17.17
741C	17.17
743(1)	17.20
(3)	17.20
761(1)	14.22
765	8.89
765A	8.89
768	17.43, 17.47
(1), (2)	17.44
(4)	17.45
(6)	17.49
768A	17.49
768B	17.49
768C	17.49
768D	17.49
768E	17.49
769(1)	17.48
738	17.39, 17.40
770A	17.65
776	16.40
832	4.3, 4.6
838(1)	4.3
839	2.13, 2.74, 17.85
840	3.32
841(1)(b)	9.1
Pt VI	3.2
Sch 15	9.21
Sch 18	4.4, 4.5, 4.6, 4.8, 4.11, 4.27, 4.61
para 1(1)	4.5, 4.6, 4.7
(5)	4.7
Sch 18A	4.22
Pt 2	4.22

Table of statutes

Income and Corporation Taxes Act 1988 – *contd*

Sch 28AA	4.70, 17.65
para 1	17.65
para 1A	17.83
para 3	17.67
para 4	17.68
(7)	17.69
para 4A	17.70
para 5	17.71, 17.76
para 5B	17.71, 17.72
para 6	17.73
para 18	17.75

Income Tax Act 2007 .... 1.46, 3.70

s 9	14.21
11	14.21
12	14.21
14	14.21
43	16.7
64	1.46
72	1.46
83	1.46
102	17.52
103	17.52
103C	1.47, 1.59
104	1.59, 17.52
(4)	17.52
105	17.52
106	17.52, 17.53
107	17.52, 17.53
108	17.52, 17.53
109	17.52
110	17.52, 17.54
111	17.52
112	17.52, 17.54
113–116	17.52
131	7.44, 7.45, 7.46, 7.47, 7.48, 7.54, 9.8
(3)	7.44
132	7.48
134	7.47
135	7.47
136	7.47
137	7.47
148	7.46
157	9.6
158	9.6
173A	9.16
186A	9.16
213–225	9.12

Income Tax Act 2007 – *contd*

s 416	1.88
(5)	1.90
(6)	1.88
466(2)–(5)	14.18
475	14.16
(3)	14.17
(6)	14.17
476	14.16
479	14.21, 14.51
480	14.51
(1)	14.21
(2)	14.21
(3)	14.21
(4)	14.21
(5)	14.21
(6)	14.21
481	14.22, 14.51
482	3.70, 14.22, 14.51
484	14.23
485	14.23
486	14.23
487	14.51
491	14.24
492	14.24
494	14.24
684	3.5, 5.17, 6.2, 6.26, 7.38, 7.39, 7.40
685	5.17
688	3.59
689	3.59, 7.39
701	3.5, 3.59, 3.62, 5.17, 5.18, 6.2, 6.26
714–719	14.51
720	13.42, 14.51
721–730	14.51
731	14.51, 16.43
732–751	14.51
752–755	14.22
756	14.22, 16.40
757–772	14.22
811	14.40
812	14.50
(2)–(5)	14.50
813	14.50
814	14.50
831	8.20
993	2.13
(2)	1.55
994	2.13

Table of statutes

Income Tax Act 2007 – *contd*
s 995 .... 3.32
  1005 .... 9.1
  1011 .... 16.12
  Pt 3 .... 16.9
  Pt 4 .... 3.54
  Pt 5 .... 2.53, 7.47
  Pt 8 .... 16.7
  Pt 10 .... 13.51
  Pt 13 .... 5.4, 5.5, 5.17, 5.18

Income Tax (Trading and Other Income) Act 2005 .... 7.11, 9.21
  s 9 .... 12.59
  13(3) 1.85
    (4) 1.85
  34 .... 1.96, 1.120
  53 .... 12.60
  175 .... 2.64
  177 .... 2.13
  178 .... 2.14
  179 .... 2.13
  182–184 .... 2.15
  185 .... 2.15, 2.16
  202 .... 2.6, 2.7
  205(1) 2.9
  209 .... 2.8
  214 .... 2.7
  215 .... 2.7
  216 .... 2.7
  217 .... 2.7
  243 .... 2.16
  264 .... 2.91
  265 .... 2.91
  276–307 .... 14.22
  Pt 4 .... 9.31, 16.40, 16.47
  416 .... 14.34
  429 .... 14.22
  433 .... 16.40
  439 .... 16.40
  453(3) 9.27
  461 .... 9.22
  465(1) 9.25
  467 .... 9.27, 14.22
  481 .... 9.33
  482 .... 9.33
  487 .... 16.47
  554 .... 14.22
  557 .... 14.22
  573 .... 14.22
  Pt 5 .... 1.70, 16.10

Income Tax (Trading and Other Income) Act 2005 – *contd*
s 619 .... 1.123, 14.19, 17.30
  620 .... 1.123, 14.19, 17.30
    (1) 17.31
  621 .... 1.123, 17.30
  622 .... 1.123, 17.30
  623 .... 1.123, 17.30
  624 .... 1.123, 1.125, 13.42, 14.31, 14.32, 17.30
  625 ..... 1.123, 14.28, 14.51, 17.30
    (1) 14.28
    (4) 16.11
  626 .... 1.123, 1.126, 14.51, 17.30, 17.32
    (1), (2) 14.28
    (3) 1.126, 14.28
    (4) 14.28, 17.32
  627 ..... 1.123, 14.30, 14.51, 17.30
  628 ..... 1.123, 14.30, 14.51, 17.30
  629 .... 1.123, 13.51, 14.32, 14.51, 16.11, 17.30
    (1), (2), (7) 14.31
  630 .... 1.123, 14.31, 17.30
  631 .... 1.123, 14.31, 17.30
  632 .... 1.123, 17.30
  633 .... 1.123, 14.34, 17.30, 17.35, 17.37
    (3)–(5) 14.32
  634 .... 1.123, 14.33, 17.30
    (1) 17.35
    (5) 17.36
    (7) 14.33
  635 .... 1.123, 14.32, 17.30
    (2) 17.35
  636 .... 1.123, 14.33, 17.30
  637 .... 1.123, 17.30
    (8) 14.35, 17.37
  638 .... 1.123, 17.30
    (1) 17.36
    (2), (3) 14.34
    (4) 17.36
  639 .... 1.123, 14.34, 17.30
  640 .... 1.123, 14.32, 17.30
  641 ..... 1.123, 14.35, 17.30, 17.37
  642 .... 1.123, 14.35, 17.30
  643 .... 1.123, 17.30
    (3) 14.35, 17.37
  644–648 .... 1.123, 17.30
  671 .... 13.41

xxv

Table of statutes

Income Tax (Trading and Other Income) Act 2005 – *contd*
s 830(1)	8.37
833(1)	8.38
(3)	8.38
(4), (5)	8.39
834	8.39
Pt 9	1.44

Income Tax (Earnings and Pensions) Act 2003 .... 10.111
Pt 2	1.94, 1.100
s 21	8.40
22	8.40
23	8.40
24	8.46
25	8.51
26	8.51, 15.30
33	8.47
(3), (4)	8.38
39	8.40
175	3.65
184	1.115
336	1.96
374	8.48
379	9.48
477	1.148
(4)	1.148
Pt 7	1.144
s 446X	3.77
447	1.148, 2.98
(4)	1.147

Inheritance Tax Act 1984 . 1.118, 11.1, 15.31
s 3(3)	13.91
3A	8.69
(1), (2)	11.49
(4)	12.66, 13.81
5(2)	13.91
(5)	15.68
6(1A)	8.67
(2)	8.67, 8.68, 8.71
(3)	8.67, 8.68
7(4)	13.81
8	13.60, 13.66
8A	13.94
(2)	13.97
(3)	13.95
(4)	13.97
8B	13.94, 13.102
(2)	13.95

Inheritance Tax Act 1984 – *contd*
s 8C	13.94, 13.96
(2)	13.97
(4)	13.98
(5)	13.98
10	2.77, 13.61, 13.110, 16.22, 16.23, 16.25
11	8.85, 13.58, 13.68, 13.110, 16.22, 16.23
18	13.24, 13.58, 13.61, 13.67, 13.89
(1)	13.59
(2)	8.69, 13.60
(3)(a)	13.61
(b)	13.61
(4)	13.59
21	13.89
23	14.90
30	13.97
32	13.97
32A	13.98
38(1)	13.40
39	13.40
39A	11.46, 12.34, 13.34, 13.56
(2)	11.47
(3), (4)	11.46
(6)	13.67
43	16.38
(2)	14.74
44(2)	13.91
47A	13.61
48	13.41
(1)(b)	9.42, 16.39
(3)	8.71, 13.41
(3A)	8.71
(3B)	8.71
(4)	8.68, 8.71
49	14.82
(1)	11.3, 11.11, 14.75
49A	11.48, 14.82
49C	14.76
49D	14.76
50	13.78, 14.77
(1)	14.77
51	14.77
(4)	14.77
52	14.77
(1)	14.77
(3)	14.78
(4)	8.72, 14.78

Table of statutes

Inheritance Tax Act 1984 – *contd*

s 53(5)	14.78
54	14.78
(2)	8.73
55	13.61
55A	13.61
56(1)	13.62
(2)	13.61
58	11.49
(3)	14.67
64	14.70
65(4)	14.73
66(1)	14.70
(2)	14.71
(3)	14.71
(4)	14.72
(5)	14.72
67	14.71
68	14.73
69	14.72
(1)	14.73
70	14.90
(6)	14.81
71(1)	14.79
(a)	14.79
(2)	14.79, 14.84
(4)	14.79
(5)	14.81
71A(1)–(3)	14.87
71B(2), (3)	14.87
71C	14.87
71D	14.88
71E(2), (3)	14.88
71F	14.89
72	14.91
74	14.84
76	14.90
(1)	14.90
81	14.93
86	14.91
87	14.91
88	14.85
(1)	14.85
89(1)	14.84
(4)–(6)	14.84
91(1)	12.14
92	13.46, 13.61
94	2.77, 8.72
(2)	8.72
103	11.1, 12.67, 13.109

Inheritance Tax Act 1984 – *contd*

s 103(1)(b)	11.49, 12.25
104	11.1, 12.67
(1)(a)	2.80, 2.83
(b)	2.79, 2.81
105	11.1, 11.32, 12.67
(1)	1.118
(a)	2.79, 2.83, 11.29, 11.30
(bb)	2.83
(d)	11.14, 11.29, 11.44, 12.8, 12.36
(1ZA)	11.3
(3)	2.79, 11.5, 11.6, 11.8, 11.15, 11.18, 11.23, 11.54
(4)(b)	11.23, 11.25
(5)	11.28
106	2.83, 11.1, 11.9, 11.28, 12.67
107	2.83, 11.1, 12.67
(2)	11.10
(3)	11.10
(4)	11.10, 11.28
108	11.1, 11.10, 12.67
109	11.1, 12.31, 12.67
(1)	11.10
(2)	11.10
(3)	11.10
110	11.1, 12.67
(a)	11.54
(b)	11.13
111	11.1, 11.24, 12.67
(b)	11.25
112	2.79, 11.1, 11.48, 12.67
(2)	11.24, 12.50
(3)	11.14
(4)	11.14, 11.19
(6)	11.21, 12.50
113	2.80, 11.1, 11.33, 11.34, 12.63, 12.67
(a), (b)	11.35
(3A)	11.38
(8)	11.39
113A	11.38
(1), (2)	11.37
(3)	11.42
(5)	11.40
(6)	11.43
113B	11.38
(1), (2)	11.41
(3)	11.42

Table of statutes

Inheritance Tax Act 1984 – *contd*
s 113B(6) 11.43
114 .... 11.1, 12.67
  (1) 2.84, 11.57
115 .... 12.1
  (1)(b) 12.25
  (2) 12.40, 12.45, 12.46,
              ,12.47, 12.61
  (3) 12.8, 12.15, 12.16
116 .... 12.1, 12.8
  (1)(c) 2.85
  (2)(a) 12.18, 12.20, 12.22
    (b), (c) 12.20
  (5A) 12.20
117 .... 12.1
  (a) 12.9
  (b) 12.9
118 .... 12.1, 12.13
  (1) 12.13
  (3) 12.13
119 .... 12.1
120 .... 12.1, 12.14
  (1)(a) 12.11
    (b) 12.10, 12.121
121 .... 12.1, 12.31
122 .... 12.1, 12.24, 12.57
  (1) 2.85
123 .... 12.1
  (1) 12.57
124 .... 12.1, 12.62
124A 12.1, 12.35
124B 12.1, 12.35
124C 12.1
125 .... 12.64, 12.66, 12.67
126 ...... 12.64, 12.65, 12.66, 12.67
  (3) 12.65
127 .... 12.64, 12.66, 12.67
  (2) 12.67
128 .... 12.64, 12.65
129 .... 12.64
130 .... 12.64
  (1)(b) 12.67
  (2) 12.65
142 .... 11.47, 13.20, 13.35, 13.36,
        13.38, 13.39, 13.44,
        13.50, 13.51, 13.88,
        13.91, 13.109
  (2) 13.40
  (2A) 13.37
  (3) 13.41

Inheritance Tax Act 1984 – *contd*
s 142(6) 13.36
143 .... 13.106
144 .... 12.34, 13.29, 13.33, 13.39,
          13.59, 13.107,
          13.109
151B 13.100
151BA 13.94
  (2) 13.99
  (5) 13.99
  (6) 13.99
  (7) 13.99
  (8)–(12) 13.100
155 .... 8.67
157 .... 8.67
158(6) 8.68, 8.73
159 .... 8.77
161 .... 16.24
162 .... 12.41
  (4) 11.54
169 .... 12.44
201 .... 14.75
203 .... 13.62
234(1) 12.57
239 .... 13.94
242 .... 13.94
247(2) 13.102
267 .... 13.60
  (1) 8.68
  (2) 8.68
267A 11.31
268 ..... 11.52, 13.41, 13.68, 13.75
  (1) 13.91
269 .... 11.3
272 .... 13.91, 13.94
Sch 1 .... 13.66
Sch 2 .... 13.98
  para 4 .... 12.65
Sch 4 .... 14.92

Inheritance (Provision for Family and Dependants) Act 1975 .... 13.51
Insolvency Act 1986 .... 7.25
s 110 .... 7.40
175 .... 7.13
386 .... 7.13
Ch III 5.4
Pt IV 5.4
s 214 .... 1.82

Table of statutes

Interpretation Act 1978	12.44
Law of Property Act 1925	
s 36(2)	13.88
196	13.88
Limited Liability Partnerships Act 2000	1.61, 12.7
Limited Partnerships Act 1907	1.56
s 4	1.57
Matrimonial Causes Act 1973	
s 24A	16.26
Mental Health Act 1983	14.37, 14.49, 14.84
Partnership Act 1890	1.40, 1.41, 11.132
s 2	1.41
4(2)	1.51, 1.56
Pension Schemes Act 1993	10.19, 10.21
Pensions Act 1995	10.31, 10.44
Pensions Act 2004	10.103
s 287	10.111
294	10.111
Pensions Act 2007	
s 12	2.33
Social Security Contributions and Benefits Act 1992	
s 6A(2)	2.33
11(1)	2.29
64	14.37, 14.84
(1)	14.49, 14.84
67(1), (2)	14.84
71	14.37, 14.84
(6)	14.49, 14.84
72(8)	14.84
Statute of Uses 1535	14.1
Taxation of Chargeable Gains Act 1992	2.94, 3.71, 15.2
s 2(1)	14.52
(2)	8.35
2A(1)	8.35
(2)(a)	6.19
(8)	3.47
4(1AA)	14.36
10	8.56, 8.60, 8.61, 8.62
(9B)	8.59
(9C)	8.59
10A	8.57, 8.58, 17.23
(1)	8.57
(2)	8.58
(3)	8.58

Taxation of Chargeable Gains Act 1992 – *contd*	
s 10B	8.56, 8.85, 17.23
12	8.63
(1)	8.35, 8.63
(2)	8.63
13	8.58, 8.59, 17.20, 17.21, 17.23, 17.25
(1)	17.20
(2)	17.22
(4)	17.20
(5A)	17.21
(10A)	17.21
14	8.88
16(4)	8.35
16A	17.82
(1)	17.82
(2)	17.83
(3)	17.83
17	2.38, 3.77, 5.13, 16.15
(1)	7.54
(a)	7.34, 17.76
(2)	7.42, 17.76
18	2.38, 3.77, 16.14
(2)	17.76
(3)	3.53
21(1)(a), (b)	12.53
24(1)	7.43, 7.44
(2)	7.41, 7.44, 7.45
(2)(a), (b)	7.41
25	8.61, 8.62
(1)	17.23
(2)	17.23
(3)	8.61, 17.23
(5)	8.61
28	6.4, 7.8, 16.18
(1)	3.41, 6.4
(2)	6.4
29	12.20, 17.76
30	4.51, 4.54, 4.55, 4.56, 4.57, 17.76
(6)	4.55
(7)	4.55
(8)	4.55, 4.56
31	4.55, 17.76
31A	4.56
32	4.57, 17.76
33	17.76
34	17.76
33A	4.58

Table of statutes

Taxation of Chargeable Gains Act 1992 – *contd*

s 37	2.35, 3.71
(1)	3.51, 3.68, 3.71
38	2.50
42	7.32
48	6.4
58	16.13
59	1.49
60	14.18
(1)	3.61
(2)	14.18
62	12.47
(6)	13.42, 13.43
68	14.17, 14.18, 16.37, 16.38
68C	13.42
(3)	13.54
69	3.21, 14.16
(2)	3.21
(2D)	14.17
(2E)	14.17
70	14.38
71(1)	14.39
(2)	14.40
(3)	14.39, 14.42
72	13.29, 14.40
73(1)(b)	13.29
76	16.37
(1A)	14.49, 14.59
77	14.47, 16.45, 17.30, 17.38
(1)	17.38
(2), (2A)	14.41, 17.38
(3A), (3B)	14.41
(4), (4A)	14.43
(5)	14.44
(8)	14.45
78	17.30
79	17.30
79B	17.25
80	14.60, 17.25, 17.30
81	14.60
82	14.60
83A	17.25
85	14.59
86	13.54, 16.45, 17.26
(1)(a)	14.52
(c)	14.52
(d)	14.52
87	8.59, 16.43, 16.44, 17.26
(4), (5)	14.57

Taxation of Chargeable Gains Act 1992 – *contd*

s 87(7)	14.57
89	14.58
(2)	8.59
90	14.59
91	13.53, 14.58
97(1)	17.27
100(1)	9.14
109	11.53
115	6.19
116(10)	6.19
(11)	6.19
122	5.4, 7.20
(1)	7.22
(2)	7.33
(4)	7.33
(5)	7.34
126	11.10, 11.28, 11.43
127	4.67, 6.17, 11.10, 11.28, 11.43
128	11.10, 11.28, 11.43
(2)	7.42, 7.54
129–134	11.10, 11.28, 11.43
135	4.55, 6.20, 11.10, 11.28, 11.43
136	4.55, 7.40, 11.10, 11.28, 11.43
137	6.18
138	6.18
138A	6.23, 6.24, 6.25
(2A)	6.25
139	7.40, 8.61
(7)	15.13
150A	2.53
150B	2.53
150C	2.53, 9.9
150D	2.53
151	4.32
152	12.20
154	2.37
161	4.31
162	2.21, 2.39, 2.40, 2.41, 2.43, 2.44, 2.45, 2.46, 2.4, 2.51, 2.52, 2.72, 2.9, 2.94, 2.95, 2.100, 5.1, 8.62, 9.10
(1)	2.40
(4)	2.42

Taxation of Chargeable Gains Act 1992 – *contd*

s 162A	2.45, 2.46
(5)	2.46
163	9.10
164	9.10
165	2.21, 2.39, 2.47, 2.49, 2.51, 2.52, 2.56, 2.93, 2.100, 9.10, 11.53, 12.24, 12.31, 14.38, 14.39, 16.17
165(1)(a)	2.48
(b)	2.49
(2)(a)(i)	2.47
(4)	2.48
(6)	2.50
(7)	2.50
166–169	9.10
169B	12.36
169D	15.27
170	9.10
(3)	4.27
(7)	4.27
(8)	4.27
(10)	4.28, 4.48
171	4.29, 4.30, 4.31, 4.31, 4.32, 4.37, 4.67, 8.61, 9.10
(1)	4.55, 4.55, 4.57
(2)	4.30
(3A)	4.30
171A	4.37
173	4.31
(1)	4.31
(2)	4.31
176	4.51, 4.52, 4.54
177	4.51, 4.52, 4.53
177A	4.45, 17.50
177B	17.50, 17.51
179	4.32, 4.33, 4.36, 4.54, 4.56, 4.72, 17.77
(1)	17.79
(2)	4.32, 4.33, 4.34, 17.78
(10)	17.78
a)	4.33
179A	4.36
181	4.35
(4)	4.35
184A	4.45, 4.49, 4.50
184B	4.45, 4.50

Taxation of Chargeable Gains Act 1992 – *contd*

s 185	8.88
190	4.36
209(1)	7.20
210	9.28
222	15.11
(1)	15.3, 15.8, 15.9
(5)	15.9, 15.16
(6)	16.29
(7)	16.30
(8)	15.14
223(1)	15.8, 16.31
(2)(a)	15.17
(c)	15.17
(3)	15.9
b)	15.17
(4)	15.18, 15.19
224(1)	15.19, 15.20
(3)	15.3
225	15.26, 15.27, 16.36
226	15.24
(6)	15.24
226A	15.27, 15.28
226B	15.27
249	3.24
251	15.50
(6)	6.20
253	7.49, 7.50, 7.51, 7.52, 7.53, 7.54, 7.55, 7.56
(1)	7.50
(3)	7.49, 7.50, 7.53
(a)	7.51, 7.56
(3A)	7.49
(4)(c)	7.53
254	7.55
260	12.29, 12.30, 14.38, 14.39, 15.27, 15.27, 15.28
(2)(b)	14.38
262	2.35
263	2.35
268	12.20, 12.30
269	11.3
279A	6.22
280	3.41, 6.4
286	16.14
(6)	2.38
288(1)	4.49
(3)	16.12
475	14.16

Table of statutes

Taxation of Chargeable Gains Act 1992 – *contd*
s 476 .... 14.16
Pt IV, Ch 2 .... 3.24
Sch 1
  para 2 .... 14.36
    (7) 14.37
Sch A1
  para 2(1) 6.10
    (2) 6.10
    (4) 3.44
  para 3(2), (3) 7.26
  para 6(1) 3.44
    b) 6.17
  para 9 .... 15.21
  para 11A 3.44, 7.24, 7.26
    (1)–(4) 7.25
  para 15 .... 6.10, 16.13
  para 16 .... 6.19
  para 21 .... 7.26
  para 22A(1) 3.9, 3.45
Sch 2
  para 6 .... 13.54
Sch 4A
  para 1–8 .... 14.59
  para 10(2) 14.59
Sch 4B 14.66
  para 1 .... 14.62
  para 2 .... 14.63
  para 5 .... 14.63
  para 6 .... 14.64
  para 11 .... 14.65
Sch 4C 14.66, 17.28
Sch 5
  para 2 .... 16.45, 17.24
    (1) 14.55
    (3) 14.55
    (4), (5) 14.56
  para 2A 14.56, 17.24
  para 9(1)–(6A) 14.53
    (10C), (10D) 14.54
Sch 5B 2.39, 2.53, 2.55
  para 1(2) 2.54
  para 2(1) 2.54
  para 13 .... 2.55
Sch 7A 4.45, 4.46
  para 1(2) 4.46, 17.51
    (6) 4.48
  para 2 .... 4.46
  para 5 .... 4.46

Taxation of Chargeable Gains Act 1992 – *contd*
Sch 7A – *contd*
  para 7 .... 4.47
    (1) 17.50
  para 9(6) 4.48
Sch 7AA 4.45, 4.50
Sch 7AC 4.51, 4.63, 4.67, 4.68
  Pt 1 .... 4.60
  para 2 .... 4.65
  para 3 .... 4.65, 4.66
    (2)(d), (e) 4.66
    (3) 4.66
  para 4(1) 4.67
  para 5 .... 4.68
  para 6 .... 4.67
  para 8 .... 4.61
  para 9 .... 4.61, 4.67
  para 10 .... 4.67
  para 20–22 .... 4.64
  para 30 .... 4.65
Taxes Management Act 1970
s 32 .... 3.71
Sch 1B
  para 2 .... 7.48
Trustee Act 1925 .... 13.10
s 33 .... 13.59
  (1) 14.85
s 37(1)(c) 14.61
Trustee Act 2000 .... 13.10
s 32 .... 13.10
Trustee Delegation Act 1999 ...... 13.10
Trusts of Land and Appointment of Trustees Act 1996 .... 12.8, 13.77, 13.79
Value Added Tax Act 1994
s 43 .... 1.67
  43A(1) 17.59
  43AA 17.60
  43B(5) 17.63
  43C 17.64
  43D 17.64
  45(1) 1.51
  49(2) 1.53, 1.68
Sch 1
  para 1A(2) 17.58
  para 2 .... 17.55
    (2) 17.55
    (4) 17.56
    (6), (7) 17.56

Value Added Tax Act 1994 – *contd*
  Sch 4
    para 5 .... 2.86
  Sch 9
    para 2 .... 17.62
    para 3 .... 17.61

Value Added Tax Act 1994 – *contd*
  Sch 9A 17.62
    para 1 .... 17.61
       (4) 17.61

Table of statutory instruments

Accounts of Small and
  Medium-Sized Enterprises
  and Audit Exemption
  (Amendment)
  Regulations 2004,
  SI 2004/16 .... 1.10
Charge to Income Tax by
  Reference to Enjoyment of
  Property Previously Owned
  Regulations 2005,
  SI 2005/724 .... 15.54, 15.55
  reg 5 .... 15.61
Corporation Tax (Treatment of
  Unrelieved Surplus Advance
  Corporation Tax)
  Regulations 1999,
  SI 1999/358 .... 3.43
CTT (Settled Property Income
  Yield) Order 1975,
  SI 1975/610 .... 14.77
Family Provision (Intestate
  Succession) Order 1993,
  SI 1993/2906 .... 13.12
Occupational Pension Schemes
  (Cross-border Activities)
  Regulations 2005,
  SI 2005/3381 .... 10.111
Occupational Pension Schemes
  (Investment)
  Regulations 2005,
  SI 2005/3378 .... 10.31, 10.110
Pension Schemes (Prescribed
  Interest Rates for Authorised
  Employer Loans)
  Regulations 2005,
  SI 2005/3449 .... 10.32
Registered Pension Schemes
  (Modification of Rules of
  Existing Schemes)
  Regulations 2006,
  SI 2006/364 .... 10.103

Registered Pension Schemes
  (Provision of Information)
  Regulations 2006,
  SI 2006/567 .... 10.87
Social Security (Contributions)
  Regulations 2001,
  SI 2001/1004 .... 10.77
  reg 21 .... 2.31
Stamp Duty (Exempt
  Instruments Regulations)
  1987, SI 1987/516 ... 13.52, 13.87
Taxation of Income from Land
  (Non-Residents)
  Regulations 1995,
  SI 1995/2902 .... 8.53
Taxation of Pension Schemes
  (Transitional Provisions)
  Order 2006, SI 2006/572 ... 10.87
Taxation of Pension Schemes
  (Transitional Provisons)
  (Amendment No 2) Order,
  SI 2006/04 .... 10.57
Value Added Tax
  Regulations 1995,
  SI 1995/2518
  art 6 .... 2.88
Value Added Tax (Group
  Eligibility) Order 2004,
  SI 2004/1931 .... 17.60
Value Added Tax (Special
  Provisions) Order 1995,
  SI 1995/1268
  art 5 .... 2.86
    (2), (2A) 2.87

Table of European legislation

Directive 2003/41/EC (Pensions Directive) 10.110

Directive (draft) (Pension Portability Directive) 10.115

Table of cases

Abbott v IRC (1995) Sp C 58 .... 1.121
Allerton Motors, Re, VTD 9427 .... 17.57
Allum v Marsh [2005] STC (SCD) 191 .... 3.12, 3.15, 3.16, 3.61
Anand v CIR [1997] SSCD 58, SpC 107 .... 13.90
Anysz v IRC [1977] STC 296, 53 TC 601 .... 17.10
Balloon Promotions Ltd v Wilson (Inspector of Taxes) [2006] STC (SCD) 167, [2006] SWTI 623, SpC 524 .... 5.15
Barclay's Bank Trust Co Ltd v IRC [1998] STC (SCD) 125 .... 11.17
Barclays Mercantile Business Finance Ltd v Mawson (Inspector of Taxes) [2004] UKHL 51, [2005] 1 AC 684, [2005] 1 All ER 97, [2004] 3 WLR 1383, [2005] STC 1, 76 TC 446, [2004] NLJR 1830, (2004) Times, 27 November, [2004] All ER (D) 389 (Nov) 17.91, 17.93
Batey (Inspector of Taxes) v Wakefield [1982] 1 All ER 61, 125 Sol Jo 498, [1981] STC 521, 55 TC 550, [1981] TR 251, [1982] RVR 11, CA 15.6
Beatty's (Admiral Earl) Executors v IRC (1940) 23 TC 574, 19 ATC 419 .... 17.19
Beckman v IRC [2000] STC (SCD) 59 .... 2.79, 11.29, 11.32
Beni-Felkai Mining Co Ltd, Re [1934] Ch 406, 18 TC 632, 103 LJ Ch 187, [1934] B & CR 14, [1933] All ER Rep 693, 78 Sol Jo 29, 150 LT 370 .... 7.15
Billingham (Inspector of Taxes) v Cooper [2000] STC 122, 74 TC 139, sub nom Cooper v Billingham (Inspector of Taxes) [2000] 06 LS Gaz R 36, 144 Sol Jo LB 85; affd sub nom Billingham (Inspector of Taxes) v Cooper [2001] EWCA Civ 1041, [2001] STC 1177, 74 TC 139 .... 17.27
Brown's Executors v IRC [1997] STC (SCD) 277 .... 11.7, 11.18
Buccleuch (Duke) v IRC [1967] 1 AC 506, [1967] 1 All ER 129, [1967] 2 WLR 207, 45 ATC 472, [1966] TR 393, 111 Sol Jo 18, [1967] RVR 25, 42, 201 Estates Gazette 109 .... 12.18
Bullock (Inspector of Taxes) v Unit Construction Co Ltd [1959] Ch 147, [1958] 3 All ER 186, [1958] 3 WLR 504, 38 TC 712, 37 ATC 292, 51 R & IT 625, [1958] TR 277, 102 Sol Jo 654 .... 8.78
Burkinyoung (Burkinyoung's Executors) v IRC [1995] STC (SCD) 29 .... 12.51
Butler (Inspector of Taxes) v Wildin [1989] STC 22, 61 TC 666 .... 14.20, 17.33
Cannon Industries Ltd v Edwards (Inspector of Taxes) [1966] 1 All ER 456, [1966] 1 WLR 580, 42 TC 625, 44 ATC 391, [1965] TR 385, 110 Sol Jo 55 .... 17.43
Chamberlain (J O) v Customs and Excise Comrs [1989] STC 505 .... 17.57
Chinn v Collins (Inspector of Taxes) [1981] AC 533, [1981] 1 All ER 189, [1981] 2 WLR 14, [1981] STC 1, 54 TC 311, [1980] TR 467, 125 Sol Jo 49; L(TC) 2817 .... 17.33
Clark and another (executors of Clark, dec'd) v HMRC [2005] STC (SCD) 823 .... 11.6

Table of cases

Coe (DJ & Mrs I R), Re, VTD 10911 .... 17.57
Cooper v Cadwalader (1904) 5 TC 101, 42 SLR 117, 7 F 146, 12 SLT
  449 .... 8.19
Copeman (Inspector of Taxes) v Coleman [1939] 2 KB 484,
  [1939] 3 All ER 224, 108 LJKB 813, 83 Sol Jo 623, 22 TC 594, 18
  ATC 109 .... 14.20, 17.33
Copeman (Inspector of Taxes) v William Flood & Sons Ltd [1941] 1 KB
  202, 110 LJKB 215, 24 TC 53, 19 ATC 521 .... 1.106, 1.121
Cottle v Coldicott (Inspector of Taxes) [1995] STC (SCD) 239 .... 12.53
Crosby (Trustees) v Broadhurst [2004] STC (SCD) 348 .... 7.52
Crossland (Inspector of Taxes) v Hawkins (1960) 39 TC 493, 39 ATC 461,
  53 R & IT 758, [1960] TR 297; on appeal [1961] Ch 537,
  [1961] 2 All ER 812, [1961] 3 WLR 202, 39 TC 493, 40 ATC 126,
  [1961] TR 113, 105 Sol Jo 424, CA 14.20, 17.33
Dalgety v IRC (1941) 24 TC 280 .... 14.20
De Beers Consolidated Mines Ltd v Howe (Surveyor of Taxes) [1906] AC
  455, 5 TC 198, 75 LJKB 858, 13 Mans 394, 50 Sol Jo 666, 95 LT 221,
  22 TLR 756, [1904–7] All ER Rep Ext 1256 .... 8.77
Dixon v IRC [2002] STC (SCD) 53 .... 12.46
Dollar (t/a I J Dollar) v Lyon (Inspector of Taxes) [1981] STC 333, 54 TC
  459 .... 1.106
Dunlop International AG v Pardoe (Inspector of Taxes) [1999] STC 909 .... 4.33
Evans (EM, PG & CP), Re, VTD 10532 .... 17.57
Falmer Jeans Ltd v Rodin (Inspector of Taxes) [1990] STC 270, 63 TC 55 ..... 17.41
Farmer and another (executors of Farmer, dec'd) v IRC [1999] STC (SCD)
  321 .... 11.27, 12.6
Faulkner (trustee of Adams, dec'd) v IRC [2001] STC (SCD) 112 .... 13.16
Fetherstonaugh v IRC [1985] Ch 1, [1984] 3 WLR 212, [1984] STC 261,
  128 Sol Jo 302 .... 11.3, 11.12
Five Oaks Properties v HMRC [2006] STC (SCD) 769 .... 4.48
Frankland v IRC [1996] STC 735; [1997] STC 1450 .... 13.59, 13.108
Fraser (A E & M E), Re, VTD 16761 .... 17.57
Furniss (Inspector of Taxes) v Dawson [1984] AC 474, [1984] 1 All ER
  530, [1984]2 WLR 226, 128 Sol Jo 132, [1984] STC 153, 55 TC
  324, HL 2.43, 3.61, 17.100, 13.69, 17.90, 17.92
G W and J A Green v Customs and Excise Commissioners (1992, Decision
  9016) 2.94
Gaines-Cooper v Revenue and Customs Comrs [2007] STC(SCD) 23, SpC
  568 .... 8.23
Gordon & Blair Ltd v IRC 40 TC 358, 41 ATC 111, [1962] TR 161, 1962
  SC 267, 1962 SLT 373, Ct of Sess 17.43
Gregario (D) & Sons, Re, VTD 9105 .... 17.57
Griffin (Inspector of Taxes) v Craig-Harvey [1994] STC 54, 66 TC 396 .... 15.10,
  15.11
Hancock (Surveyor of Taxes) v General Reversionary and
  Investment Co Ltd [1919] 1 KB 25, 88 LJKB 248, 119 LT 737, 35
  TLR 11, 7 TC 358 .... 7.3
Hardcastle (Vernede's Executors) v IRC [2000] STC (SCD) 532 .... 11.13
Harding (executors of Loveday) v IRC [1997] STC (SCD) 321 .... 13.59
Harris (A & J), Re, VTD 4882 .... 17.57

Table of cases

Harrold (Harrold's executors) v IRC [1996] STC (SCD) 195 .... 12.46
Harvey (Inspector of Taxes) v Sivyer [1986] Ch 119, [1985] 2 All ER
   1054, [1985] 3 WLR 261, [1985] STC 434, 58 TC 569, [1986] 1 FLR
   72, [1986] Fam Law 17, 129 Sol Jo 524, [1985] LS Gaz R 216 .... 16.10
Head (A D), Re, VTD 4828 .... 17.57
Hertford (Marquess) v IRC [2005] STC (SCD) 177 .... 11.13
Higginson's Executors v IRC [2002] STC (SCD) 483, SpC 337 .... 12.47
Holland (Holland's Executor) v IRC [2003] STC (SCD) 43, 147 Sol Jo LB
   267 .... 13.58
Holt (Tracey J), Re, VTD 10942 .... 17.57
Hood-Barrs v IRC [1946] 2 All ER 768, 27 TC 385, 25 ATC 375, 40 R &
   IT 77, 91 Sol Jo 84, 176 LT 283 .... 14.20
Ingram (Executors of Lady Ingram's Estate) v IRC [1997] 4 All ER 395,
   [1997] STC 1234, [1997] NPC 129, 141 Sol Jo LB 204,
   [1997] 34 LS Gaz R 29, CA; revsd [2000] 1 AC 293; [1999] 1 All ER
   297, [1999] 2 WLR 90, [1999] STC 37, 143 Sol Jo LB 52,
   [1999] 03 LS Gaz R 32, HL 15.46
IRC v Brackett [1986] STC 521, 60 TC 134 .... 17.20
IRC v Buchanan [1958] Ch 289, [1957] 2 All ER 400, [1957] 3 WLR 68,
   37 TC 365, 36 ATC 36, 50 R & IT 223, [1957] TR 43, 100 Sol Jo 502,
   L(TC) 1823 .... 14.20, 17.33
IRC v Cleary [1966] Ch 365, [1966] 2 All ER 19, [1966] 2 WLR 790, 110
   Sol Jo 190, 44 TC 399, [1966] TR 39, CA 17.10
IRC v Cosmotron Manufacturing Co Ltd [1997] 1 WLR 1288, [1997] STC
   1134, 70 TC 292, 141 Sol Jo LB 215 .... 7.6
IRC v Duke of Westminster [1936] AC 1, [1935] All ER Rep 259, 104
   LJKB 383, 153 LT 223, 51 TLR 467, 79 Sol Jo 362, sub nom Duke of
   Westminster v IRC 19 TC 490, 14 ATC 77, HL 17.89
IRC v Eversden [2003] EWCA Civ 668, [2003] STC 822,
   [2003] 27 LS Gaz R 38, 147 Sol Jo LB 594 .... 9.38, 15.38, 15.45, 15.47
IRC v Forsyth Grant (1943) 25 TC 369, 1943 SC 528 .... 12.50
IRC v George [2003] EWCA Civ 1763, [2004] STC 147, 75 TC 735,
   [2004] 03 LS Gaz R 34, Times, 9 December, [2003] All ER (D) 102
   (Dec), [2003] SWTI 2276 .... 11.5
IRC v Gray (Executor of Lady Fox) [1994] STC 360, [1994] RVR 129 . 12.18, 12.22
IRC v Horrocks [1968] 3 All ER 296, [1968] 1 WLR 1809, 44 TC 645, 47
   ATC 279, [1968] TR 233, 112 Sol Jo 786 .... 17.10
IRC v Joiner [1975] 1 All ER 755, [1975] 1 WLR 273, 119 Sol Jo 137,
   [1975] STC 200, 50 TC 449, [1974] TR 383, CA; affd [1975] 3 All ER
   1050, [1975] 1 WLR 1701, 119 Sol Jo 827, [1975] STC 657, 50 TC
   449, [1975] TR 257, HL 5.17, 7.39, 7.40, 17.10
IRC v Laird Group plc [2002] EWCA Civ 576, [2002] STC 722, 75 TC
   399, (2002) Times, 22 May, [2002] All ER (D) 306 (Apr) 5.17
IRC v Leiner (1964) 41 TC 589, 43 ATC 56, [1964] TR 63, L(TC) 2091 ...... 14.20,
                                                                                                                      17.33
IRC v Lloyds Private Banking Ltd [1998] STC 559, [1998] 2 FCR 41,
   [1999] 1 FLR 147, [1999] Fam Law 309, [1998] 19 LS Gaz R 23, 142
   Sol Jo LB 164, [1998] All ER (D) 124 .... 13.16, 13.78, 15.66
IRC v Mallender (Drury-Lowe's Executors). See Mallender (Drury-Lowe's
   Executors) v IRC

Table of cases

IRC v Morton (1941) 24 TC 259, 1941 SC 467, 1941 SLT 388 .... 14.20, 17.33
IRC v Muller & Co's Margarine Ltd [1901] AC 217, 70 LJKB 677, 49 WR
 603, [1900–3] All ER Rep 413, 84 LT 729, 17 TLR 530, HL 2.59
IRC v Parker [1966] AC 141, [1966] 1 All ER 399, [1966] 2 WLR 486,
 110 Sol Jo 91, 43 TC 396, [1966] TR 1, HL 17.10
IRC v Payne (1940) 23 TC 610, 110 LJKB 323 .... 14.20
IRC v Plummer [1980] AC 896, [1979] 3 All ER 775, [1979] 3 WLR 689,
 123 Sol Jo 769, [1979] STC 793, 54 TC 1, [1979] TR 339, HL 14.19
IRC v Prince-Smith [1943] 1 All ER 434, 25 TC 84, 168 LT 406 .... 14.20
IRC v Schroder [1983] STC 480, 57 TC 94 .... 17.19
IRC v Tennant (1942) 24 TC 215, 167 LT 159 .... 14.20
IRC v Trustees of Sema Group Pension Scheme [2002] EWCA Civ 1857,
 [2003] STC 95, 74 TC 593, [2003] 10 LS Gaz R 30, (2003) Times,
 17 January, [2002] All ER (D) 304 (Dec) 17.10
IRC v Universities Superannuation Scheme Ltd [1997] STC 1, 70 TC 193 ..... 17.10
IRC v Wachtel [1971] Ch 573, [1971] 1 All ER 271, [1970] 3 WLR 857,
 46 TC 543, 49 ATC 204, [1970] TR 195, 114 Sol Jo 705 .... 14.20, 17.33
IRC v Wiggins [1979] 2 All ER 245, [1979] 1 WLR 325, 122 Sol Jo 863,
 [1979] STC 244, 53 TC 639, [1978] TR 393 .... 17.10
Jaggers v Ellis [1997] STC 1417, 71 TC 164, [1997] 46 LS Gaz R 29 .... 12.64
Jamieson v Customs and Excise [2002] STC 1418, [2001] All ER (D) 139
 (Jun) 1.52
Jarvis (P & R), Re, VTD 3920 .... 17.57
Jasmine Trustees Ltd v Wells & Hind (a firm) [2007] EWHC 38 (Ch),
 [2007] 1 All ER 1142, [2007] 3 WLR 810, [2007] STC 660, (2007)
 Times, 12 February, [2007] SWTI 261, [2007] All ER (D) 112 (Jan) 14.61
Johnston Publishing (North) Ltd v HMRC [2007] All ER (D) 240 .... 4.34, 17.78
Jones v Garnett (Inspector of Taxes) [2005] STC (SCD) 9 (SPC 432),
 [2004] SWTI 2263; affd [2005] STC 1667, (2005) Times, 17 May,
 [2005] SWTI 903, [2005] All ER (D) 396 (Apr); [2007] UKHL 35,
 [2007] 1 WLR 2030, [2007] STC 1536, [2007] ICR 1259, [2007] NLJR
 1118, (2007) Times, 9 August, [2007] SWTI 1899, [2007] All ER (D)
 390 (Jul) 1.70, 1.124, 1.127, 2.98, 14.29, 17.3, 17.34
Jowett (Inspector of Taxes) v O'Neill and Brennan Construction Ltd
 [1998] STC 482, 70 TC 566, [1998] 16 LS Gaz R 25, 142 Sol Jo LB
 124 .... 11.15
Judge (personal representatives of Walden, dec'd) v Revenue and Customs
 Comrs [2005] SWTI 1800, (2005) SpC 506 .... 13.17, 13.78
Kawthar Consulting Ltd v Revenue and Customs Comrs [2005] SWTI
 1237 .... 17.43
Kneen (Inspector of Taxes) v Martin [1935] 1 KB 499, 19 TC 33, 13 ATC
 454, 104 LJKB 361, [1934] All ER Rep 595, 79 Sol Jo 31, 152 LT
 337 .... 8.36
Lee (I & A J), Re, VTD 2640 .... 17.57
Lee v IRC (1941) 24 TC 207, 22 ATC 393 .... 17.19
Levene v IRC [1928] AC 217, 13 TC 486, 97 LJKB 377, [1928] All ER
 Rep 746, 72 Sol Jo 270, 139 LT 1, 44 TLR 374 .... 8.22
Lewis (A S), Re, VTD 3329 .... 17.57
Lloyds TSB (Personal Representative of Antrobus) v IRC [2002] STC
 (SCD) 468, 146 Sol Jo LB 249 .... 12.2, 12.16, 12.46, 12.49

Table of cases

Lloyds TSB Private Banking plc (personal representative of Rosemary
   Antrobus, dec'd) v HMRC DET/47/2005 .... 12.16, 12.17, 12.40, 12.49
Longson v Baker (Inspector of Taxes) [2000] STC (SCD) 244; affd
   [2001] STC 6, 73 TC 415, [2001] 03 LS Gaz R 43 .... 15.7
Lowenstein v De Salis (Inspector of Taxes) (1926) 10 TC 424, 161 LT Jo
   235 .... 8.19
Lubbock Fine & Co v Customs and Excise Comrs Case C-63/92
   [1994] QB 571, [1994] 3 All ER 705, [1993] ECR I-6665,
   [1994] 3 WLR 261, [1994] 2 CMLR 633, [1994] STC 101 .... 12.55
Lyons (I), Re, VTD 2451 .... 17.57
Lysaght v IRC [1927] 2 KB 55, 13 TC 511, 6 ATC 326, 96 LJKB 462, 71
   Sol Jo 253, 137 LT 70, 43 TLR 337 .... 8.19, 8.20, 8.22
McKenna v HMRC [2006] SpC00565 .... 12.49, 12.60
MacNiven (Inspector of Taxes) v Westmoreland Investments Ltd
   [2001] UKHL 6, [2003] 1 AC 311, [2001] 1 All ER 865,
   [2001] 2 WLR 377, [2001] STC 237, 73 TC 1, 145 Sol Jo LB 55, sub
   nom Westmoreland Investments Ltd v MacNiven (Inspector of Taxes)
   [2001] NLJR 223 .... 17.90, 17.93
Mallender (Drury-Lowe's Executors) v IRC [2000] STC (SCD) 574; revsd
   sub nom IRC v Mallender (Drury-Lowe's Executors) [2001] STC 514 .... 12.41
Marks & Spencer plc v Halsey (Inspector of Taxes) Case C-446/03
   [2006] Ch 184, [2006] All ER (EC) 255, [2006] 2 WLR 250,
   [2006] STC 237, (2005) Times, 15 December, [2005] All ER (D) 174
   (Dec) 4.14, 4.20
Marks v McNally (2004) STC (SCD) 503 .... 7.45
Marren (Inspector of Taxes) v Ingles [1980] 3 All ER 95, [1980] 1 WLR
   983, 124 Sol Jo 562, [1980] STC 500, 54 TC 76, [1980] TR 335, HL 6.21,
                                                                                        6.22, 6.25
Marshall (Inspector of Taxes) v Kerr [1993] STC 360, 67 TC 56,
   [1993] 14 LS Gaz R 45, CA; revsd [1995] 1 AC 148, [1994] 3 All ER
   106, [1994] 3 WLR 299, 138 Sol Jo LB 155, [1994] STC 638, 67 TC
   56, HL 13.42, 13.43, 13.54
Martin (Moore's Executors) v IRC [1995] STC (SCD) 5 .... 12.51
Mills v IRC [1973] Ch 225, [1972] 3 All ER 977, [1972] 3 WLR 980,
   [1973] STC 1, 49 TC 367, 51 ATC 263, [1972] TR 245, 116 Sol Jo
   802, L(TC) 2467 .... 14.20
Moody v Tyler (Inspector of Taxes) [2000] STC 296 .... 3.15
Moore v Thompson (Inspector of Taxes) [1986] STC 170, 61 TC 15,
   [1986] LS Gaz R 1559 .... 15.8
National Provident Institution v Brown (Surveyor of Taxes) [1921] 2 AC
   222, 8 TC 57, 90 LJKB 1009, 125 LT 417, 37 TLR 804 .... 8.37
National Westminster Bank plc, Re, VTD 15514 .... 17.63
New Angel Court Ltd v Adam (Inspector of Taxes) [2004] EWCA Civ
   242, [2004] 1 WLR 1988, [2004] STC 779, (2004) Times, 12 April,
   148 Sol Jo LB 357, [2004] All ER (D) 294 (Mar) 4.31
Old Farm Service Station Ltd, Re, VTD 4261 .... 17.57
O'Neill v IRC [1998] STC (SCD) 110 .... 13.92
Osman v Customs and Excise Comrs [1991] 3 CMLR 262, [1989] STC
   596 .... 17.57

Table of cases

Owen v Elliott (Inspector of Taxes) [1989] 1 WLR 162, [1989] STC 44, 63
TC 319, [1989] 2 LS Gaz R 39; revsd [1990] Ch 786, [1990] 3 WLR
133, 134 Sol Jo 861, [1990] STC 469, 63 TC 319,
[1990] 23 LS Gaz R 31, CA 15.19
Phillips and others (Executors of Rhoda Phillips, dec'd) v HMRC (2006)
SpC 555 .... 11.6, 11.22
Phizackerley (personal representative of Phizackerley, decd) v Revenue and
Customs Comrs [2007] SWTI 559, (2007) SpC 00591 .... 13.63, 13.109, 15.70,
16.23
Potts' Executors v IRC [1951] AC 443, [1951] 1 All ER 76, 32 TC 211, 44
R & IT 136, [1950] TR 379, [1951] 1 TLR 152, L(TC) 1538 .... 17.36
Pritchard (Inspector of Taxes) v MH Builders (Wilmslow) Ltd
[1969] 2 All ER 670, [1969] 1 WLR 409, 45 TC 360, 47 ATC 453,
[1968] TR 429, 113 Sol Jo 285, L(TC) 2296 .... 17.42
R v Dimsey [2001] UKHL 46, [2002] 1 AC 509, [2001] 4 All ER 786,
[2001] 3 WLR 843, [2002] 1 Cr App Rep 167, [2001] STC 1520, 74
TC 263, [2001] All ER (D) 157 (Oct) 17.19
R v IRC, ex p Newfields Developments Ltd [1999] STC 373, 73 TC 532;
on appeal [2000] STC 52, 73 TC 532, CA; revsd [2001] UKHL 27,
[2001] 4 All ER 400, [2001] 1 WLR 1111, 73 TC 532, [2001] STC
901, [2001] 26 LS Gaz R 45 .... 1.90
Ramsay (W T) Ltd v IRC [1982] AC 300, [1981] 1 All ER 865,
[1981] 2 WLR 449, 125 Sol Jo 220, [1981] STC 174, 54 TC 101,
[1982] TR 123, HL 2.43, 13.29, 13.41, 17.99, 17.89, 17.103, 17.104
Ramsden v IRC (1957) 37 TC 619, 36 ATC 325, 50 R & IT 662, [1957]
TR 247 .... 17.19
Reed (Inspector of Taxes) v Clark [1986] Ch 1, [1985] 3 WLR 142,
[1985] STC 323, 58 TC 528, 129 Sol Jo 469, [1985] LS Gaz R 2016 ...... 8.13,
8.14, 8.22
Reed v Nova Securities Ltd [1985] 1 All ER 686, [1985] 1 WLR 193,
[1985] STC 124, 59 TC 516, 129 Sol Jo 116 .... 4.31
Revenue and Customs Comrs v Salaried Persons Postal Loans Ltd
[2006] EWHC 763 (Ch), [2006] STC 1315, (2006) Times, 20 April,
[2006] SWTI 1269, [2006] All ER (D) 93 (Apr) 11.16
Robson v Dixon (Inspector of Taxes) [1972] 3 All ER 671, [1972] 1 WLR
1493, 116 Sol Jo 863, [1972] TR 163, 48 TC 527, 51 ATC 179 .... 8.41
Rogers (decd), Re [2006] EWHC 753 (Ch), [2006] 2 All ER 792,
[2006] 1 WLR 1577, [2006] NLJR 644, (2006) Times, 3 May, [2006]
All ER (D) 68 (Apr) 13.4
Rogers v IRC (1879) 1 TC 255 .... 8.13
Rolls-Royce Motors Ltd v Bamford (Inspector of Taxes) [1976] STC 162,
51 TC 319 .... 4.43
Rosser v IRC [2003] STC (SCD) 311 .... 12.35, 12.45, 12.47, 12.49
Roy (J), Re, VTD 9384 .... 17.57
Rysaffe Trustees (CI) Ltd v IRC [2003] EWCA Civ 356, [2003] STC 536,
[2003] 22 LS Gaz R 31, (2003) Times, 29 April, 147 Sol Jo LB 388,
[2003] All ER (D) 295 (Mar) 11.52, 12.30, 13.69
Saunders (H) and Sorrell (TG) v Customs & Excise Commissioners (1980)
VATTR 51 .... 1.60
Scottish Provident Institution v Allen (1901) 4 TC 409 .... 8.36

Table of cases

Shah v Barnet London Borough Council [1983] 2 AC 309,
 [1983] 1 All ER 226, [1983] 2 WLR 16, 81 LGR 305, 127 Sol Jo 36 .... 8.22
Sharkey (Inspector of Taxes) v Wernher [1953] Ch 782, [1953] 2 All ER
 791, [1953] 3 WLR 549, 97 Sol Jo 573, 36 TC 275, [1953] TR 317, 46
 R & IT 562, 32 ATC 328; on appeal [1954] Ch 713, [1954] 2 All ER
 753, [1954] 3 WLR 367, 98 Sol Jo 556, 36 TC 275, 47 R & IT 545,
 sub nom Wernher v Sharkey (Inspector of Taxes) [1954] TR 273, 33
 ATC 284, CA; revsd sub nom Sharkey (Inspector of Taxes) v Wernher
 [1956] AC 58, [1955] 3 All ER 493, [1955] 3 WLR 671, 99 Sol Jo 793,
 36 TC 275, [1955] TR 277, 48 R & IT 739, 34 ATC 263, HL 4.31
Smith and others [2007] SpC 605 .... 12.30
South West Launderettes Ltd, Re, VTD 2608 .... 17.57
Soutter's Executory v IRC [2002] STC (SCD) 385 .... 13.50
Spence (W P & Mrs D K M), Re, VTD 5698 .... 17.57
Starke v IRC [1994] 1 WLR 888, 138 Sol Jo LB 55, [1994] STC 295,
 [1994] 13 LS Gaz R 37; affd sub nom Starke (Brown's Executors) v
 IRC [1996] 1 All ER 622, [1995] 1 WLR 1439, 139 Sol Jo LB 128,
 [1995] STC 689, [1996] 1 EGLR 157, [1996] 16 EG 115,
 [1995] 23 LS Gaz R 32, CA 12.44, 12.45
Strand Options and Futures Ltd v Vojak (Inspector of Taxes)
 [2003] EWCA Civ 1457, [2004] STC 64, 76 TC 220, [2003] All ER
 (D) 358 (Oct) 3.69
Summers (M J & P), Re, VTD 3498 .... 17.57
Taylor (S & L), Re, VTD 9125 .... 17.57
Thomas v Marshall (Inspector of Taxes) [1953] AC 543, [1953] 1 All ER
 1102, [1953] 2 WLR 944, 34 TC 178, 32 ATC 128, 46 R & IT 295,
 [1953] TR 141, 97 Sol Jo 316, L(TC) 1642 .... 14.20, 17.31
Toshoku Finance UK plc (in liq), Re, Kahn v IRC [2000] 3 All ER 938,
 [2000] 1 WLR 2478, [2000] STC 301, [2000] 1 BCLC 683,
 [2000] 15 LS Gaz R 39, 144 Sol Jo LB 165 .... 7.14
Trippitt (S & A), Re VTD 17340 .... 17.57
TSD & Mrs M E Williams, Re, VTD 2445 .... 17.57
Vandervell v IRC [1967] 2 AC 291, [1967] 1 All ER 1, [1967] 2 WLR 87,
 43 TC 519, 45 ATC 394, [1966] TR 315, 110 Sol Jo 910, L(TC) 2214 .... 14.20
Varty v Lynes [1976] 3 All ER 447, [1976] 1 WLR 1091, 120 Sol Jo 525,
 [1976] STC 508, [1976] TR 209 .... 15.7
Vodafone Cellular Ltd v Shaw (Inspector of Taxes) [1997] STC 734, 69
 TC 376, 141 Sol Jo LB 93 .... 3.17
Walker (D A) v Customs and Excise Commissioners [1976] VATTR 10 .... 2.94
Walker's Executors v IRC [2001] STC (SCD) 86 .... 11.3
Walton's Executors v IRC [1996] STC 68, , [1996] 1 EGLR 159,
 [1996] RVR 55, [1996] 21 EG 144 .... 12.19
West (Inspector of Taxes) v Trennery and other appeals [2003] EWCA Civ
 1792, [2004] STC 170, 76 TC 713, (2004) Times, 23 January, 148 Sol
 Jo LB 56, [2003] All ER (D) 329 (Dec) 14.46
West End Health and Fitness Club, Re, VTD 4070 .... 17.57
Westmoreland Investments Ltd v MacNiven (Inspector of Taxes). See
 MacNiven (Inspector of Taxes) v Westmoreland Investments Ltd
Wheatley (Walter (dec'd), executors of), Re [1998] STC (SCD) 60 .... 12.50

Table of cases

Wilkie v IRC [1952] Ch 153, [1952] 1 All ER 92, 32 TC 495, 31 ATC
442, 45 R & IT 29, [1951] TR 371, 95 Sol Jo 817, [1952] 1 TLR 22,
L(TC) 1565 .... 8.19
Williams v HMRC [2005] SpC 00500 .... 12.1, 12.64
Williams (personal representative of Williams, dec'd) v HMRC
[2005] STC (SCD) 782 .... 12.45
Willis (Inspector of Taxes) v Peeters Picture Frames Ltd [1983] STC 453,
56 TC 436, [1982] 12 NIJB, NI CA 17.47
Wood v Holden (Inspector of Taxes) [2006] EWCA Civ 26, [2006] 1 WLR
1393, [2006] STC 443, 78 TC 1, [2006] 2 BCLC 210, (2006) Times,
20 February, 150 Sol Jo LB 127, [2006] SWTI 236, [2006] All ER (D)
190 (Jan) 8.81
Wood Preservation Ltd v Prior (Inspector of Taxes) [1969] 1 All ER 364,
[1969] 1 WLR 1077, 45 TC 112, 47 ATC 364, [1968] TR 353, 112 Sol
Jo 927, L(TC) 2291 .... 17.42
Woodhall v IRC [2000] STC (SCD) 558 .... 13.16
Yates (Inspector of Taxes) v Starkey [1951] Ch 465, [1951] 1 All ER 732,
[1951]1 TLR 661, 95 Sol Jo 268, 32 TC 38, 30 ATC 33, 44 R & IT
237, CA 17.33
Young, Re (1875) 1 TC 57 .... 8.13
Young (Inspector of Taxes) v Scrutton [1996] STC 743, 70 TC 331 .... 14.20

Chapter 1

Starting a business – choosing an appropriate trading vehicle

Rebecca Cave CTA FCA MBA

INTRODUCTION

1.1 When an individual decides to form a business, he must decide on the most appropriate medium through which to conduct that business. The choice of the business vehicle can contribute to the ultimate successes of the business, as it will affect the tax payments, tax reliefs and the legal obligations of the business owners.

The basic choice for a new UK-based business is between a sole trader, general partnership or limited liability partnership (LLP), or private limited company. Other alternatives for trading structures are the limited partnership, the trading trust, unlimited company, public company, co-operative, or a joint venture arrangement. There are also various types of corporate vehicle that are briefly discussed in paras **1.73** to **1.79**.

WHY THE CHOICE OF TRADING VEHICLE IS IMPORTANT

1.2 Different trading vehicles are subject to different taxes (income tax, corporation tax, capital gains tax, and national insurance), which are applied at various rates (from 10% to 41%, including national insurance), and require the tax to be paid at different times, according to the business structure. The same transaction may produce a different tax charge depending on the type of trading vehicle used, because certain tax charges or reliefs apply to only companies or only to individuals and trustees (see **Table 1.4** in para **1.158**). The choice of vehicle will thus have a significant effect on the quantum and timing of the tax liabilities generated by the business venture.

1.3 *Starting a business – choosing an appropriate trading vehicle*

ISSUES UNDERLYING THE CHOICE

1.3 Some business sectors expect participants to trade in a certain form for traditional or tax-based reasons. In the IT industry consultants or contractors will not normally be directly engaged by a customer unless they operate their business through an intermediate vehicle such as a limited company or partnership. This is primarily to protect the engager from the tax and legal implications of being treated as the employer of the consultant. The consultant may however be subject to the anti-avoidance rules known as IR 35 (see **1.94**), or the additional constraints imposed by the Managed Service Companies legislation (see **1.100**).

In the absence of such external pressures the initial choice of business vehicle will turn on these issues:

- the number of people involved;
- current or future flexibility;
- administrative costs; and
- tax costs.

There are also a number of commercial considerations that should be raised with the client when discussing the trading vehicle to be used to start the business. It is important to note that one form of trading vehicle is rarely suitable for the entire lifetime of the business.

Number of people involved

1.4 The choice of business structure is partly determined by the number of people who will be involved in running and owning the business. A sole trader is restricted to single-person ownership and management. A company may have any number of shareholders, and the directors may also hold shares, but can be appointed by the shareholders to run the company on their behalf. This allows the management of the business to be separated from the ownership.

A partnership also allows a multi-person ownership and, since 2002, there is no restriction on the number of partners that may be involved in the business. Larger partnerships may appoint managers to run the business, but the partners will remain fully liable for the debts of the business unless the partnership is incorporated as an LLP (see **1.61**).

Flexibility

1.5 The future requirement for flexibility is important. As the business grows a different business vehicle may become more appropriate for the business needs, so thought must be given as to how a transition can be made from say a partnership to a limited company. There is no one business structure that suits all businesses at all times. A dynamic business will benefit from a regular review of its structure.

If the business plan involves several separate projects or products that have different chances of succeeding or failing, it may be worthwhile using a separate business vehicle for each one, to isolate these different commercial risks and to ensure that a successful project is not brought down by one that fails. This approach may lead to forming a joint venture company, creating a number of associated companies or a combination of partnerships and companies. A group of related businesses will also allow one project or product line to be extracted and sold on without disturbing the rest of the business.

1.6 A private limited company is a particularly flexible vehicle as it may be owned and run by just one individual, who will normally be the sole director. The only limitation laid down by the *Companies Act 1985* is that a company is obliged to have one director and a company secretary, who, if the company has a sole director, may not be that director (*CA 1985, s 283(2)*). From 1 October 2008 if the company has only one director that director must be a natural person and not a company. The *Companies Act 2006, s 270* will also allow private companies to dispense with the office of company secretary from October 2008, although public companies will still be required to have a company secretary. The company secretary need not hold any shares in the company, and thus need not be a part owner of the business, and need not be involved in the day-to-day running of the business.

Administrative costs

1.7 The administrative costs will tend to be higher where the business vehicle has greater reporting requirements and is subject to more regulation. The costs of running a limited company tend to be greater than those for a general partnership or sole-trader business, although the scale of the organisation and the complexity of the business will have a bearing on the total costs.

1.8 A company can be registered at Companies House and adapted for the client to trade through for as little as £50, but an ordinary partnership or sole-trader business has no such registration costs. An LLP must also be registered at Companies House and the charges are about the same as for a limited company. Limited partnerships are required to be registered with Companies House although the fee is minimal (£2).

1.9 Companies and LLPs must both file annual returns at a cost of £30, although companies can take advantage of a reduced fee by filing electronically. The filing fee must be paid whether or not the business has traded during the year.

1.10 *Starting a business – choosing an appropriate trading vehicle*

1.10 The annual accounts of companies and LLPs must also be filed annually at Companies House and certain of those accounts must be subject to an audit. Most LLPs and companies qualify as 'small' so they may take advantage of the audit exemption, under the *Accounts of Small and Medium-Sized Enterprises and Audit Exemption (Amendment) Regulations 2004, SI 2004/16*. However, some accounts will require an audit for other regulatory reasons, such as in the financial services sector. To qualify as 'small' the company or LLP must meet two of the following three conditions (*CA 1985, s 247/ CA 2006, s 382*):

- annual turnover of £5.6 million or less;
- balance sheet total value of £2.8 million or less;
- average number of employees of no more than 50.

The value of turnover and balance sheet total are likely to be increased to £6.5 million and £1.26 million respectively, possibly from early 2008, following a consultation by the DTI in March 2007. Different limits apply to trading charities.

1.11

Companies and LLPs that qualify as 'small' are also permitted to submit abbreviated accounts to Companies House, which do not include a profit and loss account for the business. This prevents competitors from discovering the business turnover, profit, or whether a dividend has been paid. However, under proposed regulations under the *Companies Act 2006* small and medium-sized companies will be required to include details of the business turnover within the abbreviated accounts. A full set of accounts including profit and loss account must always be submitted to HMIT to support the corporation tax return.

1.12 Partnerships that are not LLPs, and sole-trader businesses are not required to file an annual return, submit to an audit, or file annual accounts at Companies House.

1.13 All businesses should consider registering the trading name and any trademarks to be used with the UK Patents Office. A website address in a recognisable form of the trading name is also essential for most new businesses, and this needs to be reserved with a reputable registration agent.

Tax costs

1.14 The tax cost may be influenced not only by the differing tax rates applicable to the structure (see **1.116**) but also by the possibility of taking advantage of tax breaks only available to say, limited companies, such as:

Starting a business – choosing an appropriate trading vehicle **1.16**

- Enterprise Investment Scheme (EIS) which provides tax relief for investing in unquoted trading companies (see **Chapter 9: Tax efficient investments**);
- Enterprise Management Incentives (EMI) is a share option scheme, which can be used by small companies to attract and retain key individuals to work for the company.
- R&D tax credits which provides an enhanced tax deduction for certain costs incurred in research and development projects; or
- Land Remediation Relief, which provides enhanced tax relief for the cost of cleaning up contaminated land.

1.15 There are a number of tax sensitive decisions for a new business (listed below), which need to be addressed irrespective of the structure adopted:

- choice of accounting date;
- ownership of real property;
- ownership of vehicles;
- ownership of intellectual property;
- how to attract investors;
- how to extract profits;
- how to provide for the proprietor's pension;
- how to pass the business on;
- how to extract capital.

Different business vehicles will produce different costs and results for these issues. For example, the choice of accounting date for an unincorporated business can have a big influence on the timing and quantum of tax in the early years of the business (see para **1.32**), but is not so relevant for a corporate structure.

Commercial considerations

Credibility

1.16 A corporate structure can appear more credible to suppliers and customers, who often tend to perceive most unincorporated businesses as being

1.17 *Starting a business – choosing an appropriate trading vehicle*

small and risky, and so may feel more comfortable dealing with a company. Indeed there may be considerable pressure from customers who receive a personal service from the proprietor of the business for that supplier business to be incorporated.

1.17 A corporate structure has been thought to protect the customer from the strict employment tests that may require a contract with an individual to be treated as an employment contract, and so make the payments under that contract subject to PAYE and national insurance. Where an intermediary, such as a company or partnership or even another individual such as an agent, is placed between the customer and the contractor who provides the personal service, the burdens of PAYE and employment rights for the individual should fall on the intermediary where the IR 35 provisions apply (see para **1.94**).

1.18 An LLP can also offer customers and suppliers a sense of security as the reporting requirements mean the accounts are published for public view at Companies House. However, as this structure is still relatively new, many people are unaware of the difference between traditional partnerships and LLPs and the increased openness of the latter.

Privacy

1.19 Those who prefer to keep the financial affairs of their business as a private matter between themselves and HMRC will see the disclosure requirements of a limited company or LLP as a disadvantage. A solution to this may be to operate as an unlimited company that is exempt from filing its accounts with the Registrar of Companies (*CA 1985, s 254*). Small and medium sized companies as LLPs can protect their commercial details somewhat by submitting abbreviated accounts.

An unlimited company is not exempt from the requirement to submit an annual return to the Registrar of Companies including the names and private addresses of the shareholders and directors. It may be possible to have a nominee company hold your shares, act as company secretary or even as a director, but this extra protection for privacy has to be paid for.

1.20 From 1 October 2008 the requirement for directors to record their personal address on the public register at Companies House is removed. Directors will be able to use a service address, although Companies House will still keep their residential address on a secure register. Partnerships, which are not LLPs need make no public disclosure of their members or of their accounts.

Retention of control

1.21 The majority shareholders in a company who hold more than 50% or 75% of the shares can take the major decisions. The unanimous agreement of partners in a partnership is usually required for all major decisions unless the partnership agreement states otherwise.

1.22 Shares in a private company can be created with diverse rights as to voting, dividends, right to capital on winding-up, and so on. This offers not only great flexibility, but also the opportunity for the original proprietor to retain voting control in the company although he may not, at that stage, be entitled to the largest equity interest in the company. On the death of a shareholder the legal continuity of the business is guaranteed, but there is no automatic continuity on the death of a partner. The business of a sole trader will cease with the individual's death.

Raising finance

1.23 Companies may be able to raise additional finance from other shareholders, and minority and non-voting shareholders can provide finance that does not impinge on the majority's control over the running of the company. However, a private company cannot raise funds directly from the general public; only a public company can do this (see **1.77**).

1.24 Companies may find it easier than unincorporated businesses to raise finance from other sources due to their equity structure. A venture capitalist is unlikely to wish to become involved as a partner in a partnership, even as a limited partner. Similarly, any idea for future public flotation on a recognised stock exchange presupposes that the business is organised through a corporate structure.

1.25 The personal liability of the business owners is often thought to influence the choice of business structure. However, in practice the limited liability achieved by the business owner by operating as a private limited company or an LLP is frequently undermined by the requirement to give personal guarantees to providers of business finance, or to provide a charge over their own personal assets in return for a business loan.

Unincorporated businesses are not able to offer a floating charge over their assets as security for borrowings, whereas companies and LLPs can.

National minimum wage

1.26 The national minimum wage (NMW) is a statutory hourly wage rate that must be paid to all workers. It applies to all workers in family companies, including family members, but not necessarily to the directors. HMRC have confirmed that where a director does not have an explicit contract of employ-

1.27 *Starting a business – choosing an appropriate trading vehicle*

ment with the company he is not likely to be a 'worker' for the purposes of the NMW legislation and does not have to be paid the NMW (*Tax Bulletin, Issue 50*). Family members who work in unincorporated businesses and live at home are also exempt from the NMW. Partners in LLPs, limited or unlimited partnerships and sole traders are under no obligation to pay themselves any set wages as they are not treated as 'workers' for the purposes of the national minimum wage legislation.

Share options

1.27 Potential employees may find a corporate structure more attractive than working for a sole trader, partnership or LLP. This is because it is possible to provide employees with incentives through share options or employee share schemes with a corporate structure. In particular the Share Incentive Plan (SIP) allows an employee to receive the benefit of up to £7,500 of shares in his employing company in any one year. The Enterprise Management Incentive (EMI) can also provide significant tax advantages for holding shares.

Exit strategy

1.28 The ownership of shares in a company enables a much more controlled transfer of wealth to be made, compared with transferring the interest of a sole trader or partner in his business. Small numbers of shares in a company can be passed on to the next generation by way of gift or sale.

If shares are given to employees of the company, or to individuals who become employees when they acquire the shares, an income tax charge may arise under the employment-related securities legislation on the basis that the shares are received due to the donee's employment (see **1.144**).

1.29 In order to give away an interest in an unincorporated business, the proprietor has to bring the donee in as a partner, whether as an active or sleeping one, but this will necessitate a partnership deed and can cause complications where the transfer is to trustees.

1.30 It is easier to sell shares in a private company than to sell a partnership share in a similar-sized business. If the intention is to develop the business to the point where it can be sold, a corporate structure will normally be more appropriate.

SOLE TRADER

Structure

1.31 A sole-trader business is the simplest possible structure for a business. It only involves one person and that person is personally liable for all the debts of the business and is taxed on all of the profits. Essentially there is no legal distinction between the individual and the business. HMRC require the individual to register with them for national insurance and tax purposes within three months of the end of the month in which the business commenced. This can be done by ringing the HMRC newly self-employed helpline: 0845 915 4514, or by completing the form included with the leaflet SE1: *Thinking of working for yourself?*

Accounting date

1.32 The choice of the accounting date to which the sole trader's accounts are made up each year can have a significant effect on the timing of tax payments, particularly in the early years of the business. The accounting date can also affect the degree to which the profits made in the first year are subject to tax more than once, known as overlap profits.

Timing of tax payments

1.33 A sole trader, partner or member of an LLP may be due to pay tax on profits from the first period of trading of the business on 31 January following the end of the tax year which contains those first few months or days of his accounting period. This can represent a long delay between making the profits and paying the tax. This delay arises because the first two on-account income tax payments due on 31 January within the tax year and 31 July following the tax year, are both based on the tax liability payable for the previous tax year. Where the individual was employed immediately before commencing his business, the on-account tax payments will be zero, as all his previous income would have been taxed under PAYE.

Overlap profits

1.34 In a normal tax year, when the business is not commencing or ceasing, an unincorporated business will pay tax on the profits it makes in the accounting period that ends in the tax year concerned.

Example 1.1

The profits for the accounting period to 30 June 2007 will be assessed in 2007/08, the tax year that runs from 6 April 2007 to 5 April 2008.

1.35 *Starting a business – choosing an appropriate trading vehicle*

1.35 In the first tax year of a new business the profits arising in that tax year are assessed to tax from the date of commencement of the business to the end of the tax year. This is referred to as an actual basis of assessment. An accounting date coterminous with the tax year on 5 April will produce no overlap profits, and a 31 March year end will be treated as 5 April for tax calculation purposes.

1.36 In the second tax year, profits of the accounting period that ends in that tax year are assessed to tax. If the first accounting period ends on a date in the second tax year, but is for a period of less than 12 months, the tax charge is based on the first 12 months of the business profits from the commencement date. Alternatively if the first accounting period ends in the second tax year but is for a period of more than 12 months the tax charge is based on the profits made in a 12-month period ending on that accruing date. It can be possible for the first accounting period to be made up to a date that is more than 12 months from the commencement date and does not end in the second tax year. In this case the tax charge for the second tax year is based on the profits of that tax year itself.

1.37 The change from an actual basis of assessment (first year) to one based on the accounting year end (second or third year onwards) can mean some profits are taxed more than once (the overlap profits). These overlap profits are relieved against the final amount of profits assessed when the business ceases, or possibly when it changes the date to which its accounts are made up. Either of these events may occur many years after the overlap profits arose, but the amount of profits that will attract tax relief at that time is not adjusted for the effect of inflation. The overlap tax relief thus loses its value over time.

Tax delay versus overlap profits

1.38 A date early in the tax year, such as 30 April, will provide the longest period between making the profits and paying the tax due on them. This date will give the business some 21 months to prepare the accounts before the tax return is due. However, 30 April may produce the highest amount of overlap profits. A date late in the tax year, such as 31 March or 5 April, will produce little or no overlap profits, but allows only ten months to prepare the accounts before the tax return and tax payments are due on the following 31 January.

PARTNERSHIPS

Why use a partnership?

1.39 The decision to trade as either a sole trader or a general partnership (see **1.40**) is likely to be influenced largely by family, professional, or other commercial considerations. For example, in an industry sector where there is a

Starting a business – choosing an appropriate trading vehicle **1.42**

strong tradition of family continuity, such as farming, there may be powerful domestic reasons that induce the proprietor into taking his children into partnership.

The liability of a sole trader is unlimited in respect of his business debts. A partner will have joint, or joint and several, liability for partnership debts. This can mean, in the case of joint and several liability, any one partner could be called upon to satisfy the whole of the debts, albeit with the right to claim a contribution from his fellow partners. The liability for tax due on the partnership profits is not joint and several, as each partner is due to pay only the tax due on his or her individual profit share. In spite of this many large partnerships will retain funds within the partnership to pay the income tax due on behalf of the partners.

General partnership

1.40 A partnership may be referred to as a general partnership to distinguish it from the forms of limited partnership and limited liability partnership (LLP). The law relating to partnerships is largely included within the *Partnership Act 1890*.

How a partnership is formed

1.41 It is not a necessary requirement of a partnership to have a written partnership agreement, but the existence of such a document agreement is very good evidence that a partnership exists. Where there is no partnership agreement in existence, the *Partnership Act 1890* takes precedence. However, the existence of a partnership agreement is not, of itself, conclusive evidence of the existence of a partnership; other factors need to be present. Sharing profits raises a presumption that a partnership exists, but, again, is not conclusive evidence of a partnership.

For a partnership to exist a business must be carried on 'in common' between the parties. The *Partnership Act 1890, s 2* sets out certain transactions which do not by themselves create a partnership, such as the co-ownership of property, or an employee receiving part of his or her salary by way of a share in the profits of the business.

Profit shares

1.42 Normally, a partner in a general partnership will contribute a proportionate part of the capital to the partnership together with his or her labour and

1.43 *Starting a business – choosing an appropriate trading vehicle*

services. So where four individuals are to form a partnership with equal sharing of the profits they would normally all provide approximately equal amounts of capital to the business. A partner who only provides capital and is not involved in the day-to-day running of the partnership business is known as a 'sleeping partner'. There are anti-avoidance rules that limit the amount of tax relief 'non-active' partners can receive for losses made by the partnership. A non-active partner is one who devotes on average less than ten hours per week personally engaged in the business, so this would include a sleeping partner (see **1.47**).

Tax treatment

Income tax

1.43 The taxation of partnerships is relatively simple where there are only a few partners. For tax and national insurance purposes each partner is treated as an individual sole trader. The amount of profit or loss taxed on each partner is determined by the profit-sharing ratio the partnership operates. Capital profits and losses may be shared in different ratios to income profits and losses.

1.44 Each partner is liable to pay income tax on their own share of the partnership profits, and must report this profit share on their personal tax returns. The partnership is also issued with a tax return to report the total partnership profits and any deductions from those profits such as capital allowances which are made before the net profits (or losses), are shared between the partners (*ITTOIA 2005, Pt 9*).

1.45 When a partner joins a partnership, or the partnership starts trading there can be some double taxation of profits (known as overlap profits) made from the date of commencement or partner joining the partnership to the end of the tax year. This also applies when a sole trader starts to trade (see **1.34**). Tax relief for the overlap profits is given when the individual partner leaves the partnership, the partnership or sole trader ceases to trade, or there is a change in the accounting reference date. The first of these events may occur many years after the partner joins the partnership but there is no indexation of the value of the overlap profits to take account of inflation, so the value of the overlap relief diminishes over time.

Losses

1.46 A partner has several options over how their portion of any trading loss should be relieved; it may be carried back (*ITA 2007, s 72*), set against other income of the same year (*ITA 2007, s 64*), or carried forward (*ITA 2007, s 83*). Each partner can make an independent choice as to how to obtain tax relief for their share of a trading loss. The calculation of the tax charge for each individual partner can become complex if there are a large number of partners in the partnership and frequent changes in the profit-sharing ratios in any one tax year.

1.47 If a partner is a 'non-active' partner or a limited partner (see **1.56**), the tax relief for their share of the trading loss will be restricted where the loss is to be set against other income or gains made by that individual in the same or previous tax year (*ITA 2007, s 103C*). The loss relief is restricted to the amount of capital that partner has contributed to the partnership, with a cap of £25,000. This restriction does not apply to relevant British film-related expenditure but it could deter outside investors from investing in a trading partnership.

National insurance

1.48 Partners are self-employed earners for national insurance purposes, so must register to pay Class 2 NICs, normally collected via a monthly direct debit. If the profit share subject to income tax exceeds the minimum threshold for class 4 NICs, (£5,225 for 2007/08), class 4 NICs are assessed and collected with the income tax self-assessment.

Capital gains

1.49 In general, an acquisition or disposal by the partnership of a partnership asset will result in a series of acquisitions or disposals by each of the partners. Whether or not capital gains tax is payable will depend upon the circumstances, and reference should be made to HMRC Statement of Practice SP D12. Each partner computes his own gain or loss by reference to his interest in the partnership assets, and pays any capital gains tax due calculated according to their other gains and losses for the tax year (*TCGA 1992, s 59*).

Inheritance tax

1.50 An interest in partnership or sole-trader business potentially qualifies for 100% business property relief (BPR), although relief is denied if a binding contract for sale exists at the date of death. The partnership deed should therefore contain an option for the existing partners to acquire the business interest following death, but not a requirement that the business interest should be acquired. Alternatively, a tax liability may be avoided by claiming that the arrangements are part of a bona fide commercial bargain and were made without gratuitous intent.

Personal property held by a partner outside of the partnership and used by the partnership for its trade will qualify for 50% business property relief from inheritance tax.

1.51 *Starting a business – choosing an appropriate trading vehicle*

VAT

1.51 Although a general partnership is not a legal entity in its own right in England and Wales, for VAT purposes it has a single VAT registration which is normally issued in the name of the firm (*VATA 1994, s 45(1)*). Partnerships formed in Scotland are treated as a separate legal person (*Partnership Act 1890, s 4(2)*).

1.52 No change in VAT registration is needed if there are changes in the composition of the partnership, ie partners leaving or joining. However, such changes should be notified to HMRC on form VAT 902 as the departing partner will be regarded as a continuing partner and liable for the VAT debts of the business until the change is notified (see *Jamieson v Customs and Excise* [2002] STC 1418).

1.53 Where a sole proprietor takes another person into the business to form a partnership, or where a business carried on by two or more people in partnership is dissolved and continued by one person alone, HMRC VAT office must be informed. The change from sole proprietor to partnership or vice versa is a change of legal entity and will normally require deregistration of the existing business for VAT purposes and registration of the new, although an election can be made to transfer the VAT registration to the new entity (*VATA 1994, s 49(2)*).

Stamp duty land tax

1.54 Stamp duty land tax (SDLT) can apply to the transfer of an interest in UK land into or out of a partnership whether by:

- an existing partner;
- a person joining the partnership; or
- a person connected with an existing or new partner.

1.55 The amount chargeable to SDLT is calculated by reference to the market value of the land that has been transferred and any consideration for the transaction, based on the proportion of the land interest equal to the partners' partnership shares immediately after the transfer. However, where the partners are connected to each other because they are related (*ITA 2007, s 993(2)*), no SDLT is due on the introduction of UK land into the partnership or the introduction of a partner, unless actual consideration is payable.

Limited partnership

1.56 Limited partnerships are partnerships registered under the *Limited Partnerships Act 1907*. A limited partnership will comprise at least one general partner (whose liability is unlimited) and limited partners whose liability is limited to the amounts of their respective capital contributions. Like a general partnership a limited partnership is not a separate legal entity when formed in England or Wales. Scottish partnerships do have a separate legal entity (*PA 1890, s 4(2)*).

Why use a limited partnership?

1.57 Limited partnerships are often used to undertake property developments or investments that are too big for a single person or organisation to take on. The liability of each limited partner is limited to the capital he introduces to the venture. From 20 December 2002 there is no limit on the number of partners in each limited partnership, although it must contain at least one general partner who does not have limited liability (*Limited Partnerships Act 1907, s 4*). However, any other partner including general partners can be a limited company. Only the general partners can be involved in the management of the limited partnership.

1.58 Limited partnerships are typically used as investment vehicles, particularly in the venture capital and commercial property sectors. An investment manager will set up a subsidiary company to act as a general partner and invite third-party investors to become limited partners. Often the investment manager will then provide the general partner with services of managing the limited partnership investment business.

Tax treatment

1.59 The tax treatment of a limited partnership is much the same as a general partnership, as the partners are subject to tax on their share of the profits or losses as individuals (see **1.43**). However, the freedom to utilise trading losses has been restricted by *ITA 2007, s 104*. The amount of loss that can be used is restricted to the capital introduced by the limited partner plus any accumulated losses. This restriction is further strengthened by *ITA 2007, s 103C*, which limits the loss that can be relieved to £25,000 per tax year, although this cap does not apply to certain film partnerships.

VAT

1.60 The VAT regulations relating to partnerships detailed in para **1.51** do not apply to limited partnerships. A limited partnership does not have to have one VAT registration. The limited partners can be separately registered for VAT as decided in *H Saunders and TG Sorrell v Customs & Excise Commissioners* (1980) VATTR 51.

1.61 Starting a business – choosing an appropriate trading vehicle

Limited liability partnership

1.61 A limited liability partnership (LLP) is a corporate body with its own legal personality, and is formed by incorporating under the *Limited Liability Partnerships Act 2000*. The LLP must be registered at Companies House, just like a company, and must submit annual accounts which are open to public view.

1.62 The LLP must have a minimum of two partners, known as members, but there is no maximum. Limited companies can also be members. An existing general partnership can convert into an LLP with no tax charge arising on the conversion. Unlike a general partnership it is possible for members of the LLP to also be employed by the LLP and taxed as employees if they so wish. In this way the individuals gain access to favourable tax treatment for certain benefits which are restricted to employees, such as childcare vouchers and employer-provided training.

1.63 Another advantage of an LLP is that it is a legal body separate from its members. A general partnership only has a separate legal personality from the partners if it is formed under Scottish law. The members of an LLP have their liability limited to the amount of capital the member has contributed to the LLP.

Why use an LLP?

1.64 An LLP offers protection for all of the partners from the acts of the other partners as the members do not have joint and several liability for the debts of the LLP, as is the case with an ordinary partnership. Limited partnerships, as opposed to LLPs, offer limited liability to partners who do not participate in the management of the business.

Tax treatment

1.65 The individual members of the LLP pay income tax and national insurance on a self-employed basis on their share of the profits, just like members of a general partnership (see **1.43**). A corporate member will pay corporation tax on its share of the profits.

VAT treatment

1.66 As an LLP is a corporate body it is a recognised legal entity for VAT purposes and is separately liable for VAT registration, subject to the normal registration rules. As with general partnerships this does not normally mean that the members will be seen as supplying their services to the LLP and therefore they will not normally have to register for VAT as individual partners.

Starting a business – choosing an appropriate trading vehicle **1.69**

1.67 As a corporate body the LLP can join a VAT group that has a company or other corporate bodies, such as universities, as members, as long as the conditions in *VATA 1994, ss 43* and *43A* are met. However, there are restrictions as to when an LLP can join a VAT group when it functions as the vehicle for a joint venture arrangement. For more information on VAT grouping see *HMRC VAT Notice 700/2*.

1.68 If an existing partnership changes to an LLP, the LLP may have a requirement to apply for VAT registration. If the ordinary partnership ceases to exist, it may be possible for the VAT number to be reallocated to the LLP using the election under *VATA 1994, s 49(2)*.

Tax benefits of all partnerships

Income spreading

1.69 In some cases the tax considerations may exercise a substantial influence on the decision to form a partnership. It is relatively common for a proprietor to take his or her spouse into partnership with a view to achieving a saving on income tax. By spreading the profits of the business over two sets of lower and basic-rate income tax bands, and against two personal allowances, a considerable tax saving may be achieved, as shown in the example.

Example 1.2

Frankie is in business on her own account and makes annual taxable profits of £60,000, on which she pays £18,149.60 in tax and national insurance, leaving £41,850.40 net income, as shown below. If Frankie traded in partnership with Johnny, sharing profits equally, the total tax and NICs payable would be £14,558.60, leaving a total net income of £45,441.40, thus increasing their net income by £3,591.

Comparison of sole-trader and partnership taxation of profits

2007/08 Tax Year	As sole trader	As partnership	
	Frankie	Frankie	Johnny
	£	£	£
Profits	60,000.00	30,000.00	30,000.00
Personal allowance	5,225.00	5,225.00	5,225.00
Net taxable profits	54,775.00	24,775.00	24,775.00

1.70 *Starting a business – choosing an appropriate trading vehicle*

	£	£	£
Tax due at 10% on £2,230.00	223.00	223.00	223.00
Tax due at 22% on next £32,370.00	7,121.40	4,959.90	4,959.90
Tax due at 40% over £34,600.00	8,070.00	—	—
Class 2 NIC at £2.20 per week	114.40	114.40	114.40
Class 4 NIC at 8% up to £34,840.00, 1% above	2,620.80	1,982.00	1,982.00
Total tax and NICs payable	18,149.60	7,279.30	7,279.30
Net income after tax	41,850.40	22,720.70	22,720.70

Limits to tax saving

1.70 HMRC may challenge the profit-sharing arrangements within a family partnership when it appears that the partner whose efforts generate the highest proportion of profits for the business (often the husband), has diverted part of that income for it to be taxed as the income of another partner who took a less active role in the business (frequently the wife). The Inspector of Taxes may contend that the principal partner, by allowing the spouse to receive a disproportionate profit share, has made a settlement in which he retains an interest, and hence under provisions of the settlements legislation (primarily *ITTOIA 2005, Pt 5 Ch 5*) the diverted income should be taxed on the principal partner. This renders ineffective the transfer of income to achieve a tax saving. However, this argument may no longer hold water following *Jones v Garnett*, which tested the application of the settlements legislation to profits shared between the owners of family companies (see **1.123** to **1.128**).

1.71 To provide a robust argument against the settlements legislation being invoked it is important that all the partners have the attributes and trappings of full equity partners. Good evidence of a genuine partnership should be available, such as a partnership agreement that provides for the sharing of losses as well as profits. Trade should be conducted through a partnership bank account, on which all partners are signatories.

If the partnership is involved in the service industry, the IR 35 rules for personal services provided through intermediaries may apply (see **1.94** to **1.99**).

Estate spreading

1.72 The prospect of saving inheritance tax can influence a business proprietor to form a partnership. In the case of a partnership between husband and wife the tax saving can come from the equalisation of their estates. Where the

Starting a business – choosing an appropriate trading vehicle **1.75**

partnership is between parent and child the business arrangement can form the basis for a long-term transfer of the business down one generation.

COMPANIES

Type of company

1.73 The following types of companies may be incorporated in accordance with the *Companies Act 1985* and the *Companies Act 2006* (when it fully comes into force) or under European law:

- private company limited by shares;
- private company limited by guarantee and not having share capital;
- private unlimited company, with or without share capital;
- public company limited by shares;
- community interest company (CIC); and
- European economic interest grouping (EEIG).

In addition there are various forms of co-operative and common share ownership arrangements, which are not dealt with in this chapter.

Private limited company

1.74 The defining criterion of a private limited company, is that the liability of its members is limited to the amount, if any, unpaid on the shares held by each of them (*CA 1985 s 1(2)(a), CA 2006, ss 3(2) and 4(1)*). This is the most commonly used corporate form, and is generally used as a trading vehicle. It can also be used in joint-venture situations.

Company limited by guarantee

1.75 A company limited by guarantee is normally used by non-profit making organisations that do not have a requirement for working capital, such as trade associations, clubs, charities and trade protection societies. Membership of a company limited by guarantee is not transferable and ceases on death or earlier retirement.

Since 8 November 2006 it is possible to form a charitable incorporated organisation, under the *Charities Act 2006*. This type of charitable organisation may replace the use of a company limited by guarantee by charities. It is not considered further in this chapter.

1.76 *Starting a business – choosing an appropriate trading vehicle*

Unlimited company

1.76 An unlimited company cannot have limited in its title, as it does not confer limited liability on its members. This means the members' liability is similar to that of partners in a general partnership (see **1.44**). However, the unlimited company does have a separate legal existence and its members, unlike partners, have no direct obligation to contribute to the assets of the company while it is a going concern, save to be called upon to contribute to the company any capital unpaid on their shares. The unlimited company must have at least two members, but there is no maximum number of members. Under the *Companies Act 2006, s 7*, one or more persons may form any type of company, including an unlimited company, so the restriction of having at least two members may disappear.

Public company

1.77 A public company is a company whose memorandum contains a statement that the company is to be a public company. Under the *Companies Act 2006* the certificate of incorporation must state that it is a public company. A public company has a major advantage over a private company in that it can offer its shares or debentures to the public, which *CA 1985, s 81 (CA 2006, ss 755–760)* prohibits a private company from doing. Because of this the public limited company is subject to a number of restrictions that do not apply to private companies.

Community interest company (CIC)

1.78 The CIC is designed to be used for community-based social businesses that are run as not-for-profit. A CIC may be a private or public limited company, limited by shares or guarantee. However, its articles of association must restrict the use of its assets for the benefit of the community. The CIC must also abide by rules monitored by the CIC regulator.

European economic interest grouping (EEIG)

1.79 An EEIG is a form of incorporated partnership, made up of two or more individuals, corporate or partnership members who carry on their principal activity or have their central administration in at least two different Member States of the European Community. It is usually not suitable in start-up situations.

Limited liability

1.80 Limited liability is perceived as being an important commercial advantage of carrying on a business through the medium of a limited company. The liability of the shareholders of a limited company is limited to the amount (if any) unpaid on their shares. Thus, if the company fails, they are not normally liable to make good any deficit. In the case of an unlimited company (see **1.76**), the shareholders' liability is not limited and they will be responsible for meeting all of the company's debts.

1.81 The actual degree of protection given by limited liability to the shareholders of private companies may be negated insofar as they have given any personal guarantees for the company's borrowings. A bank lending to a small company will almost invariably require personal guarantees from the directors or shareholders, and security over the personal assets of the major shareholders to support the loan provided. Shareholders will, normally, still be protected against claims by any creditors who have not taken such a security for their debts. The incorporation of a business will not absolve the proprietors from liability for pre-incorporation debts.

1.82 Individuals considering setting up a new business within a company, or incorporating an existing business, with a view to leaving creditors high and dry in the event of its being unsuccessful, should beware the provisions of the *Insolvency Act 1986, s 214* and the *Company Directors (Disqualification) Act 1986*. Under this legislation, directors can incur personal liability, notably in circumstances of wrongful trading or fraudulent trading, or when acting as a director when disqualified.

Tax treatment

Corporate taxes

1.83 The rates of corporation tax for small companies and the main rate of corporation tax are being realigned in the years to 2009, and possibly beyond. Table 1.1 shows the rates for current and future periods as they have been announced, but not legislated for. A further alignment of the corporation tax rates for small and large companies may occur in future. In addition the income tax rates and thresholds are also due to be adjusted over the years to 6 April 2009.

1.84 *Starting a business – choosing an appropriate trading vehicle*

Table 1.1: Rates of corporation tax

From 1 April:	2006	2007	2008	2009
Small companies rate for profits up to £300,000	19%	20%	21%	22%
The main corporation tax rate above £1,500,000	30%	30%	28%	28%
Marginal rate of tax in band £300,001–£1,500,000	32.75%	32.5%	29.75%	29.5%

1.84 These movements in rates and thresholds make it difficult to compare the relative tax charges that will be incurred by running a small business through a company compared to operating an unincorporated business. At present there are tax savings to be made by operating through a limited company, but that tax saving does very much depend on exactly how the business owners extract profits from the business (see **1.102 to 1.119**).

Associated companies

1.85 If the company has associated companies, the profit thresholds which determine the tax rate (£300,000 and £1,500,000) are divided by the number of active associated companies plus one *(ICTA 1988, s 13(3))*. This rule prevents groups of companies taking advantage of the lower rates of corporation tax by spreading the total profits of the group over several associated companies. A company is associated with another if *(ICTA 1988, s 13(4))*:

- one of the two has control of the other; or

- both of the companies are under the control of the same person or persons, ie under 'common control' (see **1.88**).

1.86 A dormant company: one that has no trade or business in the accounting period, is excluded from the total of associated companies. A holding company that merely holds shares in subsidiaries and receives dividends to pass through to shareholders is not an associated company (see *HMRC Statement of Practice SP 5/94*). Overseas associated companies must be included in the total number of associated companies to calculate the UK corporation tax due.

Example 1.3

Ant Ltd makes profits of £290,000, but it is associated with Deck Ltd that makes profits of £10,000. Their corporation tax liabilities are calculated as follows:

Ant Ltd	£
£150,000 at 20%	30,000
£140,000 at 32.5%	45,500
Tax due	75,500
Deck Ltd	
£10,000 at 20%	2,000
Total tax payable by Ant Ltd and Deck Ltd:	77,500

The owners of Ant Ltd and Deck Ltd decide to merge the operations of the two companies by inserting a holding company: Mite Ltd above Ant Ltd and Deck Ltd, then hiving up the trades into Mite Ltd, to be run within two divisions: A and D. The old companies Ant Ltd and Deck Ltd are liquidated. The corporation tax of Mite Ltd is calculated as:

Mite Ltd has profits made by the following divisions	£
Division A	290,000
Division D	10,000
Total profits	300,000
Corporation tax at 20%	60,000

The owners of Ant Ltd and Deck Ltd save tax of £17,500 (£77,500-£60,000) per year by operating the two trades as divisions of one company rather than as separate companies.

Operate as divisions

1.87 For most small companies there will usually be a tax saving by operating as just one company with trade separated into divisions. However, this strategy must be reviewed as the profits rise.

1.88 *Starting a business – choosing an appropriate trading vehicle*

Example 1.4

Flowerpot Ltd has two divisions: W and B, and its total corporation tax is calculated as follows:

Profits are made by the following divisions:	£
Division W	1,375,000
Division B	125,000
Total profits	1,500,000
Corporation tax at 30%	450,000

If Flowerpot Ltd were to form two subsidiaries; William Ltd and Ben Ltd, and transfer the trades of the divisions into those new companies leaving Flowerpot Ltd as the dormant holding company, the total corporation tax would be calculated as follows:

The Flowerpot Group has the following results:	£
William Ltd	
£1,375,000 at 30%	412,500
Ben Ltd	
£125,000 at 20%	25,000
Total tax payable:	437,500

The Flowerpot Group would save tax of £12,500 (£450,000–£437,500) per year by operating as a group of two trading companies rather than as one company with two divisions.

Definition of control

1.88 Control is defined for the purpose of determining associated companies in *ICTA 1988, s 416*: control is the ability to exercise or the entitlement to acquire, control over the company's affairs, including the ownership of, or entitlement to acquire:

- over 50% of the company's share capital; or
- over 50% of the company's voting rights; or
- the right to receive over 50% of the company's distributable income; or
- the right to receive over 50% of the company's distributable assets.

To determine whether two or more companies are under 'common control' you must look at what other companies are controlled by the proprietor and his or her associates, as the powers and rights of the associates are deemed to belong to the proprietor for this purpose (*ICTA 1988, s 416(6)*).

Definition of associates

1.89 The following people will be associates of the proprietor:

- any relative (meaning spouse, parents, children, siblings including half-siblings and remoter relatives in direct line, but not aunts, uncles, cousins, step and divorced relatives);
- any business partner (meaning anyone the proprietor is also in business with by way of a partnership);
- the trustee(s) of any settlement in which the proprietor (or any living or dead relative – as defined above) is or was the settlor; and
- the trustee(s) of a settlement or personal representative of an estate holding the company shares in which the proprietor has an interest.

1.90 In determining whether the control test is satisfied, *ICTA 1988, s 416(5)* provides that any rights or powers which a nominee of a person possess on his behalf, or may be required to exercise on his direction or behalf, are attributed to him. The 'may' in this sentence is interpreted by HMRC as being 'must', so HMRC have no discretion on whether to attribute powers, and they must examine all possible combinations. HMRC successfully argued this point in the case: *R v IRC, ex p Newfields Development Ltd* [2001] STC 901, where the rights and powers of a trustee were deemed to be held by the settlor.

Since the *Newfields Development* case HMRC have been looking more closely at the control of close companies, particularly where shares are held by family trusts, and in circumstances where there is significant commercial interdependence between family companies.

1.91 The attribution of rights of associates is limited in certain situations by Extra-Statutory Concession (ESC) C9, which relaxes the rules of common control and reduces the scope of the associates to be taken into account, but only for the purpose of determining the profit thresholds for corporation tax. Where there is no substantial commercial interdependence between companies controlled by relatives, those companies are not considered to be associated. However, the relaxation of attributed powers does not apply to:

- the person's spouse and minor children;
- the person's business partners; and

1.92 *Starting a business – choosing an appropriate trading vehicle*

- the trustee of a settlement where that person is the settlor, or the settlor's spouse or minor child.

1.92 Business partners are associates, so the rights of those associates must be attributed to each other. A company controlled by an individual who is a member of a partnership is associated with any other companies controlled by the other partners of the same partnership. Each partner must either know exactly how many companies all the other partners control, or not claim the small companies rate of corporation tax for his own personal company. This rule particularly bites where individuals are partners in large film partnerships or in professional partnerships, where they may not know much about the business dealings of the other members of the partnership.

Example 1.5

A company controlled by Anita will be associated with the company controlled by her husband Peter. If Peter and Anita are not married the companies they control will not be associated.

Example 1.6

Companies controlled by brothers Ben and Jerry would be associated but for the operation of ESC C9 that ignores all relatives other than spouses and minor children where the companies are not substantially commercially interdependent.

Close investment-holding companies

1.93 Close investment-holding companies are ineligible for the small companies' rate of corporation tax, and must be taxed at the main rate of corporation tax on all their profits. The definition of a close-investment holding company in *ICTA 1988, s 13A* excludes trading companies and those that hold property for rent to third parties, and affects companies that are mainly concerned with passive investments such as shares or securities. Where a company holds a property only for the personal use of the directors of that company, that company will be treated as a close investment-holding company. Property investment companies and trading companies are not treated as investment companies.

Personal service companies

1.94 Owner-managed companies whose shareholders personally perform the service contracts on behalf of the company can fall foul of the wide-ranging anti-avoidance legislation for provision of personal services through intermediaries, known as the IR 35 rules (*ITEPA 2003, Pt 2, Ch 8*). These rules do not prohibit the payment of dividends, but can mean that any dividends or payments to other employees must be paid out of income that has been subject to tax under PAYE and NICs.

1.95 The IR 35 rules can apply where the intermediary is a company, partnership, or even an individual, but different qualifying conditions exist in each case:

- Intermediary is a personal service company: the worker who performs the services must either hold a material interest in the company, broadly defined as 5% or more of the ordinary share capital, or receive payments from the company that can be taken to represent remuneration for the services performed for the final client.
- Intermediary is a partnership: the individuals who perform the personal services must share 60% or more of the profits of the partnership.

Sole traders who do not themselves act as intermediaries cannot fall under the IR 35 legislation.

1.96 The IR 35 legislation is designed to increase the tax burden of businesses that fall within it, and thus reduce the tax advantage from working through one's own service company rather than as a direct employee for the final client. The tax advantages are principally the ability to receive income free of NICs paid as dividends and to gain tax relief for expenses on the wholly and exclusively basis (*ICTA 1988, s 74(1)* and *ITTIOA 2005, s 34*) rather than the wholly, exclusively and necessarily basis required for tax relief of expenses incurred by an employee (*ITEPA 2003, s 336*). The IR 35 rules seek to apply PAYE and NIC to the proceeds of contracts that would be treated as employment contracts if they had been performed by the individual working directly for the client and not through the intermediary.

1.97 Whether income received by a personal service company falls within the IR 35 rules will depend on the performance of the hypothetical contract represented by the actions of the worker, the final client, and any agent in between. There are few clear dividing lines, but HMRC will give an opinion on agreed written contracts if all relevant details are submitted. This HMRC opinion is not binding, as the written contract will not necessarily reflect the performance of the hypothetical contract on which the legislation is based.

1.98 Although the IR 35 rules may remove many of the benefits of operating through a personal service company, some are retained:

- Tax relief can be claimed for the cost of travel to a temporary workplace, which would not apply if the worker were employed directly by the client.

1.99 *Starting a business – choosing an appropriate trading vehicle*

- If the company has some intrinsic value this can be relieved through capital gains tax taper relief and the annual capital gains exemption when the company is sold.
- NIC savings can be made by the company making pension contributions into funds set up for the director and his dependants.

1.99 All business proprietors who are potentially affected by IR 35 need to make the following judgments:

- What proportion of income is caught by the IR 35 rules?
- What additional costs will the business incur by keeping records to comply with the rules?
- Do the benefits of operating through a company outweigh the immediate costs?
- Will the business make losses under the IR 35 rules that cannot be relieved?
- What is the risk of the proprietor's view of which income falls under IR 35 being challenged by HMRC?

Managed service companies

1.100 From 6 April 2007 a company whose business consists wholly or mainly of providing the personal services of a worker to others can be defined as a managed service company (MSC) under *ITEPA 2003, Pt 2, Ch 9*, if the following conditions also exist:

- More than half of the income of the MSC is paid on to the worker in some form.
- The manner of payment of this income to the worker increases the worker's net receipt above the amount he would have received if all those payments were treated as employment income.
- A person who carries on a business of promoting or facilitating the use of companies to provide the services of individuals (an MSC provider) is involved with the company.

1.101 The consequences of being an MSC are serious for the MSC provider and the company. All non-employment income extracted from the MSC (such as dividends) is deemed to be earnings for both PAYE and national insurance purposes. The tax and NICs are also payable when the payment to the worker is

Starting a business – choosing an appropriate trading vehicle **1.104**

made, not at the end of the tax year as under the IR 35 provisions. The MSC provider, as well as the directors or office holder of the MSC, and their associates, may also become liable to pay any PAYE and NICs not paid by the MSC. Where the MSC provisions apply to a company the IR 35 provisions do not also apply.

Profit extraction

Extract as dividends

1.102 Although the lower rates of tax applicable to corporate profits when compared to profits accruing to an individual can be an incentive to incorporation (see **Table 1.3** at **1.138**), those profits cannot easily be placed in the hands of shareholders without suffering a further charge to tax. The obvious way of distributing such profits is by the payment of dividends.

A company can only pay a dividend if it has sufficient realised profits at the time that the dividend is paid. It may be necessary to prepare interim accounts to show that the profits are available. If there are insufficient profits available the dividend payment may be challenged by HMRC as a loan to the shareholder, or remuneration.

1.103 Dividends from UK companies are subject to tax at 10% for taxpayers whose total income is less than the higher rate threshold (£34,600 for 2007/08). Dividends are thus effectively tax free in the hands of individuals who pay only the basic or starting rates of income tax, as the dividend tax credit will cover the income tax due. Higher rate taxpayers pay tax at 32.5% on the gross dividend income, so they pay an effective income tax charge of 25% of the net dividend paid, after taking into account the 10% dividend tax credit.

Extract as bonus or salary

1.104 Profits extracted in the form of remuneration give rise to both income tax and NIC charges that make this method of profit extraction relatively expensive, once the NIC threshold of £5,225 (for 2007/08) is exceeded.

In the following examples it is assumed the employee has already received a salary of £5,225 that covers his personal allowance for the year. The salary plus the employer's NI charge of 12.8% is fully deductible for tax purposes, so there is no corporation tax charge where a salary only is paid. The dividend must be paid out of post-tax profits, so a corporation tax charge must first be deducted from the gross profits.

Example 1.7

Company pays corporation tax at 20% (calculation to nearest £)	Bonus £	Dividend £
Gross profits before tax	100,000	100,000
Less salary	88,653	Nil
Less employer's NIC at 12.8%	11,347	Nil
Corporation tax charged at 20%	Nil	(20,000)
Payable to employee/shareholder before deductions	88,653	80,000
Deemed tax credit: 1/9	N/A	8,889
Employees NIC at 11% up to £29,615 (£34,840 – £5,225) +1% above £29,615	(3,848)	Nil
Gross receipt for employee before income tax	88,643	88,889
Income tax at 10% on £2,230 / £34,600	(223)	(3,460)
Income tax at 22% on £32,370	(7,121)	–
Income tax at 40%/ 32.5% above £34,600	(21,617)	(17,644)
Net cash available to employee after setting-off tax credit	55,834	67,785
Effective total tax rate on gross profits of company	44.17%	32.22%

Example 1.8

Company pays corporation tax at 30% (calculation to nearest £)	Bonus £	Dividend £
Gross profits before tax	100,000	100,000
Less salary	88,653	Nil
Less employer's NIC at 12.8%	11,347	Nil
Corporation tax charged at 20%	Nil	(30,000)
Payable to employee/shareholder before deductions	88,653	70,000
Deemed tax credit: 1/9	N/A	7,778
Employees NIC at 11% up to £29,615 (£34,840 – £5,225) +1% above £29,615	(3,848)	Nil
Gross receipt for employee before income tax	88,643	77,778
Income tax at 10% on £2,230 / £34,600	(223)	(3,460)
Income tax at 22% on £32,370	(7,121)	–
Income tax at 40%/ 32.5% above £34,600	(21,617)	(14,033)

Starting a business – choosing an appropriate trading vehicle **1.109**

Net cash available to employee after setting-off tax credit	55,834	60,285
Effective total tax rate on gross profits of company	44.17%	39.72%

1.105 These examples show that paying a dividend is more tax efficient than a bonus or salary payment at the 20% and 30% rates of corporation tax, when all taxes, including national insurance, are taken into account.

1.106 It should be noted that if remuneration is paid to a director or employee who is not actively involved to a significant extent in the running of the company, HMRC will seek to disallow the deduction of excessive remuneration: *Copeman v Flood* (1940) 24 TC 53; *Dollar v Lyon* [1981] STC 331.

Extract value by rent

1.107 Where a property is held by the proprietor or their family personally, but used for the company for its trade the company may pay rent for the use of that property. The rent received must be declared on the individual's personal tax return, and be subject to income tax on the net amount after deduction of expenses such as loan interest, repairs and insurance.

1.108 The payment of rent to an individual can be a useful way to extract funds from the company, and it has the following advantages:

- rent payments do not carry national insurance charges;
- the rent can be paid whether or not the company has made a profit in the period, unlike a dividend;
- the rent payments are tax deductible for the company;
- the property can be placed in the hands of a member of the family who does not work directly for the business, and hence direct some income from the company to that individual where it may be taxed at a lower rate;
- the rent paid does not effect the business property relief (BPR) available on the value of the property, which will be 50% whether or not a market rent is paid.

A lease should be drawn up between the company and the property owner, and if the property owner is a director of the company the rents should be set at a reasonable market value. The grant of a lease may incur a Stamp Duty Land Tax charge.

1.109 The proprietor of the business needs to balance the potential advantage of holding the property outside the company, in terms of profit extracted from

1.110 *Starting a business – choosing an appropriate trading vehicle*

the company, 50% BPR available on death and 75% taper relief available to an individual owner on sale, compared to the 100% BPR available on the value of the property if it is held within the company. For further discussion of planning techniques available with BPR see **Chapter 11: Business property relief.**

Extract value by interest

1.110 Where a shareholder or director has loaned money to the company, perhaps by not withdrawing amounts voted as dividends or remuneration, the company can pay that individual interest on the outstanding balance. The interest charged by the individual to the company should be set at a commercial rate, which could be several points above the bank base rate. However, if HMRC perceive the interest charge materially exceeds a commercial rate they may seek to treat the excess interest as a salary or dividend distribution.

1.111 The payment of interest has the following advantages as a profit extraction method:

- the interest can be paid whether or not the company has distributable profits, unlike a dividend;
- the interest payments do not carry national insurance;
- the interest payments are tax deductible for the company (but see para **1.112** below);
- payments are only made to those individuals who have outstanding credit balances with the company, rather than all of the shareholders, as with a dividend.

Where the interest is paid on a short-tem loan from the individual to the company, the company can pay the interest due without deduction of tax. However, if the period of the loan can exceed one year, the company should deduct tax at 20% (the savings rate), when the interest is paid.

1.112 Where the company is a close company and the individual is a shareholder of that company, the company can only get a tax deduction for the interest due when it is actually paid, if the interest is paid more than 12 months after the end of the accounting period in which it was due.

Extract value by benefits in kind

1.113 Value may be extracted from the company in the form of benefits in kind made available to directors and employees or to shareholders who do not actually work for the company. Where the benefit is provided to a non-working

Starting a business – choosing an appropriate trading vehicle **1.115**

shareholder, or an associate of that shareholder, the value of the benefit is not taxed as employment income, but is treated as a distribution under *ICTA 1988, s 418*.

Extract value by way of a pension

1.114 Pension contributions can also be a tax efficient way of extracting value from a company. The pension contribution paid by the company into a scheme for a director or employee or the company will normally be tax deductible. For further discussion of the tax treatment of pension contributions see **Chapter 10: Pensions**.

Extract as a loan

1.115 Funds held within a private company may be loaned to directors, shareholders or employees with the following restrictions:

- The *Companies Act 1985* prohibits loans to directors of more than £5,000, although this rule is routinely ignored by private companies (*CA 1985, s 334*).
- A loan to an employee who earns over £8,500 or to a director, which exceeds £5,000 at any point in the tax year, will generate a benefit in kind under *ITEPA 2003, s 184* equivalent to the interest due on the loan calculated at the official rate (set at 6.25% since 6 April 2007), less any interest actually paid.
- Loans to shareholders or directors of close companies can give rise to a charge under *ICTA 1988, s 419* if the loan is not repaid within nine months of the company's accounting period.
- The charge under *ICTA 1988, s 419* is an amount equivalent to 25% of the monies advanced, but it does not apply if:
  - the amount of the loan does not exceed £15,000; and
  - the borrower works full-time for the close company or any of its associated companies; and
- the borrower does not have a material interest in the company (being 5% or more of the ordinary shares); or
- the debt is incurred for the supply of goods or services in the ordinary course of the trade or business of the company.

When the loan is repaid the company must make a claim for repayment of the *s 419* charge within six years from the end of the financial year in which repayment is made.

1.116 *Starting a business – choosing an appropriate trading vehicle*

1.116 When examining the company's accounts, it may not be clear to the tax inspector whether a particular transaction has in fact repaid the outstanding loan at year end or a further loan has arisen since that date. It is thus advisable for the board minutes approving any loan clearing bonus or dividend to clearly state the accounting treatment in the directors' loan account.

Extract by way of purchase of own shares

1.117 Limited companies may now issue redeemable shares and purchase their own shares under certain conditions. The amount by which the purchase price for the shares exceeds the amount paid on subscription must be treated as a distribution (*ICTA 1988, s 209*). The shareholder who receives value for the shares will have to pay income tax on the net proceeds as if they were a dividend. However, the proceeds are treated as a capital payment subject to capital gains tax, if the conditions of *ICTA 1988, s 219* can be met for the transaction. The company should always apply to HMRC for clearance under *ICTA 1988, s 225* before undertaking any purchase of its own shares. For a full discussionion of the tax implications of the company purchasing its own share see **Chapter 3: Company purchase of own shares.**

Extract value on death

1.118 Any holding of shares in an unquoted trading company qualifies for 100% business property relief (BPR) from inheritance tax (*IHTA 1984, s 105(1)*). The same applies for any size of partnership share and for a sole-trader business, which by its nature is not divided into shares. If the share that qualifies for BPR is gifted to an individual before death the gift will be a potentially exempt transfer for inheritance tax, so no inheritance tax is paid unless the donor dies within seven years of the date of the gift. However, the share which was the subject of the gift must qualify for BPR at the date of death or the tax relief will not apply. So the company must still be unquoted and trading within the definitions of those terms as they apply under the *Inheritance Tax Act 1994*.

1.119 Where an asset, such as land, buildings, plant or machinery, is held by an individual and used for the purpose of a business, the value of that asset will qualify for 50% BPR if:

- the business is the individual's own sole-trading business; or
- the business is a partnership in which the individual is a partner; or
- the business is an unquoted trading company in which the individual is a controlling shareholder.

Control for IHT purposes is measured by the voting power on all questions affecting the company as a whole, which if exercised would yield a majority of the votes capable of being exercised on them. Majority control in a small company may be undermined by weighted voting rights in the articles, or by sell and buy arrangements in the shareholders' agreements. Such rights are deemed to apply for the purposes of BPR even if they actually only come into effect in certain circumstances. For further discussion of BPR on gifts or transfers of business assets see **Chapter 11: Business property relief**.

Tax benefits of a company

Income spreading using salaries

1.120 To obtain a tax deduction for business expenses incurred by an incorporated or unincorporated business, those expenses must be incurred wholly and exclusively for the purposes of the trade or profession (*ICTA 1988, s 74(1)(a)* for corporation tax; *ITTOIA 2005, s 34* for income tax). This applies to salaries, bonuses, wages, pension contributions and other employee benefits just as it does to any other business expenses.

Having said this, a wage paid to a spouse or child is often seen by business owners as a legitimate way to redistribute some of the profits of the business into hands of those who will pay tax on a lower rate on that income. A spouse who otherwise has no other income can be paid up to the earnings threshold for national insurance (£100 per week for 2007/08), and pay no tax or NICs on that income. If the wages exceed the lower earning limit (£87 per week for 2007/08), the individual will also receive a national insurance credit that counts as Class 1 NICs for qualification for state benefits.

1.121 Wages paid to relatives of the principal owner of the business are particularly vulnerable to attack by HMRC as being a disguised distribution of profits, and not a business expense wholly and exclusively incurred for the business. HMRC will want to know not only that the wage was actually paid to the individual (*Abbott v IRC* (1995) Sp C 58), but also that it fairly represents the value of the work done by that individual (*Copeman v William Flood & Sons Ltd* (1940) 24 TC 53).

1.122 It is advisable that all employees who are close relatives of the main proprietor should have service contracts in place that set out their duties and remuneration in commercial terms. The salary paid to any family members employed by the family company should also be at least equal to the national minimum wage unless the individual acts purely as a director or company secretary.

1.123 *Starting a business – choosing an appropriate trading vehicle*

In Example 1.2, Frankie could have reduced the total tax paid by the business by employing Johnnie rather than taking him into partnership, but the employer's national insurance at 12.8% on all earnings over £100 per week, plus the employee's NI at 11% eliminates much of those savings (see **Table 1.3** at **1.138**).

Income spreading using dividends

1.123 Any problem over obtaining a tax deduction for the relative's wages may be circumvented by paying a dividend instead of a salary, if the family member holds shares in the company. However, HMRC are alive to the use of dividends as a substitute for remuneration and the diversion of income from the main worker to other less active shareholders by means such as:

- dividend waivers;
- paying separate dividends on different classes of shares; or
- gifting shares to the non-working spouse.

In any of these cases HMRC may argue that a settlement has been created by the main worker in favour of the relative who received the dividends, on the basis that the main worker has made a gift of income to the relative. The anti-avoidance rules in the settlements legislation (*ITTOIA 2005, ss 619–648*) would then apply so the diverted income is taxed as if it was that of the donor.

1.124 Such an argument was the basis of the case *Jones v Garnett (Inspector of Taxes)* [2007] STC 1536, which was seen by many as a test case for the splitting of dividend income between a husband and wife within a family company. In brief, the facts of this case were: Mr Jones set up Arctic Systems in 1992 through which he offered his services as an IT contractor. He was the only director and held one of the two ordinary shares issued by the company. Mrs Jones purchased the other ordinary share from the company formation agents, and also become the company secretary.

They decided to minimise the tax and national insurance payable by taking only small salaries from the company, and paying out most of the profits as dividends. As Mr and Mrs Jones held one each of the two shares in issue, the dividends were paid to them equally. Splitting the total dividend income in this way meant the tax credit attached to the dividends covered the basic rate income tax due, leaving no further tax to pay. If Mr Jones had paid himself a higher salary, or had been the only person receiving a dividend, he would have paid far more tax as much of his income would then have been taxed at the higher tax rate of 40%.

1.125 This structure of a husband and wife both holding shares in the company, so they can both receive some of the dividends, has been standard

Starting a business – choosing an appropriate trading vehicle **1.128**

practice for many family companies since the introduction of independent taxation for spouses in 1990. However, HMRC argued that the whole arrangement of Mrs Jones receiving her share in the company, and the dividends paid on that share, amounted to a settlement created by Mr Jones. As Mr and Mrs Jones were married, Mr Jones was deemed to retain an interest in that settlement under *ITTOIA 2005, s 624*, and thus Mr Jones, as the settlor, should be taxed on the income arising under that settlement (the dividends paid to Mrs Jones). Extra tax would then be due as Mr Jones would be taxed at the higher rate on the majority of the dividend income.

1.126 The House of Lords actually agreed with HMRC that there was a settlement. However, they established that the gift at the heart of the settlement was the ordinary share acquired by Mrs Jones at an undervalue (for only £1), and this share included future rights to capital on liquidation, and full voting rights, so was not 'wholly or substantially a right to income' (*ITTOIA 2005, s 626(3)* – condition B). This meant that the conditions A and B in *ITTOIA 2005, s 626*, (commonly known as the spouse exemption) were both met, and as the gift was made between spouses, the income was not caught by the settlement rules in *ITTOIA 2005, Ch 5*. Mr Jones could not be taxed on the dividend income correctly received by Mrs Jones.

1.127 The House of Lords decision in *Jones v Garnett* does not mean family companies can spread dividend income between the family members without restriction, as the government has announced the law will be changed to prevent income shifting using 'non-commercial arrangements'. Guidance on the application of the existing settlements legislation following *Jones v Garnett* has been issued by HMRC as an update to their Trusts, Settlements and Estates Manual: http://www.hmrc.gov.uk/practitioners/tsem4000.pdf. The tax return helpsheet: 270 Trusts and Settlements has also been updated and will be available with the 2007/08 return.

1.128 When setting up a company in which a husband and wife, civil partners, or other family members are to hold shares, the following actions may reduce the risk of attack under the settlements legislation:

- The shares issued should be ordinary shares with full voting rights and rights to capital on a winding-up.

- Where the shareholders are a married couple or registered civil partners the ordinary shares should be gifted from one spouse to the other.

- Both spouses should be made directors of the company so they are equally responsible for the decisions the board of directors takes for the business, including suggesting the level of dividends to be paid.

- Record the duties undertaken by each family member for the company to show that each shareholder plays a key role in the operation of the business.

1.129 *Starting a business – choosing an appropriate trading vehicle*

1.129 If the business is starting from scratch it may well be more tax efficient to trade within the medium of a partnership or sole-trader business for the first two years, then transfer the business to a company and sell any free goodwill built up in the business to the new company. The taxable value of the goodwill will be reduced by 75% by taper relief if the business has been run for two complete years, if the transfer occurs before 6 April 2008. The company will be able to claim a tax deduction for the cost of the goodwill where the original business commenced after 31 March 2002 (*FA 2002, Sch 29, para 118*). For a further discussion of the tax reliefs available on incorporation of a business see **Chapter 2: Incorporation.**

1.130 If the company is subject to the IR 35 rules (see **1.94**), the payment of dividends may not be effective in reducing the effective total tax paid by the shareholder and company on the income received. However, operating through a company has other commercial advantages and disadvantages, as discussed in paras **1.16** to **1.30**.

Company versus another medium

Timing of tax payments

1.131 Any comparison of the tax savings available by operating through a company rather than as a sole trader or partnership needs to take into account the timing of tax payments. Salary payments have the shortest time-lag for collection of the tax due, as they must be subject to PAYE and NIC deductions at the point of payment. Benefits in kind may also be taxed immediately through inclusion in the PAYE code, and the employer will have to pay NICs on most benefits within three months of the end of the tax year.

Individuals

1.132 A sole trader or partner can delay the payment of tax on profits from the first period of trading as the first two on-account payments, due on 31 January within the tax year and July 31 following the tax year, are both based on the tax liability for the previous tax year. Any short fall in these two on-account payments is made up on 31 January following the tax year of assessment. If the first trading period produces a loss, the first tax payable for the new business may be due over 33 months from the start of the business. This time-lag will also depend on the accounting date chosen for the business (see **1.32**).

However, the tax advantage on starting a business is mirrored by a disadvantage when the self-employed business ceases and the trade is transferred into a company. There is generally a bunching of profits assessable to tax on cessation of the sole-trader business, which is only partly relieved by the set-off of overlap profits. See Example 1.9.

Example 1.9

Joan has been in business on her own account for several years and plans to incorporate her business from 1 January 2007. She has overlap profits of £50,000 and has made up accounts to 30 April each year. Her taxable profits and the tax due for the final periods of her self-employed trade are as follows:

Period end	Taxable profit	Chargeable to tax	Assessed in tax year	Tax payable
	£	£		£
April 30 2005	150,000	150,000	2005/06	55,000
April 30 2006	200,000			
Dec 31 2006	170,000	370,000		
Overlap profits		50,000		
		320,000	2006/07	123,000
Total profits	520,000	470,000		178,000

When Joan starts to draw a salary from her new company from 1 January 2007 she will be taxed under PAYE and thus have no time-lag for payment of that tax.

Companies

1.133 A new company will not have the same opportunity to delay tax payments. Small and medium-sized companies pay corporation tax nine months and one day after the end of the accounting period in which that tax liability arises. Large companies which have taxable profits in excess of £1.5 million a year must pay their corporate tax liability in four instalments commencing six months and 14 days from the start of the accounting period which gives rise to the tax liability.

Hybrid structures

1.134 A way to mitigate the problem of bunching of tax payments is for the sole trader to start a parallel trade within the new company and run off old contracts within the old self-employed business. The self-employed trade is then run down to the point where overlap relief will cover the majority of the profits in the last period of trading.

1.135 *Starting a business – choosing an appropriate trading vehicle*

1.135 Alternatively, the individual could form a partnership with the new company and gradually move the share profits over to the company. Such a hybrid trading structure may also be constructed as an LLP that has a company as one of the members. These partnership structures can be used in the long term to allow the business owners to take advantage of the lower rates of corporation tax on retained earnings available to a company, yet maintain the flexibility of the partnership or LLP for the partners' drawing and benefits.

National insurance

1.136 The national insurance burden can be a significant influence on the decision whether or not to take income in the form of earnings from a company, and if it is not possible to take NIC-free income, then whether to incorporate at all. National insurance is payable on remuneration at levels over £100 per week (for 2007/08), and there is no upper limit on the remuneration that bears Class 1 NIC, although the rate payable by the employee drops to 1% once the upper earnings threshold is reached (£670 per week for 2007/08). Class 4 NICs payable by the self-employed are also unlimited in a similar fashion, but the Class 2 flat rate has been reduced to £2.20 per week to reflect the minimum social security benefits it provides.

Table 1.2 illustrates the massive gulf at the higher level of earnings between the contributions payable in respect of employed and self-employed persons.

Table 1.2: Comparison of employed and self-employed NIC 2007/08

Earnings or profits per annum before personal allowance of £5,225	Employed (not contracted out) NI Contributions above £5,225			Self-employed NI Contributions above £5,225		
	Employee (11% to £34,840 + 1%)	Employer (12.8%)	Total	Class 2 (£2.20 per week)	Class 4 (8% to £34,840 + 1%)	Total
£	£	£	£	£	£	£
10,000.00	525.25	611.20	1,136.45	114.40	382.00	496.40
20,000.00	1,625.25	1,891.20	3,516.45	114.40	1,182.00	1,296.40
40,000.00	3,309.25	4,451.20	7,760.45	114.40	2,420.80	2,535.20
80,000.00	3,709.25	9,571.20	13,280.45	114.40	2,820.80	2,935.20
160,000.00	4,509.25	19,811.20	24,320.45	114.40	3,620.80	3,735.20

1.137 The difference in the burden of NICs between the employed and self-employed is difficult to justify, as the only difference in terms of social security benefits is the entitlement to jobseekers allowance, which is not

Starting a business – choosing an appropriate trading vehicle **1.139**

available to those who have been self-employed. Nevertheless, NICs represent a very considerable fiscal impost in their own right, and their impact needs to be carefully considered by any individuals thinking of incorporating their business. The employer's NIC burden is purely a tax on employment, as the contributions paid do not secure rights to state benefits such as the state retirement pension for the employee. The employer must also pay Class 1A NICs on almost all benefits in kind provided for employees where those benefits are also taxable.

Combination of NIC and personal or corporate tax rates

1.138 The combined effect of the differing rates of NICs and tax on profits from unincorporated businesses and companies is shown in **Table 1.3**. These calculations assume that all the profits are retained in the company. Any tax credits that could be claimed by the sole trader have been ignored but the personal allowance of £5,225 (for 2007/08), has been taken into account.

Table 1.3: Comparison of tax charges for 2007/08

Profits per year	Tax and NIC payable by individual after personal allowance	Effective tax rate for sole trader or partner	Tax payable by the company (no associated companies)	Effective tax rate for the company
£	£	£	£	£
10,000	1,287.90	12.87%	2,000	20%
30,000	7,278.90	24.26%	6,000	20%
60,000	18,149.20	30.25%	12,000	20%
120,000	42,749.20	35.62%	24,000	20%
360,000	141,149.20	39.21%	79,500	22.08%
1,600,000.00	649,549.20	40.60%	480,000.00	30%

The effective rate of tax indicates that the corporate status does confer a clear tax benefit at all levels of profit above about £15,000. Although this break-even point will alter as the small companies rate of corporation tax increases to 21% from 1 April 2008, and 22% from 1 April 2009 (see **Table 1.1** at para **1.83**).

Combination of personal taxes

1.139 Considering the break-even point for tax on profits in isolation is meaningless, as the company director will normally have to extract funds from the company in order to live. The sole trader or partner is taxed on all the profits he makes whether or not he extracts those profits from the business, but the

1.140 *Starting a business – choosing an appropriate trading vehicle*

proprietor of a corporate business has the flexibility to control the level of personal tax he pays by extracting just enough income to keep his total taxable income within the basic rate band.

That profit extraction, whether by way of remuneration, benefits in kind, dividends or other methods, will generally be chargeable to income tax, and also in most cases national insurance.

Profit extraction strategy

1.140 There are tax savings that can be made operating a trading business through a company, particularly where the profits range up to £300,000 (see para **1.138**). However, the margin of tax advantage will depend on the method by which the proprietor extracts profits from the business. Where profits are extracted from the company as remuneration, which is subject to national insurance, the impact of the combined employers' and employees' NICs are capable of resulting in the overall fiscal cost being in excess of that which would be suffered without incorporation (see **1.136**).

1.141 The payment of dividends does not carry national insurance, so that can be a tax-efficient method of profit extraction for a basic-rate taxpayer. However, in certain cases dividend income may be reclassified as earnings and taxed as such (see para **1.94**), which will tip the balance back in favour of an unincorporated business.

Small salary, high dividends

1.142 Where a controlling director can take a small salary and extracts the balance of his income requirements from the company in another form that does not attract NICs such as dividends, interest or rent (see **1.107** to **1.110**) significant NIC savings may be made. However, this strategy is only tax efficient for certain companies, as the dividend is not tax deductible and so does not reduce the corporation tax payable, as a salary payment does. The tax efficiency also depends on the marginal tax rate of the shareholder.

The example below compares the standard profit extraction strategy for a small company of paying a low salary with the balance of profits taken out of the company as a dividend, with the taxation of the same business as a partnership.

Example 1.10

2007/08 Tax Year

	As a company F&J Ltd £	As a partnership Frankie £	As a partnership Johnnie £
Profits	60,000.00	30,000.00	30,000.00
Wages of up to personal allowances	10,450.00	5,225.00	5,225.00
Net taxable profits	49,550.00	24,775.00	24,775.00
Tax at 20%	9,910.00		
Net income to extract as dividend	39,640.00		
Tax credit attached to dividend	4,404.44		
Gross dividends	44,044.44		
Tax due at 10% on £22,022.22 dividend or £2,230 profits each	4,404.44	223.00	223.00
Less tax credit on dividend	(4,404.44)	—	—
Tax due at 22% on next £22,545 profits	—	4,959.90	4,959.90
Tax due at 40% over £34,600 profits	—	N/A	N/A
Class 2 NIC at £2.20 per week	—	114.40	114.40
Class 4 NIC at 8% on profits of £24,775	—	1,982.00	1,982.00
Net wages received (£5,225.00 each)	10,450.00	—	—
Total tax, including CT and NICs payable	9,910.00	7,279.30	7,279.30
Net income, including wages, after tax	50,090.00	22,720.70	22,720.70

As a partnership Frankie and Johnnie have a net income after tax of £45,441.40. If they run their business through a company and cover their personal allowances with a small salary, they will have a net dividend income of £39,640 plus a net earned income of £10,450, giving a total of £50,090. The structure of a company could thus increase their net income by £4,648.60, but the exact savings will depend on the method of extracting profits from the company.

Benefits in kind

1.143 A definite view on the potential tax saving gained by incorporating a business cannot be made without undertaking individual calculations which take into account the likely levels of pension contributions, drawings or remuneration required, and the benefits in kind to be provided through the business. Certain benefits, such as childcare vouchers and relocation costs can be provided tax free through a company, but would not be tax deductible for a sole

1.144 *Starting a business – choosing an appropriate trading vehicle*

trader, or partner. On the other hand, a car paid for by a partnership or unincorporated business may incur far lower tax charges than one provided for business and private use by the company.

Employment-related securities

1.144 To take profits out of the company as dividends the individual must first hold an appropriate proportion of the company's shares. Where the individual already works for the company, holds a directorship, is related to someone who is employed by the company, or is about to be employed by the company, any shares acquired in that company will almost certainly be 'employment-related securities' as defined in *ITEPA 2003, Pt 7*. Where this is the case, tax charges can arise at the point when those shares are acquired, or when benefits connected with those shares, such as dividends, are received.

1.145 Where employees are awarded shares, it is clear that those shares are employment-related, but shares acquired in many other situations are also caught by deeming provisions. Even gifts of shares between family members or others are caught unless the gift is made in the course of the normal domestic, family or personal relationships of the donor. Where such a gift of shares is made there should be some contemporaneous recording of the motive for the gift, and preferable a suitably worded deed of gift.

1.146 The tax charges on acquisition of employment-related securities normally only apply where:

- the shares have unusual terms (restricted securities, conditional securities or convertible securities); or
- the value of the shares is abnormal (high or low) as against a market value.

1.147 An income tax charge on dividends paid on shares classified as employment- related securities arises under *ITEPA 2003, s 447*, as the dividends paid on those shares are a benefit received in connection with those shares. However, the provisions in *s 447* only apply where something has been done on or after 2 December 2004 that affects the shares as part of a scheme or arrangement, the main purpose of which (or one of the main purposes) is the avoidance of tax or national insurance (*ITEPA 2003, s 447(4)*). If this is proven, the market value of the benefit from the share (the net dividend received) becomes chargeable as employment income instead of as dividend income. As employment income, the amount of the dividend must be subject to NIC and taxed under PAYE at the individual's marginal rate (up to 40%) rather than at the rate that applies to dividend: 10% or 32.5%, with a 10% tax credit.

1.148 The burden of proof would be on the taxpayer to demonstrate that whatever was done to the share (such as issuing the share or an alteration of terms), these actions were not intended to avoid tax and NICs. It is thought that paying a dividend on a share is not something that is '... done which affects the employment-related securities as part of a scheme or arrangement the main purpose (or one of the main purposes) of which is the avoidance of tax or national insurance contributions' (*ITEPA 2003, s 447(4)*). The action also needs to taken on or after 2 December 2004 to fall within *ITEPA 2003 s 447*. The ability of the provisions in *ITEPA 2003, s 447* to apply to dividends issued by owner-managed companies has not yet been tested in the courts. However, it is possible that a decision to pay dividends in the place of salary in a small company could be caught as a scheme or arrangement to avoid tax or NIC.

Disadvantages of dividends

Pension contributions

1.149 Dividends do not count as earnings for pension contribution purposes. The maximum pension contribution an individual may make per tax year and receive tax relief for is £3,600 (gross) or 100% of their UK earnings, if higher. So where individuals are trying to maximise their personal pension contributions for a year, they may prefer to be paid an increased salary or bonus rather than a dividend.

1.150 However, a more tax efficient strategy for owner-managed companies is to have the company pay the pension contribution as the employer. The company may pay a contribution of up to the annual allowance (£225,000 for 2007/08), irrespective of the level of salary paid to the employee. The pension contribution paid by the employer will not receive income tax relief, but it will qualify for a corporation tax deduction if the company can show the payment was made wholly and exclusively for the business. For further discussion of this point see **Chapter 10: Pensions**.

Flexibility

1.151 Where the directors and shareholders are different individuals it is difficult to use dividends to replace salaries to reward the directors separately from the non-working shareholders. Dividend waivers are commonly used to remedy this problem, although great care should be taken where these involve the shareholder's spouse or minor children to avoid the possibility of the settlements legislation applying to the arrangement (see **1.123**). It is essential that any dividend waiver is made before the dividend is paid.

Different classes of shares may be issued to working and non-working shareholders, although this strategy can create problems, as the shares issued to the employees are likely to be employment-related securities (see **1.144**).

1.152 *Starting a business – choosing an appropriate trading vehicle*

Administration

1.152 When paying a dividend certain administrative formalities have to be observed; dividend certificates, directors' minutes and resolutions must be prepared and filed. If dividends have not been properly declared in accordance with company law formalities, HMRC may challenge the payment and seek to treat the dividend as remuneration subject to Class 1 NICs, and require PAYE to be applied.

Retention of profits

1.153 Normally at least some of the profits will be retained within the business for future investment or to use as working capital, and these profits will add to the capital value of the business. A small company will generally have the advantage in this area as its profits will have been subject to corporation tax at just 20% for profits up to £300,000, whereas profits retained within the business of a partnership, sole trader or LLP will have been subject to tax at marginal rates of up to 40% plus national insurance at 8% up to £34,840, and 1% beyond that threshold.

1.154 The proprietor will need to assess the medium and long-term life of the business and the difficulties of extracting such capital value in the long term. There is a potential double capital gains tax charge where appreciating assets are held within the company, and a potential double charge on retained earnings, both of which will crystallise when the company is liquidated (see **1.157**). If the company is sold rather than liquidated, this will not actually crystallise the double capital gains tax charge. However, the share price may reflect the gains held in the company and a charge on retained earnings will in effect arise at that time.

Long-term intentions

Continuing the business

1.155 The relative importance of the long-term disadvantage of the double charge on capital gains will depend upon the timescale that the proprietor has in mind for retaining the business. If he plans to run the company for many years the cash flow advantage from the lower tax rates on profits may outweigh the capital tax disadvantage at the time of liquidation or sale. Alternatively there may in fact be no liquidation or sale because the business will be passed down to the next generation and continued within the family.

The decision in each case will depend very much on the precise circumstances of the business and the objectives of the proprietor. He will need to take a long view of the trends for both corporation tax and income tax rates, and weigh up the pros and cons of each course of action with considerable care.

Dissolving the company

1.156 Having once incorporated a business, it is not so easy to dissolve the company without incurring tax charges. Although certain tax reliefs apply when assets are transferred into a corporate body in return for shares, there are none that provide tax relief for the reverse process of distributing assets and moving a trade into individual hands. The directors/shareholders may purchase the business assets and trade from the company at their full market value, but this leaves cash within the company. The cash may be extracted as a dividend, or as capital distribution after the company has been put into liquidation or possibly as part of a purchase of own shares (see **1.117**).

For a more detailed discussion of the processes involved in the liquidation of a company see **Chapter 7: Winding-up the family or the owner-managed company**.

Double tax charge

1.157 The received wisdom for capital gains tax planning has been to keep valuable assets used for the business outside the company if possible, to avoid the double tax charge when the company sells the asset and the shareholder extracts the proceeds. The potential double charge springs from:

- the charge to corporation tax in respect of a capital gain realised on disposal of the asset by the company; and

- the further charge to capital gains tax arising in the event of the shareholder wishing to liquidate the company and extract the net proceeds of the disposal of the asset; or

- a further charge to income tax when the shareholder extracts the proceeds of the sale from the company as a dividend.

The individual only obtains the benefit of the gain on the disposal of the asset by the company by suffering, at least to some extent, a duplicate tax charge.

Where the company pays corporation tax at 20% and the individual takes the net proceeds of the sale as a dividend, the total tax paid may not be greater than the individual would have paid on the disposal of the asset held outside of the company.

1.158 *Starting a business – choosing an appropriate trading vehicle*

Example 1.11

Company		£
Chargeable gain		10,000
Less corporation tax at 20%		(2,000)
Available for distribution		8,000

Distributed to	**Basic-rate taxpayer** £	**Higher-rate taxpayer** £
Gross dividend including tax credit	8,888	8,888
Tax due at 10%/32.5%	888	2,888
Less tax credit at 10%	(888)	(888)
Income tax payable	Nil	2,000
Corporation tax paid on the gain	2,000	2,000
Total tax paid on gain	2,000	4,000
Effective tax rate on gain	20%	40%

1.158 Example 1.11 shows that a basic-rate taxpayer will suffer tax of 20% where the company disposes of the asset, and a higher-rate taxpayer will suffer total tax of 40% on the same disposal. The maximum rate of capital gains tax the individual would pay on an asset held personally is 40% and disposed of before 6 April 2008. However, that maximum rate is rarely paid as various tax reliefs may be available to both the individual and the company, as summarised in **Table 1.4** below:

Table 1.4

Tax relief	**Individuals, trustees and partners**	**Companies**
Taper Relief (withdrawn from 6 April 2008)	75% reduction in gain of business assets held for two complete years held since 1998. 40% reduction for non-business assets held for at least 10 years	Not available

Starting a business – choosing an appropriate trading vehicle **1.159**

Tax relief	Individuals, trustees and partners	Companies
Indexation allowance	Reduces effect of inflation between 31 March 1982 and 6 April 1998 for disposals made before 6 April 2008.	Reduces effect of inflation since 31 March 1982
Annual exemption	£9,200 for 2007/08	Not available
Substantial shareholding exemption	Not available	Exempts gain or loss on shares if at least 10% stake is held for one year within two years of sale
Roll-over of gains on replacement of business assets in the following categories	Land and buildings Fixed plant and machinery Ships, aircraft and hovercraft Satellites and space stations Goodwill Milk and potato quotas Ewe and sucker cow premium quotas Fish quota Lloyds syndicate rights	Land and buildings Fixed plant and machinery Ships, aircraft and hovercraft Satellites and space stations
Hold-over relief	Gifts of business assets and gifts on assets on which IHT is chargeable	Not available
Enterprise Investment Scheme	Unlimited gain may be deferred by investing in EIS shares	Not available
Corporate Venturing Scheme	Not available	Gains made on CVS shares can be deferred by reinvesting in new CVS shares
Transactions within a marriage/group	Transfers between a married couple or civil partners who are living together are treated as no gain/no loss	Transfers within a group of companies where there is a 75% relationship are generally treated as no gain/no loss.

1.159 Where real capital gains are likely to arise, the potential double tax charge must be considered when incorporating a business that holds appreciating assets which are used for the trade. In such cases it may be sensible to leave

1.160 *Starting a business – choosing an appropriate trading vehicle*

the asset in the private hands of the proprietor and rent or lease the asset to the company. On the subsequent sale of the asset the individual should achieve full business asset taper relief, provided the company is trading or is the holding company of a trading group and at least one of the following applies:

- the company is unquoted; or
- the individual is an officer or employee of the company or of another company within the same group; or
- the individual can control at least 5% of the voting rights in the company.

1.160 Where the asset is land or buildings on which there is an outstanding mortgage, the individual who retains the property will obtain relief for the interest paid against rent received from the company. The fact that rent has been received for a property used for business purposes does not affect the availability of business asset taper relief on the gain arising on the eventual disposal of that property. However, the desire to reduce a potential capital gains tax charge must be balanced against the 100% protection for inheritance tax which is offered by business property relief when the asset is held within a trading company (see **1.118**).

Chapter 2

Incorporation

Mark McLaughlin CTA (Fellow), ATT, TEP

The contents of this chapter include material adapted from the book *Incorporating a Business* (2nd edition) by Roger H Jones FTII, TEP

INTRODUCTION

2.1 The choice of the most tax-efficient trading medium (ie sole trader, partnership or limited company) is a complicated subject, involving many different considerations. A separate chapter of this book has therefore been dedicated to choosing an appropriate trading vehicle when a new business commences (see **Chapter 1: Starting a business**).

2.2 This chapter covers tax issues in connection with the process of incorporation. The subject has been a popular one for many years. The 'heyday' for business incorporations probably followed the *Finance Act 2002*, with the introduction of a 0% starting rate of corporation tax. Much has changed since then, including the withdrawal of the starting rate and an increase in the small companies rate of corporation tax. In an increasing number of cases, it has therefore become attractive for owner managers to disincorporate an existing company's business, and to operate as a sole trader or partnership instead. Disincorporation has its own set of tax problems associated with it, which are also briefly mentioned at the end of this chapter and covered in some depth in a separate chapter of this book (see **Chapter 5: Disincorporating a business**).

2.3 Whilst this chapter does not deal with non-tax issues arising from incorporation, it should be borne in mind that there are a number of legal and commercial issues arising from incorporation. These issues broadly include:

- Company formation (eg appointment of directors, allotment of shares etc).
- Shareholders' agreement (if there is one).
- Statutory obligations such as in terms of annual company returns and accounts submission to Companies House.

2.4 *Incorporation*

- Formalities of transferring the unincorporated business (eg documenting the transfer, accounting for the incorporation, notifications to HMRC, the transfer of employees between businesses, etc).

- Professional fees (ie in connection with the incorporation process, and the costs of preparing company accounts, which are often higher than for unincorporated businesses).

- Other practicalities (eg company accounts and financing, notifying customers, suppliers, insurance companies, employees, amending trade and telephone directories, etc).

2.4 A subject as wide as incorporation cannot be covered in detail in a single chapter. Readers are directed to the latest edition of *Incorporating a Business* by Roger H Jones (Tottel Publishing) for more comprehensive coverage.

INCOME TAX

2.5 The incorporation of a business involves the cessation of a former sole trade or partnership. It must be remembered that the company is a totally separate entity, chargeable to corporation tax and not income tax. It is therefore necessary to apply appropriate cessation adjustments to the unincorporated business. The cessation will, of itself, cause certain adjustments to the tax computation especially as regards stock and capital allowances (see **2.13, 2.17**).

Cessation computation

2.6 The general position under current year basis (CYB) is that the income tax assessment for a given year is based on the profits of the accounting period ended in that year. Adjustments are needed in the opening years to get to this position. Similar adjustments are necessary when a business ceases. There is no gap between the basis periods at cessation. The profits forming the basis of the assessment for the final tax year will be those earned in the period beginning immediately after the end of the basis period for the preceding year and ending on the date of cessation (*ITTOIA 2005, s 202*). Depending on the accounting date and date of cessation, this could be a period of more or less than 12 months.

2.7 Unless the incorporation takes place on the usual accounting date, the accounts to cessation of the sole trade (or partnership) will be for a period other than 12 months. Use of a different date for the final accounting period will not normally trigger the change of basis period rules. The cessation rules of *ITTOIA 2005, s 202* automatically take priority over the rules governing a change of accounting date (*ss 214–217*) for the year of cessation.

Overlap relief

2.8 Where 5 April has been used as the annual accounting date of a business, the total profits assessed will automatically equal the total profits earned. There will be no overlap between any income tax basis periods. Accounts drawn up to 31 March (or 1, 2, 3 or 4 April) may be treated as coterminous with the tax year end (*ITTOIA 2005, s 209*).

Drawing up accounts to 5 April (or 31 March) has the advantage of simplicity. The profit earned during a tax year suffers income tax in that same year. No basis period adjustments are necessary. For this reason alone, many small sole traders will choose this accounting date.

2.9 In using an accounting date other than one coterminous with the tax year end, there will be one or more years in which the basis periods for two adjacent tax years overlap. The logic to creation and use of overlap relief is that the profits earned throughout the life of a business are all subject to tax once, and once only. An adjustment may be made on a change of accounting date during the life of the business. Any remaining overlap relief can be useful in the tax year in which the business ceases.

Overlap relief is given as if it were an additional trading deduction incurred in that period (*ITTOIA 2005, s 205(1)*). In most instances, the use of overlap relief simply reduces the assessable profit in the final year. Depending on the relative size of the profit and the overlap relief, a loss may be created. Equally, if a loss already arose in the period of cessation, the overlap relief will augment that loss. A loss created or enhanced by overlap relief is treated in exactly the same fashion as any other trading loss. The usual loss relief claims may be made.

2.10 In any other case other than a 31 March accounting date, there is no substitute for looking at the realised profits, projected future profits, amount of overlap relief and dates in each case. A wrong decision can result in a substantial additional income tax liability on cessation or, at least, a cash flow disadvantage. The proprietor is not going to welcome that as a penalty for incorporation. There is also the issue of adjustments which vary the profits. Particular issues here include stock valuation and capital allowances (see below).

Payment of tax

2.11 Very few sole traders (and partnerships) seem to make any provision for tax in their business accounts. For the most part, tax liabilities falling due now are paid out of profits earned now.

Example 2.1

Chris drew up accounts to 30 June each year. Ignoring incorporation, the tax due for 2007/08 would be payable by two payments on account on 31 January 2008 and 31 July 2008, with a balancing payment on 31 January 2009. He will quite

2.12 *Incorporation*

probably meet the 31 January 2009 bill out of incoming funds at the end of 2008, despite the fact that he began earning the relevant profits as long ago as 1 July 2006 (the basis period for 2007/08 is 1 July 2006 to 30 June 2007).

2.12 The proprietor needs to be warned in advance of the change in timing of tax payments which is occasioned by incorporation:

- Chris's sole-trader self-assessment for 2007/08 was based on profits earned in the period 1 July 2006 to 30 June 2007. Tax is payable in instalments falling due between 31 January 2008 and 31 January 2009. Payment of the tax therefore falls much later than the inflow of the corresponding funds.
- If the incorporated business draws up accounts to 30 June 2008, tax is payable on 1 April 2009, a delay of only nine months.
- If Chris draws a taxable salary from the company, income tax and NIC is normally payable only 14 days after the month of payment (or 17 days, if paid electronically).

The cashflow considerations of funding the income tax (and NIC) liabilities of the unincorporated business up to the date of cessation should not be overlooked or underestimated. Forward planning (eg projecting tax liabilities and payment dates) based on the anticipated date of incorporation should be implemented as far as possible in advance.

Treatment of stock and work in progress

Stock

2.13 The basic position regarding the transfer of stock upon incorporation is that it is always deemed to pass between connected persons at an arm's-length price (*ITTOIA 2005, s 177*). The meaning of 'connected persons' is defined in *ITTOIA 2005, s 179* and is rather wider than the usual definitions (in *ICTA 1988, s 839* or *ITA 2007, ss 993–994*).

2.14 However, the transferor and transferee (ie sole trader or partner and new company) may jointly elect (under *ITTOIA 2005, s 178*) that the stock is instead to be treated as transferred at the higher of cost or the amount actually paid. Since the sale price or market value must be included in the cessation accounts of the unincorporated business to determine the final profit, but is also deductible in arriving at the profits of the company, there is scope for planning. If the unincorporated business pays tax at 40% but the company at only 20% (say), the stock should be transferred at a low value to reduce the income tax profits at the expense of corporate tax profits increasing but taxed at lower rate.

The choice of transfer value is not infinitely variable though. It seems that it must either be market value or cost (or net realisable value, if lower).

Where an election is appropriate, it must be made within two years of the end of the chargeable period in which the transfer occurs. However, it will often be practical to submit the election with the tax return covering the cessation period of the unincorporated business. Note that such an election is only permissible where stock is 'sold or transferred for valuable consideration'. It appears that if the stock is gifted to the company (which is not an impossible position in certain types of incorporation) then market value must prevail with no option available.

Work in progress

2.15 For the vast majority of businesses, everything so far mentioned about stock applies equally to work in progress. There are, though, distinct rules concerning the valuation of work in progress on discontinuance of a profession or vocation. These are to be found in *ITTOIA 2005, ss 182–185*.

The basic position is that where there is valuable consideration (eg on a business transfer in exchange for shares) the work in progress is taken to have that value, which must be the market value. On a gift, market value must prevail. HMRC is normally prepared to accept whatever value is attributed to work in progress, unless it is blatantly unreasonable. HMRC will not seek to make any adjustment so long as the value attributed to work in progress follows the basis consistently used for accounting purposes. Accounts prepared in accordance with UITF 40 will usually be required. If there is occasion to deal with the incorporation of a professional partnership, ICAEW Technical Release TAX 7/95, 15 February 1995, includes a guidance note on the taxation implications of transfers of work in progress on the incorporation of such a business.

2.16 There is a further provision relating to the cessation of a profession or vocation in that the taxpayer may elect for the closing work in progress on cessation to be taken as having its cost value (*ITTOIA 2005, s 185*). Any realised excess is then treated as a post-cessation receipt under *ITTOIA 2005, s 243*.

Capital allowances

Plant and machinery

2.17 Writing down allowances (WDA) and first year allowances (FYA) are not available in the final chargeable period. The final chargeable period is (for the main pool or long-life asset pool) the chargeable period in which the

2.18 *Incorporation*

qualifying activity is permanently discontinued (*CAA 2001, s 65(1)*). WDA is prohibited by *CAA 2001, s 55(4)*, and FYA is prohibited by *CAA 2001, s 46(2)*, General Exclusion 1.

2.18 In virtually every case, the new company will be connected with the proprietors of the unincorporated business. In most cases, the company's shareholders and directors will be identical to the sole trader or business partners. Connection follows under *CAA 2001, s 575*. The disposal value of plant and machinery is to be interpreted in accordance with the table in *CAA 2001, s 61*. This bears careful consideration because there may be important planning advantages. The result is that there will be a balancing allowance or balancing charge. A balancing allowance occurs when the disposal value is less than the written down value of the pool (*CAA 2001, s 55(2)*) and is given as a deduction in the income tax computation in a similar fashion to a WDA or FYA. A balancing charge occurs when the disposal value is more than the written down value of the pool (*CAA 2001, s 55(3)*) and is treated as an addition to profit.

2.19 The parties do not necessarily have to suffer the balancing allowance or charge. Instead the transferor and transferee (the previous sole trader and the company) may make a joint election under *CAA 2001, s 266* that the plant and machinery are transferred at a price which gives rise to neither a balancing allowance nor a balancing charge. So what does that really mean? There is nothing in *CAA 2001, s 267* to override the rules in *CAA 2001, ss 46, 55* that prohibit a WDA or FYA in the final chargeable period. And the trade of the former sole trader *is* discontinued at the point of incorporation. So, the plant and machinery is actually transferred at the tax written down value at the *start* of the final period of account of the sole trade.

2.20 The absence of any capital allowances at all in the final period of account means that great care should be taken in selecting the date on which to incorporate. A tidy-minded adviser may favour incorporation at the traditional accounting date and make a *CAA 2001, s 266* election 'because it's easier'. This may result in the trader getting no capital allowances in the last period when, perhaps, there are substantial profits taxed at 40%. The pay-off, of course, is that the company gets a higher writing down allowance in its first period of trade but it pays tax at only 20%. Is this good planning, especially if the client bought a large piece of equipment just before incorporation in anticipation of first year allowances to mitigate the tax on the profits? When there might be 100% FYA on a low emission car one needs to be very careful that this is not prejudiced by the act of incorporation. Pre-incorporation planning must encompass the effect on capital allowances.

Remember that capital allowances are given for a period of account (not a year of assessment). Where accounts have traditionally been drawn up to 31 March, incorporation on that date will mean the loss of FYA or WDA for a full accounting period. How about incorporating at 30 April instead? The final period of account in which no capital allowances can be given is therefore only one month – a far more acceptable proposition. How short might the final period actually be? In theory, perhaps as little as a day (though this might be unduly provocative to HMRC); a month is probably realistic.

2.21 The above analysis applies to incorporation by the *TCGA 1992, s 162* route. There is an alternative. This is to ignore the incorporation relief in that section and go for the alternative afforded by *TCGA 1992, s 165*. This relates to a gift of business assets, though payment of some proceeds is possible. The company could actually pay the sole trader for the plant and machinery. Where there are actual proceeds, then they are taken as the disposal value under *CAA 2001, s 61(2)*, Table Item 1. Market value is not substituted even where the vendor and purchaser are connected. The sale proceeds could be left outstanding on loan account with the company. The proprietor can then draw down on the loan account at a later date without further tax charge.

Capital allowances changes

2.22 The government issued a consultation document in July 2007 ('Business tax reform: capital allowances changes') on a new regime for plant and machinery allowances from April 2008. The proposed new regime means, for example, that the main rate of WDA will reduce from 25% to 20%. In addition, most FYAs will disappear (although 100% allowances will continue to be available for qualifying 'green' expenditure), to be replaced by a new 'Annual investment allowance' (AIA) of 100% for the first £50,000 of qualifying expenditure for businesses of any size, with WDAs being available on any excess expenditure over that limit. The rate of allowances on fixtures integral to a building will be only 10%, but the rate of WDA for long-life assets will increase from 6% to 10%.

At the time of writing (November 2007), the draft legislation introducing the above changes was not yet available. It therefore remains to be seen how the new rules will interact with business incorporations, and the extent to which anti-avoidance legislation will affect the company's entitlement to AIA. However, it is likely that some form of 'connected persons' rule will be introduced to prevent unincorporated businesses from incorporating in order to obtain the allowance.

Industrial and agricultural buildings

2.23 A sole trader or partnership using an industrial building (or qualifying hotel) will get WDAs (ie IBAs) on qualifying expenditure. At present, those

2.24 *Incorporation*

WDAs need not cease when the trade of the unincorporated business ends. However, following changes introduced in *Finance Act 2007*, IBAs are gradually being phased out, and will cease to be available altogether from 1 April 2011 onwards. In addition, the *Finance Act 2007* changes withdrew balancing adjustments and the recalculation of WDAs on the sale of an industrial building with effect from 21 March 2007. However, those measures are subject to an exception in respect of qualifying enterprise zone expenditure, and also transitional rules in respect of a 'relevant pre-commencement contract' (ie broadly a written contract made before 21 March 2007, where certain conditions are satisfied) (*FA 2007, s 36*).

2.24 Similar provisions to those mentioned above apply in respect of agricultural buildings.

2.25 The withdrawal of the balancing adjustment rules means that in most cases following incorporation the company, as the purchaser of a second-hand industrial building, will simply take over the allowances to which the previous owner would have been entitled, until they cease to be available on 1 April 2011.

2.26 In relation to pre-21 March 2007 incorporations, a balancing adjustment for IBAs is only required on the happening of a balancing event (*CAA 2001, s 314*). The main balancing events are as follows (*CAA 2001, s 315*):

- sale of the relevant interest;
- if the relevant interest is a lease, the ending of the lease except where the person entitled to it acquires the reversionary interest;
- the building is demolished or destroyed;
- the building ceases altogether to be used.

Upon incorporation, three alternatives arise:

- the building is sold to the company;
- the building is retained by one (or more) business proprietors and a long lease is granted to the company;
- the building is retained by the proprietors and a short lease or mere licence to occupy is granted to the company.

Where there is a sale of the relevant interest, proceeds from the balancing event will primarily be the proceeds of sale (*CAA 2001, s 316*, Table Item 1). Where the parties to the transaction are connected, which will almost invariably be the case on incorporation, market value is substituted (*CAA 2001, ss 567, 568*). If the transfer is by way of gift, then market value is imposed (*CAA 2001, s 573*). For this purpose, the sale proceeds or market value cannot exceed the first cost

Incorporation **2.31**

of the building; where they do, the capital gains tax position must be considered. Accordingly, a balancing adjustment is calculated.

2.27 The vendor and purchaser may override the need for a balancing adjustment by joint election under *CAA 2001, s 569* that the transaction be deemed to take place at a value equal to the residue of qualifying expenditure at that time. Such an election must be made within two years of the end of the chargeable period, but in practice is often submitted with the business proprietor's tax return for the year of incorporation.

2.28 In the case of agricultural buildings, unlike IBAs, a balancing adjustment does not automatically arise on the sale of the relevant interest in an agricultural building. The basic position is that the residue of allowances simply passes to the purchaser (*CAA 2001, s 375*). That is to say, the former business proprietor gets WDAs up to the date of incorporation. The company gets WDAs of the same amount for the remainder of the chargeable periods throughout the original 25-year life of the building. If the incorporation takes place in the middle of a chargeable period, the allowance is apportioned for that period between the transferor and transferee. There can be a balancing event, but only where both parties to the transaction specifically elect for one (*CAA 2001, s 382*). Where a former business proprietor retains the relevant interest in the business, the rights to ABAs remain with him. Consideration must then be given to payment of rent.

National Insurance contributions

2.29 The impact on National Insurance contributions (NICs) must be taken into account in any consideration of incorporation. In some ways, it may seem paradoxical that one should want to move from self-employment where the 'mainstream' rate (Class 4) is now 8% to employment where the mainstream rate (Class 1 primary and secondary) is 23.8%. Of course, self-employed earners over the age of 16 and under pensionable age are also liable to pay Class 2 contributions at a flat rate (*SSCBA 1992, s 11(1)*), at a rate (for 2007/08) of £2.20 per week.

2.30 In an owner-managed company, where earnings fall between the Class 1 NIC 'Primary Threshold' and the 'Upper Earnings Limit', the total NIC payable is at a rate of 23.8%, a not inconsiderable sum. It is well in excess of the 8% NIC payable by a self-employed person. To avoid the disadvantage, one must be prepared to withdraw funds other than by way of salary. At this level, of course, the employee will be paying only basic rate income tax so that the total impost is not as great as that for a higher rate taxpayer. Nevertheless, a dividend is still to be preferred.

2.31 Unless the incorporation of the business takes place on 6 April, there will be a tax year in which the proprietor is both self-employed (as a sole trader

2.32 *Incorporation*

or partner of the existing business) and an employed earner (as director/employee of the new company). There may be a liability for Class 1, Class 2 and Class 4 contributions. Fortunately, there are rules to limit the maximum amount of contributions payable where an individual has more than one employment or both employment and self-employment.

Where both Class 1 and Class 2 contributions are payable, the liability for primary Class 1 contributions and Class 2 contributions is not to exceed an amount equal to 53 primary Class 1 contributions payable on earnings at the UEL for the year (*Social Security (Contributions) Regulations 2001, SI 2001/1004, reg 21*). However, the position is complicated because there is required to be made a further adjustment in respect of the additional rate of 1% which has no upper earnings limit.

2.32 The possibility of total contributions exceeding the relevant maxima may not be identified during the course of the tax year. Thus, contributions actually paid may be excessive. Overpaid contributions may be recovered from HMRC. Where the situation of overpayment is foreseen, it is possible to make application to defer payment of Class 1 and/or Class 4 contributions. In theory such applications should be made before the beginning of the tax year to which they relate. This may make it an impractical option in the case of incorporation unless this occurs early in the tax year. If an application is successfully made and the contributions actually paid prove insufficient then the shortfall must be satisfied by direct payment to HMRC.

None of the foregoing has any effect on the new company as secondary contributor. There are no provisions to limit the secondary contributions in respect of an employed earner. This is also true for Class 1A (and Class 1B) contributions which are payable only by the employer.

An employed person (whether self-employed or an employee) pays NIC during his working life and generates a contribution record against which the basic National Insurance Retirement Pension (NIRP) is paid after retirement age.

2.33 Class 1 Contributions start at the PT. However, 'payment of contributions' for NIRP purposes includes receipt of earnings equal to or exceeding the 'Lower Earnings Level' (LEL), but on which no contributions are actually paid (*SSCBA 1992, s 6A(2)*). On earnings lying between the PT and LEL, a credit is available in order to establish a contribution record for NIRP even though no contributions are actually due. This is a very useful planning tool in remunerating small company directors. Note that the company must still have a PAYE scheme in operation and submit an annual return in order to record the earnings for this purpose, even if no income tax or NIC is actually payable.

From 6 April 2009, there is to be an 'upper accrual point' for National Insurance contributions, above which contributions will continue to be paid but additional state pension entitlement will not be enhanced (*Pensions Act 2007, s 12*). This appears to strengthen the case for dividend payments following incorporation, unless of course future changes make dividends potentially less attractive than they are at present.

Capital Gains Tax

2.34 The Pre-Budget Report 2007 on 9 October 2007 announced fundamental changes to the CGT regime, with effect from 6 April 2008. The introduction of a standard CGT rate of 18% came as a complete surprise to most taxpayers and advisers. The proposed changes of most potential interest to business owners considering incorporation are the withdrawal of taper relief and indexation allowance. The time delay between the changes being announced and the introduction of the new CGT regime provided an opportunity for business owners to consider whether to incorporate before 6 April 2008 where, for example, maximum business asset taper relief had accrued in respect of free goodwill. Of course, businesses will continue to incorporate after 5 April 2008, for commercial reasons if not for tax savings.

2.35 What assets might the business own? There could be stock, tools and equipment, land and buildings, goodwill and investments. In all but the smallest businesses, there will be CGT considerations on the transfer of a business to a company. Many items of tools and equipment (including motor vehicles), fixtures and fittings in buildings etc will have attracted capital allowances as plant and machinery. Income tax adjustments will be necessary. This does not stop assets of this type being chargeable to CGT (though chattels having a value of £6,000 or less and motor cars are exempt (*TCGA 1992, ss 262, 263*)). However, *TCGA 1992, s 37* excludes from the CGT computation any consideration taken into account as a receipt in computing income. An actual gain in respect of this type of asset will therefore only arise where it is transferred for a value greater than original cost (which will be rare). There may be income tax consequences to certain buildings too (eg hotels, industrial buildings) and agricultural buildings) but, in most instances, we need to consider the CGT aspects on transfer of land and buildings.

2.36 The subject of goodwill and whether it can be transferred is a subject in itself. In many instances, goodwill will not appear on the balance sheet of an unincorporated business. Ensure that it is of a type which is transferable.

2.37 A gain realised on the disposal of one asset, which has been used in a trade, may be deferred against the acquisition of a second asset where the new asset is a wasting asset, also used in a trade (*TCGA 1992, s 154*). In that case, no adjustment is made to the base cost of the second asset. The gain on the first asset is calculated according to normal rules and simply deferred until the earliest of:

- the disposal of asset number two;

2.38 Incorporation

- the cessation of use of asset number two in a trade;
- the expiry of ten years from the acquisition of asset number two.

If an asset carrying a deferred gain is transferred to a company on incorporation, there is a disposal. The original deferred gain comes back into charge. And, there is nothing you can do about it. None of the reliefs examined below cope with this. The deferred gain now chargeable arose on an earlier disposal and cannot be expunged by the incorporation reliefs. The tax will be due and payable. When preparing to incorporate a business, always check whether there have been previous claims to rollover chargeable gains on business assets within the last ten years. Especially note whether any such gains were merely deferred and not 'properly' rolled.

2.38 The transfer of assets from an unincorporated business to a company is a disposal for the purposes of CGT. Further, it is invariably a disposal between connected persons. For this purpose, a company is connected with another person, if that person has control of it or if that person and persons connected with him together have control of it (*TCGA 1992, s 286(6)*). Where the transactions are between connected persons, the rules of *TCGA 1992, s 18* prevails, in particular that the transaction is to be treated as a bargain not made at arm's length. This in turn brings *TCGA 1992, s 17* into play, to the extent that the consideration for the business proprietor(s) disposal of the assets is to be treated as their market value, and the company's corresponding acquisition value is also to be treated as market value. So, for the purposes of the CGT computation, the chargeable assets of a business are treated as passing at market value. However, the actual consideration may be:

- shares in the company, which may be of more than one class;
- loan stock in the form of a debenture or similar (although this is rare in the case of small private companies);
- cash, often left outstanding on a director's loan account;
- Cnothing, it being quite common to gift the assets of a business to the company.

2.39 If there were to be a large chargeable gain, with tax payable, this would amount to a significant disincentive to incorporation. Various reliefs exist to alleviate this problem and the rest of this chapter explores them:

- *TCGA 1992, s 162* ('Rollover Relief on Transfer of Business');
- *TCGA 1992, s 165* ('Relief for Gifts of Business Assets').

These two are the most used, the latter of which is more flexible. However, in addition there is EIS CGT deferral relief (*TCGA 1992, Sch 5B*) sometimes referred to as 'The Third Way'.

Section 162 relief

2.40 The relief is mandatory if specified conditions are met and does not require a claim. The cost of the new assets (ie the company shares) is deducted from the chargeable gain. Correspondingly, the base cost of the new assets is reduced by the amount left out of the CGT computation on incorporation. There are provisions for apportionment where the consideration is not wholly in shares. The relief applies where three conditions are satisfied (*TCGA 1992, s 162(1)*):

- a person who is not a company (ie sole trader or partner) transfers to a company a business as a going concern;
- together with the whole assets of the business, possibly excluding cash; and
- the business is so transferred wholly or partly in exchange for shares issued by the company to the person transferring the business.

The relief is therefore very specific. All of the assets of the business (apart from cash which is, of course, not a chargeable asset) must be transferred to the company and this must be done wholly or partly in exchange for shares. In fact, cash is not the only item which may be left out. HMRC Concession D32 indicates that relief under *s 162* is not precluded by the fact that some or all of the liabilities of the business are not taken over by the company. 'Cash' in this context is accepted by HMRC as including sums held by the business in a bank deposit or current account' (CGM 65719).

Example 2.2

Janine decides to incorporate her retail gift shop. A very simplified balance sheet shows the assets to be stock £30,000, shop premises £100,000 (cost £80,000) and goodwill £20,000 (cost nil). The entire business is transferred to a newly formed company Super Gifts Ltd and 1,000 ordinary £1 shares are issued to her.

(a) The market value of the 1,000 shares is £150,000 being the total value of the assets transferred in (market value applies as this is a connected persons transaction).

(b) The consideration (shares issued) is apportioned in a just and reasonable manner, thus:

Stock	£30,000
Shop premises	£100,000
Goodwill	£20,000

2.41 *Incorporation*

(c) The chargeable gains are:

	£	£
Shop – consideration	100,000	
Less: Cost	(80,000)	20,000
Goodwill, consideration	20,000	
Less: Cost	nil	20,000
Total gain		£40,000

The whole of this gain will be rolled over under *s 162*.

(d) The CGT base cost of the shares, for a future computation on disposal is:

Market value	150,000
Less: Gain rolled over *s 162*	(40,000)
Base cost	£110,000

2.41   However, the gain will not always be fully relieved. The business must be transferred as a going concern and must therefore reflect liabilities to be satisfied by the company. An undertaking to satisfy these liabilities amounts to further consideration. Concession D32 prevents the assumption of liabilities from being treated as consideration for the purposes of the *s 162* computation. However, this does not mean that the liabilities can be ignored in determining the market value of the assets transferred. Where the liabilities are relatively high, the net asset value of the business (which equals the value of the shares issued) may be low. If the chargeable assets have large inherent capital gains (watch for goodwill off the balance sheet) then it may be impossible to roll all of the gain – the base cost of the shares cannot go below zero.

Example 2.3

Colin is a sole trader publican at the Railway Tavern. The balance sheet is thus:

	£
Freehold property	300,000
Fixtures and fittings	25,000
Stock	25,000
	350,000
Less: Bank loan	(225,000)
Creditors	(50,000)
	£75,000

Incorporation **2.42**

Represented by:
Capital account   £75,000

The property originally cost £200,000, and there is goodwill off balance sheet of £75,000 for which Colin paid nothing.

He formed the Railway Tavern Ltd on 1 September 2007 and 1,000 ordinary £1 shares were issued to him.

(a) The market value of the shares issued is £150,000 being the total net value of the assets transferred in (ie £75,000 balance sheet net assets, plus £75,000 goodwill).

(b) The chargeable gains are:

		£	£
Property:	Consideration (market value)	300,000	
	Less: Cost	(200,000)	100,000
Goodwill:	Consideration (market value)	75,000	
	Less: Cost	nil	75,000
			175,000
	Less: Rolled over under s 162		(150,000)
Chargeable gain			£25,000

Subject to taper relief and annual exemption, this gain is immediately taxable.

(c) The CGT base cost of the shares is:

Market value	150,000
Less: Gain rolled over s 162	(150,000)
	£nil

2.42 In the above situation where all the assets are transferred, only shares are issued and yet a chargeable gain still arises. Occasionally, though, other consideration might be taken. This could be in the form of loan stock issued by the company or more simply the creation of a director's loan account with a credit balance. In these circumstances, the gain which may be rolled over is limited to the fraction A/B of the amount of the gain on the old assets, where:

- A is the cost of the new assets (shares); and
- B is the value of the whole consideration received by the transferor in exchange for the business (*TCGA 1992, s 162(4)*).

2.42 *Incorporation*

Example 2.4

Linda runs a grocery business as a sole trader and decides to incorporate, with effect from 1 October 2007. The net asset value of her business is as follows:

Freehold property	200,000	(cost 100,000)
Fixtures and fittings	4,000	(cost 10,000)
Stock	6,000	(cost 6,000)
Goodwill	30,000	(cost nil)
Debtors	5,000	
	245,000	
Less: Trade creditors	(20,000)	
	£225,000	

Linda transfers the business to The Corner Shop Ltd which issues 1,000 ordinary £1 shares to her and a director's loan account of £40,000 is created.

(a) The market value of the shares issued is £185,000 being the net asset value of the business transferred in, less the loan account.

(b) The chargeable gains are:

	£	£
Property: Consideration	200,000	
Less: Cost	(100,000)	100,000
Goodwill: Consideration	30,000	
Less: Cost	nil	30,000
		130,000

Amount rolled over under s 162:

A/B x 130,000 =

$\dfrac{185,000}{225,000} \times 130,000 =$ (106,889)

Chargeable gain £23,111

Subject to taper relief and the annual exemption.

The CGT base cost of the shares is:

Market value	185,000
Less: Gain rolled over *s 162*	(106,889)
	£78,111

Incorporation **2.44**

2.43 The application of *s 162* is relatively inflexible, for two main reasons. First, it requires the transfer of all the business assets (with very limited exceptions) to the company. Second, most of the inherent value of the business is locked into the share capital of the company and cannot readily be extracted. Some commentators recommend that, if there is a substantial capital account in the unincorporated business, then the proprietors should be advised to draw down on it before incorporation. Presumably such a capital account exists in the first place in order to fund continuing trading operations. If this is the case, then there is every likelihood that the funds withdrawn will be reintroduced into the company shortly afterwards by means of a credit to a director's loan account.

Perceived challenges to this process are often said to stem from *Furniss (Inspector of Taxes) v Dawson* [1984] STC 153, in that the transactions are preordained and the intermediate one has no real purpose. The net effect of which is to re-characterise the transaction as if the business had been transferred for a consideration partly in the issue of shares and partly in cash. A counter-argument might be demonstrated by the incorporation agreement (assuming that there is one) showing the intention to transfer the entire assets of the business in return for shares. In which case, the withdrawal of cash from the capital account must be part of the net business assets and is therefore now encapsulated in the share capital. Could a similar challenge stem from the principle in *Ramsay (WT) Ltd v IRC* [1981] STC 174, notably that there is a circular series of transactions leaving the business in the same position as before it started? It is better not to risk it by being too provocative.

It may be necessary to remove and retain part of the pre-incorporation capital account, for example to meet the tax liabilities of the unincorporated business. Provided that the final accounts of the unincorporated business have made full provision for outstanding tax liabilities, this should not be a problem.

2.44 It may be worthwhile thinking carefully about the consideration to be given by the company. If it is entirely the issue of shares, then the whole gain on the transfer of the business assets is (usually) deferred but then their full value is locked into the company. If some other consideration is given, there will be a chargeable gain, but does it need to be a taxable gain?

Example 2.5

The facts are as in the previous example. The net asset value of Linda's business upon incorporation on 1 October 2007 is £225,000. The gross chargeable gains are £130,000.

2.45 Incorporation

Would Linda be better advised to create a loan account of (say) £63,600 as well as taking 1,000 ordinary shares?

(a) The market value of the shares is £161,400 being the net asset value of the business transferred in, less the loan account.

(b) Chargeable gains (gross), as before   130,000
Amount rolled over under *s 162*:
A/B x 130,000 =
$\frac{161,400}{225,000} \times 130,000 =$ (93,253)

Chargeable gain	36,747
Business asset taper relief (75%)	(27,560)
	9,187
Annual exemption (to cover)	(9,187)
Taxable gain	£nil

Linda has therefore created a director's loan account of £63,600 on which she is later free to draw with no additional tax liability.

(c) The CGT base cost of the shares is:

Market value	161,400
Less: Gain rolled over *s 162*	(93,253)
	£68,147

This is only £9,964 below the previous example, but Linda has an additional credit of £23,600 to her loan account.

The above planning opportunity will be diminished from 6 April 2008, following the withdrawal of taper relief as originally announced in Pre-Budget Report 2007 on 9 October 2007. However, the opportunity remains to make use of the CGT annual exemption in the manner described.

2.45 As mentioned, the CGT incorporation relief in *s 162* is mandatory. No claim is required. If the individual making the disposal of chargeable assets to the company meets the conditions laid down, then the relief is given.

However, *TCGA 1992, s 162A* permits a specific claim to disapply *s 162*. When this provision was introduced (in *Finance Act 2002*), it helped to overcome a potential problem involving the interaction of incorporation relief and taper relief, namely that the shares in the company issued on incorporation are a new asset and the qualifying holding period for taper relief must begin again. If the shares were sold shortly after incorporation then any previously earned entitlement to business asset taper relief on the assets transferred would be lost. This problem will disappear with the withdrawal of taper relief from 6 April 2008, but is still a potential issue for incorporations before that date.

2.46 If *s 162* relief is to be overridden, the business proprietor making the disposal to the company must make a claim usually by the second anniversary of 31 January following the year of assessment in which the disposal took place. This is shortened to the first anniversary if the shares are sold before the end of the year following incorporation. If the business was transferred from a partnership to a company, each individual partner may separately choose whether or not to make a *s 162A* claim (*TCGA 1992, s 162A(3), (4), (7)*).

The effect of the election is that the gain on disposal of business assets to the company is calculated in the usual way, taking (if before 6 April 2008) the benefit of taper relief. There is no deferral and tax is payable on the net gain. The base cost of the shares issued on incorporation is therefore market value. Presumably, a disposal within two years will not show a huge gain so that the tax payable on a share disposal would be minimal. If, having made a claim under *s 162A*, there is a transfer of shares between spouses it is ignored. The sale of shares by the recipient spouse is treated as made by the donor spouse (*TCGA 1992, s 162A(5)*).

Section 165 relief

2.47 Many incorporations use the relief in *TCGA 1992, s 165* instead. Although the relief is headed 'Relief for Gifts of Business Assets' it does not simply apply to gifts. It would be better termed a relief for transfers of business assets at undervalue.

A business asset for this purpose is defined as including an asset, or interest in, an asset used for the purposes of a trade, profession or vocation carried on by the transferor (*TCGA 1992, s 165(2)(a)(i)*). Any chargeable asset used in a sole trade or partnership by the asset owner is therefore encompassed.

2.48 The relief applies where the asset owner disposes of it by a bargain which is not at arm's length (*TCGA 1992, s 165(1)(a)*). As mentioned, the transfer of assets from an unincorporated business proprietor to the company will normally be such because it is a connected party transaction. The effect of the relief is that a chargeable gain otherwise arising is reduced by the 'held over gain' and the amount of the company's CGT base cost is also reduced by the held over gain (*TCGA 1992, s 165(4)*).

2.49 Incorporation

2.49 Unlike s 162 (application of which is mandatory in the relevant circumstances), a specific claim is required for the gift relief to apply (*TCGA 1992, s 165(1)(b)*). The claim must be made jointly by both the individual making the transfer and the company. HMRC require the claim to be made on the form contained in Helpsheet IR295 to the self-assessment tax return. No shorter time limit is specified, so the general time limit of five years following 31 January following the year of assessment in which the transfer takes place applies. In practice, claims will nearly always be made long before this (normally on the business owner's tax return for the year of incorporation), because otherwise CGT on the gain would become payable. Note that *s 165* contains no requirement that the transfer shall be the whole of the business or even all of the assets used in the business. It is simply 'an asset' used in a trade, profession or vocation. Thus there is a flexibility which is absent from the *s 162* process.

2.50 The amount of the gain which can be held over is as follows:

- in the case of a pure gift (no proceeds at all), the gain which would otherwise arise in deeming the proceeds to be market value (*TCGA 1992, s 165(6)*), or

- in the case of a transfer at under value, the amount by which the deemed gain exceeds the excess of the actual consideration over the costs deductible in the CGT computation (*TCGA 1992, s 165(7)*).

The costs deductible are those given by *TCGA 1992, s 38* only and, therefore, specifically exclude indexation allowance, which the Pre-Budget Report 2007 announced ceases to be available from 6 April 2008 in any event.

Example 2.6

Grant runs a musical supplies business. He decides to incorporate it but wishes to retain a number of assets personally. He will, however, transfer to the company the business premises now valued at £180,000. The CGT base cost is £75,000.

(a) Capital gain arising:

	£
Consideration (market value)	180,000
Less: Cost	(75,000)
	£105,000

(b) If Grant gifts the property to the company the whole of the gain is held over. The base cost of the property for the company is:

	£
Market value	180,000)
Less: Held over gain	(105,000)
Base cost for future disposal	£75,000

(c) If Grant sells the property to the company for £50,000.

Actual proceeds	50,000
Less: Allowable cost	(75,000)
Excess	£nil

The result is as in (b) above. This is probably not a realistic option as Grant is missing the opportunity to take a further £25,000 tax free; the proceeds might as well be £75,000 – the result is similar.

(d) If Grant sells the property to the company for £125,000.

Actual proceeds	125,000
Less: Allowable cost	(75,000)
Excess	£50,000
Gross gain	105,000
Less: Excess	(50,000)
Gain held over	£55,000

The excess is also the chargeable gain subject to taper relief (if the disposal is before 6 April 2008) and the annual exemption.

The base cost of the property for the company is:

Market value	180,000
Less: Held over gain	(55,000)
Base cost for future disposal	£125,000

2.51 Unlike *s 162*, there is no fixed process to follow. An incorporation using *s 165* relief may therefore typically proceed on the following basis:

- Form the company (or acquire a shelf company) and issue shares by cash subscription. Typically, the number of shares will be small.

- Some time later, on incorporation, transfer the required assets to the company either by pure gift or by sale for proceeds of a personally determined amount. Note that the company's undertaking to satisfy any liabilities of the unincorporated business will amount to proceeds for this purpose.

2.51 Incorporation

- At the outset, the company is unlikely to have substantial cash, so the proceeds are often left outstanding on loan account.

- Some time later, when the company is trading profitably, the proprietor may draw down from the loan account effectively taking the proceeds without further tax cost.

There is perhaps less need in these circumstances for a formal incorporation agreement (which is essential for the *s 162* process). Any property transfer will be evidenced by a conveyance. However, because of its intangible nature, there ought to be a document evidencing the transfer of goodwill. Do not forget also that other items, such as stock and plant and machinery attracting capital allowances, may need to be sold to the company at particular prices. All in all, some sort of document is still a sensible requirement.

Section 162 and section 165 compared

		Section 162	*Section 165*
1	How the relief is given	Mandatory. If certain conditions are satisfied the relief is given automatically.	Optional. Claim required.
2	Method of incorporation	Fixed method: form company, issue a few shares; transfer entire business and assets to company; company issues more shares (and loan/cash) to the transferor of the business as consideration.	Method more flexible: form company, issue required number of shares; transfer only assets required to company; company may pay for assets; price flexible.
3	CGT base cost of shares	Market value less gain rolled over.	Subscription price, minimal.
4	Base cost of assets in company	Market value. Incorporation was a connected party transaction; s 162 depresses the share base cost, not that of the assets.	Market value less gain held over.

5	Flexibility	Can be overridden by a claim under *s 162A*. Partners in a partnership can separately choose to make this claim or not.	Claim may cover all assets or selected ones. Partners in partnership may make different claims to suit personal circumstances.
6	Funds potentially available	Value of assets locked into share capital of company unless cash/loan note issued. Amount which can be withdrawn relatively low.	Shareholder/director free to draw on loan account created as consideration for asset transfer. The amount may be quite high.
7	Debtors / other assets	Other assets, such as debtors, must go into the company.	Debtors may be left out of company. Care though if creditors exceed debtors and both are excluded from the transfer. The company's satisfaction of the creditors amounts to consideration for other assets transferred.
8	Losses	Permits the carry forward of losses under *ITA 2007, s 86* (previously *ICTA 1988, s 386*)	Cannot carry forward losses under *ITA 2007, s 86* (previously *ICTA 1988, s 386*)

2.52 For the most part, there is a straight choice between incorporation by the *s 162* route or the *s 165* route. There is no right or wrong answer. All the circumstances of the business, its asset values etc must be considered along with the future intentions of the proprietors. An appropriate decision must be made. What you cannot do is to pick the best bits of *s 162* and *s 165* and use them both. We have seen that there may be circumstances in which *s 162* can leave a residual chargeable gain. This is not eligible for a claim under *s 165* because there are actual market value proceeds (the shares).

Enterprise Investment Scheme

2.53 A further opportunity in the CGT legislation to defer realised gains is afforded by EIS reinvestment relief under *TCGA 1992, Sch 5B*. This relief is

2.54 *Incorporation*

related to investments in EIS companies and is perhaps better referred to as deferral relief. Some refer to it as 'The Third Way'.

It has to be said that the EIS legislation (both for the income tax relief in *ITA 2007, Pt 5* and the CGT reliefs in *TCGA 1992, ss 150A–150D* and *Sch 5B*) is extraordinarily complicated. There are pitfalls aplenty and anyone seeking to use these reliefs should exercise great care. Even if a qualifying investment is successfully made, there is plenty of scope for things to go wrong after the event due to a plethora of anti-avoidance rules. A detailed analysis of the EIS reliefs is beyond the scope of this chapter.

2.54 In broad terms, CGT deferral relief is potentially available where, inter alia, an investor subscribes in cash for new ordinary shares which are fully paid up; in a qualifying company which carries on a qualifying trade; and the company uses the money received in a trade within specified time limits (*TCGA 1992, Sch 5B, para 1(2)*). If those and other relief conditions are satisfied, then a capital gain realised by the investor may be reduced by the amount of the investment (or a smaller amount specified in a claim) (*TCGA 1992, Sch 5B, para 2(1)*).

2.55 Can use be made of EIS deferral relief upon incorporation? With care, it would seem possible. The route must be:

- Form the company and issue a small number of shares for cash. It is preferable that the initial shareholder is not (one of) the proprietor(s) of the business to be incorporated. This is for complex technical reasons which might lead the share issue to be regarded as a bonus or rights issue and not a new subscription.

- The business proprietor then enters into an agreement to sell the assets of the business to the company for cash. The deal must be at market value, realising a chargeable gain. It is preferable that the company borrows money to do this, rather than have the proceeds left outstanding on loan account.

- The business proprietor then uses all or part of the cash consideration to subscribe for new ordinary shares in the company and claims deferral relief under the provisions of *TCGA 1992, Sch 5B*. It is important that cash must change hands to avoid falling foul of the anti-avoidance provisions in *Sch 5B, para 13*. Further, the second and third steps above must not be combined. The shares must be subscribed for in cash – linking the steps would mean an asset/share exchange and the relief would not be due.

- The amount subscribed must be sufficient to cover the gain (ie the gross gain, pre-taper relief for incorporations before 6 April 2008) on disposal of the original business assets. However, should the deferred gain come

Incorporation **2.59**

back into charge when taper relief is still available, a deduction (by reference to the original disposal) is permitted.

However, the above is not necessarily a tried and tested route and HMRC could argue that the rather circular series of transactions is part of a scheme for the avoidance of tax. There is an advance clearance procedure, largely for establishing the qualifying nature of the company, though one could try to seek comment on the actual investment. Also remember that the EIS legislation is complex – if you think you understand it, you probably don't.

Goodwill

2.56 The planning opportunity afforded by the business owner selling goodwill upon incorporation is relatively well known. The basic process of incorporation under *TCGA 1992, s 165* is as follows:

- Sell the goodwill to the company either for full value or undervalue, leaving the proceeds outstanding on loan account.
- The first step is perceived to have created a capital gain which is reduced or extinguished by business asset taper relief (ie for incorporations before 6 April 2008) and the annual exemption. Indexation relief (again for pre-6 April 2008 incorporations) will then be available up to 5 April 1998. Any unrelieved gain is then held over under *s 165*.
- Once the company starts to make profits, the proprietor can draw down on the loan account (representing the proceeds of sale of goodwill) without incurring further tax liabilities.

2.57 Best practice for advisers who use the above route would be to follow the CG34 procedure and, shortly after the transaction took place, seek guidance on the valuations of the capital assets transferred to ensure that the CGT computations submitted are accurate so that the correct tax (if any) may be paid on the due date.

2.58 Some advisers may have experienced an unpleasant surprise following the goodwill sale, in the form of a letter from HMRC Shares & Assets Valuation. Typically, this will say that HMRC have sought guidance on the valuation of the goodwill transferred to the company and stated that, in their view, this is little or nothing. What has been forgotten?

Nature of goodwill

2.59 What is goodwill? The HMRC manuals cover the major issues extensively (see Capital Gains Manual at paragraph 68000 et seq.). Readers who wish to steer clear of the potential pitfalls are strongly advised to refer to that commentary.

2.60 *Incorporation*

The courts have tried to define goodwill, with varying success. Perhaps the leading commentary is that of Lord MacNaghten (in *IRC v Muller & Co's Margarine Ltd* [1901] AC 217, HL):

> 'What is goodwill? It is a thing very easy to describe, very difficult to define. It is the benefit and advantage of the good name, reputation and connection of a business. It is the attractive force which brings in custom. It is the one thing which distinguishes an old established business from a new business at its first start.'

2.60 Following case law, HMRC favour a kind of zoological classification, likening the behaviour of business customers to certain types of animal (see CGM 68011). Developing the theme there are, in essence, three components to goodwill though they are not separable and, where the different types are present in one business, they become parts of an inseparable whole.

- **Personal goodwill** – This is inherent in the technical skills, personal attributes etc of the business proprietor. Customers come to the business because they want the attention of the individual. Commonly cited examples are the celebrity chef or well-known photographer. HMRC takes the view that this type of goodwill cannot be sold. It is inseparable from the individual. In the field of incorporation, one might argue that the individual can be 'tied' to the company by means of a service contract. However, it is difficult to see how this amounts to a transfer of goodwill. The rewards offered under a service contract must represent payment for the continuing use of personal skills (which remain with the individual). Such a contract would also inhibit the tax planning opportunities afforded by trading in the corporate medium.

- **Inherent goodwill** – This attaches, not to the skills of the individual proprietor, but rather to the location. Customers go to the business because of its location. It might be the case with a hotel; customers go to it because of its pleasant surroundings, ease of access etc. Equally, customers will go to a retail shop because of where it is, convenience factors etc. This type of goodwill can be transferred, but only with the premises. A business of this type could endeavour to change premises but might often find that some of its customer base (assuming continuation of a similar business there) remains at the old location.

- **Free goodwill** – This is the form of goodwill sought on incorporation of a business. It is not fixed with any particular attribute of the business. It is the measure of the business value over and above its net assets. It might include a transferable customer list, brand name, general reputation etc. The reason it is so easy to overlook is that, unless purchased in the first place, it rarely appears on the balance sheet of an unincorporated business.

2.61 Advisers who have had goodwill valuations challenged by HMRC Shares & Assets Valuation possibly valued the goodwill by reference to the 'super profit' of the business.

Example 2.7

Mike is the chef proprietor of a successful restaurant business. Last year, the gross profit was £200,000. The super profit might be established thus:

Gross profit	200,000
Less: Drawings (say)	(50,000)
Less: Interest on capital (say)	(20,000)
Super profit	£130,000

Goodwill valued at 1–2 times super profit (say £125,000 – £250,000)

The problem? Most of the goodwill is personal (attaching to Mike and his reputed skills as a chef), or inherent (attaching to the location of his premises). Mike's adviser forgot this and merely included £200,000 (on a multiplier of $1^1/2$) in the CGT computation relating to incorporation of the business. After business asset taper relief and annual exemption, this gave a tax bill of just under £17,000, which Mike thought acceptable for the ability to draw £200,000 from the new company without further tax charge. So now the adviser is faced with explaining to Mike why HMRC will not agree.

2.62 In the above example, could Mike's adviser have done anything better? As regards the personal goodwill, the answer is probably not. Mike does not want a service contract with the company. The advantage of taking a dividend and not a salary has been explained to him and he wants to exploit this. In any case, it is questionable whether a service contract would make any difference. It merely gives the company an opportunity to exploit Mike's goodwill: it does not effect a transfer.

As regards the goodwill inherent in the restaurant premises, the answer is 'perhaps'. Mike had various personal reasons for not placing this in the company. HMRC appear to accept that some measure of inherent goodwill attaches to a lease (CGM 68031), so Mike could have leased the premises to the company. This does not, however, transfer all of it.

2.63 HMRC seem to take the view that much of the goodwill attaching to any small business derives from the skills, abilities and other personal attributes of the proprietor. In other words, the transfer of goodwill might be a nice idea, but in many instances the scope to do it may be severely limited. You may have to face the fact that the goodwill must be left outside the company.

2.64 Incorporation

2.64 In the above example, Mike's new company is paying him £200,000 and HMRC Shares & Assets Valuation maintain that the value of the free goodwill truly transferable is well below this. The majority of the goodwill remains outside the company. What then is the nature of the payment?

The capital gain will be calculated by reference to the market value of the goodwill as the parties are connected. How should the excess be handled? At this stage the company has not traded and, in the absence of any borrowings, has no funds. Its payment is therefore, to all intents and purposes, an IOU represented by a credit balance on a loan account. HMRC's view, as stated in *Tax Bulletin, Issue 76* (April 2005), is that the excess could fall to be treated in alternative ways, as follows:

- **Employment earnings** – HMRC have indicated that if goodwill was '… deliberately overvalued when it was sold to the company' the excess payment will be taxable as employment income (ie as earnings or, exceptionally, a benefit). The same applies to payments by the company for future services to be provided by the former business owner. Earnings will be subject to PAYE, and any benefit is reportable on form P11D. In either case, HMRC consider that the excess payment is liable to Class 1 National Insurance contributions.

- **Distribution** – It will normally be the case that goodwill is transferred before the company has commenced trading. HMRC consider that, in the majority of cases in which goodwill is transferred, any excess value will be received in the capacity of a shareholder, rather than an employee of director. A payment of excess value would therefore be treated by HMRC as a distribution by reason of *ICTA 1988, ss 209(2)(b)* or *209(4)*.

HMRC's analysis of the tax treatment of payments for goodwill in *Tax Bulletin, Issue 76* is based on the premise that the goodwill has been deliberately overvalued. They appear to accept that goodwill valuations are not an exact science, and consider that distributions (within *ICTA 1988, s 209(4)*) can be 'inadvertent'. HMRC will therefore allow the transaction to be 'unwound'.

However, there are caveats to this let-out. Firstly, 'reasonable efforts' must be made to carry out the transaction at market value using a professional valuation (ie an 'independent and suitably qualified valuer on an appropriate basis'). Secondly, there can be no unwinding on intentional overvaluations. Thirdly, there must be no tax avoidance motive. If a distribution is unwound, the shareholder must repay the excess value to the company. This may give rise a loan to a participator under *ICTA 1988, s 419*, leading to tax chargeable on the company. There might also be an income tax charge on the individual under *ITEPA 2003, s 175*.

2.65 One could endeavour to ensure that the document of transfer expresses the proceeds as being £x 'or such lesser amount as may be agreed with HMRC' though, on enquiry, this would seem likely to provoke a challenge.

Valuation of goodwill

2.66 The valuation of goodwill is a specialist area. HMRC deal with such valuation issues through its Shares and Assets Valuation office. As mentioned, on incorporation it will be necessary to identify the value of free goodwill which is readily transferable to the company. The usual method of valuation is by reference to the maintainable profits of the business. Allowance should be made for proprietor's remuneration, measured as the likely salary which an arms' length manager of the business might expect to be paid. Differential weighting might be applied over a period of time giving more significance to recent profits than the older ones.

2.67 Finally, there is the vexed question of a multiplier to use. Comparisons of quoted companies in similar fields of business are of little relevance. The business being transferred is non-corporate and probably quite small. The well-advised purchaser will assess the risk and, on an arms' length basis, may make an offer well below what the business proprietor considers reasonable. However, this is the principle to be adopted and in many small trades a multiplier of 1 or 2 only is probably realistic.

2.68 Where the amounts involved are material, an independent expert valuation will be worth considering, particularly in view of HMRC's comments in *Tax Bulletin, Issue 76*. At a minimum, a record of the considerations taken in establishing the figure adopted should be maintained as a defence should there be a Revenue enquiry, which is likely to involve HMRC Shares and Assets Valuation.

Intangible fixed assets

2.69 A major reform of the tax treatment of intangible fixed assets was introduced in *Finance Act 2002, Sch 29*. To take advantage, it is essential to operate as a corporate medium. Previously, intangible assets fell within the chargeable gains regime. The effect of the current provisions is to take specified intangible assets of companies out of this regime and into the normal trading rules. In the context of business incorporations, the most common form of intangible asset is goodwill, although the rules also apply to 'intellectual property' as defined (*FA 2002, Sch 29, paras 2, 4*). If the intangible fixed asset rules apply, the company may obtain a deduction for expenditure, and receipts from disposal are treated as taxable. However, HMRC may challenge tax relief claims for purchased goodwill, etc where its value appears to be excessive, and there are anti-avoidance rules to prevent the perceived abuse of the intangibles rules.

2.70 There are rules to prohibit relief in respect of expenditure on transactions between related parties (*FA 2002, Sch 29, paras 95, 118*). For unincorpo-

2.71 *Incorporation*

rated businesses established before 1 April 2002 (ie before the intangible fixed assets rules were introduced), it is therefore not possible to incorporate the business, have the company make a payment for goodwill acquired from the former sole trader or partnership and then write off the expenditure in the new company over time.

2.71 However, there are certain exceptions to the general rule prohibiting the company from claiming a deduction under the intangible fixed assets upon acquisition from a related party, such as upon incorporation. One such exception is where the sole trader or partnership acquired the goodwill after 31 March 2002 from an unrelated third party (*Sch 29, para 118(2)(b)*).

A further, important exception from the related party prohibition of intangibles relief is where the unincorporated business (or any other person) itself created the asset after 31 March 2002 (*Sch 29, para 118(2)(c)*). This exception will become increasingly significant with the passage of time, as more sole traders and partnerships which commenced trading before 1 April 2002 grow their businesses and enhance the value of free goodwill.

Stamp duties

2.72 Stamp duty is not a tax levied on profits, income or gains. It is not even a tax on transactions. Stamp duty is charged on 'instruments', broadly defined as documents, transferring title to property. It is a tax on documents. However, goodwill ceased to be an asset liable to stamp duty in respect of instruments executed on or after 23 April 2002, and the transfer of debtors ceased to be liable to stamp duty from 1 December 2003. Assets such as stock or plant and machinery may pass by delivery, free of stamp duty.

In the context of incorporation and small owner-managed or family companies, a stamp duty charge may be encountered in some cases if the unincorporated business is exchanged for shares, such as when relief is sought under *TCGA 1992, s 162*. There is no stamp duty on the issue of shares as such; only in the event that the business assets transferred include shares will there be a stamp duty liability (at 0.5%) on their value. In addition, since 1 December 2003 stamp duty has only applied to instruments relating to shares. However, if there is a contract or agreement for the sale of goodwill and other business property (some of which attracts duty under *FA 1999, Sch 13, para 7*) the consideration must be apportioned on a 'just and reasonable' basis (*FA 2002, Sch 37, para 1*).

2.73 Stamp Duty Land Tax (SDLT) applies to all transactions in respect of interests in and rights over UK land and buildings and will be triggered by the payment of substantive consideration (whether on contract or at completion). SDLT is in point regardless of whether or not the transactions are effected inside or outside the UK.

2.74 If land and buildings are transferred to the company upon incorporation, invariably both parties will be connected persons. If so, the land and buildings are deemed to pass at market value for SDLT purposes (*FA 2003, s 53*). The rule for connection is found in *ICTA 1988, s 839*. Thus, for example, a controlling holding will be connected with the company. Whilst there may be some incorporations where the company has diverse shareholdings which will be outside the test in *ICTA 1988, s 839*, these are likely to be the exception rather than the rule.

2.75 If property is, for any reason, retained outside the company then rent may be paid. In most cases, this will be in respect of an informal licence without the need for a lease. A licence to use or occupy land is an exempt interest (*FA 2003, s 48(2)(b)*). However, care must be taken to distinguish a licence from a lease, as the distinction is important for SDLT purposes. The Stamp Duty Land Tax Manual states (at SDLTM 00320): 'Note that a document which describes itself as a licence may in fact be a lease, especially if the practical consequence is that the grantee has exclusive occupation.'

2.76 If a new lease is granted, SDLT will be charged on both the premium payable, if any, and also on the rent payable. There is a single SDLT charge of 1% charge on the net present value of all rental payments due under the lease where this exceeds £125,000 for residential property or £150,000 for non-residential property. Where there is a premium for grant of a lease, this is subject to the usual SDLT charge, with one exception. This is where the average annual rent for the lease exceeds £600. In that case, the 0% band is unavailable so that the whole of the premium becomes chargeable at 1%. In other words, only one 0% band can be obtained, in respect of the net present value of the rent.

Inheritance Tax

2.77

Incorporation is a commercial transaction. There should be no gratuitous intent to it. In theory therefore there is no charge to IHT or it should be excluded by *IHTA 1984, s 10*. Where there is a gratuitous reduction in an individual's estate, most lifetime transfers are potentially exempt transfers (PETs). However, note that if a close company makes a transfer of value and this is apportioned to the participators, this is not a PET and IHT is immediately chargeable (*IHTA 1984, s 94*).

Whilst the interests of the shareholders in the newly formed company will, in most instances, be identical to the interests of the proprietors in the unincorporated business, this is not exclusively the case. To the extent that anyone other than the original business proprietor or spouse takes shares, the real problem is

2.78 *Incorporation*

that the transfer of value made in such circumstances is not a PET. It is a chargeable transfer, as the recipient of the gift is a company, not an individual. In most instances, the transfer of value in such circumstances will be relatively small. However, the proprietor needs to be aware of the erosion to his IHT nil-rate band.

Business Property Relief

2.78 A separate chapter of this book is devoted to Business Property Relief (BPR) (see **Chapter 11**). Every business proprietor must be aware of this relief and the impact that incorporation might have on it. The rate could be halved and the assets encompassed by it restricted.

2.79 Provided that the business of the sole trader is not excluded by the investment activity test in *IHTA 1984, s 105(3)*, the whole of the value should qualify for BPR in the event of death or chargeable transfer for IHT purposes, unless there is any 'excluded property' as defined in *IHTA 1984, s 112*. As regards the business itself, a partner is in broadly the same position as a sole trader. 100% BPR should be available in respect of a chargeable transfer of the business interest. As *IHTA 1984, s 105(1)(a)* refers only to an interest in a business, the extent of participation is irrelevant. Thus, a partner with a 5% share in a business (say) can obtain exactly the same relief pro rata to value as a partner with a 90% share.

There is no relief for the asset held outside the partnership, unless the partnership interest itself is relevant business property. Again, there is no minimum participation limit in the partnership. So a partner can get BPR in respect of property let to a partnership of which he is only a small minority partner. The rate of relief is 50% (*IHTA 1984, s 104(1)(b)*). However, the loan account of a retired partner does not qualify for BPR (*Beckman v IRC* [2000] STC (SCD) 59).

2.80 Shares in unquoted trading companies generally qualify for BPR when there is a chargeable transfer for IHT. BPR is available both to working and passive shareholders. It is not necessary for the shareholder to be a director of the company. There is no minimum size of holding, nor any specification as to the type of share. The rate of relief is 100% (*IHTA 1984, s 104(1)(a)*). However, if business property is subject to a binding contract for sale at the time of a chargeable transfer, then BPR is not available (*IHTA 1984, s 113*). Beware company articles or shareholder agreements that impose buy and sell arrangements on the members of the company. This pitfall is covered in greater detail in **Chapter 11**.

2.81 As with a partnership, a business proprietor who becomes a shareholder may retain property outside the company. The property may qualify for

BPR if it is used for the purposes of a business carried on by the company, the shares held are themselves relevant business property, and the transferor controlled the company. The rate of relief is 50% (*IHTA 1984, s 104(1)(b)*). Thus for assets used but not retained within the business vehicle, the situation may worsen. A sole trader would get 100% BPR if the asset comprised part of the business but a shareholder gets 50% relief only if he controls the company.

2.82 A loan to a company does not qualify for BPR. Whilst the incorporation transactions may lead to a positive balance on a director's loan account, this should not be left in place indefinitely. It gives a means of drawing cash from the company without further tax charge but, if it is still in place when the shareholder dies or wishes to make a chargeable transfer of shares, the value is excluded from BPR. The solution may be, if the funds are required in the company and IHT is a concern, to capitalise the loan for more shares. The freedom to draw down is then, of course, lost.

2.83 The availability of BPR depends on the holding of a certain type of business asset. Additionally, it must be held for a minimum period of two years (*IHTA 1984, s 106*). This does not necessarily mean that the same relevant business property must be held throughout. The two-year minimum holding period need not be satisfied by the same relevant business property. It is possible to carry forward the qualifying conditions into replacement property. So, where one item of qualifying business property is replaced by another, the conditions for BPR remain satisfied. There may even be a gap in ownership. The two-year minimum holding period is satisfied if both assets are held for a total of two years within five years before the transfer of value (*IHTA 1984, s 107*).

As far as the main business interest is concerned, incorporation should have no effect on the availability of BPR should the proprietor die or wish to transfer all or part of the business. Incorporation will involve a switch from a business held personally (qualifying under *s 105(1)(a)*) to shares in a trading company (qualifying under *s 105(1)(bb)*). All other conditions being satisfied, one replaces the other and the availability of BPR continues throughout. There is no need to establish a new minimum holding period for the shares.

Agricultural Property Relief

2.84 A separate chapter of this book also covers Agricultural Property Relief (APR) (see **Chapter 12**). However, in broad terms APR is available in respect of the agricultural value of agricultural property, being the value which it would have if it were to be used perpetually for agriculture. Much agricultural property will also satisfy the conditions for BPR. Where, on the face of it, both reliefs are available, APR takes precedence (*IHTA 1984, s 114(1)*). However, this does not prevent a claim for BPR on the excess over the agricultural value.

2.85 *Incorporation*

2.85 If, on incorporation, the land is placed within the company then the business proprietor ceases to own it. Rather, he has shares in the new company the value of which reflects the value of the land held therein. These shares are clearly not agricultural property in themselves but their value will reflect the underlying agricultural property. If that is the case, then APR may be available on the share value to the extent that that value is attributable to the underlying agricultural land providing that the shares give the transferor control of the company (*IHTA 1984, s 122(1)*). Assuming that this will be a trading company, it is more than likely that BPR will be available in respect of the shares as well. This will relieve the excess value of the shares over the agricultural value of the land holding. If the control test is not satisfied, then BPR should be available on the whole value. Loss of APR should therefore be no real disaster. If the agricultural land is held outside the company, on a new incorporation it is perhaps best to ensure that a formal tenancy is put in place. This would satisfy the conditions of *s 116(1)(c)* and, all other things being equal, 100% APR is maintained.

Value Added Tax

2.86 Most businesses will be registered for VAT. The disposal of the assets of a business is to be treated as a supply made in the course or furtherance of that business. Accordingly, VAT will be chargeable on the sale of such items as stock, plant and machinery, fixtures and fittings (*VATA 1994, Sch 4, para 5*). VAT is even due on goodwill. However, the general rule is that no taxable supply is made and no VAT should be charged where the assets of a business are transferred to another person (eg a successor company) in connection with the transfer of all or part of the business as a going concern.

Therefore, the transfer of a business as a going concern is neither a supply of goods nor a supply of services for VAT purposes. This applies where the assets are to be used by the transferee in carrying on the same kind of business as that carried on by the transferor; and where the transferee is a taxable person, or immediately becomes one as a result of the transfer. If only part of the business is transferred as a going concern, the same rule applies where that part is capable of separate operation (*VAT (Special Provisions) Order 1995, SI 1995/1268, art 5*). The transfer of a going concern (TOGC) rule is mandatory provided all the statutory conditions are satisfied.

2.87 However, there is an exception to the TOGC rules. This is where the assets being transferred include land and buildings which are potentially taxable (ie on which the transferor has exercised the option to tax, or if there is a sale of the freehold of a new or incomplete building liable to VAT at the standard rate). Such property is standard rated, unless the business purchaser opts to tax the property from the date of the transfer, notifies HMRC (by the date of the transfer) of an election to waive exemption in respect of the property concerned, and notifies the vendor that the purchaser's option will not be disapplied (*Special Provisions Order, SI 1995/1268, arts 5(2), (2A)*).

2.88 When the ownership of a business is transferred to a different legal entity it is possible for the transferee to take over the transferor's original VAT registration number. This treatment is broadly available if registration of the original business is cancelled from the date of the transfer, and the new business is not already registered, but is liable or entitled to be registered. The process is effected by completion of form VAT 68 (*VAT Regulations 1995, SI 1995/2518, art 6*).

However, it should be noted that transferring a VAT registration number from one business to another transfers the responsibility for any debits and credits both before and after the transfer to the new owner. The decision to transfer a VAT number must be taken in the light of any adverse history or potential liability which may be assumed by the company.

2.89 Alternatively, if it is decided to break the link with the old business, the company may apply for fresh registration. The former business proprietor must deregister immediately after the transfer. It is not necessary for the transfer of all the assets of a business to take place for it to be a TOGC. However, what is transferred should be sufficient to enable continued operation of the same business as was carried on by the transferor.

2.90 It is crucial for all businesses to establish whether there is a TOGC or not. There is no safe option – if VAT is charged on a transaction which turns out to be a TOGC, both parties will have misstated their VAT liabilities where, at worst, HMRC can both require the vendor to account for the amount he has incorrectly treated as output tax and deny input tax recovery to the purchaser. If VAT is not charged, but HMRC decide there is no TOGC, the transferor will have a VAT liability which it may be impossible to recover from the transferee.

Investment businesses

2.91 Very often, the nature of an investment business will be the letting of property. Whilst for income tax purposes the receipt of rents from property is treated as a 'property business' (*ITTOIA 2005, ss 264, 265*), the real problem with the tax legislation is that there is no satisfactory definition of what is a 'business'. There is abundant case law on activities in the nature of a trade, but nothing on activities in the nature of a business. It is clear that a business is rather wider than (but includes) a trade, as well as a profession or vocation. Active management is a characteristic of a business, as is the profit motive.

2.92 *Incorporation*

2.92 Why, in any case, would anyone want to incorporate such an activity anyway? For example, for IHT purposes no BPR would be available in respect of shares in the company. Against this is the potential double tax charge of corporate operation. The company pays tax on its gain; the shareholder pays tax on extraction of the profit.

An unincorporated property letting business will derive gross rents against which may be set various expenses to arrive at a net property business profit. An individual receiving this will be chargeable to income tax at his highest marginal rate as it arises. Getting the profits into a company has the obvious attraction of the ability to withdraw profits by way of dividend rather than salary, just as with any trading company.

2.93 There are two traditional routes of relieving the capital gains arising on incorporation of a business. These use either the general relief for gifts of business assets in *TCGA 1992, s 165*, or the specific incorporation relief in *s 162*. A claim under *TCGA 1992, s 165* is a non-starter. This permits the holdover of a capital gain where an asset is transferred at undervalue and the asset is used for the purposes of a trade, profession or vocation. Whatever property letting may be, it is not a trade, profession or vocation.

2.94 By contrast, *s 162* provides a mandatory rollover of the gain where a person who is not a company transfers to a company a business as a going concern, together with the whole assets of the business. This must take us back to the question 'what is a business?' As already noted, there is no definition in *TCGA 1992*.

HMRC's Capital Gains Manual (at CGM 65714–65715) tries to extract a meaning from various pieces of case law. CGM 65713 (rather unhelpfully) says it is a question of fact whether a particular activity does constitute a business. It is not easy to draw the line. It does, however, go on to say that HMRC will resist claims that the passive holding of investments or an investment property amount to a business.

It is worth noting that for VAT purposes the letting of property can amount to a business activity (see *D A Walker v Customs and Excise Commissioners* [1976] VATTR 10, and *G W and J A Green v Customs and Excise Commissioners* (1992, Decision 9016)). For example, in the former case, the letting of three semi-detached houses on assured tenancies was considered to be a business in VAT terms.

2.95 *TCGA 1992, s 162* not only requires transfer of the business, but of the business 'as a going concern'. It is difficult to see how the letting of property could be a going concern. This predicates something more than transfer of a mere collection of assets. There must be an active infrastructure to go with it. On that basis, it seems unlikely in many cases that a property letting business could

Incorporation **2.98**

be transferred to a company with the benefit of *s 162* relief. However, some commentators have adopted a more optimistic view that active property letting is arguably a business activity (see, for example Malcolm Gunn 'It's my business', *Taxation*, 8 November 2007).

A cautious approach is advocated. If incorporation was successfully challenged by HMRC on enquiry, a very large unrelieved gain could ensue with no cash to meet the liability. However, there is a limited exception to all of this. This is the possibility that the properties concerned meet the conditions to be treated as furnished holiday lettings.

2.96 One should also bear in mind the impact of SDLT. Where land and buildings are transferred to a company which is connected with the transferor, SDLT is charged by reference to market value (*FA 2003, s 53*). A significant SDLT liability may therefore arise should it be desired to transfer properties to a company.

2.97 At the time of writing (November 2007), the government proposed to withdraw CGT taper relief from 6 April 2008. For prior disposals, if any of the properties are commercial properties, one should bear in mind that, from 6 April 2004, these will generally qualify for business asset taper relief. This very valuable relief would be lost if the properties were transferred to a company. An alternative way of dealing with the situation was to form an investment company and lease or license the properties to the company at a minimal rent. The company would then sublet the properties to the end users (who should be sole traders, partnerships or qualifying companies who use them in their trades) at a full rent. The property owner would still get business asset taper relief to offset any gain on sale, the interposition of the property company being seemingly irrelevant as it is the end use that governs business asset taper relief.

The majority of the rents are received in the company and taxed at the lower corporate rates. This will not be a close investment holding company, subject to corporation tax at 30%, if all the properties are let to third parties. SDLT on the initial letting of the property must be borne in mind as a cost of the arrangement.

Disincorporation

2.98 The government appears intent on ensuring that small and owner-managed companies pay what it considers to be 'the right amount of tax', their main concerns apparently being the ability of companies to distribute its profits to shareholders as dividends, resulting in a loss of National Insurance contributions compared with the payment of a salary or bonus.

In addition, a company can be a convenient asset in terms of passing on an income-producing asset (ie shares) between family members. Following the success of the taxpayers in the 'Arctic Systems' case (*Jones v Garnett*) at the

2.99 *Incorporation*

House of Lords, the government almost immediately announced that measures would be introduced to counter what it calls income splitting. According to a Parliamentary statement, 'income splitting' is what the government consider to be '… non-commercial arrangements (arrangements that they would not reasonably enter into with an arms-length third party) to divert income (which would, in the absence of those arrangements have flowed to them) to others'.

The resulting legislation to counter this perceived abuse is expected to be introduced in *Finance Act 2008*. This follows other measures aimed at the small and owner-managed company, such as the 'IR35' rules affecting personal service companies. There are also specific provisions to treat dividends as employment income in certain circumstances (*ITEPA 2003, s 447*). Alternatively, HMRC may assert that dividends which they consider to be 'thinly disguised general earnings' are liable to PAYE income tax and National Insurance contributions (ERSM 90210). More recently, the small companies' rate of corporation tax has been gradually increased, rising to 22% from 6 April 2009.

2.99 One should also consider the possibility that the company may run into trading difficulties, or will one day have served its purpose. Its useful life has ended. What happens next?

2.100 A separate chapter of this book has been devoted to the subject of disincorporation. However, in broad terms any business proprietor heading for incorporation must understand and appreciate that he may have a one-way ticket. In principle, all the considerations for incorporation, such as the cessation of trade, capital gains, VAT and inheritance tax apply to disincorporation. The problem is that, whilst there are reliefs to ease the way into the company, there is precious little to help on the way out. Perhaps the biggest single problem is CGT. *TCGA 1992, ss 162* and *165* are there to defer capital gains arising on the incorporation of a business. There is no equivalent to deal with such liabilities on the way out. Bear in mind that these could be enormous with inflation, development of the business inside the company and understanding that the underlying assets may have a low base cost because of deferred gains when the company was incorporated.

2.101 Factors to consider include the following:

- cessation of trade;
- losses;
- close investment holding company status;
- extracting the business as a going concern;
- extracting cash from a solvent company;
- liquidation; and

- striking off.

All of the foregoing assume a solvent company at the end of its useful life. There may be failed companies giving rise to alternative considerations.

2.102 For a more detailed analysis of disincorporation, see **Chapter 5.**

Chapter 3

Company purchase of own shares

Mark McLaughlin CTA (Fellow), ATT, TEP

INTRODUCTION

3.1 This chapter is mainly concerned with the purchase by an unquoted trading or holding company of its own shares from an individual shareholder, particularly in respect of family and owner-managed companies. As a general rule, when a company buys back its own shares from a shareholder, any 'premium' (ie payment in excess of the capital originally subscribed for the shares) constitutes a distribution (*ICTA 1988, s 211(1)*). For tax purposes, the transaction generally falls to be treated as an income distribution (*s 209(2)(b)*), such as on a purchase of own shares by a quoted company. However, there is an exception in the case of unquoted trading companies (*s 219*). If certain conditions are satisfied, the transaction is automatically excepted from income distribution treatment. The effect is that the vendor is treated as receiving a capital payment instead (unless the vendor is a share dealer, in which case the receipt is treated as trading income). This treatment provides shareholders with a potentially tax-efficient exit route from the company.

For disposals before 6 April 2008, in many cases the prospect of taper relief at the business asset rate possibly reducing an individual shareholder's gain by 75% means that the effective capital gains tax rate could be as low as around 10% for a higher rate taxpayer. This compares favourably with an income distribution for a higher rate taxpayer, who would be taxable on the grossed-up distribution at 22.5% (ie 32.5% less a tax credit of 10%), giving an effective tax rate of 25% on the net distribution. At the time of writing (December 2007), a single capital gains tax rate of 18% is to be introduced from 6 April 2008, and taper relief (and indexation allowance) will be withdrawn. However, a capital gains tax rate of 18% rate is clearly still better than a 25% income tax rate for a higher rate taxpayer. Hence capital treatment can be a crucial requirement for the shareholder.

A company purchase of own shares can be useful in a variety of situations, particularly in the context of family or owner-managed businesses. For example, a controlling director shareholder may wish to retire and make way for younger management, some or all of whom may be family members. Alternatively, shareholder disputes over the running of the company's trade may be resolved by using a company purchase of own shares to provide dissenting parties with an opportunity to depart from the company and realise the value of their shares. In both cases, this route may seem particularly attractive if a direct purchase of the shares (eg by other shareholders, family members or managers) is not possible due to insufficiency of funds. A company purchase of own shares also provides the personal representatives or legatee with an opportunity to realise the value of shares following the death of a shareholder.

A number of conditions must generally be satisfied in order to qualify for capital gains treatment on a company purchase of own shares, including a 'trade benefit' test, as well as requirements as to residence, length of ownership of the shares and the degree (if any) to which the vendor remains connected with the company. In some cases, it may not be possible to satisfy all the requirements. The business owners may therefore wish to consider alternative exit strategies for the vendor shareholder, eg a management buyout. Such considerations are outside the scope of this chapter.

3.2 The tax legislation on company distributions is contained in the *ICTA 1988, Part VI*. This legislation contains provisions specifically dealing with the purchase of own shares by an unquoted trading company (*ICTA 1988, ss 219–229*). The purchase of own shares rules exclude from distribution treatment payments made by a company on the redemption, repayment or purchase of its own shares, if certain conditions are satisfied. This chapter outlines those rules, and considers planning points and potential pitfalls in relation to them. All statutory references in this chapter are to *ICTA 1988*, unless otherwise stated.

3.3 It is important to note that a purchase of own shares must comply with company law requirements to be valid. In practice, the Companies Act requirements are often an after-thought, and have the potential to be overlooked completely by the uninitiated. As this book is mainly concerned with tax law rather than company law, priority is given to tax considerations. However, whilst company law is discussed later in this chapter, strictly speaking it should be a primary consideration, as the implications for 'getting it wrong' can be unfortunate to say the least.

3.4 Guidance on the tax treatment of a company purchase of own shares is contained in HMRC's 'Company Taxation Manual' (at CTM 17505 onwards), mainly in respect of income distribution treatment, and 'Capital Gains Manual' (at CTM 58600 onwards) relating to capital gains treatment.

Checklist

3.5 Aside from the company law requirements mentioned above, the following checklist is intended as a brief summary of the conditions to be

3.6 Company purchase of own shares

satisfied for a company purchase of its own shares to be excluded from income distribution treatment, and to be treated as a capital payment instead (within *ICTA 1988, ss 219–229*). These conditions are considered further in this chapter.

Table 3.1: Conditions for company purchase of own shares within *s 219(1)(a)*

Company status – the purchasing company must be an unquoted trading company, or the unquoted holding company of a trading group (*s 219(1)*).

Purpose of the payment – either the 'trade benefit' and 'no scheme or arrangements' tests are met (see **3.12**), *or* the payment is applied by the recipient in discharging an inheritance tax liability within two years after a death (in the latter case, the further conditions below do not need to be satisfied) (*s 219(1)(a)*).

Residence – the vendor shareholder must be UK resident and (for individuals) be ordinarily resident for the tax year in which the purchase takes place (*s 220(1)–(4)*).

Period of ownership – the shares must have been owned for a minimum of five years. However, if the shares were acquired by Will or intestacy, this ownership period is reduced to three years (*s 220(5)–(9)*).

'Substantial reduction' – the vendor shareholder's interest in the company must be substantially reduced (eg if the vendor retains some shares after the purchase) (*s 221*).

No 'continuing connection' – the vendor must not be connected with the company (or group company) immediately after the purchase (*ss 223, 224, 228*).

If these conditions are satisfied, capital treatment is automatic. This assumes of course that the transaction is valid under company law.

An application can be made to HMRC under *s 225* for advance clearance that capital treatment will be available to the vendor shareholder. This is normally accompanied by an application for clearance under *ITA 2007, s 701* (previously *ICTA 1988, s 707*) that the anti-avoidance rules regarding 'transactions in securities' in *ITA 2007, s 684* (previously *ICTA 1988, s 703*) do not apply.

3.6 Alternatively, a 'negative' clearance application can be made that the transaction should be treated as an income distribution. It can be possible to break the conditions for capital treatment, if distribution treatment is preferable. For example, this could be achieved by the vendor leaving the sale proceeds outstanding as a loan, so that the 'no continuing connection test' is broken. Alternatively, the shares could be bought in stages, so that the 'substantial reduction' test is not met. Breaching the capital treatment conditions is further considered later in the chapter.

IHT and 'undue hardship'

3.7 The purpose of the company purchase of its own shares (or redemption or repayment) for which this chapter is mainly concerned is broadly that the payment is wholly or mainly to benefit a trade carried on by the company or group, and is not part of a scheme or arrangement a main purpose of which is to allow the owner to participate in company profits without receiving a dividend, or tax avoidance.

However, it should be noted that there is a second, alternative allowable purpose. This is that substantially the whole proceeds from the share transaction relating to an unquoted trading company or holding company of a trading group (apart from any payment towards a CGT liability arising in respect of it) are applied in discharging an IHT liability of the recipient on a death, within two years of that event (*ICTA 1988, s 219(1)(b)*).

3.8 If this purpose is relevant, it is not necessary for the vendor to demonstrate that the transaction was for the benefit of the company's trade, and the other conditions which apply to the first purpose need not be satisfied by the vendor of the shares. However, there is a further specific condition to the second purpose, which is broadly that the relevant IHT liability could not otherwise have been paid without 'undue hardship' (*ICTA 1988, s 219(2)*).

The remainder of this chapter considers the conditions to be satisfied for a purchase of own shares to fall within *ICTA 1988, s 219(1)(a)*.

Company status

3.9 The purchasing company must be an unquoted trading company or the holding company of a trading group (*ICTA 1988, s 219(1)(a)*). The terms 'unquoted company', 'trading company' and 'trading group' are specifically defined for the purposes of the purchase of own shares rules, and broadly have the following meaning (*s 229(1)*):

- An 'unquoted company' is a company which is neither quoted nor a 51% subsidiary of a quoted company. A 'quoted company' is a company whose shares (or any class of them) are listed on the stock exchange. However, shares listed on the Alternative Investment Market are regarded as unquoted for these purposes (CTM 17507).

- A 'trading company' is a company whose business consists 'wholly or mainly' (ie more than 50%) of carrying on one or more trades. This differs from the definition of trading company for taper relief purposes (ie for periods before 6 April 2008), which requires that the company's activities do not include to a substantial extent activities other than trading activities

3.10 Company purchase of own shares

(*TCGA 1992, Sch A1, para 22A(1)*). Hence it is possible that a company may satisfy the 'wholly or mainly' test of trading status on a purchase of its own shares, and yet a gain on the disposal of those shares may be denied business asset taper relief in the hands of an individual shareholder for disposals up to 5 April 2008 because the company's non-trading activities are 'substantial' (defined by HMRC as 20% or more of certain measures, such as non-trading income; see CGM 17953p).

- A 'trading group' is one in which the business of its members taken together consists wholly or mainly of carrying on one or more trades, and in this context 'group' means the company itself and its 75% subsidiaries.

3.10 There is a distinction between 'trade' and 'business' which must be recognised. For example, property investment activities may amount to a business, but on general principles does not constitute a trade. In addition, a 'trade' for the above purposes specifically excludes dealing in shares, securities, land or futures. Finally, it is not sufficient that the company was formerly trading, or intends trading in the future. It must be a trading company when the transaction takes place (*Tax Bulletin, Issue 21* (February 1996)).

Purpose of the payment

3.11 This condition contains two separate limbs, both of which must be satisfied (*ICTA 1988, s 219(1)*). These limbs are considered separately below.

The 'trade benefit' test

3.12 The first limb of the 'purpose' condition mentioned above is that the company's purchase (or redemption or repayment) of shares must be wholly or mainly for the purpose of benefiting a trade carried on by the company, or by any of its 75% subsidiaries. This requirement is referred to in this chapter as the 'trade benefit' test.

As indicated in the Checklist at **3.5**, in addition to the 'trade benefit' condition in *ICTA 1988, s 219(1)(a)*, there are various other conditions for a company purchase of own shares to be excluded from income distribution treatment. Those further conditions are contained in *ss 220–224* (see below), and are relatively unambiguous. By contrast, a particular difficulty with the 'trade benefit' test is that it is not defined anywhere in the legislation. However, this test was considered in *Allum v Marsh* [2005] STC (SCD) 191, which is discussed below.

Statement of Practice 2/82

3.13 The 'trade benefit' test is also the subject of guidance by HMRC in SP 2/82 ('Company's purchase of own shares: *ICTA 1988*'), which includes examples of situations in which the trade benefit test would normally be regarded as satisfied:

- *Disagreements between shareholders over the company's management, which has or could have an adverse effect on the company's trade.* As a general rule, the company must buy back all the dissenting shareholder's shares and remove him entirely. However, there are possible exceptions to this rule, such as if the company cannot afford them all, but buys back as many as it can afford and intends buying the rest as soon as possible, or if the retiring director shareholder wishes to retain up to 5% for sentimental reasons.

- *An 'unwilling shareholder' wants to end their association with the company.* The trade benefit test may be satisfied if the purpose of the share buyback is to ensure that the shares are not sold to someone who could be unacceptable to the other shareholders. SP 2/82 provides examples of 'unwilling shareholders':

    – 'business angels' (ie outside shareholders who wish to withdraw equity finance);

    – retiring controlling director shareholders wanting to make way for new management;

    – personal representatives of deceased shareholders wishing to realise the shares; and

    – legatees of a deceased shareholder not wishing to hold shares in the company.

Retaining an interest in the company

3.14 SP 2/82 indicates that if the vendor shareholder retains an interest in the company (eg if the company is not buying all the vendor's shares, or if the vendor is retained as a director or consultant) the trade benefit test will probably not be satisfied. However, the possibility of a retained interest is not ruled out as mainly benefiting the company's trade in certain circumstances. For example:

- the company does not currently have the resources to purchase all the shares of a retiring controlling shareholder immediately; or

- a retiring director wishes to retain no more than 5% of the company's shares for sentimental reasons.

It should be remembered that Statements of Practice only represent the views of HMRC, and are not legally binding. Nevertheless, taxpayers and their advisers should be aware of SP 2/82 and its contents. An Annex to SP2/82 helpfully contains the suggested format of advance clearance applications on a purchase of own shares, including a statement of the expected 'purpose and benefits' of the purchase, trading and otherwise.

3.15 Company purchase of own shares

3.15 Despite the non-statutory nature of the trade benefit test, prior to *Allum v Marsh* (see below) case law had not offered much guidance on its meaning. In *Moody v Tyler (Inspector of Taxes)* [2000] STC 296, the taxpayer resigned as the director of a family company in 1989. The company lent him £50,000. In 1995 the company purchased 2,247 shares from his holding for £50,000. Those monies were offset against the loan. The taxpayer appealed against an assessment to tax as an income distribution, on the basis that the purchase had been made wholly or mainly to benefit the trade carried on by the company within *s 219(1)(1)*. The General Commissioners dismissed the appeal, and the Court of Appeal upheld their decision. Whether the trade benefit test had been satisfied was a pure question of fact, and there was no basis upon which the court could interfere with the Commissioners' decision. In any event, it is interesting to note that the purchase of own shares in this case was in breach of company law, as the proceeds were used to cancel the vendor's outstanding loan account with the company. As noted elsewhere in this chapter, consideration for the transaction must be paid in full, in cash, on completion.

Allum v Marsh

3.16 The more recent case of *Allum v Marsh* [2005] STC (SCD) 191 offers some assistance on the application of the 'trade benefit' test. In that case, the company's purchase of the taxpayer's shares was held not to be for the benefit of the company's trade. The taxpayers, Mr and Mrs A, were the directors of an unquoted trading company. They held all the shares except one held by R, their son. When the taxpayers were approaching age 70, a property developer expressed an interest in purchasing the company's premises. Mr and Mrs A wished to retire from the business and dispose of their shares without selling them outside the company, so that R could run the company and continue trading. The property sale was completed. The company voted to purchase Mr and Mrs A's shares, and to repay an outstanding directors' loan. In the following year, the company's trading operations reduced considerably. Suitable trading premises were not found, and the company's business was carried out from a limited facility shared with another company. HMRC assessed the taxpayers on the sale proceeds for their shares as an income distribution, on the grounds that the conditions for capital gains tax treatment in *ICTA 1988, s 219(1)(a)* were not satisfied. HMRC considered that the company's purchase of its own shares had not benefited the company's trade. The taxpayers appealed.

The Special Commissioner, Dr Brice, dismissed the taxpayers' appeal. In determining whether a company purchase of its own shares had been made 'for the purpose of benefiting a trade', it was necessary to take account of consequences closely linked to the payment, so that unless those consequences were merely incidental, they had to be regarded as a purpose for which the payment had been made. The offer to purchase the property had been made when Mr and Mrs A were approaching age 70, and wished to retire. The company's decision to purchase the taxpayer's shares had been inextricably linked to its need for the sale proceeds from the property to enable it to do so. The company had been left without permanent premises from which to trade, without the benefit of the directors' loan, and without Mr and Mrs A's services. Those consequences were so closely linked to the company's purchase of the shares that they had to be regarded as a purpose for which the payment was made. The purchase of the shares had therefore not been made wholly or mainly for the purpose of benefiting the trade, but to enable the directors to retire.

Factors to consider

3.17 The Special Commissioner considered a number of principles established in the case *Vodafone Cellular Ltd v Shaw* [1997] 69 TC 376, to decide whether the company's payment for the shares was made wholly and exclusively for the purposes of the trade, or whether there was some element of personal advantage:

- 'For the purposes of the trade' was taken to mean to serve the purposes of the trade, and not for the purposes of the company or for the benefit of the company.
- Was the payment made for the purposes of the taxpayer's trade? To answer this question, it was necessary to discover his object or subjective intentions in making the payment.
- The taxpayer's object in making the payment must be distinguished from the effect of the payment.
- The taxpayer's subjective intentions are not limited to his conscious motives. Consequences which are so inevitably and inextricably linked to the payment must be taken to be a purpose of the payment, unless they are merely incidental.
- The primary question to ask of the taxpayer is 'what was the particular object of the taxpayer in making the payment?'

The Special Commissioner concluded that the purchase of shares was not made 'wholly or mainly' to benefit the company's trade, but to facilitate the retirement of Mr and Mrs A. The purchase allowed the trade to continue, but Dr Brice said that surplus funds could have been paid to Mr and Mrs A, and the trade could still have continued.

3.18 Whilst advance clearance from HMRC on the tax treatment of a purchase of own shares is not mandatory, it will clearly be beneficial to do so, at least in terms of obtaining certainty in cases where the trade benefit requirement is in any doubt.

3.19 *Company purchase of own shares*

'Scheme or arrangement' test

3.19 The second limb of the 'purpose' condition mentioned above is that the company purchase (or redemption or repayment) of its own shares must not form part of a scheme or arrangement, a main purpose of which is either to enable the share owner to participate in the company's profits without receiving a dividend, or the avoidance of tax (*ICTA 1988, s 219(1)(a)*).

'Scheme' or 'arrangement' is not defined for these purposes in the legislation. Both terms require consideration of the motive for the transaction. This is largely a question of fact. However, it may be more difficult to discern whether the 'main purpose' test is breached. It is therefore important that any clearance application made by the company to HMRC in respect of the transaction contains complete and correct details. Otherwise, any clearance given by HMRC cannot subsequently be relied upon.

Residence of vendor

3.20 A further condition for exception from income distribution treatment on a company purchase of its own shares is that the vendor (and any nominee, if appropriate) must be resident and ordinarily resident in the UK in the tax year of purchase (*ICTA 1988, s 220(1)*). However, the 'ordinarily resident' requirement is disregarded if the vendor is a company (*s 220(3)*).

3.21 If the vendors are trustees, the capital gains tax rules for determining their residence and ordinary residence apply (*TCGA 1992, s 69*). A detailed consideration of those rules is outside the scope of this chapter. However, it should be noted that the rules for determining the residence status of trustees changed from 6 April 2007. Trustees are resident in the UK from that date if all of the trustees are UK resident, or if the following conditions are satisfied (*TCGA 1992, s 69(2)*):

- at least one trustee is UK resident; and

- a settlor was resident, ordinarily resident *or* domiciled in the UK at the 'relevant time' (ie broadly when the settlement was made, or immediately before the settlor's death if the settlement was made by Will, intestacy or otherwise).

3.22 Before 6 April 2007, trustees were broadly treated as resident and ordinarily resident in the UK unless two conditions were satisfied:

- all or a majority of trustees are not resident or not ordinarily resident in the UK; and

- the general administration of the trust is ordinarily carried on outside the UK.

Thus a UK resident trust before 6 April 2007 may have inadvertently become an offshore trust from that date (eg by one of the trustees not being resident in the UK and the settlor not meeting the above UK residence or domicile requirements when making the settlement). Previously, a majority of trustees needed to be non-resident and the general administration of the trust carried on abroad. However, note that the trustees need only be resident in the UK for the purposes of this chapter for the tax year in which the share purchase takes place.

3.23 The residence and ordinary residence status of personal representatives is somewhat more straightforward, as their status follows that of the deceased immediately before death (*s 220(3)*).

Period of ownership

3.24 The general rule is that the vendor must have owned the shares throughout the five-year period ending with the share purchase (*ICTA 1988, s 220(5)*). However, this basic requirement is modified in certain respects, depending on the circumstances:

- In the case of transfers to the vendor from a spouse or civil partner, periods of ownership may be combined for the purposes of the five-year test, unless the parties are no longer living together other than by reason of death (*s 220(6)*).
- If the vendor acquired the shares by will or intestacy, or is the deceased's personal representative, periods of ownership by the deceased (or his personal representatives) may be combined, and the required period of ownership is reduced from five years to three years (*s 220(7)*).
- If the shares were acquired as part of a company reconstruction (eg the 'stand in shoes' provision on a share for share exchange) within the capital gains tax legislation (*TCGA 1992, Part IV Ch 2*), the same treatment applies in terms of the ownership test. There are certain exceptions from this relaxation, in respect of allotments for payment and stock dividends within *TCGA 1992, s 249* (*s 220(9)*).

If the vendor's shares were acquired at different times, care may need to be taken in matching the disposal with those acquisitions. For the purposes of the ownership test a FIFO ('first in, first out') basis applies, so that earlier share acquisitions are taken into account before later ones. This rule is helpful, as it gives the longest possible period of ownership for the purpose of this test. In

3.25 *Company purchase of own shares*

addition, any previous share disposals are matched with earlier acquisitions on a LIFO ('last in, first out') basis, so that later acquisitions are taken into account first (*s 220(8)*).

3.25 Apart from the above exceptions, if the company has been incorporated for less than five years, the shareholder cannot satisfy the five-year ownership test. This includes on the incorporation of a sole trader or partnership business.

The 'substantial reduction' test

3.26 Two separate arithmetic tests must be satisfied for the exception from income treatment in *ICTA 1988, s 219(1)(a)* to apply, which are relevant if the vendor retains an interest in the company following the share sale. The interests of 'associates' (see below) are taken into account for these purposes. The first test is that the vendor's interest as a shareholder in the company must be substantially reduced (*ICTA 1988, s 221(1)*). The combined interests of the vendor (and any associates) are taken into account for this purpose. The term 'substantially reduced' broadly means that the nominal value of shares owned by the vendor and associates immediately after the purchase, expressed as a fraction of the company's share capital at that time, does not exceed 75% of the corresponding fraction immediately before the purchase. This test is illustrated below.

Example 3.1

Lee owns 4,000 shares in Express Retail Ltd, an unquoted trading company. The company's issued share capital is 10,000 ordinary £1 shares. Express Retail Ltd agrees to purchase 2,000 of Lee's shares. The relevant fractions are as follows:

Before the purchase: 4,000/10,000 (40%)

After the purchase: 2,000/8,000 (25%)

75% (the substantial reduction threshold) x 40% = 30%. Lee holds 25% of the company's shares following the purchase.

Lee's remaining holding of 2,000 therefore represents a substantial reduction based on his original holding. Note that his interest in the company has actually been reduced by 37.5% (ie (40% − 25%)/40%), but Lee's shareholding in the company has reduced by 50%.

3.27 A second test must also be satisfied, broadly in terms of the vendor's interest in the company's profits. Even if the substantial reduction test is met in terms of share capital, it is not regarded as satisfied if the vendor shareholder's interest (expressed as a fractional share) in the company's profits available for distribution exceeds 75% of the corresponding fraction immediately before the purchase. 'Profits available for distribution' has the meaning given in *Companies Act 1985*, except that the amount is increased by £100 per company plus any fixed distributions to which the shareholder may be entitled. Added to that figure is the excess of all sums payable on share purchases (or redemptions or repayments) over distributable profits available immediately before the purchase (*ICTA 1988, s 221*).

Groups of companies

3.28 If the purchasing company is a group member, the vendor's interest as a shareholder in the group (together with any associates) must be substantially reduced. A 'group' is a company (which is not itself a 51% subsidiary) plus its 51% subsidiaries (*ICTA 1988, s 222(9)*). There are two tests to be satisfied.

The first test is a calculation, which involves aggregating the nominal value of shares (expressed as a fraction of the issued share capital) of each company in the group in which the vendor owned shares immediately before or after the purchase, and dividing that aggregate by the number of group companies in which the vendor owned shares immediately before, or immediately after, the purchase. The vendor shareholder's interest in the group is substantially reduced if it does not exceed 75% of his interest before the purchase.

3.29 The second test to be satisfied is expressed in terms of the vendor's entitlement to a share of the group's 'profits available for distribution' (see above). This test involves aggregating the vendor's share of such profits from each group member to which there was a notional entitlement immediately after the share purchase, and dividing that aggregate by each company's profits available for distribution in which the vendor owns shares immediately before, or immediately after, the purchase (including 51% subsidiaries of such companies). The vendor's entitlement to distributable group profits is substantially reduced if it does not exceed 75% of his interest before the purchase.

3.30 There are anti-avoidance provisions to extend the group for these purposes in two specific circumstances. First, if an unquoted company acquired all or a significant part of the business of the purchasing company (or group member) less than three years before the purchase (or redemption or repayment) of the shares, that outside company (and any 51% subsidiaries) is treated as a member of the same group as the purchasing company (*ICTA 1988, s 222(10), (11)*).

Secondly, a company that has ceased to be a group member continues as such if there are any arrangements under which it could rejoin the group (*s 222(12)*).

3.31 *Company purchase of own shares*

The 'no continuing connection' test

3.31 In addition to the 'substantial reduction' test, there is a further arithmetic test to be satisfied in order to qualify for exception from income distribution treatment on a purchase of own shares. This test requires that the vendor must not be connected with the company (or a group company) immediately after the purchase (*ICTA 1988, s 223*).

3.32 'Connection' is broadly defined in terms of direct or indirect ownership or entitlement to acquire (now and in the future) more than 30% of the company's ordinary share capital, loan capital (except in limited circumstances involving moneylending companies), voting power or the entitlement of equity holders to assets available for distribution on a winding up of the company. The rights of associates are also taken into account for these purposes. The vendor is also connected with the company if he controls it. 'Control' in this context has the meaning given in *ITA 2007, s 995* (previously *ICTA 1988, s 840*) (ie broadly a person's power to secure that the company's affairs are conducted in accordance with his wishes, through shareholdings, voting or other powers in respect of the company) (*ICTA 1988, s 228*).

Anti-avoidance

3.33 There are anti-avoidance provisions to prevent the 'substantial reduction' and 'no continuing connection' arithmetic tests being circumvented:

- The purchase must not at any time be part of a scheme or arrangement with a view to the vendor (or an associate) having an interest immediately after the share purchase that would breach the arithmetic tests (*ICTA 1988, s 223(2)*).
- A transaction within one year after the purchase is deemed to be part of a 'scheme or arrangement' for the above purposes (*s 223(3)*).

Disposals by associates

3.34 There is a relaxation in the arithmetic tests. An associate of the vendor may dispose of shares to the company, to enable the vendor to satisfy the substantial reduction test. In those circumstances, the arithmetic tests do not apply to the company's purchase of the associate's shares, to the extent that the number of shares purchased enables the vendor to comply (*ICTA 1988, s 224*).

Meeting the conditions

3.35 In many cases, in order to satisfy the 'trade benefit' test it may be necessary for the vendor shareholder to dispose of their entire shareholding.

However, the purchasing company may have insufficient funds to acquire the vendor's shares without causing cashflow difficulties. It may therefore be argued that it would be of greater benefit to the company's trade to purchase the shares in tranches. However, to avoid income distribution treatment the two arithmetic tests mentioned above (ie the 'substantial reduction' and 'no continuing connection' tests) must be satisfied. In addition, if the shares are being purchased in stages, HMRC clearance would be required for each transaction. In addition to the 'arithmetic' conditions being met, HMRC would also need to be satisfied that the 'trade benefit' test was passed in each clearance application.

'Loan back' by vendor

3.36 If the company wants to purchase all the vendor's shares but cannot afford to do so, HMRC accept that there is no reason why the vendor should not lend part of the consideration back to the vendor immediately after the purchase. Clearly, the 'substantial reduction' requirement is satisfied. However, the 'no continuing connection' test must also be considered, ie the vendor (and any associates) must not have interests in the company of more than 30% of the combined issued share and loan capital. A loan back to the company may breach this requirement, particularly if the market value of the shares is relatively high and the remaining issued share capital is relatively small.

3.37 In *Tax Bulletin, Issue 21*, HMRC helpfully point out that it is acceptable for the company to satisfy the connection test by making a bonus issue before the purchase of own shares takes place, in order to increase its issued share capital, as illustrated below.

Example 3.2

Martin owns 2,500 shares in Express Widgets Ltd, an unquoted trading company. His shareholding represents 25% of the company's issued share capital of 10,000 shares. Martin wishes to retire, and Express Widgets Ltd therefore agrees to buy Martin's 2,500 shares on 31 March 2008 for their market value of £100,000. Martin has owned his shares for six years, and the shares qualify as a business asset for CGT taper relief purposes. The parties agree that they would like the transaction to fall within *ICTA 1988, s 219*, with the transaction giving rise to a chargeable gain for Martin, on which full business asset taper relief can be claimed.

However, the company is experiencing temporary cashflow difficulties. Martin therefore agrees to loan £50,000 of his proceeds back to the company. However, this would mean that Martin held loan capital of £50,000. The company's

3.38 *Company purchase of own shares*

combined share and loan capital would be £57,500 (ie £7,500 plus £50,000). Martin would therefore be connected with the company.

The company's accountants therefore suggest that before the purchase of own shares takes place, the company should make a bonus issue of 20 shares for each share held, out of its distributable reserves. Martin now holds 52,500 shares out of 210,000 in issue. The company then purchases Martin's 52,500 shares for £100,000, and Martin loans £50,000 back to the company.

Martin now holds loan capital of £50,000. The company's combined share and loan capital is £207,500 (ie £7,500 original share capital, plus £150,000 bonus share capital, plus Martin's loan of £50,000). Martin's interest in the company is less then 30%.

'Phased' purchases

3.38 For a purchase of own shares to be valid under company law, the company must make full cash payment on purchase. The transfer of a company asset, or alternatively leaving the proceeds outstanding on loan account, strictly does not represent 'payment' for these purposes. In such circumstances, the shares are not treated as cancelled and the vendor retains legal ownership of the shares (CTM 17505). The tax implications of any payments already made to the shareholder would then need to be considered.

3.39 An alternative to the 'loan back' following the purchase of the vendor's entire shareholding is a 'phased' purchase, ie the purchase of shares in tranches. Clearance applications will be required in respect of each purchase. HMRC accept (subject to the 'trade benefit' test being satisfied) that it is possible for the vendor to make a series of disposals phased over a period (ICAEW Technical Release 745). However, for the transactions to be eligible for capital gains treatment, the 'substantial reduction' and 'no continuing connection' tests must be satisfied on each occasion.

Contracts with multiple completion

3.40 As indicated above, a company purchase of its own shares by instalments is prohibited under company law. However, a company may enter into a single, unconditional share sale contract with the vendor, with completion taking place on different dates in respect of separate tranches of shares within the agreement. The effect is that the 'substantial reduction' test mentioned above need only be considered once (ie at the contract date), and not at the date of each completion. The vendor must also satisfy the 'no continuing connection' test. However, if the vendor loses beneficial ownership of the shares at the contract date (see below), he will only remain connected with the company if there is ongoing ownership of or entitlement to more than 30% of its issued ordinary shares, loan capital, voting rights and/or assets on a winding up. The rights and powers of any associates must also be taken into account (see below). Completion of the contract in stages does not create a debt for connection purposes. In the event that the company defaults on a stage of the purchase, the vendor could sue under breach of contract for the right to enforce specific performance.

3.41 HMRC may be prepared to accept that a multiple completion contract is possible, provided that beneficial ownership passes at the contract date (ICAEW Technical Release 745). The date of disposal for capital gains purposes is when the unconditional contract is made (*TCGA 1992, s 28(1)*), notwithstanding that payments are made at later dates. This means that the tax liability arising from the disposal could fall due before the consideration for all the shares is received. However, this may not be a significant problem where, for example, full business asset taper relief is available to the vendor shareholder for share disposals before 6 April 2008. In addition, if the consideration is payable over a period exceeding 18 months, the capital gains legislation allows tax on a chargeable gain to be paid by instalments over a period of up to eight years, if appropriate (*TCGA 1992, s 280*).

It should be noted that loss of beneficial ownership of the shares effectively means that the vendor shareholder is unable to participate in dividends paid after the contract date, or exercise voting rights in relation to the shares. The vendor shareholder would need to consent to the waiver of rights to any dividends or other shareholder rights when entering into the agreement and will therefore probably wish to take legal advice to ensure that the contract offers appropriate safeguards to protect his position. A single contract with multiple completion normally only requires a single clearance application to HMRC under *s 225*.

Income or capital?

3.42 This chapter has so far mainly been concerned with the conditions to be satisfied by the individual shareholders of unquoted trading companies for a purchase of own shares to be excluded from income distribution treatment, and to be treated as a capital payment instead. This emphasis on capital treatment is understandable, such as for disposals up to 5 April 2008, given that full taper relief at the business asset rate can reduce the effective CGT rate for a higher rate individual taxpayer to 10% or less after only two complete years' ownership of the shares.

However, it will sometimes be preferable for the transaction to be treated as an income distribution. For example, taper relief may be diluted in some cases, such as in the circumstances highlighted below.

3.43 Company purchase of own shares

3.43 In the case of an income distribution, a purchase of own shares by a company with surplus Advance Corporation Tax (ACT) at 5 April 1999 will give rise to notional (or 'shadow') ACT, which must be taken into account before any offset of actual ACT, in accordance with the shadow ACT provisions (*SI 1999/358*).

Status of the shares

3.44 For company share repurchases before 6 April 2008, the definition of 'qualifying company' for taper relief purposes means that an individual is generally eligible for business asset taper relief in respect of any holding of unlisted trading company shares (*TCGA 1992, Sch A1, para 6(1)*). However, for periods prior to 6 April 2000, the requirement was broadly that the individual must either hold at least 25% of the voting rights, or alternatively hold at least 5% of the voting rights and be a full-time working officer or employee of the company.

The latter, more stringent requirement may result in the dilution of taper relief entitlement, although its effect lessens over time. However, certain periods of share ownership do not count for taper relief purposes at all. This can affect close companies which have not been 'active' for periods of time (*TCGA 1992, Sch A1, para 11A*). Certain taper relief anti-avoidance rules can also have the effect of excluding periods of ownership from both the 'qualifying holding period' and 'relevant period of ownership' (*Sch A1, para 2(4)*). These excluded periods are ignored when counting the ten years up to the date of the share disposal.

Company status

3.45 The definition of 'trading company' for the purposes of a company purchase of own shares requires that the company is 'wholly or mainly' trading (*ICTA 1988, s 229(1)*). This is a less stringent test than for CGT taper relief purposes in respect of disposals before 6 April 2008, which requires that the company's activities must not include non-trading activities to a substantial extent (*TCGA 1992, Sch A1, para 22A(1)*). 'Substantial' in this context is considered to mean more than 20% (CG 17953p).

3.46 The circumstances in which HMRC will provide a ruling on the status of a company for taper relief purposes was significantly narrowed down following *Tax Bulletin, Issue 84* (August 2006), which announced changes to the facility for obtaining such rulings. Previously, it was possible to apply to HMRC for a ruling under Code of Practice 10 on the status of a company for a particular period. However, HMRC will now only provide a post-transaction

Company purchase of own shares **3.47**

ruling where a 'significant number of shareholders' have made a disposal, and only if the company itself has 'genuine doubt or difficulty' as to its trading status (CG 17953r). In some cases, a disposing shareholder with genuine concerns over the trading status of the company may therefore wish to seek a 'negative clearance' from HMRC that the conditions for capital treatment are not satisfied.

Example 3.3

Edward has owned 50% of the shares in Dotcom Ltd, an unquoted company, for nearly six years. The company traded very successfully and quickly grew during that time, accumulating a significant amount of surplus cash at bank, some of which was invested in quoted shares. In August 2007, following a disagreement with Eric, his fellow 50% shareholder, both parties agree that Edward will resign as a director and that Dotcom Ltd will purchase his shares for £500,000.

Edward is concerned that Dotcom Ltd is not a 'trading company' for taper relief purposes. Faced with the uncertainty of 75% business asset taper relief and an effective CGT rate of around 10% at one extreme, and 15% non-business asset taper relief and an effective CGT rate of around 34% at the other, he discusses with his accountant the possibility of ensuring that the conditions for capital treatment are not satisfied.

Following a successful 'negative clearance' application to HMRC, Dotcom Ltd buys back Edward's shares. The resulting income distribution gives rise to a higher rate income tax liability equal to around 25% of the net distribution (see below).

Comparing tax rates

3.47 It should be noted that full non-business asset taper relief potentially accrues for the first time in April 2007, in respect of shares held before 17 March 1998 (*TCGA 1992, s 2A(8)*). For a higher rate taxpayer entitled to full non-business asset taper relief (in the circumstances outlined above, or possibly on a sale of shares to another shareholder), an effective CGT rate of around 24% (ie 40% CGT rate reduced by 60% non-business asset taper relief) compares favourably with the effective 25% liability on an income distribution. The latter income tax rate is illustrated in the example below.

Example 3.4

Sarah is a higher rate taxpayer, and owns 20% of the shares in Alpha Ltd. She wishes to retire, and the company buys back her shares on 1 October 2007 for £250,000. Sarah originally subscribed for the shares at par in 1990, at a cost of

3.48 *Company purchase of own shares*

£100. The conditions for capital treatment are not satisfied. Her income tax liability on the sale is calculated as follows:

	£
Proceeds	250,000
Less: Subscription cost	(100)
Net distribution	249,900
Tax credit (1/9)	27,767
Gross distribution	277,667
Income tax liability:	
£277,667 x 32.5%	90,242
Less: Tax credit	(27,767)
	62,475
Effective income tax rate: £62,475 / £250,000	25%

3.48 For disposals before 6 April 2008, where taper relief relevant ownership periods are less than ten years (but more than five years, such that the minimum ownership period requirement in *ICTA 1988, s 220(5)* is capable of being satisfied), if mixed (business and non-business) taper relief entitlement applies a comparison of the tax rates on a company purchase of own shares based on income or capital treatment may be worthwhile if the parties are in a position to influence the tax treatment of the transaction (see below).

If the consideration for the shares is relatively low and/or the cost is relatively high, the individual vendor shareholder may not be liable to higher rate tax. In those circumstances income distribution treatment is likely to be more beneficial, as no further income tax would be due on the distribution. However, in practice such cases are likely to be relatively few.

Income distribution treatment

3.49 As indicated in the above example, the amount of the income distribution is broadly the consideration for the shares, less the original subscription price (*s 209(2)(b)*). In some cases, share capital may be issued at a premium, representing new consideration (eg following a share exchange on a previous takeover of the company). The amount of such a premium is generally treated as part of the share capital when considering the amount of any repayment of share capital (*ICTA 1988, s 211(5)*; see CTM 17510–17520).

3.50 There are potential traps to avoid in the distributions legislation:

a previous bonus issue of shares followed by a repayment of share capital may result in the application of the distribution rules in certain circumstances, eg in relation to bonus issues of redeemable shares (see *ICTA 1988, s 211(1)*). The effect is that on a subsequent purchase of own shares, share capital is only treated as repaid to the extent that the repayment exceeds the earlier bonus issue. Thus if the amount of the bonus issue exceeds the amount that would otherwise be treated as a repayment of share capital, the whole payment for the purchase of own shares will be treated as an income distribution (see CTM 17530).

A purchase of own shares followed or accompanied by a bonus issue of shares can result in the latter being treated as an income distribution in certain cases, including close companies, irrespective of capital treatment having applied to the earlier share repurchase, or clearance having been given under *ICTA 1988, s 225 (s 210(1))*. The effect is that a distribution can arise up to the amount of share capital repaid from the purchase of own shares. This can apply even if the recipient of the bonus issue is not the same as the vendor on the company purchase of own shares (see CTM 17540).

3.51 As a result of income distribution treatment, the proceeds received by an individual vendor shareholder may partly represent a return of share capital for capital gains tax (CGT) purposes, and partly an income distribution. The fact that the transaction is an income distribution does not prevent it from being a disposal for CGT purposes as well. The amount charged to income tax is excluded from the taxable consideration when calculating the CGT position (*TCGA 1992, s 37(1)*). The net proceeds in the CGT computation would be matched with the original amount paid for the shares. This will often mean that no capital gain or loss arises, as illustrated below.

Example 3.5

In January 2004, Jason subscribed for 10,000 ordinary £1 shares in Delta Ltd, an unquoted trading company, representing 50% of the company's share capital. The company is successful. On 31 March 2008, Delta Ltd agrees to purchase Jason's shares for £500,000. Unfortunately for Jason, the company's purchase of his shares does not qualify for capital gains treatment, as the five-year ownership condition has not been satisfied. The transaction is therefore treated as an income distribution. His CGT computation is as follows:

	£
Proceeds	500,000
Less: Treated as a distribution (£500,000 – £10,000)	(490,000)

3.52 *Company purchase of own shares*

	£
Net distribution	10,000
Less: Cost	(10,000)
Chargeable gain / (allowable loss)	Nil

3.52 However, in some situations (eg if the vendor shareholder held the shares at 31 March 1982, and the shares had a high value at that time) an allowable capital loss may be generated.

Example 3.6

Gerald subscribed for 100 ordinary £1 shares in Beta Ltd in 1980, representing 75% of the company's share capital. The company's trade is successful, and Gerald's shares are worth £200,000 at 31 March 1982. On 31 March 2008, Beta Ltd agrees to purchase Gerald's shares for £800,000. The conditions for CGT treatment in *s 219* are not satisfied in respect of the transaction.

	£
Income distribution	
Proceeds	800,000
Less: Subscription cost	(100)
Net distribution	799,900
Tax credit (1/9)	88,878
Gross distribution	888,778
CGT computation	
Proceeds	800,000
Less: Charged to income tax	(799,900)
	100
Less: Value at 31 March 1982	(200,000)
Allowable loss	(199,900)

3.53 The rule regarding disposals between connected persons (ie which restricts loss relief to transactions with the same connected person) in *TCGA 1992, s 18(3)* does not apply in the above circumstances. This is because the 'connected persons' rule applies when a person 'acquires' an asset, whereas in the above example for company law purposes Beta Ltd would be required to cancel the shares, so in that sense would not 'acquire' anything (*FA 2003, s 195(2)*). The tax treatment for company or trustee vendor shareholders is considered later in this chapter.

3.54 If an individual vendor subscribes for ordinary shares in an unquoted trading company and a capital loss arises such as in the circumstances outlined above, it may be possible to offset the loss against the taxpayer's total income for the same and/or the preceding year. This income tax relief is subject to a number of conditions (in *ITA 2007, Pt 4, Ch 6*, previously *ICTA 1988, ss 574–576*), a detailed consideration of which is outside the scope of this chapter. However, there appears to be no reason why an eligible loss cannot relieve total income, including the distribution arising from the company purchase of its own shares.

Capital gains treatment

3.55 The conditions for automatic capital gains treatment were described earlier in this chapter. If those conditions are satisfied, the income tax distribution rules are disapplied, and the entire proceeds are treated as a capital receipt instead. For individual vendor shareholders, this presents an opportunity to claim CGT reliefs, allowances and exemptions, if applicable. For example, the CGT liability of an individual shareholder may be reduced or extinguished by a high base cost (or March 1982 value), indexation allowance (up to April 1998, for disposals before 6 April 2008), capital losses, taper relief (for disposals before 6 April 2008), and the annual CGT exemption. Even if the CGT liability is not completely extinguished, capital treatment can result in a relatively low effective tax rate, as illustrated below.

Example 3.7

The facts are in **Example 3.6** above, except that the conditions for capital gains treatment in *s 219* are satisfied in relation to Gerald's disposal of 100 ordinary £1 shares to Beta Ltd for £800,000 on 31 March 2008. In addition, the conditions for business asset taper relief (BATR) have been satisfied throughout Gerald's relevant ownership period. His CGT position for 2007/08 is as follows (Gerald is a higher rate taxpayer on his entire gain):

	£
Proceeds	800,000
Less: Value at 31 March 1982	(200,000)
	600,000
Less: Indexation (to April 1998 @ 104.7%)	(209,400)
	390,600
Less: BATR (75%)	(292,950)
	97,650
Less: Annual exemption	(9,200)

3.56 *Company purchase of own shares*

	£
Chargeable gain	88,450
CGT at 40%	£35,380
Effective CGT rate	4.42%

3.56 If maximum business asset taper relief applies to disposals before 6 April 2008, it will be noted that the effective CGT rate for a higher rate taxpayer can be considerably lower than the often-publicised 10% 'headline' rate, depending on factors including allowable costs, and the availability of indexation allowance (until April 1998) and the annual exemption. The effective CGT rate is potentially lower still, to the extent that the gain falls with the basic rate limit. Capital gains treatment will therefore be the preferred path for many vendor shareholders of unquoted trading companies. This will probably remain so in most cases after 5 April 2008, particularly if the proceeds are substantial. However, it should be remembered that capital treatment under *ICTA 1988, s 219* is mandatory if the relevant conditions are satisfied. Otherwise, income tax distribution treatment will automatically apply instead.

Clearance applications to HMRC

3.57 As noted above, the legislation on the purchase (or redemption or repayment) by an unquoted trading company of its own shares in *ICTA 1988, ss 219–229* contains various conditions which must be satisfied before the tax treatment allowed by *s 219* can apply. Provision is therefore made (in s 225) for the company (or its agent) to make a written clearance application in advance to HMRC.

It is worth noting two general points in relation to clearance applications under *s 225*. Firstly, a clearance application is not necessarily required in order for *s 219* to apply (ie the application of *s 219* is mandatory, and the conditions for capital treatment are either satisfied, or they are not). However, if a complete and correct clearance application is submitted to HMRC, this does provide certainty of treatment. Secondly, clearances applications can either be 'positive' under *s 225(1)(a)* (ie that *s 219* does apply) or 'negative' under *s 225(1)(b)* (ie that it does not). Negative clearance applications are discussed further below.

3.58 To assist companies and agents in preparing clearance applications under *ICTA 1988, s 225*, HMRC included as an Annex to SP 2/82 pro-forma applications for clearance for the purchase of own shares under *ICTA 1988, s 219(1)(a)* (ie relating to the benefit of a trade), and *s 219(1)(b)* (ie relating to the payment of inheritance tax). The pro-forma clearance application relating to the former payment is included below, based on the Annex in SP 2/82.

HMRC state that the format of the clearance letter does not represent an exhaustive list, but that it would be helpful if applications followed the order set out below, each item being expanded as necessary and any further information being added at the end. The application must give particulars of all 'relevant transactions' (*s 225(2)*), and must fully and accurately disclose all material facts and circumstances material, as otherwise any resulting clearance given by HMRC is treated as void (*s 225(5)*).

3.59 An application to HMRC under *ICTA 1988, s 225* for advance clearance that capital treatment will be available to the vendor shareholder is normally accompanied by an application for clearance under *ITA 2007, s 701* (previously *ICTA 1988, s 707*) that the 'transactions in securities' anti-avoidance rules do not apply. Those rules are of relevance to most owner-managed businesses as they relate to close companies (ie under the control of five or fewer persons). They broadly apply to company distributions not otherwise taxable as income (*ITA 2007, ss 688, 689*, previously *ICTA 1988, s 704C, D*) unless HMRC are satisfied that the transaction was for bona fide commercial reasons, and that obtaining a tax advantage was not a main object.

As mentioned, in practice, a joint clearance application will normally be made under *s 225*, and also *ITA 2007, s 701* concerning the transactions in securities provisions. A single letter is used for both clearances, which should be sent to the Clearance & Counteraction Team, Anti-Avoidance Group Intelligence. Contact details can be obtained from HMRC's website (http://www.hmrc.gov.uk/cap/). No extra copy is required as the same person will deal with each of the clearances asked for. A single response will be given covering all of these.

'Negative' clearance applications

3.60 As mentioned elsewhere in this chapter, capital gains treatment in *ICTA 1988, s 219(1)(a)* applies automatically if the relevant conditions are satisfied. This will often be the preferred tax treatment for vendor shareholders. However, particularly in the case of family or owner-managed companies, it is often possible to structure the company purchase of own shares so that the relevant conditions are breached.

Breaking the conditions for capital treatment

3.61 A breach of the rules for capital gains treatment can be caused in various ways. For example:

3.62 *Company purchase of own shares*

- The vendor could sell the shares in stages under separate contracts, or immediately lend the sale proceeds back to the company for a time, such that the 'substantial reduction' and/or the 'no continuing connection' tests are not satisfied.

- The vendor could breach the residence condition by transferring the shares to a nominee who is not resident or ordinarily resident in the UK. The acquisition of shares by the nominee does not trigger a disposal by the vendor for CGT purposes, as transactions between them are specifically disregarded (*TCGA 1992, s 60(1)*). However, the rules for capital treatment on a purchase of own shares require that both the vendor and nominee must be resident and ordinarily resident in the UK (*ICTA 1988, s 220(1)*). The transfer of shares to a nominee prior to a company purchase could be challenged by HMRC, on *Furniss v Dawson* [1984] STC 153 principles.

- It may be argued that the purchase of own shares was not wholly or mainly for the benefit of the company's trade. For example, the vendor may be retained as a full-time director. Alternatively, it may be that the transaction wholly or mainly benefited the vendor shareholder as opposed to the company, eg that the transaction was undertaken wholly or mainly to provide funds to facilitate the retirement of a director shareholder (as held by the Special Commissioner in *Allum v Marsh*), rather than to benefit the company's trade.

3.62 There is a 'negative' advance clearance application procedure available to the company by virtue of *ICTA 1988, s 225(1)(b)*, ie to the effect HMRC are satisfied that the transaction is *not* one for which capital gains treatment in *s 219* applies. HMRC are required to give their decision within 30 days of receiving the application, or requesting further particulars.

Application for clearance under s 225(1)(a) – Purchases within s 219(1)(a)

Note: It should be clearly stated at the top of the letter the clearances requested (eg *ICTA 1988, s 225* and *ITA 2007, s 701*). It should also be confirmed whether the purchase of shares is regarded as falling within *s 219(1)* by virtue of (a) or (b). If the purchasing company has previously made any application under *s 225* it will be helpful if HMRC's reference can be quoted.

- **The company**
    - the name of the company making the purchase;
    - its Tax District and reference;
    - confirmation that it is an unquoted company as defined in *ICTA 1988, s 229(1)*;

Company purchase of own shares **3.62**

- – its status, that is, 'trading company' or 'holding company of a trading group' within the *s 229(1)* definitions or some other type of company not within the definitions.

- **Groups**

  Where the company is a member of a group (a 'group' for the purpose of this paragraph is the largest 51% group to which the purchasing company belongs (*s 222(9)*), but the meaning of 'group' is extended, where appropriate, by *ICTA 1988, s 222(10)* and *(12)*).

  - – the names of the group companies together with their Tax Districts and references:
  - – a statement or diagram showing the shareholding interests of each group company in other group companies.

- **Shareholders**

  - – A list of the current shareholders in the purchasing company, and where appropriate, in each company in a group as above, together with particulars (amount, class, dividend rights etc) of their current holdings;
  - – a statement of any relationships of the shareholders to each other;
  - – where the shareholder is the son or daughter of another shareholder, an indication that he or she is over 18 or else details of their age.

- **Prior transactions**

  Particulars of any prior transactions or rearrangements to be carried out in preparation for the purchase.

- **Purpose and benefits**

  A statement of the reasons for the purchase, the trading benefits expected and any other benefits expected to accrue, whether or not to the purchasing company.

- **Conditions in *ICTA 1988, s 219***

  Confirmation, together with all relevant information, that the purchase etc does not form part of a scheme or arrangement the main purpose or one of the main purposes of which is to enable the owner of the shares to participate in the profits of the company without receiving a dividend, or the avoidance of tax. Confirmation that the vendor will receive no other payment from the company, or details of any such payment to be made.

- **Conditions in *ICTA 1988, ss 220–224***

  - – the present residence status of the vendor and any intended change (*s 220*);

3.62 *Company purchase of own shares*

- the tax district, reference and National Insurance number of the vendor, or if not known his or her private address (*s 220*);
- the period of beneficial ownership by the vendor of the shares to be purchased (*s 220(5)*);
- confirmation, if appropriate, that the vendor's interest will be 'substantially reduced' *s 221(1)*);
- confirmation, if appropriate, that the combined interests as shareholders of the vendor and his 'associates' (see *s 227*) will be substantially reduced (*s 221(2)*);
- confirmation, if appropriate, that the vendor's interest as a shareholder in the group will be substantially reduced (*s 222(1)*);
- confirmation, if appropriate, that the combined interests as shareholders in the group of the vendor and his associates will be substantially reduced (*s 222(3)*);
- confirmation that the vendor will not, immediately after the purchase, be 'connected with' (see *s 228*) the company making the purchase or with any company which is a member of the same group as that company (*s 223(1)*);
- confirmation that the purchase is not part of a scheme or arrangement within s *223(2)*.

- **Accounts and other financial information**

The application should be accompanied by:

- copies of the latest available financial statements for the purchasing company and for any group companies (see paragraph 2 above), and in the case of a group the financial statements for the group;
- a note of any material relevant changes since the balance sheet date or confirmation that there are none;
- details of any loan or current account which the vendor maintains with the company or with any group company.

APPENDIX*

Schedule of transaction(s)

- Details of the shares to be purchased, the name of their present owner, the purchase price and the method of payment.
- Details of any other transactions between the company and the vendor at or about the same time.

- Confirmation that the company's Articles of Association allow it to purchase its own shares.

---

* Adopting the layout suggested in 'Working Together' (Issue 6) in connection with *ICTA 1988, s 707* applications.

Company law

3.63 A company purchase of its own shares must comply with certain *Companies Act* requirements. HMRC can only consider a request for clearance on a transaction which appears to be a valid purchase of own shares (*Tax Bulletin, Issue 21* (February 1996)). A detailed consideration of company law issues is outside the scope of this chapter. However, compliance with the law is fundamental to the transaction, and the tax treatment is dependent on the legal analysis. The main company law considerations (ie for an unquoted or 'off market' purchase) are therefore set out below. Professional advisers who are unfamiliar with company law should obtain the necessary legal advice. Failure to comply with the legal requirements could make the transaction void and legally unenforceable, and render the company and its officers liable to sanctions.

A new Companies Act (*Companies Act 2006*) was given Royal Assent on 8 November 2006. The Act was to be introduced in stages between October 2007 and October 2008. *Companies Act 2006, Pt 18* ('Acquisition by limited company if its own shares') was originally scheduled to be introduced on 1 October 2008. However, the government announced on 7 November 2007 that the commencement date for certain *Companies Act 2006* provisions originally due to commence on 1 October 2008 was being put back to 1 October 2009. This includes the purchase of own shares provisions in CA 2006, Pt 18. References to the new Companies Act provisions are included below.

3.64 Shares purchased by an unquoted company are treated as cancelled. From 1 December 2003, companies which are listed (including on the Alternative Investment Market) can generally hold repurchased shares 'in treasury'. Shares held in treasury are not actually cancelled, and are retained by the company. However, the rights attaching to the shares are effectively suspended whilst they are held in treasury, ie the company may not vote in respect of the shares or receive distributions in respect of them. The purchase by a company of its own shares is not treated as the acquisition of an asset (*FA 2003, s 195(2)*).

Requirements

3.65 The Companies Acts give a company power to purchase its own shares, if certain conditions are satisfied. Otherwise, the shares are not treated as

3.66 *Company purchase of own shares*

cancelled, and legal ownership remains with the vendor (Company Taxation Manual, CTM 17505). The tax implications of the company's payment to the shareholder would then need to be considered. For most owner-managed companies, this would include a potential liability for the company under the 'loans to participators' provisions (*ICTA 1988, s 419*), and for the vendor as a taxable benefit under the beneficial loan rules (*ITEPA 2003, s 175*). Companies Act 1985 specifies a procedure for share buy-backs. Companies Act 2006 restates some provisions of its predecessor, and changes others.

3.66 The following is a brief outline of the main company law requirements.

- **Power to purchase own shares**

    Companies Act 1985 gives a company the power to purchase its own shares, if authorised to do so by the Articles of Association (*CA 1985, s 162(1)*). Most 'modern' Articles include such a power. However, for some older companies (eg those incorporated under *Companies Act 1948*), it may be necessary for the shareholders to pass a special resolution to allow the company to make the purchase.

    Companies Act 2006 does not include a requirement in the company's Articles to purchase its own shares, although the members may restrict or prohibit a purchase of own shares through the Company's articles if they wish. This is helpful, because as mentioned the Articles of some older companies do not contain the necessary authority. The share purchase must not leave the company with only redeemable and/or treasury shares (*CA 1985, s 162(3), CA 2006, s 690*).

- **Authority for purchase**

    Companies Act 1985 requires the share purchase contract to be agreed by the company's members through a special resolution beforehand (*CA 1985, s 164(5)*). The contract (or a detailed memorandum of its terms) must be available for inspection for at least 15 days before the meeting, and also at the meeting.

    Companies Act 2006 also requires a contract for an 'off-market' company purchase of own shares to be approved in advance (*CA 2006, s 693*). However, that Act allows a company to enter into a contract to purchase its own shares, on condition that the shareholders approve the contract terms by a special resolution (*CA 2006, s 694(2)*). If the contract is not approved, the company may not purchase the relevant shares and the contract lapses. A copy of any written contract (or a memorandum of its terms) must be made available to the members. For resolutions at meetings, it must be available for inspection at the company's registered office for at least 15 days prior to the meeting, and also at the meeting itself (*CA 2006, s 696(2)*).

- **Payment for the shares**

    The shares purchased must be fully-paid, and the company must pay for the shares on completion (*CA 1985, s 159(3); 2006, s 691*).

- **Distributable profits**

    A company must purchase its own shares out of distributable profits, or out of the proceeds of a fresh share issue to finance the purchase (*CA 1985, s 162(2), CA 2006, s 692(2)*). An amount equal to the par value of the shares bought back must be transferred to a capital redemption reserve account.

    However, a private company may purchase its own shares out of capital, if certain conditions are satisfied (*CA 1985, ss 160(1), 171–177, CA 2006, ss 692(1), 709–723*), consideration of which is outside the scope of this chapter.

- **Cancellation of shares**

    Following the company share repurchase, the relevant shares are treated as cancelled. The company's share capital is reduced by the nominal value of the cancelled shares (*CA 1985, s 160(4); CA 2006, s 706*). This rule does not apply to treasury shares (see above).

- **Return to Companies House**

    The company can enter into the contract when the resolution is passed. A return must be made to the Registrar of Companies within 28 days, stating the number of shares purchased, their nominal value and the date of purchase (*CA 1985, s 169(1), CA 2006, s 707*).

    Except in the case of treasury shares which are not cancelled, the company must also notify the Registrar of Companies of the cancellation of the shares within 28 days, together with a statement of the company's share capital (*CA 2006, s 708*). *Companies Act 1985* imposes this notification requirement only in relation to treasury shares which are cancelled (*CA 1985, s 169(1A)*).

- **Inspection of contract**

    Companies Act 1985 requires that the share purchase contract (or a memorandum of its terms) must be retained at the company's registered office for at least ten years from completion of the contract (*CA 1985, s 169(4)*).

3.67 *Companies Act 2006* also stipulates a ten-year retention period. However, it also provides that a copy of the contract (or any variation) may alternatively be kept for inspection at a specified place (in regulations made under *CA 2006, s 1136*). The company must notify the registrar of the place

3.68 *Company purchase of own shares*

where the contract is available for inspection. Contracts (or memorandums of terms) relating to private companies must be made available for inspection by any of its members (*CA 2006, s 702*).

Corporate vendors

3.68 Whilst this chapter is mainly concerned with individual owner-managers of unquoted trading companies, it should be noted that a company purchase of own shares by a UK company from another UK company (after 19 April 1989) has potentially different tax implications.

In those cases, if the purchase gives rise to a distribution, the disposal proceeds are not reduced by the amount of the distribution for the purposes of calculating corporation tax on chargeable gains. This is because, in HMRC's view, the distribution does not suffer a tax charge as income within *TCGA 1992, s 37(1)* (*SP 4/89*). This view follows from the distributions legislation (*ICTA 1988, s 208* 'UK company distributions not generally chargeable to corporation tax'), which provides 'except as otherwise provided by the *Corporation Tax Acts*, Corporation Tax shall not be chargeable on dividends and other distributions of a company resident in the United Kingdom, nor shall any such dividends or distributions be taken into account in computing income for corporation tax'. HMRC accept that this treatment only applies to a purchase of own shares, not to a redemption or reduction in share capital (*CG 58625*).

3.69 HMRC's view on the treatment of a purchase of own shares from a corporate shareholder in SP 4/89 was upheld by the Court of Appeal in *Strand Options and Futures Ltd v Vojak* [2003] EWCA Civ 1457. In that case, HMRC had previously confirmed that chargeable gains treatment did not apply to the taxpayer company, so that proceeds from the purchase of part of its shareholding in another company would be treated as a distribution for tax purposes. The Court of Appeal held that a true interpretation of the effect of *ICTA 1988, s 208* (except where otherwise expressly provided by the Tax Acts) was to exempt from corporation tax all company distributions, whether as income or giving rise to a chargeable gain. The distribution element should be brought into account in computing the taxpayer's chargeable gains.

Trustee vendors

3.70 As explained in this chapter, a company purchase of own shares is generally treated as a distribution for tax purposes. Under company law, such a transaction usually gives rise to a capital receipt. Certain types of capital receipts by trustees are treated as income receipts in their hands, and are liable at 'special trust rates' (ie the rate applicable to trusts of 40%, or the dividend trust rate of 32.5%). This includes the receipt from a company which is buying back its own shares from the trustees. The tax treatment of such a disposal by trustees was called into question following changes to what has now become *ITA 2007, s 482* (previously *ICTA 1988, s 686A* ('Receipts to be treated as income to which *s 686* applies')), which were made in *FA 2006*. The original legislation in *s 686A* provided that what was taxable was only the distribution element, excluding the original subscription price for the shares. However, the effect of an omission in the wording of the *FA 2006* amendments was to treat the whole payment to the trustees (ie including the original subscription price) as being taxable, rather than just the distribution element. The circumstances in which capital gains treatment applied were not distinguished either. This omission was corrected in *FA 2007*, which ensures that 'qualifying distributions' are liable to income tax (ie the 'profit' element, excluding the original subscription price). The amendment has effect from 6 April 2006.

Following the introduction of *ITA 2007*, the correct position is stated in *ITA 2007, s 482* ('Types of amount to be charged at special rates for trustees') as amended by *FA 2007*. A 'qualifying distribution' covers most types of distribution (*ICTA 1988, s 14(2)*). However, a company purchase of own shares which satisfies the conditions for capital treatment is specifically excluded from the meaning of 'distribution' (*ICTA 1988, s 219(1)*). Hence a capital payment under trust law, and for tax purposes by virtue of *s 219*, on a company purchase of own shares should not be subject to income tax as a distribution.

3.71 There was some concern that where the vendor of shares is a trust, a 'double' charge to income tax and CGT could arise effectively on the same transaction, for reasons other than those outlined above. For CGT purposes, *TCGA 1992, s 37(1)* provides that disposal proceeds are excluded from the chargeable gains calculation if '… charged to income tax as income of, or taken into account as a receipt in computing income of, *the person making the disposal …*' (emphasis added). In the case of a settlor-interested trust, the person making the disposal will be the trustees, but the income tax liability will arise on the settlor. In strictness, relief under *s 37* would therefore be unavailable in the settlor's CGT computation (the settlor being liable to CGT on the trustees' gains), as the person making the disposal would be different than the person incurring the income tax charge. However, HMRC have apparently confirmed that relief is available under *TMA 1970, s 32* ('Relief for excessive assessments') to vacate the CGT assessment. A similar problem potentially arises in respect of life interest trusts which are not settlor-interested, whereby the trustees are liable to CGT on the gain, but the income tax liability otherwise belongs to the life tenant. HMRC are reported to consider that because a purchase of own shares is generally capital under trust law, the income tax liability will not usually belong to the life tenant. The trustees would therefore be liable to the income tax instead, and the protection of *TCGA 1992* would then be available. However, as a precaution, the trust deed should not define the life

3.72 *Company purchase of own shares*

tenant's entitlement to income by reference to 'taxable income' (see John Barnett 'A problem of trust' *Taxation*, 9 June 2005).

OTHER POINTS

Associated persons

3.72 For the purposes of the company purchase of own shares rules providing for capital treatment if the conditions in *ICTA 1988, ss 219–228* are satisfied (eg in respect of the 'substantial reduction' and 'no continuing connection' tests), the interests of associated persons' need to be considered. Such interests are added to those of the vendor for these purposes. 'Associated persons' include the following (*s 227*):

- Spouses or civil partners living together.
- Parents and minors under the age of 18.
- A person connected with a company is associated with that company, and with any other companies which it controls.
- If a person connected with one company controls the other, the two companies are associated.
- Settlement trustee shareholders are broadly associated with any settlor(s), their associates and with any person who has an actual or potential beneficial entitlement to a significant interest in the shares (subject to certain exceptions relating to pension schemes and employee trusts).
- The personal representatives of a deceased shareholder are associated with any person who has an actual or potential beneficial entitlement to a significant interest in the shares.
- If a person is accustomed to acting on the directions of another person in respect of the company's affairs, the two persons are associated.

An interest is 'significant' in the context of trustees and personal representatives if its value exceeds 5% of the beneficial interest in the settlement or estate concerned.

Returns of own share purchases

3.73 The company must submit a return to HMRC within 60 days of making a payment for the purchase of own shares to which capital treatment is considered to apply (*ICTA 1988, s 226*). This requirement applies whether or not clearance was requested and obtained from HMRC that capital gains treatment applies to the payment (CTM 17580).

In practice, if a clearance application was made this requirement can often be satisfied in a short letter to HMRC drawing the inspector's attention to the clearance letter and outlining any changes between the proposed transactions in the letter and the actual transactions that took place. If a clearance application was not made, the Inspector will need to know the date of the purchase, the name of the vendor, the number of shares, the amount of consideration, and the grounds on which the 'trade benefit' test are considered to be satisfied.

3.74 An Inspector who has reason to believe that a company payment subject to capital gains treatment forms part of a 'scheme or arrangement' may issue a notice requiring the company (or any connected person) to provide certain information relating to the transaction within a period of not less than 60 days (*s 226(3)*). Penalties may be charged for failing to comply with the return and information requirements. The maximum initial penalty is £300, plus a maximum daily penalty of £60 in cases of continued failure to provide the information.

Stamp duty

3.75 The purchasing company is liable to a stamp duty charge of 0.5% on returns to Companies House under the *Companies Act 1985, s 169 (FA 1986, s 66)*. This stamp duty liability is rounded up to the nearest multiple of £5. The return provides details of the share buyback. Form G169 is a stampable return, and the duty is charged on the consideration for the shares. Note that the return itself is stampable, rather than the share transfer form. The company must deliver the return to Companies House within 28 days from the first date on which the shares were delivered to the company.

Professional fees

3.76 Professional costs incurred on the company purchase (or redemption or repayment) of its shares are generally not an allowable deduction from Sch D Case I or II profits for corporation tax purposes. This is either on the basis that such fees are capital expenditure in respect of the company's share capital, or that they are specifically excluded from relief under the 'wholly and exclusively' rule (*ICTA 1988, s 74(1)(f)*). It may seem somewhat anomalous that HMRC can give clearance that a purchase of own shares is wholly or mainly for the benefit of the company's trade, and yet a deduction for the professional costs of securing that benefit should be denied. However, it does not automatically

3.77 *Company purchase of own shares*

follow (at least in HMRC's view) that the related professional costs are considered to be 'wholly and exclusively' for the purposes of the trade (see CTM 17600).

Professional advisers may therefore wish to word their fee notes carefully, to distinguish between allowable and non-allowable services, with a view to minimising any disallowance for the latter.

Valuation of shares

3.77 The market value rule for transactions between connected persons for CGT purposes in *TCGA 1992, s 18* does not apply to a company purchase of own shares, even in the case of a family company, as there is no acquisition by the company corresponding to the disposal by the shareholder. However, market value may still be substituted if the purchase is not considered to be at arm's length (*TCGA 1992, s 17*; see CGM 58645). A purchase at what HMRC considers to be overvalue may be referred to Shares Valuation. The end result may be that HMRC seek to tax the excess over an arm's-length value (eg as an income distribution within *s 209(4)*, or possibly as employment income within *ITEPA 2003, s 446X*). However, reports by HMRC officers to Shares Valuation on this basis are understood to be rare (SVM 35070).

Chapter 4

Groups

John Baldry LLB LLM (London); Partner, Kirkland & Ellis International LLP

INTRODUCTION

4.1 This chapter deals with the principal considerations which arise for companies which fall to be treated (under tests which differ according to the tax in question) as members of a group for one or more corporation tax purposes. This brings with it both benefits and opportunities for the careful and less desirable consequences for the unwary.

Unlike some other taxing jurisdictions, such as the US, the UK does not operate a consolidated system of group taxation, at least for corporation tax, and nor does it seem that such a reform is likely to be introduced in the near future. Rather, the UK tax system respects each company within the group as distinct legal entities, each subject to the general tax regime, but then overlays various additional substantive and administrative rules in order to take into account the fact that the companies are in reality part of one economic unit.

The principal day-to-day issue for a group of companies will be how to deal with situations where certain members of the group are making profits and others losses. This is dealt with through the group relief rules. Companies may also be concerned about the transfer of assets, businesses or assignment of debts between members of the group. The tax code attempts to provide for all these scenarios, but in doing so also provides certain anti-avoidance rules which must be carefully negotiated in order not to cause immediate or future tax concerns.

That is not to say, however, that the rules achieve, or even attempt to achieve, neutrality between the position where an economic entity operates through one company, and where it operates through many companies. Inefficiencies may arise because the group has many companies (for example losses may become stranded by being carried forward in a non-profit making member of the group when other members are profitable), or fortuitous planning using subsidiaries may lead to tax advantages not available if the enterprise had been carried on through a different corporate structure (for example a business to be sold is carried on in a separate subsidiary so that substantial shareholdings relief is available on the sale).

4.2 *Groups*

The tax consequences of a particular group structure are myriad and infiltrate through every area of tax. The main focus of this chapter is on the basic rules which a practitioner or in-house tax adviser to a group is likely to come across, both in the operation of the group, and transactions undertaken by it. It therefore deals principally with group relief, capital gains tax groups, transfers of trades, pre-entry loss provisions, depreciatory transactions and the substantial shareholdings exemption. On the administrative side, group payment arrangements are also dealt with.

There are also a plethora of anti-avoidance rules which are applicable to groups in a number of areas of corporate tax legislation, including the various specialist regimes, for example those relating to intellectual property and derivatives. A detailed consideration of those rules is outside the scope of this work, and is best dealt with in those works which consider the areas concerned. Some of the rules in those regimes which apply specifically to groups are, however, noted.

DEFINITIONS

4.2 Certain of the provisions which apply for the various definitions of a 'group' of companies have common elements. They are therefore considered together in this section.

75% Subsidiary

4.3 For the purposes of most group tests, *ICTA 1988, s 838(1)* provides the definition for one body corporate being a 75% subsidiary of another. A body corporate will be a 75% subsidiary of another body corporate if and so long as 75% of its ordinary share capital is owned directly or indirectly by that other body corporate.

There are two points to note here. First, ordinary share capital is itself defined in *ICTA 1988, s 832* and means all share capital of the company, whatever it is called, other than capital the holders of which have the rights to a dividend at a fixed rate but have no other rights to share in the profits of the company. Essentially, therefore, this removes fixed rate preference shares from the test. Other preference shares, however, count as ordinary share capital.

Secondly, the test is an indirect one. Therefore if A owns 100% of B and C, each of which owns 50% of D, D will be a 75% subsidiary of A, even though it is not a 75% subsidiary of B or of C.

The basic tests of capital ownership for grouping purposes are often referred to as the 'nominal' ownership requirements, referring to the 'nominal' amount of share capital which is required to establish the group, as contrasted with the economic tests discussed below.

ICTA 1988, Sch 18

4.4 *ICTA 1988, Sch 18* provides what are often referred to as the 'economic' tests for ownership. Without these, it would obviously be easy to manipulate the ownership of companies so that they fell within a particular group, but where the real economic interest in the company lay elsewhere.

4.5 The basic premise of *ICTA 1988, Sch 18* is to establish what a shareholder (an 'equity holder') would receive by way of share of profits or assets if all the profits or assets were distributed by the company. For these purposes, equity holder means any person who holds ordinary shares in the company or is a loan creditor of the company in respect of a loan which is not a 'normal commercial loan'; *Sch 18, para 1(1)*.

4.6 For *ICTA 1988, Sch 18* purposes there is a self-contained definition of ordinary shares, which is not the same as that in *s 832* referred to above. The effect is similar, but more prescriptive. Here the definition of ordinary shares is 'all shares other than fixed rate preference shares'. There is a lengthy definition of 'fixed rate preference shares'; *Sch 18, para 1(3)*. In summary

- the shares must be issued for 'new consideration';
- they must not carry conversion rights, except into (broadly) other fixed rate preference shares or quoted shares in the company's parent;
- they must carry dividends of a fixed amount or fixed rate percentage of their nominal value;
- the dividends must represent no more than a reasonable commercial return on the consideration received by the company for the issue of the shares;
- they must not carry rights to repayment of an amount exceeding the new consideration given, except in so far as those rights are comparable with those for fixed dividend shares listed on a recognised stock exchange.

4.7 As regards the definition of 'normal commercial loan', again there is a list of requirements (*ICTA 1988, Sch 18, para 1(5)*). In summary:

- the loan must have been for 'new consideration';
- it must not carry conversion rights except (broadly) those which could be carried by a fixed rate preference share within *Sch 18, para 1(3);*
- it must not carry interest which depends on the results of the company's business, or the value of its assets, or which exceeds a reasonable commercial return on the consideration lent;

4.8 *Groups*

- it must not carry a right to repayment in excess of the amount of new consideration lent, except in so far as that right is comparable with those for debt listed on a recognised stock exchange.

4.8 In order to deal with situations where shares carry rights to dividends which are limited or which may change by reason of arrangements which exist, or which may change because of the existence of options which may be exercised, *ICTA 1988, Sch 18* contains a number of provisions which provide for the recalculation of the distribution of profits. Not all of these apply to all group tests; in particular the group relief test is more stringent than the capital gains tax test. Further reference is made to the differences in these tests in the relevant sections below.

GROUP RELIEF

4.9 The group relief rules allow the transfer ('surrender' in the statutory terminology) of various types of losses, including but not limited to trading losses, from one member of a group (the 'surrendering company') to another (the 'claimant company'). The rules are concerned with income type losses rather than capital losses (which are dealt with in a different way, see further below). One consequence of the introduction of the various specific regimes over the last decade or so (loan relationships, intangibles etc) has been that the non-trading losses under such regimes also fall to be dealt with under the group relief regime.

4.10 It is important to remember that group relief operates on an annual basis. It is this fact that causes many inefficiencies to arise in groups of companies. A company can only claim losses in any year to the extent that it has profits to absorb them. If, therefore, a company in a group has surplus losses in a year which cannot be surrendered to other members of the group, then its only option will be to carry those losses forward to use against its own profits. This may result in the losses being stranded and becoming more or less worthless, particularly, for example, in the case of a holding company which ends up with a brought forward non-trading deficit on its loan relationships.

Qualifications for membership of a group

4.11 The basic group relief provisions are to be found in *ICTA 1988, Pt X, Ch IV, s 402* et seq. For the purposes of the group relief provisions (which apply to all types of losses available for group relief) two companies are members of a group of companies if one is the 75% subsidiary of another, or both are 75% subsidiaries of a third company; *s 413(3)*. *ICTA 1988, s 413(7)* introduces the economic tests of ownership referred to in the discussion on *ICTA 1988, Sch 18*

Groups **4.13**

above, so that a company will not be treated as a subsidiary of another company at any time where the parent company would not be entitled to 75% of the profits available for distribution to equity holders or 75% of the assets of the company available for distribution to equity holders on a winding up. For these purposes, the full provisions of *Sch 18* apply, so the effect of options will need to be taken into account.

4.12 In addition, *Ch IV* has its own anti-avoidance provision in *s 410* where there are arrangements under which the relationships between two group members (the 'first company' and the 'second company' may change. In particular the section applies where there are arrangements in existence whereby:

- the first company (or any successor company under *ICTA 1988, s 343*, see further the discussion at para **4.38** below) could cease to be a member of the same group of companies as the second company and could become a member of the same group of companies as a third company; or

- any person or persons together have or could obtain control of the first company but not of the second; or

- a third company could begin to carry on the whole or part of a trade which is carried on by the first company either as successor to the first company or as successor to another company which has begun to carry on part of that trade.

4.13 The most obvious application of *ICTA 1988, s 410* is when a group member is being sold to a third party. In such a case, there will come a point where the transaction between the seller and purchaser is at a stage where arrangements will be considered to have come into place, and group relief will no longer be possible. It is not always easy to determine at exactly what time that will be. Although the terminology of *s 410* is very broad, there is a necessity for 'arrangements', and it is accepted generally that this means arrangements with another party or parties. There is some guidance to be found in HMRC manuals, in particular at CTM 80165 (and the other paragraphs referred to therein) and SP 3/93 as to HMRC's view, which is that such arrangements may or may not be legally binding and may or may not be in writing. It is often the case that it is unclear where a sale of a group member will take place until very shortly before signing, the parties' negotiations being continuous until that point with the prospect of no transaction taking place at all. In that case, it would usually be relatively safe to conclude that there were no arrangements in place until agreement had been reached. Obviously once a written agreement is reached, even though it may be conditional, there will be arrangements in place, and group relief will not be possible during a period between sale and completion. In joint venture arrangements, ESC C10 provides HMRC's practice in relation to arrangements between joint venture parties which might otherwise fall foul of *s 410* and also deals with share mortgages.

4.14 *Groups*

Residence qualifications for group relief

4.14 Since the *Finance Act 2000*, it is possible for members of a group to be resident outside the UK and to 'trace' groups through ownership of foreign bodies corporate. However, it is obviously not the intention of the legislation to give worldwide relief for losses, and therefore *ICTA 1988, s 402(2)* provides that the surrendering company (the group member with the loss) and the claimant company (the group member with the profit against which the loss is to be offset) must either be resident in the UK, or carry on a trade in the UK through a permanent establishment. From 1 April 2006 this is extended by *s 402(2A)* in certain cases involving companies in the European Economic Area following the *Marks & Spencer* group relief case, although this is subject to restrictive conditions (see further below).

Types of loss available for group relief

4.15 The types of loss which may be surrendered by way of group relief are set out in *s 403* and are trading losses, excess capital allowances, non-trading deficits on loan relationships, charges on income, Schedule A losses, management expenses and non-trading losses.

4.16 It should be noted that trading losses, excess capital allowances and non-trading deficits on loan relationships may be surrendered even where the surrendering company has other profits against which they could be set. However, charges on income, Schedule A losses, management expenses and non-trading losses on intangibles may only be group relieved to the extent they exceed the surrendering company's gross profits for the period.

Limits on group relief

4.17 *ICTA 1988, s 403A* deals with the limits on group relief, and despite the impenetrable drafting the principle is fairly simple. The basic limitation is the lower of the amount of the loss (the 'surrenderable amount') and the claimant company's total profits. The limitations are applied by reference to the 'overlapping period', which is the part of the accounting period which is common to both the surrendering company and the claimant company in relation to the claim in question; *s 403A(8)*.

4.18 If all members of the group have the same accounting period, then such complications do not arise, but otherwise it is necessary to apportion amounts of profits and losses between accounting periods of the claimant and surrendering companies. The basic rule is that this is to be done on a time basis; *ICTA 1988, s 403B(1)*. However, where that would give rise to a result which is 'unjust or unreasonable in relation to any person', then the apportionments may be made on such other basis as may be just and reasonable; *s 403B(2)*. It is worth bearing this provision in mind where a business is very seasonal or where unusual events during an accounting period have given rise to particular losses, and it would be more advantageous to the taxpayer to attribute those losses to a particular part of an accounting period. Further guidance may be found in the HMRC manuals at CTM 80260. It should be noted however, that HMRC interprets any person as including HMRC. If therefore, they believe a taxpayer has deliberately manipulated profits or losses in accounting periods to take advantage of this rule, then they may seek a different apportionment.

4.19 If, in any period, a company is a 'dual resident investing company' then that company may not be a surrendering company for the purposes of group relief. This is an anti-avoidance provision which is intended to prevent the double usage of losses by companies which are resident in more than one country; see HMRC manuals at CTM 34500 and following paras for history and HMRC's view. *ICTA 1988, s 404* contains a restrictive meaning of 'trading company' which excludes trading companies if their main function or one of their main functions is one set out in *s 404(6)* (mainly holding company, finance company and analogous activities).

They may, however, have unexpected application to certain companies which are incorporated in tax-haven jurisdictions, but which may technically be considered within the charge to tax of that territory, and which are also tax resident in the UK by reason of their management and control being exercised in the UK. This is particularly the case in jurisdictions which apply tax to certain types of companies but exempt others. In such cases it may be wise to seek guidance from HMRC if group relief is to be of particular significance in the group in question. There is nothing to prevent such companies being claimant companies for group relief purposes.

Relief for overseas losses of non-resident companies

4.20 In the *Marks & Spencer group relief case* (Judgment C-446/03), Marks & Spencer successfully claimed before the ECJ that as a matter of principle the UK group relief laws breached EU law as whilst they would allow losses of a UK company arising from a branch in France (for example) to be relieved against another UK group member's profits, it would not allow relief if, as in the case of Marks & Spencer, those losses arose in a French company.

4.21 *ICTA 1988, s 403F* applies with effect from 1 April 2006 (with certain transitional provisions) to permit losses from companies resident in the European Economic Area (or EEA permanent establishments of non-EEA resident companies) to be surrendered to other members of a UK group. Apart from the

4.22 *Groups*

conditions therein, it is also subject to its own anti-avoidance provision in *s 403G* where arrangements were entered into to ensure that losses would be available for group relief (for example by taking certain corporate actions to ensure that the conditions discussed below were satisfied).

4.22 The four conditions for group relief to be permitted in this situation are:

- the equivalence condition;
- the EEA tax loss condition;
- the qualifying loss condition; and
- the precedence condition.

All four conditions must be satisfied in order for a loss to be relieved. The detail of the tests is set out in *ICTA 1988, Sch 18A*. In broad terms the principles of the conditions are as follows.

The loss must be equivalent (ie it must correspond in all material respects) with a type of loss which would be surrendered under the domestic rules (the equivalence condition).

It must be calculated in accordance with the relevant rules under the relevant territory for the calculation of losses or other amounts eligible for relief (the EEA tax loss condition).

The loss must not have been relieved or be able to be relieved in a previous, current or future periods (the qualifying loss condition). It is this condition which effectively reduces the use of the overseas loss to cases where the loss has become legally (and not just practically) impossible to use. This might occur, for example, where the time limit for the use of losses has expired in the overseas country, or the company in question had ceased trading and been liquidated.

The final qualification is that there is no other territory (not limited to EEA countries) in which effective relief could be given for the relevant loss.

Once those conditions have been satisfied, *ICTA 1988, Sch 18A, Pt 2* provides for rules for the recalculation of the amount of the loss in accordance with UK tax rules and the assumptions to be made in making the surrender as regards accounting periods etc.

Administrative requirements for group relief

4.23 Claims for group relief are part of the corporation tax self-assessment regime (CTSA) and are dealt with by *FA 1998, Sch 18, para 66* ff. A claim must be made in the CTSA return or in an amendment to that return. The surrendering company must give its consent to the claim, and consent must be given at or before the time of the claim and the claim must contain a copy of that consent, otherwise the claim for group relief will be ineffective; *Sch 18, para 70*. Revised claims may only be dealt with by amendment of the CTSA return, and strictly this is by withdrawal of one claim and resubmission of another rather than by amendment of the claim; *Sch 18, para 73*.

There are separate time limits for the claiming or withdrawal of a claim for group relief from the general CTSA return amendment rules, which are set out in *Sch 18, para 74*. The basic rule is that the claim must be made by the first anniversary of the CTSA filing date for the company, but this is extended if there is an enquiry into the return or an appeal in relation to the return to 30 days after the completion of the enquiry or the final determination of the appeal. This obviously gives time for consequential amendments to the group relief claims which may be affected by other matters which are the subject of the enquiry or appeal.

Payment for group relief

4.24 Payments for group relief are ignored for corporation tax purposes provided they do not exceed the amount of the loss. Obviously, the benefit to the claimant company is that amount multiplied by the effective corporation tax rate for the period in question, and so it will usually be that, lesser, amount which is paid, if any payment is made. The company law relating to corporate benefit and maintenance of capital should be taken into account when deciding whether or not and how much to pay for group relief.

CHARGEABLE GAINS GROUPS

4.25 The provisions relating to corporation tax on chargeable gains in groups principally deal with the transfer of assets from one company in a group to another, and provide for the transfer to be on a 'no-gain-no-loss' basis. The corollary of this is that a potential 'exit charge' is created if the transferee company leaves the group within six years of the transfer, subject to certain exceptions which are discussed further below.

Qualifications for membership of a group

4.26 Grouping for capital gains tax purposes is dealt with in a conceptually different way to groups for group relief purposes. The legislation works in terms of first determining a particular capital gains tax group with one parent com-

4.27 Groups

pany. This is principally so that it can then be determined whether a company has left a particular group for the purposes of applying the exit charge. However, this way of viewing the group does create complications in trying to determine whether a group is the same group or not, for example if a new parent company is formed and the existing parent company transferred to it.

4.27 A group for chargeable gains purposes is therefore defined as a company (the 'principal company of the group') and all its 75% subsidiaries; *TCGA 1992, s 170(3)*. No company which is itself a 75% subsidiary of another company can be a principal company of a group. In economic ownership terms, a group does not include any company which is not an 'effective 51% subsidiary' of the principal company. *Section 170(7)* provides the definition of 'effective 51% subsidiary' with the usual tests of profits available for distribution and beneficial entitlement to assets on a winding up, and *s 170(8)* brings in the tests in *ICTA 1988, Sch 18* discussed above in relation to group relief. For these purposes, *Sch 18* is modified so that loans from banks in the normal course of their business are excluded from the meaning of 'loan creditor' for the definition of equity holders, and the 'arrangements' and options provisions are also ignored for the purposes of the chargeable gains group tests.

4.28 Because the definition of a group revolves around identifying a particular group rather than simply the relationship between two companies, it is necessary to identify when the group has remained the same group. *Section 170(10)* provides that a group will remain the same group for as long as the principal company of the group is the same. If the principal company becomes a member of another group, then the two groups are also regarded as the same group.

Residence qualifications

4.29 As with the group relief provisions discussed above, *FA 2000* introduced changes to the definitions of chargeable gains groups so that it is possible for the principal company of a group to be a company resident outside the UK, and for members of the group to be non-UK resident companies. This can give rise to issues where the constitution of groups changes by reason of a transaction taking place entirely outside the UK, and the parties involved overlook a charge to capital gains tax because no-one envisages that such a transaction would cause a UK tax effect. At the same time as the *FA 2000* amendments to the constitution of groups, residence qualifications were inserted into the transfer provisions in *TCGA 1992, s 171* to ensure that the provisions did not permit transfers outside the UK tax net on a tax free basis.

Transfer provisions

4.30 The principal provision on transfers is in *TCGA 1992, s 171*, which provides that where a transfer is made between two members of a chargeable

Groups **4.32**

gains group, and they are either resident in the UK, or the asset is (or will be) a chargeable asset in relation to them, then the transfer is deemed for corporation tax to be one at a consideration which will give rise to neither a gain nor a loss.

The use of the phrase 'disposes of an asset to another company', as well as the general framework of the provisions, means that there must be both a disposal and an acquisition of an asset for the provisions to apply, and a disposal without an acquisition (such as the redemption of shares), or an acquisition without a disposal (such as the subscription for shares) will not be within *s 171*. There are also some specific exclusions in *s 171(2)* and *(3A)*. Of note is the exclusion for transfers to dual resident investing companies. The point made in **para 4.19** above in relation to unexpectedly dual resident companies is worth remembering.

4.31 It may be the case that the assets which are the subject of the transfer are trading assets for one of the companies but capital assets for the other. If the transferee is acquiring the asset as part of its trading stock, then *s 173(1)* deems him to have acquired it as a capital asset and then immediately appropriated it to trading stock. This will give rise to a charge under *TCGA 1992, s 161* either as a capital gain, or, by election, by an adjustment to the trading profits of the acquirer.

If the transferor is the trader, then *s 173(2)* deems the transferor to have appropriated the stock from trading stock immediately before the transfer. *TCGA 1992, s 161* treats the transferor as having acquired it for the value which is taken into the accounts in respect of it, and *s 171* then applies to the transfer. There is no specific statutory provision which provides what figure is to be placed in the trading accounts on the deemed appropriation from trading stock in such a case. It might be thought that the most appropriate value would be market value, on the basis of the principle in *Sharkey v Wernher* (1955) 36 TC 275. Although it is not clear, given the appropriation is deemed for the purposes of *ss 171* and *173* rather than an actual appropriation, any other figure is likely to lead to an argument with HMRC.

Although the provisions of *s 173* open up the possibility of planning by, for example, the triggering of losses, it should be borne in mind that attempts to rely on trading or non-trading status have not received much sympathy before the courts when taxpayers have sought to rely on different group members having a different status. See, in particular, *Reed v Nova Securities Ltd* [1985] STC 124 and *New Angel Court Ltd v Adam* [2004] STC 779.

Company ceasing to be a member of a group

4.32 Without anti-avoidance measures, the intra-group transfer provisions would obviously be open to abuse as assets could effectively be transferred to

4.33 *Groups*

third parties by the mechanism of a company. However, rather than adopt any mechanism which depends on there being arrangements in place at the time of the transfer, or any reliance on any motive test, the chargeable gains legislation imposes a charge on any transferee company leaving the group within six years of the transfer under *TCGA 1992, s 179*. As the charge is one which arises in the acquiring company, it is obviously extremely important on any acquisition of a company out of a group to discover whether there have been any transfers of assets into that group, and obtain indemnification if possible.

The conditions for the charge (commonly referred to as an 'exit charge') are:

- there has been a transfer from Company B to company A;
- at the time of the transfer Company A and Company B were either resident in the UK or the asset was a chargeable asset in relation to the charge;
- within six years of the time of the acquisition, company A ceases to be a member of the group.

If at the time Company A leaves the group, either it, or an associated company also leaving the group, owns the asset (or an asset into which a gain on the asset has been rolled under the replacement of business assets rules) otherwise than as trading stock, then company A is deemed to have sold and immediately reacquired the asset on its acquisition from Company B.

There are several points worth making in relation to the basic application of *s 179*. First, as mentioned above, it is a blanket charge and does not depend on the circumstances of the original transfer being tax motivated or carried out at otherwise than market value. Secondly, it technically does not depend on the original transfer falling within *TCGA 1992, s 171* in the first place, although if company A has acquired the asset at market value another chargeable event on company A leaving the group is usually a mere technicality. Thirdly, the asset may no longer be owned by company A but may have been transferred on to another company leaving the group at the same time (leading to the mistaken conclusion that *s 179(2)* applies (see further below)), and fourthly, in fact the asset which was the subject of the original transfer to Company A may no longer be owned by the group at all, but *s 179* will still impose a charge if a gain on the disposal of the asset has been rolled into another asset under *TCGA 1992, s 151*.

Companies leaving a group at the same time: Johnston Publishing

4.33 The primary exemption from the charge under *TCGA 1992, s 179* is contained in *s 179(2)* which prevents a charge arising on a transfer between two associated companies when those associated companies leave the group together. For these purposes, companies are associated if, by themselves, they would form a group; s 179(10)(a). There has long been a concern as to whether this requires the companies to be associated only at the time of leaving the group, or at both the time of the original transfer and at the time of leaving the group.

If the group structure has not changed between the time of the intra-group transfer and the time of the sale outside the group, and both transferee and transferor are sold in consequence of the sale, then there should be no concern as to the non-application of s 179(2). It must be noted however that in this context leaving the group at the same time effectively means leaving the group as a consequence of the sale of one company (which may be transferor, transferee, or a parent company). Selling the transferor and transferee separately but as part of the same sale will not be effective; see *Dunlop International AG v Pardoe (Inspector of Taxes)* [1999] STC 909.

4.34 If, on the other hand, transfers are made between members of the group, and then the group relationship changes, then, following *Johnston Publishing (North) Limited v RCC* [2007] All ER (D) 240, this may well cause great difficulty in relying on the exemption. In *Johnston*, a number of companies were transferred by one company in the group (Company B) to another (Company A). Companies B and A were in the same group at that time. At a later point it was decided to sell Company A, and Company B was transferred into the same sub-group as Company A. Company A sought to rely on *TCGA 1992, s 179(2)*. The companies leaving the group on the subsequent sale would not have formed a group by themselves at the time of the earlier transfer (because the intermediate holding companies were not also being sold), but of course they did form such a group at the time of the subsequent sale.

The Special Commissioners, upheld on appeal by Lindsay J. in the High Court, held that s 179(2) required that the second use of 'associated' in s 179(2), referring to 'an acquisition by one from another of those associated companies' must be given some meaning, and the only specific meaning was that it was intended to refer back to the time of the original acquisition so that it had to be established at both times. It is fair to say that this interpretation is contrary to the view of the majority of practitioners, but unless and until it is overturned on appeal, this point is one which practitioners are going to have to take great pains to deal with. In practice, it is perhaps of less importance since the introduction of the substantial shareholdings exemption, but of course the work necessary to ensure that exemption applies is not always insubstantial.

Merger exemption; TCGA 1992, s 181

4.35 The merger exemption in *TCGA 1992, s 181* is sometimes overlooked, but it can be useful. The exemption applies where Company A (the transferee)

4.36 *Groups*

leaves the group as part of a merger carried out for bona fide commercial reasons and the avoidance of tax was not the main or one of the main purposes of the merger. This principally assists in cases where two groups exchange interests in each other's businesses, either via the transfer of business to a newco, or to one of the group companies involved in the transaction. The value of the interests acquired by each group must be substantially the same, and the consideration must be substantially in the form of the acquisition of the interest in the business, or applied in acquiring such an interest (ignoring any small amounts): *s 181(4)*.

Reallocation of s 179 gains under TCGA 1992, s 179A

4.36 Assuming it is not possible to avoid a gain under *s 179* on a subsequent sale of the transferee company, *TCGA 1992, s 179A* (introduced by *FA 2002*) provides for the possibility of the transfer of that charge to another company which was a member of the group at the time the *s 179* gain would otherwise accrue to the transferee (ie when it leaves the group, not immediately after the acquisition). This is done by means of an election between the transferee company and the company to which the charge is to be transferred. This can be a useful tool from a purchaser's point of view on a company acquisition, although it does not remove credit risk on the seller given that the target company is likely to be one on which a secondary liability for any unpaid tax on a chargeable gain could be visited under *TCGA 1992, s 190*.

Notional transfers prior to a sale; TCGA 1992, s 171A

4.37 Prior to the introduction of *TCGA 1992, s 171A*, it was common for groups to marshal their gains and losses by the transfer of assets intra-group prior to their disposal to third parties. This type of planning was generally accepted by HMRC, and effectively allowed group relief for allowable (capital) losses. The same effect is now achieved by *s 171A*, which, rather than using a group relief method, operates by way of election to deem a transfer (which would have previously been an actual one) to another group member prior to the sale to a third party. The election must be entered into by both the group companies concerned, and may be entered into provided that *s 171* itself would have applied to the transfer.

TRANSFERS OF TRADES UNDER ICTA 1988, S 343

4.38 The transfer of a business between members of the group will of course have more tax implications than just tax on chargeable gains. There may be brought forward trading losses in the transferring trading company which may be lost, or there may be capital assets on which capital allowances have been claimed where a disposal would lead to a balancing charge or a balancing allowance. *ICTA 1988, s 343* aims to avoid those events where a trade is transferred between parties under common ownership, and avoids the effects of the statutory discontinuance of the trade under *ICTA 1988, s 337*. It is subject to its own anti-avoidance provisions.

Common ownership requirements

4.39 The common ownership requirement in *ICTA 1988, s 343* is stated in a different way to the grouping tests. *ICTA 1988, s 343* is intended to be broad in application, and can itself be viewed as an anti-avoidance provision. The test is to be found is *s 343(1)(a)* which is that 'the trade or an interest amounting to not less than a three-fourths share in it belongs to the same person'. The test is applied at the time the transferor company transfers the trade to the transferee company, for one year before, and for two years after the transfer.

Although *s 343* itself only applies to transfers between companies (as it applies for corporation tax), the 'common ownership' requirement can be traced through persons other than companies. *Section 344* provides the detailed rules for common ownership. Basically, ownership is traced through the ordinary share capital of the company carrying on the trade. 'Ordinary share capital' for this purpose bears its *ICTA 1988, s 832* meaning discussed above in relation to group relief. A trade is therefore regarded as belonging to the persons owning the ordinary share capital of the company carrying on the trade, or if it is carried on in a subsidiary, by the persons owning the ordinary share capital of the parent.

There is also a particular rule, in *s 344(4)*, which treats for this purpose persons who are related (being husbands, wives, civil partners, ancestors or lineal descendants, and brothers and sisters) as the same person. Shares owned by non-charitable trusts are treated as owned by the persons entitled to the income under the trust; *s 344(1)*, and for these purposes if there is more than one such person, they are treated as the same person; *s 344(4)*.

Effect of application

4.40 *ICTA 1988, s 343* applies for two specific purposes only. First, it prevents a disposal event under the capital allowances legislation, and effectively gives future allowances to the purchaser in the same amounts as would have been given to the seller; *s 343(2)*. Secondly, it allows the carry forward of losses in the trade under *ICTA 1988, s 393(1)* to continue to be carried forward by the purchaser; *s 343(3)*.

4.41 *Groups*

Anti-avoidance

4.41 ICTA 1988, s 343(2) (the capital allowances provision) does not apply if the transferee company is a dual resident investing company (see the discussion at **para 4.19** above).

Where liabilities of the transferor company are not assumed by the transferee, and these exceed the value any assets of the transferor not transferred, the loss carry-over under *s 343(3)* is restricted to the amount of losses over and above that excess. This provision is designed to prevent the hiving down of trades and associated losses where the liabilities of the trade remain with the transferor (for example in an insolvency proceeding), and the subsequent sale of a company with those losses.

Other issues on a transfer of trade

4.42 It should be noted that *ICTA 1988, s 343* makes no provision about trading stock. The basic provision in *ICTA 1988, s 100* will therefore apply by reason of *s 337* and an amount will have to be brought into account in respect of the disposal of it, which is either the value obtained on transfer, or the market value if the parties are connected (subject to the ability to elect otherwise).

4.43 If only part of a trade is transferred under *ICTA 1988, s 343(8)*, a question arises as to whether the transferor continues to carry on the remaining trade as part of the previous trade, or whether there has been a discontinuance of that part (which will not be assisted by *s 343* unless that part is also transferred); see *Rolls-Royce Motors Limited v Bamford* [1976] STC 162.

4.44 If the transferee already carries on a trade, the transfer of the new trade may be an expansion of the existing trade, it may result in two separate trades being carried on by the transferee, or it may represent a discontinuance of the previous trade (which, again, will not be assisted by *ICTA 1988, s 343*).

PRE-ENTRY GAINS AND LOSSES

4.45 It will be obvious from the discussion above in relation to chargeable gains groups that there is room for manipulation of the rules by reason of companies joining groups having either made a gain or loss in the accounting period in which they join (which is then offset by a later disposal of an asset in the acquiring group or used to offset a gain on an asset about to be disposed of in the acquiring group), or by the acquisition of companies with assets which have inherent unrealised gains or losses. These are referred to as pre-entry (ie into the new group) gains and losses.

The provisions which have been enacted to counter various sorts of these activities have changed over time. The main provision in *TCGA 1992, Sch 7A* (given effect by *s 177A*) (loss buying) was enacted by *FA 1993*, and remains in force. It was joined in 1998 by *TCGA 1992, Sch 7AA* (gain buying). *FA 2006* inserted two new provisions, *TCGA 1992, s 184A* (loss buying avoidance schemes) and *s 184B* (gain buying avoidance schemes). *FA 2006* also repealed *TCGA 1992, Sch 7AA*, as it was felt to have been superseded by *TCGA 1992, s 184B*. The same was not felt to be true of *TCGA 1992*, Sch 7A, and therefore that provision now exists in tandem with *s 184A* (which takes precedence over Sch 7A).

Pre-entry losses – TCGA 1992, Sch 7A

4.46 *TCGA 1992, Sch 7A* restricts two types of losses (each, a 'pre-entry loss'). First, allowable losses which accrued to a company before it became a member of a chargeable gains group, and secondly, the 'pre-entry proportion of any allowable loss accruing to that company on the disposal of any pre-entry asset'; *Sch 7A, para 1(2)*. There is no motive or commerciality test in *Sch 7A*. The provisions are therefore commonly applicable to groups of companies, and can therefore result in a significant compliance burden in relation to the second leg of the restriction.

The first leg of the restriction is fairly obvious, and is only relevant for the accounting period in which a company becomes a member of a new chargeable gains group. It is more likely, but not exclusively so, to have resulted from active tax avoidance than the second leg.

The second leg operates, as its description suggests, to apportion the loss on the disposal of an asset which a company owned when it joined the group between the periods before and after it joined the group. The 'pre-entry proportion' is calculated according to the formula in *Sch 7A, para 2*. Although this seems impenetrable at first, the basic idea is to apportion the loss by reference to the time each item of allowable expenditure was incurred to the date of disposal. Although this can give a quite complicated computation, it is obviously fairer to the taxpayer than the simpler alternative of calculating the pre-entry proportion simply by reference to the time of ownership of the asset. There is also an alternative method of calculation by reference to the market value of the asset which can be made by election under *Sch 7A, para 5*. There are particular rules for pooled assets (the most common example being shares).

4.47 Once the pre-entry proportion of an allowable loss has been discovered, it is, as mentioned above, a pre-entry loss. In principle, the restrictions on the two types of pre-entry loss are the same, but they are dealt with separately in the relevant provisions. Those restrictions are to be found in *ICTA 1988*,

4.48 *Groups*

s Sch 7A, para 7. Pre-entry losses which have accrued prior to the time the company joined the group may be deducted from chargeable gains which have arisen on:

- a disposal by the company before the date on which it became a member of the relevant (new) group;
- the disposal of an asset which was held by the company before it became a member of that group; or
- the disposal of an asset which was acquired after the date the company became a member of the group from a person who was not a member of that group at the time of the acquisition, and which was used in a trade carried on by that company which trade had been carried on from immediately before the date it joined the group until the time of the disposal of the asset.

In the case of a pre-entry loss which is a pre-entry proportion of an allowable loss, it may be deducted from chargeable gains where:

- the gain is made on a disposal by that company before it became a member of the group, and the company is the company by reference to which the asset is a pre-entry asset;
- both the pre-entry asset and the asset on which the gain is made were held by the company before it became a member of the relevant group;
- the gain accrues to the company on an asset which it acquired from a person who was not a member of the group at the time it acquired it, and the asset was used in a trade carried on by that company which trade had been carried on from immediately before the date it joined the group until the time of the disposal of the asset.

The order in which losses are to be offset against gains is set out in *Sch 7A, para 6.*

4.48 The rules which apply when companies join capital gains tax groups, in particular in the circumstances in which *TCGA 1992, s 170(10)* deem there to be a continuity of groups. There are two provisions which apply in this case. First, if the company joining the group (the 'relevant company') does so in the same accounting period as a principal company of the first group becomes a member of the second group (and would therefore be treated as one group under *s 170(10)*), or, regardless of timing, if the principal company of the first group was under the control of a member of the second group before it became a member of it, then *s 170(10)* is disapplied by *Sch 7A, para 9(6).*

Secondly, if neither of those situations is relevant, it is necessary to look to *Sch 7A, para 1(6).* That sub paragraph disapplies *s 170(10)* generally, subject to the provision in *para 1(7)* which deals with the insertion of new holding companies, where *s 170(10)* remains. *Para 1(6)* works by treating all the members of the first group as becoming members of the second group at the time they actually joined the second group, and not, by reason of *s 170(10)*, when they joined the first group.

However, what *para 1(6)* does not do is set out what happens when there are successive changes of groups. On its plain wording, it deems all members of the first group to join the second group at that time. There is simply no mechanism for dealing with what happens to the member of the first group if at a later time, the second group joins a third group. *Para 1(6)*, applied literally, then deems all members of the second group (including those from the first group) to join the third group at the actual time they do so. This arguably has the effect of removing the pre-entry loss barrier between members of the first and second groups once they join the third group. This interpretation was rejected by the Special Commissioner, Dr J F Avery-Jones CBE, in *Five Oaks Properties v HMRC* [2006] STC (SCD) 769, essentially on the basis that the purpose of the legislation did not require *para 1(6)* to negate *s 170(10)* at all in those circumstances, and therefore the 'relevant group' was not necessarily the latest group one was dealing with. With respect to the Special Commissioner, that analysis does rather strain the structure of the schedule, and although it doubtless has a more logical effect than the interpretation argued for by the taxpayer, in the author's view the plain words of the provision ought to have been applied. It is no part of a court's function to amend mistakes in, or sloppy drafting of, legislation by interpretation, especially against a taxpayer.

Pre-entry losses – s 184A

4.49 *TCGA 1992, s 184A* is a broader provision than *Sch 7A* in that it is drafted to apply in wider circumstances. It does, however, contain a motive test, and so to that extent is likely to apply in a much more restricted range of circumstances than *Sch 7A*. *Schedule 7A* remains in force. Note however, that the tax advantage in question does not have to be secured for the company making the loss.

Section 184A applies wherever there has been a 'qualifying change of ownership' and a 'qualifying loss' arises in relation to a 'pre-change asset'. A qualifying change of ownership includes where a company has joined or left a group of companies and also where a company becomes subject to different control; *s 184C(6)* (control for this purpose bearing its wider meaning in *ICTA, s 416; TCGA 1992, s 288(1)*). If the provisions apply, a qualifying loss may not be deducted from gains accruing to the company other than those on pre-change assets.

Pre-entry gains

4.50 As mentioned above, *TCGA 1992, Sch 7AA* was repealed by *FA 2006*, and replaced by *s 184B*. *Schedule 7AA* is not dealt with further in this chapter.

4.51 *Groups*

Section 184B applies in the same circumstances to *s 184A* save that there must have been a 'qualifying gain' made on a pre-change asset rather than a qualifying loss. Again, the motive test should mean that this will not apply otherwise than in avoidance cases, subject to the usual questions of interpretation as to what is meant by tests encompassing 'one of the main purpose' language, as is the case in both *s 184A* and *s 184B*.

DEPRECIATORY TRANSACTIONS

4.51 The fortunate aspect of these parts of the tax legislation is that it is now irrelevant for disposals to which the substantial shareholdings exemption in *TCGA 1992, Sch 7AC* applies. Its existence should not, however, be forgotten. The two sets of provisions are *TCGA 1992, ss 176* and *177* on the one hand, and *TCGA 1992, s 30* et seq on the other.

TCGA 1992, ss 176 and 177

4.52 *TCGA 1992, s 176* is a basic anti-avoidance provision which aims to restrict the creation of losses by the reduction in the value of shares or securities prior to their disposal by means of a 'depreciatory transaction'. It only restricts the creation of losses, and does not result in a gain being imposed.

For the purposes of *s 176*, a depreciatory transaction is either a disposal of assets between two group members at an undervalue, or any other transaction which involved the company to be disposed of, or one or more of its 75% subsidiaries, where that transaction involved two or more group members. The classic application of *s 176* is squarely within the main heading and occurs where assets are transferred intra-group at an undervalue, and the transferor company is then sold at a loss.

Where the section applies, any allowable loss is reduced to the extent 'just and reasonable'.

4.53 *TCGA 1992, s 177* is aimed at the reduction in the value of a target by basic dividend stripping in the form of a payment of a dividend by the target company. It applies where the recipient has a holding of 10% or more of any one class of shares. The consequences are the same as the application of *s 176*.

TCGA 1992, s 30 ff

4.54 Unlike *s 176*, *s 30* can result in the imposition of an actual charge to tax, and has historically therefore given more concern to tax advisers than *s 176*.

Groups **4.56**

It has also given them more headaches, being somewhat tortuously drafted. This is partly because the provisions are drafted generally, and then further refined in the context of groups. Approached in this way, they are slightly easier to understand.

The basic criteria for *s 30* to apply are that in the context of a disposal of an asset:

- the value of the asset (or of a 'relevant asset') has been materially reduced; and
- a tax-free benefit has been or will be conferred on the person making the disposal, a connected person, or, where there is an avoidance motive, any other person.

For this purpose 'relevant asset' means an asset owned by a company associated with the disposing company. This only applies in limited circumstances, and if there is a charge under *s 179*, this element of the provision is excluded.

4.55 *TCGA 1992, s 31* limits the application of *s 30* in the cases of dividends paid within a group prior to a sale of the dividend paying company. It provides that reductions in the value of an asset which are attributable to the payment of a dividend are only taken into account to the extent the dividend is paid out of 'chargeable profits'. Chargeable profits are a construct for the purposes of the section, and the conditions are found in *s 30(6)*, *(7)* and *(8)*. The first condition is that there must either be:

- a disposal within *TCGA 1992, s 171(1)*;
- an exchange of securities within *TCGA 1992, s 135 or s 136*;
- a revaluation of assets in the accounts of the company.

Each of the asset, the securities, and the revalued asset, are then referred to as the 'asset with enhanced value'. The second condition is that there is no disposal of the asset with enhanced value, other than a *s 171(1)* disposal before the *s 30* disposal. The third condition is that after the *s 30* disposal the asset with enhanced value is owned by a person other than the company making the disposal or the person connected with it.

The policy behind the legislation can therefore be seen – there is an assumption that there has been a transaction which has given rise to profits of the company which can be distributed, but which have not arisen from what might be called the normal business of the company. Only a dividend based on these profits is a 'bad dividend' for the purposes of the provision.

4.56 *TCGA 1992, s 31A* applies if the only reason that *s 30* did not apply is that the third condition in *s 30(8)* was not satisfied. This would typically occur if

4.57 *Groups*

the actual disposal was to a related party other than on a *s 171(1)* transfer (which would mean the second condition was not satisfied) – most obviously to a non-resident member of the group.

Section 31A attempts to cure this problem by creating a *s 179* type charge if at any time within six years from the date of the *s 30* disposal (ie the disposal which has not been caught because *s 30(8)* has not been satisfied), the asset holding company ceases to be a member of the group. How often this charge is ever picked up during the compliance process is uncertain.

4.57 TCGA 1992, *s 32* contains a further relaxation of *s 30* in the case of reductions in the value of an asset which occur as a result of a transfer falling within *s 171(1)*. Only if the disposal is for an amount less than the cost and less than the market value of the asset will the transaction be caught, subject to an overriding motive test.

4.58 Note that in relation to chargeable intangible assets, *FA 2002* inserted a new *s 33A* into *TCGA 1992* following the introduction of the intangibles tax regime, with some modifications to the basic provision to deal with the way the new regime operates.

SUBSTANTIAL SHAREHOLDINGS EXEMPTION

4.59 The scope of the capital gains tax charge was radically changed for companies by *FA 2002* by the introduction of the substantial shareholdings exemption. As mentioned above, this made many of the loss buying and depreciatory transactions effectively redundant, certainly as far as M&A practitioners were concerned. The regime does however have some uncertainties. These are usually largely factual, as the regime only applies to disposals of trading companies or groups by trading companies or groups. The 'trading' issue is therefore of paramount importance, and is often the subject of a clearance application under Code of Practice 10 other than in very obvious cases. It should be noted that the exemption is not limited to actual disposals to third parties, disposals for chargeable gains purposes in general are exempted (the losses are of course correspondingly unallowable).

Basic application

4.60 Despite the drafting of *TCGA 1992, Sch 7AC, Pt 1*, the basic exemption is very simple. There are requirements to be met as regards the shareholding, the disposing company (referred to unhelpfully as the 'investing company' in the legislation), and the company whose shares are being disposed of (the 'company invested in').

4.61 A 'substantial shareholding' is where a company has a holding of not less than 10% of the company's ordinary share capital, is beneficially entitled to at least 10% of the profits available for distribution to equity holders, and is beneficially entitled to 10% of the assets available for distribution on a winding up. *ICTA 1988, Sch 18* (as modified) applies for the purposes of the latter two tests; *Sch 7AC, para 8*. The holdings of groups are generally aggregated for this purpose; *para 9*.

The shareholding must have been held throughout a 12-month period beginning not more than two years before the day on which the disposal takes place.

Investing company requirements

4.62 Perhaps slightly oddly, the disposing company must be a sole trading company or a holding company of a trading group in order for the exemption to apply. This criterion must be satisfied for the 12-month period ended at the time of disposal, and it must also be satisfied immediately after the disposal. Therefore a disposal of its sole trading subsidiary by a non-trading holding company will not satisfy the exemption, but the disposal of such a subsidiary by a trading holding company would satisfy the exemption. The lessons for group structuring could hardly be clearer.

Investee company requirements

4.63 The requirements for the company invested in are essentially the same, other than that that company may be the holding company of a trading subgroup (this is really due to the fact that the concept of group in *TCGA 1992, Sch 7AC* is by reference to chargeable gains tax groups, so there can be only one group, hence the adoption of the subgroup).

Meaning of trading

4.64 'Trading company', 'trading group' and 'trading subgroup' are defined in *TCGA 1992, Sch 7AC, paras 20, 21* and *22* respectively, but the essence of the primary definition in each is the same – the company (or group or subgroup as a whole) means 'a company carrying on trading activities whose activities do not include to a substantial extent activities other than trading activities'. There is an extended meaning of 'trading activities' which is expressed to include preparatory activities and activities in preparing for acquiring a trade or a company which carries on a trade, as well as activities in the course of or in furtherance of a trade.

4.65 *Groups*

In practice, it is usually obvious which activities of a company, group or subgroup are or are not trading, the most frequently seen non-trading activities being property leasing (including intra-group of course), financing (by companies other than those which can qualify as financial traders), and the holding of large amounts of cash (perhaps arising from a disposal) on a temporary basis. What is often less obvious is whether those activities will be 'substantial' to the extent that they taint the rest of the activities of the company, group or subgroup. In the case of the wider group, intra-group activities can usually be ignored (on the basis that the provisions refer to the activities of the members of a group 'taken together', and the problem usually arises where there is intra-group activity between a company or subgroup which has to be examined, and other members of a wider group.

In relation to non-trading activities, and whether they are substantial, HMRC take a similar approach to that taken for taper relief. For these purposes 'substantial' means more than 20%. HMRC has published guidance on their approach at CG 53116 and the following paragraphs. The 20% test is applied to turnover, the value of assets, management time spent and the company's history. The latter test is intended to avoid a 'snapshot' approach to the tests, by looking at them over a period of time.

Because of the difficulties in applying the trading tests, it had become fairly standard practice to seek a ruling from HMRC under Code of Practice 10. Code of Practice 10 rulings are usually available for up to four Finance Acts, and thereafter the legislation is no longer considered new enough to warrant the system being available. However, HMRC has relaxed this approach in relation to substantial shareholdings and introduced a new facility with effect from June 2007, see Revenue & Customs Brief 41/07.

The subsidiary exemptions

4.65 *TCGA 1992, Sch 7AC, paras 2* and *3* contain subsidiary exemptions. *Sch 7AC, para 2* deals with disposals of 'assets related to shares' (see *para 30*), which is intended to cover disposals of options and convertible securities where the main exemption would be met. As the HMRC manuals state, this is effectively to ensure that companies do not have a choice as to whether to dispose of assets which are within the capital gains tax charge or those which are not (and indeed, the same applies generally to the legislation, as otherwise companies would have the choice of creating capital losses).

4.66 *TCGA 1992, Sch 7AC, para 3* contains a further subsidiary exemption, which is rather impenetrably drafted, but its effect can be very useful, and it should not be overlooked. The substantial shareholding condition must still be met. *TCGA 1992, Sch 7AC, para 3(2)(d)* then applies a 'look back' provision to

Groups **4.67**

the previous two years as regards the exemption to find a time when it would have been satisfied (ie applying all the tests of the exemption at that time). *TCGA 1992, Sch 7AC, para 3(2)(e)* then looks to the two years before disposal and tests the 'company invested in' requirement, and deems that requirement satisfied if that company was controlled by the disposing company or companies connected with the disposing company.

TCGA 1992, Sch 7AC, para 3(3) then limits the application of the *para 3* exemption in cases where the investing company requirement immediately after disposal is not met, where the failure to meet that requirement is due to the disposing company being wound up or dissolved or the fact it is about to be wound up or dissolved.

In practice, therefore, *para 3* applies particularly where the status of the company invested in (or indeed the group, but this may be less likely) has changed prior to the disposal, or where the disposing company is in the process of being wound up.

Interaction with other provisions

4.67 The application of *TCGA 1992, Sch 7AC* is more complicated in group situations where there has been a reorganisation prior to sale. The overall aim of the legislation is to ensure that ownership which is split between different members of a group, whether in amount or in time, is taken together for the purposes of the Schedule; *Sch 7AC, paras 9* and *10*.

The first point to make is that *Sch 7AC* does not displace *TCGA 1992, s 171*, and that provision operates in its usual way as a disposal for a consideration which results in neither a gain nor a loss accruing; *Sch 7AC, para 6*.

The second point, where the difficulty arises, is its application of *s 135* to intra-group share exchanges. *Schedule 7AC, para 4(1)* effectively gives priority to the substantial shareholdings rules over *TCGA 1992, s 127*. However, removing *s 127* leaves one with a transaction under *s 171*, over which the exemption does not have priority. That is not, it would seem, what was intended by the legislation.

The answer to this was given by HMRC at the time the provisions were passing through the legislative process, and is, in summary, that there is a disposal for substantial shareholdings purposes, with the result that on a disposal by company A to company B of company C in return for an issue of shares by company B to company A, company A has a substantial shareholdings exempt disposal, company B acquires company C at market value, and company A acquires the shares in company B at the value it held the shares in company C (ie *s 127* does

149

4.68 *Groups*

apply for that purpose). That is perhaps a sensible result, but it is very difficult to reach that conclusion on the wording of the legislation, and HMRC's circular explanation has to be read to be believed.

This does, however, mean the position remains the same as if *Sch 7AC, para 4(1)* had not prevented *s 127* applied to the transaction as a whole, and means that companies which carry out such internal share for share reorganisations should ensure that clearance is obtained so that they know what their base costs in the various subsidiaries are. The previous position, where companies can, to at least a limited extent, indulge in base cost planning in the context of reorganisations (subject to the commercial purpose test) remains the same.

Anti-avoidance

4.68 *TCGA 1992, Sch 7AC* has its own anti-avoidance provision, contained in *para 5*, which is perhaps considered less than it should be in practice. It is necessary for it to apply that the sole or main benefit that could be expected to arise be that a gain which would otherwise have accrued be exempt, but note that this is not a motive test, rather it is an objective test based on the facts of the case.

The other conditions in *para 5* are that the disposing company 'acquired' control of the target and there was a significant change in trading activities of the target company when the disposing company controlled the target. The main target of this provision can therefore be seen as artificial manipulation of the trading requirement for the company invested in.

OTHER RELEVANT PROVISIONS FOR GROUPS

4.69 The aim of this section of the chapter is to provide an overview of other provisions which are relevant to groups, although detailed consideration of the regimes is outside the scope of this chapter.

Transfer pricing

4.70 The amendment of the transfer pricing legislation in *ICTA 1988, Sch 28AA*, to include transactions between UK companies rather than just between UK and overseas companies has undoubtedly increased the burden on many groups. The pricing of each transaction between group members needs, strictly, to be justified on the basis of arm's-length principles. It should be remembered that this applies in relation to all sorts of transactions, including loans.

There is an exemption for small and medium-sized companies in *Sch 28AA, para 5B*, which applies to transactions between companies resident in the UK and between companies resident in the UK and companies resident in a territory which is party to a double tax treaty with an anti-discrimination provision and subject to certain designation powers of HM Treasury.

Should an adjustment under the transfer pricing provisions apply, then there is the possibility of a compensating adjustment under *Sch 28AA, para 6*. Obviously, any of these provisions needs to be considered in the context of the wider tax attributes of the companies concerned and the group as a whole.

Loan relationships

4.71 The loan relationships legislation contains a number of provisions which apply between connected parties and/or members of groups of companies.

The provisions in *FA 2006* were substantially amended by *FA 2004* to cope in particular with the introduction of International Accounting Standards (IAS) accounting. Loan relationships between connected companies (and therefore group companies) will now be taxed on a mandatory 'amortised cost' basis of accounting; *FA 1996, s 87*.

4.72 The rules in *FA 2006, Sch 9*, also require careful examination where groups and connected companies are concerned. The main provisions are as follows:

FA 2006, Sch 9, para 2 may apply to delay an interest deduction where the payee does not accrue the interest under the loan relationships regime and it is not paid within 12 months of the accounting period in which it would have otherwise accrued.

FA 2006, Sch 9, para 4A may cause there to be a deemed release by a creditor company of an amount where it acquires a loan relationship for less than its face value and the debtor is a connected party. The debtor company may therefore suffer a tax charge on that deemed release.

FA 2006, Sch 9, para 5(3) may prevent a charge arising between connected companies on the release of a debt.

FA 2006, Sch 9, paras 6 and *6A* contains the rules for impairment losses between parties having a connection or becoming connected. Essentially a loss may only be brought into account if it falls within these paragraphs, whatever happens in the commercial accounts. The situations are limited to debt for equity swaps where the parties were not otherwise connected but only for ordinary share

4.73 *Groups*

capital). *Paragraph 6(6)* deals with the debits and credits to be brought into account where a loan relationship between connected parties is the subject of a 'related transaction' (ie a form of disposition).

FA 2006, Sch 9, para 12 provides for the continuity of treatment where a loan relationship is transferred between members of a group of companies (within the capital gains tax meaning). It broadly is intended to provide for a tax neutral transfer, whatever the actual value paid on the transfer.

FA 2006, Sch 9, para 12A has a provision which is very similar in construct to *s 179*. It provides for a deemed assignment and reacquisition at market value where a company has acquired a loan relationship under *para 12* and leaves the group within six years. This will obviously only give rise to a charge in practice where the value of the loan relationship was not equal to the carrying value at the time of the transfer.

FA 2006, Sch 9, para 17 applies to deeply discounted securities, and provides for a deferral of the discount accrual where the parties are connected until the time of redemption of the security. It is effectively the equivalent of *para 2* for discount.

Derivative contracts

4.73 The derivative contracts regime in *FA 2002, Sch 26* also contains provisions which apply between connected parties and groups. In particular *Sch 26, paras 28* and *30A* contain provisions which are broadly equivalent to *FA 1996, Sch 9, paras 12* and *12A* mentioned above.

Intangibles

4.74 *FA 2002, Sch 29, Pt 8* contains its own particular group regime in relation to intangible assets, which is similar to the chargeable gains tax system. *Part 9, para 55* provides for tax neutral transfers within a group and *para 58* provides for a de-grouping charge, and there is an exemption for companies leaving the group together in the same way as for chargeable gains.

FA 2002, Sch 29, Pt 12 provides for general rules in transactions between related parties, and *para 94* of that part provides for deferral of accrual of debits if they are not paid within 12 months of the accounting period in which the debit would otherwise accrue (whether or not the recipient accrues the receipt within the charge to corporation tax).

GROUP PAYMENT ARRANGEMENTS

4.75 *FA 1998, s 36* permits HMRC to enter into 'arrangements' for the payment of tax for a group to be made by one designated member. This is done by way of contract with HMRC, and the standard form contract is published on HMRC's website, together with guidance notes.

The arrangements are purely administrative, and *s 36(3)* specifically provides that it shall not affect the liability of any company for corporation tax. The group payment arrangements (GPA) contract provides that HMRC will not pursue individual companies for tax until after the final filing date for corporation tax for all the companies in the group.

The contract only provides for arrangements between the companies and HMRC, and does not deal with arrangements between the companies themselves. It is obviously necessary for there to be some arrangements between the group members and the representative member for the payment of tax. Tax advisers need to take account of these arrangements in the context of company sales and purchases and ensure that agreement is reached, and/or an indemnity obtained in respect of the apportionment of payments under the GPA.

Chapter 5

Disincorporating a business

Peter Rayney FCA, FTII, TEP, National Tax Technical Partner, BDO Stoy Hayward LLP

BACKGROUND

5.1 A number of proprietors will have found that trading through a company is not all it 'was cracked up to be' – for example, paying substantial amounts of tax on company cars, operating PAYE on their own 'drawings', additional accountancy fees and Companies Act compliance and reporting, and so on. Unfortunately, for many, it may have been a case of 'incorporating in haste and repenting at leisure!'.

A number of small businesses may therefore consider disentangling themselves from a company structure by 'disincorporation'. However, this solution may not be a simple one – primarily because the process of 'disincorporating' a business does not have any CGT relieving provisions. While the CGT legislation recognises that it would be inequitable to charge CGT on transferring an existing sole-trade/partnership business into a company (for example, by providing for the relevant gains to be held over under *TCGA 1992, s 162*), there are no equivalent provisions for a disincorporation.

PLANNING A DISINCORPORATION

5.2 Many (old) sad tax anoraks (like me) will remember that there once were proposals to introduce special CGT reliefs for disincorporation, which were set out in the joint 1987 Inland Revenue/DTI Consultative Document 'Disincorporation'. The main tax proposals were the elimination of capital gains tax at both the company and shareholder levels. (Broadly, the company's chargeable assets would be transferred to the shareholders at their indexed base cost and shareholding gains arising on the disincorporation would be deferred until the shareholder(s) disposed of their interest in the successor business.)

Sadly, these initiatives never saw the light of day. Despite the continuity of ownership, the current tax rules do not facilitate the transfer of the company's assets (including goodwill) on a 'tax-neutral' basis. Consequently, there may be some CGT to pay on getting the trade and assets out of the company into the shareholder's hands, enabling them to continue to carry on the business as a sole trader/partnership.

The potential tax charges and events which arise on a disincorporation would be similar to those which would occur on any 'third-party' sale of a company's business and assets. (although it should normally be possible to avoid any capital allowance clawbacks). However, for the smaller 'one-man-band' type business, disincorporation may be implemented within minimal tax costs especially where is little or no 'freely transferable' goodwill (see below).

LEGAL MECHANICS

5.3 From a company law viewpoint, the disincorporation of a business is likely to take place by means of a members' voluntary winding-up or simple dissolution.

Members' voluntary liquidation

5.4 This type of liquidation is largely controlled by the company's shareholders and it can only be used where the company being liquidated is solvent (*Insolvency Act 1986, Ch III, Pt IV*). Generally, a special resolution of the shareholders is required to place the company in voluntary liquidation. Before this is done, the directors must make a statutory declaration of solvency. After having made a full inquiry, the directors must declare that the company will be able to pay its debts within 12 months following the commencement of the winding-up.

The liquidator can then wind up the company which, under a disincorporation, would entail the transfer of the business and assets to the new unincorporated business, owned by the shareholder(s). The liquidator will pay off the creditors and distribute the surplus to the shareholder(s). The distribution to the shareholder(s) should be a capital one (under *TCGA 1992, s 122*), although there is a possibility that HMRC may tax the amount as income under the Transaction in Securities' anti-avoidance provisions now contained in *ITA 2007, Pt 13, Ch 1* (see below).

Dissolution

5.5 Where a 'dissolution' process is used, the company will first transfer its trade and assets to an unincorporated business. The transfer can be challenged by any minority shareholder or creditor who feels that this is prejudicial to their interests. Liabilities can either be settled by the company or assigned to the successor business (provided agreement is obtained from the relevant creditors). The company will then be dissolved under *CA 1985, s 652*. A

5.6 *Disincorporating a business*

dissolution therefore involves fewer legal formalities and minimises costs. However, unlike a liquidation, it is not legally possible for a company to distribute its share capital (or any other non-distributable reserves) – although this should not be a material problem where the share capital is very small. However, any sizeable 'unauthorised distributions' may be collected by the Office of the Treasury Solicitor – which has announced that it will not seek to collect amounts of less than £4,000!

Under Extra-statutory Concession C16, HMRC is normally prepared to treat a distribution made to the shareholders prior to dissolution as having been made under a formal winding-up. The company is required to give certain assurances to the Inspector beforehand. Such a distribution should therefore be treated as a capital distribution for the shareholder, subject again to the risk of HMRC making a counteraction under *ITA 2007, Pt 13, Ch 1*.

CASE STUDY – TORQUAY TOWERS LTD AND MR BASIL

5.6 Basil has run his small bed and breakfast business since 1990 through his 100% owned company, Torquay Towers Ltd. He would now like to run the business as a sole trader, since this is more appropriate to its future scale of activities. The disincorporation date is 31 December 2007 (when the trade will be transferred to Basil and the company will be wound up).

The likely balance sheet at 31 December 2007 (reflecting the estimated trading profits to date) is shown in **Table 5.1**.

Table 5.1

	Note	£000	Book value £000	Market value £000
Freehold property	1		120	220
Goodwill	2		–	20
Fittings, plant and equipment	3			
Cost		20		
Less: Depreciation	4	(8)	12	15
Stock	4		10	12
Debtors			7	
Bank overdraft			(4)	
Creditors	5		(9)	
Represented by share capital (£100) and reserves			£136	

Notes:

1. The freehold property has not been subject to depreciation – and represents the cost of the premises when it was acquired in March 1990.

2 The goodwill value is considered to represent 'free' goodwill (and is not attributable to the premises or Mr Basil personally!).

3. The tax written down value of the plant etc on 1 July 2007 was £9,000.

4. Stock and plant etc will be transferred at their book values.

4. No tax provision has been made in the above figures.

In the six months to 31 December 2007, the tax adjusted trading profit (before making any cessation adjustments) is expected to be £40,000.

Assume the trade and assets are sold to Basil on 31 December 2007, so he can continue to operate the business as a sole trader. Provided the appropriate tax elections are made in relation to trading stock (under *ICTA 1988, s 100(1C)* and plant (*CAA 2001, s 266*) the corporation tax computation for the six months to 31 December 2007 would be as follows:

	£000
Tax adjusted trading profit (no cessation adjustments)	40
Chargeable gains on sale of Goodwill (no base cost – market value = chargeable gain)	20
Taxable profits	60
Corporation tax liability @ 20%	£12

The goodwill would be transferred on the cessation of trade.

Main corporation tax consequences

Deemed consideration of trade

5.7 There is a deemed cessation of trade for corporation tax purposes on its transfer to Mr Basil, even though the actual trade is continuing (albeit under different ownership) (*ICTA 1988, s 337(1)*).

Termination of corporation tax accounting period

5.8 The cessation of trade automatically brings to an end the current corporation tax accounting period (CTAP) of Basil's Towers Ltd. The company will therefore have a six-month CTAP to 31 December 2007 (*ICTA 1988, s 12(3)(c)*).

5.9 *Disincorporating a business*

Unused trading losses

5.9 If Basil's Towers Ltd had any unused trading losses, these would effectively be lost on the disincorporation since they cannot be carried forward beyond the deemed cessation of trade (*ICTA 1988, s 393(1)*). There is no provision for their transfer to the unincorporated successor business.

If the company had a current year trading loss in the final CTAP, this could be offset against any other corporation tax profits, including chargeable gains of the current and preceding one year (*ICTA 1988, s 393A(1)*). However, the current trading loss could not be matched against chargeable assets transferred/ distributed to the shareholders during the course of the winding-up/dissolution, since these would arise in the subsequent CTAP (see below). In such cases, a sale of the chargeable assets to the shareholders at open market value before 'cessation' should be considered to achieve the appropriate loss offset.

The possibility of making a terminal loss relief claim should only be considered after all other forms of loss relief have been exhausted (*ICTA 1988, s 393(2), (2A)*).

Transfer of closing trading stock

5.10 As Basil Tower's Ltd (the transferor company) is 'connected' with Basil (see *ICTA, s 100(1F)*), who will continue to carry on the trade, the deemed 'market value' rule in *ICTA 1988, s 100(1A)* will apply to the transfer of closing stock. (Based on the facts of the case study, the amount of stock held by the company's 'bed and breakfast' trade is relatively small, so this is not a material issue here).

However, in most cases, it should be possible for the parties to make a joint election under *s 100(1C)* to transfer the stock at its actual transfer value (or, if higher, the book value). (In the unlikely event of the company being subject to UK-to-UK transfer pricing, the stock must be transferred at an arm's-length market value (*ICTA 1988, s 100(1ZA)*.)

Capital allowances: plant and machinery

5.11 The normal 'capital allowance' cessation rules apply. No writing-down allowances are given in the final basis period and a balancing adjustment is calculated (*CAA 2001, s 61* and Table Item 6). The balancing adjustment will generally be computed by reference to the actual transfer value.

However, if both parties make an election under *CAA 2001, s 266* the cessation rules will not apply and the plant can be transferred at its tax written-down value (*CAA 2001, s 267*). In this context, an election to transfer the plant at its tax written-down value may not be advantageous if the 'disincorporated' company is going to have unrelieved trading losses. In such cases, the balancing charge can be used to absorb the loss, thus increasing the tax value of the plant for the successor business.

VAT

5.12 Assuming the business is VAT registered, the general rule is that where a trade ceases, the 'registered person' is deemed to make a taxable supply of all the goods then held by the business. However, since the business will be transferred to the shareholder(s) who will continue to carry it on as a sole trader/partnership, there should be no VAT levied on the transfer (by virtue of the 'transfer of going concern' provisions in VAT (Special Provisions) Order 1995, Art 5. Given the recent delays currently being experienced with VAT registrations, it may be considered appropriate to elect to continue to use the business's existing VAT registration number (on form VAT 68), particularly as the history of the business will be well-known to the shareholder(s).

Capital gains on transfer of assets

5.13 Chargeable gains will arise when the assets are transferred to the shareholders. The chargeable assets of the company (including goodwill) are deemed to be disposed of at market value for tax purposes (*TCGA 1992, s 17*).

The property held by Torquay Towers Ltd would be distributed in specie during the winding-up to avoid SDLT. However, this will still trigger a chargeable gain in the subsequent CTAP by reference to the property's market value.

	£000
Freehold Property:	
Market value	220
Less: Base cost	(120)
Indexation, say £120,000 x 70%	(84)
Chargeable gain = Taxable profits	16
Corporation tax liability @ (say) 20%	£3.2

Property

5.14 In those cases where the shareholder personally holds the trading premises and has granted the company a (non-exclusive) licence to occupy it, no further action is normally required. In such cases, the property will still continue to accrue taper relief at the beneficial business rate on its continued use for the trade (subsequently carried on through a sole trade or partnership).

5.15 *Disincorporating a business*

However, where the property is owned by the company, the CGT cost 'disincorporating' may prove to be prohibitive, particularly if a substantial capital gain is likely to arise. If the tax cost of transferring the property is manageable, then it may often be preferable to 'distribute' it to the shareholders in specie during the winding-up. This will normally avoid any SDLT charge (see *FA 2003, Sch 3, para 1*) and ranks as a capital distribution in the shareholder's hands. However, any assumption of a property loan/mortgage by the shareholders would represent 'consideration' for the transfer with a consequent SDLT charge.

If the property is sold to the shareholders on or just before the trade ceases (this may be done, for example, to access trading losses that might otherwise remain unused), then SDLT will be payable at the relevant rate (maximum of 4% for property sold for more than £500,000).

From 21 March 2007, the *Finance Act 2007* provides that there is no clawback of industrial buildings allowances (IBAs) claimed on the disposal of properties. In such cases, the transferee owner(s) will effectively stand in the company's shoes and continue to claim IBAs on the transitional basis until 31 March 2011.

Goodwill

5.15 Clearly, business goodwill will follow the transfer of the trade and may trigger a significant capital gain, depending on the market value agreed with HMRC. However, where the business was established after 31 March 2002, the gain will be treated as a taxable (trading) credit under the Intangibles regime in *FA 2002, Sch 29*.

Given HMRC's recent stance with regard to goodwill valuations on business incorporations (where the trader has opted to sell goodwill to the newly incorporated company at its full market value), it will be interesting to see whether the same approach is adopted on a disincorporation. For many small businesses, HMRC have typically contended that the value of transferable goodwill is low or insignificant. This is because, HMRC argue, most if not all of the goodwill attaches to the proprietor personally and so is not capable of being transferred. (The over-analytical approach adopted by HMRC in relation to goodwill was recently questioned by the Special Commissioner in *Balloon Promotions v Wilson (Inspector of Taxes)* (SpC 524).) It is however likely that many very small 'one-man-band' type businesses will have minimal goodwill which should facilitate a relatively easy disincorporation.

On the other hand, there will be a number of businesses which have built up significant 'free' goodwill attributable to the reputation built up by the business, its name and trade connections and so on. Any potential uncertainty surrounding the value of goodwill in these cases must be carefully factored into the tax cost likely to arise on the disincorporation. Agreeing the value of goodwill with

HMRC – Shares Valuation could well turn out to be a protracted process and may be uncertain. In some cases the CGT involved may well make the disincorporation unacceptable.

Tax liabilities arising on shareholders

5.16 The company will be wound-up or dissolved as part of the disincorporation and the amounts/assets distributed will normally represent a capital distribution in the hands of the shareholder(s). The amount will therefore be subject to CGT (provided HMRC do not successfully invoke the Transaction in Securities anti-avoidance legislation).

Inevitably, a disincorporation will normally involve a classical 'double tax' charge, since the tax suffered by the shareholder on the capital distribution creates a further tax liability on the appreciation in the value of the company's chargeable assets which has already been taxed in the company.

Following the Pre-Budget Report 2007 proposals, (business) taper relief will only be applied to capital distributions made before 6 April 2008. Hence, those contemplating disincorporating in the near future, would be well advised to ensure that any capital distributions are made whilst taper relief is still available. Post-6 April 2008 disposals are likely to attract CGT at a flat rate of 18%.

Based on the case study, the estimated CGT payable by Mr Basil on the liquidator's distribution is shown below

	£000	£000
Net reserves at 31 December 2007 (before disincorporation)		136
Realisations:		
Goodwill – surplus on transfer		20
Freehold property – surplus on distribution in specie – £220,000 less £120,000		100
		256
Less: Corporation tax liabilities – say £12,000 + £3,200 (say)	(16)	
Liquidator's fees and other costs (say)	(8)	(24)
Surplus available to distribute		£232
Satisfied thus:		
Capital distribution – cash		12
Distribution *in specie* – market value of property		220
		£232

5.17 *Disincorporating a business*

Based on the above, Mr Basil's estimated CGT liability (ignoring his negligible base cost) would be around £20,000 calculated as follows:

	£000
Capital distributions	
Cash	12
Market value of property	220
Total amount	232
Less: Business taper relief @ 75%	(174)
Chargeable gain	58
Less: Annual exemption	(9)
	49
CGT liability @ (say) 40%	£19.6

POTENTIAL IMPACT OF TRANSACTIONS IN SECURITIES RULES

5.17 The 'Transaction in Securities' provisions now contained (for income tax purposes) in *ITA 2007, Pt 13, Ch 1* must always be considered in relation to transactions involving the company's shareholders. Following the House of Lords decision in *IRC v Laird Group plc* [2002] STC 722, the better view is that (by itself) the winding-up and distribution of the company's assets by a liquidator would not fall within the ambit of this legislation. On the other hand, *CIR v Joiner* [1975] STC 657 considered that these provisions would apply where a company's shareholders continue to carry on the trade in a new company *after liquidation*, having extracted the old company's distributable reserves as capital (rather than income). This view is also supported in HMRC's Company Taxation Manual (CTM 36850).

Even though the trade is being transferred into personal ownership (rather than a commonly-owned company), it is probably prudent to assume that HMRC would seek to counteract the 'tax advantage' from the liquidation/dissolution (ie extracting the reserves in an income tax-free form as a capital receipt) under *ITA 2007, s 684*. However, provided it can be demonstrated that the disincorporation was motivated by sound commercial reasons, the normal 'let-out' in *ITA 2007, s 685* should be available. (Mr Basil would appear to have a very good chance of obtaining clearance under *ITA 2007, s 701* – since he is only extracting a minimal amount of cash which will probably be reinvested in the business.)

5.18 The practical application of *ITA 2007, Pt 13, Ch 1* clearly depends on HMRC's interpretation of the facts in each case. For example, HMRC is likely to challenge those cases where they suspect the shareholders have only 'disincorporated' to extract the company's reserves at a beneficial CGT rate (assisted by business taper relief). On the other hand, where all (or substantially) all the company's funds need to be re-invested in the successor sole trade/partnership business, a more benign approach is likely to be taken. The overall tax costs of the 'disincorporation' may also be an important factor in HMRC's deliberations.

The shareholders will need to obtain certainty on the tax treatment of the capital distribution and should therefore apply for advance clearance under *ITA 2007, s 701* that HMRC agree that the 'genuine commercial purpose' test is satisfied.

Not all disincorporation exercises will be as simple or as inexpensive as those of our case study – Basil Towers Ltd. Where property is held within the company and/or there is clearly significant business goodwill, the 'double-tax' costs may make it very costly, possibly persuading those involved to maintain the corporate 'status-quo'.

Chapter 6

Current tax planning issues for owner managed company sales

Peter Rayney FCA, FTII, TEP, National Tax Technical Partner, BDO Stoy Hayward LLP

IMPACT OF PRE-BUDGET REPORT 2007 PROPOSALS

6.1 Owner managers who are contemplating a sale of their company, or are actively in the process of selling it, currently face a number of uncertainties. These were largely created by the Pre-Budget Report 2007 proposals for the abolition of taper relief from 6 April 2008. For many years, most of us have taken business taper relief and the expectation of an effective CGT 'exit' rate of 10% for granted. However, following the Pre-Budget Report 2007 proposals, the tax bill for the sale of a typical owner-managed company is likely to increase substantially from 6 April 2008. The main change proposed is the abolition of CGT taper relief from 2007/08, which is being replaced by a flat CGT rate of 18%. Indexation relief, which often provides an additional beneficial reduction, is also being removed from 6 April 2008.

The message is clear – if an owner manager wishes to enjoy the beneficent 10% effective CGT rate, they must ensure that any sale of their company takes place before 6 April 2008. For those who have not even started the sale process, this is likely to be unachievable. Probably their best option is to consider how they might 'bank' business taper relief before it is abolished.

This article assumes that the Pre-Budget report 2007 CGT proposals will be enacted in full. However, given the overwhelming criticism of the proposed abolition of taper relief (and the 10% effective CGT rate for business assets in particular), it is possible that these proposals may be amended or even ditched before they reach the statute book. The indications are that Mr Darling will not wish to make such a drastic U-turn on his first Pre-Budget Report although he has opened up a dialogue with business leaders to discuss his proposed CGT regime! One thing is clear though – *vendors can only be certain of their tax treatment by taking action before 6 April 2008.*

SALE OF COMPANY BEFORE 6 APRIL 2008

6.2 Many owner managers will be accelerating the sale of their company before 6 April 2008 to 'lock' into the beneficial 10% CGT rate. However, they will need to ensure that their company satisfies the relevant 'trading company/group' criteria for business taper (throughout the relevant share ownership period).

However, a sale before 5 April 2008 would only be effective in fixing the fully (business) tapered CGT rate of 10% to the extent that the sale consideration is taken in the form of cash (or fixed deferred consideration which is left outstanding as a simple debt ie which is not evidenced by a formal loan note). In contrast, where the sale consideration is received in shares of or loan notes in the acquiring company, the deferred gains will invariably arise under the post-5 April 2008 regime when the 'consideration' shares/loan notes are sold/redeemed. Under current proposals, it is likely that such gains would be taxed at a flat CGT rate of 18%. The precise tax treatment of earn-out consideration will depend on the facts of each case.

Given the relatively large disparity that has existed between the 'dividend' tax rate (effective 25% rate for a higher-rate taxpayer) and the business tapered CGT rate of 10%, HMRC have begun to apply the 'Transaction in Securities' anti-avoidance rules in (what is now) *ITA 2007, s 684* more vigorously. It is therefore very important for the vendor shareholders to make use of the statutory clearance procedure under *ITA 2007, s 701*. Provided the main aspects of the transaction have been fully disclosed, the vendor can obtain some certainty before the sale that HMRC are satisfied that the transaction is being made for good commercial reasons and will not subsequently be challenged under this legislation.

BASIC DEAL STRUCTURING ISSUES

6.3 Generally, vendors can either sell their shares in the company or arrange to sell the trade and assets out of the company. In the majority of cases, the vendor shareholders will seek to structure the deal as a sale of their shares (which is therefore the main focus of this chapter). This is attractive for a number of reasons. The sale proceeds are received directly in their hands and (before 6 April 2008) would normally subject to the attractive business taper rates in calculating their capital gain. After 5 April 2008, the CGT rate is likely to be 18%.

A share sale also limits the vendor's commercial exposure, subject to the protection obtained by the purchaser through warranties and indemnities under the sale agreement.

6.4 *Current tax planning issues for owner managed company sales*

In contrast, an asset deal frequently gives rise to an element of double taxation. This is because capital gains and 'clawbacks' of previously claimed capital allowances typically arise on the company's sale of the assets (such as goodwill and plant). A further tax charge then arises when the company's post-tax sale proceeds are extracted by the shareholders. Vendors generally tend to be 'forced' to sell the trade and assets out of their company in 'distress' sale situations.

Purchasers have tended to prefer to acquire the trade and assets since this involves less commercial risk and the prospect of obtaining tax relief on the assets purchased, such as on goodwill and other intangible assets. However, in recent years, asset deals are likely to be more expensive in terms of Stamp Duty Land Tax (SDLT), where the acquisition contains a substantial element of UK land and property. For example, if the amount paid for (say) a trading premises exceeds £500,000, the SDLT cost would be 4% of the amount paid. (Goodwill and all transfers of intellectual property or debts no longer attract any stamp taxes.) On the other hand, share purchases only attract stamp duty at ½% but this is levied on the *total* value of the company (reflecting the value of non-dutiable assets but reduced by the company's debt and liabilities).

BASIC CAPITAL GAINS TAX (CGT) RULES ON SHARE SALES

Date of disposal

6.4 The vendor will normally generate a capital gain when they sell their shares. A disposal of an asset will be recognised for CGT purposes when an unconditional contract is executed for its sale (*TCGA 1992, s 28(1)*). In the case of a conditional contract, the date of disposal is deferred until the relevant condition precedent is satisfied (or waived) (*TCGA 1992, s 28(2)*). A condition precedent refers to an event which is outside the control of the contracting parties – for example obtaining satisfactory tax clearances or relevant regulatory approval etc. (On the other hand, a 'condition subsequent' is merely a term of the contract required to be fulfilled by one of the parties and does not create a conditional contract for CGT).

Cash consideration is immediately chargeable to CGT in the tax year of disposal (*TCGA 1992, s 28*). Tax must be paid on any *fixed* (ie ascertainable) deferred consideration, even it if is conditional, although the HMRC will refund the tax when it is satisfied that the conditional amount will not be paid. Instalment relief may be available for the tax payments, given the difficulty of paying the tax before the full cash proceeds are received (*TCGA 1992, ss 48 and 280*). However, fixed deferred consideration is usually best structured through the use of loan notes, as this enables the relevant tax to be held-over (subject to the timing point mentioned in **6.2**).

Calculation of capital gain

6.5 In broad terms, an individual or trustee vendor's capital gain is calculated as the amount by which the sale proceeds (net of allowable incidental costs of disposal) exceeds the amount they originally paid for the shares – often referred to as the 'base cost'.

For disposals made before 6 April 2008, this gain may then be subject to further reductions for indexation relief and taper relief. If the sale proceeds are less than the vendor's base cost, a capital loss arises (which can be offset against other capital gains made by the vendor).

Special rebasing rules apply where the vendor held their shares at 31 March 1982. In such cases, they can normally deduct the market value of their shareholding at 31 March 1982 (instead of their pre-31 March 1982 acquisition cost) as their base cost.

Indexation allowance (for pre-6 April 2008 disposals)

6.6 If the vendor acquired their shares before April 1998, they are entitled to an indexation allowance. Broadly, this gives a measure of relief for inflation – by taking the increase in the Retail Prices Index (RPI) between the disposal date (or, if earlier April 1998) and the date the shares were acquired (or March 1982, where rebasing is used). No indexation relief can accrue beyond April 1998 since indexation relief is effectively frozen at this date. The relevant RPI increase is represented as an 'indexation' factor (expressed as a decimal, calculated to three places), which is then applied to the shareholder's base cost. The resultant amount is then deducted in arriving at the shareholder's gain (see calculation in **Example 6.1**).

Taper relief (for pre-6 April 2008 disposals) and the annual exemption

6.7 For disposals made before 6 April 2008, if the shareholder has a chargeable gain (after deducting indexation relief), this will often be reduced by a further deduction – known as taper relief. Individual vendors are also entitled to an annual CGT exemption (£9,200 for 2007/08) which can be applied against their net chargeable gains. The annual exemption for trustees is half the 'individual' exemption – special rules limit this amount even further where a number of trusts have been created by the same individual.

6.8 *Current tax planning issues for owner managed company sales*

The vendor's taxable gain is then taxed at their marginal tax rate (being treated as the highest slice of their taxable income of the tax year). Thus, significant gains would normally be taxed at 40%.

A simple CGT computation for a pre-6 April 2008 share sale is shown in **Example 6.1**.

Example 6.1 – CGT computation for sale of shares (before 6 April 2008)

In February 2008, Jennifer Eccles sold her 75% shareholding in The Hollies Ltd for £2,000,000, incurring incidental legal and professional disposal costs of £30,000. She acquired her 75% shareholding in June 1983 for £100,000. Jennifer's marginal tax rate is 40%.

Jennifer's capital gain is calculated as follows:

	£
Sale proceeds	2,000,000
Less: Incidental disposal costs	(30,000)
	1,970,000
Less: Acquisition cost (June 1993)	(100,000)
Indexation relief	
£100,000 x 0.153 (RPI increase between June 1993 to April 1998)	(15,300)
Chargeable gain	1,854,700
Less: Business asset taper relief	
1,854,700 x 75%	(1,391,025)
Chargeable gain (after taper relief)	463,675
Less: Annual exemption	(9,200)
Taxable gain	454,475
CGT @ 40%	181,790

Proposed CGT treatment for post-6 April 2008 disposals

6.8 The Pre-Budget Report 2007 proposals will radically change the CGT regime for disposals taking place after 5 April 2008. The main changes are:

- the abolition of taper relief and indexation relief; and
- a single flat CGT rate of 18%.

Current tax planning issues for owner managed company sales **6.9**

The Chancellor's proposed CGT reforms have received widespread criticism from business leaders. At the time of writing, it is quite possible that some concession may be given to those owner managers selling on 'retirement' (it has been rumoured that part of these gains may be completely exempt).

To put the impact of these changes in context, if Jennifer's sale (in **Example 6.1**) is delayed beyond 5 April 2008, her likely CGT liability would be computed as follows:

Example 6.2 – CGT computation for sale of shares (after 5 April 2008)

Assume the same facts as in example 1 above, except that Jennifer sells her shares in (say) May 2008. (It is assumed that no 'retirement' relief is available.)

Her capital gain is likely to be in the region of £335,000 (which is considerably more than she would pay on a pre-6 April 2008 sale (see **Example 6.1**). Her CGT would be calculated as follows:

	£
Sale proceeds	2,000,000
Less: Incidental disposal costs	(30,000)
	1,970,000
Less: Acquisition cost (June 1993)	(100,000)
Capital gain	1,870,000
Less: Annual exemption (say)	(9,500)
Taxable gain	1,860,500
CGT @ 18%	£334,890

TAPER RELIEF ON SHARE SALES (BEFORE 6 APRIL 2008)

Basic principles of taper relief

6.9 Taper relief is only applied to a *chargeable gain* on the disposal of an asset after deducting any available capital losses. Taper relief is calculated on an increasing scale, based on the number of *complete* years for which the asset is held and the 'business/non-business' status of the asset over the relevant period of ownership. Two types of taper relief are available – business and non-business.

It may be that the shares only qualify as a business asset for only part of the ownership period. In such cases, the shareholder will have a mixed-taper profile, with the gain being apportioned between business and non-business

6.10 *Current tax planning issues for owner managed company sales*

elements, with the relevant taper relief being applied to each part – in each case, the actual business/non-business taper relief is based on the total period of ownership.

Relevant period of ownership

6.10 The relevant period of ownership for taper relief purposes is deemed to begin on 6 April 1998, for assets already held at the date; otherwise it starts when the asset is acquired. The relevant period of ownership ends when the asset is disposed of, subject to a maximum period of ten years. The ownership period is counted as the number of complete years (ie 365 day periods) (*TCGA 1992, Sch A1, para 2(1)(2)*).

If the shares have been acquired from a spouse, the 'combined' ownership period of both spouses is taken (*TCGA 1992, Sch A1, para 15*). However, the taper relief status of the pre-transfer period depends on whether the *recipient* spouse had a business or non-business period during that period.

Business taper relief

6.11 Vendors will be interested in ensuring that their gain is eligible for the more favourable business asset taper reduction. Under the current regime, the maximum business taper reduction of 75% is given after just two *complete* years of share ownership, provided the relevant conditions are satisfied. Where the gain qualifies for full business taper, this means that the effective CGT rate is around 10% (ie chargeable gain after taper reduction of 25% (100%-75%) at the individual's/trustee's marginal CGT rate of 40%).

The accrual of business asset taper relief is illustrated below:

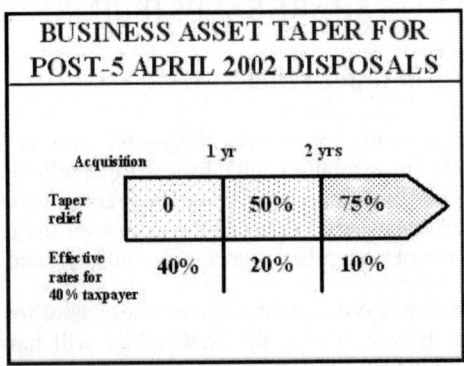

Since 6 April 2000, shares in *unlisted* companies (which includes AIM companies) will accrue business asset taper relief provided the underlying company is either

- a trading company; or
- holding company of a trading group.

Trading company/group test

6.12 The 'trading company/group' test is quite stringent since it requires the company/group to be wholly engaged in carrying on trading activities. This is subject to a special *de minimis* rule which enables a company/group to carry on non-trading activities provided they do not exceed 20% of their total activities. Vulnerable non-trading activities would include property letting to third parties, investment in shares etc, loans to shareholders/connected companies, and surplus cash not required for future trading activities. HMRC generally test whether non-trading activities are within the 20% benchmark by looking at a range of measures, such as:

- turnover;
- the asset-base of the company;
- expenses;
- time spent by management and employees.

Thus, for example, the turnover/sales income from a company's non-trading activities would be compared with the total turnover generated by the company and so on. It may be necessary to build-up the correct picture over time and this may involve striking a balance between all these factors (*see IR Tax Bulletin, Issue 62*). Although many considered that substantial surplus cash could invalidate a company's trading status, HMRC now seem to have a more relaxed approach in this area. It would appear that provided the cash had been generated from a company's trading operations and it has not been applied for an investment purpose, then it should be treated as a trading asset.

In the past, vendors were able to obtain a degree of certainty from HMRC as to whether 'their' company satisfied the 'trading' company criteria for business taper. This was achieved by making a COP 10 application to HMRC prior to a sale, which analysed the company's activities and requested the Inspector to confirm whether the company was a trading company/group. However, since the FA 2006 received Royal Assent, HMRC have indicated that they will no longer give business taper-based COP 10 clearances (under the 'four-year' rule) (see *Tax Bulletin, Issue 84*).

6.13 *Current tax planning issues for owner managed company sales*

Non-business taper relief

6.13 Where the shares are not eligible for business taper, they will qualify for the less beneficial non-business taper relief (which is effectively the 'default' taper relief). For 'non-business' shares, no taper relief accrues for the first three complete years of ownership. Once three years have elapsed, non-business taper is given at the rate of 5% per year reaching a maximum of 40% after ten years. This would mean an effective CGT rate of 24% for a 40% taxpayer (ie chargeable gain after taper relief of 60% (100% less 40%) at marginal CGT rate of 40%).

Where the shares were held at 6 April 1998 (the taper base date), then a 'bonus year' of non-business taper is given. This means that non-business taper would start to accrue from 6 April 2000 (ie after just two years of ownership). The build-up of non-business taper relief for shares held at 6 April 1998 (together with effective CGT rates) is shown below:

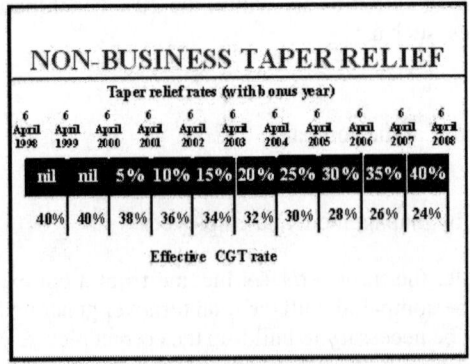

Potential dilution of business taper relief before 6 April 2000

6.14 Prior to 6 April 2000, the legislative conditions for business asset taper were far more stringent. This means that some shareholders' taper relief may be restricted by the more stringent 'business asset' criteria that existed in the two years to 5 April 2000. Broadly, a vendor can only count this period as a *business* one for taper relief purposes provided they held at least:

- 25% of the voting rights; or
- 5% of the voting rights *and* worked for the company (as a director/employee) on a full-time basis.

Current tax planning issues for owner managed company sales **6.16**

Failing that, this period (or part of it) would be counted as a 'non-business' period for taper relief. This means that the vendor's taper relief would be split between the 'business' and 'non-business' elements of their gain when they sold their shares, effectively giving them a 'diluted' taper rate.

It is fairly common for spouses of the proprietor-shareholders to hold shares in owner managed companies to benefit from the tax-efficient spreading of dividends for income tax purposes. However, for established shareholdings, unless the spouse has worked for the company on a *full time* basis, the spouse's shares are likely to have a reduced taper rate on sale – this is because they will have a 'non-business' taper period in the two-year period to 5 April 2000.

However, the 'proprietor' spouse will invariably have held their shares as a business asset (since 6 April 1998). It is therefore possible for the couple to correct this taper relief disadvantage by arranging for the 'non-working' spouse to (unconditionally) transfer their shares to the other.

Special business taper rules for shares in listed companies

6.15 Shares held in *listed trading* companies can qualify for business asset taper provided the shareholder *either*:

- is an employee or director of that company (or any fellow (51%) group member, or
- holds at least 5% of the voting rights in the investee company.

There is a special relaxation for 'minority' shareholdings held by directors/employees (which applies from 6 April 2000). In such cases, provided the director/employee (together with any associates, such as spouses and close relatives) holds a non-material interest (ie not exceeding 10%), business taper relief will accrue, regardless of the company's/group's status. This means that business asset taper relief could be available on minority shareholdings in an investment company.

TREATMENT OF SALE CONSIDERATION SATISFIED BY SHARES/LOAN NOTES IN THE ACQUIRER

Deferral of capital gain

6.16 Vendors may sell their shares for a consideration satisfied in cash, loan notes or shares issued by the acquiring company. Very often the vendor is likely

6.17 *Current tax planning issues for owner managed company sales*

to be offered a combination of cash and loan notes/shares. In some cases, vendors may also be given additional deferred consideration in the form of an 'earn-out'.

Consideration shares in the acquirer

6.17 Many private company takeovers, particularly by quoted companies, will entail the purchaser issuing new shares to the vendor shareholders as part of the sale consideration.

Many company takeovers, particularly by plcs, will entail the purchaser issuing new shares to the vendor shareholders as part of the sale consideration. This enables the vendor to defer his capital gain until the shares are sold. The CGT reorganisation rule in *TCGA 1992, s 127* is applied here so that the vendor does not make any disposal of his old shares and is treated as receiving his new 'consideration' shares at the same time and cost as his old shares.

The vendor will only realise their gain when the consideration shares are sold. Following the Pre-Budget Report 2007 proposals, taper relief will only be a relevant factor in the determination of their CGT liability where the consideration shares are sold before 6 April 2008. The CGT reorganisation rule permits the vendor's period of ownership for taper purposes to continue after the sale. Whether this 'post-sale' period qualifies as a business or non-business period for taper relief purposes, depends on a number of factors. For current deals, the continued accrual of a business taper period typically depends on one of the following conditions being satisfied.

Condition 1 – The acquiring company must be (and remain) a trading company or holding company of a trading group. However, employee/director minority shareholdings (no more than 10%, of the share capital (taking into account shares held by close relatives and other 'associates') qualify for business asset taper relief, irrespective of the company's trading or non-trading status.

Condition 2 – The acquiring company must be a 'qualifying company' in relation to the individual vendor, which means that:

- the company's shares must be unlisted (which embraces AIM companies); or

- the individual shareholder is an employee (either part or full time) of any 'group' company (or a qualifying 'joint-venture' company owned by the group) (*TCGA 1992, para 6(1)(b) Sch A1*); or

- the individual holds shares carrying at least 5% of the voting rights (in the acquirer).

If the vendor has a mixture of business and non-business periods at the date of the final disposal, his gain is apportioned on a pro-rata basis for taper purposes, producing a lower 'diluted' taper rate.

Where the consideration shares are disposed of after 5 April 2008, no taper relief is given. Instead, the vendor can expect a CGT rate of 18% on their disposal gain.

Loan notes

6.18 In many deals, the vendor may agree to accept deferred payment for part of the sale consideration by taking loan notes in the acquiring company. As a general rule, where the purchaser satisfies part of the consideration by issuing loan notes, an appropriate part of the vendor's gain is deferred until the loan note is redeemed for payment. This rule is subject to HMRC being satisfied that the loan note has been issued for genuine commercial reasons and not mainly to avoid tax (*TCGA 1992, s 137*). The vendor would normally apply for a *TCGA 1992, s 138* clearance to seek advance confirmation of this point from HMRC.

The mechanics of the tax deferral and hence any available taper relief position depends on the type of loan note issued by the purchaser.

Dealing with QCBs

6.19 Broadly, most 'non-convertible' loan notes will represent QCBs. The capital gains deferral mechanism for a QCB is governed by the rules in *TCGA 1992, s 116(10)*. These provide that the *chargeable gain* on the loan note consideration is computed at the date of sale. This gain is then postponed and becomes taxed only when the loan note is encashed (or disposed of outside the cases specified in *TCGA 1992, s 116(11)*).

Unfortunately, the deferred capital gain can also triggered where the purchasing company defaults on a QCB loan note which is cancelled or settled via a 'compromise arrangement'. No capital loss relief is available as a QCB is not a chargeable asset for CGT (*TCGA 1992, s 115*). In these dire circumstances, HMRC generally permit the worthless loan note to be 'gifted' to a charity without triggering the held-over gain. Having said all that, vendors should always seek to obtain 'commercial bank' guarantees for their loan notes to avoid these types of 'nightmare' scenarios!

Taper relief will only be applied to the postponed gain if it crystallises before 6 April 2008. However, the taper relief is only calculated up to the original sale date rather than the date of redemption (*TCGA 1992, Sch A1, para 16*).

6.19 *Current tax planning issues for owner managed company sales*

Where a company has been sold in the past few years, it is likely that most shareholders will be on 'maximum' business asset taper of 75% (having amassed two complete years of qualifying ownership before the sale). In such cases, taking a loan note in the form of a QCB was often considered beneficial. This is because vendors considered that they had captured their maximum (business) taper relief entitlement (and would not be potentially subject to any post-sale dilution in taper). However, the proposed abolition of taper relief will have altered their expectations unless the loan note can be encashed before 6 April 2008!

Example 6.3 – Deferral of QCB gain

In June 2006 Bobby Joe sold his 100% shareholding in Equals Ltd to Viva plc. He had formed Equals Ltd in April 1999, subscribing for 1,000 £1 ordinary shares at par. Equals Ltd has always been a trading company for taper relief purposes.

On the sale in 2006, Bobby received sale consideration of £3 million, £2 million of which was paid in cash on completion and £1 million was satisfied by a Viva plc loan note. All relevant tax clearances were applied for and given on the sale.

The Viva plc loan note carried an interest coupon of 8% and was redeemable at any time after 31 December 2007. It was agreed that the £1 million loan note would be structured as a Qualifying Corporate Bond (QCB).

If Bobby redeems his loan note *before* 6 April 2008, he would (based on the facts) qualify for full business taper relief up to the June 2006 sale. His *postponed* chargeable gain would be computed as follows:

	£
QCB consideration	1,000,000
Less: Part disposal base cost*	(333)
£1,000 x (£1m/(£2m + £1m))	
Chargeable gain	999,667

* The CGT base cost is apportioned between the cash proceeds (£2m) and the loan note (£1m).

When the redemption takes place (before 6 April 2008), business taper relief would be applied to Bobby's *chargeable* gain (*TCGA 1992, s 2A(2)(a)*) and therefore his CGT liability (for 2007/08) would be £96,287, calculated as follows:

	£
Chargeable gain	999,667
Less: Business taper relief @75%	(749,750)
Tapered gain	249,917
Less: Annual exemption	(9,200)
Taxable gain	240,717
CGT at 40% (Bobby's marginal tax rate)	£96,287

However, If Bobby encashed his loan note after 5 April 2008, his postponed chargeable gain would be dealt with under the new CGT regime (as announced in the Pre-Budget Report 2007 proposals). From 6 April 2008, CGT taper relief ceases to be available and all capital gains are taxed at a flat rate of 18% (irrespective of the period of ownership).

At the time of writing, there is no draft legislation as to how the new CGT rules would work. However, it is very likely that the gain crystallising on Bobby's redemption would simply be taxed at the flat CGT rate of 18%. Assuming the loan note was redeemed in (say) March 2009, Bobby's CGT liability would be £178,230, calculated as follows:

	£
Chargeable gain	999,667
Less: Annual exemption (say)	(9,500)
Taxable gain	990,167
CGT at 18%	£178,230

Non-qualifying corporate bonds (non-QCBs)

6.20 Different rules apply where the purchaser issues non-QCB loan notes. The terms of such loan notes will be designed so as to fall outside the criteria for a QCB. Thus, for example, a non-QCB loan note would be one which is convertible into the acquirer's shares or contains the right to subscribe for additional shares or securities. Where such notes are issued in exchange for shares they are deemed to be a security (and therefore do not necessarily have to be 'marketable', readily transferable and so on) (*TCGA 1992, s 251(6)*).

Non-QCB loan notes represent a security for CGT purposes and are treated as being exchanged under *TCGA 1992, s 135* – ie in exactly the same way as a share exchange. The appropriate part of the vendor's original base cost in the target company's shares is therefore treated as given for the non-QCB security at the original acquisition date(s).

Non-QCBs were often used under the taper relief regime where the vendor had not accrued their full (business) taper relief entitlement at the date of sale (since with a QCB, their taper relief clock 'stopped' at the sale date. With a non-QCB, the vendor's taper accrual would continue up to the redemption of the loan note, which usually ensured that maximum taper relief was given. However, the vendor would be exposed to a dilution in their taper relief where part of their post-sale period was a non-business one for taper relief. Clearly, such taper relief issues are only relevant where the non-QCB is encashed or otherwise disposed of before 6 April 2008.

After 5 April 2008, the gain arising on the redemption of a non-QCB (which would normally be computed by reference to an appropriate part of the vendor's original base cost), is likely to be taxed at the flat CGT rate of 18%.

Where the vendor is unable to obtain a commercial bank guarantee for the loan note, many feel that a non-QCB would be a more prudent alternative – this avoids the QCB-type risk of triggering a CGT charge on the cancellation of the loan note (for example, where the acquiring company becomes insolvent).

EARN-OUT DEALS

Basic tax treatment of 'cash-based' earn-outs

6.21 Owner-managed companies are sometimes sold on an 'earn-out' basis with deferred consideration being provided, calculated on a formula basis relating to the post-sale profits over (normally) the next two or three years. This will generally enable the vendor to enjoy extra consideration, calculated by reference to a formula based on the level of profits achieved by the Target company in the two or three years following the sale. An earn-out also limits the purchaser's 'downside' risk as the vendor will receive little or nothing if the anticipated profits are not met.

Under the principles established in the case of *Marren v Ingles* [1980] STC 500, the expected net present value of the earn-out right falls to be included as part of vendor's taxable consideration for the disposal of the shares.

Where the disposal occurs before 6 April 2008, the gain (enhanced by the value of that right) qualifies for the appropriate taper relief at the share sale date in the usual way.

6.22 As and when the earn-out payments are received, further CGT charges will arise in respect of the earn-out *right* itself (representing capital sums derived from the right to receive the earn-out and not the disposal of shares). Any pre-6 April 2008 gain on the earn-out payments (based on the earn-out payment received less the appropriate deductible base value of the right) will *not* be eligible for business asset taper. The right constitutes a *non-business* asset and therefore taper relief at the lower rate will only be available after three complete years from the share sale date. (In the case of a three-year earn-out period, only the final CGT disposal of the right is likely to qualify for 5% taper.)

One of the main potential problems arising from the *'Marren v Ingles'* treatment is the risk of being tax on an unrealised gain, ie the vendor would suffer tax on the *value of the right* (when their shares are sold).

In an extreme case, if the earn-out falls (well) below expectation, this could result in a capital loss arising on the disposal of the right in a subsequent tax year. In such cases, it is now possible to make an election under *TCGA 1992, s 279A* to carry the subsequent loss back to reduce the vendor's original capital gain.

Earn-outs satisfied in shares/loan notes

6.23 An earn-out may also be structured so that it must be satisfied in the form of shares and/or loan notes in the acquiring company (when the relevant earn-out consideration is determined). This enables the 'deferral' mechanism in *TCGA 1992, s 138A* to apply (automatically without the need for an election) and thus avoids the 'up-front' tax charge based on the value of the right. The vendor is then treated as exchanging his original shares (normally partly) in exchange for a deemed *(non-QCB) security* (representing the earn-out right).

6.24 For share/loan note-based earn-out deals concluded before 6 April 2008, *TCGA 1992, s 138A* has the effect of extending the vendor's taper period in the same way as an actual non-QCB. Provided the acquiring company or group has the requisite 'trading' status and one of the individual qualifying conditions are satisfied (for example, where the acquirer is listed and the vendor is continuing to work for the Target company, as will often be the case under an earn-out arrangement) (see **6.17**), this will qualify as a business period. When the actual 'earn-out' consideration shares or loan notes are issued, there will be a further CGT deferral into those shares/loan notes for CGT purposes.

However, taper relief will only be given where the actual earn-out consideration shares or loan notes are sold/encashed before 6 April 2008. The taper treatment of the earn-out consideration shares or loan notes would follow the relevant rules outlined above for exchanges involving shares and loan notes.

From 6 April 2008, taper will cease to accrue on the deemed *TCGA 1992, s 138A* debenture and the earn-out consideration shares/loan notes since it will no longer be relevant.

6.25 *Current tax planning issues for owner managed company sales*

Share/loan note-based earn-outs straddling the CGT changes

6.25 Although they have generally been unpopular hitherto (largely due to the 'up-front' tax charge arising under the *Marren v Ingles* ruling), cash-based earn-outs may now be more palatable where they are concluded (in anticipation of the CGT changes) before 6 April 2008

If a substantial part of the 'earn-out right' value at the sale date can be agreed with HMRC – Shares & Asset Valuation team, this would be taxed (along with any initial cash sale proceeds) at the effective rate of 10%. Broadly, any excess of the actual earn-out payments over the initial value of the right would then be subsequently taxed under the flat rate of 18%.

Where a sale has already been concluded with an earn-out satisfied in loan notes, the normal 'deferral' rule in *TCGA 1992, s 138A* would apply. In broad terms, the effect is twofold

- there is no initial CGT charge on the value of the right; and
- the CGT on the gains relating to the 'earn-out' loan notes is taxed when they are redeemed.

Where all or substantially all the 'earn-out' loan repayments would fall to be taxed under the post-5 April 2008 18% flat rate regime, vendors should consider whether it would be advantageous to make a *s 138A(2A)* election to disapply the *s 138A* deferral. The election for earn-out sales in 2006/07 and 2007/08 must be made by 31 January 2009 and 31 January 2010 respectively.

APPLICATION OF ITA 2007, S 684 ANTI-AVOIDANCE RULES

6.26 Under these provisions, an owner-managed company will invariably constitute what is known as a '*s 684*' (circumstance D) company and the sale of the company would constitute a 'transaction in securities'. HMRC are particularly likely to seek to apply this legislation where the vendor

- still retains a material equity interest in the company post-sale; or
- sells the company to a connected party (such as a trust or connected company).

If HMRC succeed in applying *ITA 2007, s 684* (previously *ICTA 1988, s 703*), all or part of the vendor's sale proceeds would effectively be taxed as a distribution/dividend at a higher (25%) tax rate.

Current tax planning issues for owner managed company sales **6.26**

This legislation does not apply where (amongst other things) the sale has been motivated by genuine commercial reasons (rather than tax avoidance motives). Vendors should always make use of the advance clearance procedure in *ITA 2007, s 701* (previously *ICTA 1988, s 707*), which enables them to obtain comfort before the deal takes place that HMRC are satisfied that the transaction is being made for commercial reasons and not for tax avoidance so that *ITA 2007, s 684* would not be applied.

Chapter 7

Winding-up the family or owner-managed company

Peter Rayney FCA, FTII, TEP, National Tax Technical Partner, BDO Stoy Hayward LLP

BACKGROUND

7.1 The shareholders of a family or owner-managed company may decide to wind it up voluntarily, perhaps following a sale of the assets and trade or a planned closure of the business. In such cases, there will often be a surplus available for distribution to the shareholders after the interests of the creditors have been satisfied. It will be essential to ensure that the surplus funds are distributed in a tax-efficient manner (see **7.20–7.29**). Where a company is wound up voluntarily, there may be time to implement appropriate corporate tax planning measures to increase the amount ultimately available to the company's shareholders.

In some cases, the existing shareholder(s) may simply wish to 'disincorporate'. This would normally entail winding the company up and transferring its trade and assets to the shareholder(s). The shareholders would then continue to carry on the trade through a sole trader or partnership structure (see **Chapter 5: Disincorporating a Business**).

7.2 If the company is wound up by a receiver or creditor, then the shareholders are likely to lose most if not all of their capital stake. It will then be necessary to consider what tax relief can be claimed in respect of their shares and any irrecoverable shareholder loans (see **7.44–7.52**). If the company is insolvent, the actions of the receiver/liquidator will be dictated by commercial requirements but, where possible, these should be conducted on the most tax efficient basis to enhance the amount available for both creditors and shareholders. However, there is no point in planning to reduce tax liabilities that are never going to be paid due to insufficiency of funds.

CONSEQUENCES FOR THE COMPANY

Pension provision

7.3 Before the company ceases trading the proprietors'/directors' pension provision should be considered. Unless full provision has been made, there will be a tax advantage in making 'top-up' payments to an approved scheme. Provided the pension contributions are *paid* in the final corporation tax accounting period (CTAP) (ie up to cessation of trade), a trading deduction can normally be claimed with no spreading of contributions. This will also reduce the funds remaining for distribution and hence the shareholder's exposure to tax.

Where a company has not made any pension provision for its proprietors/directors, it may be possible for it to enter into a Hancock annuity arrangement. The company would purchase an annuity from an insurance company before the trade ceases. Following the case of *Hancock v General Reversionary & Investment Co Ltd* (1918) 7 TC 358, the purchase of an annuity to fund a future pension was held to be deductible against profits – it was not a capital payment. The insurance company would then be responsible for paying the pension.

7.4 HMRC have confirmed that Hancock annuities can still be purchased post-A Day as long as they comply with the new pension rules. A specially purchased Hancock annuity for a retiring employee (before 75 years old) would normally be set up through a registered scheme in the same way as any other pension scheme, especially if a tax-free lump sum is to be provided. Tax relief for the employer contribution is subject to the 'wholly and exclusively' rule. (It is also possible for the company to purchase a Hancock annuity through a registered scheme.)

Under a Hancock-type arrangement, all benefits will have vested, so it does not have to satisfy the annual allowance rules. The lifetime allowance does apply. If the retiring employee is over 75 or has exhausted their lifetime allowance, then benefits could be provided by an employer-financed retirement benefit scheme.

Termination of CTAP and closure costs

7.5 The company's trade will usually have ceased before it is wound up and this will have a number of important tax consequences.

The cessation of the company's trade will bring about a termination of the company's current corporation tax accounting period ('CTAP') (*ICTA 1988, s 12(3)(c)*). Generally, this will accelerate the date on which the company pays its tax liability. Companies which do not pay their tax in instalments, must pay

7.6 *Winding-up the family or owner-managed company*

the corporation tax for the final CTAP within nine months following the end of that period. For other companies, the final instalment date is effectively brought forward, being due three months and 14 days after the end of the CTAP. Any unprovided expenses incurred after the cessation of trade (known as 'post-cessation' expenses) can only be offset against post-cessation receipts (see **7.11**), which reduces the prospect of obtaining relief (*ICTA 1988, s 105*).

In drawing up the tax computation to cessation, particular care must therefore be taken to ensure that specific provisions are made for all known trade expenses that have been incurred up to the date of cessation. This will include provisions for warranty claims and bad and 'impaired' trading and loan relationship debts.

7.6 HMRC will disallow any expenses incurred in connection with the cessation of trade. However, following the Privy Council's decision in *IRC v Cosmotron Manufacturing Co Ltd* [1997] STC 1134, HMRC will normally allow relief for contractual redundancy or severance payments made on cessation of trade. The rationale being that the payment is made under a pre-existing contractual or statutory obligation incurred as a consequence of the employees being employed for the purposes of the trade (*Tax Bulletin, Issue 39*).

Termination payments that do not qualify under the above principle, such as ex-gratia payments, can be specifically relieved under the statutory trading deduction rules. Specific statutory relief is given for statutory redundancy payments and any additional redundancy payments (up to three times the amount of the statutory redundancy payments). Such payments are treated as paid on the date of cessation *if* they are paid after the trade ceases (*ICTA 1988, ss 90, 579(2)*).

Sale of plant and industrial buildings

7.7 The cessation of trade will give rise to a deemed disposal of plant and machinery for capital allowance purposes, resulting in a balancing adjustment (*CAA 2001, s 61(2)*, Table, item 6). If the plant is sold either before or shortly after the trade ceases, the disposal value will generally be the net disposal proceeds (*CAA 2001, s 61(2)*, Table, item 1).

The sale of an industrial building no longer gives rise to any balancing adjustment. For a post-20 March 2007 disposal, the vendor avoids any recapture of industrial buildings allowances ('IBAs') where the building is sold for an amount exceeding its tax residue. However, as part of the phasing out of IBAs, the purchaser can continue to claim IBAs on the building (on the transitional basis) until their abolition on 31 March 2011.

Capital gains on property sale

7.8 The sale of the company's chargeable assets may also produce capital gains, giving rise to a significant tax liability. Broadly, the disposal of a property, etc is recognised for capital gains purposes when an unconditional contract for the sale is made (*TCGA 1992, s 28*). If the company has significant trading losses in the final CTAP, the company should enter into the sale contract for the property on or before it closes down the trade (although completion can take place afterwards). This would enable any gain on the property sale to be sheltered by the current trading losses (that might otherwise be forfeited on cessation).

Inevitably, there will be situations where it is not possible to sell the property until some time after the trade has ceased so that any gain cannot be offset by the trading losses generated in the final CTAP to cessation. Furthermore, the gain might be taxed at the full 28 % (30% up to 31 March 2008) tax rate if the company becomes a close investment holding company. In these cases, it may be beneficial to crystallise the gain before the trade ceases by arranging for the property to be sold to the owner-manager and then possibly licensed back to the company. The sale of the property would attract SDLT. Where appropriate, it might be possible for the property to be distributed *in specie* to the owner-manager. This would be treated as a distribution (taxable at an effective rate of 25% in the owner-manager's hands), but would be exempted from any SDLT charge. The company's disposal would be deemed to take place at market value.

Sale of trading stock

7.9 Where the company's trading stock and work in progress is sold to an *unconnected* UK trader, the actual sale proceeds will be credited in the trading account for tax purposes. In such cases, HMRC cannot impute a market value for tax purposes (*ICTA 1988, s 100(1)(a), (1A)(a)*).

Trading losses

7.10 The liquidator must consider how to make best use of any remaining tax adjusted trading losses. Trading losses can only be carried forward for offset against profits of the same trade (*ICTA 1988, s 393(1)*)). Consequently, any unrelieved tax losses cannot normally be carried forward beyond the date of cessation except where they can be offset against post-cessation receipts.

The main reliefs which are likely to be relevant for (tax adjusted) trading losses are as follows:

7.11 Winding-up the family or owner-managed company

- the offset of trading losses for the final CTAP to cessation against the company's other profits (before charges on income) of that period (*ICTA 1988, s 393A(1)(a)*);
- the offset of any remaining trading loss by carrying it back against the total profits (after deducting trading charges on income) for the previous year (*ICTA 1988, s 393A(1)(b)*);
- tax adjusted trading losses arising in the final 12 months before cessation of trade can be carried back against the company's total profits (*after* deducting trading charges on income) against the CTAPs falling within the *three* previous years on a LIFO basis (*ICTA 1988, s 393A(2A), (2B)*) – a company's CTAP terminates on cessation of trade – if an earlier CTAP straddles and ends in the final 12-month period, any trading loss for that CTAP is time apportioned and added to the terminal trading loss claim;
- trade charges for the final 12-month period can be used to augment the terminal loss claim.

Trade charges for CTAPs partly straddling the final 12 months are apportioned. However, trade charges are now likely to arise only in rare cases. For CTAPs straddling 1 April 2002 and later CTAPs, patent royalties recognised for accounting purposes on or after that date are normally included within the trading loss calculation (under the *FA 2002* intangible fixed assets regime).

Setting off trading losses against post-trading receipts

7.11 Income receipts arising after a company has ceased to trade are assessable as 'non-trading' post-cessation receipts (*ICTA 1988, ss 103* and *104*). This would include the write-back of excessive provisions (upon which tax relief was originally claimed), the unanticipated recovery of a bad debt that had been provided against or written-off and the release of trading liabilities after the trade has ceased.

Post-cessation expenses can be deducted against post-cessation receipts. However, if the company had unused trading losses at the date of cessation, HMRC accept that they can (exceptionally) be carried forward and offset against post-cessation receipts (see HMRC Business Income manual (at BIM 80535) which indicates that '*any unrelieved losses and unused capital allowances of the discontinued business*' can be deducted for the purposes of *ICTA 1988, s 105*.

(Until 5 April 2005, *ICTA 1988, s 108* allowed for post-cessation receipts to be carried back for up to six years to be treated as received *immediately prior* to the cessation, enabling them (for example) to be offset by trading losses brought forward under *ICTA 1988, s 393(1)*. However, *ICTA 1988, s 108* was repealed by *ITTOIA 2005*.)

Close investment holding company status

7.12 Where a close company ceases to carry on a trade or property investment business, it will usually be treated as a close investment holding company (CIHC) (*ICTA 1988, s 13A*). A CIHC cannot benefit from the lower small companies rate of corporation tax, nor can it claim small companies' marginal relief, whatever the level of its profits. In such cases, the company's post-cessation income and gains would be taxed at the main corporation tax rate.

If the company is not a CIHC throughout the CTAP which ends on the commencement of its winding up, it will not be treated as a CIHC for the next CTAP (*ICTA 1988, s 13A(4)*). However, where the company has ceased trading before it is wound up, this exemption is unlikely to apply. The company will normally have already become a CIHC before it goes into liquidation.

Pre-liquidation tax liabilities

7.13 The liquidator will need to take account of pre-liquidation tax liabilities as either preferential or ordinary claims (*IA 1986, ss 175, 386*). Broadly, preferential creditors have the right to repayment of their debts ahead of the *unsecured* creditors. Since 15 September 2003, preferential creditors have been confined to liabilities broadly representing unpaid employee remuneration, etc for the four months before the winding-up. Previously, certain 'government' debts were also counted as preferential debts which included unpaid PAYE and National Insurance contributions, etc for the 12 months prior to the receiver's/liquidator's appointment and unpaid VAT arising within the previous six months. However, unpaid PAYE and NIC ceased to be a preferred creditor from 15 September 2003 onwards.

7.14 Assessed taxes are not preferred debts, so any unpaid pre-liquidation corporation tax would rank as an unsecured creditor. Corporation tax arising during the liquidation is, however, normally treated as a liquidation expense (*Re Toshoku Finance UK plc, Kahn (liquidators of Toshoku Finance UK plc) v IRC* [2000] STC 301).

A practical approach will normally be required by the liquidator of the insolvent company when dealing with the company's tax affairs. He must inform HMRC of his appointment and determine the outstanding corporation tax position. Where the company is insolvent or has substantial brought forward tax losses, HMRC may be prepared to agree a 'nil liability' position without the need to submit detailed tax computations (but a CT600 must be submitted). However, if the liquidator wishes to agree an amount of trading losses for the purposes of a loss relief claim, HMRC will require detailed computations and accounts.

7.15 *Winding-up the family or owner-managed company*

Post-liquidation tax liabilities

7.15 The commencement of a winding-up terminates the company's current CTAP and a new accounting period will begin. Each successive accounting period will last for 12 months, with the final accounting period ending on the date the winding-up is completed (*ICTA 1988, s 12(7)*). Similar rules apply (from September 2004) where a company goes into administration.

Corporation tax liabilities which arise during the course of the winding-up would be treated as an expense or disbursement of the liquidation (see *Re Beni-Felkai Mining Co Ltd* (1933) 18 TC 632). In most cases, the only taxable income received during the winding-up period is interest receivable on realised funds. However, interest received from HMRC on overpaid corporation tax is exempt from tax (where the amount is less than £2,000).

As a necessary disbursement of the liquidation, the tax liabilities must (together with any overdue tax) be met in priority to the claims of all creditors and the liquidator's remuneration. However, where appropriate, the liquidator can apply to the court for an Order of Priority to be made to ensure that his remuneration and expenses can be dealt with equitably.

Legal formalities

Members' voluntary liquidation

7.16 The shareholders of a solvent company can proceed to wind up the company voluntarily. Generally, a special resolution of the shareholders is required to place the company in voluntary liquidation. Before this is done, the directors must make a statutory declaration of solvency. After having made a full inquiry, the directors must declare that the company will be able to pay its debts within 12 months following the commencement of the winding-up.

A member's voluntary liquidation must be dealt with by a licensed insolvency practitioner. Under a liquidation, a company can only be restored to the Register within a period of two years after the winding-up has been completed (although claims for death or serious injury can be made at any time). Such an order can be brought by a member or creditor or any other interested person. It therefore provides greater protection as regards dealing with creditors. The creditor who surfaces after the company has been liquidated has only two years to put the company back on the register and even then can only overturn distributions made if the liquidator did not take proper steps to contact creditors. Quite often, the costs of a formal voluntary liquidation may seem relatively high compared to the value of the company's assets.

Dissolution under *CA 1985, s 652*

7.17 A solvent company may be dissolved as a result of the company's name being struck off the register by the Registrar of Companies under *Companies Act 1985, s 652*. This route is sometimes preferred to a liquidation. HMRC are prepared to treat a dissolution under *CA 1985, s 652* as a 'winding-up' for tax purposes under ESC C16 (see 7.21). However, *CA 1985, s 652A* imposes additional stringent requirements on the directors such as the need to notify all shareholders, employees, creditors, etc with tough penalties for non-compliance. Furthermore, it is necessary to wait at least three months after the trade has ceased before an application can be made.

7.18 Where a dissolution is used, it is vital that any remaining assets must first be stripped out of the company, otherwise they will pass to the Crown under the '*bona vacantia*' rule in *CA 1985, s 654*.

This is an important consideration, as the strict legal position is that share capital (and other non-distributable reserves) cannot be repaid to shareholders on a dissolution. This means that any share capital, etc, would fall to be 'vacant goods' and would therefore pass to the Crown.

For example, if a company had share capital of £20,000 and distributable reserves of £80,000, only £80,000 could be repaid to its shareholders under a dissolution (which would be treated as 'capital' under ESC C16). The share capital of £20,000 would strictly pass to the Crown. Consequently, if the entire £100,000 was paid out, the company would have made an unauthorised distribution of £20,000. This would fall to be recoverable by the company, and the right to recover the £20,000 would pass to the Crown once the company was 'struck-off'. The Office of the Treasury Solicitor has indicated that, in practice, it will not seek to recover unauthorised distributions of less than £4,000.

7.19 The principle of *bona vacantia* should be borne in mind when weighing up the costs of appointing a liquidator as opposed to using the seemingly less expensive ESC C16 'dissolution' route.

In contrast to the 'two-year' period allowed for liquidations, a dissolved company can be restored by a court order within 20 years from the publication of the striking off notice in the Gazette (*CA 1985, s 653*). Any member or creditor who 'feels aggrieved' can apply to the court for such an order. It would therefore be possible for a creditor to come forward at any time during the 20-year period to overturn a transfer of assets to the members.

7.20 *Winding-up the family or owner-managed company*

DEALING WITH SURPLUS AVAILABLE TO SHAREHOLDERS

Capital distributions

7.20 Where a company has surplus funds (ie after its creditors have been paid), it is necessary to decide how these can be extracted for the shareholders' benefit in the most tax efficient manner.

Distributions made in the course of dissolving or winding-up the company are treated as 'capital distributions' and are therefore chargeable to CGT (*TCGA 1992, s 122*). A distribution made to shareholders during the course of the winding-up does not count as an 'income' distribution for tax purposes and therefore no tax credit is available to the recipient shareholder (*ICTA 1988, s 209(1)*).

7.21 Under ESC C16, HMRC will treat a distribution made prior to a dissolution as having been made under a formal winding-up, and therefore as a capital payment. Certain assurances must be given to the Inspector beforehand. Normally, the Inspector will require that any remaining tax liabilities are paid and also confirm that, once the assets have been distributed, the company will request the Registrar of Companies to strike the company off the register. Although ESC 16 merely requires the company and its shareholders to *agree* to pay any corporation tax, in practice, HMRC insist that it is actually paid otherwise they will object to the 'striking-off' application.

Inspectors now appear to insist on the formal signatures of both the company secretary (on behalf of the company) and *all* the shareholders (as opposed to the company's agents) on the application for ESC 16 treatment (see *Taxation*, 25 July 2002, p 453).

7.22 Strictly speaking, a company cannot distribute its share capital and other non-distributable reserves under the 'striking off' procedure – this can only be done under a formal liquidation. It is therefore recommended that the 'striking off' procedure is only used where the share capital is relatively small (see **7.18**).

A shareholder is treated as making a disposal for CGT purposes when he becomes entitled to receive the capital distribution from the company (*TCGA 1992, s 122(1)*). The commencement of the liquidation does not trigger any deemed disposal for the shareholder.

Capital distributions made before 6 April 2008 are eligible for taper relief (see **7.23**). Taper relief is given against the indexed gain (with the indexation relief being frozen at April 1998, where appropriate). Under the Pre-Budget Report 2007 proposals, capital distributions made after 5 April 2008 do not carry any taper relief (or indexation entitlement).

Taper relief on capital distributions made before 6 April 2008

Non-business and 'inactive' periods

7.23 Taper relief is only given on capital distributions made before 6 April 2008. In such cases, the vast majority of proprietorial shareholders should have accrued full business taper up to the point when the company ceases to trade.

Some established minority shareholders would, however, suffer a restriction in business taper for the two years to 5 April 2000 if they did not qualify under the more stringent *Finance Act 1998* regime. This will be the case where they held less than 25% of the voting rights or less than 5% if they worked for the company on a full time basis. From 6 April 2000, all unlisted shareholders will 'clock up' a business period for taper relief until the company stops trading.

7.24 Once the company ceases to trade, the shares become a 'non-business' asset under general taper relief principles. Thus, the gain on any (pre-5 April 2008) distribution would normally be subject to time apportionment for business/non-business taper relief to be applied.

For capital distributions paid *after 16 April 2002*, it is, however, important to note that *TCGA 1992, Sch A1, para 11A* might be used to exclude the 'post-trading' period completely if the (close) company becomes 'inactive'. For these purposes, the 'winding-up' of the affairs of a company would be regarded as an *activity* and so this would count as a period of ownership for taper relief purposes. This would include the formal winding-up of the company by a liquidator as well as where the directors (or some other person) deals with the post-cessation business affairs of the company, such as selling assets and paying creditors. However, where a company is in liquidation, but there are *no* winding-up activities, this will be an 'inactive' period (*Tax Bulletin, Issue 61*).

7.25 The mere holding of cash on current or deposit account or the making of loans to an associated company or participator would not be regarded as a period of activity (*TCGA 1992, Sch A1, para 11A(1)–(4)*).

On this basis, there appears to be at least a tenable argument that where, for example, a company ceases to trade and is subsequently dissolved under *CA 1985, ss 652–652A*, the period after the trade ceases should be ignored for taper purposes. However, where the company's activities and assets are being formally wound up under the *Insolvency Act 1986*, this is generally regarded as a 'non-trading' activity.

Apportionment between business and non-business periods

7.26 When a pre-6 April 2008 capital distribution is made (resulting in a CGT disposal), taper relief would generally be computed by reference to the

7.27 *Winding-up the family or owner-managed company*

period for which the shares have been held as 'business' and (if applicable) 'non-business' assets over the relevant period of ownership. The gain is deemed to have accrued evenly over the relevant period for apportionment purposes (*TCGA 1992, Sch A1, paras 3(2),(3) and 21*). However, any period of 'inactivity' is excluded under the *TCGA 1992, Sch A1, para 11A* rule mentioned in **7.24**.

The indexed gain is therefore time-apportioned over the relevant period of ownership between the 'business' and (if applicable) 'non-business' periods. As indicated above, some minority shareholders may also have a non-business period of two years (or less) before 6 April 2000.

7.27 The more beneficial business asset taper relief is applied to the 'business' element of the gain, calculated by reference to the *total* relevant period of ownership. Similarly, non-business taper relief is applied to the 'non-business' portion of the gain, based on the entire ownership period (see **Example 7.1**) (from 6 April 2000, the bonus year for shares held before 17 March 1998 is only given when computing 'non-business' taper).

The apportionment of the gains and the increase in taper relief for each additional *complete* year produces some interesting results, which must be considered when planning the timing of a capital distribution.

Timing of capital distributions

7.28 Capital distributions must be paid before 6 April 2008 to obtain taper relief. As a general rule, accelerating the capital distribution increases the gain qualifying for business asset taper relief. Thus, the sooner the winding-up can be completed, the better. However, in practice, the actual tax effect will depend on the length of the shareholder's business period and the size of their gain. The distribution of the cash usually depends on the speed of collecting debts and realising other assets. Where cash is likely to be collected over a lengthy period, taper relief could be improved by making interim distributions.

7.29 Where substantial delays are anticipated in the making of capital distributions, the shareholder(s) may find it beneficial to trigger their CGT disposal before 6 April 2008 by transferring their shares to a settlor-interested trust. The resultant capital gain would be based on the market value of the shares (no 'hold-over' relief is available). This should be done before the trade ceases to give maximum taper relief. (Furthermore, since this will be a chargeable transfer for IHT, this will ensure BPR is given on the transfer. Some care must be exercised over timing issues since the transfer of the shares into the trust does not realise any cash. Assuming the transfer takes place before 6 April 2008 sufficient cash may be realised by the liquidator (or directors) and paid out to shareholders before the 31 January 2009 CGT payment date. (The trust receives

Calculation of taxable gain on capital distribution

Pre-6 April 2008 distributions

7.30 The shareholder's capital gain or loss on the receipt of a capital distribution is effectively computed as a disposal of his interest in the shares, as follows:

	£
Capital distribution	X
Less Base value of shares	
Cost/Deemed March 1982 value	(X)
Unindexed gain/loss	X
Less Indexation (frozen at April 1998)	(X)
Chargeable gain	X
Less Taper relief (apportioned between post-5 April 1998 business and non-business periods)	(X)
Taxable gain (subject to any annual exemption)	X

Post-5 April 2008 distributions

	£
Capital distribution	X
Less Base value of shares	
Cost/Deemed March 1982 value	(X)
Taxable capital gain/loss (before any annual exemption) taxed at flat CGT rate of 18%	X

Example 7.1

Taper relief on capital distribution gain

7.31 Ferdinand Ltd ceased trading on 6 April 2007 after selling its trade and assets. The company was then immediately wound up with a capital distribution of £650,000 being paid on completion of the winding up on 6 October 2007.

7.32 *Winding-up the family or owner-managed company*

Mr Rio incorporated Ferdinand Ltd in March 1979 with 100,000 £1 ordinary shares and his shareholding was worth £200,000 at 31 March 1982.

His capital gain on the capital distribution would be computed as follows:

		£
Capital distribution		650,000
Less March 1982 value		(200,000)
Indexation (March 1982 to April 1998 (max)) £200,000 × 104.7%		(209,400)
Indexed gain		240,600
Less Taper relief (see below*)		(176,018)
Capital gain (before annual exemption)		**£64,582**

*Taper relief

Business period 6/4/98–6/4/2007	= 9.0 years
Non-business period 7/4/2007–6/10/2007	= 0.5 years
	9.5 years

Business taper relief
£240,600 × 9/9.5 years = £227,937
£227,937 × 75%   = 170,953

Non-business taper relief
£240,600 × 0.5/9.5 years = £12,663
£12,663 × 40% (10 years, including bonus year)   = 5,065

Total taper relief   £176,018

Multiple capital distributions

7.32 If a shareholder receives more than one capital distribution, all but the last one will be treated as a part disposal in respect of the shares. The normal

$$\frac{A}{A + B}$$

part disposal formula in *TCGA 1992, s 42* will be used to apportion the base cost of the shares where:

A = the amount of the interim capital distribution

B = the residual share value at the date of the interim distribution.

Winding-up the family or owner-managed company **7.32**

In practice, a relatively relaxed approach is taken with regard to agreeing interim valuations of shares (for the purpose of calculating 'B') where the liquidation is expected to be completed within two years of the first distribution (SP/D3). For example, if all the distributions are made before the CGT is calculated, HMRC will normally agree that the residual share value at the date of any interim distribution equals the total amount of subsequent distributions, without any discount for the delay in the receipt of the subsequent payments.

Depending on the amounts involved it may be beneficial to phase the timing of the capital distributions over as many tax years as possible. This will enable the shareholders to benefit from more than one annual exemption. Although all parties may be anxious to conclude the liquidation as quickly as possible, by timing the liquidation shortly before the start of the tax year, it may be possible to pay capital distributions over three separate tax years (but paid over a period of only (say) 18 months). Where there are a number of shareholders, the benefits from using multiple annual exemptions may be considerable.

Example 7.2

Tax treatment of multiple capital distributions

Brooking Ltd went into liquidation on 10 March 2007, having ceased trading on 6 February 2007. After the trade ceased, the company leased out its trading premises on a short lease until the property was sold during the liquidation.

Mr Brooking formed the company in September 1989, subscribing for all the 20,000 ordinary £1 shares at par.

The liquidator made the following distributions to Mr Brooking from the residual profits and initial capital. (The final distribution is made before 6 April 2008 to ensure taper relief.)

	£	£
6 July 2007	45,000	
31 March 2008 (final)	24,000	
Mr Brooking's CGT computations would be as follows:		
2007/08:	£	
6 July 2007		
Capital distribution	45,000	

7.32 *Winding-up the family or owner-managed company*

	£	£
Less Part disposal cost £20,000 × £45,000 / (£45,000 + £24,000)	(13,044)	
Indexation (Sept 89–April 98 (max)): £13,044 × 39.5%	(5,152)	
Chargeable gain (before taper relief)	26,804	
Less: Taper relief (see below)	(19,681)	
		£7,123
31 March 2008	£	
Final capital distribution	24,000	
Less Cost: £20,000 less £13,044 used in July 2007	(6,956)	
Indexation (Sept 89–April 98 (max)): £6,956 × 39.5%	(2,748)	
Chargeable gain (before taper relief)	14,296	
Less: Taper relief (see below)	(10,138)	
		4,158
Total gains		11,281
Less: Annual exemption		(9,200)
Taxable gain		2,081

Taper relief

		6 July 2007		31 March 2008
Business asset period	6/4/1998–6/2/2007	106 months		106 months
Non-business asset period	7/2/2007–6/7/2007	5 months	7/2/2007–31/3/2008 (say)	14 months
		111 months		120 months

Business asset taper relief	£	£
£26,804 × 106/111 × 75% (9 yrs)	19,198	
£14,296 × 106/120 × 75% (9 yrs)		9,471
Non-business asset taper relief		
£26,804 × 5/111 × 40% (10 yrs, incl bonus year)	483	
£14,296 × 14/120 × 40% (10yrs, incl bonus year)		667
Taper relief	19,681	10,138

Small capital distributions

7.33 'Small' interim distributions are deducted against the shareholder's base cost, thus effectively postponing any gain (*TCGA 1992, s 122(2)*). For these purposes, a distribution not exceeding £3,000 is always taken as small. In all other cases, the distribution is accepted as 'small' provided it does not exceed 5% of the value of the relevant shareholding at the relevant date. However, HMRC do not insist on deducting the small proceeds against the cost where it is beneficial for the shareholder to crystallise a capital gain, for example, if it can be covered by an otherwise unused annual CGT exemption (*Tax Bulletin, Issue 27*).

Where the capital distribution exceeds the allowable CGT base cost, the 'small proceeds' rule does not apply. Instead, the shareholder can elect to offset the capital distribution against his base cost (*TCGA 1992, s 122(4)*). Once the base cost has been fully used, the balance of proceeds and any subsequent distributions will be fully chargeable to CGT.

Distributions in specie

7.34 If a liquidator distributes assets to the shareholders in lieu of their entitlement to a cash distribution, this will still constitute a capital distribution for tax purposes (*TCGA 1992, s 122(5)*). This will always be treated as a transaction at market value because the shareholders are connected with the company (*TCGA 1992, s 17(1)(a)*).

In contrast to a capital distribution for cash, a distribution *in specie* involves two disposals – one by the company in respect of the asset disposed of (which should be exempt from stamp duty or stamp duty land tax (as appropriate)) and one by the shareholder in respect of his shares. As there is no tax credit available on a capital distribution, this gives rise to an acute form of the 'double charge' effect.

7.35 *Winding-up the family or owner-managed company*

PRE-LIQUIDATION/DISSOLUTION DIVIDEND VERSUS CAPITAL DISTRIBUTION

Benefits of CGT treatment

7.35 Where a capital distribution is made before 6 April 2008, it will be entitled to a taper relief reduction. Since business taper relief is likely to be available in many cases, the receipt of a capital distribution in the winding-up is likely to be preferred (to a pre-liquidation 'income' distribution at an effective rate of 25%).

The potential advantage secured by taper relief clearly depends on the post-5 April 1998 ownership period for taper purposes and the potential dilution of taper caused by the delay in paying out the capital distribution.

Post- 5 April 2008 capital distributions

7.36 Capital distributions made after 5 April 2008 do not attract any taper relief. The capital gain is simply taxed at the flat rate of 18% (the timing of the distribution and the length of any 'non-trading period' ceases to have any effect on the tax rate).

When pre-liquidation dividends are beneficial

7.37 Pre-liquidation dividends would be subject to income tax at the effective rate of 25% on the amount received (due to the availability of the 10% tax credit). However, a flat CGT rate of 18% applies from 6 April 2008 (based on the Pre-Budget Report 2007 proposals). Consequently, under this regime, it will always be more tax efficient to extract the maximum possible amount as a capital distribution.

Different considerations apply to the planning under the pre-6 April 2008 taper regime. In such cases liquidation dividends may be preferred where, for one reason or another, the shareholders cannot benefit from (full) business taper – for example – where the company does not qualify as a trading company (or holding company of a trading group) for all or part of the 'taper' ownership period. However, for long-standing shareholders, as non-business taper relief steadily increases, the tax differential between 'income' dividends and 'capital gain' distributions becomes quite small.

Indeed the minimum effective tax rate in 2007/08 for non-business taper is 24% (for a higher-rate taxpayer). At this point, capital distributions are marginally beneficial.

Winding-up the family or owner-managed company **7.37**

On the other hand, where the shareholders have only held their shares for a relatively short period, pre-liquidation dividends can generate larger tax savings.

An income dividend must be paid before the company is wound up (ie before the liquidator is appointed or, if the company is being struck off, *before* steps are taken to dissolve it). The optimum income dividend/capital distribution mix will depend on the shareholder's indexed based cost, etc.

Example 7.3

Planning a pre-liquidation dividend

Pardew Ltd sold its commercial property letting business as a going concern on 6 October 2007. It was then decided to immediately put the company into liquidation and distribute the remaining cash to its sole shareholder, Mr Alan. (Given the substantial level of share capital it would be unwise to proceed via a dissolution – see **7.11**.)

Mr Alan incorporated Pardew Ltd in June 2001, subscribing for 100,000 £1 ordinary shares at par. Pardew Ltd acquired its first property for letting in May 2002 and has always carried on the business of commercial property letting. It is not, therefore, a 'qualifying company' for business taper relief. Mr Alan will therefore only be entitled to taper relief at the 'non-business' rate.

Pardew Ltd's current summarised balance sheet (after providing for dissolution expenses) is as follows:

Current assets	£
Debtors	29,000
Cash	601,400
	630,400
Less Current liabilities	
Corporation tax and sundry expenses	(54,600)
	£575,800
Financed by:	
Share capital	100,000
Reserves	475,800
	£575,800

7.37 *Winding-up the family or owner-managed company*

Capital distribution

If the reserves are distributed and share capital repaid to Mr Alan on completion of the winding-up on (say) 6 December 2007, this will be treated as a capital distribution, chargeable to CGT, as follows.

	£
Capital distribution	575,800
Less Base cost of shares	(100,000)
Gain	475,800
Less Non-business taper relief £475,800 × 15% (5 years)	(71,370)
Capital gain	404,430
Less Annual exemption	(9,200)
Chargeable gain	£395,230
CGT thereon at 40%	£158,092
Effective CGT rate on indexed gain $£158,092/£475,800 \times 100$	33.2%

Mix of pre-liquidation dividend and capital distribution

If the reserves were paid to Mr Alan *before* the commencement of the liquidation, this will be treated as an ordinary 'income' dividend in his hands, taxed at an effective rate of 25%. However, it would not be efficient to pay the full amount of reserves out as a pre-liquidation dividend. Ideally, a shareholder should receive a capital distribution on liquidation equal to the combined amount of his CGT *indexed* base value and any other CGT exemptions. This part of the capital 'return' carries no CGT liability (however, virtually all the taper relief would have to be forgone as this relief is based on the *chargeable* gain).

The 'excess' amount that should be extracted as an income dividend is calculated as follows:

	£	£
Total amount to be returned		575,800
Less Amount to be returned as a 'capital distribution' with no CGT liability:		
Base cost of shares	(100,000)	
Taper relief on annual exemption – £9,200 × 15%/85%	(1,624)	
Annual exemption	(9,200)	

	£	£
Capital distribution to retain	(110,824)	Say (110,800)
Therefore pre-liquidation dividend should be		465,000

Mr Alan's tax liability would then be:

	£
Dividend	465,000
Add: Tax credit (10/90)	51,667
Gross dividend	516,667
Income tax @ 32.5%	167,917
Less Tax credit	(51,667)
Dividend tax liability	£116,250

The capital distribution of £110,800 would be paid once the company is wound up. No CGT liability would arise as it would be covered by Mr Alan's CGT base cost, taper relief and annual exemption. Since Mr Alan would only be entitled to 15% non-business taper, the tax saved by paying a pre-liquidation dividend in 2006/07 is £41,842 (ie £158,092 *less* £116,250).

LIQUIDATION AND *ITA 2007, S 684* ISSUES

Phoenix company arrangements

7.38 Under the pre-6 April 2008 business asset taper relief regime, some owner-managers were tempted to retain profits in their companies with the view to liquidating them after the full taper rate of 75% has been accrued. The tax-driven aim here would be to extract the retained reserves as a capital gain on liquidation at an effective CGT rate of around 10% (ie chargeable gain representing 25% of full gain on capital distribution taxed at 40%). Although this tax differential reduces after 5 April 2008, there would still be a tax advantage in doing this with an 18% CGT rate. The business could subsequently be carried on under identical or similar ownership via a new company – often called a 'phoenix company'. There may of course be tax charges and stamp duty land tax arising on the transfer of the assets to the new company.

However, such planning aspirations are fraught with a number of technical difficulties. Under the taper regime, HMRC may be able to argue that the accumulated profits give rise to 'non-trading' assets on the company's balance sheet. If the 'surplus' cash reserves have been retained over a lengthy period before a subsequent 'capital' distribution to the shareholders, the argument

7.39 *Winding-up the family or owner-managed company*

would run that they are never going to be required for a trading purpose (HMRC are likely to adopt a far more stringent approach to surplus cash in such cases as opposed to where cash is built up within a 'continuing' trading company. If HMRC succeeded on this point, the company would not qualify as a trading company for a substantial part of the shareholders' ownership period. This would mean that their taper relief would be (largely) diluted by the consequential 'non-business' period. The benefits of obtaining a capital gains' receipt would then be squandered.

Section 684 and the Joiner case

7.39 It has been firmly established that (what is now) *ITA 2007, ss 684* and *689 (previously ICTA 1988, s 703)* can apply where a company (with retained profits) is liquidated with its business being sold to another company under the same or substantially similar ownership. This is broadly what happened in *IRC v Joiner* [1975] STC 601. However, in that case, the House of Lords held that the arrangement was only caught by the 'transactions in securities' legislation because an agreement which varied the shareholders' rights to a capital distribution on a winding-up constituted a 'transaction in securities'.

7.40 The *Joiner* case also concluded that simply putting a company into liquidation was not sufficient (by itself) to be a transaction in securities. The Revenue subsequently issued a statement that (what is now) *s 684* would *not be* applied to an 'ordinary liquidation'. This effectively means a genuine winding-up of a company, whether it comes to an end or its business is taken over by another entity that is under substantially different control, is unlikely to be vulnerable to a challenge.

On the other hand, HMRC are likely to challenge the transfer of a business to another 'commonly controlled' company in the course of a winding-up. A similar stance may be taken where the shareholder(s) seek(s) to 'disincorporate' their company to enable them to continue to carry on the trade as a sole trade or partnership.

In contrast, HMRC are likely to accept cases where the businesses are being transferred as part of a genuine reconstruction operation within *TCGA 1992, ss 136* and *139* using *Insolvency Act* 1986, *s 110*.

RELIEF FOR SHAREHOLDERS OF INSOLVENT COMPANIES

Negligible value claim

7.41 Where the shares are worthless, a shareholder can make a 'negligible value' claim. There is no specified form for making the claim, but it should clearly identify the shareholding which is claimed as becoming of negligible value, the date on which the capital loss is deemed to arise (see below), and the claim is being made under *TCGA 1992, s 24(2)*.

HMRC should accept a 'negligible value' claim where the shares are 'worth next to nothing' (see *Capital Gains Manual* CG 13124). This will enable the shareholder to be treated as disposing of their holding for no or virtually no consideration (indexation cannot be used to increase or create a capital loss). The deemed disposal does not take place until the claim is made (*TCGA 1992, s 24(2)(a)*). However, *TCGA 1992, s 24(2)(b)* permits a negligible value 'capital loss' claim to be backdated to an earlier date specified in the claim, which must be within two years before the start of the tax year in which the claim is made. Importantly, a 'backdated' claim can only be made if the shares were (held by the claimant and) also worthless at that earlier date.

7.42 Sometimes, negligible value claims are negated because HMRC successfully show that the shareholder's base cost is substantially less than the amount paid for the shares. This is often the case where the shares have been subscribed for shortly before the date of the negligible value claim and are deemed to have been acquired at a (low) market value (either by way of the 'non arm's length bargain rule' in *TCGA 1992, s 17(2)* or on a share reorganisation within *TCGA 1992, s 128(2)*).

It is perhaps worth noting that the Inspector has the discretion to accept certain types of negligible value where the claim is free from any doubt or difficulty (such as the need to agree share valuations). These are for capital losses of under £100,000 on shares in UK unquoted companies that, at the date of the claim or any earlier specified date:

- were in an insolvent liquidation; or
- had ceased trading with no assets.

7.43 If a shareholder does not make a negligible value claim, their capital loss will then be deemed to arise when the company is finally dissolved. In practice, this would be when the liquidation is completed or when the company is finally dissolved – a disposal arises for CGT purposes when the shares are finally extinguished (*TCGA 1992, s 24(1)*).

Example 7.4

Backdated negligible value claim

Mr Cohen's company, Craven Cottage Ltd, went into liquidation in July 2000. The liquidation was completed in July 2007 without Mr Cohen receiving any distributions from the liquidator.

7.44 *Winding-up the family or owner-managed company*

Mr Cohen formed the company in June 1986 subscribing for 10,000 £1 ordinary shares.

A negligible value claim is made in January 2008, which backdated the deemed disposal of his shares to March 2007 (ie 2006/07).

The calculation of the allowable loss arising in 2006/07 is as follows:

	£
Capital distribution	–
Less Cost	(10,000)
Allowable loss	(10,000)

Income tax relief for capital losses on shares

Application of *ITA 2007, s 131* relief to companies in liquidation

7.44 In certain circumstances, shareholders may be able to make a claim to offset the capital loss arising on their shares against their other *taxable* income (under the share loss relief provisions in *ITA 2007, s 131* (before 6 April 2007, *ICTA 1988, s 574*).

For shares issued after 5 April 1998, *s 131* relief is only available if the company is a qualifying company for EIS purposes. Income tax relief is particularly valuable, as capital losses cannot be relieved unless and until the shareholder makes a capital gain.

In relation to liquidations, income tax relief can be claimed in respect of a capital loss arising on:

- a capital distribution during a winding-up;
- The cancellation (extinction) of the shares under *TCGA 1992, s 24(1)*; or
- a negligible value claim under *TCGA 1992, s 24(2)* (*ITA 2007, s 131(3)* – before 6 April 1998, *ICTA 1988, s 575(1)*).

7.45 In many cases, it may be beneficial to establish that a deemed capital loss has arisen by making a negligible value claim. This treats the shares as having been disposed and immediately reacquired at their negligible value. As far as timing is concerned, the deemed capital loss can be specified to arise at the date of the claim or at any time within the two years before the start of the tax year in which the claim was made (provided the shares were also 'negligible' at that time). Where *s 131* is claimed for a deemed 'negligible value' loss, a clear

Winding-up the family or owner-managed company 7.46

claim must also be made under *TCGA 1992, s 24(2)*. This was confirmed by the Special Commissioner's decision in *Marks v McNally* (2004) STC (SCD) 503, where a share loss relief claim was denied because of the failure to show unambiguously that the capital loss was being claimed under *TCGA 1992, s 24(2)*.

Strictly, *s 131* relief cannot be claimed for a capital loss arising on the dissolution of the company. However, by concession, the relief can be claimed where:

(a) the company has no assets and is dissolved; *and*

(b) the shareholder has not received a capital distribution in the course of the dissolution or winding-up of the company *or* where an anticipated final distribution has not been made; *and*

(c) a negligible value claim has not been made under *TCGA 1992, s 24(2)* (ESC D46).

If reliance cannot be placed on the concession to obtain relief on a dissolution, then a negligible value claim must be made while the shares still exist.

'Subscriber share' requirement

7.46 Shareholders can only obtain share loss relief (against their taxable income) if they originally *subscribed* for the shares. Therefore, relief cannot be claimed for shares acquired 'second-hand'.

Special identification rules deal with cases where the claimant shareholder has a 'mixed' shareholding – ie has 'subscriber' shares qualifying for *s 131* relief and other shares acquired by purchase, gift, etc. In such cases, *ITA 2007, s 148* provides that (from 6 April 2007) the shares are deemed to be identified on the same basis as under the normal (pre-6 April 2008) CGT identification rules – which is broadly a last in, first out (LIFO basis). Thus, if a capital loss arises on a July 2007 disposal of 5,000 shares which were part of a mixed holding of 20,000 shares – 10,000 purchased on 8 July 2006 and 10,000 originally subscribed for on 18 June 1990 – then no *s 131* relief could be claimed on them. This is because the 5,000 shares would be identified with the July 2006 acquisition (which were not acquired via a subscription). Where it is necessary to identify shares out of a 'frozen' pool at 6 April 1982 (treated as a single asset), the individual shares within the pool are also identified on LIFO basis for this purpose. However, on a liquidation all the shares would generally be treated as disposed of at the same time.

Where the shareholding is made up of BES shares, EIS 'income tax' relief shares and EIS 'CGT deferral' shares, these 'subscription' shares are broadly identified on a FIFO basis.

7.47 *Winding-up the family or owner-managed company*

Detailed conditions for s 131 relief

7.47 The 'insolvent' company must also satisfy numerous conditions. In the context of an insolvency or winding-up, the shares will qualify for relief under *ITA 2007, s 131* relief if they either:

- Qualified for EIS relief under *ITA 2007, Pt 5* (or before 6 April 2007, *ICTA 1988, Ch 3, Pt 7*); or

Main requirements	
1.	Company must be unquoted (ie none of the company's shares or securities must be marketed to the general public)
2.	Company must be an eligible trading company (broadly, a 'qualifying company' for EIS relief purposes)
3.	Business of company must be carried out wholly or mainly in the UK throughout the relevant period

- Satisfied the relevant conditions for 'non-EIS shares' in (what is now) *ITA 2007, ss 134–137*.

Main requirements	
1.	Company must be UK resident and unquoted (ie none of its shares or securities must be marketed to the general public)
2.	Company must: (a) have been actively trading at some time within the three years before the disposal date (without subsequently becoming an investment, share or land dealing company); and (b) have traded for at least six years before it ceased trading, although a shorter period will qualify provided the company did not engage in any of the 'excluded' investment, share or land activities in (a) above before the disposal date
3.	Company's trade must be carried out wholly or mainly in the UK throughout the relevant period

Operation of s 131 relief

7.48 *Section 131* relief for disposals (or deemed 'negligible value' disposals) is claimed against the shareholder's income for the tax year of the disposal *and/or* the previous tax year. Where a claim is made for both years, the claim must specify the year against which the *s 131* deduction is to be claimed first. Otherwise, the claim must specify the relevant year being claimed (*ITA 2007, s 132*). Under self-assessment, any carry back claim is treated as a claim for the later year. The relief is calculated as the reduction in the previous year's tax liability as a result of the claim. The consequent reduction in the previous year's tax liability is treated as an additional 'payment on account' of the later year (*TMA 1970, Sch IB, para 2*).

The claim must be made within 12 months after the 31 January following the tax year in which the loss is incurred (*ITA 2007, s 132(4)*).

RELIEF FOR SHAREHOLDER LOANS

Capital loss relief for irrecoverable loans

Outline of *TCGA 1992, s 253* relief

7.49 Generally, a simple debt is outside the scope of CGT and therefore if it becomes irrecoverable, relief would not be available for the creditor's loss. However, an individual shareholder (or indeed any other individual lender) can make a claim under *TCGA 1992, s 253* to obtain a capital loss equal to the *principal* element of their irrecoverable loan (which can include credit balances on current accounts). Corporate lenders generally obtain relief under the loan relationship regime unless they are 'connected' with the borrowing company.

The claimant will receive a capital loss equal to the amount that the Inspector has agreed is irrecoverable. The capital loss *cannot* be offset against income under *ICTA 1988, s 574* (as it does not relate to shares).

The capital loss on an irrecoverable loan arises when the claim is made. However, it is also possible to establish the loss at an earlier time, being within the two previous tax years before the start of the tax year in which the claim is made, provided the loan was also irrecoverable at that earlier date (*TCGA 1992, s 253(3), (3A)*).

Conditions for *s 253* relief

7.50 To make a competent claim under *TCGA 1992, s 253*, a number of conditions must be satisfied, the most important of which are:

(*a*) The loan must be irrecoverable and the claimant must not have assigned their right of recovery;

(*b*) The amount lent must have been used wholly for the purposes of a trade (which can include capital expenditure and trade setting-up costs) carried on by a UK resident company. This trade application test is also satisfied

7.51 *Winding-up the family or owner-managed company*

where the borrowing company has lent the monies to another 'fellow' group company for use in its trade. The fellow group company must be in a 75% group relationship – the wider 'group' definition (which includes non-resident companies) applies for loans made after 31 March 2000. Since 6 April 2003, that group company must be a 'trading company'. (Relief is also available where the borrowed amount is used to repay a loan that would have qualified.)

The relief is not therefore available for loans to investment companies or to purchase 'investment' assets.

(c) The loan must *not* constitute a 'debt on security' (broadly, a debt on security represents a loan held as an investment which is both marketable and produces a return or profit to the holder) (*TCGA 1992, s 253(1), (3)*).

7.51 In judging whether a loan has become 'irrecoverable' at the date of the claim (or earlier date), HMRC are likely to examine the prospects of its recovery based on relevant balance sheets and other information. The Inspector would seek to determine whether there is a reasonable likelihood of the loan (or part of it) being repaid, having regard to the borrowing company's current and probable future financial position. In practice, where the borrower is insolvent and has ceased trading and it is clear that the loan (or part of it) would not be repaid, a *s 253* claim would usually be accepted for the relevant amount. On the other hand, relief may be denied where the borrowing company is still trading (albeit making losses). Similarly, if the borrower was in a parlous state when the loan was made, the Inspector may refuse the claim on the grounds that the loan had not *become irrecoverable* as required by *TCGA 1992, s 253(3)(a)*.

7.52 In *Crosby (Trustees) v Broadhurst* [2004] STC (SCD) 348, the Special Commissioners agreed that relief was available on an irrecoverable loan that had (as part of the terms of the borrowing company's sale) been waived before the formal claim was submitted to the Inspector. They did not accept the Inspector's view that the loan had to be in existence at the time the claim was made.

Any subsequent recovery of part or all of the debt will be treated as a chargeable gain arising at the date of repayment. Capital loss relief cannot normally be claimed on intra-group loans under *TCGA 1992, s 253*.

Guarantee payments

7.53 Where an *individual* shareholder has provided a personal guarantee which is called in by the lender, they will be able to claim capital loss relief on any payment made under the guarantee. Claims for guarantee payments made by an individual must be made before the fifth anniversary of the 31 January following the tax year in which the payment is made.

Winding-up the family or owner-managed company **7.54**

Capital loss relief may also be available where a group company makes a payment under a guarantee in relation to a borrowing by a fellow group company. The claim must be made within six years of the accounting period end in which the payment is made. The group guarantor company would become entitled to the rights of the original lender and can therefore claim capital loss relief if it is prevented from claiming a deduction under the loan relationship legislation (*TCGA 1992, s 253(3), (4)(c)*).

Example 7.5

Capital loss relief for irrecoverable loan

Wright Ltd has traded profitably for a number of years. However, the company has experienced a downturn in trading during the last three years. In May 2002, Mr Billy, the controlling shareholder, had to make a cash injection of £80,000 to the company to ease its ailing finances. However, in December 2007, the company's bankers called in the receiver and the company was subsequently wound up. No part of Mr Billy's loan account was repaid.

Mr Billy can therefore claim under *TCGA 1992, s 253* for the £80,000 to be treated as an allowable loss for CGT purposes.

If Mr Billy realises a capital gain of, say, £50,000 in 2007/08, he should be able to relieve it with his capital loss on the loan, provided he makes the claim by 5 April 2010. To do this, Mr Billy must be able to satisfy the Inspector that the full amount of the loan (or substantially all of it) was irrecoverable by 5 April 2008.

CONVERTING LOANS INTO NEW SHARES

7.54 Given the potential advantages of income tax relief by making a claim under *ITA 2007, s 131* (previously *ICTA 1988, s 574*), shareholders may be tempted to 'capitalise' their loans by subscribing for further shares. However, if the company is *insolvent*, the amount subscribed for the new shares is unlikely to be reflected as part of the shareholder's CGT base cost. This is because *TCGA 1992, s 17(1)* deems the shares to be acquired at their (negligible) market value (where the amount subscribed is greater than market value).

Alternatively, the capitalisation of the loan for new shares may constitute a 'reorganisation' for CGT purposes. This would be the case where, for example, all shareholders subscribe for additional shares in proportion to their existing holdings. On a 'reorganisation', *TCGA 1992, s 128(2)* effectively provides that

7.55 *Winding-up the family or owner-managed company*

the amount subscribed will only be reflected in base cost to the extent that the relevant shareholding increases in value, which in such cases is unlikely.

Given the above difficulties in securing a CGT base cost, it will normally be disadvantageous to substitute share capital for shareholder loans (where the company has a deficiency of net assets). The shareholder should be able to claim capital loss relief for his irrecoverable loan under *TCGA 1992, s 253*, whereas if it is 'converted' into shares there is unlikely to be any relief.

Losses incurred on Qualifying Corporate Bonds (QCBs)

7.55 In some cases, the shareholder may hold a loan note evidencing the debt. This will invariably constitute a Qualifying Corporate Bond (QCB) and represent a 'debt on security'. However, provided the loan was made *before 17 March 1998*, an allowable capital loss can still be claimed for the irrecoverable part of the debt under the provisions of *TCGA 1992, s 254* for CGT loss relief.

However, to qualify the QCB must comply with the 'qualifying loan' rules and the funds concerned must have been lent wholly for the purposes of a trade carried on by the borrower. It follows that if the holder received the QCB as consideration for the acquisition of shares relief will not be available (*TCGA 1992, ss 253, 254*).

No CGT loss relief is available for QCB loans made after 16 March 1998.

Loans made by companies

7.56 Capital loss relief under *TCGA 1992, s 253* is not available where the lender is able to claim a deduction under the loan relationship rules (*TCGA 1992, s 253(3)(a)*). In many cases, a corporate lender should be able to claim a 'non-trading' loan relationship deduction for an impairment loss on a 'non-trading' loan (ie where the loan is effectively written off or provided against as an irrecoverable bad debt). A trading deduction would only be available where the loan was made in the course of a trade.

However, if the borrower is a *connected person*, such as a fellow group member or a 'parallel' company under common control, then it is not generally possible to claim a tax allowable impairment loss (*FA 1996, Sch 9, para 6*). In this context, *FA 1996, Sch 9, para 6C* provides a mechanism for a lender to obtain relief *only* on amounts which become subject to an impairment 'write-off' after it ceases to be 'connected' with the borrowing company. This means that amounts remaining outstanding when the borrower goes into liquidation cannot be relieved. It should be noted that GAAP usually requires impairment of debts that are not expected to be recovered. Hence the lender is likely to have already impaired most, if not all, of the loan balance prior to the commencement of liquidation, etc. Relief will only be available on such amounts that remain 'unimpaired'.

7.57 The legislation in *FA 1996, Sch 9, para 6C* works by preventing any tax deduction being taken for impairment losses that were denied relief whilst the companies were 'connected'. It is helpful to understand why the 'connection' test in *FA 1996, s 87(3)* would be broken where the 'connected party' debtor goes into insolvent liquidation or administration. In broad terms, *FA 1996, s 87A* provides that a person has control of a company for this purpose if they are able to conduct the company's affairs in accordance with their wishes through holding the requisite shares, voting power or powers conferred by the Articles of Association or any other documents (such as a shareholders' agreement). Where the borrowing company goes into liquidation or administration, this 'control' nexus would be broken since the liquidator/administrator would take over the management of the company's affairs. A parent company would therefore lose its ability to control the affairs of its subsidiary (for example, by appointing and removing directors) and hence would no longer 'control' the company within *FA 1996, s 87A*.

Exceptionally, where the lending company is able to deduct an impairment loss for amounts becoming impaired post-liquidation, it will be allowed as a non-trading (or trading) deduction by virtue of *FA 1996, Sch 9, para 6C*.

Chapter 8

Tax planning for the non-resident and non-domiciled

Robert Maas FCA FTII FIIT TEP, Tax Partner, Blackstone Franks LLP

INTRODUCTION

8.1 Chargeability to UK tax depends on three concepts, residence, ordinary residence and domicile. A person who is resident, ordinarily resident and domiciled in the UK is liable to UK tax on worldwide income and assets. If a person does not meet all three of these tests then some of his income or assets may well escape UK tax.

The starting point is accordingly these three concepts.

RESIDENCE

8.2 There is no statutory definition of residence for tax purposes. There are a large number of court decisions on whether or not a person was resident in the UK but it is difficult to draw much firm guidance from them. HMRC have sought to do so in their booklet IR 20, 'Residents and non-residents – Liability to tax in the UK'. This is an extremely useful booklet. It is unwise to seek to decide a person's residence without first becoming familiar with this booklet, not only because it highlights areas to which HMRC attach particular importance but also because the HMRC interpretation is to an extent concessionary.

Broadly speaking, a person is resident in the UK if he normally lives here. Whether or not he does so is a question of fact.

8.3 The HMRC view seems to be that in order for a person to cease to be resident in the UK he needs to go abroad permanently or for a settled purpose. Once he has left the UK he will become UK resident again only if he returns to the UK for more than 90 days a year on average. In deciding whether or not a person has left the UK, HMRC will consider all the relevant evidence, including the pattern of presence in the UK and elsewhere (Revenue & Customs Brief

Tax planning for the non-resident and non-domiciled **8.4**

01/07). It is not wholly clear what this means. Prior to the issue of this statement in January 2007, most people thought that HMRC's approach to residence was an arithmetical one, ie that a person was UK resident if he was physically present in the UK for 183 days or more in a tax year or if he was physically present here for more than 90 days a year on average.

8.4 IR 20 gives the following guidance:

- To be regarded as resident in the UK a person must normally be physically present in the UK at some time in the tax year (para 1.2). The use of the word 'normally' needs to be borne in mind.
- A person will always be resident in the UK in any tax year in which he is physically present in the UK for more than 183 days. There are no exceptions to this (para 1.2).
- It is possible to be resident in the UK and some other country (or countries) at the same time (para 1.4). However, if the other country is one with which the UK has a double taxation treaty the agreement is likely to contain a 'tie-breaker clause' which might prevent the UK as treating the individual as UK resident for the purpose of the agreement. Double tax agreements do not usually deal with income from third countries.
- Strictly speaking a person is UK resident for the whole of a tax year if he is resident here for any part of it (para 1.5). However, extra-statutory concession E11 provides that if an individual ceases to reside in the UK and he has left for permanent residence abroad (or comes to the UK to take up permanent residence or to stay for at least two years) he will be taxed only for the part of the year up to the date of his departure (or from the date of his arrival). This is known as the split year concession. It will not apply if the individual remains ordinarily resident in the UK (see below) after his departure or was ordinarily resident in the UK prior to becoming resident here. IR 20 states that ESC E11 applies if a person has been resident in the UK and 'leaves to live abroad permanently or for a period of at least three years' (para 1.6). There is a corresponding CGT concession (ESC D2) but this is much more limited. It does not apply where a person leaves the UK (unless he was not resident and not ordinarily resident here for the whole of at least four out of the last seven tax years preceding that in which he leaves the UK). It applies to a person coming to the UK only if he has not been either resident or ordinarily resident in the UK at any time during the five tax years preceding that in which he becomes resident here.
- An individual is regarded as resident and ordinarily resident in the UK if he usually lives in the UK and only goes abroad for short periods – for example, on holiday or on business trips (para 2.1).
- A person who leaves the UK to work full-time abroad under a contract of employment is treated as not resident and not ordinarily resident in the UK if his absence from the UK and the employment abroad both last for at

8.5 *Tax planning for the non-resident and non-domiciled*

least a whole tax year (and visits back do not breach the 183 or 91 day rule) (para 2.2). This is considered further below.

8.5 *Tax Bulletin, Issue 52* deals with the position of mobile workers, namely people such as lorry or coach drivers who drive their vehicles to and from the Continent, those who work on cross-channel transport and salesmen who make frequent short business trips abroad. HMRC consider that even though such a person may be here for less than 91 days on average he will be resident and ordinarily resident here if he usually lives in the UK and makes frequent and regular trips abroad in the course of his employment or business. They regard a person as usually living in the UK if his home and settled domestic life remains here. It is probable that this is the test that they also apply to decide whether a person who goes abroad for a longer period has left the UK. It should be particularly noted that HMRC regard someone 'travelling to France most Sundays or Mondays in connection with their employment but returning to the UK by or at the following weekend' as a mobile worker (*Tax Bulletin, Issue 52*).

CEASING TO BE UK RESIDENT

8.6 There are four ways that a person who is UK resident can cease such residence:

- leaving to go abroad for one tax year under a contract of employment;
- leaving to go abroad for at least three tax years;
- not being physically present in the UK at all during a tax year;
- becoming resident in a country with which the UK has a double tax agreement and being deemed to be non-tax resident for the purpose of that agreement.

Contract of employment

8.7 The individual needs to work full-time abroad under a contract of employment spanning at least one complete tax year. If this condition is met he is regarded as ceasing to be both resident and ordinarily resident in the UK from the date of his departure.

HMRC have given guidance on what they mean by 'full-time' for this purpose in *Tax Bulletin, Issue 6* (February 1993). In general where a job involves a standard pattern of hours they would expect the individual to put in what a layman would clearly recognise as a full working week. They say that 'there is no fixed minimum number of hours for this purpose but 35–40 hours is obviously a typical UK working week'. However, it is probable that it is sufficient to look at a normal working week in the country where the person is working if this is less than the norm in the UK.

8.8 Where a job does not have a straightforward structure they would look at the nature of the job and, where appropriate, would take account of local conditions and practices in that particular occupation. This probably means that they would expect the individual to put in the number of hours that a person doing a similar job would normally be expected to work.

HMRC also say that where a person has several part-time jobs overseas concurrently, particularly if they were with the same employer or group of companies, it might be reasonable to aggregate the time spent on them. This might also be done where the person simultaneously works abroad both as an employee and as a self-employed person.

They also warn that where a person has a main employment abroad but also works in the UK in some unconnected occupation (eg he has a directorship of a UK company) they would want to consider whether the extent of the UK activities might cast doubt on the full-time nature of the overseas employment.

8.9 If the employment is terminated prematurely and a new employment contract entered into with someone else, HMRC would want to review the position but might be prepared to aggregate the two employments (para 2.3). They might aggregate them even if the individual returns temporarily to the UK between the employments, planning to go abroad again. However, it would clearly be safer to try to obtain the new employment whilst the individual is living abroad.

A person will also be regarded as having ceased to be UK resident and ordinarily resident if he leaves the UK to work full-time in a trade, profession or vocation and he meets conditions similar to those in paragraph 2.2 (para 2.4). It is not clear what this means. Does it merely mean that the self-employment overseas must span a complete tax year or might it mean that there needs to be a contract requiring the person to be abroad for such a period?

8.10 If a person is treated as non-resident under either para 2.2 (employed) or 2.4 (self-employed) his spouse will also be treated as non-resident if she accompanies him (or later joins him) even though the spouse is not in full-time employment – provided that the spouse is abroad for at least a complete tax year (ESC A11).

Where a person is regarded as non-UK resident under this test he can still visit the UK for up to an average of 90 days. However, it is hard to envisage a genuine full-time employment that allows three months holiday every year.

8.11 *Tax planning for the non-resident and non-domiciled*

Leaving the UK permanently or indefinitely

8.11 HMRC say in IR 20:

'If you claim that you are no longer resident and ordinarily resident, we may ask you to give some evidence that you have left the UK permanently or to live outside the UK for three years or more. This evidence might be, for example, that you have taken steps to acquire accommodation abroad to live in as a permanent home, and if you continue to have property in the UK for your use, the reason is consistent with your stated aim of living abroad permanently or for three years or more. If you have left the UK permanently or for at least three years, you will be treated as not resident and not ordinarily resident from the day after the date of your departure providing your absence from the UK has covered at least a whole tax year and your visits to the UK since leaving have totalled less than 183 days in any tax year and have averaged less than 91 days a tax year.' (para 2.8)

8.12 HMRC's Inspector's Manual (IM) (which was withdrawn recently) said:

'If an individual goes to live outside the UK, acquires a permanent home abroad, has a reason for having accommodation for use in the UK which is consistent with the aim of permanent residence abroad, [and] returns to the UK only on visits which do not average 91 days or more a tax year, he will be regarded as having ceased to be resident and ordinarily resident. For tax years before 1993–94 an individual also had to cease to retain accommodation in the UK.

Where an individual claims that he had ceased to be resident and ordinarily resident in this country, his claim may be admitted on a provisional basis at the outset ... if the grounds on which it is based are adequately proved, but in no circumstances can a final decision be made until the individual's absence from the UK has extended over a period which includes a full tax year. If adequate proof is not immediately available a decision on the claim is postponed for up to three years from the date of departure and the position is determined by reference to what has actually happened since the date of departure.' (IM 41)

These quotations suggest that HMRC regard a person as ceasing to be UK resident from the time of his departure if he goes abroad with an intention to live outside the UK for three years or more (and in fact fulfils that intention). However, he must go abroad 'for a settled purpose'. This probably requires an identifiable change in the person's lifestyle and possibly a specific reason for going abroad.

No presence in UK during tax year

8.13 If a person does not set foot in the UK at all during a tax year it is unlikely that he is resident here for that year. He could well be ordinarily resident though – but see *Reed v Clark* below.

There are two early cases, *Re Young* (1875) 1 TC 57 and *Rogers v CIR* (1879) 1 TC 255, in which the taxpayer was held to be resident in the UK even though he did not set foot here at all during the tax year. These cases involved master mariners, whose voyages lasted for over a year and whose home and family were in the UK. As the taxpayers lived in the UK when not on a voyage these decisions are understandable. In the former case the Lord President commented that 'every sailor has a residence on land'.

8.14 In *Reed v Clark* (1985) 58 TC 528, Nicholls J said that:

> 'The word "reside" is a familiar English word and is defined in the Oxford English Dictionary as meaning "to dwell permanently or for a considerable time, to have one's settled or usual abode, to live in or at a particular place" ' and that 'the task of the fact finding tribunal ... was to consider and weigh all the evidence and then, giving the word "residing" its natural and ordinary meaning, reach a conclusion on the factual question of whether or not the taxpayer was residing in the UK in the year of assessment'.

In that case he felt that:

> 'I am in no doubt that the true and only reasonable conclusion from the primary facts found by the Commissioners was that Mr Clark was not residing in the UK in the tax year 1978/79. For the whole of that year his home and place of business was in Los Angeles.'

This suggests that it is possible for a person to be UK resident in a tax year in which he does not set foot in the UK if he is normally resident here and does not have a settled abode somewhere else during that year.

Deemed non-residence

8.15 Most, but not all, of the UK's full double tax agreements contain a 'tie-breaker' clause to treat an individual as resident in one only of the countries concerned where he would otherwise be treated by each as resident there under its domestic laws. A fairly standard example is that with the United States which provides that where an individual is both resident in the UK under UK law and resident in the US under US law then:

8.16 *Tax planning for the non-resident and non-domiciled*

- he is deemed to be resident only in the country in which he has a permanent home available to him;
- if he has a permanent home available in both countries he is deemed to be resident only in the country with which his personal and economic relations are closer (often called his 'centre of vital interests'); and
- if either his centre of vital interests cannot be determined or he does not have a permanent home available to him in either country he is deemed to be resident only in the country in which he has a habitual abode;
- if he has a habitual abode in both countries (or neither) he is deemed to be resident only in the country of which he is a national; and
- if he is a national of both (or neither) the tax authorities of the two countries must endeavour to settle the question by mutual agreement.

(Article 4(4), US/UK Double Tax Agreement)

8.16 The notes to the OECD model double tax convention expand on the second point above:

'It is necessary to look at the facts in order to ascertain with which of the two States his personal and economic relations are closer. Thus, regard will be had to his family and social relations, his occupations, his political, cultural or other activities, his place of business, the place from which he administers his property, etc. The circumstances must be examined as a whole, but it is nevertheless obvious that considerations based on the personal acts of the individual must receive special attention. If a person who has a home in one State sets up a second in the other State while retaining the first, the fact that he retains the first in the environment where he has always lived, where he has worked, and where he has his family and possessions, can, together with other elements, go to demonstrate that he has retained his centre of vital interests in the first State.'

Some double tax agreements include a provision that relief from UK tax is due to a resident of the other country only to the extent that the person is liable to tax on the income in that other country. This particularly applies where the other country taxes the income on a remittance basis. Such countries include Australia, Canada, Ireland and Jamaica. Conversely the US agreement does not grant exemption from US tax where the income is taxed in the UK on a remittance basis and has not been remitted.

The 91-day test

8.17 Where a person has left the UK (or has never been UK resident) he is treated as UK resident in any year in which he is physically present here for 183 days or more or for any year in which his visits to the UK exceed on average 90 days ('the 91-day test').

Tax planning for the non-resident and non-domiciled **8.19**

This average is calculated over the period from a day of departure using the formula:

$$\frac{\text{Days in the UK}}{\text{Total period since leaving UK}} \times 365$$

If the period since the person left the UK exceeds four years (or the person has never been UK resident) the calculation is done by reference to the last fours years only.

8.18 For the purpose of the 91-day test (but not the 183-day one) HMRC are prepared to ignore days spent in the UK because of exceptional circumstances beyond the individual's control such as the illness of himself or a member of his immediate family (SP 2/91 and para 2.10 IR 20). SP2/91 states that 'each case where this relaxation of the normal rules may be appropriate will be considered in the light of its own facts'. In the self-assessment era the notes to the Non-residence page of the tax return indicate that it is now for the taxpayer to make this judgement himself. It would probably be sensible to flag up in the 'white space' on the return what days have been ignored and why.

HMRC do add a caveat to para 2.10 that: 'If during your absence the pattern of your visits varied substantially year by year, it might be appropriate to look at the absence as being made up of separate periods for the purpose of calculating average visits. This might be necessary if, for example, a shift in the pattern of your visits suggested a change of circumstances, which altered how we viewed your residence status'.

8.19 In calculating the days in the UK 'the normal rule is that days of arrival and departure from the UK are ignored in counting the days spent in the UK' (para 1.2, IR 20). This is concessional. In *Wilkie v IRC* (1952) 32 TC 495 Donovan J, concluded: 'there is nothing in the language … to prevent hours being taken into the computation, but that … since what has to be determined is the period of actual residence it is legitimate to do so.' In that case Mr Wilkie arrived in the UK around 2 pm on 2 June 1947. He intended to leave on 30 November 1947 but owing to the cancellation of his plane was compelled to remain until he was able to fly out around 10.00 am on 2 December. HMRC claimed that he had been in the UK for more than 182 days as both 2 June and 2 December were days in the UK. Mr Wilkie was held to be non-resident for 1947/48 as he was in the UK for only 182 days and 20 hours, which is less than 183 days.

HMRC say that they derive the 91-day test from decided cases. However, it seems to give a generous interpretation to such decisions. In *Cooper v Cadwalader* (1904) 5 TC 101 the taxpayer was held to be resident even though he was here for only about two months a year. In *Lowenstein v De Salis* (1926) 10 TC

8.20 *Tax planning for the non-resident and non-domiciled*

424 he was here on average for between two and three months a year. In *Lysaght v IRC* (1927) 13 TC 511 the taxpayer was here for 101 days in one year and 94 in the next.

Available accommodation

8.20 Up to 1992/93 a person was regarded as resident in the UK in any year in which he visited the UK however short the period if he had accommodation available for his use in the UK. This 'available accommodation' rule was excluded for the purpose of *ICTA 1988, s 336* (now *ITA 2007, s 831*) by *F(No 2)A 1993*. At that time the Minister indicated that the available accommodation rule had been abolished completely as: 'it has been held in the courts in the case of *Lysaght v IRC* (1927) 13 TC 511 … that the language of *s 336* has 'illustrative value' in relation to the definition of residence elsewhere in the *Taxes Act 1988*.'

However, the view of HMRC is that this does not mean that the existence in the UK of accommodation available for the person's use is no longer relevant. They still regard both the existence of available accommodation in the UK and whether or not the taxpayer has accommodation overseas as relevant in relation to the question of whether or not he has left the UK for a settled purpose. It is not, however, decisive; it is simply one of the factors to be taken into account. Accommodation does not have to be owned by the taxpayer for it to be available for his use. It is a question of fact whether it is so available.

Ordinary residence

8.21 A person is ordinarily resident in the UK if he is resident here year after year (IR 20 para 1.3).

HMRC practice is to treat a person who comes to the UK intending to live here permanently or to remain here for at least three years (four if he comes to study) as being ordinarily resident from the date that he arrives in the UK (para 3.1). They treat someone who comes here without such an intention as ordinarily resident from the beginning of the tax year after the third anniversary of his arrival or, if earlier, the beginning of the tax year in which the person decides to stay in the UK for three years or more (para 3.10). If a person already owns accommodation in the UK or acquires accommodation (buys or takes a lease of three years or more) in the year of arrival he will also be treated as ordinarily resident from the date of his arrival (assuming that he becomes resident here) (para 3.11). If he disposes of the accommodation and leaves the UK within three years he can however be treated as not ordinarily resident. A person who acquires accommodation after his arrival will be treated as ordinarily resident from the beginning of the year in which he acquires such accommodation (para 3.11).

8.22 In *Reed (Inspector of Taxes) v Clark* (1985) 58 TC 528 Nicholls J said:

'The approach which I have found most helpful is to start from the contrast, which has been commented upon more than once, drawn in *s 49* itself between ordinary residence and departure abroad for occasional residence. In the section occasional residence is the converse of ordinary residence. This seems to me to conform to the common usage of the phrase "occasional residence" – a person's occasional residence is contrasted with his usual (or ordinary) residence.

'For the meaning of ordinary residence one need look no further than the recent decision of the House of Lords in [*Shah v Barnet London Borough Council* [1983] 2 AC 309]. In that case the issue was the meaning of the phrase "ordinary resident" in the context of a student's entitlement to receive an educational grant under an Act and regulations excluding a local authority from being under a duty to bestow an award upon a person who had not been ordinarily resident in the United Kingdom throughout a specified period of three years. In delivering the leading speech, with which Lord Fraser, Lord Lowry, Lord Roskill and Lord Brandon concurred, Lord Scarman observed that 'ordinary residence' was not a term of art in English law and that in *Levene v IRC* (1928) 13 TC 486 and *Lysaght v IRC* (1927) 13 TC 511 the House of Lords construed those words in their tax context as bearing their natural and ordinary meaning as words of common usage in the English language. Lord Scarman said (at pages 343–44) "Unless, therefore, it can be shown that the statutory framework or the legal context in which the words are used requires a different meaning, I unhesitatingly subscribe to the view that 'ordinary resident' refers to a man's abode in a particular place or country which he has adopted voluntarily and for settled purposes as part of the regular order of his life for the time being, whether of short or of long duration". He added that a settled purpose did not require an intention to stay indefinitely, but that the purpose, while settled, might be for a limited period only: "all that is necessary is that the purpose of living where one does have a sufficient degree of continuity to be properly described as settled."

On that basis it seems to me plain that a British resident's departure abroad for a period of a few weeks or months with the firm intention of returning at the end of the period to live here as before would be likely always to be for the purpose only of occasional residence. At

8.23 *Tax planning for the non-resident and non-domiciled*

the opposite end of the scale, it seems to me equally plain that the departure of such a resident abroad for a limited period of (say) three years would not necessarily be fore the purpose only of occasional residence just because from the outset he had a firm intention of returning at the end of the period to live here as before ... For my part I think this latter conclusion is also true of residence abroad for just over one year in duration. The difference between these examples is one of degree, and there is an area in which different minds may reach different conclusions. In my view a year is a long enough period for a person's purpose of living where he does to be capable of having a sufficient degree of continuity for it to be properly described as settled. Hence, depending on all the circumstances, the foreign country could be the place where for that period he would be ordinarily and not just occasionally resident'.

Accordingly, the HMRC three-year rule is not necessarily correct.

The Gaines-Cooper case

8.23 The Special Commissioners' decision in *R Gaines-Cooper v CIR* (2007) STC (SCD) 23 has caused many people to question whether HMRC have changed their approach. In particular HMRC claimed that in applying the 91-days test the Commissioners should look at nights in the UK, not ignore days of arrival and departure. Furthermore Mr Gaines-Cooper was held to be resident in the UK in some years even though he spent well under 90 days in the UK. This is what prompted HMRC to confirm in Revenue & Customs Brief 01/07 that they have not adopted a new approach.

The facts of that case are complex and it is not intended to consider them here. The case emphasises that much of IR 20 is concessional. The courts and the Commissioners must apply the law. The cannot take any account of HMRC concessions (other than in the context of judicial review). In such circumstances it is not surprising that HMRC should argue the case on the basis of the law where this conflicts with their normal practice. An unfortunate side effect of relying on HMRC concessions is that if agreement cannot be reached with HMRC an appeal to the Commissioners inevitably carries with it a need to forfeit the benefit of such concessions.

It should also be noted that both parties asked the Commissioners to look at the overall position over a period of 11 years, so it is not surprising that they did not hold him to be non-resident in years when his visits to the UK were minimal. Indeed HMRC view this as a case where the taxpayer, although living part of his time abroad and part of his time in the UK for over 20 years, had never left the UK, so the length of his visits were irrelevant.

Domicile

8.24 Domicile is also not defined. It is not a tax concept. It is a general legal concept. It ties a person to a system of law. It is accordingly an important concept in matrimonial and family law.

Domicile is largely a question of intention. It is the country (or State in the case of a country with a Federal system where each State has its own legal system) that a person regards as his homeland.

A person starts life with a 'domicile of origin'. This is not the place where he was born. It is his father's domicile at the time of his (ie the son's) birth. If his father is not known it will be his mother's domicile.

A person's domicile can change during his lifetime. However, it is a fairly enduring concept. It is not easy to change one's domicile. If a person does acquire a new domicile and subsequently abandons his new country, his domicile of origin will revive.

8.25 There is an inference that a person retains his original domicile. It is for the person who alleges a change of domicile to prove it. This differs from the normal tax approach where it is for the taxpayer to disprove HMRC's contention.

To change one's domicile one must go to a new country with the intention of living there permanently or indefinitely. It is obviously difficult to prove intention. Indeed there are no published tax cases where HMRC have sought to show that a person who started life with a non-UK domicile of origin has become UK domiciled and that person is still alive. This is because if the individual can go before the Special Commissioners (who have exclusive jurisdiction in relation to residence and domicile) and give evidence of his intention, HMRC know that it is virtually impossible for them to show a change of domicile.

This does not mean that HMRC do not challenge domicile; it means that they defer doing so until after his death as at that stage he is no longer able to say what his intention was, so the Commissioners have to discern that from the surrounding facts.

8.26 A person who starts life with a non-UK domicile of origin does not become UK domiciled merely by living in this country for many years (although for inheritance tax purposes only, he is deemed to be domiciled here if he has been resident here for 17 out of the last 20 tax years). This is a common misconception. Many people who have lived in the UK even for 40 or 50 years are not domiciled here because they have retained an intention to return to their home country. Indeed, the probability is that a person who started life with a

8.27 *Tax planning for the non-resident and non-domiciled*

foreign domicile and came to the UK for a specific purpose, such as to study, to work or to marry, has retained his domicile of origin as it is unlikely that such a person has formed a decision never to return to his home country.

Conversely, of course, a person who started life with a UK domicile of origin will have difficulty in convincing HMRC that he has obtained – and retained – a foreign 'domicile of choice', particularly if the claim to be non-UK domiciled is made at a time when he is living in the UK. That is not to say that it is not possible to do so. It depends on the facts. A UK domiciled person who goes to, say, the US to study and while there marries and decides to stay there may well acquire a US domicile of choice. If his employer were to send him to the UK to work, or he takes a job in the UK, he will retain his US domicile whilst he is in the UK provided that his intention is always to return to the US at some stage.

8.27 Whilst the UK and the US are referred to above, this is a form of shorthand. They are in fact both federal countries. A person cannot actually be domiciled in the UK. He must be domiciled in either England and Wales, Scotland or Northern Ireland. It is important to realise that. If the hypothetical taxpayer envisaged above had gone to New York to study and now feels that when he retires he will not return to New York as it is too cold but will retire to Florida, his English domicile of origin will have revived when he came back to England as he would have abandoned his intention to live permanently in New York and could not have acquired a Florida domicile of choice as he would have to actually live there for a period before he could do so.

The tax significance of the three concepts

8.28 The most important concept for income tax is residence. A person is taxable on world-wide income if he is resident in the UK. He is taxable only on UK income – and even then there are some exemptions – if he is not resident here. This is subject to a major caveat. A person who is resident in the UK but not domiciled here (or not ordinarily resident here) is taxable on non-UK source income only to the extent that it is brought into the UK. The remittance basis does not apply to income arising in the Republic of Ireland. That is taxable in the UK on the same basis as UK income. The EU Commission believes that this provision breaches EU law as it restricts freedom of establishment. It is currently taking a case against Ireland to the ECJ and has asked the UK to justify the provision, preparatory to launching a case against the UK.

Furthermore, one of the main income tax anti-avoidance provisions, *ICTA 1988, s 739*, (transfer of assets abroad), only applies if a person is ordinarily resident in the UK.

8.29 Capital gains tax is triggered by either residence or ordinary residence. Again, capital gains on overseas assets realised by a person who is not domiciled in the UK are taxable here only to the extent that they are remitted to the UK.

8.30 Inheritance tax depends almost wholly on domicile. A person who is domiciled in the UK is taxable here on world-wide assets. A person who is not domiciled here is taxable only on UK assets. Residence is irrelevant with one exception. If, at the time of death or an inter vivos gift, the decedent or donor has been resident here during more than 17 of the previous 20 tax years he is treated, for inheritance tax purposes only, as if he were domiciled here. A point to watch is that a person who is resident here at any time in the tax year is treated as resident throughout that year for this purpose. Accordingly, a person who comes to the UK on 5 April and makes a gift on 7 April 15 years later is deemed domiciled in the UK even though he has only been resident here for 15 years and three days.

The remittance basis

8.31 Where income and gains are taxable on a remittance basis it is up to the taxpayer to demonstrate that he has not remitted income or gains. If he cannot do so, HMRC will regard all remittances as representing overseas income up to the amount of such income that has arisen since the individual came to the UK. They will then treat further remittances as a mixture of capital gains and capital in proportion to the amount of gains and capital in the bank or other account from which the funds were remitted.

To avoid this presumption a non-UK domiciled individual should maintain a number of overseas bank accounts and should take care to ensure that the money in the separate accounts are not mixed. It is extremely difficult to show the source of a payment out of a mixed fund. In this context it is important to realise that income does not lose its nature by being invested. For example, suppose a person has £100,000 of income overseas which he invests in overseas shares and that five years later he sells the shares for £150,000. The £150,000 is £100,000 of income and £50,000 of capital gain, not £100,000 of capital and £50,000 of capital gain. Accordingly, an individual who wants to avoid remitting capital needs to monitor very carefully what is paid into his overseas bank accounts.

8.32 At a minimum a non-domiciled individual needs to maintain two overseas bank accounts, one for income and the other for capital. He then needs to ensure that all income arising overseas is paid into the income account. It can be difficult to convince some overseas banks of the importance of keeping a rigid separation between the two. In particular it is unwise to credit the interest on a capital deposit account to that account and then immediately transfer it to the income account. This is not necessarily fatal as it may well be possible to convince the Special Commissioners that what has been transferred out is the same funds as were paid in. However, it becomes more difficult to do this if other transactions take place in the account between the time of the credit and the time of the transfer out, particularly if the account is overdrawn. It also of course needlessly presents HMRC with the opportunity to argue the point.

8.33 *Tax planning for the non-resident and non-domiciled*

8.33 If a person generates capital gains overseas, he also ideally ought to have one or more capital gains accounts. It needs to be appreciated though that the sale proceeds of an asset is itself a mixed fund. It is not possible to demonstrate which part is the original capital and segregate it from the gain. The whole of the sale proceeds need to be paid into the capital gains account. There are two caveats to this. The first is that if a share is sold at a loss no part of the proceeds can be gain; the whole amount must be original capital (unless of course the initial purchase price represented income or earlier capital gains). Accordingly, where a share or other asset is sold at a loss the whole of the proceeds ought to be paid into the capital account (which represents freely remittable funds). The second is that it probably does not matter if small gains are paid into the capital accounts. This is because if capital gains are remitted the amount remitted is deemed to be gains of the year they are remitted.

A person is not taxable on (and does not need to declare) capital gains which total in aggregate less than £9,200 pa. Accordingly, if the total capital gains paid into the capital account are below this figure it is irrelevant whether or not they are remitted. If they exceed that figure there is a problem only if the gains form a large proportion of the capital in the account. For example, if an individual has an overseas bank account that contains £1 million of initial capital and £100,000 of capital gains, only one-eleventh of any remittance is regarded by HMRC as capital gain so that person could remit £101,000 from the account without triggering a tax liability (assuming that he realises no UK gains during the tax year) as only £9,182 would constitute capital gains.

8.34 If a person makes a large number of disposals of overseas assets it may be sensible to pay the disposal proceeds into one capital gains account where the taxable gain element of a disposal is high in proportion to cost, into a different bank account where the proportion is relatively low and perhaps into the capital account where it is small. Remittances would be made from the capital account until it is exhausted, then from the second capital gains account (as the taxable proportion is lower) then from the first capital gains account, and finally from income.

HMRC take the view that it is impossible to remit a loss. Accordingly, a person who is taxed on the remittance basis will obtain no relief for losses.

8.35 The position in respect of taper relief is not wholly clear. What a person is taxed on is 'the amounts, if any, received in the UK in respect of those chargeable gains' ie chargeable gains accruing in 1965/66 or a later year of assessment (*TCGA 1992, s 12(1)*). The normal rule is that CGT is charged on the total amount of chargeable gains accruing to the person chargeable in the year of assessment after deducting any allowable losses (*TCGA 1992, s 2(2)*). Taper relief applies where 'there is, in any person's case, an excess of the total amount referred to in subsection (2) of section 2 over the amounts falling to be deducted from that amount in accordance with that subsection' (*TCGA 1992, s 2A(1)*).

Tax planning for the non-resident and non-domiciled **8.36**

There are no special rules where a person is not UK domiciled. On the face of it, if an overseas loss cannot be remitted, it cannot be an allowable loss. This seems to be confirmed by *s 16(4)* which provides that losses of a non-domiciled person from overseas assets 'shall not be allowable losses'. Accordingly, it appears that overseas losses need not be taken into account in calculating taper relief on overseas assets (although UK losses are of course still deductible before calculating taper relief).

Remittances from mixed funds

8.36 As indicated earlier, HMRC take the view that 'remittance out of a mixed fund represents a remittance of income to the extent that the fund contains income available for remittance'. Their authority for this is *Scottish Provident Institution v Allen* (1901) 4 TC 409. Scottish Provident lent sums to people in Australia. Their Australian agents maintained a single account for Scottish Provident into which was paid both the interest and loan repayments. When they remitted funds to Scottish Provident in Scotland the amounts remitted were against specific loans. For example a loan of £25,000 was made on 21 May 1886. This was repaid on 1 June 1891. On 1 February 1898 the agents remitted £25,000 to Scottish Provident with a covering letter stating that it was the repayment proceeds of the 1886 loan.

In the Court of Exchequer the Lord President said:

> 'During the period of nearly seven years throughout which the £25,000 remained in Australia, after it was repaid by the borrower, and before the remittance was made, it was, as I understand, inmixed with the funds of the Institution in Australia, having been paid into its banking account there; it is not stated in the case that the £25,000 remitted to this country on 1 February 1898, was in fact the £25,000 repaid by the borrower nearly seven years before, and it appears to me that the statements in the case do not require, or warrant, the inference that it was so. In so far as inference from the facts stated is admissible, the natural and proper inference from the known course of business seems to me to be that the money remitted was the interest accruing from funds invested in Australia. Income of the other cases the remittance was made shortly after the repayment in Australia by the borrower, the most favourable case for the Institution being that of the £28,000 which was remitted to Australia for investment on 14 November 1888, and repaid by the borrower there on 14 November 1898, while £28,000 was remitted to this country by the Institution's representatives there on 16 November 1898. Even that sum, however, was inmixed with the funds of the Institution in Australia for two days, and no information is given in the case as to

8.36 *Tax planning for the non-resident and non-domiciled*

the state of the Institution's bank account in Australia, or as to the other operations upon it, at or about that time. In particular it is not stated as in the case that the £28,000 was in fact the amount of the loan repaid on 14 November 1898, and I am unable to find in the facts stated in the case any sufficient ground for drawing the inference that it was so.

... I am of opinion, upon the statements in the case, that the Commissioners were right in drawing the inference that they were [inmixed], and in holding that they must be regarded as interest arising from securities in Australia received in this country during the year of assessment, not as capital sums withdrawn from investment in Australia and returned to this country. The interest was not kept separate from the other funds of the Institution in Australia and so invested there as to preserve its identity as interest, and in the absence of evidence to the contrary, it appears to me that the drafts upon the bank account for the purpose of making new investments should be presumed to have been upon the capital of loans repaid, the interest in natural course being forwarded to this country. If, in terms of the agreement with a borrower in Australia, the interest on his loan had been remitted by him to the Institution in this country, it would not, in my judgement, have been doubtful that it (the interest) was assessable to income tax here and it does not appear to me to make any difference that, for the purposes of administration, the interest was paid to representatives of the Institution in Australia, by them lodged in the bank there, and remittances not proved to have been repayments of capital, made to this country. Further, I consider that money which was truly interest would not, for the purposes of the present question, cease to possess the character of interest by being invested by the Institution for a time on loan in Australia, on the contrary, I think that if and when the money so invested was repaid, remitted to, and received in this country, it would be chargeable with income tax here, as it was in fact interest or money invested in Australia.

The whole income of the Institution in Australia has consisted, and still consists, of interest arising from money invested there and this interest, whether brought home or not, was, I understand, regularly and properly included in the annual revenue accounts of the Institution as part of its income, and so far as received or accrued up to 31 December 1894, the date of the last septennial investigation, was taken into account as the surplus to be divided amongst the members by way of bonus or otherwise, while the interests received since 31 December 1894, will form part of the surplus to be dealt with at the next investigation. When, ... the question is, whether particular remittances, the real origin and character of which as capital or interest are not definitely established, should be regarded as consisting of capital or of interest, the fact that the amounts were entered in the accounts of the Institution, and treated as income in this country, may be admissible evidence upon that question. It further appears to me, that, under the circumstances, indefinite remittances to this country must be presumed to consist of interest, not of capital, so long as the amount of capital remitted to Australia for investment still remains invested there. For these reasons I am of the opinion that the decision of the Commissioners is right.'

Lord McLaren commented:

'Where a capitalist company, as in the present case, has invested large sums for a period of 15 years in a Colony and has an agent employed not only to receive interest but also to receive the capital of the investment when paid up, and to reinvest it, even if unappropriated remittances are made to this country, I think every one would agree that they must be dealt with according to the ordinary course of business, and these remittances must be presumed, to be paid in the first place out of interest so far as they are income, and in the second place out of principal or capital. I think that rule results from the fact that no prudent man of business will encroach upon his capital for investment when he has income uninvested laying at his disposal.'

This decision seems to be based on what the judges believed that a prudent businessman would do. It may be arguable that what such a person would do is irrelevant in a non-business context. In *Kneen (Inspector of Taxes) v Martin* (1934) 19 TC 33 Slesser LJ thought that there is no presumption one way or the other than an amount remitted is or is not income. It seems clear from that case that whether, and to what extent, an amount remitted is income is a question of fact, not of law, to be decided in the light of each individual case.

What to do with a mixed fund

8.37 If a taxpayer has created a mixed fund there are a number of options open to him.

- He could regard the entire fund as unremittable and earmark the money for spending outside the UK.

- He can gift the money to someone else outside the UK. The someone else could be his spouse, his children or a UK charity. Provided it can be shown that the gift is made outside the UK and that it is a genuine gift (not

8.38 *Tax planning for the non-resident and non-domiciled*

an arrangement to enable the donor to have the use of the funds in the UK) the donee can bring the money into the UK without triggering any UK tax consequences. The gift will never have constituted income or gains of the donee so cannot be a remittance of income or gains by the donee. It is important that the gift can be shown to be made outside the UK. The safest way to do this is for the money to be transferred from a non-UK account of the donor to a non-UK account of the donee and for the donee to subsequently (ideally not on the same day) to transfer the funds from her non-UK account to her UK account. If the gift is between spouses the donee should not pay the money into a joint bank account and ideally should not spend it on items that generate a joint benefit, such as household outgoings – although this is probably acceptable if it can be shown that both spouses contribute to the household expenses and the money used by the donee for her contribution does not exceed her appropriate share of the joint expenses.

- He could utilise the 'source' rules. *ITTOIA 2005, s 830(1)* defines relevant foreign income (which includes income to which the remittance basis applies) as 'income which arises from a source outside the UK'. The House of Lords held in *National Provident Institution v Brown (Surveyor of Taxes)* (1921) 8 TC 57 that in order to be chargeable to income tax for a particular year in respect of income from any source, the person must possess that source of income in that year. Accordingly, if the mixed account is a bank deposit account and the only income it contains is bank interest, the account could be closed and the funds transferred to a different bank. The entire funds can then be remitted to the UK in a later tax year as the source from which the interest arose will no longer be held in that tax year. The source rule does not apply to employment income. The source rule also does not apply to capital gains.

- He could distribute an amount equal to the income element in the fund to non-residents. This is based on the premise that HMRC regard a distribution from the fund as income to the extent that there is income in the fund. Whilst the individual would be justified in completing his tax return on this basis it is by no means clear that if HMRC were to challenge the position the Commissioners would hold that the HMRC practice reflects the law.

Deemed remittances

8.38 It is specifically provided that if overseas income is used to satisfy a UK-linked debt the funds so used are deemed to have been remitted to the UK (*ITTOIA 2005, s 833(1)*). A debt is UK linked if it is:

(a) a debt for money lent to the individual in the UK, or for interest on money so lent;

Tax planning for the non-resident and non-domiciled **8.41**

(b) a debt for money lent to the individual outside the UK and brought into the UK; or

(c) a debt incurred to satisfy a debt within (a) or (b) (or another debt within (c)).

(ITTOIA 2005, s 833(3); ITEPA 2003, s 33(3), (4))

8.39 In the case of a UK debt it is irrelevant whether the money lent is brought into the UK before or after the income used to satisfy the debt arises – but if the money lent is not brought into the UK until after the income is used to satisfy it, the income is deemed to be remitted when the money is brought into the UK, not when it is used to satisfy the debt *(ITTOIA 2005, s 833(4), (5))*. At first sight this looks impossible. However, the legislation deems a person to use overseas income to satisfy a debt if:

(a) the borrower uses the income in such a way that the lender holds money or property representing the income on behalf of (or on account of) the borrower in such circumstances that it is available to the lender to satisfy the debt (by set-off or otherwise); and

(b) under an arrangement between the lender and borrower the amount for the time being owed by the borrower, or the time at which the debt is to be satisfied, depends in any respect (directly or indirectly) on the amount or value that the lender holds on behalf of the borrower.

(ITTOIA 2005, s 834)

Employment Income

8.40 Employment income is taxable on a remittance basis only if the employee is not UK domiciled (but is both resident and ordinarily resident) in the UK, the employment is with a foreign employer (other than an Irish one) and the duties of the employment are performed wholly outside the UK *(ITEPA 2003, ss 21–23)*. For this purpose duties performed in the UK can be treated as performed outside the UK if they are 'merely incidental' to the performance of overseas duties *(ITEPA 2003, s 39)*.

8.41 In *Robson v Dixon (Inspector of Taxes)* (1972) 48 TC 527 Pennycuick V-C observed that the words 'merely incidental' are upon that ordinary usage apt to denote an activity (here the performance of duties) which does not serve any independent purpose but is carried out in order to further some other purpose'. In that case an airline pilot who was based in the Netherlands made 38 take-offs and landings in the UK out of 811 in the year. The UK landings were held not to be merely incidental to the Netherlands ones. HMRC interpret this as

8.42 *Tax planning for the non-resident and non-domiciled*

meaning that duties performed in the UK that are of the same type as those performed overseas are not merely incidental even if performed for only a very short time (*Tax Bulletin, Issue 76*). Visits to the UK to report a group's head office are likely to be merely incidental to the overseas performance of the subject of the report.

8.42 A non-UK domiciled employee should consider whether he can use a dual contract arrangement under which he is employed by an overseas company for non-UK duties and a UK company for UK ones. HMRC do not like such arrangements and are likely to look at them closely. Nevertheless they accept that they are effective in appropriate circumstances. The appropriate circumstances are where the substantive duties can genuinely be segregated. HMRC have said that:

> 'Given the way in which modern business operates and the ease and speed of communication, some employees may find it increasingly difficult to avoid performing substantive UK duties under their overseas contracts. For example, an employee who is responsible under their overseas contract for servicing the business of overseas clients may have to respond to a telephone call or e-mail from a worried overseas client with an urgent problem when the employee is in the UK. Formulating and communicating a response to such a problem would be regarded as a fundamental duty under the overseas contract. It follows that the performance of such duties in the UK will not be merely incidental to the performance of duties outside the UK as they will be of equal importance to the overseas duties. It is the quality of the UK duties and not the time devoted to their performance that determines whether they are merely incidental.'
> (*Tax Bulletin, Issue 76*)

8.43 It is questionable whether that is wholly correct. For example, if a person carries out overseas duties and sends a report to his UK office and next time he is in the office he responds to a telephone call from the client and the response could have been equally made by someone else in the office who had read the report, answering the telephone is unlikely to be a duty of the overseas employment. In other words the duties are normally segregable if the employee can deal with the UK and overseas aspects wearing two different hats, but would not be segregable if the only person who can perform the UK activity is the person who performed the overseas one, eg because it requires information that is in his head or they are both part of an ongoing negotiation.

8.44 It is generally sensible to list the duties of the overseas employment in detail in the employment contracts. This not only makes clear what those duties are but it highlights when the contract is drawn up the extent to which segregation is practical. Where some duties can be segregated and some cannot, it is advisable to limit the overseas employment to the segregable ones and leave the

Tax planning for the non-resident and non-domiciled 8.48

remaining duties in the UK employment. It does not matter that that includes overseas duties; the key thing is that the overseas employment should not include any UK duties.

8.45 Where a dual contract arrangement is used it also needs to be borne in mind that the remuneration for the overseas employment needs to be paid outside the UK (as payment in the UK is equivalent to a remittance).

Care also needs to be taken with expenses. If the UK company reimburses expenses incurred on the overseas contracts, HMRC are likely to contend that the arrangements are a sham. If a group has a policy of channelling all expenses through the UK and recharging them to the appropriate company there should be no problem though.

8.46 Where an employee has two or more employments with the same employer or with associated employers (ie under common control), and any of the duties are performed in the UK the emoluments must be aggregated and re-apportioned between the UK and overseas duties in such manner as is reasonable having regard to the nature of, and time devoted to, the UK and overseas duties respectively, and all other relevant circumstances (*ITEPA 2003, s 24*).

Accordingly, if a dual contract arrangement is used, the split of the salary between the two needs to be done on a basis that can be justified. HMRC's starting point is likely to be to expect the split to reflect the time involved in the respective duties. They are unlikely to accept that overseas work deserves a higher daily rate because it is inconvenient, but should accept that it does so because the employee works longer hours when he is overseas.

8.47 In addition to the rules on UK linked debts referred to earlier, earnings are treated as remitted to the UK if they are paid, used or enjoyed in the UK or transmitted or brought to the UK in any manner or form (*ITEPA 2003, s 33*). Accordingly, if the employee uses overseas earnings to purchase assets such as a car or a painting and brings them into the UK the earnings used to purchase the assets are regarded as remitted to the UK (Employment Income Manual, para 40302). This contrasts with the normal rule on remittances under which an asset brought into the UK will not trigger a remittance unless it is sold here. HMRC indicate that in general the purchase of investments abroad should not be regarded as a remittance even if the share certificate is brought into the UK, as they will not be enjoyed here, but the sale of such investments in the UK will constitute a remittance.

Travelling expenses

8.48 An employee who is non-UK domiciled is not taxed on travelling expenses (including accommodation) from and to his home country in the five

8.49 *Tax planning for the non-resident and non-domiciled*

years from the date he comes to the UK (not any later date on which he starts the employment) provided that the cost of the travel is either borne by his employer or is paid by the employee and reimbursed to him by his employer (*ITEPA 2003, s 379*). This relief applies only if the employee did not visit the UK in the two years prior to coming to the UK to work and was not resident in the UK in the two years preceding that in which he came to the UK. There is no limit on the number of journeys qualifying for relief in the five-year period.

Where this relief applies it also extends to the costs of two return journeys per year made by each of the employee's spouse and his infant children either accompanying him when he came to the UK or to visit him in the UK (*ITEPA 2003, s 374*). Again, the cost must either be borne by the employer or paid by the employee and reimbursed to him by his employer.

Self-employment income

8.49 It is virtually impossible for a person who is resident in the UK to carry on a trade outside the UK as a sole trader. This is because a trade is carried on where its control and management takes place. If the proprietor is UK resident the trade will inevitably be controlled and managed from the UK. In such circumstances overseas income will simply be a receipt of the UK trade.

It is possible for a trade carried on in partnership to be controlled and managed outside the UK if one of the partners is non-UK resident. In such circumstances the UK resident partner share of profits will be taxed on a remittance basis.

TAXATION OF NON-UK RESIDENTS

Investment income

8.50 As indicated above, the UK taxes non-UK residents only on income arising in the UK. Even then not all UK income is taxable. The tax chargeable on a non-UK resident is limited to the tax that would be payable on the individual's UK employment income, trading income and property income (plus, where applicable, deemed income from the release of a loan to a participant of a close company, gains from certain UK insurance policies, disposals of futures and options involving guaranteed returns, non-trading income from intellectual property and film and sound recordings) if he were not entitled to personal allowances, plus any tax deducted at source from other types of income (*FA 1995, s 121(1)*).

This means that the following types of UK income are not taxable except to the extent of any withholding tax:

Tax planning for the non-resident and non-domiciled **8.51**

- interest (there is a 20% withholding tax unless the interest is bank interest or short interest, ie on a loan which is not capable of exceeding a year);
- purchased life annuity payment;
- profits from deeply discounted securities;
- distributions from unauthorised unit trusts;
- transactions in deposits;
- royalties and other income from intellectual property (there is a 20% withholding tax);
- certain telecommunication rights;
- annual payments not otherwise chargeable to tax (there is a 20% withholding tax);
- dividends from UK companies;
- UK social security pensions;
- certain other UK pensions and employment related annuities;
- social security income (other than income support or jobseekers allowance, although these are unlikely to be paid to non-residents);
- some trading transactions carried out by an independent broker in the normal course of his business;
- any other types of income tax that the Treasury may exclude by regulation.

(*FA 1995, s 128(3)*)

The above types of income are however taxable if they are received through a UK representative of the non-resident who is carrying on a trade in the UK on behalf of the non-resident through a branch or agency (*FA 1995, s 128(2)*).

Employment income

8.51 A person who is not UK resident is taxable on employment income only to the extent that it relates to duties performed in the UK. This limitation also applies to an individual who is resident in the UK but not ordinarily resident here in the tax year in which it is earned (*ITEPA 2003, s 25*). The applicable earnings are obviously calculated by apportioning the person's salary between that attributable to UK and non-UK work.

Most of the UK's double tax agreements prevent the UK from taxing the UK earnings of a resident of the other country if that person is present in the UK for 183 days or less in any 12-month period commencing or ending in the year of

8.52 *Tax planning for the non-resident and non-domiciled*

assessment concerned, the employer is not UK resident and the remuneration is not borne by a UK permanent establishment. This exclusion does not normally apply to entertainers and sportsmen.

If a person is resident but not ordinarily resident in the UK he is also taxable here on earnings for duties performed outside the UK to the extent that they are remitted to the UK (*ITEPA 20043, s 26*).

Trading income

8.52 A non-resident who carries on a trade in the UK through a branch or agency is taxable on the profits of that branch or agency. It is unclear whether it is possible for a non-resident to carry on a trade here as a sole trader other than through a branch or agency. This is because a trade is normally carried on at the place from which it is controlled and managed, and it would be fairly unusual for that not to take place where the proprietor is resident.

It used to be thought that a trade could not be carried on in the UK if all of its sales contracts were made outside the UK. However, the courts now tend to look at the overall substance of the trade. Where the substance of the trade is primarily in the UK – such as a trade of dealing in UK property – it is sensible for a non-resident to seek to ensure that all contracts are entered into outside the UK and also to evidence that he makes decisions in relation to the trade in his home country.

Property income

8.53 The basic rule is that the rental agent (or the last agent in the chain if there is more than one) must deduct tax at 22% from the rent and account for it quarterly to HMRC (*ICTA 1988, s 42A* and the *Taxation of Income from Land (Non-Residents) Regulations 1995, SI 1995/2902*)). He can calculate this deduction on the rents that he receives less any expenses he pays on the landlord's behalf during the quarter that he reasonably believes are deductible in calculating the taxable income of the UK property business. He cannot deduct expenses paid direct by the landlord. In most cases the largest expense is likely to be loan interest and this is normally either paid by the landlord or the rents are paid into a bank account with the lender. It is rare for it to be paid by the agent. Accordingly, where there are borrowings the tax deduction is likely to exceed the tax actually due on the profits of the UK property business. Where there is no agent the tenant is obliged to deduct tax at 22% from the rent and to account for it to HMRC.

8.54 Alternatively, the non-resident can elect to be taxed directly under the Non-Resident Landord's Scheme. This requires the approval of HMRC. When approved, HMRC will authorise the agent or tenant not to deduct tax from the rents. Until he receives such authorisation the agent must deduct tax. Most non-resident landlords opt to use this scheme. It ensures that only the right amount of tax is paid. The non-resident has to file an annual tax return and must pay tax in accordance with the normal self-assessment rules, which of course require interim tax payments to be made based on the previous year's income.

A non-resident individual should normally consider holding UK property through a non-UK company. There are two reasons for this. The individual will pay tax on rental income at rates of up to 40% if the income exceeds the basic rate tax band, whereas an overseas company pays income tax at the 22% basic rate. The second is that as the property is situated in the UK it is within the scope of UK inheritance tax if it is held by the individual but will be outside the scope of IHT if held through an overseas company.

Capital Gains Tax

8.55 An individual is chargeable to CGT if he is either resident or ordinarily resident in the UK at any time during the tax year in which the gain is realised. Split year treatment does not apply where an individual leaves the UK, except where that person was non-resident and non-ordinarily resident for the whole of four out of the seven preceding tax years. It does apply where a person leaves the UK, but only if he was not resident or ordinarily resident in the UK at any time during the five tax years preceding that in which he came to the UK (ESC D2).

8.56 There are two important exceptions to this basic rule. The first is that if a non-UK resident is carrying on a trade, profession or vocation in the UK through a branch or agency he is liable to tax on gains on the disposal of UK assets which are used in (or held for the purpose of) the branch or agency at the time the gain accrues, or were used (or held for) such a purpose at an earlier time or have been acquired for use for such a purpose. For the charge to apply the trade must be carried on at the date of the disposal (*TCGA 1992, s 10*). The provision can be overridden by double tax agreements. The same rule applies for corporation tax (*TCGA 1992, s 10B*).

8.57 The second is that a taxpayer who becomes non-resident for less than five years is chargeable to CGT on his return on gains realised during his period of non-residence (*TCGA 1992, s 10A*). For this charge to apply the individual has to be resident or ordinarily resident in the UK at some time during a tax year ('the year of return') (and not be treated as if he were not UK resident under a double tax treaty throughout that year), must have been non-UK resident and ordinarily resident for at least five tax years, and prior to his year of departure (the last tax year for which he was UK resident or ordinarily resident before the year of return) must have been resident or ordinarily resident for four out of the preceding seven tax years (*TCGA 1992, s 10A(1)*).

8.58 *Tax planning for the non-resident and non-domiciled*

8.58 Where *s 10A* applies the individual is treated as realising in the year of return capital gains equal to the aggregate of the gains that arose to him during his period of non-residence and gains that would have been deemed to arise to him during that period under *TCGA 1992, s 13* (gains of overseas company with a UK shareholder) or *TCGA 1992, s 86* (gains of overseas settlement with a UK settlor). He is similarly treated as realising any losses that accrued to him during the period of non-residence (or would have been deemed to so accrue under *s 13*) (*TCGA 1992, s 10A(2)*). It should be noted that if losses actually realised by the taxpayer exceed the taxable gains the excess loss is an allowable loss deemed to accrue in the year of return.

There is an exception for assets that were acquired during the period of non-residence, or at some time in the year of departure, and disposed of during the period of non-residence (but not in the year of return). This exception does not apply if the asset was acquired under a no gain/no loss acquisition, it was an interest created by (or arising under) a settlement or a gain on another asset was rolled over into that asset (*TCGA 1992, s 10A(3)*).

8.59 Where the year of departure was 2005/06 or later (or is 2004/05 and that taxpayer was resident or ordinarily resident in the UK and not Treaty non-resident at some time between 16 March and 5 April 2005) and the individual would have been resident or ordinarily resident in the UK but was excluded for doing so by a double tax treaty, deemed gains taxable on the individual under *s 13* or *ss 87* or *89(2)* (gains of overseas settlement) are not taxable on him. However, the double tax treaty is to be interpreted so as to permit actual gains arising to the individual in the period of non-residence to be taxed on his return (*TCGA 1992, s 10(9B) & (9C)*). This prevents an individual seeking to establish residence in a treaty country which did not itself tax capital gains for a year, realising a large gain, and then returning to the UK in the following year. Belgium was a popular country. It is questionable whether that device was in any event effective. It is hard to see why another country should want to argue that a person was resident there in circumstances where it would collect no tax by doing so and could see that the reason for claiming residence there was to seek to avoid UK tax. Furthermore it is by no means clear that taxing an amount equal to a gain is the same thing as taxing the gain.

8.60 To prevent a non-resident being able to escape a CGT charge under *s 10* where he carries on a trade in the UK, there is a deemed disposal if either he takes the asset outside the UK or ceases the UK trade prior to selling the asset. Where an asset held by a non-resident for the purpose of a UK trade is removed from the UK, and so ceases to be a chargeable asset, it must be treated as being disposed of and re-acquired at its market value immediately before it left the UK (*TCGA 1992, s 25(1)*). This does not apply if the asset is taken outside the UK contemporaneously with the person ceasing to carry on his UK trade (or if it is an oil exploration asset) (*TCGA 1992, s 25(2)*).

Tax planning for the non-resident and non-domiciled **8.63**

8.61 If an asset ceases to be a chargeable asset by virtue of the owner ceasing to carry on a trade, profession or vocation in the UK through a branch or agency he is deemed to have disposed of the asset and re-acquired it at its market value immediately before the trade ceased (*TCGA 1992, s 25(3)*). This does not apply if the asset again becomes a chargeable asset in the same tax year or accounting period (*TCGA 1992, s 25(5)*). For example it would not apply if the non-resident set up a new UK trade before the end of the tax year. In the case of a company the charge also does not apply if the trade is transferred to another company by way of an intra-group transfer within *TCGA 1992, ss 139* or *171* (*TCGA 1992, s 25(5)*).

This provision will of course also prevent a UK resident who carries on a trade in the UK from emigrating and avoiding tax on the trading assets by ceasing the trade and selling the asset after he becomes non-UK resident. However, this is a question of timing. Neither *s 10* nor *s 25* will apply if a person ceases to carry on the trade while UK resident but defers selling the assets previously used for the trade until he becomes non-resident. Section 25(3) will not apply in such circumstances as if the owner is UK resident when the trade ceases the asset will not cease to be a chargeable asset as it is still within the scope of CGT by virtue of the owner being resident and ordinarily resident in the UK.

8.62 Provided that a person intends to remain non-resident for more than five tax years, it is still possible to emigrate while owning UK assets which are not trading assets of a UK branch or agency by deferring a sale until after the owner has become non-resident. Where a person carries on a business in the UK as a sole trader or in partnership and he intends to become non-resident, consideration should be given to incorporating the business for shares under *TCGA 1992, s 162. Sections 10* and *25* will not apply to a subsequent sale of the shares.

Alternatively such a person could cease to use the asset in the trade while he is UK resident. For example at a time when he is UK resident he could transfer the trade to a company but keep the asset personally. After emigration he could then sell both the shares and the asset.

8.63 An individual who is domiciled outside the UK but resident or ordinarily resident here is liable to CGT on a remittance basis in relation to gains on overseas assets (*TCGA 1992, s 12(1)*). As with income, the charge can be avoided by spending or gifting the sale proceeds outside the UK. However, the source rules do not apply to chargeable gains so it is not possible to make gains remittable in that way. The rules considered above in relation to deemed remittances of investment income also apply to capital gains (*TCGA 1992, s 12(2)*). The gain is deemed to arise when it is remitted but taper and indexation relief are of course calculated by reference to the date of the actual disposal. HMRC consider that if a person becomes domiciled in the UK and subsequently remits gains arising at a time when he was non-domiciled they can still tax the remittance under *s 12*. It is not wholly clear that this view is correct but anyone who wished to challenge it would need to litigate the point. The wording of the legislation is ambiguous.

8.64 Where an individual intends to become non-resident and sell an asset after he has ceased to be UK resident it needs to be borne in mind that the date of disposal for CGT is the date of contract, not that of completion. A contract does not need to be a formal written document. An offer to sell and the acceptance of that offer creates a contract. HMRC may well want to review all of the correspondence in relation to the sale to look for evidence that a contract came into existence at a time when the individual was still UK resident (or before the end of the tax year in which he ceased to be resident here).

8.65 A conditional contract does not create a disposal until the condition is satisfied. However, it is often difficult to be sure whether the contract is conditional. Lawyers draw a distinction between a condition precedent (ie one the non-fulfilment of which will mean that the contract never became enforceable) and a condition subsequent (ie one which does not destroy the contract but the non-fulfilment of which will give rise to a claim for damages). It is only the former that can qualify as a conditional contract for CGT purposes. It is accordingly safest to use options if it is wished to make a contract conditional. An option does not create a contract until the option is satisfied. There is a risk with cross-options (ie where the prospective vendor has an option to require the other person to acquire the asset and the proposed purchaser has an option to require the other person to sell it to him). HMRC have been known to contend that cross-options are equivalent to a contract as both parties are able to enforce the bargain. Accordingly, if cross-options are used it is safest for both not to be exercisable at the same time. For example the vendor could have an option to require the purchaser to buy the asset from him exercisable only during the following May and the prospective purchaser could have an option to require the vendor to sell the company to him exercisable only during the following July. There would then be no time at which both parties could bring the bargain into existence.

Inheritance tax

8.66 Inheritance tax is based partly on domicile and partly on the location of the assets. Residence and ordinary residence are irrelevant – except to the extent that continuous residence can create a deemed UK domicile (see below). A person is liable to inheritance tax on UK assets irrespective of where he is domiciled or resident. A person who is domiciled in the UK (or to be precise in one of the countries that constitute the UK) is chargeable to IHT in relation to worldwide assets.

8.67 Where a person is non-UK domiciled a holding in an authorised unit trust, a share in an open-ended investment company and a number of UK government securities are excluded from inheritance tax even though they are UK assets (*IHTA 1984, s 6(1A), (2)*). If the individual is domiciled in the Channel Islands or the Isle of Man Ulster savings certificates, national savings certificate, premium bonds and certified SAYE saving arrangements are also excluded from IHT (*IHTA 1984, s 6(3)*). So are emoluments from the foreign government and tangible moveable property of members of visiting forces if the presence of the property in the UK is due to the individual being in the UK as a serving member of such an overseas military force (*IHTA 1984, s 155*). There is also an exclusion from IHT on death for a foreign currency account with a UK bank where at the time of his death the holder is domiciled outside the UK and neither resident nor ordinarily resident here (*IHTA 1984, s 157*).

8.68 A person who is not domiciled in the UK is treated, for IHT purposes only, or if he were domiciled here (and not elsewhere) at any time if either:

- he was domiciled here at some time within the previous three years; or
- he was resident in the UK for income tax purposes in at least 17 of the 20 tax years ending with the year in which that time falls.

(*IHTA 1984, s 267(1)*).

This deeming does not apply for the purpose of *s 6(2)* and *(3)* (which deems certain securities etc to be outside the scope of IHT if they are held by a person who is not UK domiciled), *s 48(4)* (which applies *s 6(2)* to settlements) or *s 158(6)* (double tax relief) (*IHTA 1984, s 267(2)*).

8.69 The IHT exemption for transfers between spouses or civil partners is limited to £55,000 where the transferor is domiciled in the UK but the transferee is not (*IHTA 1984, s 18(2)*). This provision might well be overridden by the non-discrimination clause of a double tax agreement. It also needs to be borne in mind that any lifetime transfer of value to an individual is a potentially exempt transfer which will be taxable only if the transferor dies within seven years of making the gift (*IHTA 1984, s 3A*). Accordingly, a lifetime gift to a non-domiciled spouse – or indeed any other non-UK domiciled individual – is exempt, whatever the amount, if the donor survives for the seven-year period.

8.70 Where one spouse or civil partner only is UK domiciled, consideration accordingly ought to be given to putting the majority of the family assets into the ownership of the non-UK domiciled spouse (or into a trust for the benefit of the non-UK domiciled spouse if this can be done without a significant entry charge) during the lifetime of the UK domiciled spouse.

8.71 Non-UK property included in a settlement is outside the scope of IHT if the settlor was non-UK domiciled (and not deemed to be UK domiciled) at the

8.72 *Tax planning for the non-resident and non-domiciled*

time of the creation of the settlement (*IHTA 1984, s 48(3)*). So are units in a UK authorised unit trust and shares in a UK open-ended investment company which are held by such a settlement (*IHTA 1984, s 48(3A)*). This does not apply if an interest in possession in the property is held by a UK domiciled person and that interest was acquired for a consideration in money or money's worth (*IHTA 1984, s 48(3B)*). UK government securities within *s 6(2)* are also exempt if they are held by such a settlement and either a non-domiciled person has an interest in possession in them or all possible beneficiaries of the settlement are non-UK domiciled (*IHTA 1984, s 48(4)*).

8.72 If an interest in possession in a pre 22 March 2006 settlement comes to an end there is a deemed disposal of the settled property for IHT purposes. However, no tax is chargeable if when that interest in possession comes to an end the settlor's spouse or civil partner becomes entitled to the property, provided that she is domiciled in the UK (*IHTA 1984, s 53(4), 54(2)*). Again, this is not necessarily a problem if the interest in possession terminates during the beneficiary's lifetime as the deemed disposal is deemed to be a potentially exempt transfer by the person with the interest in possession so it does not matter that the spouse is not UK domiciled provided that the beneficiary survives for seven years.

A transfer of value made by a close company is apportioned amongst its participators and treated as a transfer of value by the participant (*IHTA 1984, s 94*). However, if the participator is non-UK domiciled this does not apply to the extent that the value apportioned to him relates to non-UK property held by the company (*IHTA 1984, s 94(2)*).

Double tax treaties

8.73 The UK has only ten tax treaties in relation to inheritance tax. Those that it does have fall into two categories, namely those that were entered into pre-1975 and originally related to estate duty (which was payable only on death) and those entered into after 1975 which originally related to capital transfer tax (the original name of inheritance tax) and thus also cover lifetime gifts.

The first category comprises the agreements with France, Italy, India and Pakistan. These treaties now apply to IHT on death only (*IHTA 1984, s 158(6)*).

The second category comprises the agreements with Ireland, Netherlands, South Africa, Sweden, Switzerland and the US.

8.74 Clearly, the individual agreement needs to be looked at in a particular case. However, they normally apply where a person is domiciled in both countries under their domestic law. The category two agreements refer to a person being domiciled in the UK in accordance with its law or treated as domiciled for the purposes of IHT. This raises an interesting question as to the application of the category one agreements where a person is not domiciled in the UK under UK law but is deemed domiciled here for IHT purposes. The probability is that such a person is automatically regarded as French (or Italian, Indian or Pakistani) domiciled for the purposes of the treaty. Where a person is domiciled in a category two country, such as the US and deemed domiciled in the UK then the tie-breaker clause of the agreement will apply in the same way as if he were domiciled in both countries.

8.75 The category one agreements (other than that with Italy which is more limited) prevent the UK charging IHT on property situated outside the UK where the decedent was domiciled in the other country and not in the UK for the purpose of the agreement. They also contain rules to determine the situs of specific assets. However, these agreements also allow the UK to charge IHT on property which 'passes under a disposition or devolution regulated by the law of some part of Great Britain'. This probably allows the UK to tax non-UK property if it passes under a UK will or is held in a UK settlement. Where the other country imposes tax on assets situated in that country, the UK has to give credit for such tax in determining the UK tax payable.

The category two agreements normally lay down more detailed rules as to what can be taxed by each country. They determine the situs of property and normally allow the UK to tax land and business property situated in the UK.

Where the UK does not have a double tax agreement with the other country it allows a credit for foreign tax paid both on death and on lifetime gifts (*IHTA 1984, s 159*).

Residence of trusts

8.76 The residence of trusts and settlements is dealt with in **Chapter 14**.

Company residence

8.77 A company is domiciled where it is incorporated, but domicile is rarely important in a corporation tax context.

A company is resident in the country in which its central control and management takes place. This was established by the House of Lords in a commendably brief judgment in *De Beers Consolidated Mines Ltd v Howe* (*Surveyor of Taxes*) (1906) 5 TC 198. De Beers was incorporated in South Africa where it operated

8.78 *Tax planning for the non-resident and non-domiciled*

diamond mines. Its Head Office was in South Africa. The company held weekly board meetings in both London and South Africa. The majority of the directors lived in the UK. Attendance at the London meetings was far greater than at the South African ones and in practice the major decisions were taken at the London meetings. The Lord Chancellor, Lord Loreburn, opined:

> 'In applying the conception of residence to a company, we ought, I think, to proceed as nearly as we can upon the analogy of an individual. A company cannot eat or sleep, but it can keep house and do business. We ought, therefore, to see whether it really keeps house and does business. An individual may be of foreign nationality, and yet reside in the United Kingdom. So may a company. Otherwise, it might have its chief seat of management and its centre of trading in England, under the protection of English law, and yet escape the appropriate taxation by the simple expedient of being registered abroad and distributing its dividends abroad. The decision of Chief Baron Kelly and Baron Huddleston, now thirty years ago, involved the principal that a company resides, for purposes of income tax, where its real business is carried on. Those decisions have been acted upon ever since. I regard that as the true rule; and the real business is carried on where the central management and control actually abides. It remains to be considered whether the present case falls within that rule. This is a pure question of fact, to be determined, not according to the construction of this or that regulation or bylaw, but upon a scrutiny of the course of business and trading.'

As the Commissioners had found as a fact that 'the head and seat and directing power of the affairs of the Appellant Company were at the office in London from whence the chief operations of the Company, both in the UK and elsewhere, were, in fact, controlled, managed and directed', the company was held to be resident in the UK.

8.78 HMRC say that 'in seeking an answer to the question where the exercise of management and control lies the first natural step is to ask who, in law, has the right and duty to exercise it' (International Manual, ITH 316). The company law cases have held that normally this is the Board of Directors.

However, as residence is a question of fact it is possible that the people legally charged with the management and control of the company did not in fact exercise it. In *Bullock (Inspector of Taxes) v Unit Construction Co Ltd* (1959) 38 TC 712 the issue in dispute was the residence of a number of Kenyan subsidiary companies of Unit Construction. These were incorporated in Kenya and their Boards of Directors met only in Kenya. In 1950 the parent company directors decided that they would in future make all the major decisions in relation to the operation of the subsidiaries, and the Boards of the subsidiaries acquiesced in this. The East African companies were held to be resident in the UK. In the House of Lords, Lord Radcliffe said:

> 'Ought we, then, to adopt this principle that evidence of what has happened in fact must be excluded by a rule of law if what has been done is inconsistent with the regulations of a company? In my opinion it would be wrong to do so. I cannot see how the corollary of such a principle could fail to be that, if you cannot look beyond what the regulations of the company provide for, it is only those regulations which need to be or indeed can be referred to when a question of residence arises. Companies could be equipped with the most comprehensive sets of constitutions providing for management to be located in this or that selected taxing jurisdiction, and, however much the written requirements were in fact departed from for reasons of convenience or otherwise, all efforts to establish the true facts relating to the actual seat of management would founder on the ground that what had been done was merely "unconstitutional" ... I cannot think that such considerations are sufficient to introduce an important qualification upon this accepted test by which you try to ascertain what are the real facts about the seat of management and control and to put in its place what seems to be the merely formal device of studying a set of written regulations. I do not believe that this would conduce to the health of revenue administration. I think it much better to adhere to the approach laid down by Lord Loreburn, LC, in the De Beers case. "This is a pure question of fact, to be determined, not according to the construction of this or that regulation or by-law, but upon a scrutiny of the course of business and trading".'

8.79 HMRC are very alert to the risk that the decisions might in reality not be made by the Board of Directors. They tell their staff, under a heading 'what is the reality', that:

> 'it has been said that the management and control test is bad because it leads to the nonsense of directors flying to Jersey for board meetings ... It is quite easy for a company operating here to incorporate in Jersey and claim to be managed and controlled there with only a minimal tax cost in Jersey provided the shareholders are not resident there.'

On the face of it the point is a valid one. But criticism of that kind is concerned as much with questions of fact as of concept and the two things must be kept separate in our minds. There is, in principle at any rate, no reason why a business which is visibly in this country should not be managed and controlled from, let us say, Jersey. But if the directors of that company are working in this country on a regular basis and probably living here as well, it may be highly unlikely that

8.80 *Tax planning for the non-resident and non-domiciled*

they will be doing anything more in Jersey than reaffirming decisions already taken here. If that is so the mere fact of having board meetings in the Channel Islands is irrelevant. The question is, where do the people concerned exercise management and control. If they really do it in this country and go through a meaningless form of words in Jersey, that will achieve nothing for them. (International Manual ITH 334)

8.80 HMRC have given guidance on residence in SP1/90 where they emphasise:

> 'In general the place of directors' meetings is significant only insofar as those meetings constitute the medium through which central management and control is exercised. If, for example, the directors of a company were engaged together actively in the UK in the complete running of a business which was wholly in the UK, the company would not be regarded as resident outside the UK merely because the directors held formal meetings outside the UK. While it is possible to identify extreme situations in which central management and control plainly is, or is not, exercised by directors in formal meetings, the conclusion in any case is wholly one of fact depending on the relative weight to be given to various factors. Any attempt to lay down rigid guidelines would only be misleading.
>
> Generally, however, where doubts arise about a particular company's residence status, the Revenue adopt the following approach—
>
> (i) they first try to ascertain whether the directors of the company in fact exercise central management and control;
>
> (ii) if so, they seek to determine where the directors exercise this central management and control (which is not necessarily where they meet);
>
> in cases where the directors apparently do not exercise central management and control of the company, the Revenue then look to establish where and by whom it is exercised.'

They also warn:

> 'In outlining factors relevant to the application of the case law test, this statement assumes that they exist for genuine commercial reasons. Where, however, as may happen, it appears that a major objective underlying the existence of certain factors is the obtaining of tax benefits from residence or non-residence, the Revenue examine the facts particularly closely in order to see whether there has been an attempt to create the appearance of central management and control in a particular place without the reality.'

Tax planning for the non-resident and non-domiciled 8.82

8.81 The latest case to come before the courts is *Wood v Holden* [2006] STC 443 which was heard by the Court of Appeal in January 2006. This is a significant case partly because it relates to a tax avoidance scheme, so the courts might be expected to seek to interpret the law so as to thwart the scheme, and partly because it draws a clear distinction between simply implementing decisions of someone else and considering what that other person proposes and deciding that it is in the best interest of the company to adopt that proposal.

8.82 A CGT avoidance scheme was formulated by Price Waterhouse Corporate Finance Ltd[? Should this be PricewaterhouseCoopers – I don't have a clue! The judge referred simply to Price Waterhouse. There is a mention of Price Waterhouse Corporate Finance, so I have assumed that is the correct full name/] in the UK which involved one non-UK company, CIL, being gifted shares in a UK company, Holdings, CIL selling those shares to its wholly owned Dutch subsidiary, Eulalia, at market value and Eulalia subsequently selling the shares in Holdings to an arm's-length purchaser. The Special Commissioners decided that CIL was non-UK resident but that Eulalia was UK resident. They felt that the taxpayer had failed to satisfy them that Eulalia was not UK resident (and both HMRC and the Woods had claimed that CIL was non-resident). This received short shrift from Park J in the High Court:

> 'There plainly comes a point where the taxpayer has produced evidence which, as matters stand then, appears to show that the assessment is wrong. At that point the evidential basis must pass to the Revenue. ... In this case ... Mr and Mrs Wood had to show to the civil standard of proof that the adjustment was wrong. I accept that the onus was on them to show that Eulalia was not resident in the United Kingdom, but rather was resident in the Netherlands. They showed that Eulalia was incorporated in the Netherlands. They showed incontrovertibly that it had been resident only in the Netherlands until it was acquired by CIL. They showed that CIL was not itself a United Kingdom company, and indeed was a company which the Revenue asserted to have been resident outside the United Kingdom. They showed that, from the time when Eulalia was acquired by CIL, its managing director was [ABN AMRO] Trust, a large Dutch company with offices in Amsterdam. They showed resolutions and consequential actions being taken in the offices in Amsterdam. They accepted that what Eulalia was doing was part of a tax scheme which was being superintended by Price Waterhouse in their Manchester offices. They called evidence from the Price Waterhouse partners who at the time were heads of the firm's departments for corporate finance and for tax in Manchester. They produced a witness statement from the head of the legal department at [ABN AMRO] Trust. They were willing for the appeal to be adjourned in order that the witness could attend in person to be available for cross-examination. They produced all the documents which existed

8.83 *Tax planning for the non-resident and non-domiciled*

(so I assume, and no one has suggested that any documents were suppressed). The documents showed guidance and influence coming from Price Waterhouse, but no more than that. Mr. and Mrs Wood were able to point out that the Netherlands Revenue had stated to the United Kingdom Revenue that the actual management of Eulalia was carried out by [ABN AMRO] Trust, "meaning that the taxable domicile of Eulalia Holding BV is located in the Netherlands". Surely at that point they can say: "We have done enough to raise a case that Eulalia was not resident in the United Kingdom. What more can the Special Commissioners expect from us? The burden must now pass to the Revenue to produce some material to show that, despite what appears from everything which we have produced, Eulalia was actually resident in the United Kingdom." '

He also thought it was not enough for HMRC to demonstrate that the steps taken were part of a single tax scheme, that there were overall architects of the scheme in Price Waterhouse Corporate Finance Ltd and that those involved all shared the common expectation that the various stages of the scheme would in fact take place. These matters were not denied. However, he felt that, taken together they did not, of themselves, lead to the conclusion that Eulalia was resident in the UK.

8.83 The Court of Appeal agreed with the judge. Furthermore, Lord Justice Chadwick added that:

'A further flaw in the Special Commissioners' approach was to treat the decisions which were made by ABN AMRO as not "effective decisions" because they were reached without proper information or consideration. But a management decision does not cease to be a management decision because it might have been taken on fuller information; or even, as it seems to me, because it was taken in circumstances which might put the director at risk of an allegation of breach of duty. Ill-informed or ill-advised decisions taken in the management of a company remain management decisions.'

Companies incorporated in the UK

8.84 From 15 March 1988, a company that is incorporated in the UK must be regarded as UK resident for tax purposes (*FA 1988, s 66*). This can, of course, be overridden by double tax treaties (*FA 1994, s 249*). As with individuals, double tax treaties normally contain a tie-breaker clause to treat a company as resident in one only of the two countries which are party to the treaty. This normally provides that the company is deemed to be a resident only of the country in which its place of effective management is situated. This is probably the same test as central management and control.

Non-resident company trading in the UK

8.85 A non-UK resident company will of course be taxable in the UK to the extent that it has taxable income arising here. A non-UK resident company is within the charge to corporation tax if, and only if, it carries on a trade in the UK through a permanent establishment in the UK. It is so taxable on all profits, wherever arising, that are attributable to its permanent establishment in the UK, including income from property or rights used by, or held by or for, the establishment, and on chargeable gains falling within *TCGA 1992, s 10B* (see above) by virtue of assets being used in or for the purposes of the trade carried on through the establishment or being used or held (or acquired for use) for the purposes of the establishment (*ICTA 1988, s 11*).

8.86 A company has a permanent establishment in the UK if, and only if, it has a fixed place of business here through which its business is wholly or partly carried on, or an agent acting on behalf of the company has, and habitually exercises in the UK, authority to do business on behalf of the company (*FA 2003, s 148(1)*). For this purpose, a fixed place of business includes a place of management, a branch, an office, a factory, a workshop, an installation or structure for the exploration of natural resources, a mine, an oil or gas well, a quarry or any other place of extraction of natural resources, a building site and a construction or installation project (*FA 2003, s 148(2)*). A company cannot have a permanent establishment in the UK by reason only of the fact that it carries on business here through an agent of independent status acting in the ordinary course of his business (*FA 2003, s 148(3)*). A company is not regarded as having a permanent establishment if the activities carried on in the UK are only of a preparatory or auxiliary character, such as the use of facilities for the purpose of storage, display or delivery of goods or merchandise belonging to the company, the maintenance of a stock of goods or merchandise belonging to the company for the purpose of storage, display or delivery or of processing by another person, or purchasing goods or merchandise for the company, or collecting information (FA 2003, *s 148(4), (5)*).

The legislation lays down rules for attributing profits to a permanent establishment (*ICTA 1988, s 11A, Sch A1*).

Where a company is not within the charge to corporation tax it will be chargeable to income tax at the basic rate on UK source income. It is not clear if it can be chargeable to income tax on trading income which does not arise through a permanent establishment.

Change of residence

8.87 There is no bar on a UK company changing its residence, although if the company is incorporated in the UK it can do so only by becoming dual

8.88 *Tax planning for the non-resident and non-domiciled*

resident or being deemed to be non-resident under a double tax agreement as a UK incorporated company is treated as resident here (with some exceptions where a company ceased to be UK resident before 1988).

8.88 There are a number of provisions that can impose a tax charge where a UK resident company ceases to be resident here or which relate to non-resident companies. The main ones are *ICTA 1988, s 337*, (company beginning or ceasing to be within the charge to corporation tax), *FA 1988, s 130* (provisions for securing payment by company of outstanding tax), *FA 1988, s 132* (liability of other persons for unpaid tax), *TCGA 1992, s 14* (non-resident groups of companies), *TCGA 1992, s 185* (deemed disposal of assets on company ceasing to be resident in the UK), *FA 1995, s 126* (UK representatives of non-residents), *FA 2000, s 98* (recovery of tax payable by non-resident company), *FA 2003, s 150* (non-resident companies: assessment, collection and recovery of corporation tax), *s 151* (non-resident companies: extent of charge to income tax), *s 152* (non-resident companies: transactions carried out through broker, investment manager or Lloyd's agent), and *FA 2006, s 27* (group relief where surrendering company not resident in UK).

8.89 It is unlawful for a UK company to cause or permit a non-UK company over which it has control to create or issue any shares or debentures, or to transfer to any person any shares or debentures of a non-UK company over which it has control, without Treasury consent (*ICTA 1988, s 765*). There is an exception where the issue or transfer is a movement of capital within the EC Directive of 24 June 1988 (*ICTA 1988, s 765A*).

Dual resident companies

8.90 As with an individual, it is possible for a company to be resident in two or more countries simultaneously because the test for residence is different in each country. Where this occurs the legislation can restrict the deductibility of specified expenditure and capital allowances to prevent double relief being obtained. Accordingly, it is normally best to seek to avoid such a status.

Companies treated as non-resident

8.91 Where a UK resident company is treated as non-resident under a double tax treaty it is treated as non-resident for all the purposes of the *Taxes Acts* (*FA 1994, s 249*). For this purpose a company is regarded as treaty non-resident if it meets the appropriate conditions, even if it has not claimed the benefit of the treaty (*FA 1994, s 249(2)*).

Chapter 9

Tax efficient investments

David Brookes FCA, Tax Partner, BDO Stoy Hayward LLP

INVESTMENT IN UNQUOTED TRADING COMPANIES

9.1 There are important tax reliefs available for investments in qualifying unquoted trading companies. It should be noted that shares that are quoted on AIM/ PLUS Markets (formerly Ofex) are regarded as unquoted for this purpose. Although Plus-Quoted shares are treated as unquoted, PLUS-listed shares are treated as quoted for tax purposes and companies which are dual listed are likely to be treated as quoted for tax purposes since HMRC's list of 'Recognised Stock Exchanges' includes most foreign exchanges (*ITA 2007, s 1005* and *ICTA 1988, s 841(1)(b)*).

The principal tax reliefs available to individuals investing in unquoted trading companies are as follows:

- Capital Gains Tax (Business Asset Taper Relief and Gift Relief) – see **9.2–9.3**
- Inheritance tax (Business Property Relief) – see **9.4**
- Loss relief – see **9.8**
- The Enterprise Investment Scheme ('EIS') – see **9.5**
- Venture Capital Trusts ('VCT's) – see **9.14**

Capital Gains Tax (CGT)

Business asset taper relief

In the Pre-Budget Report of October 2007 the Chancellor of the Exchequer announced that taper relief would be abolished in its entirety for disposals taking place after 5 April 2008.

9.2 *Tax efficient investments*

From 6 April 2008 Capital gains will simply be calculated on the proceeds of disposal less any cost and taxed at the rate of 18%. At the time of going to press, there is still no draft legislation, so the finer details of the changes are unclear.

9.2 Taper relief applies to individual investors and trustees and reduces the gain subject to taxation on the disposal of shares. The amount of relief given depends on whether the asset is a 'business' or a 'non-business' asset and how long the asset has been held since 6 April 1998. Where assets have been business assets for only part of the qualifying holding period it is necessary to apportion this gain between business and non-business periods. Only the last ten years of ownership are taken into account.

Shares in AIM/ Plus Markets trading companies are classified as 'business assets' which results in a higher rate of taper relief. Business asset taper relief can reduce the individual's effective tax rate on a disposal of shares after two years from 40% to only 10% of the gain. Unlike Enterprise Investment Scheme disposal relief (which may result in a tax-free gain on new shares which have been subscribed for), taper relief can be claimed on either newly issued shares or 'second hand' shares.

In order to qualify as a trading company, or the holding company of a trading group, it is important to ensure that any non-trading activities are not substantial (broadly no more than 20%).

For disposals on or after 6 April 2002, until 5 April 2008, the rates of taper relief are as follows:

No of whole years assets held	Taper relief %	Gain chargeable %
Business assets		
For disposals after 5 April 2002		
0	0	100
1	50	50
2 or more	75	25
Non-business assets*		
Less than 3	0	100
3	5	95
4	10	90
5	15	85
6	20	80

7	25	75
8	30	70
9	35	65
10 or more	40	60
(* assets held before 17 March 1998 receive a one year bonus)		

Taper relief is available to individuals and trustees on gains assessed to UK CGT whether or not they are resident in the UK.

Capital gains tax gift relief

9.3 It is possible for shares in an unquoted trading company held by an individual or trust to be transferred to another individual or trust at a price other than arm's length (eg a gift). In such circumstances the capital gain based on the market value of the asset can be 'held over' until the recipient sells the shares.

Both the donor and the recipient must claim gift relief within certain time limits, and the recipient has a capital gains tax base cost equal to the donor's base cost. The recipient must be resident or ordinarily resident in the UK.

It should be noted that the gift has the effect of restarting the period of ownership for taper relief purposes (except for transfers between spouses) and no taper relief is available for the previous period of ownership. Although this will not be applicable after 5 April 2007.

Inheritance tax business property relief (IHT BPR)

9.4 Subject to certain conditions, investments in AIM/Plus-Markets trading companies will attract 100% relief from inheritance tax (business property relief) provided the shares have been held for at least two years. Most trades qualify but the company's business must *not* be wholly or mainly that of:

- dealing in securities, stocks and shares;
- dealing in land or buildings;
- making or holding investments within an investment business.

Due to the attractive nature of this relief for individuals seeking an inheritance tax shelter there are a number of investment products on the market such as AIM Portfolios where investors can invest in a portfolio of AIM companies which is managed on the investor's behalf by a professional manager. The investor is the

9.5 *Tax efficient investments*

beneficial owner of the shares although not the legal owner. Inheritance business property relief should be available on the investment after two years.

There are other investment products on the market which involve shareholders holding shares in an unquoted trading company which is carrying on a qualifying trade. If the shares are subscribed for and the company's trade also qualifies under the EIS requirements it would be possible to combine the benefits of inheritance tax relief with EIS tax reliefs, as discussed in more detail below.

ENTERPRISE INVESTMENT SCHEME (EIS) RELIEF

9.5 The EIS gives a tax incentive to qualifying investors (as defined below) who subscribe for shares in certain small unquoted trading companies (this includes shares quoted on AIM/Plus-Markets).

The EIS relief has four elements, outlined below.

Income tax relief

9.6 This allows an investor to reduce the amount of his, or her, liability to income tax in the year of investment (*ITA 2007, ss 157, 158*). Relief is obtained at the lower rate of income tax, currently 20%, on the amount subscribed for the shares of qualifying companies. Investors should be able to deduct an amount equal to 20% of their investment from their liability to income tax in the current tax year. From 6 April 2006 relief cannot be claimed on more than £400,000 (previously £200,000) subscribed by an individual (in any number of qualifying companies).

An individual who subscribes for shares after 5 April and before 6 October in a tax year may claim to carry back part of the subscription to the previous tax year. The amount of the subscription that can be carried back is limited to the lower of:

- £50,000;
- half of the amount subscribed; and
- the unused balance of relief available for the previous year.

To retain this relief the shares must be held by the investor for a period that ends three years after the share issue date or three years after the trade starts, whichever is later. This will be referred to below as the three-year period.

Example 9.1

	£
Gross subscription for shares	10,000
Less tax relief at 20%	(2,000)
Net cost of investment	8,000

Capital gains tax exemption

9.7 This exempts investors from the liability to capital gains tax when they realise a gain on a disposal of their shares in qualifying companies after the three-year period, provided the EIS income tax relief was given on the shares and has not been withdrawn.

Example 9.2

	£
Realised value of shares after three- year period	20,000
Original gross subscription for shares	(10,000)
Tax-free gain	10,000

Loss relief

9.8 In the event of an investor suffering a loss arising from the disposal of the EIS shares at any time, this relief allows the offset of that loss against either capital gains or, by election, taxable income in the year of the loss (*ITA 2007, s 131*; for claims prior to 5 April 2007 *ICTA 1988, s 574*).

Example 9.3

	£
Realised value of shares	Nil
Original cost of investment	(10,000)
EIS income tax relief	2,000
Loss	(8,000)
EIS loss relief (assuming a 40% taxpayer)	3,200
Net loss (available to offset against other gains)	(4,800)

9.9 *Tax efficient investments*

Capital gains tax deferral

9.9 Individuals and certain trustees can defer all or part of their Capital Gains Tax (CGT) liabilities by subscribing for eligible shares in an EIS company (*TCGA 1992, s 150C*). There is no monetary limit on the amount of the EIS subscription and thus the gain that can be deferred in this way. The gains that can be deferred are those that have arisen in the three years before the EIS shares are issued or those that arise up to one year after that date. Such gains may be the result of the disposal of an asset or, a gain previously deferred by the individual, may have become chargeable to tax.

Investors should note that this relief is a deferral only and that the original capital gain will crystallise on the disposal of the EIS shares at any time, resulting in CGT being payable in the normal way. The investor would, however, be able to claim further CGT deferral to the extent that a qualifying reinvestment is made within the time allowed. A transfer of shares on the owner's death does not cause the deferred gain to crystallise.

Example 9.4

(assumes a higher rate taxpayer with a chargeable gain of £10,000)

	£
Gross investment in shares	10,000
Less CGT deferral at 40%	(4,000)
Less tax relief at 20%	(2,000)
Cost of investment (prior to capital gain crystallising)	4,000

EIS qualifying investors

9.10 Individual investors must meet certain conditions to be a qualifying investor (*ITA 2007, ss 162–171*). Qualifying investors must continue to qualify for the three-year period. The conditions, which are less stringent for deferral relief than for income tax relief and tax-free capital gains, can be summarised as follows:

For ***income tax relief and tax-free capital gains*** the individual:

- Must have a liability to pay UK income tax (the individual need not be UK resident).

Tax efficient investments **9.12**

- Must not be 'connected' with the company by being:
  - an employee
  - a paid director prior to the share issue
  - a shareholder who, together with associates, controls the company or is entitled to more than 30% of:
    - the company's issued ordinary share capital;
    - the aggregate of its loan capital and issued share capital;
    - its voting power; or
    - its assets in a winding up.
- Must not be a *new* director unless the complex so-called 'business angel' provisions have been met.

Finally, there is an upper limit for qualifying investments of £400,000 per person per annum from 6 April 2006.

9.11 For *deferral relief* the individual:

- Must be UK resident and ordinarily resident (and not dual resident) at both the date of the disposal giving rise to the gain and the date of the investment. This status must continue for three years from the date the shares are issued.
- Must reinvest the chargeable gain (before taper relief) in the period one year before and up to three years after it arises.
- May be 'connected' with the company as defined above.

The individual can invest any amount (restricted of course by the gross asset limit for the company itself, which must not exceed £8 million immediately after the share issue).

The level of investment required to defer the gain is the amount of the gain after indexation and before taper relief. Where a gain is deferred there is no loss of taper relief but no further taper relief accrues on the deferred gain, ie the amount of taper relief is frozen at the date of the disposal.

Receipt of value

9.12 An EIS investor must not receive 'value' from the company (or any of its subsidiaries) at any time during the period one-year before to three years after his shares are issued (*ITA 2007, ss 213–225*). The rules in this area are complex but the investor is deemed to receive 'value' if, inter-alia:

9.13 *Tax efficient investments*

- the company buys back its own shares;
- the company makes a loan to the investor;
- the investor receives an abnormal amount by way of dividend, or excessive remuneration or expenses.

Withdrawal of relief

9.13 Shares cease to be eligible and deferral relief may be withdrawn in the following circumstances:

1. where, during the qualifying period, the company is no longer a qualifying company;
2. where, during the qualifying period, the qualifying trade or research and development is not being carried on by the qualifying company or a qualifying 90% subsidiary;
3. where less than 80% of the proceeds of the issue have been applied towards a qualifying business activity within one year and the balance within the following year;
4. where not all the shares (other than, for shares issued after 16 March 2004, any of them which are bonus shares) were issued in order to fund a qualifying business.

In cases 1–3, shares cease to be eligible at the time of the relevant event; in case 4, deferral relief is deemed never to have been available.

Relief can only be withdrawn where the company concerned has given notice to the inspector where required to do so, or where the inspector has given notice to the company that, in his opinion, relief should be withdrawn.

VENTURE CAPITAL TRUSTS (VCTs)

9.14 VCTs are fully listed companies that attract individual investors who are able to claim tax reliefs on their investment. The VCTs then invest in a spread of unquoted trading companies (which for these purposes includes AIM/Plus companies) and is exempt from corporation tax on its capital gains as an investment trust (*TCGA 1992, s 100(1)*). In order to be approved by HMRC the VCT's investments must, after three years, be at least 70% in qualifying unquoted trading companies.

Each VCT may only invest up to £1 million per tax year in any one company and no holding may represent more than 15% of the VCT's total investments. These rules are designed to ensure a spread of investments.

A VCT company's investment may be in the form of a cash subscription for shares and/or loan stock with a minimum term of five years. At least 30% of the VCT's total qualifying investments and 10% of each individual investment must be in new ordinary shares.

9.15 The following VCT reliefs are available to individuals who are over 18 years of age, in respect of subscriptions of up to £200,000 per tax year.

- *Income tax relief.* For shares issued after 6 April 2006 an amount equal to 30% of the amount subscribed is deducted from the investor's income tax liability. The relief is limited to the income tax liability of an investor and is given before all other deductions. It is only available if new shares are subscribed for and held for five years (previously three years). There is no legal minimum but each VCT decides on its minimum subscription.
- *Tax-free gains.* Any gain on a disposal of VCT shares is tax-free at any time. There is no tax relief of any kind if a loss arises on VCT shares.
- *Tax-free dividends.* Dividends paid by a VCT to individuals are tax-free.

These last two reliefs are available to individuals who subscribe for or purchase shares, provided they have not exceeded their VCT annual limit of £200,000.

VCT capital gains tax deferral relief has been withdrawn for shares issued on or after 6 April 2004.

Criteria for qualifying EIS and VCT companies

9.16 There are a number of criteria that must be met for qualifying companies:

- The shares on which EIS and VCT relief can be claimed must be eligible shares, which are:
    - new ordinary shares,
    - with no present or future preferential right to income or to assets on a winding up, and
    - with no present or future right to be redeemed.

    The shares must be subscribed for wholly in cash and be fully paid up at the time of subscription.

    A VCT's investment can be in:
    - new ordinary shares, and/or
    - preference shares or loans with a minimum term of five years.

9.16 *Tax efficient investments*

If a company is to remain as a qualifying holding it must do so throughout the period the investment is held by a VCT.

- The issuing company can be a single trading company or the parent of a trading group (the Group).
- For shares issued after 5 April 2006, the gross assets of the issuing company or the Group must not exceed:

    – £7 million immediately before; and

    – £8 million immediately after, the share issue.

    There are transitional provisions which allow the previous gross asset limits of £15 million and £16 million to apply; in the case of EIS investments where the subscription took place before 22 March 2006 and VCT investments where the funds were raised by the VCT prior to 6 April 2006.

- The issuing company must not have arrangements in place at the time of the share issue, to reduce the investors' risk or pre-arrange the investors' exit.

    For EIS purposes, when the shares are issued, the issuing company must be unquoted and there must be no arrangements in place for it to become quoted. In the case of VCT investee companies that later become quoted they are deemed to be unquoted for these purposes for a further five years. Shares that are quoted on AIM/Plus are unquoted for this purpose.

- The issuing company (or one of its subsidiaries) at the time of the share issue must exist to carry on a qualifying trade and must either be:

    – carrying on a qualifying trade;

    – preparing to carry on a qualifying trade (which it must start within two years); or

    – carrying out research and development from which a qualifying trade will be carried on.

- During the issuing company's qualifying period it must not be under the control of another company and cannot itself control another company except for its qualifying subsidiaries.

    To be a qualifying subsidiary, the following conditions must be satisfied:

    – the issuing company must directly or indirectly own more than 50% of the ordinary share capital of the subsidiary;

    – no person other than the issuing company or another of its subsidiaries should control the subsidiary; and

Tax efficient investments **9.16**

- no arrangements should exist whereby either of the above conditions would cease to be satisfied.

In the case of the corporate venturing scheme (CVS), at least 20% of the ordinary share capital of the issuing company must be owned by individuals who are not directors or employees (or their relatives) of the investing company or a company connected with that company.

- In each case, the activity must be carried on commercially, and wholly or mainly (more than 50%) in the UK, if it is to be a qualifying activity. A qualifying subsidiary can trade outside the UK. However, the company using the funds, which may be the issuing company or its qualifying 90% subsidiary, must trade mainly in the UK.
- The company must employ at least 80% of the money raised for qualifying trading purposes within 12 months of:
  - the date the shares were issued; or
  - the company starting its qualifying trade, if this is later.

  The remainder must be employed within 24 months of these dates.
- The company must carry on a qualifying trade.

  There is no definition of a qualifying trade, but non-qualifying trading activities must not be carried on to any substantial extent (more than 20%). These activities are:
  - dealing in land, in commodities or futures, or in shares, securities or other financial instruments;
  - dealing in goods otherwise than in the course of an ordinary trade of wholesale or retail distribution;
  - banking, insurance, moneylending, debt-factoring, hire-purchase financing or other financial activities;
  - leasing (including letting ships on charter or other assets on hire), or receiving royalties or licence fees (exceptions are made for intangible assets created by the issuing company or its subsidiaries);
  - providing legal or accountancy services;
  - farming and market gardening, woodlands and timber production;
  - property development;
  - operating and managing hotels and nursing homes;
  - providing services to a connected person with one of the above trades.
- The *Finance Act 2007* introduced two new restrictions, as a result of European Commission rules on state aid. With effect from 19 July 2007 an EIS company must have no more than 50 full-time equivalent employees

9.17 *Tax efficient investments*

(*ITA 2007, s 186A*) and can raise no more than £2 million in total from the EIS, VCT and Corporate Venturing Scheme in a 12-month period ending beginning after 19 July 2007 and ending on the date of the relevant investment (*ITA 2007, s 173A*). For VCTs there is a transitional period and these new restrictions only apply to funds raised after 5 April 2007. Any funds raised on or before 5 April 2007 are 'protected money' and the new restrictions do not apply.

EIS FUNDS – APPROVED AND UNAPPROVED

Approved EIS funds

9.17 In the case of an approved EIS fund, the fund manager issues a prospectus. With the money received from subscribers the manager subscribes for shares on the individuals' behalf. The managers effectively retain control over the portfolio for the fund's life, which is normally three to seven years to allow the managers to make an orderly divestment of the shares. The managers are empowered to agree to reconstructions and amalgamations as well as to the sale of the investments.

If an investor subscribes through an EIS fund the usual EIS tax benefits will be available and the risk is spread across a portfolio of investee companies. There are also some important relaxations to the EIS rules, as follows:

- the £500 lower limit on the amount that an individual must subscribe for shares in a company to qualify for investment relief does not apply where the investment in the company is made on an individual's behalf by the manager of an approved fund; and

- the investor can obtain tax relief on their entire investment in the fund in the tax year in which the fund closes, ie provided that all the necessary conditions are satisfied, all shares acquired through the fund are treated as if they had been issued on the date the fund closes.

This contrasts with the position of investors in unapproved funds, who obtain tax relief on their share of the investment made by the fund only at the time the fund itself makes those investments. (It should be noted that even for an approved fund, in the case of an investor claiming EIS deferral relief the date of investment in the underlying investee company is the relevant date.)

An approved EIS fund must meet certain conditions; for example, the managers cannot start making investments until after the fund closes, and at least 90% of the funds raised must be invested in new shares in qualifying companies within 12 months of the date of closure.

Unapproved EIS funds and schemes

9.18 The managers of an unapproved EIS fund or managed EIS scheme will have made a decision not to seek HMRC approval because they do not wish to be bound by the conditions (particularly the 12-month time period for making investments). As in the case of an approved EIS fund, however, the manager subscribes for EIS shares on the individual's behalf and effectively retains control of the portfolio for the period of the fund's life.

The investors in an unapproved fund benefit from EIS tax reliefs and a spread of risk but do not benefit from the exemption from the £500 minimum investment and income tax relief is given by reference to the date the underlying investments are made rather than the date the fund closes.

REAL ESTATE INVESTMENT TRUSTS (REITS)

9.19 Real Estate Investment Trusts were recently introduced in the UK to allow investors to invest in a company which is fully listed on a recognised stock exchange and has a portfolio of investment properties but effectively be taxed as though they owned property directly.

Where a UK-REIT satisfies the various conditions and has a business consisting at least 75% of property rental, the rental income is exempt from corporation tax, as are capital gains on the disposal of rental properties. One of the key conditions is that the UK-REIT must distribute 90% of its rental profits from its tax-exempt property rental business, and pay these distributions under deduction of basic rate income tax.

9.20 As noted above, the returns received by investors broadly mirror the treatment of direct holding in property. For UK tax purposes, the relevant profits are not taxable within the REIT vehicle, and the property income distributions are taxed as property rental income in the hands of the shareholder.

If other profits of the REIT are distributed (ie profits other than from property rental) these will be taxed as a normal dividend.

The REIT shares will be subject to capital gains tax in the usual way.

INSURANCE PRODUCTS

Life assurance policies

Treatment of qualifying policies

9.21 Tax relief is available for premiums paid by a UK resident on a 'qualifying' life assurance policy made *before* 14 March 1984 (*ICTA 1988,*

9.22 *Tax efficient investments*

ss 266–267 and, for the definition of a 'qualifying policy', *Sch 15*, as amended by *ITTOIA 2005*). The relief is given by allowing the policyholder to deduct and retain 12½% of the premium, provided that the total annual premiums payable do not exceed the greater of £1,500 and one-sixth of his total income (*ICTA 1988, s 274*). The insurer reclaims the deduction from HMRC. The relief is not available for policies made after 13 March 1984, nor for those made before that date where the holder subsequently alters the policy to increase the benefits secured or to extend the term. In such cases premiums will be paid without the 12½% deduction.

The proceeds of a qualifying policy are not normally subject to income tax.

Non-qualifying policies (*ICTA 1988, ss 539–554*; see now *ITTOIA 2005, s 461*ff)

9.22 The typical example of a non-qualifying policy is the single premium insurance bond or with-profits investment bond. Not only is no relief available on the sum invested, but any gain realised by the policyholder, net of premiums paid, on the occasion of a 'chargeable event' (eg on surrender, maturity, assignment or death) may be subject to income tax at higher rate (but tax at the lower rate, or, for years prior to 2004/05 at the basic rate, is deemed to have been paid) subject to top slicing relief. Annual tax-free withdrawals are allowed up to the value of the original investment so long as they do not exceed 5% of the premium paid for each year of the policy (ie the tax-free withdrawals cease after 20 years). Single premium bonds therefore provide shelter for income in the case of higher rate taxpayers. However, for non-taxpayers they are not necessarily the most tax efficient investments since the underlying assets held by the life insurance company are subject to tax.

Taxation of insurance companies

9.23 The rate of corporation tax on the relevant profits (both income and capital) of a life assurance company is equal to the lower rate of income tax (20% in 2007/08). The policyholder is not charged on these accumulating profits.

FA 1998 changes

9.24 FA 1998 contained measures aimed at preventing 'avoidance loopholes', ie:

Tax efficient investments **9.26**

- In the case of policies held in trust it was possible to avoid any charge by the 'dead settlor trick'. From 6 April 1998 this is prevented by gains being taxed on the trustees or beneficiaries who receive benefits.
- Special rules for 'personal portfolio bonds' (ie a life policy where benefits are linked to a portfolio of assets that is personal to the policyholder). In such cases an annual tax charge on the basis of deemed gains is imposed.
- Compliance rules aimed at non-UK insurance companies who sell insurance in the UK and special rules for overseas life assurance business if the policyholder becomes UK resident.

General treatment of non-qualifying insurance policies

9.25 Gains arising from dealings in non-qualifying policies are subject to higher rate tax if there is a chargeable event. Lower rate tax (basic rate for years prior to 2004/05) is deemed to have been paid but is not recoverable.

A chargeable event occurs when there is a surrender, a death giving rise to benefits under the policy, maturity or assignment for consideration.

Example 9.5

Elizabeth, a higher rate taxpayer, takes out a non-qualifying single premium life contract in June 1997 for £20,000. She withdraws 5% each year for two years, ie a total of £2,000. She takes no further amounts.

In June 2007 she surrenders the policy for, say, £24,000.

The total withdrawals are £26,000, ie £2,000 plus surrender proceeds of £24,000.

Deduct premium paid of £20,000. No gains previously charged, so no further deduction. Chargeable gains are £6,000 top sliced over nine years.

Individuals who are non-UK resident throughout a year of assessment are not liable to UK tax on gains on chargeable events even on UK non-qualifying policies (*ITTOIA 2005, s 465(1)*, post-5 April 2005; previously this was an extra statutory concession, ESC B53). If the policy has been assigned by that individual to a trust the position is usually more adverse.

Offshore policies

9.26 A policy issued by an offshore life office that does not trade in the UK is not subject to tax on the income and gains from the investments underlying

9.27 *Tax efficient investments*

the policy. The chargeable events legislation still applies so that gains realised when the policy matures, is surrendered, or assigned for consideration will be taxable.

Trusts

9.27 Any gain on the policy is taxed as the income of an individual if immediately before the chargeable event he or a trust created by him owns the policy (*ITTOIA 2005, s 465(3)*). Note that there is still a charge on the settlor even if he cannot benefit from the trust although he has a right of reimbursement. Therefore trustees should be careful before taking out policies where the settlor is still alive.

If the settlor has died or is non-resident, then the gain on the policy is chargeable at the rate for trusts and assessed on the trustees (*ITTOIA 2005, s 467*).

However, if the trust had taken out a policy with funds left by a settlor who died prior to 17 March 1998 and the policy was issued before 17 March 1998 and has not subsequently been varied, then there is no tax payable (see *FA 1998, Sch 14, para 7*). This is the so-called dead settlor trick.

FA 2003 changes

9.28 FA 2003 introduced a number of changes to prevent marketed tax avoidance schemes in relation to life insurance policies and deferred annuity contracts. *TCGA 1992, s 210* was amended with effect from 9 April 2003 in order to prevent capital losses being generated which exceed the amount of any economic loss and also prevent gains escaping a charge to tax simply because the person making the disposal has received the policy or contract by way of gift.

Example 9.6

Miss X takes out a new life insurance policy paying a single premium of £500,000. The policy is one liable to income tax on a chargeable event gain. She sells it to Mr Y for £525,000, Mr Y surrenders the policy back to the insurance company and receives £502,000 in cash. Mr Y is treated as making a chargeable event gain of £2,000 on which he is liable to income tax (£502,000 less the amount of the premium paid of £500,000). Under the old rules for capital gains tax he was treated as receiving £502,000 but this was taken into account in calculating his chargeable gain so was disregarded for capital gains tax purposes. His cost of acquiring the policy of £525,000 was not taken into account in the income tax calculations so it is not disregarded for capital gains tax purposes. Therefore under the old legislation he made an allowable loss of £525,000. Following amended *s 210* the income tax position is unchanged but his allowable loss is restricted to £23,000, ie £525,000 less the amount he received on surrender of the policy of £502,000.

Example 9.7

Mrs Z buys a second-hand life insurance policy for £20,000. It is not a policy which attracts liability to income tax but she is liable to capital gains tax on any gain because she is not the original owner and she paid cash to acquire it. Just before maturity she gives the policy to her husband and he receives £36,000 from the insurance company. Mr Z does not have an income tax liability but makes a gain of £16,000. Under the old rules this gain was not liable to capital gains tax because Mr Z did not give any actual consideration to acquire the policy. Under new *s 210* neither of them will have any income tax liability but Mr Z is now treated as having made a gain of £16,000 liable to capital gains tax because, although he gave nothing to acquire the property, his spouse (or civil partner from 5 December 2005) has given actual consideration to acquire the policy.

FA 2004 changes

9.29 FA 2004, *s 140* sought to close an avoidance opportunity by limiting the amount of the deficiency relief that can be set off against the income of the individual in circumstances where there is a deficiency when the insurance policy, life annuity contract or capital redemption policy comes to an end. *FA 2004, s 140* amended *ICTA 1988, s 549*. As a result of the amendment, the amount of the relief to which the individual is entitled cannot be greater than the total amounts of earlier gains made on the insurance policy, life annuity contract or capital redemption policy which formed part of the individual's income in an earlier year of assessment. Earlier gains may have arisen as a result of earlier part surrenders of the policy or contract.

9.30 This amendment has effect from 3 March 2004 in relation to all new life insurance policies, capital redemption policies and life annuity contracts. It also applies to life insurance policies, capital redemption policies and life annuity contracts that existed at 3 March 2004 if:

- the life insurance policies, capital redemption policies or life annuity contracts are varied on or after 3 March 2004 so as to increase the benefits secured;

9.31 *Tax efficient investments*

- all or part of the rights conferred by the life insurance policies, capital redemption policies or life annuity contracts are assigned on or after 3 March 2004; or
- all or part of the right conferred by the life insurance policies, capital redemption policies or life annuity contracts come to be held as security in relation to a debt on or after 3 March 2004.

ITTOIA 2005 changes

9.31 As part of the Tax Law Rewrite project, many of the provisions relating to the taxation of insurance policies have been rewritten and are now found in *ITTOIA 2005, Ch 9 Pt 4*. These rewritten provisions deal with all three types of contracts/policies while at the same time attempting to preserve the different rules that relate to each specific type of contract/policy.

Group life policies

9.32 Many partnerships have inadequate life cover in the event that one of their partners dies in service before retirement. The occupational death in service approved life insurance options are not open to them because they are self-employed and each partner has therefore traditionally had to take out life cover individually on his own life for the benefit of his dependants. Increasingly, partnerships instead want to take out some form of group life cover that insures the lives of all their partners and pays benefits on more than one death. This can be obtained more cheaply on a group rather than an individual basis.

9.33 Following changes in *FA 2003*, the income tax situation has been improved because, provided a group life policy qualifies as an excepted group life policy within *ICTA 1988, s 539A* (now *ITTOIA 2005, ss 481–482*), it is now outside the scope of the income tax charge if there is a chargeable event such as a death. Previously there was an income tax charge on the second and subsequent deaths. If structured properly the group life assurance scheme can also be held in trust to pay out benefits to the dependants of the deceased partner on a discretionary basis in order to obtain maximum inheritance tax advantages. In order to qualify as an excepted group life policy a number of conditions must be satisfied.

9.34 Condition 1 provides that under the policy, sums or other benefits of a capital nature must be payable on the death of each of the individuals insured under the policy but only if the individual dies before reaching his or her 75th birthday. The same method of calculation must be used for calculating each of the death benefits payable under the policy. Generally, no sums or benefits may be paid or conferred under the policy other than on death. The recipients of the death benefits paid must be individuals or charities so, if the death benefits have been written in trust, care will be needed on payment out of those benefits to ensure that the payments are made outright rather than on trusts to the partners' dependants. This could cause problems if such dependants are minor children. It is not possible to allow another partner who has survived the deceased partner to receive any benefits on payment out unless such other partner receives the death benefits for another reason – for example, they are the spouse of an insured person who has died.

INVESTMENT AND SAVINGS PRODUCTS

Investment products and IHT planning

9.35 There are a number of insurance products or 'schemes' currently in the marketplace which centre round the idea of the investor giving a cash sum into trust but continuing to benefit from the funds, allegedly without inheritance or other tax problems.

These products generally involve some type of single premium non-qualifying endowment policy written in some form of trust.

9.36 The initial minimum premiums invested are often quite high – £50,000 is not atypical. The idea is that the investor is limited to his 5% 'tax-free' withdrawal. If withdrawals exceed 5% of the premium paid, there is the usual higher rate income tax charge on the excess subject to top-slicing relief. In addition, the life assurance company, unless based abroad, usually pays tax on the relevant underlying profits currently at the rate of 20%. However, provided the 5% limits are not exceeded, the investor is not charged to any income tax or gains even though the trust is settlor interested because the trust holds all its assets in the wrapper of the bond. Thus the underlying gains (if any) realised within the bond itself are not taxable on the settlor.

The types of scheme are described below. It should be noted, however, that FA 2006 will have a profound effect on new trust arrangements for life assurance based products, which will be subject to the new inheritance tax regime for trusts. For pre-22 March 2006 interest-in-possession trusts holding pre-22 March 2006 contracts of life assurance, even where premiums are paid on or after that date, measures exist in *FA 2006* which effectively exclude them from the new regime for the inheritance taxation of interest-in-possession trusts. Nor will ongoing premium payments affect the transitional provisions applicable to pre-22 March accumulation and maintenance trusts.

9.37 *Tax efficient investments*

Spousal interest trust

9.37 Such trusts are no longer possible to set up from 20 June 2003 due to *FA 2003, s 185*. Under the 'old scheme', the donor, eg the husband, effected a capital investment bond which was written on interest-in-possession trusts under which his wife was entitled to the interest in possession. The settlor was among the class of potential beneficiaries. Say six months later the trustees exercised their powers of appointment to terminate her interest in possession in favour of the settlor's children who would take interests in possession. The wife would no longer benefit and was treated as having made a PET when her interest in possession was ended by the trustees. If she survived seven years the initial value of the bond fell outside her estate for inheritance tax purposes. The idea was that any later growth in the bond should also fall outside the couple's estate for inheritance tax purposes whether or not she survived seven years.

The husband continued to benefit and from time to time the trustees could use their 5% withdrawal facility to make partial encashments from the bond and appoint such capital out to the settlor. Provided the encashments did not exceed 5%, there was no income tax charge on the settlor.

9.38 The idea behind this scheme was that the gifts with reservation (GWR) provisions were avoided due to the initial gift being to the settlor's spouse. Therefore, *FA 1986, s 102(5)(a)* arguably applied which says that to the extent any gift is covered by the spouse exemption then no GWR will occur.

The Revenue did not accept this analysis and argued that there was a reservation of benefit. The point went to the High Court and then the Court of Appeal in the context of family homes – see *IRC v Eversden* [2003] STC 822).

The scheme was effectively stopped by *FA 2003, s 185*. Insurance bonds taken out and settled prior to 20 June 2003 are not affected by the *FA 2003* changes.

Gift and loan scheme

9.39 The investor as settlor sets up a trust for the benefit of his children. He cannot benefit from the trust. The settlor then makes an interest-free loan repayable on demand to the trustees who use this money to invest in a bond normally written on the lives of the named beneficiaries under the trust. The idea is that the loan is not a diminution in the settlor's estate and therefore effectively no transfer of value has been made under this arrangement.

From time to time, the settlor demands repayment of part of the loan and to finance this the trustees will make a part surrender of the bond within their 5% entitlement. Normally, repayment of loans to a settlor can cause income tax problems for the settlor, but as before the idea is that the trust 'income' is restricted to the 5% withdrawal, at least while the settlor is alive.

9.40 As the settlor receives loan repayments and spends them, his taxable estate will reduce and the growth in value of the bond will be outside his estate. He can ask for the whole of the loan back at any time although this may trigger income tax charges if the bond has grown in value since the trustees will be forced to encash it.

The trust and loan documentation has to be drafted carefully to ensure that it does not breach any anti-avoidance legislation. And this is of course only an estate freezing exercise. There is no immediate inheritance tax benefit because the loan still forms part of the settlor's estate. It is the growth in value of the investment product which will be outside his estate.

The inheritance tax planning is rather inflexible. The settlor may not in fact need repayment of the entire loan but it will still form part of his estate. Alternatively, he may end up needing some of the capital growth in the bond as well but cannot get access to this. Or he may want to be repaid on the loan at a greater rate than 5% of the initial premium each year. Calling for repayment at a greater rate than 5% could, as noted above, generate income tax charges. Many clients might also feel unhappy in this economic climate about basing their inheritance tax planning on the idea that investment products they take out really will grow in value in the future!

9.41 If the settlor dies shortly after the product is taken out then some thought needs to be given as to what happens regarding this loan. It will be necessary to avoid a situation where the loan is automatically called in by his executors because this will result in the trustees being forced to encash the bond early. This could be expensive in terms of tax and commission charges. To avoid this, the settlor could leave his right to receive loan repayments to another beneficiary under his will, eg his spouse. If he leaves the benefit of the loan back to the trust then this will be a chargeable transfer under the terms of his will and (even if it does not jeopardise the inheritance tax planning) may result in unnecessary tax charges if his nil-rate band has already been exhausted.

Trust carve out

9.42 There are many varieties of the carve out idea. In some the settlor takes out a cluster of single premium non-qualifying endowment life assurance policies maturing at regular intervals. The policies are assigned by the settlor to a trust. The terms of the trust provide that the settlor can take if living at the maturity date, but otherwise he has no interest in the policy. He cannot benefit in any other circumstances. The trustees, but not the settlor, have the option of

9.43 *Tax efficient investments*

deferring the maturity date and can surrender the policies at any time. In either event the settlor receives nothing. He can only benefit if the policy actually matures.

The beneficiaries of the trust are usually his children who take immediate vested interests in possession. The idea is that if the settlor requires some income, then the trustees will let a policy mature and he will take the proceeds. If he does not require income, the policy is extended by the trustees and the settlor receives nothing. The argument is that the settlor has 'carved out' or retained a reversionary interest under the trust, but this interest is liable to be defeated in a number of ways by the exercise of powers vested in the trustees. Therefore although the retained reversionary interest is not excluded property (see *IHTA 1984, s 48(1)(b)*), it has little or no value. The beneficiaries take the benefit of an insurance policy which is shorn of a reversionary interest retained by the settlor.

9.43 HMRC appears to accept that the retention by the settlor of a reversionary interest under a trust is not a reservation of benefit (see letter to the Law Society dated 18 May 1987). The settlor has retained actual property rather than reserved a benefit in the policy gifted. There is some question as to whether HMRC may argue that the effecting of the bond, the assignment into trust and the extension of the maturity date are associated operations giving rise to a chargeable transfer at the date of the last operation, ie the extension date.

In addition, there is a potential double inheritance tax charge if the settlor dies within seven years of settling the property but in that time has received the policy proceeds back on maturity. The *Inheritance Tax (Double Charges Relief) Regulations 2005 (SI 3441/2005)* would not appear strictly to give relief in this situation.

Discounted gift schemes

9.44 There are also a number of schemes combining a carve out with a discounted gift. Under this route, the settlor takes out a life insurance linked bond and retains from the outset certain rights, typically the right to receive the 5% tax-free withdrawals, which add up to more than just a reversionary interest.

The bond is split into two defined parts, with certain rights (eg the right to withdraw a specified amount each year) belonging to the settlor outright, and all other rights under the bond are gifted to a trust for the residuary beneficiaries. These persons do not include the settlor. When the settlor makes the investment he is retaining certain rights under the trust (eg the right to withdraw a specified amount each year) and therefore the loss to his estate is not the full capital value of the bond. The gift of the residuary fund is treated as less than the face value. The discount depends on the donor's life expectancy. The longer he is likely to live and draw on the benefits, the greater the discount on the gift.

Tax efficient investments **9.46**

All of these schemes involve complex provisions, have certain disadvantages and risks and may only be suitable in very limited circumstances. Specialist advice should always be sought.

ISAs, PEPs, TESSAs and SAYE

Individual Savings Accounts (ISAs)

9.45 These were announced by the government in the July 1997 Budget: the intention being to 'build on' the experience of TESSAs and PEPs (see below) and for the new account to provide a tax-favoured environment for savings. The scheme came into effect on 6 April 1999 when the rules permitting tax credits to be repaid to individuals in respect of company distributions ceased. Initially introduced for ten years, the government has announced that ISAs will remain indefinitely. The basic features of the scheme are as follows:

- the account may comprise two elements: cash (including National Savings), and stocks and shares;
- individuals over 18 who are resident and ordinarily resident in the UK will be able to subscribe;
- subscription levels will be £7,000 per tax year of which no more than £3,000 may go in cash (these rates are set to increase to £7,200 per annum and £3,600 per annum with effect from 6 April 2008);. Both husband and wife are entitled to a full allowance;
- accounts will be administered by a manager;
- the tax relief provided is:
    - an exemption from income tax and CGT on the investments;
    - payment of a 10% tax credit until April 2004 in respect of dividends on UK equities.

Withdrawals can be made without forfeiting tax relief.

Personal Equity Plans (PEPs), Tax Exempt Special Savings Accounts (TESSAs), Save as You Earn (SAYE)

9.46 Personal Equity Plans were abolished on 5 April 1999, though existing plans remain effective and can be transferred between managers. PEPs allowed tax-free dividends and capital gains on annual investment in equities, stock and bonds of up to £9,000 per year. From 6 April 2008 all PEP accounts will automatically become stocks and shares ISAs and become subject to ISA rules.

9.46 *Tax efficient investments*

TESSAs were also abolished on 5 April 1999. They allowed tax-free savings on up to £9,000 per year, subject to restrictions. Existing TESSAs were allowed to continue, and there was provision to allow transfer into a 'TESSA only ISA' when their term expired.

SAYE schemes were abolished in November 1994, although schemes linked to approved employee share option schemes (SAYE Sharesave Schemes) remain available.

Chapter 10

Pensions

Alec Ure Associate of Alec Ure & Associates, Partner of UHD Pension Services LLP and

Gavin Moffatt Senior Technical Adviser, SBJ Benefit Consultants Limited

INTRODUCTION

10.1 There are wide opportunities for efficient tax-planning under the new tax regime from A-Day. The HMRC website contains a comprehensive Registered Pension Schemes Manual ('RPSM'), and this is a useful source of reference for practitioners. This chapter endeavours to highlight the main areas for consideration by practitioners, advisers, members and other advisers of pension products.

MEMBERSHIP AND CONTRIBUTIONS

Membership

10.2 The new tax regime from 6 April 2006 (A-Day) has opened up tax-advantaged schemes to a wide range of individuals and employers. Practitioners can provide a valuable service to employers and individuals by reviewing their existing arrangements with a view to taking best advantage of the new rules.

Registered schemes may be open (dependent on their own rules) to anyone without restriction. Tax relief is usually available on scheme investments, and is available on contributions for the employed or self-employed whatever their residence with some restrictions. Individuals can be members of more than one type of registered scheme, whether or not they are employees of the participating companies. They can choose from occupational pension schemes, personal pension schemes, stakeholder schemes etc. Employers now have better flexibility in how to plan for the pension provision of their employees.

10.3 Pensions

10.3 The old restrictions which were imposed on centralised schemes for non-associated employers have been removed, which means that employers can minimise administrative costs and overhead costs by acting in a group (for instance, in their geographical area or within their own industry).

10.4 *FA 2004, s 150(1)* describes the new criteria which apply to types of schemes; benefit provision and membership categories.

A *pension scheme* is described as follows:

'a scheme or other arrangements, comprised in one or more instruments or agreements, having or capable of having effect so as to provide benefits to or in respect of persons—

(a) on retirement;
(b) on death;
(c) on having reached a particular age;
(d) on the onset of serious ill-health or incapacity; or
(e) in similar circumstances.'

Therefore, it is important that any new or restructured schemes or arrangements meet the above conditions.

10.5 An *occupational pension scheme* is a pension scheme set up by an employer (known as a sponsoring employer) to provide benefits for, or in respect of:

- any or all of its own employees;
- any or all of the employees of any other employer,

and any other person who is not an employee of any sponsoring employer who is invited to join.

Tax relief on contributions is available for members who:

- have earnings which are subject to UK tax for a tax year;
- are resident in the UK some time during a tax year;
- are resident in the UK some time during the five tax years before the tax year when they became a member of the scheme; or
- for the tax year concerned have, or their spouse has, earnings from overseas Crown employment which are subject to UK tax,

subject to a maximum age of 75.

10.6 Some examples of the wide class of permitted members for whom contribution relief is available are:

- a non-working spouse or minor for whom contributions are paid by a third party, eg a working spouse, parent or grandparent;
- a self-employed individual in membership of an occupational scheme of which they are the sponsoring employer in the role of a sole trader or partnership in relation to their self-employed earnings.

UK earnings are widely drawn. They can include patent income, share options treated as employment income, the taxable element of a golden handshake over £30,000, and earnings of directors and members of their families who are employees of private investment or property companies.

Other considerations

10.7 Employers are free to design their schemes and arrangements as they see fit, and to include broad eligibility rights. For example, they will wish to consider whether to include waiting periods for scheme membership, and whether to permit an employee or other member to be re-admitted to membership (and if so, on what terms).

Providers

10.8 Practitioners will need to be aware of the types of provider which are acceptable for registered schemes. These are:

- an insurance company;
- a unit trust scheme manager;
- an operator, trustee or depository of a recognised EEA collective investment scheme;
- an authorised open-ended investment company;
- a building society;
- a bank; or
- an EEA investment portfolio manager.

The above financial institutions are subject to independent regulation by the Financial Services Authority or an equivalent body within the EEA. With effect from 6 April 2007, any persons which are regulated by the Financial Services

10.9 *Pensions*

Authority are now able to establish a registered pension scheme other than an occupational pension scheme (*FA 2004, s 154* as amended by *FA 2007, Sch 20, para 2*).

Removal of funding rules

10.9 There are no longer any statutory HMRC funding rules. Accordingly, the need to obtain actuarial advice arises mainly for the purpose of compliance with DWP legislation and the Pensions Regulator's requirements, which apply chiefly to defined benefits schemes. This should enable many schemes to cut their overheads, although the advice of an actuary may be required by trustees or administrators as a matter of prudence in appropriate circumstances.

Contributions

10.10 There are no limits on members' contributions to registered schemes, but practitioners will need to inform their clients of the thresholds which apply to the tax reliefs which are available. Members, employers and third parties may all contribute to a registered pension scheme. As maximum lump sum calculations are calculated at scheme level, it is now simpler to amalgamate additional voluntary contributions and other benefits within the same scheme. Members may also wish to consider salary sacrifices (within HMRC guidance) to enable them to take advantage of the high threshold of tax relievable contributions which is now available.

10.11 *Members* receive full tax relief on personal contributions up to 100% of their annual earnings, or £3,600 if higher. Any person other than the employer or a former employer who contributes in respect of a member, where relief at source (RAS) is in point, must gross up the contribution at the basic tax rate (and higher relief will be available, where appropriate, through self-assessment or PAYE coding). For example, to contribute £100 to a personal pension a payment of only £78 is required. The provider will add £22, which it reclaims from the government. Even where a member of a personal pension has taxable income below the basic rate tax threshold, or no taxable income at all, basic rate tax relief is still available assuming the residency requirement is met. Thus to contribute the maximum relievable £3,600 for a non-earning member of a personal pension, a payment of only £2,808 is required.

A person who contributes under a net pay arrangement (only available for occupational pension schemes) will have contributions deducted from earned pay before tax is calculated, thereby obtaining immediate relief at the marginal rate.

10.12 Individuals who joined a UK scheme and who were resident in the UK at some time in the last five tax years still qualify for tax relief on contributions through the relief at source provisions even though they are no longer UK resident and have no UK chargeable earnings (*FA 2004, s 189*). However, the maximum relievable contribution is limited to £3,600. This may have an impact on overseas members of personal and stakeholder pension schemes. Before A-Day relievable contributions could be based on UK chargeable earnings immediately before going abroad, and this was available for up to five years. If the gross contribution being made before A-Day was more than £3,600, the position of such members may need to be revisited.

10.13 *Employers' contributions* are allowable as deductions against their corporation tax/profits if they satisfy the 'wholly and exclusively' test in HMRC's Business Income Manual 46000–46198 (the old Schedule D requirement). If contributions exceed 210% of the amount paid in the preceding year, unless the excess does not exceed £500,000 or there is a cessation of business, spreading will normally apply. The spread will be for up to four years – the maximum period applying where the excess contributions are £2 million or more. *FA 2004, Sch 36, Pt 4, para 42* contains transitional protection for existing arrangements as at A-Day. There is a restriction of tax relief where an employer routes the funding of an employer-financed retirement benefit scheme (EFRBS) through a registered pension scheme.

Tax relievable allowances

10.14 The removal of virtually all HMRC benefit limits has broadened the appeal of tax-advantaged schemes for many from A-Day. There are tax relievable ceilings on aggregate annual input and aggregate pension fund entitlement. They are reviewable from 2010/11 and will not decrease. These are described below.

Annual allowance (AA) which is the maximum aggregate amount of annual tax-free input that can be put into a registered scheme. It was set at £215,000 in 2006/07 and it increases steadily to £255,000 by the year 2010 as shown below:

- Tax year 2007/08 – £225,000
- Tax year 2008/09 – £235,000
- Tax year 2009/10 – £245,000
- Tax year 2010/11 – £255,000

An AA charge of 40% will arise on any excess input under *FA 2004, s 227*.

10.15 *Lifetime allowance* (LA) which is the maximum aggregate amount of pension saving that can benefit from tax reliefs in a fund during an individual's

10.16 *Pensions*

lifetime. It was set at £1.5 million in 2006/07 and it increases steadily to £1.8 million by the year 2010 as shown below:

- Tax year 2007/08 – £1,600,000
- Tax year 2008/09 – £1,650,000
- Tax year 2009/10 – £1,750,000
- Tax year 2010/11 – £1,800,000

10.16 Any amount over the threshold will be subject to a charge of 25% (see below). The remainder may be paid as a pension and subjected to PAYE (40% for a high earner). Where excess monies are paid out in lump sum form, a charge of 55% arises on the amount paid out. Accordingly practitioners may wish to compare the value of a tax relievable contribution combined with investment yield in a registered scheme (and an ultimate 55% charge on any excess over the allowance) with a cash payment by the employer (which would be taxable at 40% + NIC).

A member may have a higher certified allowance under Primary Protection (PP) but this may only increase in line with the main allowance. It is of little appeal to high earners as any future payments into the fund will be highly tax-inefficient; any growth in the fund above the increase in the standard lifetime allowance would ultimately be subject to the lifetime allowance charge. The alternative form of protection is Enhanced Protection (EP). Both forms of protection are described later.

AA charge

10.17 The AA charge is normally taxable on the member at 40% on the excess. It is not treated as income for any of the purposes of the Taxes Acts. It applies whether or not the administrator or member are resident, ordinarily resident or domiciled in the UK. Excess monies may remain in the scheme subject to the ultimate LA at retirement, and any excessive tax withheld by the scheme may be refunded to the member. Where tax relief has been given on an excess in the scheme, it will be clawed back from the fund. The allowance cannot be set off against the AA from one year to another if the value of a defined benefit falls during the year. Importantly, there are some exemptions which do not count towards the allowance:

- contributions in excess of a member's earnings that do not qualify for tax relief;
- AVCs which are paid for the purpose of securing added years (as the increase in benefits will be counted);

- before the end of the year, the individual has become entitled (meaning an actual right to draw) all of the benefits;
- before the end of the tax year, the individual has died.

Input amounts

10.18 The AA applies to the pension input amount, which depends on the type of scheme or arrangement concerned. *FA 2004, s 152* identifies four types of scheme, and a summary of the method of calculation of the increase in the value of an individual's rights in the pension input period for each type is given below:

Cash balance arrangement

10.19 The difference between the pension value at the beginning of the opening period and the pension value at the end of the closing pension input period in the tax year concerned. The opening value is the amount which would be available for the provision of benefits to or in respect of the individual on the assumption that the individual became entitled to the benefits at the beginning of the pension input period. This is uprated by RPI or 5%, whichever is higher. The closing value is the amount which would be available for the provision of benefits to or in respect of the individual on the assumption that the individual became entitled to the benefits at the end of the pension input period.

Any pension debit in the period is added back, pension credit is deducted. If there has been a transfer to a registered, or recognised overseas, scheme, during the period, the amount of the sums transferred plus the market value of the assets is to be added (or deducted if there has been a transfer in). Any benefit that has crystallised in the period is to be added, unless the member has become entitled to the whole benefit or died. Any minimum payments under the *Pension Schemes Act 1993* are to be subtracted.

Other money purchase arrangement

10.20 The total of any relievable pension contributions paid by or on behalf of the individual under the arrangement, and contributions paid in respect of the individual under the arrangement by an employer of the individual, at the end of the closing pension input period in the tax year concerned. When at any time contributions paid under a pension scheme by an employer otherwise than in respect of any individual become held for the purposes of the provision under an arrangement under the pension scheme of benefits to or in respect of an

10.21 *Pensions*

individual, they are to be treated as being contributions paid at that time in respect of the individual under the arrangement.

Defined benefits (final salary) scheme

10.21 The difference between the pension value at the beginning of the opening period and the pension value at the end of the closing pension input period in the tax year concerned. The opening value is 10 x the pension value at the opening value (had it been taken then) plus the lump sum entitlement other than by commutation. This is uprated if no rights accrue during the pension input period. The alternative percentage by reference to which the opening value of defined benefits arrangements is calculated as the greatest of:

- 5%;
- the percentage by which RPI for the month in which the pension input period ends is higher than it was for the month in which it began; and
- the percentage to which regulations made by HMRC refer.

The closing value is 10 x the pension value at the closing value (had it been taken then) plus the lump sum entitlement (other than by commutation). Any pension debit in the period is added back, pension credit is deducted. If there has been a transfer to a registered, or recognised overseas, scheme during the period, the amount of the sums transferred plus the market value of the assets is to be added (or deducted if there has been a transfer in). Any benefit that has crystallised in the period is to be added, unless the member has become entitled to the whole benefit or died. Any minimum payments under the *Pension Schemes Act 1993* are to be subtracted.

Hybrid arrangement

10.22 The greater or greatest of such of input amounts A, B and C as are relevant input amounts.

- A is what would be the pension input amount if the benefits provided to or in respect of the individual under the arrangement were cash balance benefits.
- B is what would be the pension input amount if the benefits provided to or in respect of the individual under the arrangement were other money purchase benefits.
- C is what would be the pension input amount if the benefits provided to or in respect of the individual under the arrangement were defined benefits.

Pensions **10.25**

Input period

10.23 The pension input period applies in each tax year. It commences on the day that the member begins to accrue pension rights under the scheme, but it should be noted that there is wide flexibility in the choice of an end date (*FA 2004, s 238*). There is accordingly scope to make large contributions at the most tax efficient time for the contributor concerned. The end period may be the end of the scheme accounting period, the end of the tax year or any other chosen date.

10.24 Ending a pension input period early can allow for two payments to be made within one tax year which, in total, exceed the AA. For example, if a member of a money purchase scheme nominates an end date of, say, 28 February 2007 for his first input period, he will be able to make contributions up to a maximum of £440,000 in the 2006/07 tax year, given sufficient taxable earnings. A contribution of £215,000 could be made before 28 February 2007 and an additional contribution of £225,000 could be paid between 1 March and 5 April 2007. If the second input period is ended shortly into the next tax year, say, on 7 April 2007, the third input period would run from 8 April 2007 to 7 April 2008 (ending in the 2008/09 tax year), thereby enabling a contribution of £235,000 to be made as early as 8 April 2007, subject of course to sufficient taxable income being available. A further contribution cannot be made until 8 April 2008.

Note that start and end dates in the past may be nominated for a pension input period. Note also that just because large contributions can be made, for example by sacrificing bonuses and manipulating the AA, it does not always mean it is a sound course of action. If an employee uses up too much LA early on, he may not benefit fully from contributions an employer may make on his behalf later. Careful consideration will be required when dealing with large contributions.

Test for the LA charge

10.25 Payment of a pension commencement lump sum and payment of a pension, whether scheme pension, lifetime annuity, unsecured or alternatively secured pension will occasion a test against the LA to determine whether a lifetime allowance charge is due. Each benefit has slightly different characteristics when it comes to valuing it for this purpose.

Scheme pension is valued at £20 per £1 pa of pension. A different factor can be agreed with HMRC if greater contingent benefits are payable. The value of a lifetime annuity is the purchase price of the annuity. It is also possible to value the annuity paid under a money purchase arrangement not as a lifetime annuity but as scheme pension. This means that some investment linked annuities may be unsuitable for this purpose if they permit the level of annuity to fall below the

10.26 *Pensions*

original annuity level and therefore breach one of the scheme pension conditions. Although pension may be taken to be scheme pension under this method, the lump sum from a money purchase arrangement is still calculated as one third of the annuity purchase price.

10.26 The value of unsecured pension is the actual amount that is designated for income withdrawal (or short-term annuity). Unfortunately, the LA problem does not end with the test at that point. If unsecured pension is later used to buy scheme pension or lifetime annuity there will be a second LA test. The amount crystallised at the second test will be 20 x scheme pension or the purchase price of the annuity less the original funds designated as available for income withdrawal. Note that the original amount of funds designated is not indexed in any way. Therefore, if the LA has been exhausted and no income is drawn from the fund, and assuming that investment returns are not negative, there would be a LA charge upon buying scheme pension/lifetime annuity before age 75. If investment growth in an unsecured pension fund is strong, it may even outstrip 120% of the maximum GAD rate that applies each year. As before, the charge may be mitigated or even avoided by treating the annuity purchased as a scheme pension, but as a member gets older the more likely it is that the cost of an annuity will drop below £20 per £1 pa.

10.27 An alternative may be to transfer the unsecured pension fund to a drawdown arrangement under a qualifying recognised overseas pension scheme. There will be a lifetime allowance test on the funds at the point of transfer but no other lifetime allowance test will be applied in the receiving overseas scheme.

When a member reaches the age of 75 with an unsecured pension fund he is automatically moved into alternatively secured pension. At that point there is a second LA test. The amount to be tested against the LA is the amount of drawdown funds remaining at age 75 less the original amount designated. The original amount is not indexed in any way.

Contributions in specie

10.28 It is possible to transfer an asset into a registered scheme, if the rules so permit. However, this will effectively be a gift and so will not enjoy tax relief. However, an asset transferred in satisfaction of a contribution to be made may be acceptable, with tax relief being available on the amount of contribution due. In specie contributions will potentially be chargeable to CGT as a disposal but will not be subject to stamp duty or stamp duty land tax. It will be necessary to seek specialist guidance on the IHT position (for example, with regard to pre-owned assets).

Shares granted in an employer's share incentive plan or under an SAYE share option scheme may nonetheless be transferred to a registered pension scheme within 90 days of entitlement and will be treated for tax relief as if they were a contribution made by the member. Tax relief is available on the market value of the shares. Corporate advisers may want to consider possibilities for using a share incentive plan or SAYE scheme in conjunction with a company's pension scheme.

Recycling tax-free cash lump sums

10.29 *FA 2004, Sch 29, para 3A* restricts the recycling of tax-free cash lump sums from A-Day. HMRC expressed concern that some practitioners had identified that a member may take a tax-free cash lump sum and immediately re-invest it in a registered scheme. The payment would obtain tax relief, and the member could then take another tax-free cash lump sum to enable the cycle to be repeated. Such arrangements are blocked by the (revised) legislation, which removed the tax advantages relating to any cash lump sums artificially recycled. However, HMRC states that it is not intended to affect cases where an individual takes a tax-free cash lump sum as part of the normal course of taking pension benefits.

The legislation applies to contributions which are greater than 30% of the relevant cash lump sum made at the time a tax-free cash lump sum is paid. In such circumstances the whole of the relevant cash lump sum is treated as an unauthorised payment and subject to the unauthorised payments tax charge of 40% unless it is less than 1% of the lifetime allowance (in which case it is exempt). Members must notify their scheme administrator when such an unauthorised payment is made and its amount, and practitioners/advisers will wish to apprise them of this requirement.

Investment opportunities

Introduction

10.30 Pension investment funds may continue to build up tax-free. The relief provisions are described in *FA 2004, ss 186* and *187*. Additionally, the Act relaxed many of the investment restrictions which had been imposed on tax approved schemes before A-Day. In particular, the removal of the restriction on investment in residential property was a major relaxation. Therefore, a review of the investments of existing schemes is to be recommended if best advantage is to be taken of the new opportunities which have arisen. However, contrary to the true principles of simplification, restrictions have been imposed on schemes which contain an element of member-direction on their investment activity. These restrictions were inserted into the Act by *FA 2006*. The rules which apply to the new category of schemes ('investment-regulated pensions schemes' – IRPS) are described later.

10.31 *Pensions*

The rules which apply

10.31 In addition to the relaxations in the area of property acquisition, most of the restrictions on transactions between connected persons were removed. The new regime depends largely on the prudence of trustees and administrators, and compliance with their wider statutory duties. The main rules are as follows.

For large schemes, shareholdings in the sponsoring company and associated/connected companies remain limited to 5% of the fund value, a restriction imposed not by tax law but by the *Occupational Pension Schemes (Investment) Regulations 2005, SI 2005/3378*, issued under the *Pensions Act 1995*. Although *FA 2004, s 179* permits loans of up to 50% of fund value to participating employers and to companies associated with them, the *Occupational Pension Regulations, SI 2005/3378* contain a general prohibition on making loans to a sponsoring employer. However, the existing exemptions which applied to SSASs remain, and there are certain, limited exemptions for existing loans from schemes with fewer than 100 members.

- Underwriting commissions applied for the purposes of a scheme are not liable to income tax and other forms of income, such as stock-lending fees, and income derived from futures and options contracts are similarly exempt from tax, as previously.

- Borrowing must not exceed 50% of fund value (*FA 2004, ss 182–185* and *FA 2004, s 163*).

- Debts between the scheme, the employer or the member must be on commercial terms, and unpaid debts are taxed as unauthorised payments.

- All investments, including loans to third parties, must be on commercial terms, not remove value from the fund and annuities must not provide for a return of the balance of insurance funds on death except in specific authorised circumstances.

- Trading income is taxable under the self-assessment procedure.

- Income derived from investments or deposits held as a member of a property investment limited liability partnership are liable to tax, as previously.

- Non-commercial use of assets by a member or associate attracts a benefit-in-kind charge on the member.

- Member loans are prohibited (this means that personal pension schemes and retirement annuities that have no sponsoring employer are unable to make loans to their members' businesses or partnerships where a partner is the scheme member – loans to third parties are, however, permitted, but they must be on fully commercial terms).

Further information on loans

10.32 The other requirements of the *FA 2004* for loans are:

- The meaning of a 'loan' is given in *s 162;*
- employer loans are permitted up to five years duration – if it is not possible for an employer to repay a loan within the agreed period, it may be rolled over once for a maximum period of five years.
- loans must be secured against assets of at least equal value;
- any amounts which exceed 50% of total fund value (or are otherwise unauthorised employer payments) will be taxed at 40%;
- under the *Pension Schemes (Prescribed Interest Rates for Authorised Employer Loans) Regulations 2005 SI 2005/3449* a loan reference rate must be charged, being an average of the base rates of a specified group of banks (the rate is 1% more than the reference rate found on the reference date preceding the start of the period (that is, on 6 April));
- *Schedule 30* contains various loan definitions and explains the treatment of unauthorised payments;
- *Schedule 36, Pt 4, para 38,* describes the transitional arrangements for loans.

Surcharges and sanctions may be imposed if the provisions are abused and, where high levels of unauthorised payments are made, the registration of the scheme may be withdrawn.

Transitional provisions

10.33 In general, investments which were held as at A-Day in accordance with the relevant HMRC requirements at the time may be retained if they are left undisturbed. Changes to loans, borrowings, leases etc will normally mean that the new investment rules will apply.

Investment-regulated pension schemes

10.34 Following the enactment of the *FA 2004*, the government declared its intent to impose new restrictions on small schemes, and to extend those restrictions to schemes in which investments may be self-directed or controlled by members and connected persons. The current position is that the term IRPS appeared for the first time in *FA 2006* and prohibitive charges can be incurred by such schemes. If a scheme holds, say, 10% of the company shares, it will be taxed on 10% of the taxable property of the company. The area is a most complex one, which requires specialist advice. A description of the main criteria which apply is accordingly given below.

Definition of IRPS

10.35   An IRPS is a scheme or arrangement which fits one of the following descriptions:

- *An occupational scheme*: where there are 50 or fewer members and at least one meets the following condition, or 10% or more of the members of a scheme meet that condition. The condition is that one or more of those members or a person related to one of those members is or was able to (directly or indirectly) direct influence or advise on investments held by the scheme.

- *A scheme which is not an occupational scheme*: where one or more members, or a person related to the member is or was able to (directly or indirectly) direct, influence or advise on investments for the purpose of the scheme under an arrangement for that member.

- *An arrangement, within an occupational scheme which is not an IRPS*: which has one or more members or a person related to one of the members who is or was able to (directly or indirectly) direct, influence or advise on investments which are linked to an arrangement relating to that member ('linked' means the sums or assets are held for the purpose of an arrangement under the scheme relating to that member, but not merely by virtue of apportionment of scheme assets).

The tax charges

10.36   It is important to note that the use of funds to acquire, improve, convert or adapt taxable property is deemed to be an unauthorised member payment by the scheme, so triggering an unauthorised payment charge at 40% on the member, and a 40% scheme sanction charge on the scheme administrator, which may be reduced to 15% when the member has paid his/her liability. Income from such property is liable to income tax. Additionally, the administrator will be liable to capital gains on the disposal of assets. If the net income from the property is less than 10% of the value of the property then in place of the actual income the administrator will be taxed on a deemed income. The amount of the deemed income will be 10% of the value of the property.

The member may also face a further 15% unauthorised payment surcharge if the taxable property is a wasting asset (for example, a leasehold interest in property for less than 50 years or plant and machinery. In a worse case scenario, HMRC may de-register the scheme, resulting in a further charge on the administrator of 40% of the scheme value.

The meaning of taxable property

10.37 Taxable property is residential property and most tangible moveable property. Residential property (wherever based) is a building or structure, including associated land, that is used or suitable for use as a dwelling. Tangible moveable property is things that you can touch and move (for example, assets such as art, antiques, jewellery, fine wine, classic cars and yachts). The provisions apply to taxable property held directly or indirectly, except through genuinely diverse commercial vehicles. The benefit-in-kind charge on personal use of registered scheme assets will not apply to assets taxed under these measures.

There are some specific exceptions from the meaning of tangible moveable property). These are gold bullion, and items with a market value of £6,000 or less which no member of the scheme or connected person has a right to use or occupy, and in which the scheme does not hold an interest directly, and which is held by a 'vehicle' (*FA 2004, Sch 29A, para 20*) for the purpose of management or administration of that vehicle. There are also some exemptions from a charge for investments in various types of investment vehicle, including certain types of property investment vehicles unless one of the purposes for which the scheme holds an interest in the vehicle is to enable a member or person connected to a member to occupy or use taxable property of the vehicle. However, the exemption from the charge on indirect holdings for UK Real Estate Investment Trusts (unless such investment is made to enable a scheme member or a connected person to occupy or use residential property) does not apply if the holding by any relevant person is 10% or more.

The transitional exemptions

10.38 The taxable property provisions do not apply if:

- the scheme held an interest in such property on A-Day which it had acquired before that date, and which it was not prohibited from holding up to 5 April 2006; or
- before A-Day the property was held by a person other than the scheme and the scheme was not prohibited from holding the interest it held in that person at that time; or
- the scheme or a person in whom the scheme directly or indirectly held an interest entered into a contract to acquire an interest in such property before 5 April 2006 and was not at that time prohibited from acquiring such an interest, but acquires the property on or after that date.

It should be noted that the exemption is lost on a change in occupation or use, or where there is a change in the scheme's interest in any person who holds a direct interest in the property or in anyone who has entered into a contract to acquire the property (if the change would not have met pre A-Day conditions).

10.39 *Pensions*

Drawing benefits

Minimum payment age

10.39 Unless a pension is being brought into payment on grounds of ill health it must not commence before age 50. This rises to 55 on 6 April 2010. However, anyone entitled to a low retirement age before 6 April 2006 may continue to benefit from that low retirement age post A-Day if certain conditions are met. This will mainly affect sportsmen or those in hazardous occupations, but can also affect employees who may be entitled to early payment of pension as of right in certain conditions (eg redundancy).

Members of personal pension schemes and retirement annuity contracts may retain their low normal retirement age if:

- there was an unqualified right to take a pension before age 50;
- they draw all uncrystallised pension and/or lump sum rights under the scheme on the same day; and
- they hold one of the following occupations:
    - Athlete
    - Badminton Player
    - Boxer
    - Cricketer
    - Cyclist
    - Dancer
    - Diver (Saturation, Deep Sea and Free Swimming)
    - Footballer
    - Golfer
    - Ice Hockey Player
    - Jockey – Flat Racing
    - Jockey – National Hunt
    - Member of the Reserve Forces
    - Model
    - Motor Cycle Rider (Motocross or Road Racing)
    - Motor Racing Driver
    - Rugby League Player

- Rugby Union Player
- Skier (Downhill)
- Snooker or Billiards Player
- Speedway Rider
- Squash Player
- Table Tennis Player
- Tennis Player (including Real Tennis)
- Trapeze Artiste
- Wrestler

Benefits may only become payable on cessation of any related employment. The right will be lost upon a transfer of benefit, but not if it is part of a block transfer.

10.40 Members of occupational pension schemes or deferred annuity contracts with a low normal retirement age will be able to retain that right if:

- they had an unqualified right on 5 April 2006 to take a pension and/or lump sum before the age of 55;
- the provision was set out in the governing documentation of the retirement benefit scheme or deferred annuity contract on 10 December 2003;
- they draw all of their uncrystallised pension and/or lump sum rights under the scheme on the same day;
- they have left the employment to which the scheme relates; and
- they either:
  - had the right under the scheme or contract on 10 December 2003, or
  - acquired the right in accordance with the scheme provisions as they were on 10 December 2003 upon joining the scheme after that date.

Although those with a low normal retirement age may continue to enjoy this right under transitional protection, their lifetime allowance will be reduced by 2.5% for each complete year between the date they draw benefits and the date on which they would have reached normal minimum pension age (50 or 55, depending on occupation). The 2.5% reduction will not apply, however, in the case of benefits from certain public sector schemes.

Ill-health retirement

10.41 Dependent on a scheme's rules, benefits may be paid before age 50 (55 from 6 April 2010) in circumstances of ill health. A member must have left the

10.42 *Pensions*

employment to which the pension relates (either now or at a previous date) and the administrator must obtain proper medical evidence that the member is incapable of continuing in his current occupation. If scheme rules permit, ill-health pension may be temporarily suspended if the member recovers sufficiently to return to his original job.

Ill health insurance contracts, which were approved for personal pension schemes before 6 April 2001, or for retirement annuities, are not to be regarded as unauthorised payments under the new regime.

Pensions

10.42 There is no overall limit on the amount of pension which can be paid under the new regime, and, except in cases referred to above, the requirement that a member must have left employment for a benefit to be paid is removed. Pension can only be paid in one of the following forms post A-Day:

- Scheme pension (this *must* be paid under a defined benefit arrangement).
- Lifetime annuity.
- Unsecured pension before age 75 (income withdrawal or short-term annuity).
- Alternatively secured pension (ASP) after age 75 (income withdrawal).

Scheme pension

10.43 Scheme pension must be paid under a defined benefit arrangement and may be paid under a money purchase arrangement. It must meet the following conditions:

- It must be payable by the scheme administrator or by an insurance company selected by the scheme administrator.
- It must be payable in at least annual instalments until the member's death or until the later of the member's death and a guaranteed period of up to ten years.
- The level of scheme pension must not decrease from one year to the next except in permitted circumstances.
- If it is paid under a money purchase arrangement, the member must first have had the choice to select a lifetime annuity.

10.44 The circumstances in which a scheme pension may decrease are:

- Reduction of an ill-health pension upon full or partial recovery.
- A reduction applying to all pensions in payment.
- Reduction between the ages of 60 and 65 to take account of integration with the state pension (bridging pension).
- Pension sharing order or provision.
- Forfeiture of pension under provisions allowed by the *Pensions Act 1995*.
- Court order.
- Abatement under a public service pension scheme.
- Certain other circumstances relating to the Pension Protection Fund, contracted-out rights affected by the *Gender Recognition Act 2004* and admission to the Royal Hospital at Chelsea.

10.45 If the level of pension decreases other than in permitted circumstances, future instalments will be subject to unauthorised payment charges. Furthermore if the level of scheme pension is reduced to below 80% of its original level, any tax-free lump sum paid in connection with the pension will become an unauthorised payment. Care must therefore be taken in any matter which involves the reduction or cessation of a scheme pension in payment. Eg offering to commute a scheme pension in payment on grounds of triviality may give rise to a tax charge on the original tax-free lump sum, even though the pension itself may legitimately be commuted for a trivial commutation lump sum.

Lifetime annuity

10.46 A lifetime annuity may be paid under a money purchase arrangement and must meet the following conditions:

- It must be payable by an insurance company.
- The member must have had an opportunity to select the insurance company (open market option).
- It must be payable until the member's death or until the later of the member's death and a guaranteed period of up to ten years.
- It must not decrease in payment except where the variation relies on investment performance, tracks an investment index or the Retail Prices Index. A lifetime annuity may also be reduced in consequence of a pension sharing order.

Unsecured pension

10.47 Unsecured pension may take the form of a short-term annuity, purchased with pension scheme funds and payable for no more than five years (and not beyond age 75). However, unsecured pension is more likely to take the form of income withdrawal.

10.48 *Pensions*

The maximum amount of income withdrawal that may be drawn annually is 120% of a notional annuity rate calculated using tables drawn up by the Government Actuary's Department (GAD). The GAD rates are based on a single-life, non-escalating annuity for a person of the same age and gender as the member.

10.48 The minimum amount of income withdrawal nil. This makes it possible to draw a lump sum from a money purchase arrangement without actually having to draw any income, although the funds will have been crystallised for lifetime allowance purposes. The amount of income drawn can normally be varied at any time, subject to scheme rules.

Once funds have been designated as unsecured pension, the maximum level must be reviewed every five years, or earlier at the member's request on the anniversary of the start of unsecured pension.

ASP

10.49 ASP is the same as for income withdrawal under age 75 with two important differences.

- The GAD rate applicable will be the rate for a 75 year old no matter how old the member actually is.

- A minimum amount of 55% of the GAD rate must be drawn each year (a change introduced in the *FA 2007* amid Treasury fears of possible tax abuse), and the maximum amount that may be drawn is 90% of the GAD rate.

Alternatively secured pension may therefore be unattractive to anyone unless there is a genuine objection to the mortality pooling that comes with purchasing an annuity, or even just an objection to leaving money to an insurance company.

Lump sums

10.50 Under the post-A-Day tax regime a pension commencement lump sum must only be paid in connection with a pension coming into payment. The pre A-Day possibilities for cash only schemes no longer exist except where provided for under transitional protection. Similarly, members who had continued rights pre A-Day will no longer be able to take a lump sum at retirement and defer drawing the associated pension.

Pension commencement lump sums must be paid within the period of six months before and twelve months after the date on which the connected pension commences. Entitlement cannot arise after the age of 75, but a pension commencement lump sum may still be paid after age 75 if entitlement arose before then and it is paid within twelve months. How the lump sum is calculated depends on whether the arrangement it comes from is a defined benefit or money purchase arrangement.

10.51 In a money purchase arrangement the lump sum is expressed as one third of the annuity purchase price, where a lifetime annuity is provided, or one third of the sums designated for income withdrawal. This equates to 25% of funds being vested, but expressing it in such a manner ensures the lump sum calculation is tied to the amount of funds actually crystallised at the time.

Calculation of the pension commencement lump sum is more complicated under a defined benefit arrangement. The lump sum is calculated according to the formula $¼ \times (LS + AC)$ where:

- LS is the amount of lump sum actually taken; and
- AC is the amount crystallised by the scheme pension coming into payment (normally 20 times the initial rate of scheme pension in a defined benefit arrangement).

10.52 In a defined benefit arrangement where a lump sum is provided by the commutation of pension, the maximum amount of lump sum depends on the commutation rate used within the scheme. The lump sum formula may more usefully be expressed as:

$(20 \times \text{full pension} \times \text{commutation factor}) / (20 + 3 \times \text{commutation factor})$

Therefore a £10,000 pa pension in a defined benefit scheme with a commutation rate of, say, £14 per £1 pa may be partially commuted for a lump sum of up to:

$(20 \times 10{,}000 \times 14) / (20 + 3 \times 14) = £45{,}161$

The residual pension will be $10{,}000 - 45{,}161 / 14 = £6{,}774.21$ pa.

Note that the lump sum will always be $6^2/_3$ times the residual pension in a defined benefit arrangement unless transitional protection applies.

10.53 If a person has taken a lump sum prior to A-Day, this will be taken into consideration for the purpose of calculating the maximum lump sum that may be taken from the same arrangement after A-Day. Additionally, any person who has taken a lump sum prior to A-Day, but deferred his or her pension until after A-Day, will not be permitted to take a further tax-free lump sum in relation to that employment.

Any AVCs that were not commutable before A-Day because they were started after 8 April 1987 may be commutable post A-Day subject to scheme rules permitting. Where money purchase AVCs have been paid under a defined

10.54 *Pensions*

benefit scheme, the entire AVC fund may be used first to provide a pension commencement lump sum before it is necessary to commute defined benefit pension, subject again to scheme rules permitting.

Unless transitional protection applies the maximum pension commencement lump sum that may be taken tax-free is limited to 25% of the available lifetime allowance.

Protected lump sums

10.54 Where lump sum rights on 5 April 2006 are more than 25% of the value of pension rights under an occupational pension scheme on the same date, they may be protected and a different calculation will apply. For protection to be maintained all rights under the scheme must come into payment at the same time. If all pension rights are transferred out of the scheme post A-Day protection will be lost unless the transfer is part of a block transfer or rights are transferred to a buy-out policy upon scheme wind-up. If a partial transfer occurs, the protected lump sum in the ceding scheme is reduced by one quarter of the transfer value.

The calculation of a protected pension commencement lump sum, once it comes to be paid, depends on whether there has been relevant benefit accrual (additional pensionable service or additional pension contributions) post A-Day.

10.55 Where no relevant benefit accrual has occurred the protected lump sum is expressed as VULSR × CSLA / FSLA, where:

VULSR is the value of lump sum rights on 5 April 2006.

CSLA is the lifetime allowance at the time of paying the lump sum.

FSLA is the lifetime allowance for 2006/07 (£1.5 million).

Note that a measure announced in the October 2007 pre-budget report would instead permit the protected lump sum to be calculated using the same formula as applies where relevant benefit accrual has occurred (see **10.56** below). Details will be included in the *Finance Act 2008*.

10.56 Where relevant benefit accrual has occurred there is scope to take additional tax-free lump sum not just from any post A-Day accrual but in respect of any pre A-Day growth as well. The lump sum is expressed in the formula VULSR × CSLA / FSLA + ¼ × (LS + AC − VUR × CSLA / FSLA), where VULSR, CSLA and FSLA are as before and:

LS is the amount of lump sum actually taken;

AC is the amount crystallised by bringing the annual pension into payment; and

VUR is the value of uncrystallised rights under the scheme on 5 April 2006.

Note that this formula overrides the requirement to limit the tax-free lump sum to 25% of the available lifetime allowance. This protection does not apply if primary or enhanced protection is being relied on. Protection does not apply to lump sum rights greater than 25% under a retirement annuity contract on 5 April 2006.

10.57 Working out the maximum lump sum that could be paid on 5 April 2006 can be a complicated affair. Essentially it will be the HMRC lump sum limit, but note that post A-Day scheme administrators are not obliged to pay the maximum protected lump sum. If scheme rules permit they may pay a lump sum of up to the protected amount. The HMRC limit on 5 April 2006 will be calculated as 3/80 of final remuneration times company service, uplifted 80ths where the member had continued rights under the scheme, or, where the member was a post '89 member of a money purchase scheme, as 2.25 times the level of pension. The level of pension in this case can be calculated using the GAD drawdown rate applicable on 5 April 2006 or by simply dividing the money purchase fund by 20. Advisers therefore need to work out which method proves the most beneficial for their client.

The *Taxation of Pension Schemes (Transitional Provisons) (Amendment No 2) Order, SI 2006/04* provides rules for the calculation of stand-alone lump sums. A stand-alone lump sum is a tax-free lump sum which constitutes the whole of a person's rights under a pension scheme on 5 April 2006. It includes not just the scenario of a cash only scheme but also the situation where the maximum HMRC approvable lump sum is greater than the value of the commutable pension rights on 5 April 2006. As long as there is no relevant benefit accrual post A-Day (ie no further pensionable service in a defined benefit arrangement and no further contributions to a money purchase arrangement) the lump sum may be paid tax-free whatever its value has grown to by investment growth or revaluation.

Refunds of contributions, and compensation payments

10.58 Where a member has less than two years' qualifying service, refunds of contributions made by the member will be permitted, and will be taxed at 20% on £10,800 and at 40% on any excess (*FA 2004, Ch 5, s 205*). Such refunds will be permitted on leaving pensioned employment or on winding-up the scheme.

Compensation payments may be made to authorised employers in respect of a criminal, fraudulent or negligent act or omission by a scheme member (*FA 2004, Ch 3, s 178*).

Retained benefits

10.59 It will no longer be necessary to take retained benefits into account when testing HMRC limits if members' earnings (that is, P60 plus P11D) are

10.60 *Pensions*

less than £50,000 in the tax year which preceded A-Day. This will be important when calculating the HMRC maximum lump sum available on 5 April 2006 for protection purposes.

Serious ill-health

10.60 Serious ill-health commutation will still be permitted for registered schemes, out of uncrystallised benefits. The administrator must obtain written medical evidence that the member's life expectancy is less than one year and must notify HMRC. There will be no tax liability on the payment if the lifetime allowance is not exceeded. However, if a member in circumstances of serious ill-health with a life expectancy of less than a year fails to exercise an option to wholly commute their benefits, the value of the benefits foregone is liable to inheritance tax.

Trivial commutations

10.61 Trivial commutation is still permitted but this is no longer on a scheme by scheme basis. The aggregate of all existing pension benefits must be within 1% of the prevailing LA and there is only a 12-month opportunity in which to commute. All rights under a scheme must be extinguished by the lump sum triviality payment and income tax will be charged on 75% of the commuted value under PAYE. Tax is chargeable on 100% of the commuted value if it relates to pension which has already been brought into payment. A trivial commutation lump sum is only payable between the ages of 60 and 75 and if some LA remains available (although the lump sum itself does not count towards the LA). If a scheme is winding up, trivial commutation will be permitted if the employer ceases all contributions to registered schemes on behalf of the individual and the value of the pension commuted does not exceed 1% of the standard LA. In the case of a scheme wind-up there is no aggregation requirement and no minimum age.

Since all entitlements of the member under the scheme must be extinguished by the payment of a trivial commutation lump sum, this means that it would also be necessary to commute dependants' pensions or to establish them as a separate arrangement under the scheme.

Buy-out policies

10.62 Buy-out policies must be provided through a registered scheme. They may no longer be free-standing. There need be no monetary limits, and a tax-free lump sum of up to 25% of value may be paid. Defined contribution contracts must use a factor of 20:1 for determining limits. Pre-A-Day bought-out benefits remain subject to the limits that were written into those contracts. The latest report by HM Treasury on its review of the annuity market, which had originally been launched in February 2002, was published in December 2006. It extends to open market options, alternatively secured pension and changes to unsecured income levels.

The Finance Bill 2007 contained several proposals concerning the buy-out market position in the face of increased longevity, and the existing need for final salary schemes to report on the FRS17 basis. The main change has been that HMRC has expanded the range of alternative finance investment bonds to include the Islamic financial instruments known as sukuk (*FA 2005, s 48A*, inserted by *FA 2007, s 53*). Effectively, the sukuk will be a qualifying investment for investment savings accounts and child trust funds, subject to satisfactory listing requirements and, for ISAs, meeting the five year requirement. This is achieved by treating the exchange, by Order, as a recognised stock exchange.

Transfers

10.63 Benefits may be transferred freely between registered pension schemes and even pensions that have come into payment may be transferred to other arrangements as long as certain conditions are met. None of these transfers occasions a test against the LA, but where benefits are transferred to a qualifying recognised overseas pension scheme the amount of the transfer value is tested against the LA. Any excess over the LA is simply taxed at 25%; it is not possible to draw the excess as a LA excess lump sum in this situation.

Primary protection and enhanced protection

10.64 The two methods of protecting accrued rights are described below. Members have until 5 April 2009 to choose which form of protection suits them better, but it is advisable to make an earlier decision in order to ensure that protection is not lost. Registration should be done online on the relevant HMRC form. Whichever protection is chosen (or both), it is necessary to value the accrued rights as at A-Day. The valuation of rights which have not yet come into payment depends on the type of arrangement from which they derive. Details of calculation are contained in the RPSM. Rights already in payment are valued as 25 times the annual rate of pension being paid (disregarding any lump sum already paid). Payments in the form of income drawdown are valued as 25 times the maximum annual rate of drawdown that could be received on 5 April 2006.

Enhanced protection

10.65 This enables members to avoid the LA and AA charges completely. No further relevant benefit may accrue to the individual from A-Day. The value of

10.66 *Pensions*

aggregate uncrystallised rights on 5 April 2006 must not exceed an amount calculated as 20 x MPP, where MPP is, broadly, the maximum permitted pension that would be allowed by reference to the appropriate tax regime in force before A-Day. Any excessive amount must be surrendered if EP is to apply. Practitioners will wish to ensure that their clients are aware of the actions which may inadvertently trigger a loss of EP by way of relevant benefit accrual ('RBA'), such as further contributions, new death benefit provision, higher accrual rates, non-permitted transfers etc. Note that a transfer from a defined benefit scheme to a money purchase scheme, although being a permitted transfer for EP purposes, will cause the loss of EP if the transfer value is greater than the appropriate limit allowed for relevant benefit accrual under EP. Details are provided in the RPSM.

Primary protection

10.66 This allows further benefit to accrue post-A-Day, and provides a protection for accrued rights by way of an uplift to an individual's LA in the form of a LA enhancement factor which is the percentage by which the value of rights on 5 April 2006 exceeds £1,500,000 and is expressed in the following formula:

$(RR - SLA)/SLA$

where:

RR is the value of pension rights on 5 April 2006.

SLA is the standard lifetime allowance for the 2006/07 tax year (£1,500,000).

Any other further benefit will almost certainly attract a LA charge. Examples of how this works in practice are contained in the RPSM.

Death benefits

General rules

10.67 General death benefit rules apply on the death of a member for children's and dependants' pensions, which are subject to PAYE but are not subject to the LA. Children's pensions must cease at age 23 unless dependency continues by reason of disability. There are transitional arrangements which protect pensions in payment at A-Day and pensions from arrangements for a person who had retired by A-Day. Unvested pensions that are not yet in payment may be paid to dependants either in pension form or, if a member has not yet reached age 75, as a lump sum.

Pensions **10.69**

Permitted benefits

10.68 The main permitted benefits and the conditions which apply are:

- There are no limits on the level of the payment of a tax-free defined benefit payment.
- If a member dies before age 75 with vested or partly vested funds, the tax treatment depends on whether or not income has been secured.
- If income is unsecured, dependants' pensions may be taken in similar form until age 75 at which age they will be subject to secured pension or alternatively secured pension rules, or undrawn funds can be repaid with lump sums being taxed at 35%.
- If income has been secured, a ten-year guarantee may apply from date of vesting (this means that no guarantee will be possible if income had not been secured before the end of that period).
- Where value protection is in place, lump sums must be paid before age 75.
- Lump sums may be paid to any person, except for trivial commutation and winding-up lump sums which have to be paid to dependants.
- Tax-free charity lump sums may be paid on the death of a member or dependant, with an alternatively secured pension fund and no dependants, on or after age 75.
- A limit is imposed on the amount of dependants' benefits in order to prevent avoidance of the LA when it is valued incorporating an element for the dependant's pension and for the calculation of the maximum tax-free cash sum.
- Where a member dies after age 75, the aggregate of dependants' benefits must not exceed the member's pension at the date of death, and future pension increases are restricted in order to avoid getting around the initial limit.
- Dependants' pensions no longer need to be paid for life, in circumstances of cessation of marriage or dependency, and a spouse may include an ex-spouse to whom the member was married when the benefit came into payment.

Tax charges

10.69 The tax treatment of lump sums is complicated and is described below.

A 35% tax charge arises on the administrator on:

10.70 *Pensions*

- a pension protection lump sum death benefit ('value protection' on death before 75 with pension from defined benefits);
- an annuity protection lump sum death benefit ('value protection' on death before 75 with annuity from money purchase); and
- an unsecured pension fund lump sum death benefit (return of fund on death before 75 under income drawdown by a member or a dependant in a money purchase scheme).

The rules may provide for the tax to be recovered from the payment.

No 35% charge arises on a defined benefit lump sum death benefit if:

- the member had not reached age 75 at date of death;
- the benefit is paid in respect of a defined benefit arrangement;
- the benefit is paid before the end of two years from date of death; and
- the benefit is not a pension protection lump sum death benefit; a trivial commutation lump sum death benefit; or a winding-up lump sum death benefit.

No 35% charge arises on a money purchase uncrystallised funds lump sum when it does not exceed the amount of the uncrystallised funds.

Lump sums which are not paid to the legal personal representatives must be notified to that person. If the LA is exceeded a LA charge of 55% on the excess will fall on the beneficiary.

Excepted group life policies

10.70 Practitioners may wish to seek specialist advice on excepted group life policies (EGLPs). These products can be an attractive alternative to in-house pension scheme death benefit cover if properly drawn. There is no income tax charge, LA does not apply, they can provide tax-free lump sum death benefits and be efficient on IHT where a discretionary trust is in place. Employer contributions are tax-relievable under the 'wholly and exclusively' test and there is no benefit-in-kind charge on the member.

10.71 EGLPs are not subject to the punitive taxation that applies to employer-financed retirement benefit schemes. There is no need to register an EGLP with HMRC and no need to comply with HMRC reporting requirements. Since EGLPs sit outside the registered pension scheme tax regime, they could therefore be used to provide lump sum life cover for:

- Employees whose group life cover already exceeds their lifetime allowance.

- Employees whose group life cover, together with lump sum death benefits from other registered pension schemes, exceeds their lifetime allowance.
- Employees with enhanced protection where payment of the lump sum insured would jeopardise enhanced protection.
- Employees with enhanced protection where payment of life assurance premiums would jeopardise enhanced protection.
- Employees with primary protection where primary protection may not fully protect against a lifetime allowance charge.
- New employees who have enhanced protection and would lose it if they became members of a registered pension scheme for life assurance benefits.

A similar policy may be put in place where it covers only one employee.

Pension term assurance

10.72 *FA 2007* brought in the change announced in the Pre-Budget Report to pension term assurance policies whereby tax relief on pension contributions which are paid as premiums to such policies is withdrawn. Existing policies should be reviewed. Pre-6 December 2006 applications will continue to benefit from tax relief, as will applications which had been sent to the insurance company on or before that date and receipt recorded by that insurance company by midnight on 13 December 2006.

Transitional arrangement for five-year guaranteed lump sums

10.73 A five-year guarantee may continue for a money purchase scheme, but it may not necessarily be tax-free. For a defined benefit scheme, it is tax-free if the sum is within the LA.

Transitional arrangement for lump sums arising before A-Day

10.74 Protection is given to lump sums paid by schemes in existence before A-Day in respect of members and dependants who died before that date, and the period within which a lump sum can be paid is extended to two years from the date on which the scheme administrator could reasonably have known of the death of the member or dependant instead of from the date of death.

10.75 *Pensions*

Enhanced protection – lump sums

10.75 A defined benefit pension scheme may pay a death-in-service lump sum calculated as a multiple of salary at date of death. This can continue under EP even though the salary may have increased. It must be tested against the appropriate limit to determine whether RBA has occurred, if it has not the EP is unaffected. For a money purchase arrangement an uncrystallised funds lump sum may be paid equal to the accumulated value of the assets in a member's pension fund at the date of death, and EP would not be lost. For certainty in cases of insured lump sums, HMRC Simplification Newsletter No 8 should be consulted.

Funeral benefit

10.76 Existing one-off, tax-free payments to be made upon the death of a member to cover funeral expenses may continue in certain circumstances. If the registered pension scheme was, immediately before A-Day, an approved scheme and the member had a right under the pension scheme to such cover on 5 April 2006 *provided that* the rules of the scheme included the provision as at 10 December 2003 and the member was in receipt of benefits from the scheme on or before 5 April 2006. The payment is not included in the LA.

Hancock annuities and EFPOS

10.77 A Hancock annuity is an immediate annuity for a retiring employee. These products are still available post A-Day as registered schemes, and they are subject to the LA. Alternatively, an EFPOS (an acronym in an amendment to the *Social Security (Contributions) Regulations 2001, SI 2001/1004*) could be considered. An EFPOS enjoys exemptions from NIC charges both on the employer contribution and the benefit paid from the scheme (as for an EFRBS), although it provides only a pension.

Inheritance tax

10.78 It is prudent to avoid the prospect of a charge to inheritance tax on lump sum death-in-service benefits. For certainty, the benefit must be dispensed through a discretionary trust, meaning that the trustees have discretion to decide to whom the benefit shall be paid. Members should be asked to complete a statement of wishes form, indicating the person/s or body/ies that they would like to benefit. The trustees are not to be bound by this statement, but they will usually be guided by it.

10.79 The following special rules apply to IHT:

- In the Budget of 2006, the Chancellor stated that monies held in an ASP by an investor aged 75 or over will be subject to inheritance tax at 40% when the investor dies, deducted directly from the fund by the administrator. The charge is based on the value of the taxable property at the time the charge arises, calculated by reference to the assets over the nil-rate band and the rate of tax at the time. Funds passed to charities escape the tax, and funds paid to provide pension benefits for a spouse, civil partner or financial dependant will not be chargeable until the entitlement to the benefit ceases. Changes were forewarned in the Pre-Budget Report 2006, to ensure that ASP was used solely for the purposes of retirement income by requiring a minimum level of annual income withdrawal and prohibiting the passing on of funds on death (eg to other family members).

- *FA 2006* legislated an existing 1992 concessionary practice in relation to an IHT charge which can arise when a person aged under 75 exercises a choice which reduces his chargeable estate and increases that of another (unless on an arm's length basis, and so excepted as a transfer of value). The exemption can apply in a pension scheme where the member exercised his right not to take pension. For example, where the member was in good health when the decision was made, but subsequently his life expectancy was seriously impaired and an enhanced death benefit is paid. The Act also extends the concession to dispositions to charities.

- Accumulation and maintenance trusts and interest in possession trusts have been chargeable on establishment from 2006 if the value of the trust is higher than the nil IHT band, and a further tax charge will be levied on the tenth anniversary after they are set up. These measures also apply to existing trusts from 2008. Transfers into new trusts are taxable at 20% above the nil-rate band plus a further 6% charge every ten years. Existing trusts will only be charged at 6% – the ten-yearly charge. These rules also extend to certain divorce cases.

In mitigation of the above, there may be merit, where another family member is earning, in a member drawing maximum income and paying it directly into an arrangement for that person. The family member will obtain tax relief on the contribution and payments out of income, including income from ASP, are free from inheritance tax.

Pension sharing

Pre A-Day pension debit and credit

10.80 Pension sharing on divorce operates so as to reduce a member's pension rights by a pension debit, and to award the ex-spouse with a pension

10.81 *Pensions*

credit. Before A-Day a pension debit counted against the HMRC maximum benefit a member was allowed to accrue under the pre A-Day tax regime. The pension credit was ignored in assessing the HMRC maximum benefit of the ex-spouse.

Post A-Day pension credit

10.81 The position changed on 6 April 2006. If a person acquires a pension credit post A-Day it will count towards that person's lifetime allowance. However, in a case where the pension being shared is one that has been brought into payment on or after 6 April 2006, the person receiving the pension credit can apply for an uplift to his or her lifetime allowance. Since the pension being shared will already have been tested against the lifetime allowance once before, when it was brought into payment, it would be unfair to test it against a lifetime allowance a second time. The uplift is calculated according to the formula APC/SLA, where:

- APC is the appropriate amount of the pension credit rights at the date they were acquired (ie that part of the original member's cash equivalent transfer value which was split in favour of the ex-spouse), and

- SLA is the standard lifetime allowance at the time when the pension credit rights were acquired.

For example, if £1 million worth of pension rights are shared in the 2007/08 tax year in the proportion 50:50, the pension credit recipient can claim an uplift of £500,000 / £1,600,000 = 0.3125, which is rounded up to two decimal places, 0.32. If the person with pension credit draws benefits in the 2010/11 tax year when the lifetime allowance is £1.8 million, his or her lifetime allowance will be increased to £1.8 million × 1.32 = £2,376,000.

10.82 To receive this uplift the recipient of pension credit must notify HMRC on form APSS201 by 31 January five years after the 31 January following the tax year in which the pension sharing order took effect.

A similar uplift is available for anyone who acquired pension credit before 6 April 2006, given that pre A-Day pension credit did not count against HMRC limits. The uplift is available whether or not the pension credit relates to rights which were already in payment. The uplift is calculated according to the formula IAPC / SLA, where:

- IAPC is the appropriate amount of the pension credit rights at the date they were acquired (ie that part of the original member's cash equivalent transfer value which was split in favour of the ex-spouse), and

- SLA is the standard lifetime allowance for the 2006/07 tax year (ie £1,500,000).

10.83 To determine the amount of IAPC it is increased in line with increases in the Retail Prices Index from the month in which the pension credit was acquired up to April 2006.

Anyone seeking an uplift for pre-A-Day pension credit must notify HMRC on form APSS201 on or before 5 April 2009. Note, however, that this uplift is not available for pre A-Day pension credit if the person with pension credit is also relying on primary protection.

Post A-Day pension debit

10.84 For those subject to a pension debit before A-Day, the good news is that this does not count towards the post A-Day lifetime allowance, despite the fact that it counted towards pre A-Day HMRC limits. This means that someone with a pension debit acquires scope to fund his or her benefits up to their original level. However, if any transitional protection is being relied on that requires the calculation of HMRC maximum benefits on 5 April 2006, the pension debit may have to be taken into account for those purposes.

For the seriously wealthy this means divorce may not necessarily be all bad news post A-Day. If 100% of pension rights are given away post A-Day as part of a divorce settlement, the person giving the rights away will be able to fund up to the lifetime allowance once again essentially benefiting from contribution tax relief twice.

Inducement offers

10.85 Inducement payments are payments by employers or registered schemes to incentivise scheme members into giving up certain rights in place of alternative provision or benefit enhancement. In the past some arrangements have been accepted by HMRC as not attracting tax or NIC charges. The arrangements had demonstrated that the offer had been fairly communicated to the members, and that the relevant advisers had agreed that the payments were fair deals for all parties.

HMRC issued an Announcement on 22 January 2007 entitled 'The tax and National Insurance treatment of employer cash inducement payments to pension scheme members'. The Announcement stated that the payment of cash sums 'in connection with the surrender or exchange of rights' are employment income, and are chargeable to income tax, regardless of the age of the recipient or whether or not the recipient is retired, as they are deemed to fall within the meaning of relevant benefits payable from an EFRBS. Existing arrangements, already agreed with HMRC, are not disturbed. HMRC considers that the payment of a cash sum attracts NICs if it is deemed to be 'earnings'. Earnings

10.86 *Pensions*

'paid to or for the benefit of the individual' (payments made direct from employer to individual) attract Class 1 NICs. Where payment is made by the employer into the registered scheme it attracts neither Class 1 nor Class 1A NICs.

10.86 By way of exception, HMRC states that the above does not apply to payments that 'enhance the transfer value of the pension fund and which are included in the funds transferred between schemes'.

In further moves, the Pensions Regulator has issued guidance on the matter, requiring members to be fully informed of the implications of transferring out. The Regulator has also recommended that trustees should seek independent financial advice. In addition, the DWP issued a statement on 1 March 2007, indicating that it was considering introducing new rules to stop firms offering final salary scheme members cash inducements to give up benefits.

Reporting and tax returns

10.87 The new events reports form APSS 300 should be filed online by 31 January 2008, although nil reports are not required. The requirements are stated in the *Registered Pension Schemes (Provision of Information) Regulations 2006, SI 2006/567* and they include the administrator's general duty to report certain events to HMRC and other parties. All reporting, registration and returns must be made online from 16 October 2007. The main reportable events are:

- Unauthorised payments made to scheme members and employers, including benefits-in-kind.
- Payments in excess of 50% of the standard LA – lump sum death benefits (in aggregate) only.
- Early provision of benefits – payments before age 50 (up to April 2010), 55 (from April 2010) – to persons who were directors in any of the six years prior to the reporting current reporting year, or any connected persons.
- Payment of a serious ill-health lump sum – to persons described in the third point above.
- Suspension of an ill-health pension – where the ill-health condition is no longer met.
- Benefit crystallisation events (BCE's), enhanced LA or enhanced protection: where the amount crystallised (in aggregate) exceeds the standard LA.

Pensions **10.88**

- Payment of a pension commencement lump sum - where the sum crystallised exceeds 25% of the combined pension and lump sum, and is more than 7.5% but less than 25% of the standard LA.
- Payment of a pension commencement lump sum under primary or enhanced protection: where the amount exceeds 25% of the SLA and is protected from charge by transitional protection.
- Payment of a 'stand-alone' lump sum – transitional protection lump sums which are reportable under the terms of *SI 2006/572*.
- Transfer payment to a qualifying recognised overseas pension scheme, as defined in the *FA 2006*: the HMRC website lists such schemes.
- IRPS status – on acquiring or losing such status – some transitional protection exists for already qualified schemes.
- Making changes to scheme rules which permit unauthorised payments or widen investment beyond insurance policies or contracts of insurance.
- Making changes to the rules of pre A-Day 'split scheme' rules.
- Making changes to the legal structure of a scheme – movement between the categories of single trust, annuity contract, body corporate and other.
- Making a change to scheme membership numbers: meaning a head count as at 5 April each year.
- Making a first payment of an alternatively secured pension – on attaining age 75 or on funds becoming held after age 75.
- Transfer of a lump sum death benefit.
- Payment of a lump sum after the death of a member aged 75 or over.
- Making a scheme chargeable payment from an IRPS.
- Changing the country or territory of the scheme establishment.
- Attaining or losing the status of an occupational pension scheme.

10.88 In addition to the existing self-assessment returns:

- The new Accounting for Tax Return (AFT) is the mechanism for paying tax charges incurred. There are no notice requirements on HMRC for this return, which must be made on a quarterly basis and must be provided within 45 days of the relevant quarter end. The main areas covered are: lifetime allowance charges, repaid lump sums, taxable death benefits, taxable refunds of surpluses and de-registration charges.
- A Registered Pension Scheme Return replaces the universal issue of a self-administered tax return for trust-based schemes for earlier years. However, it only applies to the relative small number of schemes which

have taxable income to declare, and those which make in year repayment claims into scheme income received under deduction of tax.

Unauthorised transactions and certain tax charges

10.89 *FA 2004* brought in the greatest change to UK pensions tax law since WW II. The new regime is heavily dependent on direct compliance with the law. Accordingly, it is essential for practitioners to be fully aware of the current statutory requirements, as tax charges can be inadvertently incurred by the unsuspecting. Many of these charges will fall on the scheme administrator.

Unauthorised payments

10.90 Unauthorised payments are payments to or in respect of current or former members or employers (or those who are deemed to be so) which are not authorised payments. They include:

- Transfers of assets or of monies or monies' worth.
- Taking value out of a pension scheme for unauthorised reasons.
- Assignment or surrender of benefits, rights or debts.
- Value shifting of assets.
- Non-commercial transactions.
- Increases in rights of a connected person on death.
- Allocating an unallocated employer's contribution.
- Excessive benefits.
- Member use of assets.
- Taxable property held by an IRPS.
- Acquisition of wasting assets (that is, assets that have an anticipated life of less than 50 years, such as properties with less than 50-year leases, cars, racehorses, plant and machinery etc).

The main charges, surcharges, penalties and sanctions

The unauthorised payments charge

10.91 *FA 2004, s 208:* The charge is at 40% on payments to a member or sponsoring employer that are not authorised by the scheme rules. It is payable by the member, the recipient or the sponsoring employer according to the circumstances. Unauthorised payments include:

- excessive benefits;
- benefits taken at a time not permitted under the tax rules;
- unauthorised transfers;
- assignments and surrenders;
- unacceptable investment activity;
- payments to migrant members who have benefited from UK tax relief;
- value shifting;
- recycled cash lump sums;
- taxable property held by IRPS.

Any liberated funds are repatriated, and *FA 2004, s 266,* provides relief from the charge. The member has to claim the relief within a year of the repatriation of the funds.

The unauthorised payments surcharge

10.92 *FA 2004, s 209*: The member charge is 15% of the surchargeable unauthorised payment. It arises if the amount of all unauthorised payments in the surchargeable period is 25% or more of the uncrystallised and crystallised rights under the scheme. For employers the 25% percentage is calculated based on the amount of the employer payment divided by the value of the total rights under the scheme.

Members must declare the surcharge on their tax returns. A discharge is available under *FA 2004, ss 267* and *268* if 'it would not be just and reasonable for the person to be liable'.

The scheme sanction charge

10.93 *FA 2004, s 239*: The charge is 40% of the chargeable payments. It is reduced where an unauthorised payment charge above has already been paid. This reduction is the lesser of 25% of the scheme chargeable payments on which tax was paid under the unauthorised payments charge; and the actual amount of tax paid on the unauthorised payment.

The charge applies to unauthorised payments and scheme chargeable payments. A discharge is available under *FA 2004, ss 267* and *268* if 'it would not be just and reasonable for the person to be liable'.

10.94 *Pensions*

The de-registration charge

10.94 HMRC can de-register a scheme where it has failed to meet certain statutory requirements. Although this is an unlikely course of action, the most vulnerable schemes will be those which have attracted the scheme sanction charge. De-registration can occur where the total percentages of the fund used up by scheme chargeable payments exceeds 25% in any 12 month period. The rate of tax chargeable is 40% of the value of the whole fund, and it may be appealed to the Commissioners. The charge is payable by the person who was the scheme administrator immediately before HMRC de-registered the scheme.

Penalties

10.95 HMRC has power to seek penalties for failures to provide information and the provision of false information. A penalty of up to £3,000 may be incurred for making an incorrect report under the new reporting regime. Failures to make reports of unauthorised payments can incur a penalty not exceeding £300 and a continuing penalty up to £60 per day for any continuing failure.

Failure to provide a pension scheme return incurs a penalty of £100 and a continuing penalty up to £60 per day for the continuing failure. Incorrect returns or incorrect accounts may incur a penalty not exceeding £3,000. Similar penalties arise on failures to comply with a notice requiring documents or particulars.

Failure to make a quarterly return of tax may incur a penalty, calculated according to the tax payable and to the number of persons whose particulars should be included in the return. If the return is incorrect through fraud or negligence, further penalties may be imposed.

Authorised surplus payments charge

10.96 A tax charge applies where an authorised surplus payment is made by a scheme to a sponsoring employer. The charge is payable on the amount of any surplus payment authorised by HMRC, at a rate of tax of 35% on the amount of the surplus.

The tax charge on benefits in kind

10.97 This charge arises where members or their relatives occupy residential property or enjoy the use of a pride in possession asset owned by a scheme at less than a commercial rent. The rate of tax is 40% the value of the benefit in kind so enjoyed. The charge is payable by the member or any other recipient of the benefit regardless of their effective rate of tax.

Registration of enhanced lifetime allowance

10.98 Any provision of incorrect or false documents, certificates or information when registering an enhanced lifetime allowance can incur a penalty of up to 25% of the excess allowance claimed on the individual concerned.

Enhanced protection

10.99 Failure to notify HMRC within 90 days of relevant benefit accrual occurring for a person with enhanced protection can render the individual concerned liable to a penalty of up to £3,000.

Winding-up

10.100 If a scheme is deliberately wound-up to provide winding-up lump sums to the members or winding-up lump sum death benefits to others, the administrator is liable to a penalty not exceeding £3,000 in respect of each person to whom a winding-up lump sum is paid.

Transfers to the appropriate person

10.101 A penalty of up to £3,000 may be imposed on an administrator who fails to ensure that transfers to another scheme that invests in insurance policies are made to the appropriate person.

Appeals

10.102 The following appeals against HMRC action may be made to the General or Special Commissioners, normally within 30 days of the relevant event:

- against a failure to register a scheme;
- against an action to de-register a scheme;
- against a decision to exclude a recognised overseas pension scheme;
- against notices requiring documents or particulars; and
- in respect of the discharge of the LA charge.

Reviewing existing registered schemes

10.103 From A-Day all approved schemes were re-designated as registered schemes, unless they opted-out of the new regime. These schemes are subject to the overriding modification regulations until 6 April 2011 (*FA 2004, Sch 36, Pt 1, para 3*). The *Registered Pension Schemes (Modification of Rules of Existing Schemes) Regulations 2006, SI 2006/364* provide a rule of construction and give the trustees discretion over whether or not to make a payment which would fall to be treated as an unauthorised payment under the new regime. However, from a tax-planning perspective it is advisable to review existing documentation and make any desirable revisions, after seeking appropriate legal advice, at an early date. For example:

- any changes in the level of pensionable pay and the method of calculation;
- whether or not to put in place the scheme's own earnings cap as a means of controlling maximum benefit accrual;
- how the removal of HMRC limits is to impact on intended member benefits;
- whether to extend the scheme to overseas employers and employees;
- whether to widen the transfer powers and income withdrawal facilities to take advantage of the new freedoms;
- how the tax rules changes made affect benefit payments, eg transfers and income withdrawal;
- whether to change scheme indexation provisions, or remove them in the case of money purchase schemes, in accordance with the *Pensions Act 2004* relaxations.

A particular area of concern must be what the trustees should do in the event of a surplus arising which, under the existing regime, should be returned to the employer but, under the new regime, may remain within the member's LA.

10.104 It should be noted that new limits on the maximum amount of unsecured pension for members' pensions in payment will apply from 6 April 2008, at the latest. This is the legislative default date. Payments made above the new limits will attract the unauthorised payment charge and, potentially, the unauthorised payment surcharge and the scheme sanction charge. The new limit is 120% of the 'basis amount, being the annuity which could have been bought applying theoretical annuity rates from the Government Actuary's Department.

Reviewing existing unapproved arrangements

General

10.105 It is highly desirable that existing funded and unfunded unapproved retirement benefits schemes (FURBS and UURBS) are urgently reviewed. The new regime removed the pre A-Day tax advantages of such schemes, with the result that FURBS have lost virtually all attraction for investors. Transitional protection applies to funds accumulated up to A-Day, but it is not total. Members may wish to take advantage of the options available under the rules of their schemes, such as drawing or transferring benefits before fund growth attracts unwelcome tax charges. Employers will wish to consider other means of rewarding their senior employees, such as cash, share incentive schemes, share options or (where the lifetime allowance is not exceeded) assimilating their unapproved arrangements and, perhaps, life cover arrangements, into a registered scheme. In the area of life cover it is worth seeking specialist advice on EGLP as these can be an attractive form of provision for high earners (see **10.70** above). However, the withdrawal of tax relief on pension contributions which are paid as premiums to personal term assurance policies (see **10.72** above) has removed a previously available area of choice.

10.106 From A-Day all funded non-registered schemes are designated employer-financed retirement benefits schemes (EFRBS). The main new rules are summarised below:

- Contributions may continue to be made to EFRBS from A-Day. The lump sum will be adjusted to take account of the tax-free lump sum accumulated to A-Day. From the tax perspective there seems to be no attraction in taking up this option.

- The protection of the tax-free lump sum (where such payments qualified for relief either by virtue of the taxation of employer contributions on the member or the taxation of all income and gains under the fund), is only inclusive of indexation and not the fund yield on values from that date.

- The normal inheritance tax exemptions apply only to pre A-Day assets under an existing discretionary trust (for unregistered schemes with no post 6 April 2006 contributions, and those with post 6 April 2006 contributions, the inheritance tax treatment for the former shall be that in place as at 5 April 2006, limited relief shall be given for the latter for protected funds inclusive of indexation).

- No additional tax charge arises on the fund/lump sum for a FURBS which ceased contributions/input before A-Day.

- Capital gains tax is chargeable at the rate applicable to trusts, which increased from 34% to 40% on 6 April 2004. The basic rate of tax applies on the first £500 from 6 April 2005. FURBS enjoyed the 50% × annual CGT exemption/taper relief. Many FURBS did not receive annual returns and only filled them in when a chargeable event arose.

- Amounts held in the fund will not be included in the lifetime allowance.

- Income tax on the fund increased from 22% to 40% from 6 April 2006.

10.107 *Pensions*

- NIC will be payable on benefits, although it is likely that there will be no charge on any benefits which are within the limits of benefits that could be paid out of a registered scheme.
- Tax relief on employer contributions is only allowable when the benefit is paid out.

The timing of benefit payments from FURBS

10.107 The rules of each scheme will require review. HMRC produced very little guidance on FURBS – the main pre A-Day publication was last updated in 1991. The guide states that benefits outside the approved scheme regime are 'unlimited', and 'there are no tax rules which govern the structure of schemes, the type of benefits or their amount'. The guide also says that benefits may be given 'when a person retires or died, in anticipation of retirement, after a person has retired or died …' Nevertheless, the rules themselves will take precedence over benefit payments, transfers and winding-up payments. The guide also states:

> 'there are no tax problems where a cash equivalent is paid between funded schemes The funds held in the transferring scheme will have accrued from contributions, investment income and gains which have been taxed. For this reason there will not be any tax liability on the transfer payment.'

Tax charges and exemptions for EFRBS

10.108 No special CGT provisions apply to EFRBSs. Whether a benefit is paid out of cash realised from the sale of scheme assets, or by a transfer in specie of those assets, both actions are a disposal of trust assets and trigger CGT charges.

The new legislation is not specific on IHT charges for EFRBS. It is presumed that the normal provisions for discretionary settlements apply. In other words, the 6% ten-yearly charge may apply, and the exit charge up to 6% may well be triggered on death. The content of the documentation will again be paramount, and specialist advice should be sought. It was often recommended for FURBS that the employee's estate was excluded from the potential beneficiaries for reasons of certainty of IHT relief and to avoid dispute with HMRC.

Overseas tax planning

Introduction

10.109 The opening up of UK registered scheme eligibility to the employed or self-employed, including qualifying non-residents, and the advent of recognised overseas pension schemes, has brought in far wider tax-planning opportunities than those which had been available before A-Day. In addition to these significant changes, many of the restrictions on transfers to and from UK registered schemes to overseas schemes have been removed. Of course, there are specific rules to follow if tax reliefs are to be obtained and/or unwelcome tax charges are to be avoided. These rules are described below.

Background, and EU influence on investments

10.110 The relaxations of UK tax rules for overseas pension schemes, and the new cross-border opportunities, were in no small part driven by EU law. The free movement of capital, labour and services around Member States has long been a central plank of the aims of the European Commission. *EU Pensions Directive 2003/41/EC* on the activities and supervision of institutions for occupational retirement provision (IORPSs) represented the first step on the way to an internal market for occupational retirement provision on a European scale. The *Occupational Pension Schemes (Investment) Regulations 2005, SI 2005/3378* adopted a 'prudent person approach' as the underlying principle for capital investment, in accordance with the *IORPs Directive, Art 18*. Mainly, the *IORPs* guidance has been followed in a proportionate and flexible manner, namely:

- a triennial review of the statement of investment principles;
- trustees must consider 'proper advice' on the suitability of a proposed investment;
- there are specific requirements in relation to borrowing and a restriction on investment in the 'sponsors' undertaking' to no more than 5% of the portfolio (where a group is concerned, the percentage is no greater than 20%).

Significantly, the 'small scheme exemption' which is contained in *Art 5* of the Directive means that schemes with fewer than 100 active and deferred members are exempted from many of the requirements of the regulations, but are still required to have regard to the need for diversification on investment rule.

Overseas employers, and cross-border provision

10.111 EU employers may join a registered scheme, provided that there are clauses or rules in the scheme documentation to allow this, and compliance with the relevant member state's requirements. Additionally, *Pensions Act 2004, ss 287* and *294* permit cross-border activities within the EU. These activities include accepting contributions, ring-fencing of assets and preventing the disposal of assets which are held in the UK for an EU occupational pension

10.112 *Pensions*

institution. The principal regulations are the *Occupational Pension Schemes (Cross-border Activities) Regulations 2005, SI 2005/3381*. The purpose of the regulations is to enable occupational pension schemes for a qualifying person to be sponsored by a European employer in other Member States. Practitioners will wish to consider the advantages which are offered by the new rules, and to revise their clients' rules if necessary. It should be noted that *s 615* schemes may effectively continue under the *Income Tax (Earnings and Pensions) Act 2003*.

Migrant member relief

10.112 Migrant member relief is available where an individual:

- is resident in the UK but was not resident in the UK at the time he joined a qualifying overseas pension scheme;
- comes to the UK as a member of that scheme, and remains a member of the overseas scheme;
- notifies the scheme manager that he intends to claim migrant member relief (UK tax relief against UK earnings on contributions paid to the overseas scheme);
- has earnings chargeable in the UK; and
- was eligible for tax relief on contributions to the overseas scheme in the country in which they were resident immediately before coming to the UK (alternatively, where a member had received tax relief on contributions paid to the pension scheme in the country of residence at any time in the ten years prior to coming to the UK).

10.113 The overseas scheme must either be EU or EEA registered, or one that generally corresponds with a UK scheme, and must:

- notify HMRC that it is an overseas pension scheme, providing supporting evidence if required;
- undertake to notify HMRC if it stops being an overseas pension scheme;
- undertake to provide HMRC with certain information in accordance with regulations; and
- notify any member claiming migrant member relief that it has undertaken to comply with the information requirements.

Employers may claim a deduction for contributions paid to a qualifying recognised overseas pension scheme (QROPS) in respect of employees who are eligible for migrant member relief.

10.114 The new rules provide details of certain tax charges that arise in respect of 'relevant non-UK schemes', where UK tax relief has been given on contributions under migrant member relief, or under the terms of a Double Taxation Treaty, or where a transfer has been made from a UK registered scheme to an overseas scheme. Member payment charges apply under *FA 2004, Sch 34*, where the individual is resident in the UK in the year in which the payments are made or was resident in the UK in any of the immediately preceding five years.

Pension portability in the EU

10.115 The *EU portability Directive* is still in draft form. Nevertheless, practitioners will need to be aware of the latest developments as it is likely that Member States will have to ensure the fair treatment of dormant pension rights and gradually improve their transferability. The changes, when introduced, may require a review of existing pension scheme documentation. It is currently intended that the directive will apply to all work-related pension schemes both funded and unfunded, but that pension rights which existed before the directive comes into force (no later than 1 July 2008) will be excluded.

Qualifying recognised overseas pension scheme, and transfers

10.116 There is no doubt that there are considerable funds which are tied up in UK pension schemes for internationally mobile employees, expatriates and employees of overseas companies. Before A-Day there was little that could be done to move these monies to an overseas scheme. *FA 2004* introduced sweeping changes, and these have yet to be explored by many. Practitioners will wish to fully acquaint themselves with the new rules, review their own clients' status and contact specialist overseas providers and scheme administrators where appropriate.

A key opportunity for members lies in joining a QROPS. The advantages are that pension monies may be transferred to and from UK registered schemes to such schemes without tax charge, and tax reliefs are available on contributions to such schemes. Future accrual of benefits from monies which have received no UK tax reliefs will not attract the lifetime allowance charge.

The transfer rules are far more flexible than before A-Day, and are attracting increasing interest. A transfer to a QROPS is a 'relevant transfer' under *FA 2004, s 169* which includes alternatively secured pensions and pensions in drawdown, and a BCE is triggered. Additionally, there are wide potential tax savings for individual members on their benefits, dependent on their residence and/or domicility status.

10.116 *Pensions*

There are no specific UK restrictions on borrowing by QROPS. However, if a member borrows money back from funds he has transferred, it will trigger an unauthorised payment charge.

Chapter 11

Business property relief

Mark McLaughlin CTA (Fellow), ATT, TEP

INTRODUCTION

11.1 Business property relief (BPR) is an important and valuable relief from inheritance tax (IHT). It reduces the value transferred by a transfer of value of certain types of business or business property by a specified percentage. The current rates of BPR are 100% and 50% respectively. The actual rate of relief applied to a transfer depends on the type of business property. The relief applies to actual or deemed transfers. It is available for lifetime transfers, or to relevant business property included in an individual's estate on death. There are no territorial limits to the relief, so it can apply to business property situated worldwide. BPR also applies to settled property included in the death estate, and is available to trustees in respect of the periodic and exit charges that originally applied to discretionary trusts, but which now apply to most types of trust, following changes introduced in *FA 2006*.

The law on BPR is contained in *IHTA 1984, ss 103–114*. The relief must be claimed. The claimant must therefore be aware of the categories of business property that qualify, and the correct rate of BPR applicable. A number of conditions must be satisfied before the relief is available, and a number of potential traps exist for the unwary. This chapter outlines the conditions for BPR, and highlights some planning points and possible pitfalls in connection with the relief. (All statutory references in this chapter are to *IHTA 1984*, unless otherwise stated.)

Conditions

11.2 BPR applies if the value transferred by a transfer of value relates to relevant business property. The categories of business property and the rates of BPR attributable to them are broadly as listed below.

- A business or an interest in a business – 100%.

11.3 *Business property relief*

- Control holdings of unquoted securities in a company – 100%.
- Unquoted shares in a company – 100%.
- Control holdings of quoted shares in a company – 50%.
- Land, buildings, plant and machinery used by a company controlled by the transferor, or by a partnership of which the transferor was a member – 50%.
- Land, buildings, plant and machinery of a settlement in which the transferor had an interest in possession and was used in his business – 50%.

11.3 In the context of companies, the term 'unquoted' applies for BPR purposes to shares listed on the Alternative Investment Market (AIM), and to shareholdings in OFEX companies (IHTM 18336–7). Shares listed on NASDAQ Europe are (from 28 November 2001) similarly treated as unquoted for BPR purposes. In general, if a company is not listed on the UK Stock Exchange, any foreign recognised Stock Exchange or alternative market, its shares and securities will be unquoted (*s 105(1ZA)*). However, in relation to those companies and in general, it is necessary to consider whether the business carried on makes the shares or securities (or a business interest) eligible for BPR.

In the case of land, buildings, plant and machinery used by a company, it is important to note the requirement that the company must be controlled by the transferor. 'Control' for these purposes is defined in *s 269*. Note that a shareholder with a 50% shareholding and a casting vote has control for these purposes (*Walker's Executors v IRC* [2001] STC (SCD) 86).

A beneficiary with a qualifying life interest in trust property is treated for inheritance tax purposes as owning the underlying assets. A 'life interest' for these purposes means an interest in possession within *s 49(1)*. If those assets are used in the beneficiary's business, they will normally qualify for 100% BPR (*Fetherstonaugh v IRC* [1984] STC 261).

What is a 'business'?

11.4 A 'business' for BPR purposes includes a profession or vocation, but does not include a business carried on otherwise than for gain (*s 103(3)*). A 'hobby business' may therefore be excluded (see IHTM 25051), unless it is run in a proper, businesslike manner. The 'interest in a business' requirement in *s 105(1)(a)* is such that mere business assets are not of themselves eligible for BPR.

Business property is precluded from relief if the business consists wholly or mainly of dealing in securities, stocks or shares or land or buildings, or in making or holding investments. There are some limited exceptions, in respect of market makers or discount house businesses carried on in the UK. There is also an exception in group situations, if a company's business is wholly or mainly to be the holding company of one or more companies whose business is not an excluded one (*s 105(3)–(4)*). Groups of companies are discussed later in this chapter.

Caravan parks

11.5 A number of cases have considered what constitutes a 'business' for BPR purposes. This is particularly so in relation to caravan park businesses, for the purposes of determining whether they were substantially investment in nature due to rental receipts, or whether the trading (eg sales and service) components of the businesses were sufficient to enable them to qualify for business relief. In *IRC v George and another (executors of Stedman, dec'd)* [2004] STC 147, Lord Justice Carnwath accepted on the facts that a caravan site qualified, commenting that it was '… difficult to see why an active family business of this kind should be excluded from business property relief, merely because a necessary component of its profit-making activity is the use of land'.

HMRC's Inheritance Tax Manual (IHTM) provides a useful insight into its approach following the decision in George, and commentary is therefore repeated below. In practice, HMRC are likely to refer caravan park cases in which BPR is claimed to their Technical Group.

Caravan park cases following the 'George' decision (extracts from IHTM25279)

'The judgment in George is helpful in clarifying what is to be regarded as either investment or non-investment activity. It makes clear that the provision of services under the terms of a pitch agreement is a non-investment activity. This means that in cases where a large part of the business's activities (measured in both time and money) consists of providing services to residents, we would be more likely to consider that the business was neither wholly or mainly investment in nature. However, we need to be satisfied that the figures for pitch fees, for instance, are not artificially depressed in the accounts in favour of inflated figures for wages or other non-investment expenses.'

'The judgment in George also recognises that the time and money spent on maintaining amenity areas is in part designed to maintain the value of the owner's investment. It follows that the taxpayers are entitled to return a reduced level of investment income by offsetting against it part of the maintenance costs. As this could lead to the net investment income being, proportionally, a smaller part of the overall income of the business we might well conclude in a particular case that the business was neither wholly or mainly one of holding investments. On the other hand, we would also need to take into account the time spent by the owner and/or his employees in the maintenance work. When taken together with other work carried out in the business, the evidence might lead us to conclude that the majority of work done is involved in maintaining the value of the owner's investment. If so, then we would seek to deny the claim under s105 (3).'

'The judgment in George also suggests that the holding of land as an investment is separate and distinct from the service element of the business. Finally, when looking at the facts 'in the round', trading figures are only a part of the overall picture.'

'When dealing with a claim for business relief on a caravan park, you will need to obtain detailed business accounts, including breakdowns of both the income and expenditure between the investment and non-investment elements of the business. In addition, you should ask the taxpayers to state precisely what services were provided to the park residents and how long was spent by the deceased (as park owner) and his partners and/or employees providing those services.'

The 'right' business?

11.6 A detailed consideration of what constitutes a 'business' for BPR purposes is outside the scope of this chapter. However, the following points are worthy of note:

- *Property construction* – the restriction on dealing in land and buildings does not prevent a property construction business from qualifying for BPR, such as a building company holding houses or plots as stock in trade for development (IHTM 25264).
- *Hotels, nursing homes,* etc – other property backed businesses such as hotels and nursing homes will also usually qualify for relief, based on the level of services provided.
- *Holiday lettings* – short-term holiday lettings will normally be eligible for BPR, provided that the owner was 'substantially involved' with guest activities on and off the premises (IHTM 25277–8).
- *Property lettings* – difficulties can arise with property lettings. For example, in *Clark and another (executors of Clark, dec'd) v HMRC* [2005] STC (SCD) 823, a company's business comprised rents from properties it owned (ie investment income), plus trading income from management

charges in respect of a number of dwellings owned by family members. Viewed 'in the round', the company's business was held to consist mainly of investments. The company's maintenance of the rented properties was held not to constitute the separate provision of services, but was inherent in the property ownership.

- *Loans* – In *Phillips and others (Executors of Rhoda Phillips, dec'd) v HMRC* (2006) SpC 555, shares in a company which made informal, unsecured loans to related family companies were held to be relevant business property, on the basis that the company's business was making loans, and therefore did not consist wholly or mainly of making or holding investments within *s 105(3)*.

'Wholly or mainly'

11.7 The 'wholly or mainly' business test (see **11.3**) applies to a business, business interest or company shares or securities. For the purposes of determining whether a company satisfies this test, it is necessary to consider all the company's activities 'in the round'. HMRC state the following (at SVM 27570):

'It may however be readily accepted that, where the majority of both the tangible asset value and profit of the company is attributable to trading activities, relief is available.'

HMRC's likely approach in appropriate cases will be to consider the company's activities, assets and income or gains not only when business property is transferred, but also over a 'reasonable period' leading up to it (IHTM 25263). In *Brown's Executors v IRC* [1997] STC (SCD) 277, HMRC refused a BPR claim on shares, on the grounds that the business consisted wholly or mainly of making investments at the date of death. The company had traded as a nightclub, but the business was sold before the shareholder's death and the proceeds held on a short-term bank deposit pending the acquisition of a new nightclub. However, the executors' appeal was upheld.

11.8 An important point to note is that BPR is only denied if the business activities mentioned in *s 105(3)* (ie dealing in securities, stocks and shares, dealing in land or making or holding investments represent more than 50% of all business activities. Thus the shareholder of an unquoted company undertaking 51% trading activities and 49% investment business activities can benefit from full BPR if the other relief conditions are satisfied. Conversely, if trading activities represent 49% and investment business activities 51%, no BPR is due at all. In practice it may be difficult to measure the respective activities accurately. The Special Commissioner's decision in *Farmer and another (executors of Farmer, dec'd) v IRC* [1999] STC (SCD) 321 offers some guidance on the possible approach to this problem.

11.9 *Business property relief*

In that case, the deceased carried on the business of farming and letting properties which were surplus to the requirements of the farm. The net rental profits were greater than the net farming profits, but the farming assets had a higher value at death than the properties used for letting. HMRC denied BPR on the basis that the business consisted mainly of making or holding investments. However, the executors' appeal was upheld. The Special Commissioner held that it did not follow that the level of net profit was the only or principal test in *s 105(3)*. The business and its activities had to be looked at 'in the round'. The letting of properties was subsidiary to the main farming activity, and although they were more profitable in the overall context of the business, this was not conclusive. The overall context of the business, capital employed, the time spent by employees and consultants and the levels of turnover supported the conclusion that the business consisted mainly of farming.

PERIOD OF OWNERSHIP

11.9 The general rule is that no BPR is due unless the relevant business property has been owned by the transferor for a minimum period of two years (*s 106*). In terms of IHT lifetime planning, this two year minimum holding period compares favourably with the seven-year period required for potentially exempt transfers to become exempt. It makes investment in (for example) unquoted shares (see **11.3**) seem attractive to individuals whose life expectancy is likely to exceed two years but uncertain to exceed seven years due to age or ill-health, particularly while BPR is available at the 100% rate. However, such investments are generally risky in nature, and their commercial implications must therefore be carefully considered.

11.10 Changes in the business during the two-year period are not necessarily fatal for BPR purposes. The nature of the business need not be the same, but there must have been a business throughout that period (IHTM 25303). There are also certain exceptions to the basic two-year ownership requirement, in connection with replacement property, acquisitions on death and successive transfers respectively. These exceptions broadly apply as follows:

- *Replacement property* – the ownership test is treated as satisfied if the property replaced other business property eligible for relief, provided that the combined period of ownership is at least two years out of the preceding five years. However, the BPR available is restricted to what it would have been had the replacement or any one or more of the replacements not been made (*s 107(2)*). The replacement property rule may be helpful in certain circumstances:
    - Incorporation of a business – the acquisition of the business by a company controlled by the former business owner;

- Partnerships – changes resulting from the formation, alteration or dissolution of a partnership (eg retiring from one partnership to form another);
- Company reorganisations, etc – holdings of unquoted shares which would (under the capital gains tax rules in *TCGA 1992, ss 126–136*) be identified with other qualifying shares previously owned may treat their period of ownership as including the ownership period of the original shares (*s 107(4)*).

In the case of the first two bullet points, the potential restriction in BPR mentioned above is disregarded (*s 107(3)*).

- *Successions* – for the purposes of the two-year ownership requirement and the replacement property rule, business property inherited on death is generally treated as owned from the date of death. However, if the deceased was a spouse or civil partner, the ownership periods of both individuals are combined, irrespective of how long they have been married (*s 108*; see IHTM 25321).
- *Successive transfers* – BPR is broadly available for relevant business property if that property was eligible for relief when it was originally transferred to its owner (or their spouse or civil partner), and that (or replacement) property would be relevant business property on the later transfer (but for the two-year rule), provided that either the original or later transfer was made on death (*s 109(1)*). However, the BPR can be subject to limitation in certain circumstances (*s 109(2), (3)*).

BPR and interests in possession

11.11 In the context of BPR, 'ownership' generally applies in terms of beneficial entitlement. An exception to this general rule is where property is legally owned by trustees of a settlement in which there is no interest in possession (IHTM 25302). Beneficial entitlement includes a beneficiary's entitlement to an interest in possession in the settled property (*s 49(1)*). The IHT regime for interests in possession was changed significantly by FA 2006, and only certain post-22 March 2006 interests in possession (eg immediate post-death interests) are subject to the same treatment.

11.12 As noted at **11.2** above, land, buildings, plant and machinery of a settlement in which the transferor had an interest in possession and was used in his business qualify for BPR at the 50% rate. However, if the transferor has an interest in possession in the assets used for his business, those assets will normally be treated as part of his business and will be entitled to 100% relief (see *Fetherstonaugh v IRC* [1984] STC 261). HMRC consider that there is some

11.13 *Business property relief*

doubt whether the *Fetherstonaugh* decision can apply to lifetime as well as death transfers, and will refer claims for 100% BPR on lifetime transfers to their Technical Group (IHTM 25154).

Value of the business

11.13 BPR is available in respect of the net value of the business. 'Net value' is the value of business assets (including goodwill) less business liabilities (*s 110(b)*). Any assets not used in the business cannot qualify for relief. In addition, BPR is not available for assets not used wholly or mainly for business purposes throughout the preceding two years, nor are needed for future use, for future business use (see 'Excepted assets' below).

In *Hardcastle and another (executors of Vernede, dec'd) v IRC* [2000] STC (SCD) 532, the Lloyd's assets of a non-working name was accepted to qualify as business property eligible for 100% relief. Uninsured underwriting losses were held to be liabilities deductible from the value of the deceased's other estate rather than the deceased's underwriting interests. The losses were not considered to be liabilities incurred for the purposes of the business under *s 110(b)*. In *IRC v Mallender* [2001] STC 514, the deceased's Lloyd's underwriting business was also considered to be business property eligible for relief. However, a tenanted investment property used to support a security for a bank guarantee did not qualify as business property. The land was worth considerably more than the maximum sum guaranteed. The court held that the bank guarantee was the asset used in the business rather than the investment property itself.

Subsequently, in *Marquess of Hertford v IRC* [2005] STC (SCD) 177, a stately home (Ragley Hall) was operated as a business. 78% of Ragley Hall was open to the public, and 22% was occupied as a private residence. The deceased's executors claimed BPR on the value of the building as a whole, as being one of the assets of the business within *s 110(b)*. They appealed against HMRC's refusal to allow relief for 100% of the property value. The Special Commissioner held that the asset attracting business property relief was Ragley Hall in its entirety, not just 78% of it. Unfortunately, HMRC appear to view this case as an 'unusual' one, on the basis that '… it was the nature of the business in this particular case and the part that the physical structure of the hall played in that business that most influenced the Commissioner's decision.' BPR claims on buildings based on the decision are therefore likely to attract the attention of HMRC's Technical Group (see IHTM 25342).

Excepted assets

11.14 There is a potential restriction in BPR in the case of 'excepted assets', ie assets not used wholly or mainly for business purposes for at least the last two years, nor which are required for future business use (*s 112*). This section therefore has the potential to restrict BPR such as, for example, in relation to surplus cash held by an unquoted trading company. The 'future use' requirement provides a useful let-out in cases where an asset has not been used wholly or mainly for business purposes throughout the last two years. If the asset is in actual business use at the relevant point in time, it will probably be required for future business use as well. Thus shares in an investment company which have been held for at least two years can immediately qualify for BPR, if the company switches its activities to the 'right kind' of business.

Different rules apply to land or buildings, plant or machinery used wholly or mainly for the business of a company controlled by the transferor, or by a partnership of which he was then a partner, for which 50% BPR is available. The description of relevant business property in *s 105(1)(d)* only requires that the asset is in business use immediately before the transfer. The excepted asset provisions broadly require business use throughout the preceding two years, subject to relaxations for replacement property and under the rules in *s 109* for successive transfers (*s 112(3)*).

A helpful relaxation in the excepted asset rules applies to land and buildings, where part is used exclusively for business purposes but the whole of the land or building is not used wholly or mainly for business purposes (eg it was used wholly or mainly for the benefit of a transferor or a connected person). In those circumstances the part used exclusively for business purposes and the rest of the property are treated as separate assets, and BPR is applied accordingly to the business part. The value of the entire land or building is apportioned between those parts for this purpose (*s 112(4)*).

Example 11.1

Stanley owned a three-storey building on his death. The ground floor was a shop from which he operated a confectionery business. He used the second and third floors for his living quarters. The value of the whole building is £600,000, of which the upper floors are valued at £350,000. The ground floor shop is treated as a separate asset, which is not an excepted asset.

If the property is subject to a mortgage (or other loan), BPR can be maximised by arranging for the mortgage to be secured on the non-business part of the property, if possible (see **11.54**).

Investment 'business'?

11.15 In any event, investment assets will not necessarily be excepted assets. A trading company that includes a business of making or holding investments

11.16 *Business property relief*

may qualify for business property relief, provided that the investment business does not predominate. A 'wholly or mainly' test applies for these purposes (*s 105(3)*). HMRC accept that a 'hybrid' company that is mainly trading will not be subject to the excepted assets rule in respect of assets used in the investment element of the business (see Shares Valuation Manual at paragraph 27660).

However, HMRC consider that a 'business' involves a degree of activity. In our example of surplus cash, the company's holding of it generally requires no effort and involves no activity. In *Jowett v O'Neill and Brennan Construction Ltd* [1998] STC 482 (a corporation tax case), the holding of cash on interest bearing deposit was held not to constitute a business. On the other hand, a holding of investment shares or securities may constitute a business, depending on the size of holdings, the degree of active management and the reason for acquiring them.

11.16 Another corporation tax case (*Revenue and Customs Comrs v Salaried Persons Postal Loans Ltd* [2006] STC 1315) gives rise to the possibility that a company owning property and deriving a rental return from it may be considered not to be carrying on an investment business. In that case, the company's only source of income was rental income from a former business premises. The Revenue contended that the company was carrying on a business, but the Special Commissioner allowed the taxpayer's appeal. It was relevant to consider why the company received income and what it actually did to receive the income. The company had merely continued letting its old trading premises, which it had done for nearly 30 years. The circumstances in which a company letting property is found not to be carrying on a business are likely to be exceptional. However, the possible application of the decision in the *Postal Loans* case in a BPR context should be borne in mind.

'Surplus' cash

11.17 It may be relevant to ask: is the surplus cash 'surplus' at all? For example, what is the company's working capital requirement? Could the funds be applied towards repaying creditors? Or expanding the company's trade? The latter use is an express condition for the excepted assets restriction to apply (ie. that the assets are not required for present or future business use). This condition was considered in *Barclays Bank Trust Co Ltd v IRC* [1998] STC (SCD) 125. In that case, the deceased had been a shareholder in a company operating the business of selling bathroom and kitchen fittings. At the date of the deceased's death, the company held £450,000 in cash. Turnover was around £600,000. HMRC accepted that £150,000 of that cash was required by the company at that time, but maintained that the remaining £300,000 was an excepted asset. The Special Commissioner accepted HMRC's view, and dismissed the appeal against the BPR restriction. The possibility of using the money at some future point if a suitable opportunity arose was not sufficient. To be required for future use, there must be some evidence that the money will be required for a specific project or business purpose.

The *Barclays* case perhaps provides a helpful 'rule of thumb', on the footing that a cash balance equivalent to 25% of turnover was accepted as being required for the day-to-day running of the business. However, it may be possible to justify a higher proportion in practice, subject to the working capital requirements of the particular business.

11.18 By contrast, in *Brown's Executors v IRC* [1996] STC (SCD) 277, the deceased owned shares in an unquoted trading company which operated a nightclub. The nightclub was sold to third parties. Proceeds from the sale of the nightclub were held in a short-term interest bearing deposit account with a bank pending acquisition of a new nightclub business. The deceased investigated the possibility of acquiring other nightclubs, but then died suddenly. The executors appealed against HMRC's refusal of a BPR claim on the shares. HMRC claimed that the company's business consisted wholly or mainly of making or holding investments, within *s 105(3)*. However, the Special Commissioner accepted the executors' evidence that the company had been actively seeking alternative sites for another nightclub, and allowed the appeal.

The issue in the *Brown's Executors* case differs from the *Barclays Bank* case, but it does illustrate two points. Firstly, the question of excepted asset status is only relevant if the shares are relevant business property. Secondly, in the context of excepted assets and generally, it is important that clear evidence of future trading requirements for apparently 'surplus' cash is available.

11.19 As mentioned (see **11.14**), in the case of land and buildings, the excepted assets rule also contains an apportionment provision (*s 112(4)*). This rule applies if part of the asset is used exclusively in the business, where the whole of the land and buildings would otherwise be an excepted asset because it was not used wholly or mainly for business (or would be excluded from relief under a separate provision relating to land and buildings, machinery and plant in *s 112(3)*). Its effect is that the part used exclusively for business purposes and the rest of the property are treated as separate assets, and the value of the land or building as a whole is apportioned between them. This apportionment may apply where, for example, a dentist operates a practice from home. The house is mainly the dentist's residence, but rooms on the ground floor are used for a surgery, office and waiting room.

Investment 'business'

11.20 The BPR restriction for surplus cash as an excepted asset can be overcome by applying those funds towards an investment 'business'. However,

11.21 *Business property relief*

care is needed to ensure that the company's trade remains the dominant business. In addition, the question arises as to what constitutes a 'business' for these purposes. In the case of shares and securities, HMRC's Shares Valuation Manual suggests that some caution is required (SVM 27660):

'much will turn on the size of the holdings, the time spent on their management (including buying and selling) and the reason for their acquisition. For example, if a company finding itself with spare cash bought one or more holdings and held them for some time before the transfer, these could reasonably be claimed to be non-business assets. On the other hand, the greater the value of the investments in relation to the entirety value of the company, and the greater the active management required, the more likely they are to constitute a business activity.'

11.21 If the asset was used wholly or mainly for the personal benefit of the transferor or a person connected with him (eg a yacht), it is deemed not to have been used wholly or mainly for the purposes of the business concerned (*s 112(6)*). However, what is the practical effect of excluding the excepted asset? HMRC accept that in some cases (eg minority shareholdings) the exclusion of an asset would make little or no difference to the value transferred (SVM 27670). This will particularly be the case if shares are valued on an earnings basis as opposed to an assets basis, as the existence of an excepted asset may only have a minor effect on value. However, subject to the size of shareholding, a discount may also be applicable in the case of a valuation on an assets basis.

11.22 The BPR restriction for surplus cash as an excepted asset can also be mitigated by repaying trade and other creditors (eg hire purchase liabilities, long-term loans). Alternatively, following *Phillips and others (Executors of Rhoda Phillips, dec'd) v HMRC* (2006) SpC 555 (see **11.6** above), BPR can seemingly be secured by engaging in the business of making loans (eg to related businesses).

Groups of companies

11.23 Without a special rule for holding companies in group situations, their shareholders would be denied BPR under the general rule in *s 105(3)*, which excludes shares (and also businesses or business interests) from relief if the company's business is wholly or mainly dealing in securities, stocks or shares, land or buildings or making or holding investments. The exception for shares or securities in holding companies applies if the company's business is wholly or mainly as a holding company of at least one subsidiary whose business does not fall into any of the categories mentioned above (*s 105(4)(b)*).

11.24 The value of a company's shares or securities is reduced for BPR purposes if the company is a group member and one or more group companies is not within the definition of relevant business property. A company is treated as not being a group member in a valuation context unless it either satisfies the conditions for being wholly or mainly a trading company (subject to exceptions for a market maker or discount house business carried on in the UK, or holding companies as described above) or unless its business is wholly or mainly of holding land or buildings mainly occupied by group members whose business would not preclude its shares from being relevant business property (*s 111*). Thus on a transfer of shares in the holding company, the value of any 'excluded' subsidiaries would not be taken into account when considering how much of the transfer of value is eligible for BPR.

There is also an exclusion from the excepted asset rules in the case of groups. An asset will not be an excepted asset in a group situation provided that the company using it was a member of the group at the time of use and immediately before the transfer, and that the use is in a company not excluded by virtue of *s 111*, as outlined above (*s 112(2)*).

11.25 Where a group of companies carries on investment business activities, some care may be required to prevent the restriction or denial of BPR.

Example 11.2

Holdco Ltd has three wholly-owned subsidiaries, A Ltd, B Ltd and C Ltd. Each of the subsidiaries is trading. However, Holdco owns a valuable portfolio of investment properties. The value of those properties is such that Holdco is not 'mainly' a holding company within *s 105(4)(b)*. Consequently, the owners of Holdco would not be entitled to BPR on their shares under the existing structure.

If one of the subsidiaries (say, A Ltd) owned all the properties, Holdco may qualify as a holding company. However, for the purposes of calculating BPR on the Holdco shares, the value of A Ltd's shares would be excluded, as though it was not a group member. By contrast, if the assets were not investments but properties from which A Ltd and the other group members traded, the value of the A Ltd shares could be taken into account for BPR purposes as a qualifying company (*s 111(b)*).

11.26 It might be possible to arrange for an alternative allocation of investments between group members, which could result in BPR being available to the Holdco Ltd shareholders.

11.27 *Business property relief*

Example 11.3

Following on from **Example 11.2**, the investment properties are divided so that Holdco Ltd, A Ltd, B Ltd and C Ltd each hold their own separate, smaller property portfolios, which are carefully structured so that each subsidiary is mainly trading. Each property portfolio constitutes a separate business, so there is no BPR restriction in respect of their value. Similarly, Holdco is mainly carrying on the activities of a holding company. The investment property portfolios do not cause BPR to be denied, and there is no 'excepted asset' restriction because the property holdings represent a separate, smaller business on which BPR also falls to be due.

11.27 However, care is needed. The 'wholly or mainly' test in terms of qualifying activities should ideally be considered before the group asset structure is put in place. The test is particularly important in the case of the holding company, as availability of BPR for the entire group may depend on it. The test should be measured on any appropriate basis, eg turnover, profitability or asset values, and also 'in the round'. For further guidance on the potential approach and the categories of measure to consider (albeit in a different context), see **11.8** above and the Special Commissioner's decision in *Farmer and another (executors of Farmer, dec'd) v IRC* [1999] STC (SCD) 321. The position should be monitored on an ongoing basis, as trading activities may fluctuate and property values may increase, to the point where the 'wholly or mainly' test ceases to be met.

OTHER POINTS

Company liquidations, reorganisations etc

11.28 When a company is no longer required, the business owners may decide to liquidate or informally wind up the company. The company's shares or securities generally cease to be eligible for BPR when the decision is made to end the company (eg when a winding-up order or resolution has been passed). However, there is an exception from this general rule if the company's business is to continue after a reconstruction or amalgamation. This exception applies either if the reconstruction or amalgamation is the reason for the winding up, or if the reconstruction or amalgamation takes place no more than a year after the transfer of value for BPR purposes (*s 105(5)*).

With regard to company reorganisations, as indicated at **11.10** above for the purposes of the two-year ownership requirement in *s 106*, holdings of unquoted shares which would (under the capital gains tax rules in *TCGA 1992, ss 126–*

136) be identified with other qualifying shares previously owned may treat their period of ownership as including the ownership period of the original shares (*s 107(4)*).

Partnerships

11.29 There is no requirement for an asset to have been eligible for BPR throughout the period of ownership. However, it must be relevant business property immediately before the chargeable event. For example, a partner's interest in a partnership is relevant business property (*s 105(1)(a)*). Upon retirement, the partner's capital account is converted into a debt, and the retiring individual becomes a creditor of the partnership. The debt is not relevant business property (*Beckman v IRC* [2000] STC (SCD) 59). To preserve entitlement to BPR, the partner may wish to make a gift of the capital before retiring (ie an interest in the business, as opposed to a simple gift of cash; see IHTM 25250), or possibly to delay retirement by taking a lesser role on the business in return for a reduced partnership share.

BPR may be available to a business partner under two separate headings:

- As an interest in a business (*s 105(1)(a)*) – eligible for 100% BPR;
- Land, buildings, plant and machinery used by a partnership of which the transferor was a member (*s 105(1)(d)*) – eligible for 50% BPR.

If the partnership holds the land and buildings (or plant and machinery) and the partner retains an interest in the business until death, HMRC are understood to accept BPR claims on the partner's interest in the land and buildings at the 100% (not 50%) rate, on the basis that the interest is comprised in the notional transfer of his business interest within *s 105(1)(a)*. The position is thus distinguishable from the notional transfer on death of land owned outside the partnership, on which only 50% BPR is due within *s 105(1)(d)*.

11.30 However, what is the BPR rate on a lifetime transfer of the partner's interest in land and buildings held by the partnership? Unless the transfer is of the partner's interest in the partnership as a whole, it cannot fall within *s 105(1)(a)*, so would fall within *s 105(1)(d)* instead giving BPR of 50%. Thus in terms of the BPR rate it makes no difference whether the partner's lifetime transfer is of land and buildings held within the partnership or outside it, as the BPR rate in both cases is 50% (IHTM 25225). However, in the case of a retiring partner, it would seem at least arguable that the transfer of an interest in land and buildings held by the partnership as part of the partner's overall withdrawal from the business and the transfer of his qualifying interest falls within *s 105(1)(a)* and is therefore eligible for 100% relief. However, there is no indication that this view is accepted in HMRC's guidance on partnerships (IHTM 25250).

11.31 *Business property relief*

11.31 Limited liability partnerships (LLPs) are not normally treated as owned by the individual partners, in the same way that shareholders own shares in a company. Instead, a business carried on by the LLP is treated as carried on by the partners. The LLP's property is treated as that of the partners. Property occupied or used by the LLP is treated as occupied or used by the partners. The incorporation of an LLP is treated as the formation of a partnership, and a transfer of value by or to an LLP is treated as made by or to its members (*s 267A*). For BPR (and APR) purposes, there is no change in the treatment of assets held outside, but used in, the partnership. The incorporation of a partnership into an LLP is not treated as interrupting a partner's period of ownership in terms of BPR (see *Tax Bulletin, Issue 50*).

Retirement of a partner

11.32 The timing of lifetime transfers of land or buildings, plant or machinery used by the partnership is important in terms of qualifying for any BPR at all. As noted above in relation to partnership interests, the asset must have been wholly or mainly used for business purposes immediately before the transfer, by a partnership of which the transferor was then a partner. A transfer after retirement therefore attracts no BPR.

This point was illustrated in *Beckman v IRC* [2000] STC (SCD) 59. The deceased (H) and her daughter (B) had been business partners until H's retirement. H's financial interest in the business immediately before her retirement, represented by her capital account, remained the same after her retirement. However, the Special Commissioner held that her legal interest was radically changed on her retirement. Previously, she had all the rights of management conferred by the *Partnership Act 1890* and all the liabilities of a partner. Following retirement, in the absence of any agreement to the contrary, she became simply a creditor of B. Accordingly, on H's death four years later, business property relief on the sum due to her was denied. For the purposes of *s 105*, H's interest in the business ceased when she retired from the partnership that carried on that business. Partners wishing to avoid a similar outcome could consider making a gift of the capital prior to retiring, or alternatively remaining a partner with a reduced profit share.

Contracts for sale

11.33 BPR is not normally available where the subject matter of the transfer is itself already subject to a binding contract for sale at the time of the transfer (*s 113*). In that sense there is a loss of relief, in that the owner of the property can no longer claim the relief on a transfer made after a 'buy and sell' agreement has been entered into. However, arrangements between partners and shareholders can often be structured in such a way that BPR is not jeopardised.

Business property relief **11.35**

It is therefore important to recognise the types of agreement that constitute a 'binding contract for sale'. HMRC identify three key elements (see IHTM 25292) (emphasis added):

- An **agreement** for the deceased partner's business interest or shareholder's shares to pass to his personal representatives;
- A **requirement** for the personal representatives to sell to the surviving partners or shareholders; and
- An **obligation** for the partners or shareholders to buy the asset under terms of the agreement (funds for the purchase often being provided by life assurance policies).

HMRC's stated view is that such terms (referred to as 'buy and sell' agreements) prevent BPR from being due on the business interest or shares (Statement of Practice 12/80). However, BPR is not prevented by *s 113* from applying to company shares or securities, if the company's Articles of Association require the personal representatives to offer his shares for sale to the company, or to other shareholders or directors. However, there should be no obligation on any party to buy, nor should there be a mutually binding obligation to buy and sell (SVM 27370).

11.34 The types of agreement which are not 'caught' by *s 113* include those noted below:

- *'Accruer'* clauses – the deceased's interests pass ('accrue') to the surviving partners, who are required to pay the personal representatives a particular price (eg based on a valuation or formula). The agreement in these circumstances will generally be at arm's length;
- *'Options'* – the deceased's interest falls into the estate, but with an option for the surviving partners to purchase it. Agreements sometimes provide for a two-way (or 'cross') option. There is (in theory, at least) an argument that cross-options are not materially different in substance to a binding contract for sale. This argument seems unlikely in the case of genuine options, but in any event any such concerns could be set aside by using a single option (ie put or call), or by providing for successive put and call options with their own separate and distinct exercise periods.

11.35 HMRC are alert to planning involving lifetime transfers of unquoted shares, shortly followed by a sale of the company. They are likely to investigate such transfers (in the context of a possible binding contract for sale within *s 113*) if, for example, the company is sold within six months of the transfer, or possibly longer if the circumstances suggest that a sale was in prospect when the lifetime transfer was made (SVM 27380).

11.36 *Business property relief*

However, it should be noted that BPR is not denied by *s 113* if the reason for the binding contract is the incorporation of a sole trader or partnership in which the sale proceeds are wholly or mainly shares or securities in the company, or in the case of company shares or securities if the purpose of the sale is a reconstruction or amalgamation (*s 113(a), (b)*).

Lifetime gifts and BPR

11.36 An important point to consider for IHT planning purposes is whether to make gifts during lifetime, or to leave assets in the estate until death. In the case of assets eligible for 100% BPR, there are potential benefits to delaying gifts until death. These include CGT exemption and a tax-free uplift on death, no concerns about the possible clawback of BPR on lifetime gifts, and the retention of control over the asset in question.

On the other hand, there is the constant danger that BPR rates may be reduced, or that the relief may be abolished altogether. These concerns may make transferring business property into a 'relevant property' trust to 'bank' BPR seem like an attractive proposition, with the donor retaining a degree of control over the asset as a trustee. However, this type of planning needs to be considered 'in the round', taking account of factors including the loss of CGT-free uplift on death.

Avoiding a clawback of BPR

11.37 IHT charges can arise on a transferor's death if, for example, the transferee has disposed of the business property without replacement, or if the asset is no longer relevant business property. A gift of business property from one individual to another generally constitutes a potentially exempt transfer, in which case BPR is not an immediate issue. However, the availability of BPR will need to be considered in the event of the transferor's death within seven years. Alternatively, if a chargeable lifetime transfer (eg a gift to a discretionary trust) was reduced by BPR and the transferor dies within seven years, the additional IHT on death is calculated as if the transfer had not been reduced by BPR unless certain conditions are satisfied, as outlined below (*s 113A(1), (2)*).

11.38 The BPR clawback provisions do not apply if the following conditions are satisfied (*s 113A*):

- the transferee continued to own the business property until the donor's death (or until the transferee's death, if earlier); and
- the original property is still relevant business property at that time. The two-year ownership test does not apply for the purposes of this rule.

Business property relief **11.41**

The first condition above is relaxed if the transferee has replaced the original asset with other business property. BPR may still be available, subject to further conditions (*s 113B*; see below).

The second condition above does not have to be satisfied for lifetime transfers of shares or securities which were quoted at the time of the transfer, or of unquoted shares which remain as such, or of unquoted securities which, either by themselves or together with other such securities owned by the transferor and any unquoted shares so owned, gave the transferor control (*s 113(3A)*).

11.39 A potential trap exists in the meaning of transferee. A 'transferee' is defined as the person who became the owner of the property on the transfer, or where on the transfer the property became (or remained) settled on discretionary trusts, the trustees of the settlement (*s 113(8)*). For example, if the original transfer was to the trustees of a discretionary trust, the first condition above will not be satisfied if, before the transferor's death, a beneficiary becomes absolutely entitled to the trust property (eg following an appointment or termination of the trust). HMRC consider that the meaning of transferee is precise in this context (IHTM 25367).

11.40 If the BPR clawback rules apply to an immediately chargeable lifetime transfer, only the IHT on that transfer is affected by the loss of BPR. The additional tax on the transferor's death is calculated on the basis of no BPR (ie the additional tax payable on death is the difference between the IHT at death rates (after taper relief, if appropriate) on the value excluding BPR and the tax paid at lifetime rates on the reduced value). However, for the purposes of cumulating the lifetime transfer with subsequent transfers within the seven-year period before death (including the death estate), the value transferred by the transfer remains as reduced by BPR. Therefore an advantage can arise in making chargeable lifetime transfers of business property subject to 100% BPR, compared with making potentially exempt transfers which become chargeable on death (ie where the transfer must be aggregated in full).

It should be noted that if the BPR clawback provisions only apply to a part of the gifted property, BPR may still apply to the balance (*s 113A(5)*). For example, if the original transfer consisted of 1,000 unquoted shares worth £100,000, and the transferee sells 500 shares for £25,000, BPR of £50,000 remains available on the other half of the shares.

Replacement property

11.41 As indicated above, the condition that the transferee must generally own the original property at the transferor's death is relaxed in the case of replacement property. These 'replacement property' rules apply if the transferee

11.42 *Business property relief*

has sold all or part of the original property before the transferor's death and invested the whole of the proceeds in the purchase of other qualifying property. The conditions are broadly as follows (*s 113B(1), (2)*):

- the whole proceeds must be reinvested in the replacement property;
- the replacement property must be acquired (or a binding contract for its acquisition entered into) within the 'allowed period' of three years (or such longer period as HMRC may allow) after the disposal of the original property;
- the disposal and acquisition must both be made in transactions at arm's length, or on arm's length terms (eg exchanges of business property).

11.42 If the above conditions are met, the basic conditions for BPR on lifetime gifts within seven years of the transferor's death in *s 113A(3)* (see above) are taken to be satisfied in relation to the original property, provided that the following conditions are also met in relation to the replacement property (*s 113B(3)*):

- the replacement property is owned by the transferee immediately before the transferor's death (or until the transferee's death, if earlier);
- throughout the period from the date of the chargeable transfer until death (disregarding any period between the disposal and acquisition) either the original property or the replacement property was owned by the transferee; and
- the original property is relevant business property immediately before the death.

It should be noted that if the transferor has died (before the transferee) after disposal of the original property by the transferee, but before the replacement property is acquired, BPR remains available if the replacement property is acquired (or a binding contract for its acquisition entered into) within the 'allowed period' mentioned above.

11.43 A special rule applies where shares owned by the transferee immediately before the transferor's death (or before the transferee's earlier death) represent the original property received from the transferor. This rule may apply if, for example, the transferee holds shares following a company reorganisation (within *TCGA 1992, ss 126–136*), or if the shares were issued to the transferee in consideration of the transfer of business property consisting of the original property. The effect is that the shares are treated for replacement property purposes as the original property (*ss 113A(6), 113B(6)*).

The order of gifts

11.44 The making of lifetime gifts of business assets should be considered carefully, as the availability of BPR may depend upon the order of such gifts.

For example, BPR (at the 50% rate) applies to land and buildings, machinery or plant used wholly or mainly in a business carried on by a company of which the transferor then had control (*s 105(1)(d)*). The controlling shareholder of an unquoted trading company who owns its business premises may wish to make gifts of shares and the premises at different times. If the shareholder is gifting shares before the property, it is important that he retains a controlling interest in the company when the property is given away. Otherwise, BPR at 50% may be lost on the gift of the premises.

A loss of BPR in the above circumstances is not necessarily fatal for IHT purposes if the gift is to another individual, as that gift is a potentially exempt transfer which becomes exempt after seven years. It may be possible and desirable to insure against the risk of the donor's death within that time. However, if the gift is chargeable when made (ie as for most lifetime transfers into trust), the non-availability of BPR could result in an immediate, and perhaps unnecessary, IHT charge.

DEATH AND BPR

Maximising BPR

11.45 Planning involves not only taking advantage of possible tax savings, but also avoiding potential pitfalls which could, for example, result in the loss of an available relief or allowance. For example, BPR is wasted if qualifying assets are left to the spouse or civil partner, because such legacies are normally exempt in any event. There is also a danger that BPR may not be available on the spouse's later death (eg due to a change in law). Assets that may qualify for 100% BPR could therefore be given to a future generation (eg the grandchildren), or to appropriate trusts. However, consideration should be given to whether the surviving spouse requires the business assets (eg shares in the family trading company), which could provide income through future dividends.

Avoiding the loss of BPR

11.46 If an estate includes assets eligible for BPR and other assets, and the deceased's will provides for both chargeable beneficiaries (eg adult children) and an exempt beneficiary (eg a UK domiciled spouse, civil partner or a charity), it is important to ensure that specific business property (eg unquoted trading company shares) is left to chargeable beneficiaries if possible. If an estate includes property attracting BPR (or APR), special rules apply for the purposes of valuing specific and residuary gifts where part of the estate is

11.47 *Business property relief*

exempt. The rules can result in an apportionment of relief between the chargeable beneficiaries and exempt surviving spouse or civil partner (*s 39A*). If any residuary gifts (after 17 March 1986) include business (or agricultural) assets, any specific gifts of non-business assets (eg cash gifts to chargeable parties) will be entitled to a due proportion of BPR. The value of such specific gifts is the 'appropriate proportion' of their value (*s 39A(3), (4)*). This apportionment of BPR can have unfortunate consequences.

Example 11.4

Scott died on 10 October 2007. His estate of £1,600,000 consists of shares in an unquoted trading company worth £800,000, and other assets (ie cash, shares and an investment property) worth £800,000. Scott's nil-rate band (£300,000 for 2007/08) is available in full on his death.

Scott's will leaves cash and specific other (non-business) assets amounting to £500,000 to his spouse. The residue of Scott's estate, including the trading company shares (eligible for 100% BPR) is left to his adult children, together with the remaining other non-business assets worth £300,000.

The value of Scott's estate (net of BPR) is £800,000. As he left £500,000 to his spouse, his personal representatives assume (incorrectly) that the remaining £300,000 will be covered by Scott's nil-rate band, and that no IHT will be payable. However, the result of applying the 'appropriate proportion' (see above) to the spouse's exempt legacy is:

$$£500,000 \times \frac{£800,000}{£1,600,000} = £250,000$$

The residue (ie the chargeable free estate) is (£800,000 − £250,000) = £550,000. The decrease in the amount subject to the spouse exemption has resulted in a significant (and unexpected) IHT liability.

11.47 As the above example illustrates, if an exempt legacy receives a proportion of BPR, the relief is effectively wasted because the legacy is subject to IHT exemption in any event. On the death of an individual with business (or agricultural) property, a will which provides for a 'nil-rate band' legacy in non-specific terms (eg words such as 'the maximum amount of funds without incurring a liability to IHT on my death') will not have the intended effect. However, if the business property is given by a chargeable, specific gift, its value is reduced by BPR (*s 39A(2)*). BPR (or APR) can be optimised by ensuring that specific gifts of business (and agricultural) assets which attract 100% relief are made to chargeable parties in addition to the nil-rate band, if appropriate. If the deceased's will does not provide for such specific legacies, it may be possible to vary the dispositions in the will using a deed of variation within two years of the deceased's death, and including a statement in the deed that it is to apply for IHT purposes (*s 142*).

11.48 The rates of BPR available may be 100%, 50%, or some other effective rate due to the operation of the excepted asset rule in *s 112*. A married (or civil partner) testator with business (or agricultural) property may therefore wish to consider a chargeable legacy comprising all business property qualifying for 100% relief, plus property qualifying for less than 100% relief. The remainder may be left to the surviving spouse or civil partner absolutely, or possibly as an 'immediate post-death interest' (*s 49A*). If the nil-rate band legacy comprises (say) business property qualifying for 50% BPR, the maximum specific legacy to a chargeable party without giving rise to an IHT liability is equal to twice the available nil-rate band.

Example 11.5

Mr A dies on 10 November 2007 owning a controlling interest in quoted trading company shares and had made no gifts in the preceding seven years, the maximum 'nil-rate band' legacy is £600,000, calculated as follows:

	£
Shares	600,000
Less: BPR (50%)	(300,000)
	300,000
Less: Nil rate band (2007/08)	(300,000)
Chargeable	NIL

11.49 An alternative form of chargeable legacy has traditionally been to a discretionary trust. BPR is available to the trustees of a settlement (*s 103(1)(b)*). Following FA 2006, lifetime gifts to the trustees of most types of settlement are immediately chargeable transfers for IHT purposes (*s 3A(1), (2)*), and therefore the availability of BPR in connection with trusts assumes added importance generally. A trust to which the rules for 'relevant property' (as defined in *s 58*) apply, which consists entirely of business property eligible for BPR at the 100% rate, can avoid ten-yearly or exit IHT charges. BPR does not necessarily reduce the IHT rate for trusts, but it can apply to reduce the value transferred to nil.

'Doubling up' BPR

11.50 BPR can effectively be obtained twice on the same property in certain circumstances. For example, the first spouse (or civil partner) to die leaves

11.50 *Business property relief*

business property on discretionary trusts in favour of the survivor and issue. BPR (and a capital gains tax-free uplift of the business property's base cost to market value) is obtained on the first death. The surviving spouse then purchases the business property from the trustees at arm's length (under an option granted on the first death). Subject to surviving the required two-year period, (s)he may then secure BPR on that property for a second time, whether on death or on a lifetime transfer.

Example 11.6

Mr Smith died on 31 October 2007, owning the following assets:

	£
Family home	600,000
Shares in the family trading company	1,000,000
Investment properties	450,000
Building society and bank deposits	1,200,000
Portfolio of quoted shares	550,000
	£3,800,000

In his will, Mr Smith leaves the family company shares to a discretionary trust in favour of Mrs Smith, his adult children, and grandchildren. He also leaves cash from his bank and building society accounts to the trust, up to the nil-rate band (£300,000 for 2007/08), which is available in full. The residue of his estate is left to Mrs Smith absolutely, which is made up as follows:

	£
Family home	600,000
Investment properties	450,000
Building society and bank deposits (£1,200,000 – £300,000)	900,000
Portfolio of quoted shares	550,000
	£2,500,000

The chargeable legacy into the discretionary trust amounts to £1,300,000. This comprises the family trading company shares worth £1,000,000, on which BPR of 100% is available, plus cash of £300,000, which utilises Mr Smith's nil-rate band. Hence no IHT is payable on Mr Smith's death.

Mrs Smith buys the family company shares from the trustees for £1,000,000, which equates to market value in this example. The purchase is financed partly in cash of £300,000. The balance is financed by selling the investment properties for £450,000, plus part of the portfolio of quoted shares for £250,000 (no capital gains tax liabilities arise on the properties or shares, as their values were uplifted to market value on Mr Smith's death).

If Mrs Smith survives for at least two years following the share acquisition, and assuming that BPR at 100% is then available in respect of her family company shares, only her remaining estate would be liable to IHT, comprising (based on current values) the family home (£600,000), building society and cash deposits (£600,000) and the portfolio of quoted shares (£300,000). After deducting the available nil-rate band, the IHT liability on her death estate is significantly reduced. In addition, she may have benefited from the income generated by the funds held by the discretionary trust in her capacity as a beneficiary.

Protecting against future BPR changes

11.51 Given the undoubted generosity of BPR (particularly at the 100% rate) it is open to speculation how long the BPR rates will remain at their present levels. It may therefore be considered prudent to 'bank' the relief to protect against future changes in BPR. This could be achieved by making a lifetime transfer of the business property to (say) a discretionary trust (or, following FA 2006, to most other types of trust). If the value of business property exceeds the nil-rate band, a number of trusts could be considered.

Example 11.7

Mrs Jones has business property worth £900,000. She creates three discretionary trusts during 2007/08 at staggered intervals, each containing business property worth £300,000. There should be no inheritance tax liability on the transfers into the trusts, on the assumption that BPR applies at the 100% rate. Following the transfers, each trust should be protected by a nil-rate band, even if the BPR rates are changed in the future, and even if the assets cease to be relevant business property.

11.52 However, there are risks attached to this strategy. First, there is a risk that the arrangements may be challenged on the grounds of artificiality. Secondly, there is a risk that HMRC may seek to invoke the 'associated operations' rule (*s 268*), although this risk has been restricted somewhat following the decision in *Rysaffe Trustees (CI) Ltd v IRC* [2003] STC 536. These risks can be reduced by ensuring the there are genuine differences between the trusts (eg different trustees and beneficiaries), that the trusts are created as far apart as practicable, and that they are not preordained. One should also consider the implications for other tax purposes (eg capital gains tax – see below).

11.53 *Business property relief*

BPR and CGT

11.53 A disadvantage of making lifetime gifts of assets eligible for 100% BPR is often the CGT position. Whilst hold-over relief may be available under *TCGA 1992, s 165*, a tax-free uplift to market value on the death of the owner would be preferable. One possible solution in appropriate cases would be to gift the asset to an elderly relative (eg a grandparent). The gift to the elderly relative would be free of IHT and normally CGT hold-over relief will be available. On the elderly relative's death, 100% BPR should be available (the normal minimum period of ownership being relaxed because the conditions in *s 109* are satisfied). On the elderly relative's death, the property may then pass under the relative's will to the intended beneficiaries with the benefit of the capital gains tax uplift to market value.

Example 11.8

Donald is the major shareholder of Titanic Ltd, an unquoted trading company. The shares currently qualify for 100% BPR. He wishes to gift the shares to his son Michael. The shares are worth £1 million, and there is an inherent gain on them of £200,000, on which the potential CGT liability is £80,000.

Donald gives the shares (ie his desired gift to Michael) to his father Edward, who is aged in his late 80s. The gift is a potentially exempt transfer, which would otherwise be subject to full BPR. The chargeable gain is held over under *TCGA 1992, s 165*. Donald hopes that Edward will leave the shares to his grandson Michael in his will (note there must be no prior agreement or arrangement). On Edward's death, there is no IHT as 100% BPR is available. However, there is a CGT free uplift in the base cost of the shares to market value as at Edward's death. A CGT saving of £80,000 has therefore been achieved.

If Edward's will did not leave the shares to Michael, a deed of variation could achieve the same result, subject to the co-operation of the beneficiary under the will.

'Placing' debt

11.54 The value of relevant business property for BPR purposes is its net value (*s 110(a)*). 'Net value' is broadly the value of business assets, less any liabilities incurred for the purposes of the business (*s 110(b)*). For example, a sole trader's fixed and current business assets (eg plant and machinery and stock) are reduced by business liabilities (eg a bank overdraft) in determining the net value of the business.

However, the business property itself may be acquired with a mortgage or other loan. In such cases, the general rule for a debt (or 'incumbrance') charged on property is that it reduces the value of that property as far as possible (*s 162(4)*). Thus the sole trader may have previously taken out a loan secured on his house, and applied those funds in financing the acquisition of the business. On a subsequent valuation of the business for BPR purposes, it would seem appropriate to reduce the value of the sole trader's house by the debt, as opposed to the business. The loan was incurred to buy the business itself, and not for the purpose of running the business.

As stated earlier in this chapter, 'business' has a wider meaning than 'trade' and can include the making or holding of investments. However, in determining whether a business interest or company shares are relevant business property, the investment 'business' must generally not predominate (*s 105(3)*). If possible, the business or company should structure its debt so that investment business property is mortgaged, as opposed to other business property. To the extent that an investment asset is not sufficient to constitute a 'business' (ie it is an excepted asset), if extracting the asset is not practical (eg for other tax reasons, such as capital gains or the personal tax circumstances of the shareholders), those assets should be mortgaged instead if possible.

11.55 An investor can use BPR and the mortgage or charging provisions to their advantage. The owner of valuable assets could borrow on non-business assets (eg the home) and invest the proceeds in assets giving entitlement to BPR (eg AIM listed shares in trading companies), or possibly subscribe for shares in the unquoted family trading company. However, the potential IHT benefit must be measured against the commercial risk inherent in such investments.

BPR and gifts with reservation

11.56 A lifetime transfer of business property may be treated as remaining comprised in the donor's estate, if the 'Gifts with reservation' (GWR) rules apply (in *FA 1986, s 102* and *Sch 20*). An asset subject to the GWR rules can qualify for BPR, broadly if the following conditions are satisfied:

- the asset was relevant business property at the time of the gift; and
- the asset would qualify for BPR at the time of the GWR charge (ie on the donor's death or earlier release of the reservation) if the donee made a notional transfer of it.

For the purposes of the two-year ownership test, any period of ownership by the donor before the gift is treated as that of the donee. If the donee dies before the GWR charge, the period of ownership of the personal representatives or beneficiaries is also treated as that of the donee (*FA 1986, Sch 20, para 8*). If

11.57 *Business property relief*

BPR is claimed on the basis that the original property has been replaced by qualifying property, HMRC will probably refer the case to their Technical Group (IHTM 25384).

BPR and APR

11.57 Agricultural Property Relief (APR) is considered in **Chapter 12.** APR applies automatically, and for the purposes of this chapter it should be noted that if the same property qualifies for both BPR and APR in respect of a transfer, APR takes precedence (*s 114(1)*). However, the agricultural value may be lower than its value for BPR purposes, in which case it may be possible to claim APR on the agricultural value, and BPR on the excess.

Chapter 12

Agricultural property relief and woodlands relief

Toby Harris LLB CTA TEP

AGRICULTURAL ASSETS: PROPERTY

12.1 Agricultural property relief (APR) operates by reducing the value transferred by a transfer of value. The rate of reduction is 100% or 50%. The code set out in *IHTA 1984, ss115–124C* is very similar to that for business property relief described in **Chapter 11** but there are important differences of detail.

APR is available on 'agricultural property', ie primarily agricultural land or pasture. It also includes:

- Woodland and buildings used for the intensive rearing of livestock or fish, but only if the occupation of that woodland or those buildings is ancillary to the occupation of the agricultural land or pasture: see, for example, *Williams v HMRC* [2005] SpC 00500; and

- Cottages, farm buildings and farmhouses and the land occupied with them, but only if of a character appropriate to the property.

12.2 Following the Lands Tribunal decision in *Lloyds TSB Private Banking plc (personal representative of Rosemary Antrobus, dec'd) v HMRC* DET/47/2005 (*Antrobus (No 2)*), the distinction between the purchasing power (and attributes) of a 'working' and 'lifestyle' farmer may be significant for the purposes of determining the agricultural value of agricultural property. Another difficultly is the link, or nexus, between land and a farmhouse. Often the main value of APR will be, not in the land, but the house. If the link between the land and the house is not strong enough, APR will be denied on the house.

12.3 Broadly, the relief is 100% for vacant property, or property subject to a lease created or succeeded to on or after 1 September 1995; and 50% otherwise. The value to which the reduction applies is the value which the property would have if subject to a perpetual covenant prohibiting its use otherwise than as

12.4 *Agricultural property relief and woodlands relief*

agricultural property. This will typically be less than the open market value, especially where there is development potential or where the land, for any reason, commands a premium. Thus even 100% agricultural property relief will seldom eliminate the entire transfer of value attributable to the agricultural property in question. Examples of this are:

- small areas of grassland that would attract indulgent fathers of pony-riding offspring; and
- areas of land of such eye-watering beauty that they command a 'leisure' or 'vanity' premium in excess of agricultural value.

CLAWBACK

12.4 If a donor has made a lifetime gift of business or agricultural property and dies within seven years, there is a risk that APR will be clawed back. This will *not* generally be the case if the transferee retained the original property from the date of the transfer until the date of death or if he disposed of it during that period and reinvested the net proceeds of sale in replacement property. In the second case, the reinvestment must take place within three years of the sale of the original property. In contrast to the position for capital gains tax rollover relief, reinvestment during the 12 months before the disposal of the original property is not permitted.

It seems that professional costs and capital gains tax may be deducted in computing the net proceeds of sale before reinvestment; and that reinvestment into business property is acceptable even when the original property was agricultural property.

Can the donee of a potentially exempt transfer of business or agricultural property safely dispose of it four years after the gift? Yes, if it is the donor who dies within the next three years, because the donee can smartly reinvest the net proceeds. There is no requirement to retain the reinvested assets for a minimum period. On the other hand, if the *donee* dies within the seven-year period, the opportunity to reinvest and thereby prevent clawback is lost. Reinvestment by the donee's personal representatives will not prevent clawback.

Use of chargeable transfer to limit clawback

12.5 If death of donor (or donee) within seven years is likely, a chargeable transfer may be preferable to a PET. This is because, in the case of a failed PET there may be full clawback; whilst in respect of a chargeable transfer there is clawback only on the death rate uplift. A chargeable transfer does not affect cumulation. It is important to be aware of the risk of clawback where the donee has made a gift into a trust. It may be better to wait until the seven-year period has elapsed.

Once the seven years have elapsed from a PET, the donee may sell the asset without risk of clawback. Likewise, relief is available on death even though the inheritor may sell the very next day.

INVESTMENTS IN THE CONTEXT OF FARMING

12.6 In *Farmer and another (executors of Farmer dec'd) v IRC* [1999] STC (SCD) 321, the deceased was a shareholder in a company that carried on the business of letting properties as well as the business of farming. The profits of the letting business were greater than the farming profits, but the farming assets, admittedly including the farmhouse itself, were (at death) more valuable than the properties used for letting. The Revenue refused business property relief, arguing that because the profits of the letting business were greater than those of the farming the business was wholly or mainly one of making investments.

The executors appealed to the Special Commissioners and won. It was held that the nature of the business had to be considered in the round and that no single factor – such as profitability – should be determinative. On the facts, although the lettings were more profitable than the farm, the overall context of the business, the capital employed, the time spent by the employees and consultants and the levels of turnover supported the conclusion that the business consisted mainly of farming.

Farmer was a case on BPR rather than APR but it is helpful in those borderline cases where BPR may be more valuable than APR. This will be the case if agricultural land has development value, because APR is restricted, as noted at **12.1** above.

FARMING PARTNERSHIP

12.7 For discussion of partnerships and BPR, see **Chapter 11**.

In relation to a limited liability partnership (LLP) under the *Limited Liability Partnerships Act 2000* the LLP is not to be treated as owned by the individual partners. For APR there will be no change in the treatment of assets held outside, but used in, the partnership; nor will incorporation into an LLP be regarded as an interruption for these reliefs.

12.8 *Agricultural property relief and woodlands relief*

Partnership farmland

12.8 The old rule that treated partnership property as personal or moveable property was repealed by the *Trusts of Land and Appointment of Trustees Act 1996*. Land held outside a partnership – or company controlled by the taxpayer – and made available as agricultural property, attracts 100% APR (*IHTA 1984, s 116*). If held as another business asset, 50% relief is available (*IHTA 1984, s 105(1)(d)*), but free of the restriction as to agricultural value imposed by *IHTA 1984, s 115(3)*.

PERIOD OF OWNERSHIP OR OCCUPATION

Minimum period of ownership

12.9 There are two alternative rules: under *IHTA 1984, s 117(a)* relief is available where the transfer has occupied the land for the purposes of agriculture for two years, whoever has owned it; whilst under *s 117(b)* the period in seven years, during which the transferor has owned the land and it has been occupied (by anyone) for the purposes of agriculture. Slightly special rules apply to farming companies: see below.

Spouses and civil partners: a special succession rule

12.10 An exception to the minimum period of ownership requirement applies to a transferor who acquired the property on the death of his spouse or civil partner. *IHTA 1984, s 120(1)(b)* deems such a transferor to have owned the property for the period of his spouse's ownership in addition to his own period of ownership. If the aggregate is equal to or greater than two years then the test is satisfied. This aggregation applies only to periods of ownership falling either side of a transfer on the death of the first spouse. It does not apply where the first spouse made a lifetime gift of the land to the second spouse.

Successions

12.11 A legatee is deemed to have owned an inherited asset from the date of death: *IHTA 1984, s 120(1)(a)*. Where the legacy was from his spouse, the spouse's period of ownership is also deemed to be his (as has been seen above).

If the legatee acquired agricultural property from a person – whether his spouse or not – who satisfied the minimum period of ownership requirement, then that requirement is effectively waived on a subsequent transfer by the legatee as will be seen in the next paragraph.

Successive transfers

12.12 Where there are two successive transfers, and the earlier transferor satisfied the ownership or occupation requirements, these requirements are waived for the transferee (subject to certain conditions). The most significant condition is that at least one of the transfers was on death. It does not matter whether this was the earlier transfer or the subsequent one.

Example 12.1

A, who qualifies for APR in all respects including minimum period of ownership – leaves his agricultural land to B on death. B can qualify for APR on a transfer even if it occurs less than two years after A's death. Because the transfer by A to B ('the earlier transfer') was on A's death, the transfer by B ('the subsequent transfer') can be either a lifetime or a death transfer.

Example 12.2

C, who also qualifies for APR, makes a lifetime gift of his majority shareholding in a farming company to D. D will qualify for APR on a transfer on his death even if that is within two years of the gift. Because the transfer by C to D ('the earlier transfer') was a lifetime transfer, the transfer by D ('the subsequent transfer') will benefit from *s 120* only if it is on D's death. If D wishes to make a lifetime transfer which qualifies for APR he will need to build up his own period of ownership.

In both of the examples just given, it is irrelevant whether A and B or C and D are spouses or civil partners because A and C had each owned the shares for the required period. The special treatment given to spouses would only be relevant if:

- The earlier transferor had not satisfied the minimum period; and
- The earlier transfer was on death.

Revisiting the example of A and B, and supposing this time that A and B were married or were civil partners and that A had owned the land for one year only, B could benefit from APR on a subsequent transfer by holding the land until a year after A's death. This is by virtue of *IHTA 1984, s 120(1)(b)*.

Replacements

12.13 Suppose that a farmer, having owned agricultural property and occupied it for agricultural purposes, has to sell it, perhaps for road widening or to

12.14 *Agricultural property relief and woodlands relief*

distance himself from a perceived threat of spread of airborne or water-borne disease. If he reinvests no more than the proceeds of sale of his original farm in new agricultural assets, there is no need to re-qualify under the ownership and occupation tests. *IHTA 1984, s 118(1)* credits him with his past occupation period. However, if the farmer invests new funds and buys a larger unit, *s 118* relief will extend only to the replacement proportion of the new farm: see *IHTA 1984, s 118(3)*.

Residuary estates

12.14 A legatee or transferee whose minimum period of ownership has been waived or reduced by *IHTA 1984, s 120* or *s 121* must nevertheless hold the property as agricultural property to get either relief. Would there be a problem if the legatee died or made a gift before the administration of the estate is complete?

Probably not: *IHTA 1984, s 91(1)* treats the holder of an IPDI or of any other interest in possession as being entitled as from the date of the death, and therefore the administration period will count as time during which the legatee could occupy or own the land. However, as soon as the complexities of administration of this estate will allow, and liquidity is assured, the personal representatives should assent or appropriate the agricultural assets to the legatee.

AGRICULTURAL VALUE

Agricultural value

12.15 As was noted at **12.1** above, APR is available on only so much of the value transferred as is attributable to the agricultural value of the property, which is the value that it would have if it were subject to a perpetual covenant prohibiting its use otherwise than as agricultural property (*IHTA 1984, s 115(3)*). This will normally be much less than its value in the open market without such a restriction; and (as noted in the leading case next mentioned) lower than property that is merely subject to a planning tie. A restriction in a planning permission can, and quite often is, varied after a number of years.

Usually, therefore, there will be a transfer of value equal to the tax excess of market value over agricultural value.

12.16 In *Lloyds TSB (personal representative of Antrobus, dec'd) v IRC* [2002] STC (SCD) 468 (*Antrobus (No 1)*), a farmhouse, Cookhill Priory, attracted APR, as being of a 'character appropriate' to the agricultural land and pasture forming part of the estate, within *IHTA 1984, s 115(2)*.

Subsequently, in *Lloyds TSB Private Banking plc (personal representative of Rosemary Antrobus, dec'd) v HMRC* DET/47/2005 (*Antrobus (No 2)*), the Lands Tribunal was required to consider the 'agricultural value' of Cookhill Priory for the purposes of *IHTA 1984, s 115(3)*. The tribunal concluded that the agricultural value should be determined on the basis that the assumed perpetual covenant in *IHTA 1984, s 115(3)* would have prohibited use of the land in any other way and, after excluding 'lifestyle' farmers from the theoretical market, HMRC Capital Taxes pursue the point regularly, so the practitioner should allow for it in valuing a transfer. It can apply to land as well as farmhouses, as noted at **12.1** above.

Availability of relief since *Antrobus (No 2)*

12.17 The issue 'what is a farmhouse?' had been discussed in *Antrobus (No 2)* even though, strictly, it was no concern of the Lands Tribunal, having already been determined in *Antrobus (No 1)*. It was noted, in *McKenna v HMRC* [2006] SpC 00565, that the test in *Antrobus (No 2)* should be approached with caution, though in *McKenna* that was not enough to secure APR for Rosteague House, a fine house by the sea.

Special valuation issues

12.18 Where a person has both freehold land and a share in a partnership to which the land is let on an agricultural tenancy, the question arises as to whether the two interests should be valued on the assumption that they are sold together, and if so, how they should be valued.

In *IRC v Gray (Executor of Lady Fox)* [1994] STC 360, the Court of Appeal decided that, for valuation on death purposes, a freehold reversion in land must be aggregated with a partnership interest which holds a tenancy of that land (following the principle of realising the maximum practicable price without undue expenditure of time and effort: *Duke of Buccleuch v IRC* [1967] 1 506, HL). In other words, it was a single 'natural unit'. The existence of a tenancy can therefore bring about the worst of both worlds. The valuation will be initially on vacant possession principles notwithstanding the tenancy, but, by virtue of *IHTA 1984, s 116(2)(a)*, only a 50% agricultural property discount will be available rather than 100%. Note that in this case the testatrix was the freeholder and had a 92.5% interest in the partnership which held the tenancy of that freehold estate.

12.19 *Agricultural property relief and woodlands relief*

12.19 *Walton's Executors v IRC* [1996] STC 68, CA, concerned the valuation of an agricultural tenancy for capital transfer tax purposes. The W family were the freeholders. They let the farm to a partnership of Mr W and son. On Mr W's death, the Revenue claimed that the capital transfer tax value of the lease was the difference between the value of the freehold with vacant possession and its value subject to the lease. Its reasoning was that, on Mr W's death, there was a hypothetical sale of the tenancy valued at £70,000.

The taxpayer's claim, accepted by the Land Tribunal and the Court of Appeal, was that there was no hypothetical sale, as the son did not wish to sell but to continue the farming. Therefore the value of the tenancy was based on a potential profit rental basis (£6,300), ie a real-world situation. This was typically a small value in the absence of any special purchaser, who did not exist in this case.

THE LEVEL OF RELIEF

Assets qualifying for 100% relief

12.20 The circumstances in which 100% relief is available are set out in *IHTA 1984, s 116(2)(a)-(c)*.

- *Transferor has vacant possession or the right to obtain it within 12 months (s 116(2)(a))*

    This provision covers owner-occupied farms and farms where the transferor's interest entitles him to vacant possession or will do within the next 12 months. HMRC have, by concession, extended this to 24 months. Note that a partnership could, according to the terms of its agreement, have occupation rights: these must not prejudice the landowner's right to vacant possession.

- *Transferor has held his interest since before 10 March 1981 (s 116(2)(b))*

    'Working farmer' relief is still available under this heading where the transferor has held his interest beneficially since before 10 March 1981 and, had he given away that interest before then and made an appropriate claim, *FA 1975, Sch 8, para 2* would have applied in computing the value transferred without limitation by *para 5*. The main elements of these pre-1981 rules are:

    – a limit of £250,000 in value and 1,000 acres in area; and

    – the requirement that the transferor was wholly or mainly engaged in farming during five out of the previous seven years. The latter test is deemed to be satisfied if not less than 75% of his income was derived from agriculture.

Relief will be denied if at any time between 10 March 1981 and the transfer of value in question the transferor acquired the right to vacant possession, acquired the right to obtain vacant possession within 12 months, or failed to acquire either such right by reason of an act or deliberate omission.

Relief may be cut down in certain circumstances; see *s 116(4)*.

- *The property is let on a tenancy beginning on or after 1 September 1995 (s 116(2)(c))*

This relief, designed to encourage the granting of new agricultural tenancies, coincided with the introduction of the Agricultural Tenancies Act 1995 which deregulated the market for let farmland.

Where a tenant dies on or after 1 September 1995 and his tenancy vests under his will or intestacy in another person, that other person's tenancy is deemed under *IHTA 1984, s 116(5A)* to commence at the date of death for the purposes of determining whether 100% relief is available. Similar provision is made – although this is not applicable to property in Scotland – where, on the death of the surviving tenant on or after 1 September 1995, another person obtains a tenancy under a legislative right.

Where the tenant has given notice to retire in favour of a new tenant, but before such retirement takes place the landlord dies, then the new tenant is deemed to have commenced his tenancy immediately before that death, so the estate of the landlord benefits from 100% relief under this head as if the new tenancy had already commenced. This extension of the relief is subject to the condition that the tenant does indeed retire in favour of the new tenant after the landlord's death and within 30 months of the giving of notice.

Landlords and tenants may work together to bring an old arrangement under the rules. For example the landlord might add land to the tenancy, making it a new one. There are two points to watch:

The surrender of an existing lease followed by a re-grant on a non-arm's length basis in order to obtain 100% relief in the future might amount to a PET.

The arrangements could constitute dispositions for capital gains tax under the value shifting provisions in *TCGA 1992, s 29*. This might be avoided if a new lease is granted in an arm's-length transaction on the same property at a different rent but otherwise on the same terms, if that could be justified commercially.

Assets qualifying for 50% relief

12.21 50% relief is available on agricultural property which qualifies in all other respects but does not fall within any of the three heads of 100% relief. This

12.22 *Agricultural property relief and woodlands relief*

will mainly comprise property which has been let since before 1 September 1995 and will not become vacant within the next 12 (or 24) months.

Concessionary reliefs

12.22 The Extra-Statutory Concessions are relevant here.

ESC F17 treats the condition in *IHTA 1984, s 116(2)(a)* as satisfied where the transferor's interest in the property, immediately before the transfer, carried the right to vacant possession within 24 months of the date of the transfer. It also treats the conditions as satisfied where, notwithstanding the terms of the tenancy, the transferor's interest is valued at an amount broadly equivalent to the vacant possession value. See *IRC v Gray* (*Executor of Lady Fox*) [1994] STC 360, CA..

ESC F16 also gives 100% agricultural relief in respect of transfers of agricultural property which include a cottage occupied by a retired farm employee or spouse. This is subject to the occupier being a protected tenant or having a lease for life as part of his contract of employment. In practice, as fewer actually work on the land, and of those who do fewer are employed, rather than contractors, this relief will become obsolete.

THE MAIN ESTATE PLANNING LESSONS

12.23 APR is currently very generous, and will probably not survive indefinitely, though no change to it was indicated in the Pre-Budget Report 2007. Since it is available on lifetime gifts as well as transfers on death, those who currently qualify for relief might consider making lifetime gifts to insulate themselves as far as possible against future changes in the law. On the other hand, there are some advantages in delaying making gifts, which need to be considered too.

Shareholdings and partnerships

12.24 The difficulty with a limited farming company is (see *IHTA 1984, s 122*) that only a majority shareholding qualifies for APR. If the company qualifies in all respects for BPR that will not matter, but if it does not, the majority shareholder may find that his asset is in a mere investment company carrying no relief. Subject to that, several issues must be watched.

Agricultural property relief and woodlands relief **12.26**

- Selling the shares or retiring from the partnership could cause significant loss of relief. Not only will the possibility of 100% relief on the shares or partnership interest themselves be lost, but so will the 50% relief on assets belonging to the individual and used in the business of the company or partnership.
- If it is likely that shares, which qualify for APR, now will in the future cease to do so, consider making a lifetime gift now. It may be possible to hold over capital gains tax under *TCGA 1992, s 165*. The downsides to this are:
    - The possibility of clawback (see **12.2** above).
    - The lack of capital gains tax exemption on death; and the fact that the hold-over will end a period of ownership for CGT taper relief purposes and start another period. However, if the proposals in the Pre-Budget Report 2007 become law, taper relief will be lost, so in fact the farmer may wish to trigger a disposal under the present rules before 5 April 2008.
    - The gift with reservation provisions are still relevant even where a lifetime gift of business or agricultural property is made. *FA 1986, Sch 20, para 8* adapts the gifts with reservation provisions. In general terms, if the donor reserves a benefit, then the conditions for relief must continue to be met until the donor's death in order to preserve the relief and reduce the charge on death: see for example *FA 1986, Sch 20, para 8(1A)(b)*. These provisions cause difficulty where a transferee, for some reason, does not have that control.

Use of discretionary trusts

12.25 APR can reduce tax otherwise chargeable under the special inheritance tax regime applicable to 'relevant property' trusts which, since *FA 2006*, will comprise nearly all lifetime settlements. In determining whether certain conditions, such as the minimum period of ownership, are met, references to the transferor are treated as references to the trustees (*IHTA 1984, ss 103(1)(b)* and *115(1)(b)*).

A trust comprising only property that qualifies for APR at 100% can be run in a way that avoids any ten-yearly or exit charges. Although APR does not necessarily reduce the *rate* at which tax is charged under the discretionary trust regime, this is not a problem so long as the value transferred is reduced to zero: anything multiplied by zero equals zero!

12.26 The position is not so simple where:

- APR is at 50% (for example on let land); or

12.27 *Agricultural property relief and woodlands relief*

- APR is on part of the value only (say on a farmhouse).

In these cases the relief on the ten-yearly charge and on exit charges *after* the first ten-yearly charges can reduce both the rate of tax and the value transferred. A different rule applies during the first ten years of the trust. In this period APR will reduce only the value transferred, not the rate of tax. To get maximum benefit from APR, avoid distributions during the first ten years.

12.27 The transfer of farming assets into a trust, whether by lifetime gift or by will, is often one of the best estate planning methods available. Subject to the issue of agricultural value, agricultural assets can be held in such a trust almost indefinitely with 100% relief, with no ten-yearly charges (nor exit charges after first ten-year anniversary).

At the ten-year anniversary, the trustees must satisfy the relevant APR conditions. Assuming that the 100% relief applies – and that any other assets in the trust are within the nil-rate band – the ten-year anniversary charge rate will be zero. A curious feature of the regime, which may offer scope for tax planning, is that the zero rate will apply until immediately prior to the next ten-year anniversary, even though the assets are no longer business or agricultural assets, for example, because the trust fund consists of the proceeds of sale.

APR 'recycled'

12.28 APR can effectively be obtained twice on the same property in certain circumstances. This is also considered in **Chapter 13: Wills, variations and disclaimers**. Suppose that the first spouse or civil partner to die leaves business property on discretionary trusts in favour of the surviving spouse and issue. APR and capital gains tax-free uplift of the base cost to market value should be obtained on that first spouse's death. This could be pursuant to an option. The surviving spouse then purchases the business property from the trustees at market value. Subject to surviving the requisite two-year period, the spouse may then obtain business property relief a second time – either on his death or on a lifetime transfer. The capital gains tax-free uplift should also be available a second time.

12.29 Life assurance is worth considering where, as here, the effectiveness of a plan to minimise inheritance tax depends on a particular individual's surviving for a particular period. One option would be to purchase term cover for the surviving spouse for at least two years. This would be appropriate if the matter is being considered at or after the date of the first spouse's death.

Alternatively, even before the death of the first (business owning) spouse, life assurance could be taken out to cover the risk of the second spouse dying first. Obviously, if that risk materialised, it would prevent the plan for double relief from working. In this case, the cover should be against:

- the risk of the second (non-business owning) spouse dying first; *and*
- the risk of that second spouse dying within two years of the first spouse. This would be a form of term assurance, but that term would be dependent on the date of death of the first spouse, ie the life of X + 2 years.

Example 12.3

Celia Johnson was married with children and grandchildren. Her estate comprised liquid assets and savings of £2,300,000; 30% of Johnson Knitwear Ltd, which makes socks, and is worth £500,000; and Hill Top Farm which Mrs Johnson farmed under an agreement with her neighbour. The farmhouse is worth £500,000 and the land and other buildings £780,000.

By her Will made in August 2007, Mrs Johnson left the shares in the knitwear company and the farmland (but not the house) to a discretionary trust in favour of her widower, children and grandchildren. She also left so much of the liquid assets as are equal in value to the current nil-rate band into the trust. The remaining assets were left to her widower. He was also given an option to buy the business and agricultural assets from the trust at market value.

October 2007: death of Mrs Johnson

There is no inheritance tax. There will also be a capital gains tax-free uplift to market value of the base cost of all the assets. The nil-rate band for 2007/08 is £300,000 so if Mrs Johnson has made no chargeable lifetime gifts that amount would go into the trust. The remaining £2 million would go to Mr Johnson absolutely. He also, of course, acquires the option to buy the business and agricultural assets from the trust at market value.

Mr Johnson uses some of his cash inheritance to buy the business and agricultural assets from the trust – using £1,280,000 from the £2 million that he inherited absolutely. The trustees make substantial distributions to the family. Mr Johnson survives a further two years from the exercise of the option.

January 2010: Death of Mr Johnson

The assets in his estate would be:

- the farmhouse;
- the land, with 100% APR;
- the shares, with 100% BPR; and
- cash (£720,000 less any living expenses and small gifts).

12.30 *Agricultural property relief and woodlands relief*

There was never any need for the trustees to pay income to Mr Johnson: he had enough. The trust was within the nil-rate band, so distributions from it before the first ten-year anniversary attracted no exit charge on the business and agricultural property.

The business and agricultural property will benefit from a second capital gains tax-free uplift of their base costs to market value on Mr Johnson's death. Although the change to the treatment of the nil-rate band proposed in the Pre-Budget Report 2007 will reduce use of it on the first death, as between spouses, this illustration shows how it can still be helpful to use the band on the first death.

Note that when dealing with lifetime relevant property trusts the capital gains tax position is different from when they are created on death. There was some uncertainty about the availability of hold-over relief under *TCGA 1992, s 260* on non-business assets, on the basis that, if 100% relief applied, there was no chargeable transfer. However, Capital Taxes have confirmed that, in their view, a gift qualifying for 100% business or agricultural property relief is a chargeable transfer for the purposes of *s 260* (see GCM 67041). That must be right: it is chargeable, but at 0%.

Creation of several lifetime trusts to achieve protection against future changes in the reliefs

12.30 A specific arrangement uses a number of discretionary trusts to maximise the nil-rate band. It can be adapted where 100% business or agricultural property relief applies.

Example 12.4

Fred owns farmland with an agricultural value of £2,000,000. He creates six trusts over the course of 2007/08 at staggered intervals. Each trust contains assets carved out of the landholding worth £300,000, leaving Fred with only £200,000 worth at the end. Provided (see below) that 100% relief applies, none of the transfers should trigger a liability to inheritance tax. Capital gains tax should be held over: the Pre-Budget Report 2007 proposals to change that tax do not seem to restrict the operation of *TCGA 1992, s 260*, but we must await draft legislation.

Each trust should be protected by the nil-rate band rule even if:

- the business property or agricultural property relief rules are altered in the future; or
- the assets cease to be relevant business property or agricultural property.

There are several risks with a scheme of this sort: first there is its artificiality.

Second, HMRC could invoke the associated operations rule, although this risk has been curtailed following the decision in *Rysaffe Trustees (CI) Ltd v IRC* [2003] STC 536. These risks can be reduced by ensuring the there are genuine differences between the trusts – eg different trustees and beneficiaries – and that the staggered intervals are as far apart as practicable and are not preordained. Note, however, that HMRC were successful in invoking *TCGA 1992, s 268* to show that life policies, when taken out with annuities, constituted associated operations: see *Smith and others* [2007] SpC 605.

Third, where land is carved up valuation issues get complicated. The extent of the transfer is the loss of the donor's estate, so if, say, the third trust of part of the land included part of two 'natural letting units' it might depress the value of retained land. If it did, the value transferred (subject to APR) might well be different from the value of the actual parcel of land. This issue is even more important where a share or interest in land is transferred, rather than merely the separation of an enclosure from neighbouring land.

Other points to be aware of with this arrangement include the possible loss of capital gains tax rollover relief under *TCGA 1992, s 152*, and that the capital gains tax clock for taper relief will recommence for the trustees on the date of the gift, though taper relief will probably soon be withdrawn anyway.

OTHER WAYS OF USING AGRICULTURAL PROPERTY RELIEF

Gifts to elderly relatives

12.31 Where valuable assets are eligible for 100% business or agricultural property relief, the main disadvantage to a lifetime gift is the capital gains tax position. Whilst hold-over relief may be available under *TCGA 1992, s 165*, the tax-free uplift to market value on the death of the owners is clearly the much better alternative.

Consider whether the asset could be given to an elderly relative, for example a grandparent. The gift would be free of inheritance tax and normally capital gains tax hold-over relief will be available. On the donee's death, 100% business or agricultural relief should be available and the normal minimum

12.32 *Agricultural property relief and woodlands relief*

period of ownership may also be relaxed under *IHTA 1984, s 109* or *s 121*. On the death of the donee the property may then pass under the relative's will to the intended beneficiaries with the benefit of the capital gains tax uplift to market value.

Elderly relative transfers to offshore trust on death

12.32 A scheme to limit gains is discussed in **Chapter 13**. It may be effected through a deed of variation.

WILL PLANNING

12.33 Although planning through Wills is considered in **Chapter 13**, some aspects rely on detailed consideration of the special rules affecting relieved property such as farmland and are dealt with here. Leaving agricultural property to a spouse may suit family purposes but wastes that relief. A gift to a (UK domiciled) spouse or civil partner is exempt anyway. Agricultural property that may qualify for 100% relief should for tax purposes be given to the lower generations (children and grandchildren) or to appropriate trusts.

Key to the choice is the running of the farming business: a careful balance must be struck between fairness, as between siblings, and the need for 'those who work the land to own it'. Will an agricultural asset retain its character in the hands of a family member who treats it as a mere investment? Will APR remain, or remain at its present level? A gift to the next generation may 'lock into' the reliefs at present levels. Frequently, a surviving spouse does not need the business assets, such as shares in the family company, which may be illiquid. He will need the liquid assets.

12.34 If the surviving spouse may need the agricultural assets, those assets can be placed into a 'wait and see' discretionary trust and, if needed, distributed to the surviving spouse: if absolutely, more than three months after the first spouse's death but not later than two years after that date, see *IHTA 1984, s 144*; but if on IPDI terms, there is no need to wait three months.

If the testator wants to give agricultural assets to chargeable beneficiaries to supplement a nil-rate band gift, and leave the residue to the surviving spouse, he must ensure that specific property, eg the farm, is given to the non-exempt beneficiaries to avoid an apportionment of the relief between them and the exempt surviving spouse under *IHTA 1984, s 39A*.

The burden of tax can create unfairness between more than one chargeable beneficiary. A gift of shares qualifying for 100% business property relief to the testator's daughter and a gift of an equivalent cash sum to the testator's son would result in an effectively exempt gift to the daughter while the son's gift would be subject to inheritance tax.

OTHER ADVANTAGES OF DELAYING SUCH GIFTS UNTIL DEATH

12.35 If an estate owner is reasonably confident that 100% business or agricultural property relief will be available on his death, there is little incentive to relinquish control or reduce a substantial minority holding by making lifetime gifts. There can even be a disadvantage, owing to the way clawback works. The case of *Rosser v IRC* [2003] STC (SCD) 311 illustrates a situation where it would have been preferable to defer gifting agricultural property for IHT until death. Advantages of delaying gifts until death include the following:

- There is no question of clawback of business or agricultural property relief. This only applies to lifetime gifts: see *IHTA 1984, ss 124A and 124B*. There is a specific problem in relation to property that falls within *s 105(1)(d)* where the donor had the necessary control but the donees may not have it, but it has no exact parallel in APR.

- There will be full capital gains tax death exemption and tax-free uplift. Contrast this with capital gains tax holdover relief which is usually only a deferral. This may become more of an issue under the CGT changes proposed in Pre-Budget Report 2007, because rebasing, indexation and taper relief may all be lost. In relation to business assets, or farming assets qualifying as business assets, the change in tax burden could be dramatic.

- The estate owner can retain control of his shareholding. For many 'self-made men', this advantage will be hard to resist: they may feel that their children should earn their own living, not rely on inheritance.

12.36 An alternative would be for the estate owner to create a settlement in which he retains a lifetime interest in the shares. If (somewhat unusually!) he wants his children to have control of decisions in the meantime, they could be appointed trustees. The creation of the trust would be a chargeable transfer but the value transferred would be negligible because there would be little or no loss to the donor's estate (because of the retained interest).

On his death, a capital gains tax-free uplift will normally apply. The inheritance tax analysis is that a benefit has been reserved under *FA 1986, s 102* but that APR will be available.

It is important to note that holdover relief is not available at the time of making the settlement, because the trust is settlor interested (*TCGA 1992, s 169B*). However, this restriction may not necessarily be considered a problem, particularly if the transferor could benefit from a substantial amount of taper relief. During the lifetime of the Settlor the trust will be of 'relevant property'. Periodic charges to IHT will be mitigated by APR or BPR but cash in the trust could suffer IHT charges.

12.37 *Agricultural property relief and woodlands relief*

DEEDS OF VARIATION (*IHTA 1984, S 142*)

12.37 Deeds of variation are considered in detail in **Chapter 13**, but it should be noted that where death occurred less than two years ago, consider varying the gifts of agricultural property subject to 100% relief away from spouses and in favour of non-spouses, such as children, grandchildren or discretionary trusts. This will be a good use of nil-rate trusts that are no longer needed to use that band on the first to die of two spouses or civil partners.

MORTGAGING OR CHARGING AGRICULTURAL OR BUSINESS ASSETS

12.38 The placing (or moving) of debt can achieve instant tax savings and should be studied in detail.

Avoid mortgaging or charging a farm

12.39 There are three situations to consider. In the first, the farm itself is charged without other security. This should be avoided where possible because, on a transfer of value, the agricultural property relief will be restricted to the net value of the farm, ie the value of the farm less the mortgage.

If it is not possible to avoid mortgaging the farm, consider charging the farmhouse as opposed to qualifying farmland, for two reasons:

- claims to APR on land are challenged less than claims on the farmhouse; and
- APR is always restricted, see *ITA 1984, s 115(3)*, to the agricultural value and that restriction will usually affect the house more than the land.

12.40 For a farmhouse to qualify for agricultural property relief, it must be of a 'character appropriate' to the farm (*IHTA 1984, s 115(2)*). In *Lloyds TSB Private Banking Plc (personal representative of Rosemary Antrobus, dec'd) v HMRC* DET/47/2005 (*Antrobus (No 2)*), the Lands Tribunal (though that was not the issue before it) considered that, for a farmhouse to be considered as such for relief purposes, it must be occupied by the person who farms the land on a day-to-day basis. Even if the farmhouse does qualify, agricultural property relief is only given on its agricultural value. The Lands Tribunal held in *Antrobus (No 2)* that a 30% discount from market value was appropriate to reflect the agricultural value.

12.41 The second possibility is that the loan could be secured against some other asset, such as a life policy, or land not occupied for the purpose of agriculture, such as redundant farm buildings, rather than on the agricultural property itself. In such a case *ITA 1984, s 162* provides that the indebtedness is set first against the collateral security, so APR is not abated by the charge to the extent that the collateral security is sufficient to redeem the charge. This is preferable to the first scenario, even if it means that some relief may be lost.

In *IRC v Mallender and others (executors of Drury-Lowe, dec'd)* [2001] STC 514, the deceased had given security to a bank over some land in return for a bank guarantee to Lloyd's which was lodged as part of the deceased's underwriting business. Initially, the Special Commissioners had held that the land itself was business property, albeit that its value was several times the value of the guarantee. This decision was overturned by the High Court.

Remember that a guarantee that has not been called in may not be allowed by HMRC at its full value for the purposes of deduction. It may be necessary to negotiate a value to be deducted, to take account of the likelihood, at the date of death, that the guarantee would be called in. An unsecured guarantee might for this purpose be valued much lower than an a secured one: it might even die with the guarantor and not be deductible at all.

12.42 The third option is that the loan is not secured on any particular asset. This is less favourable than the second method because the loan may reduce the agricultural value of the farm on a pro rata basis. It may also be unacceptable commercially to the lender.

Timing: instant relief, at minimal cost

12.43 The movement of debt from the 'wrong' asset to the right one can achieve an instant saving of IHT because the period of ownership (for example two years for occupied farmland) is separate from the debt. The place of the debt is a 'snapshot' test as at the date of death so it does not matter how recently property was exonerated. Another good feature of this tax planning is that usually there will be no SDLT charge: just the fee of the lender for its agreement to the charge (and perhaps Land Registry fees on the taking of new security).

The mortgaging/charging suggestion can be usefully extended. An asset owner could borrow on non-agricultural property assets (eg a home) and use the proceeds to invest in assets that should give the relief.

TAX PLANNING FOR AGRICULTURAL PROPERTY: AGRICULTURAL COTTAGES AND THE FARMHOUSE

12.44 A little-known provision, *IHTA 1984, s 169*, provides that whether or not the conditions for agricultural relief are satisfied, where cottages are

12.45 *Agricultural property relief and woodlands relief*

occupied by persons employed in agriculture, their valuation will be on the basis that they are only suitable for that purpose. They can therefore be transferred at a low value.

The difficult case of *(Starke (Brown's Executors) v IRC* [1995] STC 689, CA) suggests that reference in *IHTA 1984, s 115(2)* to 'agricultural land or pasture' should be given the narrow meaning of the bare land, not the wider meaning under the *Interpretation Act 1978* as automatically including buildings on the land. Therefore it is argued by HMRC that for inheritance tax purposes, a farmhouse or building will qualify for agricultural property relief only if its occupation is ancillary to that of agricultural land. On the facts in *Starke*, a six-bedroom farmhouse on 2.5 acres did not qualify for agricultural property relief.

Starke is a special case, decided on the basis of an undertaking given during the proceedings that limited the scope of the judgment, and some weight should be given to the observations of Morritt LJ that some *nexus*, other than ownership of land, might link a house to the farmland.

12.45 In *Williams (personal representative of Williams, dec'd) v HMRC* [2005] STC (SCD) 782, it was held that broiler houses situated on land leased to a company and used for the intensive rearing of birds were not agricultural property within *IHTA 1984, s 115(2)*. The broiler houses were not 'ancillary' to the deceased's farm: they dominated it. They were not a subsidiary part of the purpose of an overall agricultural activity carried out on the land.

Example 12.5

An estate owner gives 85% of his farm to his daughter and retains 15% together with the farmhouse. If the estate owner continues to be involved in the farming business (eg through a partnership), the farmhouse may be eligible for 100% relief. It is a question of degree. One can have a 100% interest in the farmhouse and, say, a 15% interest in the partnership. It is also suggested that a service contract be entered into between the partnership and the 'farmhouse' owner as to the specific administration and other farming duties he must satisfy.

The judgment in *Starke* contains *dicta* that admit of the possibility that land may be agricultural property by virtue of some *nexus* other than direct unity of ownership. This was challenged in *Rosser,* as to which see below, where the taxpayer acted in person and the point, to judge from the report, was not fully argued. The point is still not formally decided.

12.46 In *Harrold v IRC* [1996] STC (SCD) 195, agricultural property relief was in point in considering the clawback provisions. APR was claimed under

Agricultural property relief and woodlands relief **12.48**

the seven-year occupation test but, because the house in question, though qualifying in other respects as a farmhouse, was unoccupied at the donor's death, no agricultural property relief was available. It was not occupied for the purposes of agriculture because it was not occupied at all.

In *Dixon v IRC* ([2002] STC (SCD) 53, a claim for agricultural property relief failed; in this case, the agricultural use was derisory, comprising only an orchard of 0.6 acres.

The farmhouse must be of a 'character appropriate' to the agricultural property (*Lloyds TSB (personal representative of Antrobus, dec'd) v IRC* [2002] STC (SCD) 468. In that case, a six-bedroom country house situated in approximately 126 acres of agricultural land and pasture, which had been farmed by the Antrobus family since 1907 and had been a working farm, was held to be of a character appropriate to the agricultural land and pasture within *IHTA 1984, s 115(2)*.

12.47 By contrast, in *Higginson's Executors v IRC* [2002] STC (SCD) 483, the deceased lived in a lodge in a landed estate. The house was not a typical farmhouse. The Special Commissioner held that the lodge was not a farmhouse within *IHTA 1984, s 115(2)*. For that purpose, the land and house must be part of an agricultural unit, in which the land predominated. However, in this case the lodge predominated. When sold, it commanded a substantial price, far more than a 'real' farmer would pay for an agricultural investment. It was a house with farmland going with it (and not vice versa).

In *Rosser v IRC* [2003] STC (SCD) 311 the estate owners/farmers made lifetime gifts of some 39 out of 41 acres of farmland, retaining the 'farmhouse' and a barn on the relevant death. The claim for APR on the home failed; it had, clearly, become merely a 'retirement home'. The likely moral is to leave such gifting until death which also then benefits from the CGT death exemption and market value uplift (*TCGA 1992, s 62*).

12.48 For a farmhouse to be agricultural property, it is largely a question of the purpose of occupation rather than the actual use put to it by the owner or occupier. In an extract of a letter from Peter Twiddy (whilst still Assistant Director, HMRC Capital Taxes) (*Taxation,* 15 June 2000), he described the test adopted by Capital Taxes as follows: 'The CTO asks the District Valuer to consider the appropriate test through the eyes of the rural equivalent of the reasonable man on the Clapham omnibus ...' Capital Taxes now applies the following eight tests when determining whether a farmhouse is of a 'character appropriate' to the agricultural property (IHTM 24036);

- 'Is the farmhouse appropriate judged by ordinary ideas of what is appropriate in size, content and layout in relation to the particular land and buildings, or is it a rich person's residence?

12.49 *Agricultural property relief and woodlands relief*

- Is the farmhouse proportionate in size and nature to the requirements of the agricultural activities conducted on the agricultural land?
- Within the agricultural land does the land predominate so that the farmhouse is ancillary to that land?
- Would a reasonable and informed person regard the property simply as a house with land or as a farmhouse?
- Applying the 'elephant' test, would you recognise this as a farmhouse if you saw it? (Although this test involves some subjectivity it can be useful in ruling out extremes at either end of the scale.)
- Consider all other relevant factors, such as whether land is let, the scale of the agricultural operations in context, and so forth.
- How long has the farmhouse and agricultural property been associated and is there a history of agricultural production? (The matter has to be decided on the facts as at the date of death or transfer but evidence of the farmhouse having previously been occupied with a larger area of land may be relevant evidence.)
- Weigh up all the factors and consider the matter 'in the round'.

The notorious 'elephant test' is something which is difficult to describe but you know one when you see one. However, whereas there may be a consensus as to what is an elephant and what is not, an equivalent measure of certainty will not be present when dealing with a question of fact and degree. One difficulty is in deciding to what extent any of the reported cases merely turns on its own particular facts.

12.49   The most recent authority on farmhouses is *McKenna v HMRC* [2006] SpC 00565, where an estate comprised Rosteague House, a lodge, a cottage and a stable flat and 188 acres. 52 acres were coastal slope and 100 acres were agreed to be agricultural land. HMRC denied APR on the house and the taxpayer's appeal from the decision failed.

The title went back to the thirteenth century. The house was part Elizabethan, part eighteenth-century, listed Grade II** but, by the relevant time, it needed very considerable repair. There was evidence of farming from 1365 onwards. During the twentieth century farming was mainly done by others, the owners living in London until retirement to Rosteague in 1978. As long as his health allowed, the estate owner ran the farm from the house. Eventually, it was managed by an agent. The extent of agricultural activities declined. Mr McKenna relied on a pension, not on the farm, for his living.

The estate was eventually sold, not as a farm, but as residential property. The land was incidental, being mentioned only briefly in the sales literature. Of the sale price of £3,050,000 as much as £2,030,000 might fairly be attributable to the house alone.

The Special Commissioner held that:

Agricultural property relief and woodlands relief **12.49**

- the decision in *Antrobus (No 2)* as to what constitutes a farmhouse should be approached with some caution;
- one should decide on the basis of the words of *IHTA 1984, s 115(2)* rather than apply general principles, though the idea that a farmer is the person who farms the land on a day-to-day basis is a helpful one;
- a farmhouse is a dwelling from which the farm is managed;
- the farmer is the person who farms the land on a day-to-day basis, rather than the person who is in overall control;
- it is not occupation that matters so much as the purpose of that occupation;
- if the premises are 'extravagantly large for the purpose for which they are being used' then even though used for farming they may have become 'something much more grand';
- each case turns on its own facts, to be judged by ordinary ideas of what is appropriate in size, content and layout.

On the facts, farming had been reduced and was no longer conducted from the house. The house was too grand for the amount of farming going on. Whilst a farmer need not make a profit, that did not help the taxpayer, on the facts. It was not a farmhouse.

Even if it had been, it was not of a character appropriate: it was 'at the very top end of the size of a farmhouse in Cornwall'. Applying the tests of *Antrobus (No 1)* in turn, it failed. It also failed the occupation test: neither Mr nor Mrs McKenna occupied for the purpose of farming: they were prevented by ill-health from farming.

There are still some issues unresolved, which the following example may illustrate.

Example 12.6

Mr and Mrs Gilliam retire and, as in *Rosser*, give their farm to their daughter who takes over the farming, but Mr and Mrs Gilliam stay in the farmhouse. The daughter lives elsewhere. In those circumstances, the farmhouse ceases to be agricultural property because the daughter runs the farm from other premises. The solution may be for the Gilliams to retain some partnership interest in the overall farm.

Example 12.7

Suppose instead that Mr and Mrs Gilliam occupied a farmhouse as life tenants under a pre-*FA 2006* life interest trust. The land gets separated from the trust and is now held by the daughter in her own right. The Gilliams give the land to their daughter, retiring into a bungalow nearby. The daughter moves into the farmhouse and runs the farm from there.

12.50   *Agricultural property relief and woodlands relief*

The daughter is a farmer of the type favoured by *Antrobus (No 2)*: she actually farms the land from the farmhouse. It is at least arguable that there is such a close connection between the house and the land that, on the death of Mr Gilliam or of Mrs Gilliam relief should be given on the house, but the point is undecided.

12.50   Following *IRC v Forsyth-Grant* [1943] 25 TC 369, if the grant of a farm business tenancy gives the owner a grant of herbage ('profit a prendre') with responsibility for manuring, seeding and fertilising the land, the 100% agricultural property relief will apply including the farmhouse (subject to the 'character appropriate' tests set out above). The potential availability of relief for short-term grazing lets or licences is confirmed in IHTM 24084.

Whether pasture land was 'occupied for the purposes of agriculture' was considered by the Special Commissioner in *Re Executors of Walter Wheatley (dec'd)* [1998] STC (SCD) 60. He held that grazing by horses such as draught animals could qualify because the horses would have a 'connection with agriculture'. Grazing by horses used for leisure pursuits did not so qualify. Arguably, the issue is the exact basis of occupation. If there is a tenancy, Wheatley should apply; but if a licence, the owner-occupier is producing an agricultural crop, grass, whatever eats it.

To avoid the house being an excepted asset within *IHTA 1984, s 112(2)*, because used wholly or mainly for the personal benefit of the transferor (*s 112(6)*), an arm's-length contract of employment should be considered.

TAX PLANNING FOR AGRICULTURAL PROPERTY: FALLOW LAND AND OTHER FARMING ASSETS

12.51   Fallow land (eg under an EC set-aside scheme) qualifies for APR provided that it is not used for another business purpose. Now that much arable land is not actively farmed, because of the entitlement to Single Farm Payment (as to which see below), a question arises whether it is still occupied for the purpose of agriculture; or (as some might think) only for the purpose of drawing subsidy. The farmer would do well to take seriously his duties to keep the land in good heart, even if he does not grow a crop. Most will no doubt do that anyway: it is their heritage.

Holiday lettings are not agricultural property and may well not qualify for business property relief either unless the landlord contributes active management and services. In other words, it is necessary to show that the activity in question constitutes 'trading' and not 'a mere investment'. See the Special Commissioners' decisions in *Martin (Moore's Executors) v IRC* [1995] STC (SCD) 5 and *Burkinyoung (Burkinyoung's Executors v IRC* [1995] STC (SCD) 29.

Agricultural property relief and woodlands relief 12.55

12.52 However, IHTM 25278 indicates that business property relief will normally be allowed if the lettings are short term (eg weekly or fortnightly) and there is substantial involvement with the holidaymakers both on and off the premises. This applies even if the lettings were for only part of the year.

The case of *Farmer and another (executors of Farmer, dec'd) v IRC* [1999] STC (SCD) 321 is often quoted in support of claims to BPR where the landowner, finding it hard to profit from growing crops puts his land to various uses. That case concerned an estate of over 400 acres: there is little case law to tell us the smallest acreage that may qualify for BPR because, as in *Farmer* it constitutes a 'landed estate' and is managed as such.

12.53 Milk and other quotas, for as long as still commercially relevant, will normally qualify for BRP, but since the case of *Cottle v Caldicott* [1995] Spc40, not APR.

For capital gains tax there is at present a conflict, though the changes proposed in the Pre-Budget Report 2007 will tend to resolve it. It was decided in *Caulks v Faulkes* [1992] 15 EG 15 that the quota interest was part of and indistinguishable from the land. HMRC, however, considered that milk quota exists separately from the land for capital gains tax purposes, normally with no base cost. As quotas are extinguished, these points become academic.

In *Cottle v Caldicott* it was held that the taxpayer was not entitled to deduct any part of the cost of the holding of land from the consideration for the milk quota. The milk quota was a separate personal asset (*TCGA 1992, s 21(1)(a)* and *(b)*).

12.54 Diversification to non-agricultural use (eg golf courses) will destroy APR but may well attract BPR. There is no fresh need to own for two years as business property to qualify for business property relief if it was previously owned as agricultural property and the aggregate is at least two years.

Years ago it was common to create tenancies to achieve substantial tax savings because of the double discount, ie the capital transfer tax agricultural property discount plus the reduction in value from open market vacant possession value. Since 1 September 1995, there is little point: land let on new tenancies qualifies for APR at 100%, so keep matters simple. This, however, does depend on whether one expects any changes in government policy. If APR were to be cut down, the double discount plan might revive.

12.55 In an era where vacant possession gives in effect full exemption, the grant of a tenancy is not generally advisable for inheritance tax purposes. Instead of family-type tenancies, consider a partnership with vacant possession (or at least vacant possession within 12 or 24 months). Licensing arrangements that do not constitute leases or tenancies are acceptable, for example for grazing,

12.56 *Agricultural property relief and woodlands relief*

provided that vacant possession can be obtained within only 12 months. Note that ESC F17 refers only to 'tenanted' land, not to land under licence.

The case of *Lubbock Fine & Co v Customs and Excise Commissioners* Case 6–63/92 [1994] STC 101 shows that surrenders of leases are exempt from VAT. However, bear in mind that tenants who currently have security of tenure may be reluctant to agree to a surrender. The income and capital gains tax implications of retaining a tenancy should also be taken into account.

TENANT FARMERS

12.56 A tenant farmer with cash who can afford it should consider purchasing the freehold title in order to acquire exempt IHT assets, in contrast with his other assets, reducing his liquid estate not eligible for reliefs. This is because a tenant who has been in occupation as tenant for a minimum of two years will qualify for 100% APR immediately.

Example 12.8

Evan and Ifor, brothers, inherited farms from their father. Evan farmed until his health gave out, at which point he let his farm to Ifor, telling him he would be happy to sell any time it suited Ifor to buy. Ifor carried on farming.

Road widening in their Welsh Valley took part of Ifor's farm and injected £300,000 into his bank account shortly before his 75th birthday, which was some consolation not only for the loss of the land but also for the news that, with his own failing health, he should take things easier. Why not cut back, and give up the land he rented from his brother?

Ifor took advice both of his doctor and his lawyer. The former told him he had at most 18 months to live; the latter that he should buy the freehold of Evan's land none the less. He did, dying much sooner than predicted. No tax fell due on the value of Evan's land.

FARMING COMPANIES

12.57 Farming companies (*IHTA 1984, s 122*) are at a disadvantage: the 100% relief is available only if the transferor controls the company. Contrast this with business property relief, where a 100% discount is currently available whatever the size of the holding. A holding of 50% or less in a farming company attracts no agricultural property relief, but if it can be proved that the farm is a business, 100% business property relief should be available. Control need exist only at the moment of transfer.

The company must fulfil the same requirements and minimum periods for APR as an individual. The shareholder transferor must, see *s 123(1)*, have owned the shares for whichever of the two or seven-year minimum periods is appropriate to the company.

Example 12.9

On 10 October 2006, Angela gave her farm to her niece. That was a PET. The farm consisted of a house worth £350,000 and 450 acres worth £2,500 per acre, thus having a total value of £1,475,000, of which the agricultural value was £1,370,000. Angela had used both the nil-rate band and her annual exemptions. She had occupied the farm and farmed it herself for 20 years.

The value of the transfer, reduced by APR, is £105,000.

The niece farmed the land until Angela's death on 10 February 2007, whereupon the PET became a chargeable transfer with no tapering relief. The niece can pay the inheritance tax of £42,000 over ten years by instalments. Interest (see *IHTA 1984, s 234(1)*) runs only from the due date of the instalment.

If Angela had rolled over her farming business (including the land) into a company, A Ltd, a year before the transfer in return for the transfer of her shareholding to her niece would still qualify for relief if the niece kept the shares at least until Angela's death. The niece could add together the separate occupation of both Angela and A Ltd. Inheritance tax would similarly be payable by instalments which, if paid on time, would carry no interest.

HABITAT SCHEMES

12.58 Land that is subject to habitat schemes, for the protection of the environment and preservation of the countryside, qualifies for APR even though the land is not 'occupied' for the purposes of agriculture.

SPECIAL TYPES OF FARMING

Farm sharing

12.59 Farm sharing is popular with investors in land who do not have the time or inclination to do any actual farming. The arrangement involves:

12.60 *Agricultural property relief and woodlands relief*

- a joint contractual venture between the owner of the farmland and the operator (who actually farms the land);
- provision by the owner of land, and sometimes fixed equipment and machinery;
- the supply by the operation of working machinery and labour;
- the purchase and supply by the owner of seed etc (but this is usually organised by the operator); and
- the sharing of gross outputs.

The results may be summarised as follows:

- no partnership is established;
- owner and operator have separate businesses;
- there is no landlord/tenant relationship;
- IHT 100% relief should be available.

Both parties should have vacant possession rights. In particular, the owner should be involved in policy-making decisions and exercise rights of inspection: this becomes particularly relevant in supporting the APR claim on the farmhouse, where it must be shown that the 'farmer' lives there.

HMRC appear to agree that farm sharing qualifies for capital gains tax reliefs such as rollover and (for as long as it lasts) for business asset taper relief; and constitutes trading as farmers for income tax purposes (*ITTOIA 2005, ss 9* and *859(1)*) for income tax purposes, and *TA 1988, s 53* for corporation tax).

Contract farming

12.60 Consider also contract farming, where the estate owner owns the farm and the actual farming is carried on by subcontracting, usually to someone who is self-employed. Again, the 100% relief should normally be available. Care must be taken over the invoicing arrangements, for example the purchase of seed and fertiliser is best by the owner of the land. The same issue arises over the farmhouse, particularly in the light of *McKenna v HMRC*.

SINGLE FARM PAYMENT SCHEME

12.61 The Single Payment Scheme effectively dislocated farming subsidies from production. Entitlement potentially arises in the hands of farmers and non-farmers. Entitlement is subject to various conditions and standards, such as keeping the land in good agricultural and environmental condition. A substantial payment of the entitlement in 2005 was expected to provide income support for the following eight years. Thereafter, anyone wishing to receive the subsidy must acquire the entitlement from someone entitled to receive it.

For IHT purposes, the entitlement is subject to the normal IHT rules concerning transfers of value and the death estate. The transfer of the entitlement may attract IHT as for any other asset. It is a separate asset falling outside the definition of 'agricultural property' in *IHTA 1984, s 115(2)*, and cannot therefore qualify for APR, though BPR may be available. However, transfers of entitlement by non-traders as an individual asset (as opposed to a business or interest in a business) will not qualify for BPR.

'BUY AND SELL' AGREEMENTS/ARRANGEMENTS

12.62   Neither APR nor BPR is available if the partners or company directors or shareholders have entered into a 'buy and sell' agreement under which, on retirement or the death of one of them before retirement, his personal representatives are obliged to sell and the others are obliged to buy his interest or his shares. Such an agreement, being more than a mere option, is a binding contract for sale within *IHTA 1984, s 124*.

An option arrangement can achieve the desired result. Perhaps cross-options – ie a put and a call – are equivalent in substance to a binding contract for sale, on the grounds that the terms will be beneficial to one party or the other and thus a sale is inevitable, but the argument is seldom seen. If cross-options are used, they should be made successive in time and have different exercise periods.

12.63   Automatic accrual arrangements between members of a partnership may seem similar to binding sale contracts, but IHTM 25292 states:

> '… agreements under which the deceased's interest passes to the surviving partners, who are required to pay the personal representatives a particular price …do not constitute contracts for sale. So they do not prevent the interest from qualifying from business property relief by reason of *IHTA 1984, s 113*.'

WOODLANDS – THE RELIEF

12.64   Forestry used to be very popular because of the favourable income tax treatment, but those advantages are less now than they were.

12.65 *Agricultural property relief and woodlands relief*

Some IHT relief for woodlands is contained in *IHTA 1984, ss 125–130*. It applies only to trees and underwood. Although the underlying land is excluded, its value will usually be relatively low and will be eligible for agricultural relief if occupied with, and ancillary to, agricultural land or pasture: see the detailed discussion of the need of cattle for shade in *Williams v HMRC*.

The word 'woodland' means a wood of sizeable area and to a significant extent covered by growing trees capable of being used as timber. Accordingly, a plantation of Christmas trees, which had neither the maturity, the height nor the size to be useful as timber, and which resembled bushes rather than trees, did not constitute woodland. See *Jaggers v Ellis* [1997] STC 1417. The analysis in the judgment provides useful guidance on the meaning of woodland in the inheritance tax legislation.

NATURE OF RELIEF

12.65 Inheritance tax relief, on death only, is available if claimed by notice in writing within two years of death or such longer period as HMRC will allow. It applies to woodlands other than agricultural property. The value of the timber is left out of account at death but inheritance tax may be payable on disposal (*IHTA 1984, s 126*).

Inheritance tax is payable on a disposal in relation to the last death on which the timber passes. The person entitled to the sale proceeds or who would be entitled if the disposal were a sale is liable to the tax. An inter-spouse (or civil partner) disposal is ignored. Inheritance tax is only charged on the first disposal of the trees or underwood following the death (*s 126(3)*).

Inheritance tax is calculated on the net sale proceeds or on the net value at the date of disposal if not a sale. The inheritance tax rate scale is the one which would have applied if the chargeable value had been included in the estate in relation to the latest death on which it passes and represented the highest part of that estate (*s 128*). If the inheritance tax charge crystallises after a reduction in the rates, the reduced rates apply (*Sch 2, para 4*).

12.66 Where the woodlands were being managed commercially (ie would have qualified for BPR) the amount on which inheritance tax is charged under *IHTA 1984, s 126* is reduced by 100%. However, if there is a woodland postponement election under *ss 125–127* (see below) only 50% business property relief will be available on a later sale.

Where woodland relief has been given on death, and the later disposal is also subject to inheritance tax as a chargeable transfer, there will be two computations of inheritance tax. The first will relate to the earlier death and the second to the later chargeable transfer. The inheritance tax relating to the death may be deducted from the value of the chargeable transfer to arrive at the inheritance tax liability on the latter (*s 129*). Since, by *s 3A(4)*, a potentially exempt transfer made within seven years of death is a chargeable transfer, it appears that the inheritance tax on the earlier death may be deducted not only against lifetime chargeable transfers but also against those potentially exempt transfers that ultimately become chargeable.

CONDITIONS OF RELIEF

12.67 Relief is only available if the deceased held the land beneficially for the five years preceding his death, or acquired it otherwise than for money or money's worth. The land must be situated in the UK.

Net values are after selling expenses and expenses of replanting within three years or such longer period as the Board may allow (*IHTA 1984, s 130(2)*) except to the extent that these expenses are allowable for income tax (*s 130(1)(b)*).

Where the woodlands are being managed commercially and would qualify as relevant business property for business relief under *IHTA 1984, ss 103–114*, the amount on which inheritance tax is charged is reduced by 100%, as was noted above. However, if there is an election under *ss 125–127* to leave the value of the woodlands out of account in determining the value of the estate on death, only 50% business property relief will be available under *s 127(2)* on an eventual sale. Obviously, if at all possible, it is sensible for the owners of woodland to endeavour to manage the woodlands in a commercial and active manner in order to obtain 100% business property relief. To assist this treatment, separate accounts should be kept in relation to the woodlands and these accounts should not be included in the overall farming accounts.

Example 12.10

Hawker died on 30 September 1991 and left the following estate, there having been no lifetime transfers:

	£
Sundry assets	285,000
Value of timber	80,000
	365,000

12.68 *Agricultural property relief and woodlands relief*

IHT was payable on death on £225,000, after deducting the then nil-rate band of £140,000 £90,000

On 1 May 2007, the timber was sold for £200,000 (on which 50% business relief is due) after allowing for selling and replanting expenses, so that IHT is payable on

	£
	100,000
Other assets at death	285,000
	385,000
IHT payable (at current rates)	
First £300,000 @ 0%	nil
Next £85,000 @ 40%	34,000
Less: Payable (current rates) on estate of £285,000 on death	nil
Payable on sale of timber	34,000

If no claim had been made, then IHT on death prior to 9 March 1992 would (after 50% BPR on the timber) have been on an estate of £325,000:

First	£140,000	nil
Next	£185,000 @ 40%	74,000

TRANSFERS OF WOODLANDS SUBJECT TO A DEFERRED ESTATE DUTY CHARGE

12.68 Under the estate duty regime, duty on a death on woodlands could be deferred until the heir felled or sold the timber. If the heir died before the timber was sold, estate duty on his death replaced the earlier deferred charge and could itself again be deferred. Under *FA 1986, Sch 19, para 46* any transfer which includes woodlands subject to a deferred estate duty charge is denied PET treatment so that there is an immediate lifetime chargeable transfer and the deferred estate duty is treated as discharged.

The problem with that, taken literally, would be that any single large transfer which included some small part of woodlands subject to deferred estate duty would be refused PET treatment. Extra-statutory concession F15 restricts the denial of PET treatment only to such part of the transfer as consists of the woodlands subject to the deferred estate duty. Thus there is an immediate inheritance tax charge on the woodlands subject to the deferred estate duty but the remaining part of the transfer constitutes a PET.

Chapter 13

Wills, variations and disclaimers

Toby Harris LLB CTA TEP and

Mark McLaughlin CTA (Fellow) ATT TEP

The contents of this chapter include material adapted from the book *Ray and McLaughlin's Practical IHT Planning* (7th edn)

INTESTACY

Why make a will?

13.1   There are six main advantages:

- choice of executors;
- ability for the executors to act immediately after death;
- choice of guardians;
- extension of trust rules;
- limitation of trust rules; and
- the ability to get the entitlement right and at the right time or age.

Executors and trustees

13.2   Choosing one's own executors and trustees is better than making do with the persons entitled to the equivalent office on intestacy (ie 'administrators', who may be inappropriate). An **executor's** functions include:

- collecting in the deceased's property;
- paying off any debts; and
- distributing to those persons entitled under the will.

When the executors have collected in the deceased's estate and paid the liabilities, it is common for the will to provide that they will then become trustees. This change in capacity is necessary where the will contains gifts to minors that are conditional on attaining a defined age; or where certain assets are to be held in their present state for quite some time pending sale.

Assets are transferred from the executors to trustees (even if these are the same individuals) by means of an assent. An assent can be informal, except in the case of land where a written document is necessary. The assets retained in the administration, ie not sold to pay debts, could be those assets pregnant with a high capital gain, which could then in due course be assented to the legatees free of CGT.

13.3 The **trustees'** responsibilities include:

- ensuring that the property subject to the trust is transferred to the beneficiaries at the appropriate time or occasion;
- exercising various powers given them by statute or in the will;
- managing assets of the estate (eg land) subject to the trust;
- distributing income or capital from the trust fund; and
- exercising appropriate discretions.

13.4 It is possible to appoint individuals or institutions as executors and trustees. In practice at least two individuals will be appointed with, possibly, a provision that if one dies before the testator or does not accept the office, a third person should be appointed in his stead.

Note the difficulties that arose where a firm of solicitors had become an LLP in *Re Rogers (dec'd)* [2006] 2 All ER 792. The clause appointing executors was in the common form of 'the partners at the date of my death in the firm of …' and was intended to provide succession to office but the words 'or in the firm which at that date has succeeded to and carried on its practice' was perhaps inappropriate as a reference to what had now become an LLP. Lightman J, whilst construing the will so as to allow the LLP to prove, that being the intention of the testatrix, suggested that to avoid doubt in the future 'testators will be well advised to make express provision whether on the conversion of any appointed firm of solicitors or successor firm and (if this is desired) for the appointment of employee (as well as profit sharing) members as executors'.

Administrators

13.5 These are persons appointed pursuant to statute to deal with the affairs of a deceased person, in circumstances where:

13.6 *Wills, variations and disclaimers*

- the deceased has died intestate (ie leaving no will); or
- he has left a will which fails to appoint (or effectively appoint) any executors; or
- he has left a will appointing executors none of whom take a grant of probate. This could be because the named executor had died, or was not well enough to act, or for some other reason.

13.6 An administrator's functions are similar to those of an executor. Administrators are persons having an interest in the estate of a deceased person who wish to become involved in dealing with the deceased's affairs. They obtain grant of letters of administration (contrast grant of probate) which is appropriate in the circumstances referred to above.

The power to act before probate

13.7 Executors can, to a considerable extent, act before grant of probate. An executor derives his power and appointment under the will and can act in that capacity from the moment the testator dies. The executor can:

- arrange the funeral;
- take over the deceased's affairs including the running of his business;
- terminate any continuing liability, such as tenancy;
- dispose of chattels (eg furniture and effects, jewellery or cars).

He should also take immediate possession of any valuables and secure their safety and arrange insurances where necessary since as stated, his responsibility begins from the moment the deceased dies.

13.8 By contrast, an administrator has no such power although the next of kin or proposed administrator should prudently take some of the steps mentioned such as arranging the funeral, preserving the assets, etc.

Guardians

13.9 Under the terms of a will, guardians of infant children can be appointed: clearly a most important provision, especially where the parents are separated or divorced. Normally the need to appoint guardians arises only when both parents are dead but either parent of a legitimate minor can appoint a guardian to act jointly with the surviving parent.

Extending trust powers

13.10 The trustees' implied powers under the *Trustee Act 1925*, *Trustee Delegation Act 1999* and *Trustee Act 2000* can be appropriately extended: for example, the power of applying the whole of a beneficiary's potential entitlement to capital instead of only one half as permitted under *s 32* of the Act.

Avoiding unnecessary complications

13.11 Special requirements can be embodied in a will, for example:

- directions as to burial or cremation etc;
- powers of appointment (ie distributing capital funds);
- options, eg on shares of a family company;
- powers of appropriation (to save stamp duty).

In the nineteenth century many complicated rules arose as a result of litigation which modern wills avoid, especially by the incorporation of the First Edition of the STEP Standard Provisions. These, drafted by James Kessler QC for the Society of Trust and Estate Practitioners (STEP) some years ago, contain most of the rules that will be required in a straightforward estate administration. Mr Kessler is currently revising the STEP Provisions.

Protecting the estate from improvidence

13.12 If there be still, in the twenty-first century, a single class barrier, it is the age at which children inherit! This was clearly illustrated in the parliamentary debate on the Finance Bill 2006, where the government urged the release of funds, regardless of value, to beneficiaries at 18 whilst opposition speakers did not consider that to be an appropriate age, even though 18 year-olds were then, as now, representing what some consider to be British interests in the armed forces abroad.

On intestacy, children become entitled at 18, which may be entirely inappropriate. This is because the entitlements are based on statutory provisions designed many years ago to meet the likely wishes of the average family man, at a time when the age of majority was 21. Family life has moved on: children gain some forms of independence much younger (whilst being sheltered from some forms of freedom much longer); marriage is no longer necessarily the norm.

13.13 *Wills, variations and disclaimers*

Since 1 December 1993, under the *Family Provision (Intestate Succession) Order 1993, SI 1993/2906*, the statutory legacy for the surviving spouse (or civil partner, from an appointed date) has been £125,000 where issue also survive, and £200,000 where no issue survive, but there is a surviving parent, brother or sister.

Example 13.1

Adam, one of three rival siblings, had no children but, as his mother's favourite child, had inherited the family home. He did not bother to make a will, believing that everything would go to his wife Eve. He left an estate of £300,000. Eve survived him, as did his resentful siblings.

Eve got the 'personal chattels', ie furniture, etc, £200,000 and half of the balance, ie £50,000. The siblings, entitled to £25,000 each, forced Eve to sell the house to satisfy their inheritance.

13.13 It is likely that these 'statutory legacies' will be raised, following a consultation paper by the Department for Constitutional Affairs suggesting that the above figures of £125,000 and £200,000 might be increased to £350,000 and £600,000 respectively.

When an individual considers the terms of his will it may be appropriate at that stage to consider suitable lifetime tax planning measures. For example: making potentially exempt transfers (PETs); using the nil and lower lifetime rate of inheritance tax (IHT); setting up appropriate family trusts; and undertaking suitable insurance and pension arrangements.

WILLS

The correct type of will

13.14 There are three basic types of will

- A simple will disposing of the estate by one or more outright absolute interests. The recipients will have complete control of the assets, no strings attached.
- A slightly traditional will giving a life interest from one spouse to another in the whole or part of the estate, followed by or containing one or more outright, absolute interests.
- A full tax planning will whereby the surviving spouse receives a life interest, but full and unrestricted powers are vested in the trustees. These powers enable them to advance capital and to make loans to that spouse.

Alternatively, the trustees can appoint the capital or income onto new trusts, thus terminating the spouse's life interest in whole or part. That type of tax-planning will might also include an appropriate discretionary trust fund containing three main clauses:

– income to widow(er) for life;
– if no widow(er), then discretionary trust of income and capital;
– notwithstanding the two previous provisions, a wide overriding power of appointment.

Life interest wills

13.15 Notwithstanding the IHT changes to trusts introduced in *FA 2006*, a life interest will should be drawn flexibly. The executors/trustees ('the trustees') should have wide, overriding powers of appointment, so that they can either appoint the capital in whole or part to the surviving spouse absolutely and/or terminate the life interest in whole or part and appoint the capital to one or more of the other beneficiaries named or referred to in the will, eg children or grandchildren. It should be noted that *FA 2006*, by introducing *FA 1986, s 102ZA*, has limited the original scope of this tactic.

13.16 When drafting the will trust, ensure that it is clear whether or not the surviving spouse has an interest in possession in the deceased's share of the home. Several cases illustrate the problem:

- *IRC v Lloyds Private Banking Ltd* [1998] STC 559: the deceased's will gave an interest in the house for life, because nothing was to disturb the right of the surviving spouse to live there so long as he wished.
- *Faulkner (trustee of Adams, dec'd) v IRC* [2001] STC (SCD) 112: directions in a will to the trustees to permit two persons to occupy a house constituted a present right of present enjoyment, and gave those persons a chargeable interest in possession, not a mere licence.
- *Woodhall v IRC* [2000] STC (SCD) 558: the testator gave his children the right to occupy the house and gave the trustees administrative powers to permit the children, or any of them, to occupy. Each child had an interest in possession in the property (the value divided between them).

13.17 In *Judge and anor (personal representatives of Walden, dec'd) v Revenue and Customs Comrs* (2005) SpC 506, a will declaring that the trustees during the lifetime of the widow should permit her the use and enjoyment of the property 'for such period or periods as they shall in their absolute discretion think fit' did not give her an interest in possession. She had no right to occupy the property, but the trustees had discretion (but not a duty) to allow her to. The

13.18 *Wills, variations and disclaimers*

decision also seems to call into question the correctness of SP10/79, which indicates that HMRC will normally regard the exercise of trust powers to create a permanent home for a beneficiary as constituting an interest in possession. It is argued by HMRC that SP 10/79 was not in point in *Judge*, but many advisers consider that it was relevant. The chief lessons to be learned from *Judge* are:

- do not cobble a will together from different precedents; and
- read it through carefully before sending it out for signature.

Advantages of life interest wills

13.18 A will which confers a life interest on the surviving spouse has the following advantages:

IHT – gifts with reservation provisions

13.19 This 'trick' has been curtailed by *FA 2006* but is mentioned here because it is still seen in wills that have not been revised. If a surviving spouse inherits assets absolutely which she then settles so as to reserve a benefit to herself (eg as a discretionary beneficiary) the assets remain in her estate for IHT (*FA 1986, s 102* and *Sch 20*). Prior to 22 March 2006, a life interest gift in a will could be used to overcome this. A testator could leave a life interest to his widow coupled with wide powers of the trustees to terminate that interest and, inter alia, settle the funds onto a discretionary trust. If the trustees did terminate the life interest in favour of a discretionary trust, the asset would thereupon fall into a discretionary trust in which the surviving spouse could be one of the discretionary beneficiaries.

In those circumstances, as the law then stood, the surviving spouse would not have reserved a benefit because she had made no gift, so the reservation of benefit rules did not apply. Nor would the 'pre-owned assets' income tax provisions apply. However, *FA 1986, s 102ZA* operates to treat the termination, whether by the trustees or by the surviving spouse, as a 'gift' within the GWR code, nullifying the arrangement just outlined.

IHT flexibility 'in lieu' of variations

13.20 Instruments of variation under *IHTA 1984, s 142* remain a useful fallback for cases where proper IHT planning has failed (usually because circumstances have changed by the date of death) but they are always second best. Family members may not wish to disturb the last wishes of the deceased, merely to secure a tax advantage. Besides, there are restrictions on the *s 142* variation (and it is always possible that the relief will be curtailed by legislation). Therefore, a will which includes a flexible life interest with wide powers of appointment has the best of both worlds: the will itself is flexible and can be adapted to changed circumstances but a *s 142* variation remains an option where necessary and available. The inclusion of a flexible life interest, together with wide powers of appointment written into the will itself, means that *s 142* powers of variation can be avoided.

Reversionary interests and their resettlement

13.21 The creation of the life interest will also create the subsequent interest in reversion. Prior to *FA 2006*, this enabled the parties to achieve substantial IHT, CGT and SDLT savings. This was done by the reversioner, but the scope for this has been cut down by the fact that the creation of virtually all new lifetime settlements are, since 22 March 2006, treated as chargeable transfers.

Practical use of life interests

13.22 Life interest trusts have an important practical use in retaining the capital assets in the estate for the eventual benefit of the testator's children in circumstances where it cannot be guaranteed that the surviving spouse will retain or use the assets for the benefit of the testator's children. For example, where the spouse or civil partner remarries or enters a new partnership, there is a danger that the assets will be diverted to the new husband, wife or partner or their side of the family. Similarly, with second or subsequent marriages, the testator spouse can provide for the surviving spouse by way of a life interest trust and ensure that the capital is left to his own children as appropriate.

Moreover, with a life interest, as trustees will be involved (of whom the widow(er) may well be one), opportunity can be taken of ensuring that he/she will receive proper financial and investment advice.

The fact that creation of a lifetime trust, which itself creates an interest in possession, is a chargeable transfer, may deter some settlors. They may prefer the simplicity of outright gifts. Others, if they must suffer the burden of an IHT charge, may 'go the whole hog' and create a fully discretionary trust instead.

13.23 Second wives, beware! If they have few assets, which they wish to leave tax free to children of earlier liaison(s), note that IHT on death will be based on the aggregate of their own money with the husband's trust fund in which they have a life interest. Some of the wife's nil-rate band is taken to meet the IHT on the trust fund. Consider a lifetime gift to 'collar' the nil-rate band for her children.

13.24 *Wills, variations and disclaimers*

THE APPROPRIATE TYPE OF WILL FOR IHT PURPOSES

Wills for the relevant IHT circumstances

13.24 Six suggestions are made below for six different circumstances. Remember that all families have their own peculiarities. Keep the spouse or civil partner exemption (*IHTA 1984, s 18*) in mind. In particular, at the time of writing (November 2007), the proposals announced in Pre-Budget Report 2007 to allow claims for the transfer of unused nil-rate bands between spouses or civil partners where the surviving spouse or civil partner dies on or after 9 October 2007 were expected to become law when *FA 2008* receives Royal Assent.

Married or in civil partnership – no issue

13.25 Here the usual suggestion (subject to the above comments regarding claims to transfer the unused nil-rate band) would probably be to use the IHT nil-rate band and subject thereto to provide an absolute interest (or possibly a life interest) for the surviving spouse or partner. There will no doubt be minor exceptions (for example, legacies and bequests to relatives, charities, etc).

Married – with issue – small/medium estate

13.26 Small or medium estate (say £350,000-£500,000). Use an absolute interest (and/or possibly a life interest) will in favour of the surviving spouse. However (once again subject to any claim to transfer the unused nil-rate band to the surviving spouse or civil partner, as mentioned above) the will should ensure that up to the full amount of the available nil-rate band for IHT goes to the children or other issue directly or by way of a mini discretionary trust (see below). For 2007/08, the first £300,000 of chargeable transfers (which include chargeable lifetime gifts in the previous seven years) is in effect exempt from IHT. The nil-rate band for 2008/09 is £312,000, for 2009/10 it is £325,000, and for 2010/11 it is £350,000.

It is possible to word the will so as to give chargeable beneficiaries whatever the nil-rate band (or unused balance) available on death. A maximum could be imposed, to ensure a particular beneficiary does not obtain more than the testator contemplated. Consider also gifting business/agricultural assets subject to the 100% or 50% relief, to someone other than the surviving spouse (eg children, grandchildren or a discretionary trust where the surviving spouse can be a beneficiary).

Married – with issue – larger estate

13.27 Larger estate (say more than £500,000). Where the estates are larger the proposals above, namely to take advantage of the nil-rate band, become more relevant and practical insofar as the surviving spouse does not require the whole estate for her/his personal needs. There may also be greater emphasis on the advantages of a life interest will.

Prior to the Pre-Budget Report 2007 proposals to transfer unused nil-rate bands between spouses (or civil partners), some steps towards lifetime equalisation between husband and wife may have been necessary to ensure that each spouse could use his/her nil-rate band, whoever died first. When choosing between using the nil-rate band or claiming it on the second death, consideration should be given to constituting the nil-rate band on the first death with any assets which are likely to appreciate in value more quickly than increases in the nil-rate band. Putting appreciating assets in the hands of the younger generation should defer IHT for a longer period than would be the case if they were given to the surviving spouse. However, even that advantage may well be countered by the ability of the surviving spouse (or the will trustees) to make/arrange PETs.

13.28 At this level (ie for larger estates and subject to business/agricultural property gifts) there are good reasons for the bulk of the testator's estate (ie beyond the nil-rate band – and possibly by way of flexible life interest) to pass to the surviving spouse. This is particularly true where (s)he has reasonable prospects of surviving the vulnerable seven-year period. Thus:

– IHT can be deferred until the death of the surviving spouse, a clear cash flow advantage;
– the surviving spouse can make IHT effective gifts – especially PETs (ie by way of the trustees' termination of the life interest trust; or by way of absolute gifts by the surviving spouse;
– there is greater opportunity to make gifts by normal expenditure out of income.

13.29 For CGT purposes, there are circumstances where it can be very beneficial to transfer assets, initially during lifetime, between spouses (or civil partners). For example:

– spouse A owns substantial assets showing a large capital gain;
– spouse A transfers these assets to spouse B (who is likely to die first) free of CGT and IHT;
– spouse B (dutifully) dies (NB death is not an 'associated operation');
– spouse A receives back the assets free of CGT on B's death and uplifted to the then market value.

Note, however, that there is no market value uplift if spouse B receives a life interest under a trust of the assets (*TCGA, s 73(1)(b)*) unless the trust continues after B's death, giving A a life interest and subject thereto life interests for A's

13.30 *Wills, variations and disclaimers*

children (*TCGA 1992, s 72*). The arrangements should also be carried out subtly and with the risk of challenge under *Ramsay* and under the associated operations rules in mind. To avoid that, consider an adaptation of the above whereby spouse B leaves the assets to someone other than spouse A (eg children, grandchildren, or discretionary trust for the family such as one that exploits *IHTA 1984, s 144*). This gift will also be exempt for CGT, but IHT will be payable on the death unless it is within the nil-rate band, either as gross value or because the gift attracts business or agricultural property relief.

Single (unmarried) persons

13.30 Largely non-tax considerations are applicable here, but IHT-free or exempt transfers may be appropriate (eg nil-rate band to relatives, gifts to charities, etc).

Widow(er) or divorced persons

13.31 Consider, in this situation, using a trust. Before *FA 2006*, this might have been an accumulation and maintenance trust but that, in its simplest form, is no longer possible. The choice is now between:

– *a bereaved minor's trust (BMT)* – this is the HMRC-preferred option, giving entitlement to capital at 18 and no further IHT cost or complications;

– *an '18–25' trust* – this is more flexible than the BMT, though that flexibility comes at a (moderate) cost in terms of further IHT on the fund; and

– *a full discretionary trust* – if the fund is large, say £400,000 or more, this may be the preferred choice, giving much flexibility at only moderate IHT cost, though the cost of its administration may reflect the size of the fund and the complexity.

The 'put together' family

13.32 He is widowed, so is she. Both have children and will want no more: they prefer sunshine and beaches free of schoolchildren. In each case the late wife or husband left everything to the survivor. To take account of the Pre-Budget Report 2007, if it becomes law, they should on no account marry, for tax reasons at least. They have four nil-rate bands available to them and should keep it that way.

Undecided testator

13.33 Consider the various uses of discretionary will trusts (*IHTA 1984, s 144*). As noted above, even a will that does no more than appoint executors may be better than no will at all.

Planning with agricultural or business property

13.34 Some techniques involve a detailed view of the law, such as that in *IHTA 1984, s 39A*. Business Property Relief and Agricultural Property Relief are considered in more detail in **Chapter 11** and **Chapter 12** respectively.

Variations and disclaimers: post-death planning

13.35 From the taxpayer's point of view, *IHTA 1984, s 142* has been, and continues to be, one of the most useful and popular sections in the IHT legislation, because it allows a two-year breathing space in which to rewrite the provisions of the deceased's will or the passing of property on intestacy. It is indeed useful, but it needs approaching with care.

13.36 *IHTA 1984, s 142* operates where:

- within a period of two years after the individual's death;
- the destination of any of the assets of his estate (excluding assets charged under the reservation of benefit rules);
- passing by will, intestacy or 'otherwise';
- is varied/altered or the benefits disclaimed by an instrument in writing made by one or more of the original beneficiary(ies); and
- for variations (but not disclaimers) from 1 August 2002, the instrument of variation (IOV) contains a 'statement' that the IOV is to apply for IHT.

HMRC have no discretion to extend the two-year period. The section has effect, for IHT and for certain aspects of CGT, as if the variation had been effected by the deceased or, as the case may be, the disclaimed benefit had never been conferred.

The 'instrument' is usually effected by way of a deed. This is not essential, but it is helpful as it ensures that the variation is binding as between the original beneficiary and the donee. The IOV must clearly indicate the dispositions that are the subject of it, and vary their destination as laid down by the deceased's will, or under the law relating to intestate estates. Under *s 142(6)*, a variation can apply even though the administration of the estate has been completed and the

13.37 *Wills, variations and disclaimers*

assets advanced to the beneficiary in accordance with the original dispositions. A variation must not be for a consideration in money or money's worth (unless the consideration is another variation or disclaimer). Therefore, the original beneficiary effecting the variation must not, for example, be paid costs or reimbursed income tax liabilities or have mortgage or other liabilities paid.

13.37 If the variation changes the amount of IHT payable, either in the estate of the deceased or in the estate of someone else, the beneficiaries making the variation should send a copy of the variation to HMRC. Where the variation results in additional IHT being due, the executors or personal representatives must make the statement. They may decline to do so if there are insufficient assets in the estate to cover the extra IHT (*IHTA 1984, s 142(2A)*). The personal representatives must, within six months, notify HMRC of the amount of any additional IHT payable and send a copy of the variation to them. Practitioners should refer to the useful HMRC Inheritance Tax IOV checklist IOV2 and Booklet IHT8 'Alterations to an Inheritance Following a Death'.

Multiple variations

13.38 There have been some cases in which a number of IOVs have been executed in relation to the same will or intestacy. HMRC emphasise that these cases must be considered on their precise facts, but in broad terms their views will be as follows:

- an election which is validly made is irrevocable;
- an instrument will not fall within *IHTA 1984, s 142* if it further redirects any item or any part of an item that has already been redirected under an earlier instrument; and
- to avoid any uncertainty, variations covering a number of items should ideally be made in one instrument.

13.39 However, a 'two-bites of the cherry' situation in practice may be achieved as follows:

- Execute a *IHTA 1984, s 142* variation of certain assets into a *s 144* two-year discretionary trust.
- The assets can then be redirected out of the discretionary trust without further IHT within the two-year period, (or up to ten years if the assets are within the nil-rate band).

The range of circumstances where an IOV may be used

13.40 These include:

- divesting assets from a wealthy high IHT rate individual to the next generation (particularly to enable the nil-rate band to be used);
- release by a life tenant of his interest in one part of the capital to the remainderman, and the release by the remainderman of the other part to the life tenant absolutely;
- a redirection of the beneficial interest under a will (for example a widow might renounce a life interest);
- conversion of 'tax-free' legacies into 'subject to tax' legacies adjusted appropriately etc;.
- varying the powers of executors, administrators and particularly trustees;
- correcting defects in a will; but this will not have any IHT effect unless there is also some variation of the interests taken under the will

but **not** the rearrangement of interests in a trust where that is not a disposition of the estate of the deceased but of some other person.

Example 13.2

Selwyn, a prudent investor, left an entire estate worth, say, £400,000 to his widow. Within 18 months of his death a company in which he had invested is taken over and the value of his estate increases to £600,000. If nothing is done, this increase will pass to his widow.

If she does not need the extra £200,000, she might consider (a) entering into a deed of variation under which she takes a legacy of £400,000 with residue going to, say, her children and (b) making a variation within *IHTA 1984, s 142(2)*. The value of her deceased husband's estate immediately before death would still be £400,000. Under *IHTA 1984, ss 38(1)* and *39* all of this £400,000 would be attributed to the exempt specific gift to the widow. As a result, the entire value transferred on death should be exempt and £200,000 should (in the event, namely the increase in value) pass free of IHT to the children.

Income tax problems would remain. If any income had actually been paid to the widow prior to the execution of the deed it would be treated as the widow's income for tax purposes. This could be dealt with, eg by adjusting the legacy so that the widow was given enough to discharge her income tax liability).

13.41 *ITTOIA 2005, s 671* provides that the rule as to income applies only to sums actually paid to the donor of the variation, not to income retained by the executors and paid to the new beneficiaries under the terms of the variation. It is therefore possible effectively to make the variation retrospective for income tax purposes as well as IHT and CGT.

13.42 *Wills, variations and disclaimers*

Example 13.3 – combining the previous idea with a transfer to children

Where the testator has made gifts in excess of the nil-rate band to chargeable parties eg children, these chargeable parties may redirect/vary the will in favour of the surviving spouse, who might subsequently make appropriate PETs. HMRC routinely attack such an arrangement, not so much under the *Ramsay* doctrine or *IHTA 1984, s 268* as on the basis that the variation is for a consideration in money's worth (*s 142(3)*). In the latter case the children would have made a PET gift to the mother, and the mother's transfer would presumably not be a chargeable gift because made without donative intent under a binding obligation.

Example 13.4 – extending 'the excluded property' s 48(3) benefit beyond a single generation where the testator is non-domiciled

The UK domiciled beneficiary varies the will so that he receives the assets by way of flexible life interest with remainders over; or the assets go into a discretionary trust in which the individual can be a beneficiary because the assets are excluded property (*IHTA 1984, s 48*). This is only fully effective where all the assets are non-UK situated. That may perhaps be achieved by interposing a foreign company.

As a result, the assets remain excluded property beyond the beneficiary's death. If a discretionary trust is used, no ten-year or exit charges should apply as excluded property.

Who is the settlor of an instrument of variation?

13.42 For CGT purposes, specific rules were introduced in *FA 2006* to identify the settlor following the variation of a will or intestacy, where an election is made under *TCGA 1992, s 62(6)* (see below) for the variation or intestacy to be effective for CGT purposes (*TCGA 1992, s 68C*). Previously, the House of Lords decided that it was the *beneficiary* (not the testator) who is treated as the settlor (CGT exemption therefore not applying to remitted gains, if the trustees were (or were treated as) being non-resident), see *Marshall v Kerr* [1994] STC 638, HL. The Revenue subsequently confirmed the view that the decision in *Marshall v Kerr* has no application to IHT. This is still the case following the *FA 2006* changes.

For income tax there is no saving: income is assessable on the UK beneficiary under *ITA 2007, s 720* or, in the case of a UK trust, under *ITTOIA 2005, s 624*.

Election: capital gains tax

13.43 There is a restricted power to alter dispositions on death for CGT purposes. The change effected by the IOV is not treated as a disposal but it is treated as having been made by the effective donor (following the decision in *Marshall v Kerr*, as noted above). The election under *TCGA 1993, s 62(6)* should be made only after doing the sums. It is of no help where:

- there are assets with losses; or
- it is wished to use up the small gains exemption; or
- non-UK residents are involved; or
- the principal residence has risen in value since death.

A separate statement must be included in the instrument of variation that it is intended to apply for CGT purposes.

Election: IHT

13.44 As noted, it is not always appropriate for tax purposes to elect for the variation rules to apply. The effect of not electing, for IHT, is that the beneficiary making the variation is then himself making a transfer of value. This may involve a nil or lower lifetime IHT charge than if the deceased had done this and, as the law stands, after seven years the gift will not be included in the beneficiary's cumulative total.

Where the relationship between the testator and the beneficiary is not an exempt one, eg parent to child, election should clearly be made, otherwise there may be a double charge, ie once in the testator's estate and again on the transfer by the beneficiary effecting the variation outside *IHTA 1984, s 142*, ie as a gift by the beneficiary.

13.45 Contrast the situation where there is an exempt disposition by a deceased, eg to his widow. If the widow's cumulative rate of IHT is lower (and bearing in mind that her gift can be a PET or chargeable at one half of the death rate), it will normally be better not to vary for IHT purposes. Instead, let the gift be taxed at her rate and not the deceased's – except where it is wished to use up the deceased's nil-rate band, which will be less likely if the PBR 2007 proposals are enacted.

If the deceased's disposition is not exempt, eg to a child, a statement should be included in the variation instrument to avoid a double charge. As to CGT, a statement should normally be included because of the CGT death exemption and market value uplift. If the statement is *not* made, the IHT treatment is that of a normal transfer of value; for CGT the variation is a disposal.

13.46 *Wills, variations and disclaimers*

Variation or disclaimer?

13.46 There are distinctions between variations and disclaimers:

- In a variation, the beneficiary redirects the asset as he chooses; whilst in a disclaimer he has no choice and his disclaimer merely accelerates the subsequent interest. Thus a disclaimed legacy may fall into residue.

- HMRC appear to take the view that as a matter of English law, a partial disclaimer is not possible and that the whole of the interest must be disclaimed (Inheritance Tax Manual, paragraph 16180) but there has been some challenge to this. To try to avoid this, a suitable clause for inclusion in a will might be as follows:

    'I HEREBY DECLARE that any gift or other benefit made under or in pursuance of this my Will or any codicil thereto may be disclaimed as to any part of such gift or benefit or as to the whole thereof. I accordingly authorise:–

    (a) any person benefiting under this my Will or any codicil thereto; and

    (b) my executors and trustees and any person acting in pursuance of their authority, to deal with and administer my estate in respect of any such partial (or full) disclaimer as hereby authorised.

    In furtherance of this authorisation (but not otherwise) all gifts of money or share or shares of residue shall be deemed at any relevant time to be gifts of money in separate denominations of £1 each for the purpose of enabling any relevant beneficiary of this my Will or any codicil thereto to disclaim separate parts divisible in £1 units.'

- With a variation, it makes no difference that the beneficiary may earlier have received some benefit. In the case of a disclaimer, however, it is a condition that before the disclaimer he has received no benefit. The survivorship provisions in *IHTA 1984, s 92* would be relevant here. To enable a surviving spouse to disclaim his or her interest in a home effectively for IHT (ie, not having received any interim benefit), the gift of the home could be conditional on surviving the testator for the maximum period of six months within the section.

- A variation can benefit anyone, not merely another beneficiary or a member of the family, but the interests of minor beneficiaries cannot be reduced without the court's consent. This gives rise to a fine point of will drafting. Where the testator gives a life interest (eg to spouse), the remaindermen should be restricted to the testator's children per stirpes living at the death of the testator, not at the death of the life tenant. The clause may include his issue if he dies before the life tenant, but if the

Wills, variations and disclaimers **13.50**

class is left open until the second death a variation of a testator's will by the remaindermen would be extremely difficult because of the contingent entitlement of future born issue.

Variation after second death

13.47 Personal representatives can, on behalf of a deceased beneficiary who dies before the testator or within two years of the testator's death, also vary, but HMRC may challenge on the basis of multiple variation.

No consideration

13.48 Neither a variation nor a disclaimer, to be effective in saving IHT, may be for a consideration in money or money's worth (unless the consideration is another variation or disclaimer). For example the beneficiary effecting the variation must not be paid their costs or reimbursed income tax liabilities or have mortgages or other liabilities paid off.

Gifts with reservation rules disapplied

13.49 Where a testator has died and a beneficiary of the estate effects a variation, eg by varying an outright gift to the beneficiary into a discretionary trust, the fact that the beneficiary is capable of benefiting from the varied gift (eg by being included as a discretionary object) should not constitute a reservation of benefit by the beneficiary. This is because, for IHT purposes, it is not the beneficiary but the deceased who is deemed to have created the varied gift (eg the discretionary trust).

Therefore, the reservation of benefit rules (in *FA 1986, s 102, Sch 20*) do not apply. Equally, an income tax charge on pre-owned assets from 6 April 2005 is precluded where the benefit arises from an instrument of variation. The disposition is effectively ignored for pre-owned asset tax purposes (*FA 2004, Sch 15, para 16*).

Redirection of a beneficial interest under a will

13.50 Where a will gave a widow a life interest, she might renounce it or assign the benefit of it to a third party, under a variation pursuant to *IHTA 1984, s 142*. *Section 142* used to apply even if the widow had died in the two-year period but HMRC argue that the variation must take place in the 'real world'. This approach was confirmed by the Special Commissioner in *Soutter's Executory v IRC* [2002] STC (SCD) 385 where Scottish Law applied. The effect is that

13.51 *Wills, variations and disclaimers*

once a life interest has ceased with the life tenant's death, *s 142* cannot be applied. The decision has been criticised because, although logical, *s 142* is in essence a deeming provision and retrospective to the testator's, ie the first, death. There is no case under English law to challenge the *Soutter* principle.

An alternative approach was that the executor/trustees might revoke a life interest by flexible powers in the will. That the arrangement constitutes a PET by the widow of her interest ie the *s 142* procedure is not adopted. Further, it is by *FA 1986, s 102ZA* treated as a gift so that the reservation of any benefit (typically continued residence in a house that had been left to the widow for life) negates the planning whereby the house might escape IHT seven years after the termination of the life interest.

Income tax

13.51 This power to vary the destination of the estate operates for IHT and CGT only and not for income tax. In particular, if an adult gives up his share of the estate in favour of his minor unmarried children, he will be regarded as the settlor for income tax purposes *(ITTOIA 2005, s 629)*. The income from that share is treated as the settlor's, even if accumulated during the unmarried minority of those children. That could have been avoided if the will had contained flexible powers to benefit the children. Contrast the effect of court orders made under the *Inheritance (Provision for Family and Dependants) Act 1975*, which *are* retrospective to the date of death even for income tax purposes, unlike *IHTA 1984, s 142* deeds of variation.

Although of great value therefore, in allowing second thoughts within the two-year period, *s 142* is no substitute for regularly reviewing the terms of the will in the light of its relevance to all the circumstances during the lifetime of the testator. For example, an individual with such minor children should try to persuade his parent(s) to leave the share direct to the minors (ie to have a grandparent's rather than a parent's trust).

Any income due to the beneficiary (whether received or not) up to the date of the variation will be that beneficiary's income. Where a deed of variation is to be executed in favour of a charity, it should be done as soon as possible after the death. This is because the charity, unlike the original beneficiary, will be exempt from income tax under *ITA 2007, Pt 10*.

Stamp duty and stamp duty land tax

13.52 Variations are exempt from stamp duty and adjudication requirements, provided the appropriate certificate is given under the *Stamp Duty (Exempt Instruments Regulations) 1987, SI 1987/516*. Disclaimers are also exempt from stamp duty. For stamp duty land tax purposes, variations are similarly exempt from charge if made within two years of death, and if there is no consideration other than the making of the variation (*FA 2003, Sch 3, para 4*).

Specific plan: elderly relative transfers to offshore trust on death

13.53 The will of an elderly person holding agricultural or business property, which had been given to him by a younger relative unconditionally, but perhaps with an onward gift in mind, could provide for the business or agricultural property to pass into a non-resident trust. The settlor charge would not apply to the trust, he or she being deceased, and the assets would have a base cost equal to market value at death.

On the other hand, a non-resident trust with a deceased settlor accumulates its realised gains as 'trust gains'. These are later attributed to UK-domiciled beneficiaries who receive benefits from the trust and who are subject to a surcharge if there is a delay between the realisation of the gain and the benefit. The surcharge can (under 2007/08 tax rates) increase the effective tax rate to 64% after a six-year delay, so a charge on the settlor at the time of the gain may be thought preferable. Where there are many beneficiaries, and the stockpiled gains are moderate, it is common practice to 'dribble out' the gains by making distributions to each beneficiary of an amount that is within the annual exemption of the beneficiary.

Two changes to these ideas may result from enactment, in *FA 2008*, of changes to CGT outlined in Pre-Budget Report 2007:

- some of the freedoms from CGT hitherto available to non-UK domiciled persons will be curtailed; and

- the reduction in the rate of CGT from 40% to 18% may reduce the 64% rate to 28.8%.

Example 13.5

Iain was a clergyman of otherwise modest means whose offshore trust, established by his will in 2004, included shares in the family company that had been given to him by his (very successful) children and in respect of which the already substantial gain had been held over. At his death the shares qualified for 100% BPR. The company went public in January 2006 and the trustees made gains of £700,000. Iain's children were as prolific as they had been successful and between them, now have 16 children and three grandchildren, all of whom are beneficiaries of the trust.

13.54 *Wills, variations and disclaimers*

In the year ended 5 April 2007, the trustees distributed £167,200 divided equally between Iain's grandchildren and great-grandchildren, none of whom had in that year made any personal gains. All is exempt, so there is no stockpiled gains charge under *TCGA 1992, s 91*.

On 3 May 2007 the trustees distribute a further £174,800 on the same basis. If the beneficiaries make no other chargeable gains in excess of their annual exemption, there will again be no stockpiled gains charge. Nearly half the gains have been washed out.

Alternative use of deed of variation

13.54 If the transfer into the offshore trust just described is done by way of deed of variation, rather than under the elderly relative's will, then the beneficiary effecting the variation would be the settlor for capital gains tax purposes (*TCGA 1992, s 68C(3)*, following the decision in *Marshall v Kerr* [1994] STC 638). As a result, any gains realised by the trustees would be attributable to and taxable on the donor-beneficiary concerned under *TCGA 1992, s 86*.

Although the legislation (*TCGA 1992, Sch 5, para 6*) gives the beneficiary a right of recovery against the trustees, there is some doubt over whether that right is enforceable. With the possible exception of trusts resident in a Brussels Convention country, the better view is that such rights of reimbursement will be unenforceable. Voluntary reimbursement by the trustees is not necessarily a solution, but these complex issues are outside the scope of this book.

Example 13.6

Anne owns 82% of the shares in Selfield (Agricultural) Ltd which currently qualify for 100% APR. She wants to give 30% of the shares to her only daughter Emma so as to retain control (and therefore APR) on the rest of her interest. A 30% holding of these shares is currently worth £600,000 and there is an inherent gain on such a holding, upon which the potential capital gains tax liability amounts to £75,000.

Anne's father George is still alive but widowed in his 80s. His late wife left no estate and he himself has very few assets. Anne is his only child and Emma his only grandchild. Anne gives the shares (ie the intended gift to Emma) to George free of inheritance tax as business property. Capital gains tax is held over. It is then hoped (there must be no prior agreement or arrangement) that George will leave these shares to his granddaughter Emma under his will.

On George's death, there may be no inheritance tax because his late wife did not use her nil-rate band (it does not matter that she had nothing to leave). Two nil-rate bands will be available if the Pre-Budget Report 2007 proposals become law, enough to shelter the value of the shares.

That part of the plan could have been achieved by a straight gift by Anne to Emma. However, significantly, there is a capital gains tax-free base cost uplift to market value at the date of George's death. Capital gains tax of £75,000 has been avoided.

Supplementary points

13.55 There are several points to make about the example set out above:

- If George did not leave the property to Emma by his will, the beneficiary under the will could execute a deed of variation to achieve the same result. This course depends on the co-operation of the beneficiary. Not much can be done if George's will leaves everything to the wicked stepmother or to charity and fails to change it in time.

- It was, prior to *FA 2007*, possible to achieve the result described in the example without the risk that George's will might benefit the wrong person – or indeed the risk of George's estate becoming insolvent and the property being required to pay his debts. Anne would have settled the business property on George for life with remainder to Emma. That is still possible, but the settlement will be a chargeable transfer, so the availability of APR will be tested at that point.

- If this plan is adopted instead of an immediate gift to Emma, it means gambling on the enactment of the Pre-Budget Report 2007 proposals as to transferable nil-rate band in their current form for George's life. Those involved should be made aware of this risk.

- Since this structure relies on tax-free uplift on George's death there is no particular advantage in trying to pre-empt the CGT charges outlined in the Pre-Budget Report 2007.

Checklist

13.56 In considering the effect of the variation:

- Take account of the identity of property and the needs of various beneficiaries. A widow is likely to need to own the dwellinghouse and liquid assets but may not need illiquid assets such as shares in the family company.

13.57 *Wills, variations and disclaimers*

- For IHT, consider carefully whether or not to elect. Review:
    - the effect of the seven-year cumulation provisions;
    - lifetime as opposed to death rates if there is no election; and
    - opportunities available for lifetime PETs.

    As a general rule for redirections by an exempt party under a will, elect only in order to take advantage of the nil-rate band. If the original gift is to a chargeable party (eg a child of the deceased) do elect, because no extra IHT is involved. If extra IHT is involved, consider the likely interest charge.

    Beware of a further trap. If the deceased dies with a free estate plus a life interest in assets and leaves the free estate to an exempt party, there is no aggregation with the capital supporting the life interest. However, if there is a variation so that the free estate is left to a chargeable party, extra IHT is payable on the death because of aggregation with the capital supporting the life interest.

- Consider allocating property that qualifies for business or agricultural reliefs to non-exempt beneficiaries. Note that a former quirk advantage whereby a widow(er) is left a legacy which was allocated to business or agricultural assets was countered by what is now *IHTA 1984, s 39A*).

- Try to allocate appreciating assets to younger individuals and depreciating assets to older individuals.

- Consider the cost involved including additional IHT (and interest thereon and income tax).

- A deed of variation or disclaimer is not a substitute for IHT lifetime planning, particularly in the current voluntary PET era which could always be removed in the future by the present or a future government. Note also the possibility of future restrictions on variations and similar arrangements by amending legislation.

HUSBAND, WIFE AND CIVIL PARTNER

Civil partnerships

13.57 As implied by the heading, following the *Civil Partnership Act 2004*, from 5 December 2005 registered civil partners are generally subject to the same treatment for inheritance tax purposes as married couples. References in this section to 'spouse' should therefore be interpreted to include 'civil partner' where appropriate.

The main aspects of the IHT exemption

13.58 The inter-spouse exemption in *IHTA 1984, s 18* is 'bread and butter' IHT planning. A fundamental aspect of IHT is that liability can be deferred until the death of the surviving spouse (unlike the old ED regime where duty was payable on the *first* death). Absolute transfers between husband and wife, whether during lifetime or by will, are generally exempt from IHT, subject to the domicile aspect dealt with earlier. Each has a separate estate and nil-rate band. Unlike CGT there is no requirement that the spouses be living together. The meaning of the word 'spouse' for the purposes of *s 18* is restricted to married persons, and not persons living together as husband and wife (*Holland (executor of Holland, deceased) v IRC* [2003] STC (SCD) 43).

On divorce, as opposed to separation, the exemption ceases to apply but some relief is likely to be available under *s 11*. Under *s 18* it is necessary only to show that the value transferred by the one spouse is *attributable* to property which has become the property of the transferee spouse. It is not a requirement for exemption that the consequential loss to the transferor spouse must be exactly matched by the increase to the estate of the transferee spouse. This should normally give complete exemption even in cases where before a transfer the transferor spouse had control of say a family company (whether in his own right or as related property) and after the transfer he has not.

It is, however, essential that the property become part of the donee's estate. As will be seen, practically any lifetime gift into trust made after 22 March 2006, save for a disabled person or a charity, is treated as if it were discretionary. Thus the donee is not treated as having an interest. Therefore even a transfer to a trust for a spouse fails to enjoy exemption because the spouse is not treated as owning the fund.

Settlements

13.59 The exemption used to apply where one spouse settled assets in trust for the other spouse by way of interest in possession, including protective trusts under the *Trustee Act 1925, s 33*. However *FA 2006* has restricted that. A lifetime transfer, even to an interest-in-possession trust for a spouse, is a chargeable transfer unless for a disabled person. The tenant for life does not become entitled to an interest in possession for the purposes of IHT, even though he may be so entitled for income tax and CGT.

Since the fund is not treated as forming part of the estate of the life tenant, it does not satisfy the requirements of *IHTA 1984, s 18(1)* notwithstanding the terms of *s 18(4)*. Similarly, the exemption is not usually available in the case of a discretionary trust where the trustees appoint to a beneficiary who is the spouse of the settlor.

13.60 *Wills, variations and disclaimers*

Spouse exemption would still be available if the discretionary trust in question was a will trust and the distribution created an IPDI, later than three months but within two years of death. In this situation *s 144* (as amended by *FA 2006*) would apply. Note the trap that if an outright distribution is made within three months of death the exemption will not apply (*Frankland v IRC* [1996] STC 735 and *Harding (executors of Loveday) v IRC* [1997] STC (SCD) 321).

Non-UK domiciled spouse

13.60 If, immediately before the transfer, the transferor but not the transferor's spouse is domiciled in the UK, the exemption is limited by *IHTA 1984, s 18(2)* to a maximum of £55,000. That figure of £55,000 is cumulative, taking into account any previous transfers. This is a *separate* fixed exemption (not subject to indexation under *s 8*) and does not reduce the UK spouse's nil-rate band. Note:

- Any gifts in excess of the exemption figure nevertheless constitute PETs.
- Gifts made to a spouse whilst non-UK domiciled are not 'cleansed' by the fact that the recipient spouse later becomes domiciled here, or is deemed to be so domiciled. Those 'excess' gifts remain on the donor's 'clock' and go against the donor's nil-rate band until seven years have expired from their dates.
- The foreign domiciled spouse is in a position to make gifts of excluded property outside the IHT regime. However here some care should be taken, for if excluded property is gifted to a UK domiciliary its exempt status will, of course, be lost.

The restricted exemption applies *only* where the transferee spouse is domiciled abroad and transferor spouse is domiciled in the UK. The widened definition of deemed domicile in *s 267* applies in this context and therefore the transferee spouse, who might be non-domiciled for general purposes but is UK domiciled for IHT purposes, has the full exemption available. For example a change of domicile on emigration within the previous three years will not prevent the full exemption from applying.

Conditions

13.61 The inter-spouse exemption is subject to certain conditions set out in *IHTA 1984, ss 18* and *56* namely:

- The transfer or disposition must take effect immediately, not after any period, nor when a prior interest terminates. For example, if a husband gives a life interest, say, to his brother and the remainder after such life

Wills, variations and disclaimers **13.61**

interest to his wife, the exemption will not apply because the immediate gift is to the brother. If the gift were the other way round, and absolute, this restriction would not apply to the first gift but a voluntary, unconnected, onward gift by the spouse, perhaps under the terms of mutual wills, would be chargeable under normal principles. However the exemption is not lost by reason only that the property is given to a spouse conditionally on surviving the other spouse for a specified period (*s 18(3)(a)*). This has particular relevance in the context of the survivorship clauses although they are in fact restricted to a six-month period (see *s 92*).

- The transfer or other disposition must not depend on a condition which is not satisfied within 12 months after the transfer (*s 18(3)(b)*). It is thought that if it is possible, but not certain, that the condition will be satisfied within 12 months, a 'wait and see' rule should be applied. This second rule would operate in respect of a condition that the surviving spouse acquires an asset for a third party, which is never in fact acquired. If property is left to a person (whether surviving spouse or another) subject to a condition that the recipient must 'give' certain of his or her own property to another, it seems that this latter transfer is nevertheless a gift and not excluded by virtue of *s 10*. Although the 'transferee' does not intend to make a gratuitous disposition, as the first 'giver' did so intend, it is likely that both transfers are gifts having regard to the phrase 'a transaction intended' within *s 10*. Accordingly, to comply with the condition in *s 18(3)(b)* as between spouses the condition of making the second gift should not exceed the 12-month period.

- The inter-spouse exemption does not apply to property given in consideration of the transfer of a reversionary interest, if that reversionary interest does not then form part of the recipient's estate (under *IHTA 1984, s 55*) because he has an interest in possession or future interest in the same settled property (see *s 56(1)*). This provision, intended to counter certain IHT avoidance techniques associated with dealings with settled interests, is of little practical planning effect, other than as a trap to avoid in considering the handling of settlements.

- Where a person acquires a reversionary interest in any settled property for a consideration in money or money's worth, the inter-spouse exemption does not apply on the termination of the prior interest (assuming, for instance, it was held by his wife) when the settled property passes to him as the new reversioner (*s 56(2)*).

- Spouse relief does not apply where a person makes a disposition and thus becomes entitled to a 'settlement power' for money or money's worth: *s 55A*. A 'settlement power' means (see *s 47A*) any power over settled property or exercisable over it or over the settlement itself. *Section 55A*

13.62 *Wills, variations and disclaimers*

applies not only to the acquisition of a settlement power but also to the situation where the purchaser can influence the exercise of such a power or restrict its exercise.

13.62 *IHTA 1984, s 203* is a tracing section that deserves to be better known. It provides that when a transferor has made a transfer of value to his spouse, that spouse (to an amount equal to the value of such property at the time of its transfer) is liable for any IHT for which the transferor is liable, in respect of other transfers of value. This is designed to cover the case where the transferor might wish to avoid liability to IHT having made one or more chargeable transfers, by giving the rest of the assets to his spouse.

Disposition for maintenance of family (*s 11*)

13.63 There are important exemptions for inter-family dispositions and particularly in respect of a former spouse, for example on divorce. These, and in particular the meaning of 'maintenance', were considered by the Special Commissioner in *Phizackerley (personal representative of Phizackerley, decd) v Revenue and Customs Comrs* [2007] SWTI 559.

Husband and wife estates: should we still use the nil-rate band on the first death?

13.64 For years, IHT was charged on an ascending scale which encouraged the equalisation of estates between husband and wife, but since 15 March 1988 the position is simpler. After the nil-rate band (£300,000 in 2007/08) there is only one single rate of 40% on death (half of that, 20%, for lifetime chargeable transfers).

Thus, as a general rule, there is no advantage for IHT purposes in equalising estates as between husband and wife. If changes announced in Pre-Budget Report 2007 on 9 October 2007 are enacted, it will no longer be necessary for the nil-rate band to be used on the death of the first spouse (or civil partner), due to the possibility of transferring the unused proportion of an unused nil rate to the estate of a surviving spouse who dies on or after 9 October 2007. Transfers of unused nil-rate bands are discussed further below.

Use of nil-rate band

13.65 Spouses (or civil partners) wishing to utilise the nil-rate band on the first death (as opposed to transferring it, as proposed in Pre-Budget Report 2007) should take care that the nil-rate band is used for chargeable beneficiaries or donees. Where an individual would normally regard his spouse as the primary beneficiary, he might (subject to the Pre-Budget Report) consider settling by will a sum equivalent to the upper limit of the nil-rate band upon a discretionary trust so that the surviving spouse can have the benefit of the fund and at the same time the nil-rate band can be utilised and not wasted. Distributions could be made in favour of the surviving spouse in case of need; and if they were of capital any exit charge under the discretionary trust regime in the first ten years would be by reference to the nil-rate band on the testator's death.

Distributions might be made by way of loan, which would normally expect to qualify as a deduction against the estate of the beneficiary, though this tactic should not be relied on to the point where it is clear that there is really no prospect of repayment (ie sham). The trustees could instead make income distributions subject to income tax. The use of the nil-rate band for a mini-discretionary trust in this way can be very effective. A discretionary trust with a wide class of beneficiaries and wide powers may offer added flexibility.

13.66 Remember, when using the nil-rate band as described above, that the nil-rate band can normally be expected to increase annually by reference to the retail prices index (*s 8*). However, the limit for 2008/09 has been set at £312,000, for 2009/10 at £325,000, and for 2010/11 at £350,000. The testator's will should reflect this trend to ensure that the gift matches the ceiling of the nil-rate band when he dies. The gift in the will should therefore be of an amount equivalent to the upper limit of the IHT nil-rate band in force at the time of the testator's death under *IHTA 1984, Sch 1*, as amended in accordance with the indexation provisions of *s 8*. Such a formula, while most useful for cash gifts, cannot of course operate in the same straightforward way in the case of specific legacies of assets, particularly where business or agricultural reliefs are involved and changes in values may occur.

13.67 In utilising the nil-rate band the effect of such business and agricultural reliefs is very important. Where relief is at 100% the benefit on top of the nil-rate band is unlimited. With relief at 50%, for 2007/08 the nil-rate band can become £600,000. As a general principle, because of this multiplying effect on figures, business and agricultural property should be given to chargeable parties rather than to the surviving spouse, to prevent it being wasted.

In the case of a partially exempt estate (ie because *s 18* applies in whole or in part) the gift should be of the business or agricultural property itself. It is not sufficient merely to create a specific pecuniary legacy payable out of the business or agricultural property. In this latter situation relief is denied on the value of the pecuniary legacy and therefore (at least in part) lost (see *IHTA 1984, s 39A(6)*).

Channelling of gifts and associated operations

13.68 The art of timing (whether gifts are into settlement or outright) is for a donor to make a PET or a chargeable transfer to use up the nil-rate band while

13.69 *Wills, variations and disclaimers*

the seven-year survivorship requirement is likely to be satisfied. Thus where a husband and wife wish to make such gifts to others, for example their children, it may be advisable to 'channel' the gifts through the spouse with the better life expectation or who has not used up the nil-rate band. On the face of it the associated operations provisions of *IHTA 1984, s 268* would appear specifically designed to counter such channelling transactions. It was made clear, however, when CTT was first being introduced, that in relation to outright gifts the associated operations rules would be used only in blatant or culpable circumstances, or where it was made a condition of the first gift that the other spouse would make a further gift (Mr Joel Barnett, *Hansard*, March 1975, HC Deb, Vol 888, col 56).

13.69 It is considered that this assurance also applies to gifts into settlement: see *Rysaffe Trustees (CI) Ltd v IRC* [2003] STC 536. However, the position may be less clear cut, having regard in particular to the earlier exchange of correspondence between the Institute of Chartered Accountants and the Inland Revenue of September 1985 concerning *Furniss v Dawson* [1984] STC 153 reproduced in ICAEW Guidance Note TR 588, 25 September 1985. The Revenue's response was as follows:

> 'I can confirm that we would not seek to disturb existing practices in relation to inter-spouse transfers. It should, however, be borne in mind that the circumstances of such transfers always need to be carefully examined to ensure, among other things, that the transaction has substance as well as form. (For example, an understanding between the spouses on the ultimate destination of the assets would be important in this connection.) In general the terms of the Press Release of 8 April 1975 remain valid as a description of the practice in this area.'

(That press release, reproduced in Simon's Tax Intelligence, 18 April 1975, p 180, contained notes on *FA 1975*: see at p 191 for the notes on the associated operations provisions of the then *s 44*, which reflect the Hansard statement referred to above.) IHTM 14833 also confirms that property given unconditionally by one spouse to another and subsequently transferred to a third party cannot be subject to the associated operations provisions.

It might be argued by HMRC that the gift into settlement by a spouse, say a wife, who had received a gift from her husband, was a case where the wife was acting merely as a conduit (in other words, that the husband never effectively alienated the property given). In these circumstances the husband might be regarded as the real and only settlor. Accordingly, various precautionary steps are recommended to reduce the effectiveness of any such HMRC contention.

Step 1: Record the gift

13.70 The record of the initial gift by the husband should be in a signed memorandum stressing that the gift is made to the wife as beneficial owner absolutely and unconditionally, eg as follows:

Example 13.7 – Memorandum of gift

MEMORANDUM and DEED that I the undersigned have this day of ..... 200( ) made a gift by way of [share transfer] of ... of my Ordinary Shares of £1 each in the capital of ....

Limited to my wife [names] who has countersigned by way of acknowledgement and receipt.

I RECORD AND CERTIFY that this gift is made as an outright unconditional gift to my wife for her sole absolute use and benefit.

We certify that this deed falls within Category L of the Stamp Duty (Exempt Instruments) Regulations 1987. [nb. For gifts of land and property, exemption is claimed under *Finance Act 2003, Sch 3, para 1*).

IN WITNESS whereof the parties hereto have signed this Memorandum and Receipt as their DEED in the presence of the persons mentioned below this ..... day of ...... 200( )

SIGNED and DELIVERED as a deed by   )

[HUSBAND]   )

in the presence of:)

Witness:

Address:

Occupation:

RECEIPT DATED .... 200( )

I ACKNOWLEDGE receipt of the above gift upon the terms set out above.

SIGNED and DELIVERED as a deed by   )

[WIFE]   )

in the presence of:

Witness:

Address:

Occupation:

13.71 *Wills, variations and disclaimers*

Step 2: Get independent advice

13.71 The wife should receive independent professional advice if and when she creates her settlement, and any such advice should be recorded in writing.

Step 3: Make the later gift differ from the earlier one

13.72 The wife should not settle all the assets received from her husband.

Step 4: Do not rush

13.73 The wife's gift into settlement, if in fact she decides to make it, should be after a decent interval of time, one month at the very least.

Step 5: Let some benefit flow through to the wife

13.74 If the gift from the husband produces gross income, let it sit in the wife's name long enough for that income to show up on any tax return that she might make.

Step 6: Even better, make the gift from the wife's existing resources and (maybe) reimburse her later

13.75 If possible (eg, in the case of cash) the wife should set up her settlement first, with the husband subsequently, as a separate decision and act, making a gift to the wife of a similar, but not the same, value.

Example 13.8

Mr A has made previous lifetime chargeable gifts totalling £300,000 gross. He wishes to make a gift of £100,000 gross into a discretionary trust for his son's family. This is a simple lifetime chargeable gift and the IHT (at half the death rate of 40%) would be £20,000. His wife, whose estate is worth £200,000, has not used up any of her nil-rate band. He suggests to her that she might wish to make the £100,000 gift, which she does at no cost to IHT. Mr A the following year decides to transfer £110,000 to his wife by way of exempt gift. It is considered that the wife's gift into the discretionary trust would not in practice be taxed as Mr A's under the associated operations rules of *IHTA 1984, s 268*.

The matrimonial home

13.76 For IHT purposes, as between spouses, as in other cases, a life interest in an asset that existed at 22 March 2006 is treated the same as an absolute interest (the liability being based on the capital value on the death of the surviving spouse).There was no difference for IHT between giving a life interest only in the matrimonial home to the surviving spouse and giving the property to the spouse absolutely. If the gift is by will, that is still true, provided that the spouse receives an IPDI (which she usually will).

13.77 For practical reasons, most spouses wish the survivor to have the matrimonial home absolutely, so when choosing the family assets to use up the nil-rate band, others may have to be chosen, such as shares in the family company. Indeed, there can be problems in seeking to use the matrimonial home in this way (although the risks seem to have been reduced following the commencement of *Trusts of Land and Appointment of Trustees Act 1996*).

13.78 Following the proposed introduction of claims to transfer unused nil-rate bands between spouses or civil partners, it will no longer be necessary to use the nil-rate band of the first spouse (or civil partner) to die with an interest in the family home. However, if for any reason this is what the parties want, remember:

- If the first spouse leaves his interest in the home direct to the children, subject to a right to occupy in favour of the surviving spouse, it will probably give the survivor an entitlement to the use and enjoyment of the property equivalent to an interest in possession in it (see *s 50* and *IRC v Lloyds Private Banking Ltd* [1998] STC 559). That will shift IHT on the house from the first death (exempt as passing to the survivor) to the termination of occupation by the second. The exact statutory basis is unclear: there is no formal authority for 'deeming' an interest in possession, only that it may reflect economic reality.

- No deemed life interest was found in *Judge and anor (personal representatives of Walden, dec'd) v HMRC Comrs* (2005) SpC 506, already noted. The economic control of the spouse over the asset, her veto on sale, was disregarded).

- If the house was left direct to the children, without the incorporation of conditions so as to secure occupation by the surviving spouse, the CGT private residence exemption would be at risk to the extent that all the children as owners did not live there. It may well be preferable to give the survivor the security of his or her own home absolutely, and look at other assets for nil-rate band planning.

Types of ownership

13.79 There are four main types of ownership of the matrimonial home:

13.80 *Wills, variations and disclaimers*

- Sole ownership of husband.
- Sole ownership of wife.
- Joint holding as 'joint tenants' – this is the only form of co-ownership capable of existing in law, as contrasted with beneficial ownership, ie in equity. Under this method, by reason of the *jus accrescendi* rule, the survivor takes the entire interest absolutely by operation of law. Hence it is impossible (subject to severance which cannot be by will but, as a matter of practice can be by deed of variation) to make inter vivos or death dispositions to third parties because this interest accrues automatically to the survivor.
- Joint holding as 'tenants in common' – Since 1925 it is only possible to have a tenancy in common in equity. However, this is likely to be of no practical importance as the value of the property will be represented by the respective beneficial interests and not the bare legal title. This type of holding is frequently found to be the most satisfactory from the IHT and practical viewpoints. Each spouse has a separate, say, half share which he or she can separately leave by will or dispose of during lifetime.

Husband and wife as tenants in common should make provision in their wills concerning their shares in the property. Following the commencement of the *Trusts of Land and Appointment of Trustees Act 1996*, occupation of the family home by the surviving spouse should be secure even without conferring specific rights.

13.80 When conveying or transferring from the sole name of one spouse into the sole name of the other spouse or into the joint names of both spouses, whether as joint tenants or tenants in common, remember the following practical points.

Gift of matrimonial home to a donee other than a spouse

13.81 For IHT purposes, the gift with reservation of benefit rules apply mainly to gifts during lifetime (*FA 1986, s 102* and *Sch 20*). If an owner makes a lifetime gift of his house, or part of it, and continues living there, HMRC Inheritance Tax can normally claim that by staying there after giving it away the former owner has reserved a benefit, so that the seven-year run off period for outright gifts does not apply (*s 3A(4)*), and nor does the percentage abatement of IHT on death within seven years of the gift (*s 7(4)*). The full value of the house remains in the total aggregable estate at death.

13.82 There is in fact an exemption under *FA 1986, Sch 20, para 6(1)(a)* which rules out reservation if the donee leases the property back to the donor for full consideration. Such a gift would then be a PET. It is essential to negotiate arm's-length terms for any tenancy or lease and for each party to be independently advised. Full consideration is required throughout the period of any tenancy. The rent should therefore be reviewed at stated intervals, say every four years. HMRC recognise that what is 'full' consideration must lie within a range of normal valuation tolerances and that any amount within that range can be accepted as satisfying *para 6(1)(a)* (see Revenue interpretation headed 'IHT gifts with reservation' in *IR Tax Bulletin, Issue 9*, p 98; also at [1993] STI 1409).

13.83 There are other practical problems apart from reservation: the need for the donor to go on paying a full market rent even when his income is perhaps becoming squeezed, and a continuing income tax charge on the rental for the donee. (There would also be the question of rights of holding over occupation under the landlord and tenant legislation.) If, furthermore, a lease at a market premium was chosen instead of a continuing market rental there would still be the question of income tax on the premium as well as possible rights of enfranchisement under the leasehold reform legislation. Finally, principal private residence relief from capital gains tax would not be available to the donee should he sell the property. All these ideas must also be reviewed in the light of the pre-owned assets income tax charge (*FA 2004, Sch 15*).

13.84 Commentary on other past and present arrangements to transfer interests in the family home (eg lease carve-outs, reversionary leases and 'IOU' arrangements) are outside the scope of this Chapter. Further information is contained in *Ray and McLaughlin's Practical IHT Planning* (7th edn).

Gift of a share of the home

13.85 It is possible for spouses to retain a share of the matrimonial home, perhaps a third or a quarter, and give the remaining share to their children but the spouses and the other joint owners must all occupy the home and pay their proper share of the running costs.

This method was originally non-statutory but is now in *FA 1986, s 102B*. It may work very well in the case of an unmarried son or daughter, or even a married child, living with the parents. If, however, the children already have their own homes, the required element of occupation and sharing is missing. Furthermore, if the children did live there but later moved away, the parents would from then on have to pay a full rent to avoid a reservation of benefit springing up. Nothing prevents the use of this arrangement in respect of an unequal share: however, get the paperwork right: IHTM requires all such cases to be referred to Technical Group.

Gift of cash, later invested in a home

13.86 Try basing an arrangement on a gift of cash. The parents could give their son £150,000 cash outright. Later, he could use the cash to buy a house

13.87 *Wills, variations and disclaimers*

where they all might live. However, this may lead straight to a pre-owned assets income tax (POAT) charge, unless it is precisely within the 'son of Hansard' exemption from POAT set out in *FA 2004, Sch 15, para 11(5)(c)*.

It would not be appropriate to use the cash to buy the parents' present home since HMRC could attack the arrangement on the grounds of associated operations. The income tax charge on pre-owned assets would also need to be considered, unless the cash gift was made more than seven years before the house purchase (*FA 2004, Sch 15, para 10(2)(c)*). (It would be simpler for the parents to give the son say a third of the house and for him to move in with them.)

Stamp duty and stamp duty land tax

13.87 The 'consideration' in the deed of gift or transfer is not usually valuable, being expressed as the 'natural love and affection of the donor for the donee'. As a result of the *Stamp Duty (Exempt Instruments) Regulations 1987, SI 1987/516*, no conveyance or transfer operating as a voluntary disposition inter vivos, ie as a gift, is liable to ad valorem stamp duty, but is exempt provided an appropriate certificate is included in the instrument. For stamp duty land tax purposes, a land transaction is exempt if there is no chargeable consideration, eg a gift between spouses (*FA 2003, Sch 3, para 1*). But note the mortgage trap below.

Severance

13.88 The joint tenancy of a property held by husband and wife can be severed so that husband and wife become tenants in common in equity, thereby providing greater flexibility. A simple form of notice of severance will do. An equitable joint tenancy can be severed by a joint tenant giving to the other joint tenant a notice in writing under the *Law of Property Act 1925, s 36(2)* (proviso) and *s 196*. This notice must be given during lifetime because a joint tenancy cannot be severed by will (although it can, in practice, by deed of variation under *IHTA 1984, s 142*). It is preferable for a severance to be agreed and signed by both parties.

Example 13.9 – severance notice

To [second owner]

I hereby give you notice to sever the joint tenancy that exists between us of [3, Acacia Villas, East Cheam, Surrey].

Please acknowledge this notice by signing the copy. [We will then notify the Land Registry.]

Dated 2007

Signed [first owner]

Acknowledgement

I have received a notice of which the foregoing is a copy. You may notify the Land Registry.

Signed [second owner]

Mortgages and other outgoings

13.89 Frequently the property is mortgaged; the mortgage may be either legal or equitable. Before a change can take place in the ownership of property subject to such a mortgage, the consent of the mortgagee must be obtained.

In the usual case of property subject to a mortgage with a building society or an insurance company little difficulty is experienced in practice in obtaining the mortgagee's consent to a transfer between spouses and therefore the method of transferring the property subject to the mortgage is normally adopted. Alternatively, there is nothing to prevent one spouse conveying or transferring to the other only the equity of redemption without the mortgagee's consent. There is, however, a nasty SDLT trap to beware of. Duty is still payable to the extent of the existing mortgage debt assumed by the donee (*FA 2003, Sch 4, para 8*).

The fact that a husband continues to pay mortgage instalments in respect of his wife's house or share should not give rise to any IHT charge because of the available exemptions, for example *IHTA 1984, s 18* (inter-spouse) and *s 21* (normal expenditure out of income). The same applies as to payment of other outgoings such as insurance, water rates, and ground rent if the property is leasehold.

Joint bank accounts

13.90 As a general rule, and subject as mentioned below, the use of joint bank accounts for substantial sums should be avoided. It robs the family of flexibility in disposing of value, for example to a trust of the nil-rate band, and the law on the treatment of such assets can be uncertain.

13.91 *Wills, variations and disclaimers*

Note that the courts have taken note of other cultures and the way that money is treated there: see (though not a husband and wife case) *Anand v IRC* [1997] SSCD 58 (SpC 107). However, in the case of large sums, it may be simpler and clearer for the spouses to have separate bank and building society accounts.

13.91 As between husband and wife the use of joint bank accounts for relatively small sums can be recommended on two grounds. First, as a matter of convenience for day-to-day living expenditure; and secondly, to prevent the sums in such accounts being frozen on the death of the first spouse.

Where joint bank accounts are used for making gifts to third parties, serious IHT consequences can follow having regard to the uncertainty of the treatment by HMRC and with particular reference to the following statutory provisions:

- *IHTA 1984, s 272* – the definition of 'property' as including 'rights and interests of any description …' Those rights can include, for example, the wife's statutory right to apply for the grant of letters of administration to her husband's estate, and rights to her husband's estate on intestacy (*Daffodil (administrator of Daffodil, deceased) v IRC* [2002] STC (SCD) 224;

- *IHTA 1984, s 5(2)* – the inclusion in a person's estate of property, over which he has a general power of disposal;

- *IHTA 1984, s 3(3)* – the deeming provision whereby a chargeable transfer can occur by 'omission to exercise a right'; and

- *IHTA 1984, s 268(1)* – the inclusion in 'associated operations' of an omission. Moreover, on death money in the joint account will automatically pass to the surviving spouse as a matter of law. Remember that it is not possible to sever a joint tenancy by will but only by lifetime notice or by an instrument of variation under *s 142*.

An application of these IHT provisions could result in a double charge on transfers to third parties (for example the whole credit balance in a joint account could be treated as part of a deceased spouse's estate even though subsequently the surviving spouse made gifts (eg PETs which became chargeable on the survivor's death within seven years) to third parties out of such account and can create anomalies as between the joint owners. There is scope to notify HMRC of the origin of funds: see for example form 15 election. *IHTA 1984, s 44(2)* treats a settlement by more than one settlor as being itself more than one settlement.

13.92 Do not try to use a joint account as some kind of testamentary disposition or 'will' substitute as a specific means of providing for the other joint owner on death. The reason, particularly with larger amounts, is the uncertainty of treatment for IHT described above (see for example *O'Neill v IRC* [1998] STC (SCD) 110.

Husband and wife should have separate bank accounts to make it easier to claim the normal expenditure out of income exemption, making annual exemption gifts and £250 gifts, as well as make larger PET gifts to use up the respective nil-rate bands of each spouse.

Nil-rate band transfers: background

13.93 For some time now, it has been common to draw wills that leave a nil-rate band discretionary trust in favour of the surviving spouse and immediate family so as to use the nil-rate band of the first spouse to die because under the old rules that band was otherwise lost, with an effective tax loss (at 2007/08 rates) of up to £120,000.

At the time of writing it is proposed, in the PBR 2007 changes, that the legislation to transfer unused nil-rate bands be available in respect of any surviving spouse or civil partner who dies on or after 9 October 2007. Effectively, couples who made simple wills leaving everything to each other, with remainder to children on the second death, are now in at least as good a position as those who took the trouble to obtain tax advice and who used the nil-rate band arrangement. In some circumstances those who did not take tax advice are now better off than those who did.

13.94 The legislation is to form new *IHTA 1984, ss 8A-8C* and to amend *s 151BA*, with consequential changes to *ss 239, 242* and *272*. It works by increasing the nil-rate band of the second spouse to die. The amount of the increase is fixed as a percentage, not exceeding 100, of the nil-rate band (or, where there was more than one former spouse, bands) not used on any previous occasion.

Example 13.10

Cynthia died on 6 May 2007. She had made gifts in the last seven years of her life of £50,000. By her will she left £10,000 to charity and £50,000 to her daughter Jessica, with residue to her husband Wilfred. Wilfred had not made any lifetime gifts. He died on 13 October 2007 leaving an estate of £400,000 and nominating Jessica his executrix.

Jessica may make a claim to the new relief. Wilfred's nil-rate band would have been £300,000 but there is still £200,000 unused from Cynthia's estate so the total nil-rate band available is more than enough to exempt Wilfred's estate from IHT.

13.95 *Wills, variations and disclaimers*

Example 13.11

Take the facts in the above example except that Wilfred died on 6 April 2008 and his estate was £600,000. If Jessica makes a claim, the nil-rate band available will be £312,000 plus a figure in respect of the unused nil-rate band available to Cynthia. She used one third of the band, so two-thirds is left. At 2008/09 rates, that amounts to £208,000 so Wilfred's nil-rate band will be £520,000.

Claim to the new transfer relief

13.95 The relief must be claimed: see proposed *IHTA 1984, s 8A(3)*. The rules are in the proposed *s 8B*. The claim is to be made on form IHT216 by the personal representative of the surviving spouse or civil partner within 'the permitted period' but HMRC Commissioners may allow a longer period. The permitted period is, see *s 8B(2)*, two years from the end of the month in which the survivor dies or, later, three months from the date on which the personal representatives first act as such. Form IHT216 is available via the HMRC website.

Example 13.12

Jake was 'a bit of a lad' and quite late in life was divorced from his wife and went to live with Caroline. He showered presents on her and took her away for romantic weekends and for holidays in flats above chip shops in Malaga. Caroline loved it, and to some extent, him, and whilst they were enjoying the winter sunshine in Spain arranged for Jake to sign a will. No lawyer being readily to hand, she wrote the will out herself and got a couple of people at a neighbouring table in the local café to act as witnesses.

Jake's children were not impressed. Before Caroline could even apply for a grant of probate they had lodged caveats. There was the usual interminable correspondence between the solicitors and it looked as if the case would go to court. In the end, as a result of a meeting with a mediator, a settlement was reached which allowed Caroline to apply for a grant of probate. The mediation itself took place on the second anniversary of Jake's death and it was two more months before Caroline had the HMRC Account ready. She discovered that Jake had actually been married twice before, and that his first wife had died, leaving everything to him. As a result, there was a possibility of a claim to increase the nil-rate band available on Jake's estate. Caroline had one month in which to put in the claim.

Wills, variations and disclaimers 13.97

Once a claim is made it can be withdrawn, but no later than one month after the end of the permitted claim period: *IHTA 1984, s 8B(3)*. Practitioners should claim now, not wait for the *Finance Act 2008* to become law.

Clawback of relief

13.96 It may become necessary, in relation to heritage relief and woodland relief, to look back to an earlier death to establish the tax charge. As may be imagined, the availability of the nil-rate band can affect that tax charge. Proposed *s 8C* takes account of this, where a heritage or woodland clawback charge applies.

Clawback whilst surviving spouse still alive

13.97 If the event triggering the change happens before the death of the surviving spouse, it becomes necessary to recalculate the available (or used) nil-rate band. To apply the legislation, first find the nil-rate band for the first spouse to die, defined as NRBMD in *s 8A(4)*. Next find the current nil-rate band, ie that in force at the time of the event triggering the charge. This is defined by *s 8C(2)* as 'NRBME'.

Next establish 'E': this is the excess of the nil-rate band over the chargeable transfer at the first death: effectively the unused nil-rate band.

Finally (for this stage of the computation) calculate 'TA': this is the amount on which the clawback is charged.

Then apply the fraction $\left(\frac{E}{NRBMD} - \frac{TA}{NRBME} \times 100 \right)$

to discover the percentage of the nil-rate band in respect of which a claim may be made.

Example 13.13

Lady Penelope's pink Rolls Royce, worth £100,000, was the subject of an undertaking under *IHTA 1984, s 30* when she died in November 2005. Her son had the car resprayed in May 2007 which destroyed the essential character of the vehicle and which was in breach of the undertaking, triggering a *s 32* charge. Lady Penelope had made chargeable lifetime transfers of £25,000 and left her estate, apart from the car, to Parker, whom she had married late in life.

13.98 *Wills, variations and disclaimers*

Nil-rate band, November 2005 (NRBMD):	275,000
Nil-rate band, May 2007 (NRBME):	300,000
Unused nil-rate band, November 2005 (applying the formula in *s 8A(2)* and *(4)* (E)):	250,000 viz
M+275,000	
VT=25,000	
E=(M–VT)=250,000	
TA:	100,000
Computation:	$\frac{25,000}{275,000} - \frac{100,000}{300,000} \times 100$
	$= \frac{30}{33} - \frac{11}{33} = 57.57\%$ of the nil-rate band.

If there is more than one breach of undertaking; or where there are several woodland clawback charges; TA in the calculation means the total value in respect of which the clawback has applied.

Clawback after the second death

13.98 In these circumstances proposed *IHTA 1984, s 8C(4)* reduces the nil-rate band of the first spouse to die. The mechanics of the adjustment are set out in proposed *s 8C(5)*. The nil-rate band of the first to die of the spouses or civil partners is first adjusted by applying *IHTA 1984, Sch 2* (the uprating provisions that give the benefit of any reduction in the tax that applies because the nil-rate band has been increased over time). That uprated nil-rate band is then potentially both increased and decreased. The increase can apply where the first spouse to die might himself have more than one nil-rate band available, perhaps being a widower. The reduction is the amount of any increase in that band by virtue of the nil-band transfer rules. The language is convoluted; it is with greater optimism than truth that the Explanatory Note suggests that *s 8C(5)* 'makes [it] clear' at all; but the following example may illustrate it.

Example 13.14

Sir James was first married to Zuleika who became UK domiciled in 1974 and who left her estate to Sir James when she died in March 1990. Zuleika did not use her nil-rate band. Sir James in 1996 married Sally and on his death in

Wills, variations and disclaimers **13.99**

November 2007 he left her his estate, having made only one chargeable transfer of £50,000 (a failed PET). The family seat qualified as heritage property but a sale of amenity land for £200,000 to meet Lady Sally's debts after her death in September 2010 triggered a clawback charge under the 'associated property provisions' of *s 32A*.

The nil-rate band in 1989/90 was £118,000 but none of it was used. In November 2007 it was £300,000, so the total nil-rate band available to Sir James' executor is £600,000. The nil-rate band at Sally's death is £350,000. The clawback charge is on £200,000. The reduction under clause 8C(5) is of the increase in the nil-rate band from Sir James's death to that of Sally: £50,000. Thus Sir James's executor has available a reduced (double) nil-rate band of (£600,000 – £50,000 – £200,000): £350,000.

Unexhausted pension funds: the new rules

13.99 The background to the rules is the IHT charge on that part of an alternatively secured pension fund which has not been used in benefits for the fund member and his dependants. In simplified terms, *s 151BA(2)* treats the unexhausted fund as the 'top slice' of the member's estate for IHT purposes. *Section 151BA(5)* uprates the nil-rate band that is to be applied. It is now proposed that this provision should be modified by introducing *ss 151BA(6)* and *(7)*. Again, a formula first requires the taxpayer to establish certain values.

Example 13.15

E, as before, is the unused excess nil-rate band available; and NRBM is the nil-rate band in force when the member died.

The formula $100 - \left(\frac{E}{NRBM} \times 100\right)$

produces 'the used up percentage', ie the fraction by which the nil-rate band otherwise available to the member is to be reduced.

Example 13.16

Mabel died in July 2006, when the nil-rate band was £285,000. She made no lifetime gifts but left £10,000 to her son and the rest of her estate, including her pension rights, to David. He did not draw all the pension. He had no dependants. The unexhausted portion of the pension fund, at his death on 6th January 2008,

13.100 *Wills, variations and disclaimers*

was £100,000. For Mabel's estate E=275000; NRBM=285,000 and the 'used up percentage' is 100(275/285%) ie 100–96.49=3.568%, which is the part of Mabel's nil-rate band that has been used.

13.100 Matters become more complicated where the pension fund is still not exhausted by the death of the second person benefiting from it. The proposal is to introduce *IHTA 1984, s 151BA(8)–(12)*. First, the situation is addressed where there has been an IHT charge on an alternatively secured pension fund by reference to the first to die of husband and wife. This change will affect the person's nil-rate band and restrict the amount available for transfer later: it is 'appropriately reduced' under *s 151BA(9)* where the chargeable event occurred after the death of the surviving spouse. If, however, the surviving spouse is still alive when the chargeable event happens, tax is charged when the survivor dies by adjusting the member's transferable nil-rate band using a formula (see *s 151BA(12)*) which compares the 'adjusted excess' with the 'adjusted nil-rate band maximum', expressed as a percentage.

The detail of the calculation may be enough to cow pensioners into submission – in the form of drawing income to exhaust the fund. Thus where the charge arises after both spouses have died, each may have used part of his or her nil-rate band, so there may be less available to meet the IHT charge under *s 151B*: see *s 151BA(9)*, as augmented by the definitions set out in *s 151BA(10)*.

Where the charge arises whilst the surviving spouse is still alive, the formula in *s 151BA(12)* applies. This restricts the nil-rate band available later. AE, the adjusted excess, deducts from the maximum nil-rate band the value transferred by chargeable transfers after calculating the taxable amount and after adjusting the nil-rate band itself: ANRBM. ANRBM is the nil-rate band, adjusted for ASP charges.

Compliance

13.101 Inevitably, with a new charge there is a risk that tax charges will be missed. Most taxpayers tend to think that the capital of pension funds is in some way exempt from IHT. The new rules as to transferable nil-rate bands, when affected by ASP fund charges, can reopen settled cases.

Qualified IHT clearance certificate

13.102 The clearance certificate issued by HMRC will not guarantee freedom from IHT charges where the amount of the nil-rate band that was transferred must be adjusted by the clawback effect of ASP charges. *IHTA 1984, s 239(4)* is qualified accordingly. Similarly, penalties may be imposed on a wide range of people, see *s 247(2)*, if incorrect information has been supplied, for example by failure to cut down the nil-rate band of the first spouse to die to reflect a part of that band used by him, or deemed by the ASP fund charges to have been used by him. No doubt a substantial amendment will be required to form D6 lodged with IHT 200 (which relates to pensions), quite apart from a form on which to make the claim for transfer under *s 8B*.

Record keeping for the elderly

13.103 One important self-help procedure will be for widows and widowers to make and keep a record of the extent to which their late spouses had used the nil-rate band. A simple form, along the lines of the following schedule, might be placed with the survivor's will.

Record of use of the nil-rate band for inheritance tax purposes

13.104 This record is designed to establish how much of the nil-rate band was used by any former spouse. In it, the terms 'married' and 'widowed' include being a member of a registered civil partnership and still being such a member when the civil partner died.

Example 13.17
- Have you been married?
- If so, how many times?
- Did your marriage end only on the death of your spouse?
- If so, state the date your spouse died.
- If you have been widowed more than once, state the date that each spouse died.
- If you know it, state the amount of the nil-rate band when your spouse died (or when each spouse died).
- Did your spouse leave all his estate to you?
- If not, state the value given by your late spouse to others, and specify if any was left exempt, for example to charity.
- Did your spouse make gifts to others in the seven years before death?
- If so, state the amount given and to whom, again noting any gifts that were exempt for any reason.

13.105 *Wills, variations and disclaimers*

Estate duty surviving spouse exemption

13.105 This is unaffected by the changes. Practitioners should do nothing to disturb that very useful situation, which confers freedom from both IHT and CGT.

Chattels

13.106 Practitioners should note the effect of *IHTA 1984, s 143* and take care to avoid accidental use of the 'first' nil-rate band where, for example, the surviving spouse trades down after the first death and shares out the contents of the old home.

What advice should practitioners give to testators?

13.107 We are at present in a 'limbo' period: a relief has been announced that is not yet law but that will, if enacted, be back-dated to 9 October 2007. On the one hand, advisers can reassure their clients that there is no need to panic. As an alternative, the new legislation could be seen as a special selling opportunity. There are several arguments for doing nothing at all.

Example 13.18 – both spouses still alive

Husband and wife are both still alive and have made wills that incorporate nil-rate band discretionary trusts. There is scope, under *IHTA 1984, s 144*, for the trustees of a discretionary trust to appoint funds or assets to beneficiaries within two years of the death. To avoid the difficulty that was shown in the case of *Frankland v IRC* [1997] STC 1450, the trustees should not normally take any action until three months have elapsed from the date of death. Between the third and the twenty-fourth month, however, a distribution from the discretionary trust will take effect as if it had been a gift under the terms of the will and not a distribution from the trust.

Therefore, there is no need to change the will. On the death of the first to die of husband and wife, the trustees simply wait three months and appoint the whole of the nil-rate band to the surviving spouse. There is no need to wait three months if the effect of the deed of appointment is to create an IPDI; only if the interest created is an absolute one. If the will of the surviving spouse is drafted in common form the provision as to the nil-rate band will not apply because it has been excluded where the surviving spouse is not married at the date of death. In this scenario, therefore, all that is needed is a deed of appointment by the trustees of the nil-rate band set up by the will of the first spouse to die.

Wills, variations and disclaimers **13.109**

13.108 However, not every practitioner is familiar with the drafting of deeds of appointment of assets out of discretionary trusts. Things can get left. If one of the executors is a professional person, she will probably be negligent if she fails to do what is right for the family in terms of IHT. If the executors are all family members and if they miss the various deadlines, they could be worse off than if they had simpler wills.

13.109 The debt or charge scheme is difficult to explain and where there is an *IHTA 1984, s 103* problem, as illustrated by the *Phizackerley* case) noted at **13.63**, it can get quite difficult explaining the scheme to clients. Many people may have been slightly uncomfortable with the complexity of wills containing nil-rate band discretionary trusts and they may feel much happier with simple new wills even though that will involve paying a new fee to have them prepared.

Example 13.19 – one spouse long dead

Husband died five years ago, widow still alive, nil-rate band discretionary trust in place. In this situation nothing can or should be done. By putting in place a nil-rate band discretionary trust the husband used his nil-rate band. Five years have elapsed since his death, so it is now too late to make any changes relying on *s 144*. It is also too late to consider a deed of variation because, to be effective, it also had to be made within years of death to claim relief under *s 142*.

Therefore, the only nil-rate band available to the widow (unless she remarries and survives her second husband!) is the single nil-rate band. It would be totally wrong for the family to assume that 'we just don't need that silly scheme now' and to appoint all the funds in the discretionary trust to the widow. That would just increase her estate without giving her back her late husband's nil-rate band.

Example 13.20 – one spouse died recently

Fred made a will in standard form leaving a nil-rate band discretionary trust for the benefit of his close family, with residue to his wife Hannah, still in good health. The main asset was their house, worth £800,000, held by them as tenants in common in equal shares. Fred had £100,000 of savings. He died on 3 January 2007. He had not made any chargeable lifetime gifts.

Hannah's daughter Angela was keen to look after her mother as best she could, and it was agreed that Hannah would sell the family home and move to something much less expensive nearer Angela. The house would now sell for £900,000. Fred's estate was administered promptly and the nil-rate band of £285,000 was to be satisfied initially with £100,000 from his savings and then

13.110 *Wills, variations and disclaimers*

with another £185,000 from the sale of the house. Hannah soon realised that, since so much money would be left over after the house move, she would not need to rely on any of the nil-rate band. Hannah told Angela that she would be much happier if, once the sale went through, all of the money could be released to Angela straight away. All of this was planned to take effect before Christmas 2007.

The executor was (somewhat surprisingly) looking ahead to what would go into the Tax Return for the final period of the administration. He would have to show the (forecast) gain on Fred's half of the house. In fact it began to seem that the house must have been worth slightly more than £800,000 at the date of death, so the gain on Fred's half, if realised, might not be as much as £50,000; but even so, there would be a gain and it would not be covered by 'main residence' relief because the sale would be by him as the executor or by the trustee of the nil-rate fund. Hannah's share of the gain on the house would of course be tax free.

The family sat down with their advisor after the details of the Pre-Budget Report were known. They realised that the nil-rate band was already £15,000 bigger than when Fred had died, so the tax involved at 40% was £6,000. They worked out that, since they were still within two years of Fred's death, they could effectively rewrite Fred's will so that all of Fred's estate went to Hannah. That way, the whole of Fred's nil-rate band, at the current rate, would still be available. They decided to gamble on enactment of the new rules without substantial amendment.

The assets that had already been transferred to Angela would not now be coming to her from the discretionary trust. They would be treated as given to her as a gift by Hannah and, if Hannah lived seven years, those gifts would fall out of account anyway. Apart from that, if the will was varied, the sale of the house could all be treated as a sale by Hannah and the whole of the gain, whatever it was, would become tax free.

They also worked out that if Hannah lived until 6 April 2010 the tax saving would be greater. By then the nil-rate band will be £350,000. Quite apart from the fact that Hannah's own nil-rate band (after deducting the gifts to Angela) would have increased by £50,000 from today's date, the claim to use Fred's nil-rate band would have increased by £65,000 so the true tax saving could be £26,000.

The family decided that, even though Fred's estate was almost completely administered, it would be worthwhile unscrambling everything, and rewriting the will so that Fred's nil-rate band had not been used on his death.

New will instructions

13.110 If 'second husband' and 'second wife' need wills, a careful balance must be struck between tax considerations and what the family want where each

Wills, variations and disclaimers **13.110**

party to the new marriage has assets and obligations to the children of former marriages. The new rules will allow the survivor husband and wife up to double the nil-rate band where he or she has been married more than once.

Example 13.21

David was married to Liz. They had two children. David's best friend was Edward, married to Jill. They had one son. Tragically, Edward died intestate on Boxing Day 2002. Jill put in place a deed of variation under which £125,000 was set aside for their son and the rest of the estate, about £350,000, passed to Jill. That effectively used half of Edward's nil-rate band.

David's comforting of Jill in her bereavement led to his divorce from Liz. As a preamble to, but not part of, the divorce settlement in summer 2005, David settled £75,000 on their children. David married Jill and died on 1 August 2007, leaving all his estate to her. Jill died on 17 October 2007.

Jill's executor can make claims in respect of the nil-rate band that was available to Edward and to David. From Edward's estate the provision that Jill arranged used half the nil-rate band, so half the nil-rate band is still available, which at current rates is £150,000. As far as David's estate is concerned, the gift of £75,000 was not exempt under *IHTA 1984, s 10* or *s 11*, so it reduced the nil-rate band available at the date of his death from £300,000 by one-quarter, so three-quarters of the nil-rate band is potentially still available, £225,000. However, Jill's executor cannot enjoy more than one total extra nil-rate band, so the nil-rate band available at Jill's death is £600,000.

Example 13.22 – recycling of APR or BPR

Julian was a successful engineer and by his will he left the nil-rate band to his children and the residue to Delia, his wife, who had always taken a keen interest in the family business. After Julian's death Delia encouraged the executors to allocate all Julian's shares, attracting 100% BPR, to the nil-rate trust. The shares were worth £900,000. She received the parts of the estate that did not qualify for any relief. She also received substantial cash from insurance policies and death in service benefits.

Delia used the cash to buy the shares from the trustees. That gave the trustees far more, in real terms, than the nil-rate band, so effectively the children received more than Julian could have given in simple cash terms.

If Delia lives two years from her purchase of the shares, BPR will again be available. Meanwhile, there is control over the children's inheritance.

Chapter 14

Tax planning with trusts

Robert Maas FCA FTII FIIT TEP, Tax Partner, Blackstone Franks LLP

INTRODUCTION

14.1 Trusts have always been an important tool in tax planning. They can be very flexible vehicles. They effectively allow assets to be held in suspense and for the three main attributes of an asset, capital value, income and control, to be separated out.

Not surprisingly, tax authorities do not like trusts because these attributes facilitate tax planning. There is, accordingly, a lot of anti-avoidance provisions in relation to trusts. One of the earliest UK anti-avoidance provisions was the *Statute of Uses 1535*. A use was an early form of trust. A landowner would transfer his land jointly into the name of two or three friends, for the benefit (or use) of either himself or his children. The feudal dues would then not be payable on the death of the original landowner (as he no longer owned the land) or on the death of one of the title-holders, as on his death the land passed to the others (and a new title-holder could be added to ensure that the ownership never reverted to a sole name). The *Statute of Uses* deemed the land to belong to the person for whose use it was held. The statute was nominally introduced to protect the interests of the user as instances occurred where on the original landowner's death the title-holders simply disinherited his children. It is generally accepted though that the real reason was to protect the Royal revenues and other feudal dues that fall due to the King or a local Lord on the death of a landowner.

14.2 A trust is a development of the medieval use. A settlor transfers assets to trustees to be held on the terms laid down by the settlor for the benefit of a beneficiary or a number of beneficiaries.

No formalities are needed to create a trust (other than whatever is needed to transfer legal title of the asset to the trustees). A trust can be oral unless land is involved. However, it is obviously sensible to have a formal trust deed. This both evidences the creation of the trust and avoids misunderstandings both as to the terms of the trust and the identity of the beneficiaries.

14.3 A trust can have a single trustee. However, this creates a problem if the trustee dies, as someone will need to apply to the court to appoint a new trustee. Furthermore, a trust cannot dispose of land unless there are at least two trustees, which again would require the expense of an application to the court if there is a single trustee. It is accordingly normal to have a minimum of two trustees. There is no upper limit on the number of trustees but, as trustees must act unanimously unless the trust deed specifies otherwise, and even where it does all of the trustees are entitled to be involved in decision making, a large number of trustees can make operating the trust unwieldy.

14.4 Many people are suspicious of trusts. There are too many anecdotal horror stories in circulation of where things have gone wrong. Many of these date from times when trusts were far less flexible than a modern trust and it was common to have as the trustees one's solicitor and accountant – so a lot of such stories are actually instances of professional trustees declining to follow the wishes of a settlor because the trust deed did not give them the necessary power to do what the settlor was asking them to do.

14.5 There is actually no need to have any professional trustees (although that is obviously desirable for a charity or other public trust). There is no reason – either under trust law or tax law – why the settlor and his spouse should not be the sole trustees of a family trust. Indeed, as the settlor and his spouse might be expected to be uniquely placed to determine what is in the best interests of their own children, that would in many cases be the sensible thing to do. One situation where some people think that may not be desirable is if the settlor and/or his spouse are amongst the beneficiaries of the trust, as there would be a potential conflict between their duty as a trustee to consider the needs of all of the beneficiaries and their interest as beneficiaries. There could then be a risk that a beneficiary could successfully challenge decisions of the trustees through the courts unless there is an independent trustee who was involved in the decision-making. Many parents are happy to accept the risk of being sued by their children though, as they view such a possibility as remote.

14.6 Another deterrent from the use of trusts is that a trust deed looks complicated. The average trust deed runs to 20 or 30 pages. However, this is not because the trust is complicated (although obviously some are) but because a trust is a creature of statute. As such the trustees are entitled to do only what either trust law or the trust deed itself permits them to do. If the law or deed is silent on what they need to do – such as insure the trust assets – they need either to apply to the court to approve the proposed action or to go ahead and risk challenge by a beneficiary. Accordingly, only two or three pages of a typical trust deed actually set out the terms on which the trustees held the trust property. The rest contains rules for administering the trust, such as the means for appointing and removing and remunerating trustees (a trustee is not entitled to be paid for his services unless the deed authorises it) and a long list of powers to enable the trustees to operate sensibly in relation to the trust assets and obviate

14.7 *Tax planning with trusts*

the need to obtain court approval for a whole range of things that experience has taught the draftsman that trustees frequently need or want to do.

14.7 Many trusts are created by a person's will to take effect on his death. Curiously, such trusts are normally expressed fairly briefly and most seem to operate effectively even though the will does not contain the numerous pages of powers that solicitors write into lifetime settlements. A trust created in a will is often called a will trust.

Trusts are of course not simply, or even primarily, tax avoidance devices. What they actually do in many cases is remove an obstacle that stands in the way of arranging ownership of family assets in a sensible manner. This obstacle is normally either a reluctance by the settlor to give up control over an asset in circumstances where he does not believe that his children have the expertise to exercise such control properly, or a reluctance to give a child a large amount of either income or capital at the stage where his parents do not think he has the maturity to handle such funds sensibly.

The term 'trust' (ie the terms on which property is settled) and 'settlement' (the act of creating a trust) are generally used interchangeably to refer to a trust. 'Settlement' has a different specific meaning in land law in relation to certain trusts of land but is used in the tax legislation to mean a trust as commonly understood.

Types of trust

14.8 There are two main types of trust; interest in possession (IIP) and discretionary. Under an IIP trust someone has an entitlement to the income. Under a discretionary trust no one is entitled to the income; it is at the discretion of the trustees (within the terms of the trust deed) how the income is dealt with.

There are a number of other types of trust that have been created as such by the inheritance tax legislation. These are either hybrids of IIP and discretionary trusts, or are IIP trusts which must also meet specific statutory conditions.

14.9 An 'accumulation and maintenance trust' is a discretionary trust for the benefit of an infant or infants which automatically converts to an IIP trust for the benefit of the infant when he reaches 18 (25 in the case of some trusts created before 22 March 2006) or an earlier age specified in the trust deed.

14.10 A 'trust for bereaved minors' is a will trust for the benefit of an infant child or children of the deceased settlor under which the minor must become absolutely entitled to the assets at or before age 18 and until then it is either an

Tax planning with trusts **14.16**

IIP trust of which the minor is the principal beneficiary or a discretionary trust where the discretion of the trustees is limited to paying the income to or for the benefit of the minor or accumulating it.

14.11 An 'age 18-to-25 trust' is similar to a trust for bereaved minors and, like it, can be created only by will and only by a deceased parent for his own children, but the child need not become entitled to the assets (or attain an IIP) until age 25.

14.12 An 'employee benefit trust' is, as the name suggests, a discretionary trust for the benefit of the employees of a particular employer or persons engaged in a particular trade or profession, (and their spouses or civil partners and dependants).

14.13 A 'newspaper trust' is a type of employee benefit trust which can also include UK newspaper publishing companies or newspaper holding companies amongst its beneficiaries and whose only or principal asset are shares in a newspaper publishing company or newspaper holding company.

14.14 A 'trust for a disabled person' is a discretionary trust which includes a disabled person (as defined in the legislation) as a beneficiary and provides that at least half of the settled property that is applied during his lifetime is applied for that person's benefit.

14.15 Mention should also be made of a 'charitable trust' which is a trust whose income and assets can be used only for charitable purposes (although the special tax rules relating to charities are not dealt with in this chapter) and a protective trust. This is an IIP trust which automatically becomes a discretionary trust, the beneficiaries of which are the person with the interest in possession and his family, if the person with the interest in possession does or tries to do anything which divests him of his right to the income. For example, he becomes bankrupt or tries to sell his interest.

Although there is a basic distinction between an IIP and a discretionary trust it is possible for a person to have an interest in possession in some only of the income of a trust with the trustees having discretion over the remainder, or for sub-trusts to exist within a trust under which some of the assets are held on different trusts to the remainder.

Residence of trustees

14.16 Like an individual a trust can be UK resident or non-UK resident. The residence determines which tax rules apply to the trust – and which anti-avoidance provisions might apply to the settlor or beneficiaries.

14.17 *Tax planning with trusts*

For income tax and capital gains tax purposes a trust is both resident and ordinarily resident in the UK if either:

- all of the trustees are UK resident; or
- at least one of the trustees is UK resident and at the time of creation of the settlement (or immediately before his death in the case of a will trust or other trust arising on death such as on an intestacy) the settlor was either resident, ordinarily resident or domiciled in the UK.

(TCGA 1992, s 475, 476, ITA 2007; s 69)

14.17 In applying these tests a person who acts as trustee in the course of a business which he carries on in the UK through a branch, agency or permanent establishment in the UK must be treated as if he were UK resident if he is not *(ITA 2007, s 475(6); TCGA 1992, s 69(2D))*.

If neither of these conditions are met the trust is neither resident nor ordinarily resident in the UK *(ITA 2007, s 475(3); TCGA 1992, s 69(2E))*. Different rules applied before 5 April 2007 but the above rules apply from that date irrespective of when the trust was created. Under the old rules, the test for CGT was where the majority of the trustees were resident. Accordingly, trusts with one UK trustee and the majority non-UK would have been non-UK resident but will have automatically become UK resident on 6 April 2007.

Extended meaning of settlement

14.18 A settlement is not defined as such for income tax and capital gains tax. However, the legislation states that (unless the contract otherwise requires) 'settled property' means any property held in trust and that references to property comprised in a settlement are references to settled property *(ITA 2007, s 466(2), (4); TCGA 1992, s 68)*. However, property held by a person as nominee for another person or as trustee for another person absolutely entitled as against the trustee, or for another person who would be so entitled but for being an infant or other person lacking legal capacity, is not settled property *(ITA 2007, s 466(3); TCGA 1992, ss 60, 68)*. A person is absolutely entitled to property as against the trustee if he has the exclusive right to direct how the property is to be dealt with (subject to the trustees' right to use the property for the payment of duty, taxes, costs or other outgoings *(ITA 2007, s 466(5); TCGA 1992, s 60(2))*. Where a person becomes absolutely entitled to property as against the trustees, the trustees cease to be trustees and become nominees for the beneficiary if they do not transfer the assets to him.

14.19 For the purpose of *ITTOIA 2005, s 619* (amounts treated as income of settlor) a settlement is defined to include 'any disposition, trust, covenant,

Tax planning with trusts **14.20**

agreement, arrangement or transfer of assets' (*ITTOIA 2005, s 620*). However, the courts have cut down the very wide scope of this wording a little by requiring there to be an element of bounty. This was affirmed by the House of Lords in *IRC v Plummer* (1979) 54 TC 1, where Lord Wilberforce said:

> 'These sections, in other words, though drafted in wide, and increasingly wider language are nevertheless dealing with a limited field – one far narrower than the field of the totality of dispositions, or arrangements, or agreements which a man may make in the course of his life. Is there any common description which can be applied to this? The courts which, inevitably, have had to face this problem, have selected the element of "bounty" as a necessary common characteristic of all the "settlements" which parliament had in mind.'

The *Plummer* case was a tax avoidance scheme which involved the sale of an annuity to a charity. This was held not to create a settlement.

14.20 Transactions which have been held to create a settlement include:

- The allotment of shares at a low price to children of the directors of a company coupled with the payment of a dividend on those shares (*Copeman v Coleman* (1939) 22 TC 594).

- An outright gift of shares by a father to his minor children (*Hood Barrs v IRC* (1946) 27 TC 385).

- Payments into a savings account in the name of minor children (*Thomas v Marshall (Inspector of Taxes)* (1953) 34 TC 178).

- The allotment of shares in a new company to children of a director, coupled with the payment of dividends and the parent providing the company with the opportunity to earn profits (*Butler (Inspector of Taxes) v Wildin* (1989) 61 TC 666).

- The surrender by a life tenant of his interest in a settlement so that the right to income passed to his children under the terms of the settlement (*IRC v Buchanan* (1957) 37 TC 365).

- The creation of a settlement by a grandparent for the benefit of a child coupled with its subscribing for shares in a company and the child's father generating income for the company by working for it at a very low salary (*Crossland v Hawkins* (1960) 39 TC 493).

- A loan by a settlement to the beneficiary's father carrying interest coupled with the father re-lending the money interest free to a company and the settlement distributing the interest to the beneficiary (*IRC v Leiner* (1964) 41 TC 589).

- A covenant to make annual payments to a company controlled by the covenanter until such time as the company was wound up with the payments being used by the company to pay dividends to a third party

14.21 *Tax planning with trusts*

(*IRC v Payne* (1940) 23 TC 610). The transfer was similarly held to be a settlement in *IRC v Morton* (1941) 24 TC 259 and *Dalgety v IRC* (1941) 24 TC 280, where assets were transferred to the company instead of covenanting annual payments.

- The assignment of a life policy to trustees and covenanting with the trustees to continue paying the premium (*IRC v Tennant* (1942) 24 TC 215).

- A reorganisation of share capital so that trustees ended up with preference shares carrying high dividend rights for five years (*IRC v Prince-Smith* (1943) 25 TC 84).

- The issue of preference shares to the wives of the controlling shareholders combined with the declaration of substantial dividends on those shares (*Young (Inspector of Taxes) v Scrutton* (1996) 70 TC 331).

- A gift of shares to a charity with an option to repurchase, combined with the declaration of substantial dividends (*Vandervell v IRC* (1976) 43 TC 519).

- The guarantee of a bank overdraft secured by the deposit of cash, with the bank agreeing to pay no interest on the deposit and charge only 1% pa on the overdraft and dividends being paid by a company to enable the overdraft to be repaid and the deposit to be released (*IRC v Wachtel* (1970) 46 TC 543).

- An actress entering into an agreement with a company to render her services at a nominal salary combined with a settlement by her father for her benefit of the shares in the company (*Mills v IRC* (1972) 49 TC 367).

Although some of these transactions involved the creation of settlements, it was not that settlement that was discerned by the court but a separate deemed settlement resulting from the overall arrangement.

THE TAXATION OF UK RESIDENT SETTLEMENTS

Income tax

14.21 The normal rule is that income of trustees is chargeable at the 22% basic rate, the savings rate or the dividend ordinary rate as the case may be (*ITA 2007, ss 11, 12, 14*).

However, if accumulated or discretionary income arises to the trustees (and the trust is not a charitable trust) it is instead charged at the trust rate, which is either 40% or the dividend trust rate, which is 32.5% (*ITA 2007, ss 9, 479*). Income is accumulated or discretionary income if either it is required to be accumulated or it is payable at the discretion of the trustees or of any other person (*ITA 2007, s 480(1)*). In particular income is payable at a person's discretion if he has discretion over whether, or the extent to which, it is to be accumulated, the persons to whom the income is to be paid, or how much is to be paid to any person (*ITA 2007, s 480(2)*). Income is excluded from being accumulated or discretionary income if it is deemed to be the income of some person other than the trustees, it is held for the purpose of a superannuation fund relating to undertakings outside the UK (and not held as a member of a property investment LLP) or is income from service charges (*ITA 2007, s 480(3)–(6)*).

14.22 Where trustees are taxable at the trust rate deemed income under the following provisions are also taxable at that rate.

1. A payment by a company on the redemption or purchase of its own shares.
2. Accrued income profits under *ITA 2003, ss 628(5)* or *630(2)*.
3. Offshore income gains under *ICTA 1988, s 761(1)*.
4. Deemed income of employee share ownership trusts under *FA 1989, ss 68(2)* or *71(4)*.
5. The income element of premiums on leases under *ITTOIA 2005, ss 276–307*.
6. Profits from deeply discounted securities under *ITTOIA 2005, s 429*.
7. Gains from life insurance contracts under *ITTOIA 2005, s 467*.
8. Gains on transactions in deposits under *ITTOIA 2005, s 554*.
9. Gains on disposals of options under *ITTOIA 2005, s 557*.
10. Proceeds of sale of foreign dividend coupons under *ITTOIA 2005, s 573*.
11. Deemed income from transactions in land under *ITA 2005, ss 752–772*.

Amounts within 1 above are taxed at the dividend trust rate but that under the other heads (including curiously head 10) is taxed at the 40% rate (*ITA 2007, ss 481, 482*).

14.23 Where the trust rate or the dividend trust rate applies, a deduction is allowed for expenses of the trustees which are properly chargeable to income (ie legally chargeable ignoring the express terms of the settlement) (*ITA 2007, s 484*). Any unrelieved expenses can be carried forward to subsequent years (*ITA 2007, s 485*). Expenses are set first against dividend income from UK companies (and stock dividends or the release of a loan to a participator in a close company). Any excess is set against other dividend income, then against savings income and finally against other income. The relievable expenses must be grossed up, so relief is not obtainable at the basic rate, dividend rate or savings rate (*ITA 2007, s 486*).

14.24 *Tax planning with trusts*

14.24 The trust rates and dividend trust rates do not apply to the first £1,000 pa of income. Where the settlor has created more than one settlement the £1,000 figure is divided by the number of settlements but if there are more than five the first £200 in each settlement is taxable at the basic rate, savings rate or dividend rate as the case may be (*ITA 2007, ss 491, 492*).

Where the trustees make a discretionary payment to a beneficiary the payment is grossed up at the trust rate and the beneficiary (or the settlor if the payment is made to a minor child of the settlor) is treated as having paid tax at that rate – and so can claim a refund if he is not taxable or is taxable at the basic rate only (*ITA 2007, s 494*).

14.25 The trustees must account to HMRC for the grossing up amount to the extent that it exceeds the balance of their tax pool. This is the accumulated tax suffered by the trustees. However, tax credits in respect of dividends and other notional tax is not included in the tax pool.

It will be seen that an interest-in-possession trust is taxed more lightly than a discretionary trust. Accordingly, where the beneficiaries of a trust are not higher rate taxpayers it is preferable from an income tax point of view to use an interest-in-possession trust. There are inheritance tax consequences in doing so where the trust was created before 22 March 2006, but for trusts created after that date this is no longer a problem in many cases.

14.26 Using an interest-in-possession trust does mean having to fix the division of income amongst the beneficiaries in advance. However, a well-drawn trust is a very flexible entity. There is no reason why the trustees should not have power to revoke all or part of an interest in possession and instead grant an interest in possession in that part of the income to a different beneficiary. By this means it should be possible to divide the income broadly as the trustees would have done with a discretionary settlement, but using future rather than past income to adjust the share going to each beneficiary.

Charge on settlor

14.27 In some circumstances trust income is treated as income of the settlor (and not of the trust). This can happen in three circumstances:

- where the settlor retains an interest in the settlement;
- where income is paid to an unmarried minor child of the settlor;
- where the settlor receives a capital sum from the settlement or a body connected with the settlement.

14.28 A settlor has an interest in the settlement if there are any circumstances in which the settled property or any related property (which includes the income from the settled property) is payable to the settlor or to his spouse or civil partner, or is applicable for the benefit of any such person (or will or may become so payable or applicable) (*ITTOIA 2005, s 625(1)*).

There are a number of exceptions:

- If the only circumstance in which that can happen is:
    - the bankruptcy of a beneficiary (or a potential beneficiary);
    - the assignment or charging of the trust property by a beneficiary (or potential beneficiary);
    - in the case of a marriage (or civil partnership) settlement, the death of both parties to the marriage and of all or any of the children of one or both of them;
    - the death at or before age 25 of a child of the settlor who had become beneficially entitled to the property or any related property.
- If the only circumstance in which that can happen is the bankruptcy of a beneficiary or the assignment or charging of the beneficiary's interest in the trust, whilst that person is alive and under 25.
- The settlor does not have an interest in the trust property if his spouse or civil partner dies and they are separated under an order of the court or a separation agreement, or in circumstances that the separation is likely to be permanent.
- The settlor does not have an interest in the trust property merely because his widow, widower or surviving civil partner may do so at a future time.
- The settlor does not have an interest in the settled property at a time when he is unmarried merely by virtue of the fact that he may subsequently marry (or become a civil partner of) a beneficiary (*ITTOIA 2005, s 625*).

An outright gift of property from one spouse (or civil partner) to the other is not a settlement provided that:

- the gift carries a right to the whole of the income from the property gifted; and
- the property gifted is not wholly or substantially a right to income.

(*ITTOIA 2005, s 626(1)–(3)*)

A gift is not an outright gift for this purpose if it is subject to conditions or if there are any circumstances in which the property gifted (or any related property) is payable to the donor, or is (or will or may become) applicable for the benefit of the donor (*s 626(4)*).

14.29 *Tax planning with trusts*

14.29 It is important to realise that, as an arrangement can constitute a settlement, the property gifted by the donor is not necessarily the settled property; it may simply be part of the machinery making up the settlement. Thus the fact that a gift of shares carries with it the right to dividends will not necessarily take the dividends out of the section if the arrangement is that the donor will work for the company for a nominal salary and the company will use the income generated by his work to pay dividends. That is HMRC's contention in *Jones v Garnett (Inspector of Taxes)* [2007] STC 1536.

14.30 The settlor is not taxable under these provisions in relation to income which either:

- arises under a settlement made by one party to a marriage (or civil partnership) by way of provision for the other after the dissolution or annulment of the marriage (or civil partnership) or while they are separated under an order of a court, under a separation agreement, or where the separation is likely to be permanent, where the income is payable to (or applicable for the benefit of) the other party;

- consists of annual payments made by an individual for commercial reasons in connection with the individual's trade, profession or vocation;

- consists of qualifying donations to charity (within *FA 1990, s 25* (gift aid));

- consists of a benefit under a registered pension scheme (or other specified pension scheme) (*ITTOIA 2005, s 627*); or

- is donated by the trustees to a charity in the tax year in which it arises (and it is income to which a charity is entitled under the terms of the trust) (*ITTOIA 2005, s 628*).

14.31 Income is also treated as income of the settlor (and not of any other person) if it is paid to, or for the benefit of, a child of the settlor (including a stepchild) who is under 18 and unmarried (and not in a civil partnership) (*ITTOIA 2005, s 629(1), (7)*). This does not apply if the total amount of income paid to (or for the benefit of) the child during the tax year does not exceed £100 (*ITTOIA 2005, s 629(2)*). As with *s 624*, there is also an exception for income donated to charity by the trust (*ITTOIA 2005, s 630*).

If the trustees retain or accumulate income as an addition to capital and a payment is subsequently made in connection with the settlement to (or for the benefit of) a minor unmarried child of the settlor, that payment must be treated as a payment of income up to the amount of income retained or accumulated (*ITTOIA 2005, s 631*).

14.32 Any capital sum paid directly or indirectly in any tax year by a settlement to the settlor (or to his spouse or, presumably, civil partner) is treated as income of the settlor for that year, up to the amount of 'income available' up to the end of that year. This is the income of the settlement from inception which has neither been distributed nor treated as income of the settlor under some other provision (and less tax at the trust rate on that undistributed income less any part taxed on the settlor under *ITTOIA 2005, ss 624* or *629*) (*ITTOIA 2005, s 635*). The capital sum is treated as a net amount from which tax has been deducted at the trust rate, so the taxable amount is the grossed up figure (*ITTOIA 2005, s 640*).

If the capital sum exceeds the income available the excess is carried forward and taxed as income of the settlor in future years (up to a maximum of ten future years) (*ITTOIA 2005, s 633(3), (4)*).

14.33 A capital sum for this purpose is:

- a loan;
- a loan repayment;
- any other payment which is made otherwise than as income and not for full consideration in money or money's worth; and
- any sum paid by the trustees to a third party either at the settlor's discretion, or as a result of the assignment by the settlor of his right to receive that sum, or which is otherwise paid or applied for the benefit of the settlor.

(*ITTOIA 2005, s 634*)

References to the settlor include his spouse and the settlor (or his spouse) jointly with some other person (*ITTOIA 2005, s 634(7)*).

Trust expenses which, in the absence of any express provision of the settlement, would be properly chargeable to income are deducted in calculating the available income (*ITTOIA 2005, s 636*).

14.34 If this charge is triggered by the making of a loan, and the loan is subsequently repaid, income arising after the date of repayment is not taxed on the settlor (*ITTOIA 2005, s 638(1)*). If the settlement makes a loan to the settlor, and there have been previous loans to him that have been wholly repaid, the new loan attracts the tax charge only to the extent that it exceeds the amount previously taxed on the settlor by reference to the earlier loan (*ITTOIA 2005, s 638(2), (3)*). If the capital sum is the repayment of a loan by the settlor and he subsequently makes a fresh loan which is at least equal to the capital sum, the income arising after the date of the fresh loan is not caught by the section (*ITTOIA 2005, s 638(4), (5)*). If the capital sum is a loan and a tax charge has been triggered on the settlor on the release of that loan under *ITTOIA 2005*,

14.35 *Tax planning with trusts*

s 416 (release of loan to participator in close company) the amount taxed is not also taxable under *s 633* (*ITTOIA 2005, s 639*).

14.35 If a capital sum is paid to the settlor by a body corporate connected with the settlement and an associated payment has been, or is, made (directly or indirectly) to that body by the settlement, the capital sum is treated as having been paid to the settlor by the settlement (*ITTOIA 2005, s 641*). There is an exception where the whole of the loan is repaid within 12 months and no loans to or by the settlor to the body corporate within the previous five years have been outstanding for more than 12 months (*ITTOIA 2005, s 642*). This will ensure that a director's loan account which is cleared regularly by voting remuneration or dividends will not trigger the charge. A body corporate is connected with a settlement if it is a close company (or would be if it were UK resident) in which the trust is a participator or if it is controlled by such a company (*ITTOIA 2005, ss 637(8), 643(2)*). An associated payment is a capital sum paid to the body corporate by the trust and any other sum paid, or asset transferred by the trust other than for full consideration in money or money's worth in the five years preceding or the five years following the payment of the capital sum to the settlor (*ITTOIA 2005, s 643(3)*).

It should particularly be noted that these provisions cannot apply to an interest in possession settlement as the income of such a settlement belongs to the beneficiaries and so cannot be retained or accumulated by the settlement.

Capital gains tax

14.36 Capital gains of trusts are taxable at the 40% trust tax rate, irrespective of whether the trust is a discretionary one or there is an interest in possession (*TCGA 1992, s 4(1AA)*). Furthermore, the CGT annual exemption for a trust is lower than that for an individual. For 2007/08 it is a maximum of £4,600. However, where a person is a settlor of more than one settlement (ignoring one created before 6 June 1978) the £4,600 figure is divided by the number of such settlements to determine the annual exemption of each, subject to a minimum exemption of £920 per settlement (which will apply where there are more than five) (*TCGA 1992, Sch 1, para 2*).

Accordingly, a settlement can be unattractive from a CGT point of view if the beneficiaries are basic rate taxpayers as if the assets were held directly by the beneficiary they might attract a lower tax rate on sale.

14.37 There are two exceptions. In arriving at the annual allowance of a settlement, no account is taken of any other settlement for a disabled person (see below), any settlement that is non-UK resident throughout the tax year or of any charitable settlement or sponsored superannuation scheme (*TCGA 1992, Sch 1,* *para 2(7)*). A settlement for a disabled person attracts the full £9,200 annual exemption. The settlement must secure that during the lifetime of the beneficiary at least half of the settled property which is applied is applied for the benefit of that beneficiary and the beneficiary either must be entitled to at least half of the income from the settled property or the trustees must not have power to pay income to anyone other than that beneficiary. The beneficiary must be either mentally disabled (within the *Mental Health Act 1983*) so as to be incapable of managing his own affairs, or in receipt of attendance allowance (under *Social Security Contributions and Benefits Act 1992, s 64*) or disability living allowance (within *SSCBA 1992, s 71*) by virtue of entitlement to the care component at the highest or middle rate. If a person creates more than one such settlement by the same settlor the annual exemption must again be divided by the number of settlements subject to a minimum of £920 per settlement – but disabled settlements are not aggregated with other settlements for this purpose (*TCGA 1992, Sch 1, para 1*). A non-resident settlement does not attract any annual exemption.

14.38 The transfer of property into a settlement is a disposal by the settlor and will trigger CGT on the settlor by reference to the market value of CGT assets put into the settlement (*TCGA 1992, s 70*). If the asset settled is a business asset (within *TCGA 1992, s 165*) the settlor can elect to treat the disposal as being at a no gain/no loss price in which case the settlement will be deemed to have acquired the asset at that price for CGT purposes (*TCGA 1992, s 165*). A similar election can be made by the settlor in relation to other assets if the settlement is within the IHT discretionary trust regime (*TCGA 1992, s 260*). Virtually all settlements created after 22 March 2006 (other than some will trusts) will come within this regime. If the gift to the settlement is covered by an IHT exemption – as opposed to being within the nil-rate band – hold-over relief will not apply (unless the exemption is that for transfers to be political parties, to maintenance funds for historic buildings or of heritage property) (*TCGA 1992, s 260(2)(b)*).

14.39 There is a deemed disposal by the trust (and a reacquisition by the trustees as nominee for the beneficial owner) at market value where a beneficiary becomes absolutely entitled to any settled property as against the trustee, ie where he became entitled to the asset or would do so but for being an infant or other person under a disability (*TCGA 1992, s 71(1), (3)*). Again, the tax can sometimes be deferred by making an election under *TCGA 1992, ss 165 or 260*.

It needs to be realised that a beneficiary can become entitled to assets as against the trustees, automatically as a result of a provision of the trust deed. For example if the deed provides that the assets shall be held in trust for A whilst he is under 30 and that when he reaches 30 A will become entitled to the assets, A will become beneficially entitled to the assets as against the trustee on his 30th birthday, so triggering a tax charge, without the need for any decision by the trustees.

14.40 *Tax planning with trusts*

14.40 If a loss accrues to the trust on a person becoming absolutely entitled to an asset as against the trustees and the trust cannot utilise that loss in relation to disposals of other assets before that time, the loss is treated as accruing to the beneficiary, but can only be utilised by him against gains from the same asset (or, if the asset is an interest in land from that interest or any other asset deriving from it (*TCGA 1992, s 71(2)*).

If on the death of a life tenant IHT is payable in relation to the settled property (as will apply to a pre-22 March 2006 IIP settlement and many post 22 March 2006 will trusts) the assets in which the interest subsisted are deemed to be disposed of and reacquired at their market value at the date of death – but no chargeable gain is treated as accruing to the settlement, ie there is simply an uplift in the settlement's CGT base cost of the assets (*TCGA 1992, s 72*).

If a beneficiary disposes of his interest in a settlement that disposal is exempt from CGT provided that either the interest was created under the terms of the settlement or by any other person, other than one who acquired (or derived his title from someone else who acquired) it for a consideration in money or money's worth.

Charge on settlor

14.41 The settlor is taxable on trust gains (in place of the settlement) if he has an interest in the settlement at any time during the tax year in which the gains are realised. A settlor has an interest in the settlement for this purpose if either:

- Any property which is (or may at any time be) comprised in the settlement, or any derived property (such as the income from the trust property) is (or will or may become) payable to or applicable for the benefit of the settlor or his spouse or civil partner or of a dependent child of the settlor in any circumstances whatsoever. Or

- The settlor or his spouse or civil partner or a dependent child of the settlor, enjoys a benefit deriving directly or indirectly from any property which is comprised in the settlement or any derived property (*TCGA 1992, s 77(2), (2A)*). A dependent child is one who is under 18 and unmarried (and does not have a civil partner) and includes a stepchild. A person does not have an interest in the settlement merely because it allows the settled property to be paid to a dependent child of his if at the time the gain arises he has no such children (*TCGA 1992, s 77(3A), (3B)*).

14.42 A settlor does not have an interest in a settlement merely because at the time the gain arises someone to whom he is not married, but he might later marry, is a beneficiary; or because his spouse (or civil partner) is a beneficiary if they are separated under an order of the court or a separation agreement, or in

Tax planning with trusts **14.45**

circumstances that the separation is likely to be permanent; or his widow or widower (but not his spouse) is a beneficiary (*TCGA 1992, s 77(3)*).

14.43 A settlor is also treated as not having an interest in the settlement if (and so long as) none of the settled property (and no derived property) can become payable for the benefit of himself or his spouse or civil partner except in the event of:

- the bankruptcy of a beneficiary;
- an assignment of, or charge on, the settled property (or any derived property) being made or given by any person;
- in the case of a marriage (or civil partnership) settlement, the death of both parties to the marriage or civil partnership and of all or any of the children of the family of the parties to the marriage or partnership (being a child of one or both of them); or
- the death of a child of the settlor who had become beneficially entitled to the settled property (or derived property) at or below age 25.

(*TCGA 1992, s 77(4), (4A)*)

14.44 Similarly, a settlor is treated as not having an interest in the settlement if, and so long as, some person is alive and under 25 during whose life the property (or derived property) cannot become payable to the settlor or his spouse or civil partner except in the event of that person becoming bankrupt or assigning or changing his interest (*TCGA 1992, s 77(5)*).

Gains are not attributed to the settlor in a tax year where either:

- the settlor dies in that year;
- the interest is of the settlor's spouse or civil partner only and the spouse or partner dies during the year or the two cease to be married during the year; or
- the interest is of the settlor's dependent child only and the child dies during the year (and the settlor has no subsequent dependent child during the year who can benefit from the settlement).

(*TCGA 1992, s 77(5)*).

14.45 Derived property means:

(a) income from the settled property;
(b) property directly or indirectly representing the proceeds of the settled property (or of income from it); and

14.46 *Tax planning with trusts*

(c) income from property within (a) or (b).

(*TCGA 1992, s 77(8)*)

14.46 In *West (Inspector of Taxes) v Trennery* (2003) 76 TC 713, Mr Trennery created two settlements. He transferred shares to the first. The trustees borrowed an amount roughly equal to the value of the shares and paid it to the second, at the same time removing Mr Trennery and his wife as beneficiaries of the first. In the next tax year the shares were sold and the loan repaid. It was held in the House of Lords that the funds of the second settlement (of which Mr Trennery was a beneficiary) were derived property of the first while the first continued to hold the shares. This was because the mortgage moneys represented the proceeds of the shares and thus were derived property when received by the first settlement, and they could not cease to be derived property merely because they ceased to be held in the first settlement. This gives a wide meaning to 'proceeds' of the property as the normal meaning of the word connotes a sale, whereas a mortgage is a charge on property which has not been sold.

14.47 Where settled property is held on qualifying trusts for the benefit of a vulnerable person the trustees can elect that the capital gains should be taxed as gains of the vulnerable person instead of the settlor (provided that the vulnerable person is resident or ordinarily resident in the UK and does not die during the tax year) (*FA 2005, ss 30, 31*). Such an election can reduce the rate of tax payable on the gains.

If the vulnerable person is not resident or ordinarily resident in the UK they can elect that the gain should be taxed on the trustees, not the settlor, and that their liability should be limited to what it would have been had the gains accrued to the trust and been taxable on the beneficiary under *TCGA 1992, s 77* (see below) but the beneficiary's tax were payable by the trustees (*FA 2005, ss 32, 33*).

14.48 A qualifying trust for this purpose is one the property of which is held on trust for the benefit of a disabled person or a relevant minor. In the case of a trust for a disabled person, during the lifetime of that person (or until the earlier termination of the trust) any of the trust property which is applied for the benefit of one beneficiary must be applied for the benefit of the disabled person, and either the disabled person be entitled to all of the income from the settled property or none of it can be applied for the benefit of any other beneficiary (ie it must either be paid to or for the benefit of the disabled person or accumulated). A trust for a relevant minor must be either a statutory trust under the *Administration of Estates Act 1925, ss 46* or *47(1)* (succession on intestacy) or must be established under the will of a deceased parent of the minor or the Criminal Injuries Compensation Scheme, and must provide that the minor will become absolutely entitled to the settled property and any income from it at age 18 and that until then the settled property and income therefrom can be used only for the benefit of that minor (*FA 2005, ss 34, 35*).

14.49 A disabled person is a person who by reason of mental disorder within the *Mental Health Act 1983* is incapable of managing his affairs, or who is in receipt of attendance allowance or disability living allowance by virtue of entitlement to the care component at the highest or middle rate (or would receive such an allowance if he were to meet the prescribed conditions as to residence in *SSCBA 1992, ss 64(1), or 71(6)*) (*FA 2005, s 38*). A relevant minor is a person under the age of 18 and at least one of whose parents has died (*FA 2005, s 38*).

THE TAXATION OF NON-RESIDENT TRUSTEES

Income tax

14.50 The normal rule is that non-UK residents are chargeable to income tax only on UK earnings and property income and on other income only to the extent that tax is deducted at source (*ITA 2007, ss 811–814*).

However, this rule does not apply to a non-resident trust if it has a beneficiary who is either an individual who is ordinarily resident in the UK or a UK resident company (*ITA 2007, s 812*). A beneficiary for this purpose includes an actual or potential beneficiary who is (or will, or may, become) entitled under the trust to receive some or all of any income of the trust (or capital which represents amounts originally received as income) or to whom some or all of any income of the trust may be paid or for whose benefit such income might be used in the exercise of a discretion conferred by the trust (*ITA 2007, s 812(2)–(5)*). It should be noted that the provision does not apply if all of the income beneficiaries are non-resident but trust capital can be paid to a UK resident. Accordingly, a trust with a non-resident life tenant and a resident remainderman would not be caught. Where a trust falls within *s 812* it will of course be taxable on UK source income only, as the territoriality principle will prevent the UK taxing a non-resident on non-UK source income.

14.51 The provisions in relation to UK settlements that attribute income of a settlement to the settlor in certain circumstances (*ITTOIA 2005, ss 624–629*) apply equally to non-resident settlements. So do the provisions that tax the income of a settlement (other than an interest-in-possession settlement) at the trust rate (*ITA 2007, ss 479–482*).

Where a non-resident settlement has both UK and non-UK source income the deduction for trustees' expenses is restricted in the proportion that non-UK (or other non-taxable) income bears to the total trust income (*ITA 2007, s 487*).

It also needs to be borne in mind that the anti-avoidance rules in relation to the transfer of assets to a non-resident as a result of which a person who is ordinarily resident in the UK has power to enjoy the income of the non-resident or receives

14.52 *Tax planning with trusts*

a benefit from the non-resident (*ITA 2007, ss 714–751*) apply to non-UK trusts and, where relevant, their underlying companies, in the same way as with other non-residents.

Capital gains tax

14.52 A non-UK settlement, like any other non-UK resident, is not liable to UK capital gains tax (except in relation to assets used for the purpose of a trade) (*TCGA 1992, s 2(1)*).

However, the gains of a non-UK settlement can be attributed to either the settlor or to beneficiaries.

Trust gains can be taxed on the settlor only if he is domiciled in the UK at some time during the tax year in which the gain accrues and he is either resident or ordinarily resident here at some time during that year (*TCGA 1992, s 86(1)(c)*). In addition the settlement must be a 'qualifying settlement' and the settlor must have an interest in the settlement at some time during the tax year concerned (*TCGA 1992, s 86(1)(a), (d)*).

14.53 A settlement is a qualifying settlement if it was created after 18 March 1991 or if it was created before that date and subsequent to 18 March 1991 either -

- property or income is provided directly or indirectly for the purpose of the settlement otherwise than under a transaction entered into at arm's length (and otherwise in pursuance of a liability incurred before 19 March 1991) – but any additions solely to meet a deficit on the trust expenses can be ignored;

- the trust became non-UK resident (or fell to be regarded as non-resident under a double tax agreement);

- the terms of the settlement are varied so that either the settlor, a spouse or civil partner of the settlor, a child or grandchild of the settlor or the settlor's spouse, the spouse or civil partner of a child or grandchild, or a company controlled by any such person or persons (or associated with a company so controlled) becomes for the first time a person who will or might benefit under the settlement;

- any such person as in (c) enjoys a benefit from the settlement for the first time and under the terms of the settlement as they stood at 18 March 1991 would not have been capable of enjoying a benefit from the settlement after that date; or

Tax planning with trusts **14.55**

- the settlement ceases to be a 'protected settlement' at a time after 5 April 1999

(TCGA 1992, Sch 5, para 9(1)–(6A))

14.54 A settlement is a protected settlement if it was formed before 19 March 1991 and at 5 April 1999 (and at all times thereafter) the only beneficiaries of the settlement are -

- children of the settlor (or of a spouse or civil partner of the settlor) who are under 18 (at the end of the tax year immediately preceding that in which the gain arises),
- unborn children of the settlor (or of a spouse or civil partner of the settlor or of a future spouse or civil partner of the settlor),
- future spouses or civil partners of any children (or future children) of the settlor or a spouse or future spouse (or civil partner or future civil partner) of the settlor,
- a future spouse or civil partner of the settlor, or
- person outside the defined categories (ie he is not a person whose relationship to the settlor (or any of the settlors if there is more than one) would give the settlor an interest in the settlement *(TCGA 1992, Sch 5, para 9(10A), (10B))*.

In applying these tests a person is a beneficiary if there are any circumstances whatsoever in which any of the settled property (or income therefrom) is, or will or may become, applicable for his benefit or payable to him or he enjoys a benefit directly or indirectly from any of the settled property or the income therefrom *(TCGA 1992, Sch 5, para 9(10C)(10D))*.

14.55 The settlor has an interest in the settlement if any of the settled property, or income therefrom, is (or will or may become) applicable for the benefit of (or payable to) a defined person in any circumstances whatsoever, or any defined person enjoys a benefit directly or indirectly from any of the settled property or income therefrom *(TCGA 1992, Sch 5, para 2(1))*.

The defined persons are:

(a) the settlor;
(b) the spouse or civil partner of the settlor;
(c) a child of the settlor (or of the settlor's spouse or civil partner);
(d) the spouse or civil partner of any such child;
(e) any grandchild of the settlor (or of the settlor's spouse or civil partner);

14.56   *Tax planning with trusts*

(f)   the spouse or civil partner of any such grandchild;

(g)   a company controlled by one or more of the above; and

(h)   a company associated with a company controlled by one or more of the above.

(TCGA 1992, Sch 5, para 2(3))

14.56   There are the usual exceptions where the defined person can benefit only in the event of the bankruptcy or similar event of someone who is not a defined person *(TCGA 1992, Sch 5, para 2(4), (5))*. Heads (e) and (f) do not apply to a settlement created before 17 March 1998 unless property is added to it after that date, it becomes non-resident after that date, its terms are varied after that date or a grandchild (or spouse) receives a benefit after that date he could not have received under the terms of the settlement as they stood at 17 March 1998 *(TCGA 1992, Sch 5, para 2A)*.

It will be seen that this provision is significantly wider than the corresponding income tax provision, which does not include either grandchildren or adult children of the settlor.

14.57   If the settlor does not have an interest in the settlement the trust gains are attributed to beneficiaries. The amount to be attributed in a tax year is of course the trust gains for the year (after taper relief) plus any unattributed gains of earlier years *(TCGA 1992, s 87(1), (2))*. This is attributed to beneficiaries (including, curiously, non-resident beneficiaries) who receive capital payments from the settlement in the tax year or who received capital payments in earlier years which have not yet been matched with gains. The gains are then attributed to those beneficiaries in proportion to their capital payments up to the amount of such payments. Any unattributed part of the gains is carried forward to the next tax year *(TCGA 1992, s 87(4), (5))*. Gains attributed to a beneficiary who is not domiciled in the UK are not subject to tax. Gains attributed to beneficiaries who are UK resident and domiciled are treated as gains realised by the beneficiary but are not of course eligible for taper relief (as that has already been given in arriving at the trust gains) *(TCGA 1992, s 87(7))*.

14.58   If the settlement migrates to the UK without all of the past gains having been attributed to beneficiaries the attribution continues so as to attribute those gains to beneficiaries who receive capital payments from the settlement in subsequent years *(TCGA 1992, s 89)*.

To the extent that gains are not matched with capital payments in the tax year following that in which the gain arises, the beneficiary is also liable to a surcharge on the tax. The surcharge is 10% pa for the period from 1 December following the tax year in which the gain arose to 30 November in the tax year following that in which the capital payment is made. The surcharge cannot run for more than six years though, so it is effectively limited to 24% of the gain (60% of the 40% tax rate) (*TCGA 1992, s 91*).

14.59 If the settlement distributes assets to another settlement the unallocated trust gains of the first are treated as trust gains of the second settlement and allocated to beneficiaries who receive capital payments from the second settlement. If part only of the settled property is transferred then only a proportionate part of the unallocated gains of the first settlement is transferred to the second (*TCGA 1992, s 90*).

The normal exemption for a disposal by a beneficiary of his interest in a settlement does not apply to an interest in a non-resident settlement (*TCGA 1992, ss 76(1A), 85*). Such a disposal is accordingly chargeable to CGT. In addition, where the interest is disposed of for consideration and the trustees were UK resident at any time in the tax year in which the disposal occurs, the settlor was UK resident or ordinarily resident in that year or in any of the five previous tax years, and the settlor has an interest in the settlement in that or in the previous two tax years, the trustees must be treated as having sold and immediately reacquired the relevant underlying assets of the settlement, ie the part of the assets in which the beneficiary's interest subsisted (*TCGA 1992, Sch 4A, paras 1–8*). *Schedule 4A* displaces the charge on the beneficiary, unless that would be greater than the charge on the trustees (or there would be a lower loss on the disposal) under *Sch 4A* – in which case *s 76(1A)* displaces the *Sch 4A* charge (*TCGA 1992, Sch 4A, para 10(2)*).

14.60 If a UK resident settlement ceases to be UK resident at any time the migration triggers a deemed disposal and reacquisition of all of the trust assets at the time of the migration so as to create a taxable gain while the settlement is UK resident (*TCGA 1992, s 80*). There is an exception where the migration occurs because of the death of a trustee provided that the settlement becomes UK resident again within the following six months (and the assets have not been disposed of during the period of non-residence (*TCGA 1992, s 81*).

If the tax due on the migration of a settlement is not paid within six months of the due date, HMRC can recover it from anybody who was a trustee at any time in the 12 months prior to the migration. They cannot recover the tax from a person who ceased to be a trustee some time before the migration and can show that at the time that he ceased to be a trustee there was no proposal that the trust should emigrate (*TCGA 1992, s 82*).

14.61 If it is wished to migrate a settlement it needs to be borne in mind that the *Trustee Act 1925, s 37(1)(c)* provides that a trustee should not be discharged from his trust unless there will be either a trust corporation or at least two individuals to act as trustees to perform the trust. In most cases a trust corporation is a company incorporated in either the UK or another EU country. In *Jasmine Trustees Ltd v Wells & Hind (a firm)* [2007] STC 660 UK trustees

14.62 *Tax planning with trusts*

resigned and were replaced by an Isle of Man company. It was held that the resignation was ineffective, with the result that the previous UK trustees were still the trustees, so the trust remained UK resident and all of the acts of the new trustees must have been entered into as agent for the real trustees.

14.62 If the trustees of a non-resident settlement with a UK resident beneficiary or a UK resident and domiciled settlor makes a transfer of value and that transfer is linked with trustee borrowing, the trustees are deemed to dispose of and immediately reacquire the whole (or a proportion of) the chargeable assets of the settlement (*TCGA 1992, Sch 4B, para 1*).

For this purpose trustees make a transfer of value if they:

- lend money or any other asset to any person;
- transfer an asset to any person either for no consideration or at an undervalue; or
- issue a security of any description to any person either for no consideration or at an undervalue.

14.63 The transfer of value is treated as made when the loan is made, the transfer is effectively completed (ie the transferee becomes for practical purposes unconditionally entitled to the asset) or the security is issued as the case may be (*TCGA 1992, Sch 4B, para 2*).

A transfer of value is linked with trustee borrowing if at the time of the loan or transfer there is outstanding trustee borrowing, ie either:

- any loan obligation is outstanding; or
- there are trustee borrowing that have not been either applied for normal trust purposes or triggered a tax charge under Sch 4B in relation to an earlier transfer of value.

(*TCGA 1992, Sch 4B, para 5*)

14.64 A borrowing is applied for normal trust purposes if it is used to acquire a trust asset either at arm's length or at no more than an arm's-length price, is used to repay an earlier borrowing for such a purpose, or is used to meet bona-fide current trust management expenses (*TCGA 1992, Sch 4B, para 6*).

The deemed disposal is of the whole of the trust assets unless the amount of value transferred is either:

- less than both the amount of outstanding trustee borrowing and the effective value of the remaining chargeable assets, in which case the deemed disposal and reacquisition is of the proportion of each of the remaining chargeable assets given by:

$$\frac{\text{amount of value transferred}}{\text{effective value of the remaining chargeable assets}}$$

- less than the effective value of the remaining chargeable assets (but not less than the outstanding trustee borrowing) in which case the deemed disposal and reacquisition is of the proportion of each of the remaining chargeable assets given by:

$$\frac{\text{amount of outstanding trustee borrowing}}{\text{effective value of the remaining chargeable assets}}$$

14.65 The effective value of the remaining chargeable assets is their aggregate market value less so much of that value as is attributable to trustee borrowing (*TCGA 1992, Sch 4B, para 11*). The value of an asset is attributable to trustee borrowing to the extent that the trustees applied the borrowing to acquire or enhance the value of the asset (or the asset represents directly or indirectly an asset whose value was attributable to the trustees having so applied the proceeds of trustee borrowing (*TCGA 1992, Sch 4B, para 11*).

14.66 Where *Sch 4B* applies the gains are of course attributed to the settlor (if he has an interest in the settlement) or to beneficiaries who receive capital payments from the settlement (if he does not) (*TCGA 1992, Sch 4C*).

This provision prevents avoidance of the tax charge by the trustees borrowing against the trust assets and distributing the money borrowed instead of selling the assets and distributing the proceeds. It was aimed against what was known as the 'flip-flop' scheme under which trust 1 would borrow and distribute its assets to trust 2 and in the next tax year sell the assets and use the gain to repay the borrowing. As trust 1 made no capital payment to beneficiaries and trust 2, which did make capital payments, realised no gains this was thought to avoid the tax charge. In fact in the light of the subsequent decision in *West (Inspector of Taxes) v Trennery* (2003) 76 TC 713 (see above) the scheme probably did not work but the very complex legislation in *TCGA 1992, Schs 4B* and *4C* nevertheless remains.

Inheritance tax

14.67 Trusts are within the scope of inheritance tax but are taxed under a special IHT regime – or to be more precise a number of different IHT regimes. The residence or domicile of the settlor is irrelevant, except to the extent that non-UK assets of a settlement are excluded property (and therefore outside the scope of IHT) if the settlor was non-UK domiciled (and not deemed UK domiciled) at the time that the settlement was made (*IHTA 1984, s 58(3)*).

14.68 *Tax planning with trusts*

There are two main trust regimes, the interest-in-possession regime and the standard or discretionary trust regime. The latter is a misnomer. It applies to all trusts created after 22 March 2006 including inter vivos interest-in-possession trusts. The interest-in-possession regime applies to interest-in-possession trusts created before 22 March 2006 and to some will trusts created after that date.

The standard or discretionary trust regime

14.68 There are three possible occasions of charge to IHT:

- on the settlor or creation of the settlement (the 'entry charge');
- on the settlement on each tenth anniversary (the 'ten-yearly charge');
- on distributions from the settlement or the termination of the settlement (the 'exit charge').

The entry charge

14.69 Transferring assets into settlements constitutes a gift. A gift into settlement is not a potentially exempt transfer, so it attracts IHT but at 50% of normal rates, ie the tax charge is 20% of the value of the assets put into the settlement in excess of the £300,000 nil-rate-band. As with other gifts, prior gifts within the seven years prior to the gift into settlement are aggregated with the gift into settlement to determine how much, if any, of the nil-rate-band is available to utilise against the gift.

The entry charge does not apply in the case of a will trust as the death of the deceased will have triggered IHT and the creation of the trust is simply the disposition of part of the assets on that death.

The ten-yearly charge

14.70 The ten-yearly charge is imposed on each tenth anniversary of the creation of the settlement (*IHTA 1984, s 64*). If extra assets are added to the settlement the addition is not treated as a separate settlement; there is only one anniversary date for the entire settlement.

The charge is at a special rate of 30% of half the normal IHT rate. This gives a maximum rate of 6% of the value of the assets in the settlement at the anniversary date (30% of 50% of 40% = 6%) (*IHTA 1984, s 66(1)*). In most cases the charge is significantly less than 6% as the nil-rate-band applies in the normal way.

14.71 The tax rate is based on the tax that would be payable on a gift equal to the value of the trust assets at the anniversary date by a deemed donor who had made gifts in the prior seven years equal to the gifts made by the actual settlor in the seven years prior to the initial gift into settlement (*IHTA 1984, s 66(3)*). Accordingly, if the actual settlor had made no gifts in the seven-year period the full £300,000 nil-rate-band would be available in calculating the tax payable under the ten-yearly charge. If assets have been added to the settlement in the ten-year period the gifts in the seven years prior to that addition are used as the starting point if they are greater than those in the seven years prior to the creation of the settlement (*IHTA 1984, s 67*).

The tax is calculated by computing the average rate and applying that to the value of the assets. However, if assets have been added to the settlement since the previous ten-year anniversary, that tax attributable to such assets is pro-rated by reference to the number of quarter years that the assets were in the settlement (*IHTA 1984, s 66(2)*).

Example 14.1

Joe created a settlement on 1 June 1967. On 1 June 2007 the value of the assets in the settlement was £2 million. £400,000 of those assets were added by Joe to the settlement on 31 December 2005. Joe had made no gifts in the seven years prior to the creation of the settlement or in the seven years prior to 31 December 2005.

The tax on £2 million is	£300,000 @ nil%	£ nil
	1,700,000 @ 40%	£680,000
		£680,000
The average rate is		34%
30% of 50% of 34% is		5.1%
The tax payable is		
5.1% of £1,600,000		81,600
6/40 x 5.1% of £400,000		3,060
(as the property was in the settlement for only six quarters in the ten-year period)		
Tax payable		£84,660

14.72 *Tax planning with trusts*

The exit charge

14.72 If there is other property in the settlement which is not subject to the ten-yearly charge, such as property in which there is an interest in possession, the value of that property at the time that it was put into the settlement has to be added to the value subject to the charge to calculate the effective rate of tax. So does the value at the date of the settlement of property put into a related settlement (one made by the same settlor on the same day (*IHTA 1984, s 66(4)*)). The reason is that these are in effect gifts made by the settlor in the seven years up to the creation of the settlement. If property has been distributed since the last ten-year anniversary the amount on which tax was charged on such distributions also has to be added in to calculate the rate of tax on the next ten-year anniversary (*IHTA 1984, s 66(5)*).

The exit charge is similar to the ten-yearly charge. It is payable when assets are distributed from the settlement. It is in effect the proportion of the ten-yearly charge attributable to the number of quarters (or part quarters) for which the property was in the settlement (*IHTA 1984, s 69*).

14.73 The rate of tax used for the exit charge is however based on the average rate at the previous ten-year anniversary (*IHTA 1984, s 69(1)*). On a distribution before the first ten-year anniversary the rate is that payable by a notional transferor at the time of the creation of the settlement who had made transfers equal to the value of the property settled (at the time it was settled) plus the value of any gifts made by the settlor in the seven years prior to the creation of the settlement (*IHTA 1984, s 68*).

The effect of this is that if no tax was payable on the creation of the settlement nothing is payable on a distribution of the assets prior to the first ten-year anniversary, however high the value of those assets might be at the time of the distribution. That is not wholly correct. There is a tax trap if the assets settled qualified for business property or agricultural property relief. The notional transfer by the deemed transferor is not a transfer of such property. Accordingly, it is only if the value before business or agricultural property relief fell within the nil-rate-band that the tax payable on a distribution will be nil. Of course this may not matter if the property that is distributed itself qualifies for 100% business property relief as in such a case the value to which the rate is applied is nil, so the rate does not matter.

No exit charge is payable if the distribution takes place within three months after a ten-year anniversary (*IHTA 1984, s 65(4)*).

The interest-in-possession regime

14.74 The interest-in-possession (IIP) regime applies to:

- interest-in-possession trusts created before 22 March 2006;
- some accumulation and maintenance trusts created before 22 March 2006;
- will trusts with an 'immediate post death';
- trusts for disabled persons;
- protective trusts.

It should be borne in mind that where property is added to an existing settlement that addition is actually a separate settlement held on the trusts of the existing one (except for the purpose of the ten-yearly charge) (*IHTA 1984, s 43(2)*). Accordingly, property added to a pre-22 March 2006 IIP trust after that date will be governed by the discretionary trust regime not the IIP one.

Pre 22 March 2006 IIP trusts

14.75 The settled property is treated for IHT purposes as belonging to the life tenant (or other person with the IIP) even if he has no right to capital (*IHTA 1984, s 49(1)*). There is no ten-yearly charge on such a settlement but IHT at the full rates is payable on the death of the life tenant, treating the settled property as the top slice of his estate. The trustees are liable for payment of the tax but if they do not pay it the tax can be collected from either the deceased's estate, any person who receives a benefit from the settlement after the death or, in the case of a non-resident settlement, the settor (*IHTA 1984, s 201*).

If the interest in possession terminates during the life of the beneficiary with the IIP he is treated as making a gift of the settled property. The effect is that if the property remains in the settlement, eg it becomes a discretionary settlement, he is treated as creating a new discretionary settlement, thus triggering an entry charge liability, but if the property passes to an individual the deemed gift will be a potentially exempt transfer on which IHT will be payable only if the beneficiary dies within the next seven years.

14.76 Prior to 22 March 2006 if the property remained in the settlement but a different beneficiary became entitled to an IIP this was also treated as a PET. This treatment will continue to apply if the IIP comes to an end before 6 April 2008 (*IHTA 1984, s 49C*). This effectively gives a short window within which the identity of the person with the IIP can be altered. For example an IIP in favour of a parent could be terminated by creating a new IIP in favour of his child (provided, of course, that the trust gives the power to do so).

It will also continue to apply if the IIP comes to an end by the death of the beneficiary after 5 April 2008 and the spouse or civil partner of the beneficiary becomes entitled to an IIP on the death of the beneficiary (*IHTA 1984, s 49D*).

14.77 *Tax planning with trusts*

It will also continue to apply where the settled property is an insurance contract, the person with the IIP dies after 6 April 2008 and a different person acquires an IIP on the death. This treatment will continue if a new beneficiary takes over the IIP on the second beneficiary's death and so on, provided that there is an unbroken sequence of IIPs from 22 March 2006 (*IHTA 1984, s 49C*).

14.77 Where a beneficiary has an IIP in only part of the trust assets the IIP treatment obviously applies only to that part (*IHTA 1984, s 50(1)*). If the interest is a right to a fixed annual sum (or to the trust income less a fixed annual sum) special rules apply to determine the amount in which the IIP is deemed to exist (*IHTA 1984, s 50* and the *CTT (Settled Property Income Yield) Order 1975, SI 1975/610*)).

If an IIP beneficiary disposed of his IIP (and the trust is within the IIP regime at the time) the disposal is not charged to CGT but the interest of the beneficiary is instead deemed to terminate so triggering the IHT charge that would arise on a termination of the IIP (*IHTA 1984, s 51*). No charge arises if the disposal is a gift for the maintenance of the life tenant's family (*IHTA 1984, s 51(4)*). If the IIP beneficiary sells his interest (or otherwise disposes of it for money or money's worth) the consideration is deducted from the value of the settled property in calculating the IHT (presumably because the sale proceeds remain in the beneficiary's estate) (*IHTA 1984, s 52*). No tax is of course chargeable in relation to any of the trust assets which are excluded property (non-UK assets of a settlement created by a non-UK domiciled settlor (*IHTA 1984, s 53(1)*).

14.78 There is also an exception if the trust property reverts to the settlor or his spouse or civil partner (or his widow or widower or surviving civil partner if he died within the previous two years) on the termination of the IIP and the settlor or spouse, etc is alive at that time and (except in the case of a revertor to the settlor) domiciled in the UK (*IHTA 1984, s 53(3),(4)*). The exemption does not apply if the settlor or spouse, etc acquired the reversionary interest for a consideration in money or money's worth (*IHTA 1984, s 53(5)*). The revertor to settlor exemption also applies if the reversion is brought about by the death of the life tenant (*IHTA 1984, s 54*).

Accumulation and maintenance settlement

14.79 An accumulation and maintenance (A&M) settlement is a cross between a discretionary trust and an IIP trust. The settlement must have been created before 22 March 2006, and the settled property must be held for one or more persons who will become entitled to an interest in possession in it on or before age 25, and while no interest in possession subsists the income must be either accumulated or applied to, or for the benefit of, such beneficiaries (*IHTA 1984, s 71(1)*). In addition either all of the beneficiaries must be grandchildren

Tax planning with trusts **14.82**

of a common grandparent (or surviving children of a deceased grandchild) or all of the beneficiaries must acquire their IIP within 25 years of the creation of the settlement (*IHTA 1984, s 71(2)*). No IHT charge arises on the death of a beneficiary before he obtains his IIP or on the attainment of the IIP, and after he does so the normal IHT rules apply (*IHTA 1984, s 71(4)*).

This tax treatment will cease to apply on 6 April 2008 (unless the settlement is a trust for a bereaved minor) unless at that date all of the beneficiaries will become absolutely entitled to the settled property (not merely an IIP) at or before age 18 (*IHTA 1984, s 71(1)(a)*, as amended by *FA 2006, Sch 20, para 3*).

14.80 This gives a short window in which to amend existing A&M settlements to preserve the tax benefits. However, most people do not want children to acquire substantial assets at 18 for fear that the child may be financially immature at such a comparatively young age. Accordingly, it is unlikely that many people will take the opportunity to amend their A&M settlements in this way. An A&M settlement that does not meet the new rules will come into the discretionary trust regime from 6 April 2008 (except of course to the extent that any beneficiary may have already become entitled to an IIP in part of the settled property). Where this happens there is, however, no IHT charge by reference to that event (*FA 2006, Sch 20, para 3(3)*). It can therefore be attractive to allow this to happen as it effectively results in the creation of a discretionary settlement without an IHT entry charge having had to be paid.

14.81 If the settled property ceases to qualify as an A&M settlement in any other circumstances (other than by being used to meet trust expenses) IHT is chargeable at a special rate (*IHTA 1984, s 71(5)*). This is based on the period during which the property was held on A & M trusts (but ignoring any period before 13 March 1975). It is:

- 0.25% for each of the first 40 quarters.
- 0.20% for each of the next 40 quarters.
- 0.15% for each of the next 40 quarters.
- 0.10% for each of the next 40 quarters.
- 0.05% for each of the next 40 quarters.

(*IHTA 1984, s 70(6)*).

For example, if a property is held in A&M trusts for 22 years and the assets are then distributed to an adult beneficiary (other than the one with the IIP) the charge would be 4.8% of the value of the asset (0.25% × ten years plus 0.20% for ten years plus 0.15% for two years).

Immediate post-death interests

14.82 An immediate post-death interest is an interest in possession in settled property where the settlement was created by will or under the laws of intestacy,

14.83 *Tax planning with trusts*

the beneficiary became entitled to the IIP on the death of the testator or intestate and he has remained entitled to it since that time (*IHTA 1984, s 49A*).

As with pre-22 March 2006 trusts, the beneficiary is treated as owning the assets for IHT purposes, so the discretionary trust regime will not apply even though the testator's death occurred after 22 March 2006 (*IHTA 1984, s 49*).

14.83 This provision was introduced to preserve the IHT exemption where an IIP in the testator's assets is left to his surviving spouse on his death. As the surviving spouse is deemed to beneficially own the assets the exemption for a gift to the spouse applies on the death to the assets in which the IIP is created. However, an immediate post death interest is not limited to assets passing to the surviving spouse or civil partner; such an interest can be created in favour of anybody. If the beneficiary is someone other than the surviving spouse or civil partner, IHT will of course be payable on the death, but no further IHT charge will arise until the termination of the IIP.

Trusts for disabled persons

14.84 A trust for a disabled person is one under which during the life of the disabled person no interest in possession in the settled property exists but the trusts of which secure that at least half of the settled property that is applied by the trustees during that person's life is applied for his benefit (*IHTA 1984, s 89(1)*).

A disabled person is one who, when the property was settled, was either -

(a) incapable by reason of mental disorder (within the meaning in the *Mental Health Act 1983*) of administering his property or managing his affairs,

(b) in receipt of attendance allowance under *SSCBA 1992, s 64*,

(c) in receipt of a disability living allowance under *SSCBA 1992, s 71*, by virtue of entitlement to the care component at the highest or middle rate,

(d) would have met (b) or (c) but for the exceptions for persons in a hospital undergoing treatment for renal failure or for whom certain accommodation has been provided, or

(e) any other person who satisfies HMRC that he would have met (b) or (c) had he met the prescribed conditions of residence under *SSCBA 1992, ss 64(1)* or *71(6)*, and had provisions made by regulations under *ss 67(1), (2)* or *72(8)*, been ignored (these conditions require the person to be resident in the UK, so this head will cover trusts for non-UK resident disabled persons).

(*IHTA 1984, s 89(4)–(6)*).

Where these conditions are met the disabled person is deemed to have an interest in possession in the settled property and the IIP regime accordingly applies to the settlement even if it is created after 22 March 2006 (*IHTA 1984, s 71(2)*). The qualifying conditions for trusts created before 10 March 1981 are slightly different (*IHTA 1984, s 74*).

Protective trusts

14.85 Property is held on protective trusts if it is held on trusts to the like effect as those specified in the *Trustees Act 1925, s 33(1)* (*IHTA 1984, s 88(1)*). This is a trust in which a person ('the principal beneficiary') has an IIP but if the principal beneficiary does or attempts to do or suffers any event or thing whereby he would be deprived of the right to the trust income (eg he becomes bankrupt or tries to sell his interest in the trust) the income instead comes to be held on discretionary trusts for the maintenance or support (or otherwise for the benefit of) the principal beneficiary and his spouse, children or remoter issue (or for the principal beneficiary and the persons who would become entitled to the trust property on his death if he has no spouse or descendants).

The principal beneficiary is treated for IHT purposes as continuing to have an IIP in the settled property even if the trust has become discretionary. The IIP regime will accordingly continue to apply if the trust was created before 22 March 2006. It will not however apply if the trust was created after that date unless the beneficiary's interest is an immediate post-death interest, a disabled person's interest or a transitional serial interest (ie a post-21 March 2006 IIP arising in succession to a pre-22 March one) (*IHTA 1984, s 88*).

Special trusts

14.86 Special rules apply to:

- trust for bereaved minors;
- Age 18-to-25 trusts;
- charitable trusts;
- employee trusts and newspaper trusts;
- maintenance funds for historic buildings.

Trusts for bereaved minors

14.87 A trust for a bereaved minor is one established under the will of a deceased parent of the minor or under the Criminal Injuries Compensation Scheme and which provides that:

14.88 *Tax planning with trusts*

- the bereaved minor will become absolutely entitled to the settled property (and any accumulated income) at or before age 18;
- any income applied for the benefit of a beneficiary whilst the minor is under 18 is applied for the benefit of the bereaved minor; and
- any other benefit provided out of the settled property whilst the minor is under 18 is applied for the benefit of the deceased minor.

(IHTA 1984, s 71A(1)–(3))

The statutory trust created on the intestacy of a parent for the benefit of a bereaved minor also qualifies *(IHTA 1984, s 71A(1))*. A bereaved minor is a person who is under 18 and at least one of whose parents had died *(IHTA 1984, s 71C)*.

No IHT charge arises on the bereaved minor obtaining his right to the settled property, or dying under 18, or on any capital distribution to the bereaved minor while he is under 18 *(IHTA 1984, s 71B(2))*. The special tax charge described above in relation to A & M settlements applies if the settled property ceases to be held for the benefit of the bereaved minor in any other circumstance (other than it being used to meet trust expenses) *(IHTA 1984, s 71B(3))*.

Age 18 to 25 trusts

14.88 An age 18 to 25 trust is similar to a trust for a bereaved minor but the beneficiary need not become entitled to the asset until age 25 *(IHTA 1984, s 71D)*. Many people are unwilling to take the risk that a child may be financially immature at age 18 and thus are unlikely to be attracted to a trust for a bereaved minor. Some such people may be more willing to create such a trust if the beneficiary does not take the assets until age 25.

As with a trust for a bereaved minor, IHT is not charged on the death of a beneficiary under the age of 18 (not 25) or on a distribution of capital to the beneficiary at or under the age of 18. Nor is it charged in respect of assets used to meet trust expenses *(IHTA 1984, s 71E(2), (3))*.

14.89 There is, however, a tax charge on the death of the beneficiary over the age of 18, on the distribution of assets to the beneficiary after that age, and on the beneficiary becoming entitled to the assets. The charge is calculated in the same way as the exit charge on a discretionary settlement but on the assumption that the settlement started on the beneficiary's 18th birthday *(IHTA 1984, s 71F)*. Accordingly, the maximum charge is 4.2% of the value of the assets, ie 7/10ths (or 28/40ths) (as the assets can be held for a maximum of seven years out of the ten-year period) of the value of the settled property multiplied by 30% of the rate payable on a chargeable lifetime gift (a maximum rate of 20%) by the notional transferor.

If the property ceases to be held for the benefit of the beneficiary in any other circumstances the special charge described earlier in relation to A&M settlements applies.

Charitable trusts

14.90 A charitable trust is outside the scope of IHT. The transfer of property to such a trust is exempt from IHT (*IHTA 1984, s 23*).

If settled property held in an A & M trust, a trust for a bereaved minor, an age 18-to-25 trust, an employee or newspaper trust, or old protective trusts or trusts for a disabled person, is transferred to a charity or comes to be held on charitable trusts without limit of time, the normal IHT charges that would otherwise have arisen do not apply (*IHTA 1984, s 76*).

If property is held in a temporary charitable trust (ie where the property is held for charitable purposes only until the end of a period (whether deferred by date or in some other way) a tax charge at a special rate applies when it ceases to be charitable. This is the special rate outlined earlier in relation to A&M settlements. This charge does not arise if the property is transferred to a permanent charity (or the limitation on the charitable period is removed) or to the extent that the funds are used to meet trust expenses (*IHTA 1984, ss 70, 76(1)*).

Employee trusts and newspaper trusts

14.91 An employee trust is one where the settled property is held on trusts which do not permit it to be applied otherwise than for the benefit of persons of a class defined by reference to employment in a particular trade or profession or employment by, or office with, a body carrying on a trade, profession or undertaking (or spouses, civil partners or dependants of such persons) or for such a purpose and charitable purposes. If the trust applies to employees of a particular body the class must comprise all or most of the persons who work for that body (or it must be for the purpose of an approved profit sharing scheme or approved share incentive plan) (*IHTA 1984, s 86*).

A newspaper trust is an employee trust whose class of beneficiaries also includes a newspaper publishing company or a newspaper holding company (*IHTA 1984, s 87*).

Such trusts are outside the scope of IHT. However, if any of the assets cease to be subject to the trusts the special tax charge described under A&M settlements applies (*IHTA 1984, s 72*).

Maintenance funds for historic buildings

14.92 Such funds are outside the scope of IHT. The relevant conditions are contained in *IHTA 1984, Sch 4*. If any part of the funds cease to be held for the qualifying purposes, the special tax charge described under A&M settlements applies.

Other points

14.93 If property is transferred from one settlement to another it is treated as remaining comprised in the first settlement (unless in the interim some person has become beneficially entitled to the property, eg it has been distributed to a beneficiary and remitted by him (*IHTA 1984, s 81*).

IHT planning with trusts

14.94 The changes made to the IHT trust regime by the *Finance Act 2006* mean that in some cases trusts will be used in different ways in future to those in the past. The following principles now apply to such IHT planning.

- It no longer makes any difference for IHT purposes if a new lifetime trust is a discretionary trust, an accumulation and maintenance trust or an interest-in-possession trust. This decision can now be based solely on family considerations. However, income tax considerations may affect the decision. The income of an IIP trust is taxed as income of the beneficiary so may attract tax at a lower rate than the 40% one which applies to a discretionary trust.

- It is still worth putting business assets into a trust if they attract 100% BPR and are likely to be sold at some stage. There is no IHT on the initial transfer and when the assets are sold and replaced by non-business assets the only IHT is the future ten-yearly charges and exit charge.

- Similarly it is still worth putting into trust assets worth less than the £300,000 IHT nil-rate band, which are likely to increase in value. Again this avoids the entry charge and gets the assets out of the settlor's estate subject only to the ten-yearly and exit charges.

- When the value exceeds £300,000 it may be worth selling the asset to a trust at a £300,000 undervalue leaving the sale proceeds outstanding. The outstanding amount remains in the donor's estate but the growth in value is in the trust and subject only to the ten-yearly and exit charges.
- The creation of a trust to hold non-UK assets is still virtually a must for those who are non-UK domiciled and not yet deemed domiciled here. And remember that if a person is deemed domiciled here his infant children may well not be, as they have to themselves meet the 17-year test to become deemed domiciled. Of course, a very young child probably does not have the legal capacity to create a settlement but a teenager is likely to be competent to do so. Such trusts also give capital gains tax exemption, even for gains on UK assets, in most cases.
- Bare trusts can still be used where the beneficiary is under 18 and unmarried as the beneficiary is deemed to be beneficially entitled to the assets in the trust.
- If the main concern that prevents a gift direct to the beneficiary is a fear that the beneficiary might squander the money, a gift subject to a condition, eg that management of the money is carried out by a specified third party and that the beneficiary will not call on the fund until he is 25 or 30 or whatever, is worth considering. However, that would not protect the assets from creditors of the beneficiary.
- The strategy for wills is likely to become:
    - A trust for the surviving spouse (or civil partner) should be an interest-in-possession trust with power to advance capital to the spouse or to pay capital to a second class of beneficiary. There will then be no IHT on the death and any capital appointed to someone other than the spouse will constitute a potentially exempt transfer by the surviving spouse (or civil partner) so there will be no IHT if the spouse survives for seven years after the appointment.
    - Assets put into trust for an infant child should go into a trust for a bereaved minor or an age 18-to-25 trust provided that it is intended that the child should become entitled to the assets at or before age 25.
    - If, as is likely to be normally the case, it is not wished to give an infant the assets at age 25 then a discretionary trust should probably be used. There is no charge on creating such a trust by will (as IHT already has to be paid on death where the assets go to someone other than the surviving spouse or civil partner) and no trust creation charge will arise in addition so the only additional IHT will be the ten-yearly charge and exit charge, which could well be acceptable if the child is to take the assets at say, age 35.
    - Trusts for adult children should be discretionary trusts. Again there is no trust creation charge. Depending on the age of the child, the

14.95 *Tax planning with trusts*

> total ten-yearly charges and exit charge may well be less than the 40% that would be payable on the child's death.
>
> – Trusts for other people who would in the past have been given a life interest should probably now be discretionary trusts.

- In most cases A&M trusts should be allowed to come into the discretionary trust regime from 6 April 2008. It does not appear possible to keep such a trust within the IHT regime by bringing forward the time on which the beneficiary acquires his interest in possession to a date prior to 5 April 2008.

It can be sensible to put assets into trust even if this triggers the entry charge as the £300,000 nil-rate-band can have a significant impact on the effective tax rate. For example:

Value of asset	tax on settling		ten-yearly charge		Tax on death under IIP regime
£250,000	-	-	-	-	£100,000
£500,000	£40,000	8%	£12,000	2.4%	£200,000
1,000,000	140,000	14%	42,000	4.2%	£400,000
1,500,000	240,000	16%	72,000	4.8%	£600,000
2,000,000	340,000	17%	102,000	5.1%	£800,000

A 40% rate on death has been assumed as the individual normally has sufficient assets to use up his nil-rate band. The tax under the ten-yearly charge assumes that the settlor had made no gifts in the seven years prior to the creation of the settlement.

If a person aged 60 creates a settlement of £1,000,000 now there is likely to be a maximum of four ten-yearly charges during his lifetime. Accordingly, the total IHT will be:

Entry charge	£140,000
Four annual charges	£168,000
	£308,000

This is a saving of around 25% of the tax that would be payable on death if he were to retain the asset. In reality of course the asset is likely to increase in value so the saving will be greater as the entry charge and the first couple of ten-yearly charges are likely to be payable on a significantly lower amount then the value of the assets at the time of the settlor's death.

14.95 For older settlors the saving is greater. If an 80-year old creates a settlement of £2 million and dies at age 91 the total charge will be £442,000 (plus an exit charge of around £10,000 if the assets are then distributed) compared with the £800,000 that would otherwise have been payable on death.

It should also be borne in mind that if assets pregnant with CGT are put into a trust that is governed by the IHT discretionary trust regime the CGT can be deferred until the trustees sell the asset concerned (and can be deferred again if they distribute it to a beneficiary).

Things to avoid

14.96
- It no longer normally makes sense to create a trust of which the settlor is a beneficiary. This triggers the initial IHT charge but the property remains in the settlor's estate under the reservation of benefit rules so it creates double taxation.

- Similarly it will normally no longer make sense to create a lifetime trust of which the settlor's spouse or civil partner is the main beneficiary, as a gift direct to the spouse avoids the trust creation charge of up to 20%.

- Careful thought needs to be given to the use of a trust for CGT planning where a person is non-UK domiciled but is deemed domiciled for IHT purposes; in such a case it has been sensible in the past to set up an offshore IIP trust for the settlor's own benefit to obtain the CGT and income tax advantages of such a trust. This may no longer make sense if it will trigger an immediate IHT charge – although it might still be worth selling the assets to the trust rather than gifting them.

- A similar issue arises where a person wants to let his principal private residence but wants to stop time apportionment eroding the exemption already achieved. In such cases putting the property into trust for oneself has achieved that objective in the past. Again a sale to a trust rather than a gift may still be viable.

Chapter 15

Tax planning for the family home

Jennifer Adams FCIS TEP ATT

INTRODUCTION

15.1 In an ideal world the family home would not be included as part of any tax planning exercise with other assets being taxed instead if at all. However, the current position for many taxpayers is that the family home is their major taxable asset and until a government alters the legislation with regard to the capital taxes thereon there are various tax pitfalls that need to be considered in any transaction involving the family home. For some the risk of losing the family home to fund residential care is a far greater threat than the imposition of tax and increasingly tax planning is having to take into account the release of equity from the property to fund such care or retirement.

Retirement planning could also involve the letting of property which might have originally been the family home and as such the taxpayer needs to be aware of the capital taxes position on the eventual sale of the property or death of the owner.

This chapter looks at the conditions that need to be fulfilled to ensure that what reliefs and exemptions remain available are granted on any sale, gift or inheritance of the family home, covers some problems that may arise and discusses planning opportunities that remain. In addition, the tax position of equity release and life assurance plans drawn on the family home are explored.

Capital gains tax

15.2 All statutory references in this section are to *Taxation of Chargeable Gains Act 1992 (TCGA 1992)*, unless otherwise stated.

PRINCIPAL PRIVATE RESIDENCE

Conditions

15.3 The most useful and complete exemption on the sale or a gift of the family home is to agree with HMRC that the property is designated the principal private residence (PPR). Even though it is usual to think that such a designation will allow the gain or sale to be automatically capital gains tax-free, there are two main conditions that have to be fulfilled in order for it to be so:

- the property must not have been purchased for the sole reason of making a profit (*s 224(3)*) even if the taxpayer lives in the house for a period before it is sold; and
- that to be exempt the residence must be an individual's only or main residence (*'dwelling-house'*) throughout the period of ownership (*s 222(1)*).

15.4 The first condition will only be applied where the main purpose of purchasing the property was an early disposal at a profit. The usual example of this instance is where the taxpayer already holds the lease of a property, purchases the freehold and then sells the property shortly after the freehold is purchased. The gain earned by the granting of the freehold in comparison with the sale price without will be chargeable to capital gains tax (CGT). Other examples include the gain earned on the sale of an undivided house following conversion into flats, or of barn conversions, developments of outbuildings or of the land attached to a house. Any expenses incurred on such conversions will not be deductible from the proceeds of sale unless the only relevant expenditure is the obtaining of planning permission or the cost of removal of restrictive covenants (Revenue Interpretation, *Tax Bulletin, Issue 12* – superseded by CGM 64200ff); taper relief (which is scheduled to be withdrawn from 6 April 2008, following an announcement in Pre-Budget Report 2007) will not be relevant as the asset would not have been held for the prerequisite number of years. In some cases, the development of the property may also be deemed 'an adventure in the nature of trade', thereby giving rise to an income tax charge.

15.5 The second condition is the main exempting section – that the 'dwelling-house' or part thereof must be the 'individual's only or main residence' and such residence is to be incurred 'throughout the period of ownership'. Where the property was held at 31 March 1982 periods before this date are not taken into account.

Tax cases have centred round the three main parts of the section:

- what constitutes a 'residence';
- whether the house is the 'only or main residence' of the owner; and
- what is the meaning of 'throughout the period of ownership'?

What constitutes a 'residence'?

15.6 There is no definition in the legislation as to exactly what constitutes a 'dwelling-house' but in *Batey v Wakefield* [1981] STC 521 it was decided that

15.7 Tax planning for the family home

'residence' includes not only the main building but also any other buildings that are occupied for the purpose of the main residence (eg shed, summerhouse, staff bungalow). Cases have mainly been brought to settle the question as to whether a separate property or land adjoining the property on an estate is exempt when sold. HMRC have confirmed that in deciding whether a property is to be so designated they look at such pointers as the geographical location of the two buildings to each other.

CGM 64200 confirms that care needs be taken as to in which order the property and land are sold – if the property is sold before the land then the land will be charged to CGT as the land will no longer be 'attached' to the residence. The main case on this point was *Varty v Lynes* [1976] STC 508 where a taxpayer who sold his home and part of his garden then sold the remainder of the garden 11 months later only to find that the CGT exemption did not apply.

15.7 Even though it is the sale of a second property and not the main PPR that attracts the CGT charge the Tax legislation places a restriction on the size of the property being disposed, (deemed the 'permitted area') exemption being given only to the sale of grounds attached to the residence providing that the ground does not exceed half a hectare (approximately 1.25 acres). A larger area is permitted should it be needed for 'the reasonable enjoyment' of the house as a residence. In *Longson v Baker* [2001] BTC 356 it was held that grounds used for equestrian purposes did not qualify for relief as they were not required for 'the reasonable enjoyment' of the residence.

The 'permitted area' exemption is becoming increasingly in point especially in areas of the UK where infill development is being encouraged. Following changes to planning rules in the late 1990s, rules are more lax for infill development and the increasingly common building in gardens is no longer protected as 'green space', but treated as 'brownfield land' and thereby more likely to be approved. The question of a CGT charge could arise given that often the granting of planning permission substantially increases the value of the land. The legislation does not dictate how the gain should be computed but in practice there will be a comparison between the gain which accrues following permission being granted and the gain which would have accrued if the permission had not been obtained and the relevant expenditure had not been incurred.

Whether the house is the only or main residence of the owner

15.8 HMRC views 'residence' on the basis of quality, rather than length, of occupation meaning that 'even occasional and short residence can make a residence, but the question is one of fact and degree'. For example, in *Moore v Thompson* [1986] BTC 172 a wife purchased her husband's half share of a caravan and adjoining farmhouse following divorce but as she had never lived in the farmhouse and occupation of the caravan had been 'sporadic and occasional' the PPR claim failed.

Section 222(1) gives the main exemption allowing full PPR relief if the property is the main residence and *s 223(1)* allows exemption of the last three years of ownership provided that the residence has been the owner's 'only or main residence' (see **15.9** below for further details) at some time but unusually it does not matter whether the owner has actually lived in the property or not.

15.9 The increase in the 'second home market' has meant that where two properties are held by either the one owner or jointly with the spouse or civil partner) that HMRC had to make rules to determine which of the two properties is to be deemed the main PPR. Although *s 222(1)* requires a residence to be 'an individual's only or main residence throughout the period of ownership', to enable the gain to be at least partly CGT-free periods of absence are allowed (*s 223(3)*) (this is discussed further at **15.16**)

Section 222(5) expands on the 'three-year exemption' rule by allowing a taxpayer to elect as to which residence is to be treated as the PPR. This is a valuable method of securing the exemption which must be claimed in writing within a two-year period of an event taking place. Following the imposition of self-assessment the onus is now on the taxpayer to make the election and most importantly does not depend upon which residence is in fact used as the taxpayer's main residence in practice; if the taxpayer does not elect then on sale HMRC will decide using the conditions given above as the basis for their decision.

15.10 The two-year time limit for election starts running once the second property has been purchased but it is not normally possible to backdate the claim once the two-year time limit is passed. However, *Griffin v Craig-Harvey* [1994] BTC 3 confirmed that on the purchase of another property the two-year time limit recommences as the taxpayer's circumstances have changed. Standard tax planning therefore dictates that an election should be made as soon as possible on the purchase of the subsequent property, then having made the election, the taxpayer is able to review the position at any time up to the two-year anniversary to decide whether he wishes to alter the notice and if he does the notice can be retrospective. Thus the acquisition of a third property, for example, will allow the taxpayer another chance to make a nomination with effect from the acquisition date. The nominated property can be situated in the UK or can be abroad, however only a property that the taxpayer has actually lived in at some time can be used. An election, once made, can be varied at any time. However, the variation is only effective for a period beginning no earlier than two years before it is given (see CGM 64510).

15.11 *Tax planning for the family home*

Example 15.1

Stanley and his wife own a property in Dorset which was their sole residence until Stanley was offered a full-time job in London. He therefore purchased a one-bedroomed flat in London keeping the house in Dorset. Stanley should make an election within the two years of purchase of the flat nominating the flat as the PPR as from 1 April of the tax year. A week later another variation can be submitted nominating the Dorset house as PPR as from 8 April. This planning would ensure that the London flat was the PPR for one week in April therefore attracting the three-year PPR exemption. If the Dorset residence was subsequently sold the property would have been the PPR throughout ownership bar the one week in April – the gain on which would be very small and in any event may be covered by the annual allowance.

15.11 The necessity of an election is usually an unknown but increasingly common matter for married couples (the definition of which now includes civil partners) who each own their own homes on marriage. Marriage is a change of circumstance which can trigger the start of the two-year election period previously mentioned if there is a change in the combination of houses as there can only be one PPR per couple. If one property is owned by one spouse only with no house being owned by the other then there has been no change in circumstance and therefore no need to make an election. However, where they jointly own more than one property at marriage but neither separately owns any other property, a new two-year election must be made and the election date is the date of marriage (*s* 222 and CGM 64204).

15.12 Should the taxpayer miss the two-year time limit for any reason a variation on this practice is that he rents one of the properties to a tenant for a short period of time. When the letting comes to an end the taxpayer reacquires that property and is then in a position to make an election as his property circumstances have changed. Similarly, the taxpayer could rent a property himself and that will also allow the election to be made as the rented property will normally be occupied under a tenancy rather than a licence (again this is deemed to be a change in circumstance allowing an election). Another possibility which was discussed in the judgment of *Griffin v Craig-Harvey* is for the taxpayer to transfer the main residence to the trustees of a settlement under which the taxpayer has a beneficial interest. With the proviso that the trustees allow the taxpayer to remain in the residence this will also trigger an election as there will still be two properties used as a residence.

Married couples and civil partners

15.13 When a married couple separate, whoever leaves the house then ceases to have a share in the main residence. Their share of any gain on a subsequent sale will be chargeable and is calculated as the period of non-residence less any annual exemption and/or tapering relief. The last three years will always count as exempt being that it was the PPR but if the property is sold more than three years after the date of separation then the calculation takes the proportion of gain made after the three years in relation to the total period of ownership or 31 March 1998 whichever is the latest date. The only situation where HMRC will allow greater than three years' absence is when the property is transferred to the spouse or civil partner remaining as part of the financial settlement on divorce and an election has not been made by the one partner who left the residence (ESC D6).

The problem of two properties is most usual when someone moves, cannot sell their own property and therefore owns two properties at any one time. There will be no CGT implications as the sale will be covered by the three-year PPR exemption. However, there will be a problem should the sale fall through. It is usual for a deposit to be paid to secure the purchase of the property and should the prospective purchaser then withdraw from the transaction the deposit is forfeited. There will then be a CGT charge under *s 144(7)* being 'in relation to a forfeited deposit of purchase money or other consideration money for a prospective purchase or other transaction which is abandoned as it applies in relation to the consideration for an option which binds the grantor to sell and which is not exercised.' Further, the receipt is taxed in full at the taxpayer's highest rate of tax with obviously no taper relief available (for periods prior to 6 April 2008); the only deductions being allowed are the legal costs in relation to the aborted disposal.

Job-related accommodation

15.14 Again, the problem of 'two homes' could be in point where one property is owned as the PPR and the owner is then obliged to live in job related accommodation. Without the exemption in *s 222(8)* the house not job-related would attract CGT on sale. The job-related provision is only possible if it is necessary or customary for the employee to live in accommodation provided by the employer, for the better performance of their duties. Note that the provision of accommodation by the employer must be necessary or customary – not simply a matter of choice by either the taxpayer or employer. With this provision, it is the *intention* to occupy the property in the future that is crucial; once the intention changes (for example, selling part of the house) the relief is lost.

What is the meaning of 'throughout the period of ownership'?

15.15 The second condition quoted at **15.3 and 15.5** allows full PPR relief provided the property was so used throughout the whole period of ownership

15.16 *Tax planning for the family home*

and, as has already been noted, the last three years of ownership is always exempt if the property has been the taxpayer's PPR at some time or has been elected to be so (see **15.9** for details of election). However, for some taxpayers there will be periods where the property cannot be so occupied. The Act therefore generously allows specific instances when the periods of absence are nevertheless treated as though they were periods of residence despite the individual being physically absent from the property. These instances are covered in the following paragraphs but it is important to note that relief is only granted if at some time both before and after the period of absence the property was used as the individual's only or main residence.

Delay in occupation

15.16 HMRC treat a period of up to one year as allowed should the owner not take up residence immediately on purchase (ESC D49). This 'one year' is to cover instances where the property is being constructed or renovated, or there is difficulty in selling the first property; this one year can be extended to two years if there are reasons for non-occupation outside of the taxpayer's control for example, bad weather or unforeseen structural problems but the extension will not be granted if the reason for non-occupation was shortage of funds. The ESC means that no election under *s 222(5)* is required.

Other absences

15.17 Other absences allowed include:

- three years for any reason whatsoever. The periods need not be consecutively taken but may be periods of absence which together do not exceed three years (*s 223(2a)*);
- up to four years where employment requires residence in another part of the country (*s 223(c)*); and
- any period abroad for employment reasons (*s 223(3b)*).

With the restrictions relating to employment, the condition that the property must be reoccupied following the absence is removed if the taxpayer is subsequently required to work elsewhere following the ending of a period of absence away (ESC D4). In addition permitted absences due to employment apply whether it is the husband or wife who is required to work away.

Rental and lettings

15.18 Again, the main three years' PPR exemption remains even if the owner moves and lets the property during that last three years.

If the whole or part of a private residence is let other than within the last three years, *s 223(4)* grants relief for the period of letting limited to the lower of:

- the gain attributable to the period of letting;
- the exemption applicable to the owner's occupation; and
- £ 40,000.

Example 15.2

The gain on the sale of a property is £100,000 with the agreed proportion of gain attributable to the period of letting being £56,000. The gain on the let part is limited to the lower of the amount applicable to the owner's occupation ie £34,000 (£100,000 – £56,000) and £40,000. Hence the gain equals £100,000 – £34,000 – £34,000 = £32,000

This amount will be further reduced by taper relief and the annual allowance then taxed at the taxpayer's highest rate of tax.

Where a married couple, civil partners or other joint owners let part or all of the property each is entitled to deduct their own lettings exemption of £40,000 each – hence three joint owners can deduct 3 x £40,000.

15.19 One point to make with regard to lettings is that HMRC will allow the letting of one room in the property without the PPR exemption being affected. The lettings exemption will therefore not be relevant on sale, however this is on the proviso that the lodger is treated as a member of the family meaning that they have to at least be allowed to share living rooms (Revenue helpsheet IR 283). In contrast, the PPR exemption is denied should there be more than one lodger and in this instance the letting exemption then comes into play. Some taxpayers could be tempted not to declare the presence of a lodger on their income tax return particularly if the rental income is under the 'rent a room' relief limit. They should do so, however, as this will notify HMRC that letting relief is to be a factor on any subsequent sale.

The tax cases concerning lettings have mainly centred round the situation where the taxpayers live in their own private accommodation within their private guest house or hotel. For example, *Owen v Elliott (Inspector of Taxes)* [1990] BTC 323) concerned a couple who occupied different parts of the property at different times of the year. It had been agreed that one third of the gain was exempt under PPR relief but the taxpayers went further and claimed that lettings relief was available against the balance. The Court of Appeal allowed the taxpayer's claim on the grounds that *s 223(4)* does not require the lettings to be to third parties as their homes and as such short-term lettings in the guest house were allowed.

15.20 *Tax planning for the family home*

If it is not possible to claim lettings relief because the living rooms are not shared as in the situation of a hotel where the owners living area is separate, then *s 224(1)* states that no lettings exemption is available in respect of any part of a house which has been used *exclusively* for business purposes. Therefore calculation of the gain needs to be apportioned between business and non-business use which then brings the problem of interaction with taper relief where the rates of taper relief are specified separately for business assets and for non-business assets. However, the calculation of the gain potentially becomes easier following the proposed withdrawal of taper relief from 6 April 2008.

Business use

15.20 Section 224(1) does not allow PPR relief (even in respect of the final three years of ownership) in respect of any part of a house used exclusively for business purposes and where there is such use, then the gain must be apportioned as mentioned above.

The important word to note in this situation is the word 'exclusive', where exclusive use is a question of fact although occasional use for residential purposes may not be enough to disallow the claim. To ensure that full PPR relief is allowed, whichever part of the property used for business must also be used for the home. Unfortunately, this might not be possible should the room be used as a doctor's surgery, for example.

Interaction with taper relief (2007/08 and earlier years)

15.21 For 2007/08 and earlier years (ie prior to the withdrawal of taper relief as announced in the Pre-Budget Report 2007), where there is a mix of business and non-business use *TCGA 1992, Sch A1, para 9* states that the gain must be apportioned on a pro rata basis and then taper relief is applied to each separate amount. If one or more rooms of the PPR has been used wholly for business purposes (and this includes instances where a separate studio is attached to the residence) it would be logical for the non-exempt part of the gain to be liable to the 75% taper relief available for business use where the use has been for two or more years for example. Unfortunately, logic does not prevail and the law states that the chargeable part although relating solely to business use is split using the mixed use rules. This usually results in the benefit of taper relief and PPR being reduced.

Example 15.3

Mr Jones has owned and run a small hotel business in Weymouth for some years. Due to ill-health he sold the hotel on 31 March 2007 for £1,100,000 producing a gain of £600,000 after deducting the base cost as at 31 March 1982 and indexation allowance of £500,000. 15% of the property was used solely as accommodation for Mr Jones and his family producing a gain on the business proportion of £90,000. It would have been thought that the whole of the business proportion would qualify for the 75% business asset taper relief. However, instead the calculation is as follows:

	£	
Gain	600,000	
Less Business use (85%)	(510,000)	
Exempt gain	90,000	
Business asset gain (85% × £510,000)	433,500	
Less Taper relief (75%)	(325,125)	
	108,375	
Non-business asset gain (15%)	76,500	
Less Taper relief (20%)	(15,300)	
	61,200	
	169,575	(subject to annual allowance)

15.22 The calculation above shows that the taxpayer is worse off by the granting of PPR relief because if the gain on the sale of the property had been fully chargeable tax would be due on £100,000 (ie £400,000 less taper relief at 20%) only. Lettings relief may be available if the property qualifies which would help in further reducing the amount chargeable.

15.23 Unfortunately there have been no tax cases to test the above calculation specifically with relation to residence and many would say that the application of the tax law as it stands is unjust and unfair. A point to consider is that the HMRC Capital Gains Manual (CGM) 64662 refers to business use being calculated on a 'just and reasonable basis' and perhaps if a business computation is required as above then it should be submitted on a 'just and reasonable basis' with a letter of explanation.

Dependent relative

15.24 The disposal of a property which prior to 5 April 1988 was used by a dependent relative is exempt from CGT providing that the relative was the property's only resident who lived there rent free and continued to do so until up to three years (the PPR last three year's exemption applies) before the property

15.25 *Tax planning for the family home*

was sold. The property must be provided 'rent-free and without any other consideration' (*s 226*) and although HMRC try to enforce this restriction should the dependent relative pay for such items as council tax and minor repairs the exemption should be allowed.

If there is a change of occupant after 5 April 1998 the exemption ceases even if the new occupant is another dependent relative although any period after 31 March 1982 which originally qualified for exemption will be allowed.

15.25 'Dependent relative' is strictly defined in *s 226(6)* as being any relative of the taxpayer or spouse or civil partner) who is incapacitated by old age or infirmity from maintaining himself or herself, or the taxpayers' own or his spouse's (or partner's) mother who, whether or not incapacitated, is either widowed, or living apart from her husband.

The categories are not exclusive meaning that should the taxpayer's mother for example, not fall into the second category; she may still fall into the first. The detail concerning Dependent Relative relief is covered in CGM 65550.

It is worth noting that HMRC announced a change of view in late 2007 regarding the interaction of dependant relative relief and lettings relief. Their previously held view was that the further relief provided for by TCGA 1992, s 223(4) where the residence had also been wholly or partly let out as residential accommodation was not due. However, HMRC now accept that lettings relief may be due in such cases.

Personal representatives

15.26 Section 225 (inserted by *FA 2004, Sch 22, para 5* extends the PPR exemption to any gain made on the sale of a property which had been used as the PPR immediately before and after the death of the owner by persons who are entitled to at least 75% of the net proceeds of sale of the property (incidental costs are an allowable deduction) either absolutely or for life. The person must have been in occupancy before and after the death of the deceased person so the exemption cannot apply to a child of the deceased who returned to the family home after the death of the owner. This exemption, although welcome, does not mean much in practice as the 'cost' of the property to the personal representatives is the market value on the date of death of the deceased.

Trustees – hold-over relief

15.27 The *s 225* exemption also applies where an individual's only or main PPR which is held in trust for that individual is disposed of by the trustees although in this instance there is no 75% restriction as there is for Personal

Tax planning for the family home **15.29**

Representatives. However, *FA 2004, Sch 22(6)* inserted new sections into the TCGA 1992 designed to bring to an end a number of established tax planning techniques which used trusts to exploit the interaction between PPR relief and hold-over relief under *s 260*. The changes affect all trusts – not just those that are settlor related.

An example of the type of planning that was being used is given below:

Example 15.4

John set up a discretionary trust for the benefit of his adult son and daughter and transferred a property which was not covered by PPR into the trust using his own and his wife's nil-rate bands so no IHT was relevant. If he had sold the property there would have been a CGT gain of £150,000. Hold-over relief was claimed under *s 260*. The trustees allowed the daughter to live in the property as her PPR. A few years later the daughter moved away and the house was sold. As the house was the daughter's PPR no CGT was due on either the gain made following the date that the daughter commenced living in the property or the gain held over.

This scheme is no longer possible by virtue of the new *ss 226A* and *226B* inserted by *FA 2004, Sch 22, para 6*, which state that where hold-over relief has been obtained under an earlier disposal and there is a subsequent disposal of the property on or after 10 December 2003, no PPR relief is available and instead the entire gain including the held-over part will be liable to CGT. There is exemption where the settlement is a maintenance fund for historic buildings under *TCGA 1992, s 169D* and in certain cases where it is for the benefit of a disabled person.

15.28 The effect of these provisions is to make the taxpayer choose between the two reliefs – either PPR or hold-over relief – but not both. Therefore the gain accruing prior to the transfer into the trust can no longer be protected.

Section 226A allows for a 'hold-over' claim to be revoked in respect of an earlier disposal; so if in the above example the *s 260* is then revoked it will be assumed that the claim had never been made, CGT will then be due on the transfer into the trust and when the property is eventually sold the three-year PPR relief only will be available as the daughter occupied the house as her PPR. Whether the claim should be revoked will be dependent upon the amount of tax calculated as due in each instance.

15.29 A limited transitional relief was possible for cases where the earlier disposal, subject to the hold-over claim had been before 10 December 2003. Under this relief where a claim had been made and a beneficiary occupied the

15.30 *Tax planning for the family home*

property before this date, the gain was time apportioned, PPR being available only on that part of the total gain realised by the trustees (including the held-over gain) calculated as from the date of acquisition to 10 December 2003. Obviously the longer the trustees held the property in the trust as an asset the greater the chargeable gain accruing as the benefits of the allowable 36 months' PPR disappeared after 10 December 2006.

Non-domiciliaries and the UK family home

15.30 A person may be resident but non-domiciled in the UK and in this situation the purchase of a UK family home is still subject to the PPR rules previously covered. The only complication would be if the non-domiciliary has more than one residence worldwide; then an election as detailed at **15.9** should be made.

Care is required on the financing of the purchase of the property by a non-domicile as funds should not be brought into the UK from abroad as earnings which are charged to tax on the remittance basis (*ITEPA 2003, s 26*). Ideally, therefore, interest payments on a mortgage should be met from UK sourced earnings or the finance should be via capital (capital being not taxed on the remittance basis). It should also be borne in mind that measures affecting the remittance basis of taxation were announced in the Pre-Budget Report 2007.

HMRC has produced a flow chart (CG 64270) to help in deciding whether PPR is available on the sale of a property. The chart can be found on the HMRC website at www.hmrc.gov.uk/manuals/cg4manual/objects/64270.gif

INHERITANCE TAX

15.31 All statutory references in this section are to *IHTA 1984* unless otherwise stated.

Introduction

15.32 According to the Halifax Building Society research indicates that currently more than 18 million homes in the UK are valued at greater than the current IHT nil-rate band of £300,000 per individual. In addition, they calculate that one in three houses used as the family home will be subject to IHT within 20 years as the product of rapid increases in house prices that have not been matched by increases in the IHT nil-rate band exemption. The next section of this chapter covers the possibilities that remain for tax planning post the implementation of the main rules that affect IHT planning being the 'Gift with reservation' (GWR) charge and the 'Pre-Owned Assets Tax' (POAT) charge. The text will first detail the rules for each charge, commenting on the types of schemes that they were introduced to circumvent and end with a discussion as to what tax planning opportunities remain for both lifetime and will tax planning.

Lifetime planning

Gift with reservation of benefit (GWR)

15.33 The ideal in IHT lifetime planning with reference to the family home would be to gift the property out of the estate saving a large IHT bill on death but at the same time being able to remain in residence. However, the GWR rules which came into being in the *Finance Act 1986* (*FA 1986*) will not allow a simple transfer of a whole or part of a property to another whilst the donor remains in residence as should the transaction take place the property is treated as remaining in the donor's estate on death.

FA 1986, s 102 and *Sch 20* inserted the GWR rules into the legislation and were brought in to take effect as from 18 March 1986. The rules are based on the old estate duty regime rules and charges to tax property which has been disposed of but remains subject to a reservation in favour of the donor.

15.34 The donor's retention of a share in the property will not, by itself, amount to a reservation but where an individual disposes of the whole property or just a part and the 'enjoyment' of the property is not assumed by the donee outright to the exclusion of the donor the GWR rules will then apply. When the donor subsequently dies the property will be treated as remaining in the estate. The 'enjoyment' stipulation was inserted later than the original rules came into being by the FA 1999 following the success of the 'Ingram' scheme (see **15.46**).

The donee has to 'occupy' the property for the GWR rules to not apply but the property does not necessarily have to be their main home – an often quoted example is where a child of the donor lives in the country but periodically uses the gifted property situated in London. The rules do not stipulate as to what percentage of the property can be given away; HMRC's current stance is that no greater share can be given than that equates to the number of co-owners for example, four owners should receive 25% and HMRC have stated that they may investigate should the donor take less than his or her equal share. Where the reservation, once made, is subsequently released during the donor's lifetime, he/she is treated as having made a disposition of the property by a potentially exempt transfer (PET) and must live for seven years for the gift to be free of any IHT charge.

15.35 HMRC do allow a 'de minimis' in *FA 1986, s 102(1)*) that to not be subject to GWR 'the property must be enjoyed to the entire exclusion, *or*

15.36 *Tax planning for the family home*

virtually the entire exclusion, of the donor and of any benefit to him by contract or otherwise'. The then Inland Revenue issued some guidance as to their interpretation of the phrase *'virtually to the entire exclusion'* at the time that the rules were implemented in a Revenue Interpretation (*Tax Bulletin, Issue 9* – now contained in RI 55), stating that the phrase covers cases in which the benefit to the donor is insignificant in relation to the gifted property. It will only be when various cases come before the courts that a more detailed interpretation will be possible but it does seem that there is some flexibility in the ruling as the following are given as being allowed:

- a house which becomes the donee's residence but where the donor subsequently:
    - stays, in the absence of the donee, for not more than two weeks each year; or
    - stays with the donee for less than one month each year;
- social visits, excluding overnight stays made by a donor as a guest of the donee, to a house which he had given away (the extent of the social visits should be no greater than the visits which the donor might be expected to make to the donee's house in the absence of any gift by the donor);
- a temporary stay for some short-term purpose in a house the donor had previously given away, for example:
    - while the donor convalesces after medical treatment;
    - while the donor looks after a donee convalescing after medical treatment;
    - while the donor's own home is being redecorated;
- visits to a house for domestic reasons, for example babysitting by the donor for the donee's children;
- a house together with a library of books which the donor visits less than five times in any year to consult or borrow a book.

If, after the gift occurs the benefit to the donor is, or becomes, more significant than the examples given above, the GWR conditions are likely to apply. It should be noted that the same exceptions are allowed for the POAT charge (see **15.41**).

15.36 Examples of instances where the benefit could be deemed to be significant will be gifts of:

- a house where the donor stays more than the time given above:
- a house in which the donor stays most weekends, or for a month or more each year;

Tax planning for the family home **15.37**

- a second home or holiday home which the donor and donee both use on an occasional basis;
- a house with a library in which the donor continues to keep his own books, or which the donor uses on a regular basis, for example because it is necessary for his work.

The main point to note with regard to the GWR rules is that to not be caught the disposal needs to be of a sale for full consideration (market value). If the sale is for less than the full consideration (ie at an undervalue) then GWR may be in point unless it can be proved that there has been some element of a donation. HMRC's stance on sales at an undervalue is given in IHTM 14316. It states that a sale for less than full consideration, if not a bad bargain, will be a gift and property that is disposed of by way of a gift will be deemed to have been disposed of at an undervalue. The text goes further by giving specific examples stressing in particular the 'enjoyment' factor; the one example relevant to the family home is reproduced below:

Example 15.5

In 1989 the donor sold a house, then worth £100,000, to his son for £25,000. This is a disposition partly by way of sale and partly by way of gift. The donor dies in 1993.

- If the donor has been excluded from enjoyment of the property throughout the period, the gift is a PET chargeable on his death. The loss to his estate is the value of the entirety of the property less the consideration received (£100,000 less £25,000 = £75,000).
- If the donor was not excluded from enjoyment of the property, for instance because he resided at the property following the disposition, the disposal by way of gift is a GWR. The value of the property disposed of by way of gift is 75% of the value of the whole property. Thus, if the property is still subject to a reservation immediately before the donor's death, 75% of its death value is treated as property to which the donor was beneficially entitled.

FA 1986, s 102B(4) allows a 'co-occupation' exemption by granting the donor the right to remain in occupation so long as there is full consideration in money or money's worth. Being similar to the POAT rules this exemption is possible if the donor pays all of most of his or her expenses (see **15.41**).

Pre-owned assets tax (POAT)

15.37 On 6 April 2005 the GWR rules (see **15.33**) were reinforced by an income tax charge named the 'Pre-Owned Asset' charge based on the assumed

15.38 *Tax planning for the family home*

market rental value of an asset formerly owned by the user (or for which he has provided funds to purchase) but which he still has enjoyed use unless sold to an unconnected person in a bargain at arm's length. For the definition of 'market rental value' see **15.43**.

In a consultation document published on 11 December 2003 HMRC stated that:

> '... income tax will in future be charged on the benefit people enjoy when they have arranged free continuing use of major capital assets that they once owned. Arrangements like this are often made to get round the IHT gifts with reservation (GWR) rules. Essentially these GWR rules are intended to stop people from giving their assets away, so that for IHT purposes they are out of the estate when they die, while still continuing to enjoy the practical benefits of owning them during their lifetime.'

15.38 It was the extensive and well-publicised use of the 'double trust' scheme used in relation to the family home (see **15.50**) coming hard on the heels of HMRC losing the *Eversden* case (see **15.47**) that forced the introduction of this legislation. Included within the POAT charge is land and property previously owned by the chargeable person and disposed of in whole or in part after 17 March 1986.

For a transaction to be caught by the POAT regulations the chargeable person must 'occupy' property, either alone or with others, and either the 'disposal' or 'contribution' conditions must also be met (see **15.40**) (*FA 2004, Sch 15, para 3(2), (3)*).

15.39 The POAT rules for 'occupy' are similarly wide as those for GWR (see **15.33**). The Guidance Notes on POAT issued by HMRC in March 2005 expressly adopt the RI 55 rules for 'occupy' with the added stipulation that the chargeable person would be regarded as in occupation not only if they were resident in the property but also if they used it for storage or had sole possession of the means of access and used the property from time to time. If the chargeable person's occupation or use of the property is limited in its nature or duration it may not come within the provisions; each case will obviously ultimately be decided on the facts and circumstances relating to it. There is one difference between the POAT rules and the GWR rules in this situation in that the chargeable person is not regarded as occupying a property from which they receive rental payments from the person actually in occupation.

15.40 The 'disposal' condition is satisfied where after 17 March 1986 (the commencement date for IHT and the GWR rules) the individual who owned the property disposed of all or part of his property in a transaction which is not deemed to be an excluded transaction.

Tax planning for the family home **15.41**

The 'contribution' condition is satisfied where the individual has made a gift of cash after 17 March 1986 and the cash was used either directly or indirectly towards the acquisition of a property which the donor then subsequently occupied or used.

There are 'exclusions' and 'exceptions' to the charge. The following are possible transactions related to the family home which are 'excluded' transactions as detailed in *FA 2004, Sch 15, para 10*:

- The property is sold to an unconnected person by an arm's-length transaction.
- The property is sold to a connected person but at an arm's-length transaction.
- The property is transferred to a spouse or a former spouse (now including civil partners) under a court order. This also includes the situation where the transfer was made to a trust in which the spouse or former spouse is beneficially entitled to an interest in possession. The exemption comes to an end if and when the interest in the trust is terminated.
- The property is gifted to an interest-in-possession trust of which the donor is the beneficiary – this is because the value of that life interest generally forms part of the donor's estate, either based on the pre-*Finance Act 2006* treatment of such trusts, or otherwise under the GWR rules.
- A cash gift made at least seven years before the date on which the 'contribution' condition is satisfied. This would include the instance where a cash sum is given to the donee who seven years later uses the money to purchase a property in which the donor subsequently resides.

15.41 Exceptions are allowed as follows:

- Where the donor is caught by the GWR rules (see **15.33**) so that the asset will be included in his estate on death. As a transaction cannot be caught by both rules if GWR rules apply then that takes priority. The usual example given where both GWR and POAT rules may apply is where a donor has gifted 100% of the family home but continues to live there. Paying rent at the full market value rent would not attract either charge but should the rent paid fall below the market rate (and a review must therefore be made every year to fall within this charge) GWR will be charged in priority to POAT.
- Where the donor gifts a property to another and then has to return to the property to live for reasons of ill-health.
- 'De minimis'. In this instance no charge will be levied unless the aggregate taxable value of the charge exceeds £5,000 per spouse or civil partner each year and you cannot transfer any unused exemption to the other

15.42 *Tax planning for the family home*

spouse or civil partner. If the value exceeds the £5,000 de minimis the full amount is used as the value on which to base the charge. 'Taxable value' is defined as the price the property might reasonably be expected to fetch if sold in the open market, without any allowance for a reduction for the fact that the whole property is being placed on the market at one and the same time. The problem here is that it will be necessary to formally value the property (with the costs that will entail) to decide whether it falls within the 'de minimis' amount; however, it is not necessary to make an annual revaluation but rather the property is to be valued on a five-year cycle (see **15.42**).

- Negligible benefit. *FA 1986, s 102B(4)(b)* states that the donor should 'not receive any benefit, other than a negligible one, which is provided by or at the expense of the donee for some reason connected with the gift'. This covers the situation where a parent gives a part-share of a property to a child who continues to reside with the parent. Protection is allowed under both POAT and GWR so long as each continues to live in the property. Should the child leave then the parent will be subject to the GWR rules in priority to POAT. The rationale for the exemption from both charges is that in this situation the parent derives no benefit from living in the property although each party to the transaction should pay their 'fair share' of the expenses otherwise a benefit may be seen to accrue. To come within this rule it is recommended that the property expenses be shared fairly in the proportions in which the house is owned. Personal living expenses such as the cost of food bills should be divided equally, unless some other apportionment based on actual use is used. Documentation should be prepared on a year-by-year basis which will show how the expenses are met; this is an important matter that must be undertaken as HMRC are known to enquire closely particularly if more than 50% of the home is gifted. It is acceptable for the donor to pay all the bills; the problems arise when calculating how much the donee can pay without falling foul of the POAT charge.

If the donee subsequently moves out of the property leaving the donor with exclusive occupation the donor will then be taxed at the full market consideration for the then use of the donee's share of the property.

Valuation

15.42 The value on which the POAT charge is based is the 'annual rental value (see *'Basic charge'* below). Regulation 4 of the Guidance Notes covering POAT provides for a valuation as at 6 April 2005 if the scheme is already caught by the POAT charge. Before the first five-year anniversary the valuation of the property will be that set at the first valuation date or the date the scheme commenced. Thereafter the valuation at the latest five-year anniversary will apply. Unfortunately this means that should property values fall taxpayers will have no option but to use the 6 April 2005 value for the next five years for example; the only saving grace is that at least the taxpayer knows how much the charge will be for that period. HMRC have confirmed that the *de minimis* limit of £5,000 does not need to be time-apportioned where a benefit is enjoyed for less than a full tax year.

An example of how the 'five-year' rule works in practice is given as follows in the HMRC Guidance which also shows that no charge to tax under this Schedule can arise in relation to any person for any year of assessment during which they are not resident in the UK as follows:

Example 15.6

A is first chargeable on 6 April 2005. A valuation is obtained then. He becomes non-UK resident for three years from 6 April 2006 to 6 April 2009. The charge does not apply during this period. He returns to the UK on 7 April 2009. A new valuation is made then and this is the start of the next five-year anniversary.

The basic charge

15.43 The basic tax charge in the case of property will be the 'annual rental value' which is calculated as below:

$$\frac{R \times DV}{V}$$

Where:

- R is the rental value for the taxable period;
- DV is the value at the valuation date of the interest disposed and
- V is the value at the valuation date

The 'rental value' is the amount of rent that would normally be due on a let undertaken year on year on a non-tenant repairing lease where the tenant pays the taxes, rates and charges and the landlord pays for the repairs and/or insurance.

The 'taxable period' is the tax year in which the transaction took place.

The 'valuation date' is 6 April in the relevant year of assessment or, if later, the first day of the taxable period. As noted at **15.42**, no revaluation is required until the next five-year anniversary.

15.43 *Tax planning for the family home*

Example 15.7

In August 2000, Mr Smith gifted his home to his daughter and intends to remain living in the house. It was decided that a fair rent would be £150 per week. The annual market rent value of the house for 2005/06 was £10,200 and the value at the valuation date is £300,000.

The appropriate rental value is therefore:

$$\frac{10,200 \times 300,000}{300,000} = £10,200$$

No deduction can be made for the rental payments, as they are not made under any legal obligation

The following may assist in deciding which of the GWR or POAT rules apply in any given situation:

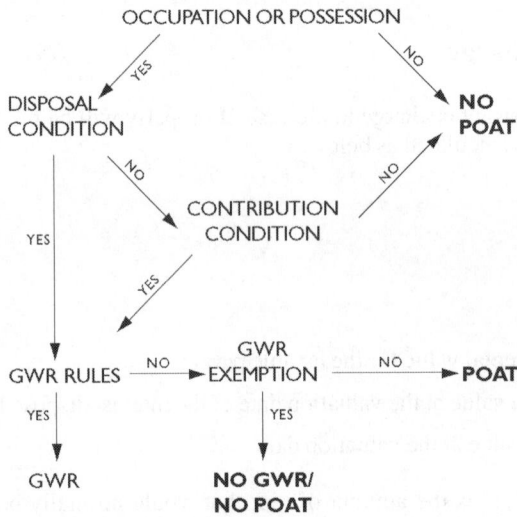

Using the flow chart above, the following example shows the interaction of GWT and the POAT in one situation that is becoming increasingly common in relation to the family home and discusses what are planning possibilities are available.

Example 15.8

Mr James is an elderly widower who is 'property rich/cash poor' living in a large property with no other assets and although he is of good health he does not think that he could cope with a move and therefore wishes to remain in the property. His son and daughter-in-law have two children and cannot afford to buy their own residence. Mr James therefore intends to renovate the house and turn a part of the house into a self-contained annexe flat in which he will live and when finished will comprise one quarter of the whole property. For safety there is to be an internal door between the two different parts of the house – the annexe and the main part of the house – as well as an outside door for each. He then intends to dispose of the house 50% by sale to his son so as to fund the alterations and to release some equity in the house and then gift the son the balance.

- **Will there be occupation or possession?**

    The answer is yes and the occupation will be of the whole property as there is access from the annexe to the main part of the house. The question will be whether there has been a gift subject to reservation of the whole of the property, or an outright gift of part of the property.

- **Does the disposal condition apply?**

    The answer is yes.

- **Do the GWR rules apply?**

    The answer is yes on the 50% share that is gifted because the son and daughter-in-law will not occupy the property to the complete exclusion of Mr James. The transaction will be at an undervalue (50%) and the GWR rules state that the amount of the reservation will be 50% of the market value at Mr James's date of death.

- **Do the POAT rules apply?**

    The answer is yes as there has been a disposal of the whole property but the price received means that it has not been sold at the full market value. The rental value charge to be levied will be calculated in the same proportion as the undervalue amount relating to the whole price received – namely 50% of the market rent.

Planning possibilities

15.44
- It might be able to be argued that the occupation is of the flat only and for this to have a chance of succeeding the door between the flat and the main part of the house will need to be boarded up. The GWT charge on death

15.45 *Tax planning for the family home*

will then be on 50% of the value of the flat. The POAT charge will be levied on the amount of rental for the flat rather than on a proportion of the whole house.

- The flat could again be made self-contained and the remainder of the property could be transferred with the proviso that Mr James continues to own the flat. The main house would need to be valued at the true market value with the son and daughter-in-law making a contribution for the value of the main house and any balance of the market value unpaid for would be treated as a gift. GWR will not apply because Mr James does not retain any benefit from the main part of the house. There will also be no POAT charge because the property Mr James occupies is his own. The value of the flat will still fall to be included in his estate on death but this value will be lower than the charge that would have applied under the GWR or POAT rules.

- Mr James could keep the separate door and continue to occupy the flat as part of the main house paying his share of the expenses. He would then transfer the remainder of the house to his son and daughter-in-law. This would then be covered by the exemption under both the GWR and POAT rules which states that there is no benefit if the expenses are met. As with the plan in point 2 the value of the flat would remain to be taxed on Mr James's death but could be covered by the exempt amount.

Tax planning schemes

15.45 There have been a number of tax planning schemes marketed intending to circumvent particularly the GWR rules on the transfer of the family home and it was the *Eversden*-type scheme (see **15.47**) in particular that forced HMRC to implement the POAT regulations. What all the lifetime tax planning schemes had in common was that, in substance, nothing practically changed – the owner was still the owner of the house, he still lived there, he still benefited from living in the house but by the signing of a few forms he was able to save potentially many thousands of pounds of IHT yet still remain in control. A brief outline of the types of scheme that are no longer possible (or if they are, are no longer advantageous) now follows with detail of the impact of the new rules.

Lease carve out – the *Ingram* scheme

15.46 This was the first scheme following the implementation of the GWR rules that brought to the Revenue's attention that there were ways round the charge which possibly they had not originally appreciated. Changes were introduced in FA 1999 specifically to negate the decision in *Ingram (Executors of Lady Ingram's Estate) v IRC* [1997] STC 1234 so that the GWR rules operated as was originally intended. In this type of scheme the donor transfers title of the property to a nominee, who then grants a lease of at least 20 years back to the donor at a peppercorn rent. Hence the retained lease, which enabled the donor to continue to occupy the property rent-free, following the gift, supposedly did not amount to a reservation of benefit in relation to the gift of the freehold interest for the purposes of the GWR rules.

The new provisions adopted a different test for 'reservation' of interest focusing on 'occupation' and 'enjoyment' of the property itself. Following the implementation of the GWR and POAT rules, if the transfer was affected after 9 March 1999 then the GWR charge remains in place which means that no POAT charge is relevant. HMRC have expressly confirmed that pre-9 March 1999 transfers are not caught by the GWR rules, rather they will be subject to the POAT rules the value being the value attributable to the property disposed of rather than the value of the lease.

Settlement of property into an interest-in-possession trust – the *Eversden* scheme

15.47 *IRC v Eversden* [2003] STC 822 was used as a test case by the Revenue against what they perceived as a tax avoidance scheme and centred on the question of whether the GWR provisions were displaced by an exempt transfer between spouses.

The main steps of the *Eversden* arrangement were:

- Creation of an interest-in-possession trust into which 95% value of a property was placed with the settlor's spouse as the life tenant. The settlor held the remaining 5% of the property in his/her own name.

- Spouse dies – IHT paid on the interest-in-possession trust fund value.

- Trust becomes a discretionary trust for a class of beneficiaries including the settlor.

- Trust property is sold and 95% of the total proceeds are reinvested – part in another property for the use of the settlor and part in a bond; settlor also invests his/her 5% in the property and bond.

- Settlor therefore has an interest of 5% in the property and 5% in the bond – settlor allowed to reside in the property

- Discretionary trust comprised 95% value of property and 95% of bond.

- Settlor dies.

15.48 HMRC contended that the trust fund was taxable on the settlor's death under the GWR rules but the Court of Appeal held that:

15.49 *Tax planning for the family home*

- discretionary beneficiaries could not have an interest in possession.
- GWR provisions do not apply to a gift to a spouse.
- The creation of the settlement was an exempt transfer and not a PET and as such could not be a caught by the GWR rules.
- The settlor's right to reside in the property was by virtue of the 5% interest in the property.

HMRC quickly put legislation in place to ensure that such schemes would no longer be possible (*FA 1986, s 102(5A)*) so that if the transfer is undertaken after 20 June 2003 the property will be subject to the GWR rules.

If the transfer had been effected pre-20 June 2003 the property would not be caught by the GWR rules and would only be replaced by a POAT charge should the settlors spouse's interest in possession cease during his or her lifetime as the settlor would still retain the 5% interest.

Reversionary lease schemes

15.49 Simplicity was the obvious attraction with these types of schemes – A grants B a long lease on the family home which takes effect some time in the future, ideally after A's actuarial life expectancy but not more than 21 years after the date of grant. The grant of the lease was a PET and as A still owned the freehold as he was allowed residency the value of which would be reduced by the grant of the lease, preferably to below the nil-rate band amount on death. In a May 1998 Newsletter the Revenue stated their misgivings to the viability of such schemes and quoted *FA 1986, s 102* largely on the basis that under this scheme the donee does not assume 'immediate possession' and 'enjoyment' of the gift unlike the donor hence, they argued, a GWR must arise.

The Guidance Notes on the POAT charge published in March 2005 confirmed that HMRC now consider that for such schemes entered into post-9 March 1999 where the freehold interest was acquired more than seven years before the gift, the continued occupation by the donor would mean a POAT charge unless the donor elects for the GWR rules to apply (see **15.33**). Pre-9 March 1999 transfers are not caught by the GWR rules but will be subject to the POAT rules.

Double trust or home loan scheme

15.50 There are a number of variants of these types of marketed schemes and in practice the introduction of stamp duty land tax (SDLT) on 1 December 2003 put paid to many of the 'double' or 'two trust' schemes available. The main ingredients of such schemes being:

Tax planning for the family home **15.51**

- Creation of an interest-in-possession trust of a nominal sum (say £10 or £100), with the settlor and spouse as life tenants and remainder to the children. The property remained part of the donor's estate on death; the transfer being exempt from CGT due to PPR exemption.
- Sale of the settlor's property to the trustees for full market value; contracts are exchanged (for IHT purposes this is not a transfer of value).
- However, the sale is not completed as the purchase price remains outstanding as an unsecured loan (ie on an IOU) payable by the trustees to the settlor when the settlor dies.
- Settlor creates another life interest trust with the children as life tenants.
- The IOU is assigned by the settlor to the second trust from which the settlor was excluded as a beneficiary (this is a PET – if the settlor survives seven years the value of the property is passed out of his estate free of IHT. No CGT implication).
- Settlor continues to occupy the property – hence continued availability of the CGT PPR exemption.
- The purchase price is then owed by the trustees of the first trust to the trustees of the second trust.
- Settlor dies – the original £10 or £100 plus the current value of the property is included in the estate, reduced by the value of the IOU owed to him (CGT could be due if the sum repayable exceeds the amount of the original sale proceeds as it would now not be the repayment of a debt to the original creditor under *TCGA 1992, s 251*; however, such refinements such as charging market interest could ensure that no charge was made); as the IOU could not be called in by the loan trustees no GWR would be due.

By allowing the property to 'rest on contract', there was no stamp duty liability when the property was acquired by the trustees of the first trust. The settlor continued to live rent-free in the property which he previously owned. There were also no GWR problems as these only apply to the gift of an asset and in this instance the asset has been sold at full market value.

15.51 These plans, although very popular pre-1 December 2003, lost their attraction as Stamp Duty Land Tax (SDLT) is now charged as from the date of the original sale of the property (step 2) rather than within 30 days of the completion of the sale as was previously levied under stamp duty (deemed to be after step 8) – this adds an additional cost which in itself renders the scheme worthless.

Further, as from 6 April 2005 the POAT charge now applies to such schemes because the fact that the IOU remains unpaid until after the settlor's death (which is crucial to avoid the GWR charge) means that there is an element of

15.52 *Tax planning for the family home*

undervalue in the transaction and hence the POAT rules apply. Further, the trustees in the first trust are connected with the settlor.

15.52 Guidance Notes published in March 2005 formally set out HMRC's view regarding home loan schemes enacted pre-6 April 2005 stating that if the loan is subject to the GWR charge there may also be a charge under POAT as the reservation of benefit is in the loan and not the house. As well as the loan being present the settlor has also made a disposal which has resulted in a reduction in the estate. Should the donor not wish to be subject to the POAT charge then the IOU needs to be appointed back to him or written off and this would result in no reduction in the value of his estate and also no POAT charge from the date the debt is written off or appointed back to him; the settlor could elect for the GWR charge to apply (see next section) in which case there is no POAT charge.

Elections

15.53 Since the introduction of POAT the regulations have been criticised for being poorly targeted. The government's answer was that if taxpayers were unwittingly caught by the rule, they could elect to pay IHT on their death instead.

Since POAT is payable where the value of an asset exceeds, roughly, £100,000, and IHT does not start until the estate of a person who has not been married or part of a civil partnership exceeds the nil-rate band (£300,000 in 2007–08, or possibly higher if a surviving spouse or civil partner dies on or after 9 October 2007 and all or part of their nil-rate band was unused on the first death, following proposals announced in the Pre-Budget Report 2007), it is clearly advantageous for those whose estates are valued at between those figures to pay IHT instead wherever possible. In addition, whilst IHT is payable on death, POAT is an annual tax on income payable whilst the taxpayer is still alive.

15.54 *SI 2005/724* permits an election so that the transaction is taxed under the GWT rules rather than being charged under the POAT rules so that the relevant property will be included in the estate on death. The Guidance rules state that the election needs to be made on or before the 31 January after the year of assessment as POAT is an income tax charge This means that for a charge first arising in 2005–06, 31 January 2007 was the last date by which a person could opt into paying IHT under the GWR rules instead of paying POAT.

FA 2007, s 66 allows HMRC to use its discretion to accept late elections. The guidance available on the HMRC website at 'BN28 pre-owned assets: late elections' gives the circumstances for which late election will be allowed – they are mostly for instances beyond the taxpayer's control, for example serious illness of the taxpayer or immediate family; the rules are deemed to have come into force on 21st March 2007. An election cannot be revoked once a person has died.

Double charges

15.55 Following on from making the election, there are regulations in place relating to the POAT charge (*SI 2005/724*) which include provisions to avoid a double charge to IHT where the chargeable person elects that the GWR provisions apply in their stead. A double charge could be a problem where the chargeable person makes a gift of property that is a potentially exempt transfer (PET); if the transaction comes under the POAT rules and the taxpayer subsequently elects for the GWR rules to apply instead then the PET will be chargeable should the taxpayer die within seven years. A double charge will arise firstly on the original transfer that is added to the death estate and secondly on the property subject to the reservation. In effect IHT will be charged twice on what is the same economic value. The regulations use the transfer that will produce the higher overall amount of IHT and delete the other transfer. In other words two calculations are undertaken – one including the now chargeable gift in the estate calculation and the other including the value of the GWR – whichever produces the higher tax liability will be taken.

Current lifetime IHT planning and the family home

15.56 A point should be made as a warning to anyone intending to enter into any form of lifetime IHT tax planning. The HMRC *IHT & Trusts Newsletter* of August 2007 has stated that as from August 2007 until 31 March 2008, when looking at forms IHT200 received on a death, HMRC will be paying particular attention to lifetime transfers whether those transfers have been notified at the date of transfer or not. The newsletter gives examples of the areas that they will be reviewing and in relation to property will look at redistributions of property inherited by the deceased as they may have been a result of a past gift.

It should be remembered that any effective tax planning exercise should not only consider the IHT implications but security of tenure should be paramount for the donor and if any payment is to be made (for example, rent after gifting the family home out of his or her estate) that the rent is affordable and will continue to be so.

15.57 The implementation of the GWR and POAT rules effectively brought the whole era of lifetime capital tax planning to an end and what is left cannot be sure to remain in place. As the opportunities for lifetime IHT planning have been so severely restricted (despite the Pre-Budget Report 2007 announcement

15.58 *Tax planning for the family home*

of a transferable nil-rate band from 9 October 2007 on the death of a spouse or civil partner, which is expected to become law in Finance Act 2008) it is now even more important that nothing impedes what routes are still available particularly in the realm of tax-efficient will planning. What remains is outlined below:

- Basic plan – sell the family home. A simple solution is that of selling the house and making a cash gift to the donee out of the proceeds of an amount that will reduce the taxable estate to less than the exempt amount; the remaining money can then be used to purchase a smaller less costly property. The gift of cash is deemed to be a PET, therein no GWR problems as there is no retained benefit but the donor does have to live for seven years for the gift to be totally IHT-free. This assumes that the taxpayer finds a house in the area they wish to live in for less than the amount and does not need the proceeds for any other reason such as day-to-day living expenses.

- Sell the property to the intended recipient for the market price and then the seller leases the property back paying the full market rent to live there. The monies received could then be gifted in the form of PETs or spent. A variation of the 'sale and lease back' scheme is the commercial 'home reversion scheme' (see **15.59**).

- On the assumption that the donor has enough money to live on he/she could gift the property out of the estate and then pay the full market rent to live there. The gift will be a PET assuming the donor lives the seven years.

- Share the house with the donee – thus able to give 50% of the share of the property so long as the donee stays and the donor pays their share of the expenses.

- Mortgage the house (a form of 'equity release': see **15.58**) investing the money in assets that do not attract IHT, for example business property relief is available on shares in unlisted trading companies (possibly the children's own company?), as well as agricultural property relief on agricultural land which is let out. After two years, the investments will qualify for 100% relief from IHT and the mortgage will reduce the value of the house for IHT purposes, the downside being that mortgage interest will be charged. The funds borrowed could also be gifted as a PET.

Equity release schemes

15.58 Equity release is an easier form of lifetime tax planning that reduces the estate for IHT purposes but does not have the added complications of the schemes discussed below.

There are two main methods in which equity can be released from property:

- **Home reversion schemes** – selling the whole or part of the home.
- **Lifetime mortgages** – taking out a mortgage on the home.

Whichever method is used, the capital released is used to provide a lump sum, income or both. The income can be in the form of a purchased life annuity or other form of investment, purchased either by or from the scheme or by the applicant independently. Depending upon the type of scheme chosen, cash can be taken in a lump sum or in regular instalments.

Home reversion schemes

15.59 These involve selling all or part of the applicant's home to a reversion company or a group of independent investors, whilst retaining the right to continue living in the property as a life tenant paying a nominal rent. In return, the applicant will receive a cash lump sum, a monthly income or both. When the property is sold, the reversion company or group will receive the proceeds of sale relating the percentage of the property sold which will include a proportion in the increase of the value of the property, if any. The applicant's estate will receive back the value of the remaining share. The purchase price of the property will not be at the market value as the applicant will still be living in the property at a peppercorn rent. The advantage of a home reversion scheme is that the applicant can choose to sell only a proportion of the house and the balance remains in the estate. Home Reversion plans are not currently as popular as lifetime mortgages (see below), as although a greater lump sum can generally be released, many people prefer to retain full ownership of their properties.

A lifetime mortgage

15.60 This is where the applicant borrows against the value of the property just as with an ordinary mortgage but this mortgage is used to provide an income, a lump sum, or both. The loan plus any accrued interest is repaid out of the applicant's estate on death or on vacation of the property should the applicant go into long-term care.

IHT position

15.61 POAT is charged where there is a disposal of property but the original owner is still able to reside in the property – which is the point of commercial Home Reversion equity release plans. *FA 2005, Sch 15, para 10* confirms that where there is a disposal of the *whole* of the property in an arms-length transaction there is no POAT charge (this is the situation whether the transaction is made with a connected or unconnected person or cohabitee). The *Charge to*

15.62 *Tax planning for the family home*

Income Tax by Reference to Enjoyment of Property Previously Owned Regulations 2005, SI 2005/724, reg 5 adds a difficulty by providing exemption if the transaction is of part only of the property at arm's length to an unconnected person (thereby exempting all commercial transactions but charging other non-commercial transactions).

A sale at arm's length effected pre-7 March 2005 is exempt even if made between connected parties.

Planning via a will

15.62 As mentioned above, lifetime inheritance planning schemes are difficult to implement effectively. However, it might be that the best IHT planning is not during the taxpayer's lifetime but by use of the will; this could also ensure that the taxpayer will not be subject to questions by the Local Authority on the grounds that he or she has voluntarily divested of assets should he or she require residential care at a later date.

The family home is the largest single asset ever owned by many taxpayers. Prior to the Pre-Budget 2007 announcement of a proposed transferable nil-rate band to surviving spouses or civil partners from 9 October 2007 where all or any part of the nil-rate band was unused on the first death, it was often necessary to constitute the nil-rate band of the deceased spouse or civil partner with their interest in the family home. This had the potential to cause complications and uncertainty. Fortunately, married couples with smaller estates will particularly benefit from the ability to transfer the unused nil-rate band of the first spouse or civil partner to die, if those proposals become law in *Finance Act 2008*. What follows is mainly for the benefit of those who are unwilling or unable to avail themselves of a transferable nil-rate band.

Nil-rate band (NRB) scheme

15.63 The most effective long-term planning for the family as a whole is the use of the nil-rate band discretionary trust. Under this method each spouse or civil partner creates a discretionary trust by will equal to the amount of the NRB (or unused NRB); the beneficiaries being the surviving spouse or civil partner, the children and any other beneficiaries the testator might wish to benefit. The surviving spouse or civil partner must not have an interest in possession, a general power of appointment or disposition over the part of the estate that was the deceased's share since either will cause that share to be treated as part of the surviving spouses' or civil partner's estate and defeat the object of the exercise – hence the use of a discretionary trust.

15.64 If the main or sole asset in the trust is the family home care should be taken that SP10/79 (power of trustees to allow a beneficiary to occupy a dwelling-house) is complied with by not giving the trustees power to create 'an exclusive or joint residence, albeit revocable, for a definite or indefinite period, ... with the intention of providing a particular beneficiary with a permanent home'. If such a power is allowed, HMRC will normally regard the exercise of the power as creating an interest in possession which again defeats the object of the exercise.

15.65 Each spouse or civil partner should hold the house as tenants in common so that the beneficial ownership and value of each half share of the property passes through the first spouse's or civil partner's estate to the discretionary trust. The surviving spouse or civil partner will have the right to occupy the home by virtue of ownership of their own half-share of the home and legal ownership will pass automatically to the surviving spouse or civil partner as tenant in common. The NRB Trustees have a problem in that they own a beneficial 50% share of a property effectively subject to a sitting tenant; they cannot sell because they do not entirely own it, and they probably cannot generate an income from it either, even on court application. As such the trustees' only option is to retain it as an asset of appreciating value.

15.66 The drafting of the will in these circumstances should be undertaken with care – HMRC will try to contend that despite a Will trust being designated a 'discretionary' trust it is in fact an interest-in-possession trust in favour of the surviving spouse or civil partner if it is felt that the trustees have granted the right to exclusive occupation – the classic case under this heading is *IRC v Lloyds Private Banking* [1998] STC 559. On the particular facts of the case (which centred around the specific wording of the will), it was held that the will effectively gave to the surviving spouse such a high degree of security that he had, in effect, a life interest in the part of the property not already owned. As a result the whole of the house fell to be taxed on the death of the surviving spouse.

15.67 If a NRB discretionary trust is provided as above, the remainder of the estate (subject to any property allowed agricultural or business property relief which is either left outright to the children or in trust but not to the surviving spouse or civil partner as there is little point in leaving assets to an exempt beneficiary) can be left to the survivor on flexible life interest trust with the remainder to the children. Thus maximum flexibility is achieved over the whole estate whilst still retaining the spouse or civil partner's exemption. The trust deed could enable the trustees to vary the ultimate beneficiaries by not treating the children equally or holding the share in trust until there were grandchildren. Best of all the entire structure is easily collapsible should the estate turn out to be less than the exempt amount. In addition this method of planning ensures that there will be no such problems should a beneficiary child become bankrupt or die.

15.68 *Tax planning for the family home*

The debt scheme

15.68 A refinement on the NRB discretionary trust above which also reduces the problem of the possibility of the trust being designated an interest-in-possession trust is via the use of the 'Debt' scheme. The legal fees in preparing such a scheme mean that it is now possibly only relevant for properties valued at a minimum of £800,000 with a total estate value of over £1 million. The scheme entails the placing of a monetary legacy or the half share of the family home under tenants in common equal to the NRB in the discretionary trust with any residue going absolutely to the spouse or civil partner. However, instead of receiving cash the trustees accept an IOU loan owed personally by the surviving spouse or civil partner who then receives the assets of the estate (to the value of that IOU) in consideration, namely the half share of the family home. The benefit of the IOU is then assigned by the executors to the trustees in satisfaction of the legacy. The debt is repayable on demand thereby avoiding any risk of the surviving spouse or civil partner being deemed to have an interest in possession and hence being included as part of their estate. In order for the debt to be allowed against the estate of the surviving spouse or civil partner's subsequent death *IHTA 1984, s 5(5)* will need to be satisfied by giving full consideration for the debt which allows the debt to be incurred for consideration in money or money's worth. However, this should not be a problem as it will almost inevitably be the case that the survivor will have given full consideration in that the value received from the original estate will exceed the amount of the debt. The saving under the scheme arises because the value of the house will be subject to a charge in order to satisfy the NRB legacy.

15.69 The advantages of the scheme are that:

- The surviving spouse or civil partner is able to continue in occupation of the house as it has been left to him/her absolutely.

- The house remains owned by the surviving spouse or civil partner and benefits from either the PPR relief should the house be subsequently sold or a base cost uplift if retained until death.

- When the remaining spouse or civil partner dies the debt owed to the NRB Trust will reduce the size of the estate.

The main disadvantage of the scheme is that Stamp Duty Land Tax is payable on the value of the half-share of the property given because the property is effectively being sold to the survivor in exchange for that part of the IOU which reflects the half share value of the home.

15.70 The above was the ideal solution but a recent case, *Phizackerley (personal representative of Phizackerley, dec'd) v Revenue and Customs Comrs* [2007] SWTI 559, threw some doubt on the effectiveness of such planning. In this case the family home was Dr and Mrs Phizackerley's main asset and importantly, as Dr Phizackerley was the earning spouse his earnings paid for its purchase. The house was purchased in joint names so Dr Phizackerley made a gift of half of the house to his wife at the date of purchase. The IOU scheme (the *'Debt scheme'*) was used in that when Mrs Phizackerley died her will created a NRB discretionary trust (which, as the will and death were before the Chancellor's announcement of the increase in the NRB amount for spouses or civil partners) leaving the remaining assets to her husband absolutely. Then when her husband subsequently died the executors claimed that the value of the estate be reduced by the value of the IOU owed to his late wife's trustees. HMRC, however, brought the case based on anti-avoidance legislation contained in *FA 1986, s 103* saying that the IOU could not be deducted from the estate on the grounds that the debt had originally been incurred in exchange for property once owned by Dr Phizackerley. According to HMRC, he had apparently received back the half-share of the house that he had originally gifted to his wife in exchange for the IOU. The Revenue won the case and the whole of the house was included in Dr Phizackerley's estate and hence taxable in full. If Dr Phizackerley had died first HMRC would not have won their case as Mrs Phizackerley would not have given the IOU and the property did not originate from her.

The *Phizackerley* case centred on correct will drafting rather than the Debt scheme itself per se and as such the scheme still works if the residue passes into spouse-exempt interest-in-possession trusts. The IOU is then incurred by the trustees of the Trust rather than the surviving spouse. The principle of the 'Debt' scheme (or indeed the 'Charge' scheme detailed in the next section), if properly executed, has not yet been challenged by HMRC in the courts.

The charge scheme

15.71 The 'charge' route is a variation of the 'debt' scheme by which the trustees are given the power to accept a charge in satisfaction of the legacy secured on the assets contained in the residue of the estate – which could include the deceased's share in the family home. The surviving spouse or civil partner will normally have no personal liability for the charge which can be index linked to take account of future increases in the NRB. Alternatively, the charge could be expressed as a proportion of the value of the house calculated periodically thereby benefiting from any capital appreciation, or it could be made to track a publicly available index of house prices for comparable properties. Once again, on the death of the surviving spouse or civil partner IHT will be payable on the house but the value of the property will be reduced by the charge to below the NRB as this time the survivor does not incur the debt. HMRC has also confirmed that SDLT is not due on this arrangement.

The usual question raised by HMRC is whether the discretionary trust actually exists and HMRC are known to be looking for cases where the discretionary trustees have never taken any steps to 'activate' the trust but simply allowed the

15.72 *Tax planning for the family home*

surviving spouse or civil partner to take all the assets thereby doing nothing to protect the interests of the beneficiaries of the discretionary trust. It is therefore important that the trustees behave like trustees which would include, for example, minuting an annual review to see whether or not they should call in the charge; minuting the original decision to accept a debt instead of assets into the trust and whether or not to charge interest on the loan; completing form 41G notifying HMRC of the trust's existence etc.

Insurance schemes

15.72 There are a number of different IHT mitigation products on the market that are insurance schemes involving the use of trusts. Following the *Finance Act 2007* and the changes contained therein with regard to trusts, such schemes were thought by many to be no longer possible. However, the Association of British Insurers has worked with HMRC and has agreed that the products are still viable. The schemes fall into two types – discounted gift schemes and loan trust schemes. Both can be implemented with use of the family home.

Discounted gift schemes

15.73 These involve the applicant investing a large capital sum into an insurance company bond which allows the applicant to withdraw income of usually 5% per year being a series of single premium policies maturing on successive annual dates. The residue is gifted into a bare trust. A bare trust is present where the beneficiary has an untenable interest in the whole of the trust property subject to only the trustee's expenses of administration. The capital value of the gift is discounted using actuarial values and is returned to the settler either on survival or if alive, on maturity of the scheme. The transaction is a PET and as such will be exempt if the applicant survives the seven years; GWR and POAT charges do not apply. If the applicant dies within the seven years the gift is valued at a discount as the applicant had an absolute right to income for the remainder of their life.

Loan trust schemes

15.74 These establish a trust for the family by making a large loan to the insurance company. The monies are then invested in non-qualifying life assurance bonds (eg a managed bond) and partial surrenders each year of 5% income tax free are used to repay the loan over 20 years. With the scheme the amount of the gift remains in the estate but the growth in the bond will not as it has been granted to the beneficiaries in the trust. Again, there is no GWR problem in

Tax planning for the family home **15.74**

addition, the settlor is not a beneficiary of the trust and the actual making of the loan is not a settlement therefore there is no POAT charge.

Example 15.9

An example of the use of an insurance product used in conjunction with the family home is where:

- A mortgage is taken out on the family home.

- This amount is placed with an insurance company in a discounted gift trust.

- The 5% taken out every year is calculated to service the interest on the mortgage plus possibly extra income which is tax-free.

With no disposal of assets there is no GWR or POAT and there should be no question of 'deprivation of assets', if asked, on assessment for long-term care costs. Should the house be sold during the owner's lifetime PPR will be available. The only IHT concern would be should the donor not live the prerequisite seven years for the residue to be exempt under the PET rules.

The final point with regard to insurance schemes is that term or whole of life assurance policies paid by either the taxpayer or his or her beneficiaries can be used to fund any IHT liability that does fall due out of 'normal income'.

Chapter 16

Separation and divorce

George Duncan Solicitor CTA TEP, Partner, Charles Russell

INTRODUCTION

16.1 This chapter will examine the main tax issues typically raised by separation and divorce. It does not deal with the breakdown of civil partnerships but these will, broadly speaking, raise similar tax issues. Tax planning in this context is, usually, planning in the sense of planning to avoid disasters, rather than planning to secure an advantage.

AN OUTLINE OF THE STEPS INVOLVED IN A DIVORCE WHERE SIGNIFICANT FINANCIAL ISSUES EXIST

16.2 In broad outline the typical pattern will be as follows.

First, sadly, the relationship will break down leading to the permanent separation of the parties. The date of permanent separation is significant for certain tax purposes. It is a question of fact and will be referred to in various documents lodged with the court in the process of the matrimonial proceedings. It is not possible to specify a date of permanent separation for tax purposes different from that which has been acknowledged in documents submitted to the court.

16.3 The question whether a separation is permanent tends to be judged with the benefit of hindsight.

Separation for these purposes is separation in the family law sense. It is possible, though rare, for a couple to be separated in the family law sense if they are living separate lives under the same roof but also possible for a couple not to be separated if they are resident in different jurisdictions, for example where one of them has gone to live overseas for employment purposes and the other has stayed at home.

Permanent separation will, typically, be followed by the commencement of court proceedings for the dissolution of the marriage.

16.4 The parties and their advisers will then try to agree 'minutes of order'. This is a document that will be submitted to the court by consent of both parties as being a form of order which both parties consider it would be appropriate for the court to make. The minutes of order are *not* a binding contract on which anyone can sue. They are simply an agreed recommendation to the court.

The judge will often make a consent order in the form of the minutes which have been supplied to him but only if he considers it just to do so.

16.5 The court has wide powers when dealing with marriage breakdown. The court may order either party to the marriage to make periodical payments to the other party for that party's own benefit or for the benefit of children of the marriage. It can also order the payment of lump sums and the transfer of property between the parties, and sharing or attachment of pensions. Attachment orders are merely a type of periodical payments or lump sum order. It also has power to vary the terms of pre-existing settlements but only if they are 'nuptial' or 'antenuptial' settlements.

Sometimes the court order will be made on the basis of undertakings given by one or both of the parties that they will do things which the court could not directly order itself.

The making of the court order dealing with financial matters will typically be preceded by the decree nisi and then, on the application of either party, followed by the decree absolute. The decree absolute ends the marriage for all legal purposes and it is then that the court order takes effect. Maintenance pending suit orders can take effect before decree nisi or absolute.

16.6 Property adjustment orders made before decree absolute take effect only on decree absolute.

It is possible under certain circumstances for financial matters to be left unresolved at decree absolute, in which case an order of the court dealing with financial matters may be made after decree absolute. Any order for payment of a lump sum or adjustment of property made after decree absolute will normally come into immediate effect.

There are of course many variations to this general pattern. If agreement cannot be reached on financial matters between the parties then there will be a contested court hearing and the court will make whatever order it thinks just. In some cases the parties will enter into a binding separation agreement which may or may not be followed by divorce proceedings. Couples who separate may also make their own financial arrangements independently of the court but, in that case, the court might order different financial arrangements if it thought it just to do so.

16.7 *Separation and divorce*

INCOME TAX

Maintenance payments

16.7 Tax relief for maintenance payments was at one time a key issue on marriage breakdown. However tax relief was greatly restricted by *FA 1988* and has subsequently become even more restricted so that it is currently seldom an issue. Relief for 'qualifying maintenance payments' survives in a very truncated form in *Income Tax Act 2007 (ITA 2007), Pt 8, Ch 5*, though only in a case where either of the parties to the marriage or civil partnership was born before 6 April 1935 or, in the case of certain child support maintenance payments, where either the person who made the payment or the person to whom it was made was born before that date. The amount of this truncated relief is a tax reduction of 10% of the lesser of the total amount of qualifying maintenance payments made by the individual in question which fall due in the tax year in question and the minimum specified in *ITA 2007, s 43* (£2,440 for 2007/08).

16.8 In other cases maintenance payments attract no tax relief in the hands of the payer and are tax free in the hands of the recipient. It is irrelevant whether the maintenance payments are secured or not. This treatment applies also to maintenance payments made by order of an overseas court (though they may attract tax relief overseas).

It should be noted that this exemption for maintenance payments does not extend to income arising under an outright alienation of capital by either party to the marriage. If one party makes an outright transfer of capital to the other then the income arising from that capital will be taxed in the hands of the recipient in the normal way.

It sometimes happens that, in a financial settlement, one party to the marriage will accept that future income distributions from a family trust will take the place of maintenance payments, but in that case those income distributions will be taxable in the normal way.

Tax reductions for married couples and civil partners

16.9 The married couples allowance now survives only in a truncated form (though it has been extended in a similar truncated form to civil partnerships). It is now represented by a tax deduction given under *ITA 2007, Pt 3, Ch 3* and applies where, for the whole or part of a tax year, the couple are living together. It is therefore available in full for the tax year of permanent separation but not thereafter. It is available only where one of the spouses or civil partners in question was born before 6 April 1935.

The settlement rules now contained in ITTOIA 2005

16.10 The settlement rules are now contained in the *Income Tax (Trading and Other Income) Act 2005 (ITTOIA 2005), Pt 5, Ch 5*. These rules will not often be an issue in a financial settlement made on the occasion of marriage breakdown. Since tax relief for maintenance payments has almost ceased the settlement rules could be an issue only in the case of a settlement of capital. It is however established by case law that the settlement rules can apply only when there is an element of bounty and, in most cases, it will be hard to argue that there is any element of bounty in a settlement made by one party to a marriage under the compulsion of a court order or as a result of arm's-length negotiation (or both).

The settlement rules could however be an issue in a case where a capital settlement is made for the benefit of the children of the marriage as well as, or instead of, one of the spouses. In *Harvey v Sivyer* [1986] Ch 119 Nourse J explained an earlier decision of the House of Lords on the basis that the natural relationship between parent and young child was one of such deep affection and concern that there must always be an element of bounty by the parent, even where the provision is on the face of things made under compulsion.

16.11 It follows, as one would expect, that no income tax advantage may be obtained by maintaining a minor child through the making of a capital settlement on the occasion of a divorce: distributions from such a settlement for the benefit of a minor child would be likely to be caught by *ITTOIA 2005, s 629*. The possibility of the application of the settlement rules should always be considered where a capital settlement is made on the occasion of marriage breakdown, especially where the children of the marriage may benefit. However, the possibility of the settlor's spouse (or civil partner) benefiting under the settlement will not in itself lead to the application of the settlement rules if the parties are separated under an order of the court or a separation agreement or in other cases where the separation is likely to be permanent (see *ITTOIA 2005, s 625(4)*).

Capital gains tax

16.12 The financial arrangements made in the context of divorce and relationship breakdown will often involve the transfer of assets between the parties. They may also involve the sale of assets to third parties to raise funds and the transfer of assets into or out of a settlement. The legislation contains no specific exemptions and major liabilities often arise. Planning for CGT currently needs to take into account the fact that, if the proposals in the Pre-Budget Report 2007 are enacted, gains realised after the end of 2007/08 tax year will generally be charged at a lower rate than previously but will no longer qualify for taper relief.

16.13 *Separation and divorce*

For both income tax and CGT, a married couple or civil partners are treated as living together unless:

- they are separated under an order of a court of competent jurisdiction;
- they are separated by deed of separation; or
- they are in fact separated in circumstances in which the separation is likely to be permanent.

See *TCGA 1992, s 288(3), ITA 2007, s 1011*.

Disposals between spouses before the end of the tax year of permanent separation

16.13 Disposals before the end of the tax year of permanent separation take place at 'no gain no loss' in accordance with *TCGA 1992, s 58*. See CGM 22202. Taper relief on such transfers is also continuous as between the spouses, with special rules for determining whether the asset in question qualifies for the higher rate of taper relief as a business asset (*TCGA 1992, Sch A1, para 15*).

Thus it will often be advantageous to accelerate the transfer of assets standing at a gain to a time before the end of the year of permanent separation. However, such transfers, while they will avoid any immediate CGT liability for the transferring spouse, may store up future problems for the recipient spouse who will thus take with a reduced CGT acquisition cost.

Transfers between the end of the tax year of permanent separation and decree absolute

16.14 During this period transfers no longer qualify for 'no gain no loss' treatment. However the spouses will still be connected persons within *TCGA 1992, s 286* with the result that transfers will be deemed to take place at open market value in accordance with *TCGA 1992, s 18*.

Transfers between spouses after decree absolute

16.15 Following decree absolute the couple will no longer be connected persons for CGT purposes (unless they are connected for some other reason). However, it will be wise to assume that, one way or another, transfers of assets between them made under a court order or as part of the financial arrangements made between them in the context of the divorce will fall within *TCGA 1992,* *s 17* and thus be treated as taking place at open market value, unless they are, as a question of fact, the result of arm's-length bargains.

Hold-over relief

16.16 The view of HMRC is that where there is a disposal of an asset from one spouse to another after the end of the year of assessment in which they separate but prior to decree absolute this is, where there is no recourse to the courts, usually made in exchange for a surrender by the donee of rights which they would otherwise be able to exercise to obtain alternative financial provision. HMRC thus takes the view that the value of the rights surrendered represents actual consideration of an amount which would reduce the gain potentially eligible for hold-over relief to nil. They accept that, exceptionally, there may be a substantial gratuitous element in the transfer so that hold-over relief will be available in the case of an appropriate asset.

16.17 HMRC formerly took this view in the case of transfers under a consent order. However, they now accept that, because a court order reflects the exercise by the court of its independent statutory jurisdiction and is not the consequence of any party to the proceedings agreeing to surrender alternative rights in return for assets, there is no actual consideration. Thus hold-over relief under *TCGA 1992, s 165* may be available for transfers of assets under a court order, even a consent order. This may be an extremely useful relief in the case of business assets, including shares in unlisted trading companies, and agricultural land. However hold-over relief reduces the acquiring spouse's acquisition cost and may thus store up problems for the future. The relief requires the consent of the acquiring spouse. (See CGM 67192.)

The time of the CGT disposal

16.18 It will be important to establish this. This is not only because disposals made before the end of the year of permanent separation will qualify for 'no gain no loss' treatment but because the timing of the disposal will determine when any CGT has to be paid and the availability of exemptions and reliefs, including the annual exemption, taper relief and loss relief. Moreover, the value of the asset may change as time goes on.

In the case of assets transferred outside the framework of a court order the normal rules apply. The date of disposal will thus be the date of actual transfer except in a case where the transfer was made in accordance with a binding contract, in which case the date of the contract will be the date of the disposal (unless it was a conditional contract, in which case the date of disposal will be the date when the condition is fulfilled). This is governed by *TCGA 1992, s 28* in the usual way.

16.19 *Separation and divorce*

16.19 The position is more difficult where the disposal is made in accordance with a court order. The view of HMRC, as set out in CGM 22426, is as follows:

- Where a disposal is made under a court order following decree absolute, the date of disposal is the date of the court order.
- Where the disposal is made under a consent order made before decree absolute, the Inspector is to accept the agreement of the parties or obtain documentation and advice as necessary.
- Where the disposal is made under another court order before decree absolute, the date of disposal is the date of the court order.

16.20 If there is little or no tax at stake, the inspector may accept the agreement of the parties (CGM 22425).

It is submitted that, since in a normal case any requirement to transfer an asset embodied in a consent order will take effect only on decree absolute, the date of the disposal will be the date of decree absolute.

It will be seen that there is some scope for planning here. If desired and with goodwill the disposal of an asset could be accelerated by actually transferring the asset (in which case any subsequent court order could leave its ownership unchanged). Alternatively the disposal could be deferred by slowing the litigation.

The receipt of lump sums under court orders

16.21 There is no CGT on the receipt of a lump sum under a court order in itself. The authority for the payment of the lump sum comes from the court order, not from the disposal of any asset. HMRC accepts that this principle extends to lump sums ordered by the court when discharging previous orders for periodical payments (see *Revenue Bulletin, April 2001*).

See below for the special circumstances applying to disposals of the main residence.

Inheritance tax

16.22 Until the enactment of *FA 2006*, IHT was rarely an issue in the context of divorce and relationship breakdown. This was for a number of reasons.

First, dispositions made on divorce for the benefit of a former spouse, whether under the court order or as a result of arm's-length negotiations, are normally accepted as being within *IHTA 1984, s 10* (dispositions not intended to confer gratuitous benefit). See IHTM 04165.

Such dispositions may also fall within *IHTA 1984, s 11* (dispositions for the maintenance of family). This applies to dispositions made by one party to a marriage in favour of the other party or of a child of either party which are either:

- for the maintenance of the other party; or
- for the maintenance, education or training of the child for a period ending not later than the year in which he attains the age of 18 or, after attaining that age, ceases to undergo full-time education or training.

16.23 The provision expressly extends to dispositions made on the occasion of the dissolution of a marriage. However the provision is still somewhat limited in its effect, especially in the light of the decision of the special commissioner in the recent *Phizackerley case* (2007) SpC 591 that the provision of housing, in the context of a transfer from husband to wife, was not the provision of maintenance.

Dispositions falling within either *IHTA 1984, s 10* or *s 11* are not transfers of value for IHT purposes.

16.24 In any case, since a married couple are still husband and wife until decree absolute the spouse exemption will still apply to outright transfers made up to decree absolute, even after permanent separation, unless restricted by the domicile of the recipient spouse. Correspondingly, on decree absolute the related property rule ceases to apply (*IHTA 1984, s 161*).

Major difficulties have, however, been caused by the changes made by *FA 2006* to the IHT treatment of settled property. It often happens that, as part of the financial arrangements made on divorce or relationship breakdown, an interest-in-possession settlement will be established. Typically, this will take the form of a life interest for the spouse/former spouse with remainder to the children of the marriage.

16.25 The difficulty is that, even though the transfer of capital into the settlement will often (though not necessarily) fall within *IHTA 1984, s 10* and thus not be a transfer of value the settled property will, under the new rules, be 'relevant property' exposed to the ten-yearly and exit charges, notwithstanding the former spouse's interest in possession.

This change discourages the establishment of such settlements and causes particular difficulties in the context of the former matrimonial home, on which see below.

Stamp duty land tax and stamp duty

16.26 SDLT is rarely an issue in the context of separation and divorce.

16.27 *Separation and divorce*

There is a very wide exemption contained in *FA 2003, Sch 3, para 3*, which provides that a transaction between one party to a marriage and the other is exempt from charge to SDLT if it is effected:

- in pursuance of an order of the court made on granting in respect of the parties a decree of divorce, nullity of marriage or judicial separation;
- in pursuance of an order of a court made in connection with the dissolution or annulment of the marriage, or the parties' judicial separation, at any time after the granting of such a decree;
- in pursuance of:
  - an order of a court made at any time under *Matrimonial Causes Act 1973, s 24A;* or
  - an incidental order of a court made under *Family Law (Scotland) Act 1985, s 8(2)* or by virtue of *s 14(1)* of that Act;
- at any time in pursuance of an agreement of the parties made in contemplation or otherwise in connection with the dissolution or annulment of the marriage or their judicial separation.

(This statement of the legislation omits some wording obsolete because of changes to matrimonial law.)

16.27 Even in the absence of this exemption, SDLT would not often be an issue because, in the context of separation or divorce, there would usually be no chargeable consideration for SDLT purposes given for the transfer of an interest in land. SDLT would, however, in the absence of this exemption, be an issue if, for example, land was transferred subject to a mortgage.

It should be noted that this exemption does not extend to transfers made to third parties, for example to a child of the marriage, as part of financial arrangements made on the occasion of separation or divorce.

There is a similar wide exemption from stamp duty contained in *FA 1985, s 83*.

Pre-owned assets tax

16.28 This is seldom an issue.

The disposal of any property is an 'excluded transaction' in relation to any person if, inter alia:

- The property was transferred to his spouse or civil partner (or, where the transfer has been ordered by a court, to his former spouse or civil partner).

Separation and divorce **16.31**

- It was a disposal by way of gift (or, where the transfer is for the benefit of his former spouse or civil partner, in accordance with a court order), by virtue of which the property became settled property in which his spouse or civil partner or former spouse or civil partner is beneficially entitled to an interest in possession (see *FA 2004, Sch 15, para 10(1)*).

PARTICULAR ISSUES

The matrimonial home and the CGT main residence exemption

16.29 The breakdown of a relationship will almost invariably lead to one or both parties to the marriage leaving the matrimonial home. It will also often lead to the transfer of the former matrimonial home, or of an interest in it, from one spouse to the other, or from one spouse into a settlement for the benefit of the other. Relationship breakdown will also often be followed by the sale of the former matrimonial home to a third party. The situation is even more complicated if the couple have owned or occupied more than one property.

The first step will be to establish to which (if any) of the properties in question the main residence exemption applies. It should be borne in mind that, in the case of an individual living with his spouse or civil partner, there can only be one main residence for both, so long as living together and, where a notice as to which residence the exemption is to apply to affects both the individual and his spouse or civil partner, it must be given by both (see *TCGA 1992, s 222(6)*).

16.30 Moreover, in the case of an individual living with his spouse or civil partner, if there is a disposal of, or of an interest in, a dwelling house which is their only or main residence from one to the other, then the recipient inherits the transferor's history of entitlement to the exemption (see *TCGA 1992, s 222(7)* and CGM 64950). If the exemption is restricted in the hands of the transferor, this problem thus passes on to the transferee.

There may be scope for planning if a property is to be transferred that has qualified for the exemption during part only of its ownership by the transferor but which will qualify without restriction in the hands of the transferee: if the transfer can be effected within the 'no gain no loss' rule but outside *s 222(7)* the chargeable element of the gain falls away.

16.31 In most cases, the main residence exemption will attach to the former matrimonial home, though if the couple have occupied more than one residence they may have made a joint election for the exemption to attach to a residence which is not, on the face of things, their main residence.

16.32 *Separation and divorce*

In this context the 'three-year rule' contained in *TCGA 1992, s 223(1)* is extremely helpful. If the main residence exemption attaches to the former matrimonial home then, if a spouse has ceased to occupy that former matrimonial home as a result of the breakdown of the relationship, he or she has 36 months in which to transfer his or her interest in the property before losing entitlement to the exemption (though bearing in mind that it may be restricted in some other way, for example by a previous period of non-occupation).

16.32 Once a couple have separated permanently, each becomes separately entitled to the main residence exemption and may make a separate election for the exemption to attach to a separate property, if otherwise entitled to do so. Prompt action may be needed to make the best use of the exemption.

Example 16.1

Mr and Mrs A own two properties, a house in the country and a flat in London, in each case as beneficial tenants in common in equal shares. Both have appreciated greatly in value. They divide their time between the two but have made a joint election for the London flat to qualify for the exemption, on the basis that it is increasing in value more quickly and that it is likely to be sold first.

The relationship breaks down and as a result Mr A ceases to occupy the London flat. He acquires rented accommodation in London for his own use. However he continues to make regular use of the country house at weekends (when Mrs A is not there).

It is less than two years since these changes happened. It is anticipated that, when a settlement is negotiated between the parties, Mr A will assign to Mrs A his interest in both the country house and the London flat. Mr A also intends, at a later stage, to purchase a further London property for his future occupation, in which case he will give up his rented accommodation.

Mr A will probably be well advised to make an immediate election in favour of the country house. This will prevent his exemption from attaching to his rented accommodation where it would be wasted. It will give him at least three years' worth of the exemption in respect of the country house, where it will be more useful. This will not prejudice his entitlement to the exemption in respect of the London flat which will continue to apply for up to three years after his departure from it. When he acquires his new property in London, he should consider whether to make a fresh election in favour of that property, to make sure that it attaches to that property, if he thinks it will be more useful there.

Extra-Statutory Concession D6

16.33 In cases where the transfer of a property, or of an interest in it, will not in any case be exempt under the three-year rule, it may be advantageous to claim the benefit of Extra-Statutory Concession (ESC) D6. This concession provides that, where a married couple separate or are divorced and one partner ceases to occupy the matrimonial home and subsequently as part of a financial settlement disposes of the home, or an interest in it, to the other partner the home may be regarded for the purposes of the CGT legislation as continuing to be a residence of the transferring partner from the date his or her occupation ceases until the date of transfer, provided that it has throughout this period been the other partner's main residence. Thus, where the husband leaves the matrimonial home while still owning it, the usual CGT exemption or relief for the taxpayer's only or main residence would be given on the subsequent transfer to the wife, provided she has continued to live in the house and the husband has not elected that some other house should be treated for CGT purposes as his main residence for this period.

16.34 The limitations of this concession should be noted. In particular it applies in relation to transfers between spouses, thus not to a sale on the open market, and it requires the spouse who claims the benefit of the concession to give up the main residence exemption in respect of any other property for the period in question, thereby potentially storing up CGT problems for himself in the future. It is therefore much less beneficial than the three-year rule, in cases where that rule applies.

The position where the former matrimonial home is to be retained following separation of the couple for occupation by one spouse only and where the non-occupying spouse wishes to keep a stake in the property

16.35 Here one enters difficult territory.

One traditional approach is to seek a *Mesher* order. Under this type of order, one spouse will have the sole right to occupy the property (perhaps with the children of the marriage) during his or her life or until the happening of a specified event, such as all the children of the marriage attaining a specified age or completing their tertiary education, but on the death of the occupying spouse or on the happening of that event, the property is to be sold and the proceeds divided between the two spouses (or their estates).

In such a case, the view of HMRC is that the making of such an order results in the property becoming settled property for CGT (see CGM 65367).

16.36 There will thus be disposals by both spouses of their entire interests in the property. However, this will usually be of no consequence for CGT pur-

16.37 *Separation and divorce*

poses. Almost invariably, the occupying spouse will qualify for the main residence exemption and, usually the non-occupying spouse will be protected by the three-year rule.

Once the property has become settled property then, since usually the occupying spouse will occupy as his or her main residence, the main residence exemption will apply, subject to the making of a claim as required by *TCGA 1992, s 225*.

16.37 A *Mesher*-type order is thus attractive from the point of view of CGT, except in a case where there has been a very long interval since the departure of the non-occupying spouse from the former matrimonial home with the result that he is exposed to CGT on the disposal he is deemed to make on the making of the order.

Once the house is settled property, the interests of the former spouses in the property will be interests in settled property and thus, in a normal situation, exempt from CGT under *TCGA 1992, s 76*.

A similar result follows if the property is expressly settled upon the occupying spouse for life or some lesser period.

16.38 However, since *FA 2006*, such an arrangement has become unattractive from the point of view of IHT. Although the definition of settled property for CGT purposes is quite distinct from the definition of a settlement for IHT purposes (these definitions being contained in, respectively, *TCGA 1992, s 68* and *IHTA 1984, s 43*), if property is settled property for the purposes of CGT, it will usually be hard to deny that it is comprised in a settlement for the purposes of IHT. The occupying spouse will normally insist, for his or her own protection, upon an exclusive right to occupy the property. Any arrangement under which one person has the exclusive right to occupy a property rent free but without being the exclusive beneficial owner seems likely to constitute a settlement for IHT purposes, unless the occupation is under the terms of a lease other than for life.

If the property has become comprised in a settlement for IHT purposes then it will be 'relevant property' and thus exposed to the ten-yearly and exit charges. These charges will, as the law currently stands, be at a maximum rate of 6%. They may, however, be irksome depending upon the value involved, particularly because, by definition, there will normally be no liquid funds comprised in the settlement from which the charges could be paid.

16.39 Furthermore, although the former matrimonial home will thus be relevant property, the capital interests of the former spouses in it will also be within their estates for IHT purposes as reversionary interests in settled property to which the settlors are entitled (*IHTA 1984, s 48(1)(b)*) (assuming both spouses previously had interests in the property).

One alternative approach would involve the transfer of the property into the outright beneficial ownership of the occupying spouse, the non-occupying spouse being given a charge over the property redeemable only on the happening of the events under which a sale of the property would have been triggered under a *Mesher*-type order. The amount needed to redeem the charge would be linked to the value of the property at that time.

However, in the tax treatment of such a charge, one enters especially difficult territory. It is reasonably clear that the 'profit' realised by the non-occupying spouse on the redemption of the charge would be subject, one way or another, either to income tax or to CGT, subject to whatever of the usual reliefs and exemptions were available.

It is, however, harder to see precisely how the gain would be charged to tax, or how it would be calculated.

16.40 Depending upon the drafting of the charge, it might qualify as a 'deeply discounted security' within *ITTOIA 2005, Pt 4, Ch* 8. In that case there would be a charge to income tax on the difference between the redemption proceeds and the amount paid to acquire the security (*ITTOIA 2005, s 439*). However it might, depending upon the drafting, qualify as an 'excluded indexed security' under *ITTOIA 2005, s 433*, on the basis that its value was linked to the value of an asset within the scope of CGT and thus not be a 'deeply discounted security'.

Another possibility is that *s 756* of the *Income Tax Act 2007* (previously *s 776* of the *ICTA 1988*) might apply on the basis that the charge was property deriving its value from land and was acquired with the sole or main object of realising a gain from disposing of the land.

(It would seem very hard to apply *s 756* to a beneficial interest in the former matrimonial home under a *Mesher*-type order, since this would normally be, in substance, retention of a pre-existing beneficial interest in the property).

16.41 If the profit realised on redemption of the charge was not subject to income tax then it would, clearly, be subject to CGT. It is generally assumed that the profit would be subject to CGT rather than to income tax.

One of the difficulties would lie in establishing the acquisition cost of the charge since its market value on creation would clearly reflect the delay before it was due to be redeemed and the uncertainty as to when this would happen, as well as the possibility of an increase in value.

16.42 *Separation and divorce*

Thus, the choice seems to lie between incurring small but recurrent charges to IHT or what might be a more substantial income tax or CGT charge at a future date, but when there would be funds to pay the tax.

PARTICULAR SITUATIONS

Extracting funds from companies and settlements

16.42 Financial arrangements made in the context of relationship breakdown and divorce will often involve the extraction of funds from companies and trusts. There are no special exemptions which apply in this situation and all of the usual tax difficulties in extracting funds from companies and trusts will need to be considered.

If one spouse has much of his or her capital tied up in a trust or company structure, and if the other spouse is seeking to obtain a lump sum that can only be paid if funds are extracted from that structure, then the spouse seeking the lump sum can be expected to press for funds to be distributed to the other spouse first. In that case, any adverse tax consequences will fall upon that other spouse and the funds will reach the recipient spouse in a 'clean' form.

16.43 If funds seem likely to reach the recipient spouse with tax liabilities attached to them then, clearly, those tax liabilities must be quantified in order to ascertain the adequacy of the capital payment.

This will be especially significant if funds are to be extracted from an offshore trust. A capital payment to a beneficiary out of an offshore trust may attract an income tax liability under the *Income Tax Act 2007, s 731* (previously *Taxes Act 1988, s 740*) or a CGT liability under *TCGA 1992, s 87*.

16.44 If one spouse is UK domiciled and the other not, and if funds are to be extracted from a settlement subject to *TCGA 1992, s 87*, then it will usually be desirable for a distribution to be made to the non-UK domiciled spouse, who cannot be liable under that provision.

Permanent separation and decree absolute may have a beneficial effect upon the liability to income tax or CGT of a spouse who is a settlor in relation to a settlement.

16.45 Following permanent separation, the fact that the permanently separated non-settlor spouse may benefit under the settlement will not in itself be sufficient to bring that settlement within the 'onshore' settlement rule (see above) nor within the rules attributing chargeable gains of an onshore settlement to a settlor with an interest in that settlement (*TCGA 1992, s 77*).

The fact that a former spouse of a settlor is a beneficiary or potential beneficiary of an overseas settlement will not, in itself, be sufficient to bring that settlement within *TCGA, s 86* leading to the attribution of its gains to a spouse who is a settlor in relation to that settlement (*TCGA 1992, Sch 5, para 2*).

Spouses with non-UK domicile

16.46 If one or both spouses have non-UK domiciles and are taxable on the remittance basis then the greatest care should be taken that the financial arrangements made in the context of relationship breakdown and divorce do not involve any remittance of funds to the UK such as to give rise to a UK tax liability. In particular, if the financial arrangements involve the transfer of funds taxable on the remittance basis between spouses, great care should taken that this transfer is effected before the funds are brought into the UK, if indeed it is necessary to bring them into the UK, so that the remittance is not made by the spouse in whose hands the remittance might give rise to a tax liability.

The assignment of life policies

16.47 The financial arrangements made in the context of relationship breakdown or divorce will often involve the assignment of life policies, or interests in life policies, between spouses.

If a non-qualifying life policy or, in certain limited circumstances, a qualifying life policy is assigned for money or money's worth then there may be a charge to higher rate tax in accordance with *ITTOIA 2005, Pt 4, Ch 9*.

For the purposes of that chapter, however, an assignment of rights under a policy or of a share in such rights is ignored if it is made between spouses or civil partners living together (*ITTOIA 2005, s 487*).

16.48 The Revenue previously took the view that the transfer by one spouse to the other of all or some of the rights under a policy as part of a divorce settlement was invariably for money or money's worth, thus potentially leading to a higher rate income tax charge. However, HMRC now accept that transferring ownership of the rights conferred by a life insurance policy under a court order is not for money or money's worth and no gain can arise because of it (see the note published in *Tax Bulletin,* December 2003, currently available on the HMRC website). This change of policy followed the change of policy in relation to CGT hold-over relief.

It follows that, if it is desired to avoid the higher rate income tax charge that may arise on the assignment of a life policy or of an interest in a life policy for money or money's worth, and if such an assignment is intended to take place in the context of a divorce, it would be as well to make sure that the assignment took place in pursuance of a court order.

16.48 *Separation and divorce*

This HMRC change of practice may enable an immediate tax charge to be avoided but it is not all good news since the recipient spouse is, sooner or later, likely to be faced with an income tax charge when a 'chargeable event' arises in relation to the policy in question, if the policy is of a type subject to this charge.

Chapter 17

Anti-avoidance

Robert Maas FCA FTII FIIT Tax Partner, Blackstone Franks LLP

INTRODUCTION

17.1 When considering any form of planning, it needs to be borne in mind that often your idea is not original. It may well have been thought of before, often by HMRC, in which case Parliament may have taken steps to prevent it achieving your desired object.

The UK has a very large number of statutory anti-avoidance provisions. Many of these are free-standing but in addition some statutory provisions contain in-built anti-avoidance rules. Accordingly, it is often difficult to identify where an anti-avoidance rule might impact on a proposed transaction. This chapter will highlight some of the most important provisions but can do no more than scratch the surface in identifying the snares that need to be circumvented.

17.2 It is equally difficult to recognise avoidance. Broadly speaking, anything that results in the payment of less tax than the Chancellor of the Exchequer envisaged ought to be due as a result of introducing a particular provision is likely to be avoidance.

People and businesses are perfectly entitled to seek to avoid tax. However, the tax planner needs to accept that HMRC and the Treasury both regard tax avoidance as immoral and are likely to seek hard to thwart it.

17.3 Unfortunately, HMRC seem to give mixed messages on avoidance. They clearly feel that avoidance of payment of a very large amount of tax by a single taxpayer, or the use of a device which is marketed to a number of taxpayers, is wholly unacceptable to them and they will attack it vigorously. Nevertheless, they seem to tolerate avoidance of small amounts by a large number of taxpayers and attack the use of such strategies infrequently, seeking specific anti-avoidance legislation to stop the use of such planning when the loss of tax becomes too great. However, it is dangerous to assume that they will always regard small scale tax avoidance as a sort of sport for the masses and seek to challenge tax avoidance only when it becomes the preserve of the elite.

17.4 *Anti-avoidance*

A good example is the shockwaves created by the Arctic Systems case (*Jones v Garnett* [2006] STC 1667) where, having seemingly long tolerated tax avoidance by use of income splitting by spouses, HMRC suddenly started to seek to apply the settlement anti-avoidance provisions which were specifically designed to prevent, amongst other things, the transfer of income from one spouse to another in an attempt to reduce the overall family tax burden.

17.4 It also needs to be remembered that under a self-assessment system the taxpayer is expected to himself identify the effect of anti-avoidance rules and apply them in declaring his taxable income. It is not a case of trying something in the hope that HMRC will not pick it up. Deliberately understating one's income by ignoring an anti-avoidance provision is fraud. You need to be able to reasonably form a view that the provision does not apply to the transactions carried out before you are entitled to take the stance that it has no effect on what your client has done.

17.5 The other key point to bear in mind is that the dividing line between tax avoidance and tax evasion can sometimes be a narrow one. That is not to say that one shades into another – there is a clear distinction between the two – but rather that successful tax avoidance often depends both on transactions taking place in a particular sequence and on being able to evidence what occurred. Where an avoidance scheme is not properly carried out there can be a temptation to fill in the missing pieces when challenged by HMRC either by pretending that things happened when they did not or creating backdated documents. Such tactics are fraudulent and turn the attempted avoidance into evasion. This is a difficult area, however.

For example, if a meeting actually took place but no one thought to minute it there is nothing illegal in writing up the minute some time after the event, provided both that the minute actually reflects what took place and if HMRC ask when the minute was drawn up the correct date is supplied. The longer after a meeting took place the record of what happened is made, the greater the risk that memories may have faded, which might affect the reliability of the minute. On the other hand to minute the declaration of a dividend in circumstances where the directors would undoubtedly have voted a dividend had it been suggested to them at the time but it was not, is not a tardily prepared record of what took place; it is simply a lie.

ICTA 1988, SS 703–707 – TRANSACTIONS IN SECURITIES

17.6 The first of the main anti-avoidance provisions, *ICTA 1988, s 703*, applies where:

- in one of five specified circumstances (A-E); and

- in consequence of a transaction in securities (or of the combined effect of two or more such transactions),

a person is in a position to obtain, or has obtained, a tax advantage (*ICTA 1988, s 703(1)*). The provision requires the tax advantage to be countered by either an assessment, the nullifying of a right to repayment, the return of a repayment already made, or the computation or recomputation of profits or gains or liability to tax on such basis as HMRC by notice may specify. As the counteractions all seem to require HMRC to do something this is not a provision that the taxpayer can be expected to apply against himself. It is, however, a provision where HMRC are fairly adept at identifying the possibility of applying it.

17.7 The specified circumstances that are most likely to apply are circumstances D and E. Circumstance D is where, in connection with the distribution of profits of a company which is either under the control of not more than five persons or whose shares are not listed (and actually dealt in) on the London Stock Exchange, a person receives (in such a way that he does not pay tax on it as income) a consideration which either:

- represents the value of assets available for distribution by way of dividend;
- is received in respect of future receipts of the company; or
- is, or represents the value of, trading stock of the company.

Circumstance E is where in connection with the transfer (directly or indirectly) of assets of a company to which circumstance D applies to another such company (or in connection with any transaction in securities in which two or more paragraph D companies are concerned) a person receives non-taxable consideration (ie not taxable as income) which is or represents the value of assets available for distribution by a paragraph D company and which consists of any share capital or security issued by such a company.

Circumstances A to C apply to dividend stripping and bond washing. They broadly apply where a person receives an abnormal amount by way of dividend and the receipt is taken into account in calculating an exemption from tax, the set-off of losses or some other relief, or the person becomes entitled to a deduction in calculating profits for a fall in value of shares brought about by the payment of the dividend.

17.8 The provision does not apply if the taxpayer can show that:

- the transaction or transactions was carried out either for bona fide commercial reasons or in the ordinary course of making or managing investments; and

17.9 Anti-avoidance

- that none of them had as their main object (or one of their main objects) to enable a tax advantage to be obtained.

(ICTA 1988, s 703(1))

17.9 There is an advance clearance procedure. Application for clearance is made to:

> Mohini Sawhney,
> Clearance and Counteraction Team,
> Anti-Avoidance Group Intelligence,
> First Floor,
> London,
> WC2B 6NR

The provision needs to be considered on any transaction that involves a company. It would be unwise not to seek advance clearance for any such transaction that involves a person receiving cash in a capital form and retaining shares in the company, or in a successor company to it.

17.10 Transactions that have been held to come within *ICTA 1988, s 703* include:

- The sale by an individual of shares in a company to another company in which he is also a shareholder (*IRC v Cleary* (1966) 44 TC 399). It was irrelevant that the sale was at market value; what matters is that it resulted in cash passing from the purchaser company to its shareholder in a form that was taxed less heavily than if that cash had been distributed by the payment of a dividend. The sale of, for example, a property will not trigger the section as that does not involve a transaction in securities.

- A scrip issue of redeemable shares and their subsequent redemption by the company (*IRC v Parker* (1966) 43 TC 396). In the *Parker* case the redemption took place eight years after the scrip issue but the two together were nevertheless held to have given rise to a tax advantage as they resulted in money coming out of the company as capital rather than as dividend. *Section 703* is no longer needed to counter such a transaction as the redemption of a scrip issue of shares is now a distribution, and as such triggers tax as if the redemption proceeds (less any amount subscribed for the shares) were income.

- A reduction of share capital followed later by a scrip issue (*IRC v Horrocks* (1968) 44 TC 645). The scrip issue was contingent on the reduction in capital though.

- The sale of a company, Kenyon, to another company, Pelkem, in exchange for shares, with Kenyon then paying a dividend to its new parent (*Anysz v IRC* (1977) 53 TC 601). It was held that the Pelkem shares

Anti-avoidance **17.11**

were received in connection with the payment of the dividend. The courts may well have been influenced by the fact that Kenyon had entered into a scheme to defer tax on the distributed profit and the dividend left it insolvent, so the real tax advantage was the non-payment of corporation tax on the profit rather than the advantage that was taxed, namely the obtaining by Mr Anysz of the capital value of Pelkem instead of his receiving the Kenyon dividend.

- The liquidation of a company with the liquidator entering into an agreement (the liquidation agreement) with the shareholders under which the liquidator agreed to sell the company's business to another company controlled by those shareholders in exchange for a loan note, the loan note and the surplus cash then being distributed to the shareholders (*IRC v Joiner* (1975) 50 TC 419). The House of Lords viewed the transaction in securities as the liquidation combined with the liquidation agreement, leaving open whether a liquidation on its own can be a transaction in securities by virtue of which a tax advantage is received.

- The sale by a company of most of its stock to a new company controlled by the same shareholders, leaving it with one very valuable item of stock only, followed by the sale of the company for cash (*IRC v Wiggins* (1978) 53 TC 639). The provision was held to apply because the shareholders received a greater amount from selling their shares than they would have ended up with had they sold the stock item, paid corporation tax and distributed the balance by way of dividend.

- Most of the recent cases have been concerned with whether a dividend is abnormal within the terms of circumstances A to C (*IRC v Universities Superannuation Scheme Ltd* (1997) 70 TC 193; *IRC v Trustees of Sema Group Pension Scheme* [2003] STC 95). Both of these cases involved dividends to tax-exempt funds.

ICTA 1988, SS 739–744 – TRANSFERS OF ASSETS ABROAD; ICTA 1988, S 13 – GAINS OF NON-RESIDENT COMPANIES; AND TCGA 1992, SS 86–90 – GAINS OF NON-RESIDENT SETTLEMENTS

17.11 There is a temptation to seek to avoid tax by the use of tax haven vehicles to carry out transactions, particularly UK property transactions. Such planning is unlikely to work where the client is both UK resident and UK domiciled (although some intricate schemes using double tax agreements might be effective). Certainly no transactions involving the use of overseas vehicles ought to be contemplated without first considering the impact of these provisions.

17.12 *Anti-avoidance*

17.12 ICTA 1988, s 739 applies where, by virtue of (or in consequence of) a transfer of assets by virtue or in consequence whereof (either alone or in conjunction with associated operations) income becomes payable to a person resident or domiciled outside the UK either alone or in conjunction with associated operations, an individual who is ordinarily resident in the UK has power to enjoy any income of a person resident or domiciled outside the UK which would be chargeable to income tax if it were received by that UK resident (*ICTA 1988, s 739(2)*). Broadly speaking a person has power to enjoy income if he or his spouse or civil partner can benefit from it either currently or at some future time, whether in an income or capital form, and even if he can only benefit if some other person exercises a power (or a series of other people do so). The tax charge arises when the income arises, not when the benefit is received, except where there is no legal power to enjoy the income but the UK resident nevertheless in fact receives a benefit, when the tax charge obviously arises when the benefit is actually received.

17.13 The sort of thing that it will catch is where a UK resident carries out a property dealing transaction through an offshore company (the dealing profit will become taxable on the individual), carries out a property investment transaction through an offshore company (the rental income will be taxable on the individual), or sets up an offshore company that charges a management fee to the individual's UK company (the offshore company's profit will be taxable on the individual).

17.14 It should be noted that the tax charge is often higher than if the individual had carried out the transaction through a UK company (because the *ICTA 1988, s 739* tax may be at 40% whereas corporation tax would have been only 20%).

It should also be noted that the taxpayer is expected to self-assess the tax charge. The second part of question 6 to the tax return (Have you or could you have received or enjoyed directly or indirectly, or benefited in any way from, income or payments of a foreign entity as a result of a transfer of assets made in this or earlier years) is specifically directed at *ICTA 1988, ss 739* and *740*. It would be fraudulent to answer 'No' if a person either receives or has power to enjoy such income.

17.15 *ICTA 1988, 740* applies where by virtue (or in consequence of) a transfer of assets, either alone or in conjunction with associated operations, income becomes payable to a person who is resident or domiciled outside the UK and an individual ordinarily resident in the UK (who is not liable to tax under *s 739* by reference to the transfer) receives a benefit provided out of assets which are available for that purpose by virtue (or in consequence) of the transfer or any associated operations (*ICTA 1988, s 740(1)*).

17.16 This ensures that UK tax cannot be escaped by having the offshore company (or other vehicle) owned by an overseas trust of which the UK resident's children or grandchildren are the beneficiaries but he and his spouse (or civil partner) are specifically excluded from being able to benefit from the trust. *ICTA 1988, s 740* taxes the income only when it is actually received by the UK beneficiary (whether as income or capital) or he receives a benefit from the income. It does not matter if the beneficiary has power to enjoy the income if it is retained within the overseas company or settlement.

This effectively means that offshore vehicles can be used to defer, albeit not avoid, UK tax if the UK resident is prepared to forgo any benefit to himself or his spouse and build up a nest egg overseas for younger generations. However, most people cannot see a lot of point in building up funds overseas in circumstances that they will attract a UK tax charge as and when there is a need or wish to use those funds.

17.17 Neither *ICTA 1988, s 739* nor *s 740* applies if either:

(a) the transfer and any associated operations all took place before 5 December 2005 and the individual can show that either:

    (i) the purpose of avoiding liability to tax was not the purpose (or one of the purposes) for which the transfer, or associated operations, or any of them were effected; or

    (ii) the transfer and any associated operations were bona fide commercial transactions and were not designed for the purpose of avoiding liability to tax;

(b) the transfer and any associated operations all took place after 4 December 2005 and the individual can show that either:

    (i) it would not be reasonable to draw the conclusion, from all of the circumstances of the case, that the purpose of avoiding liability to tax was the purpose (or one of the purposes) for which the relevant transactions (or any of them) were effected; or

    (ii) all of the relevant transactions were genuine commercial transactions and it would not be reasonable to draw the conclusion, from all the circumstances of the case, that any one or more of them was more than incidentally designed for the purpose of avoiding liability to tax; or

(c) some only of the relevant transactions took place before 5 December 2005 and:

    (i) the conditions in (a) above are met in respect of all the pre-5 December 2005 transactions; and

    (ii) the conditions in (b) above are met in respect of all the post-4 December 2005 transactions.

(*ICTA 1988, ss 741–741C*)

17.18 *Anti-avoidance*

For the purpose of these exemptions, tax means any UK tax (for which HMRC is responsible). It does not include foreign taxes. It is not limited to income tax though.

17.18 For the purpose of (b) (and (c)(ii)) above, the intentions and purposes of any person who designs or effects any of the relevant transactions or who provides advice in relation to any of those transactions must be taken into account. Furthermore a relevant transaction is a commercial transaction only if it is effected in the course of a trade or business (or with a view to setting up a trade or business). The making and/or managing of investments is not a trade for this purpose (except to the extent that the manager is an independent person dealing at arm's-length with the owner of the investments). A transaction cannot be a commercial transaction if it would not have been entered into between independent persons dealing at arm's-length or if it is not made on arm's-length terms (*ICTA 1988, s 741A(4)–(7)*).

The transfer of assets that triggers these provisions need not be from the UK resident to the non-resident. Any transfer will suffice. Subscribing for shares in a company is a transfer of assets (or at least paying for them is). So is transferring funds to trustees on the creation of a settlement.

17.19 Examples of transactions that have been held to fall within these provisions are:

- The transfer of assets to an overseas company in consideration of the issue of debentures to the UK resident transferor (*Admiral Earl Beatty's Executors v IRC* (1940) 23 TC 574). The fact that the debentures would one day be redeemed gave power to enjoy the income of the company as it could be used to make that repayment.

- The transfer of assets to an overseas company in return for A shares and a promissory note. The A shares carried the voting rights but no rights to income (this belonged entirely to the B shareholders, the sons of the transferor) (*Lee v IRC* (1941) 24 TC 207). Mr Lee was held to have power to enjoy the whole of the company's income as he had power as A shareholder to remove the directors and thus to indirectly control the application of the income (as he could appoint directors who would act on his bidding). Interestingly in *IRC v Schroder* (1983) 57 TC 94) it was held that a power to appoint and remove trustees did not give the transferor power to enjoy the income of a trust as there is a strong inference that trustees will act in accordance with their fiduciary duties whereas the duties of a director are owed only to the company.

- A sale to an overseas company with the purchase price being left outstanding (*Ramsden v IRC* (1957) 37 TC 619). The receipt of income by the company increased its ability to settle the debt.

- Working for an offshore company owned by the individual's sons for a salary of less than the market rate (*IRC v Brackett* (1986) 60 TC 134). Mr Brackett had power to enjoy the income of the company because it paid him a salary, it provided a fund to buy properties from him (at a market price) which he had been able to sell elsewhere, and it discharged his normal obligation (which was very much in his mind) to provide for his children.

Falling foul of these provisions can result in double taxation. It was held in *R v Dimsey* [2001] STC 1520 that deeming the income to be that of the UK resident individual did not prevent it also being income of the non-UK actual recipient – and being taxed on both if the non-resident was within the scope of UK tax in relation to the income.

17.20 If the transferor or person who receives the benefit that triggers the operation of these provisions is non-UK domiciled, he is not chargeable to tax in respect of the income to the extent that he would not have been chargeable on it if he had received it direct; ie to the extent that it arose overseas and was not remitted to the UK (*ICTA 1988, s 743(3)*). Where the income has been taxed on the recipient at the basic, lower or dividend rate the UK individual is given credit for that tax (or in the case of a dividend, deemed tax) (*ICTA 1988, s 743(1)*).

The provisions in relation to capital gains are not identical. *TCGA 1992, s 13*, charges CGT on gains realised by a non-UK company. It does so by apportioning those gains to the participators in the company (and re-apportioning as necessary where there is a chain of companies) and treating the part apportioned to a UK resident as if it were a capital gain realised by that resident. No tax charge arises if the part apportioned to a shareholder and persons connected with him does not exceed 10% of the gain (*TCGA 1992, s 13(4)*). No apportionment can be made if the company that realises the gain would not have been a close company if it were resident in the UK (*TCGA 1992, s 13(1)*).

17.21 It should be noted that the tax charge applies irrespective of whether or not the gain is distributed by the company to its shareholders, but if it is distributed within the following three years (either as capital or as a dividend) credit is given for the tax paid on the gain against that payable on the distribution (*TCGA 1992, s 13(5A)*).

It should also be noted that a gain apportioned to a person under *s 13* is not eligible for taper relief (*TCGA 1992, s 13(10A)*). This is because as the gain is made by a company it is calculated using company tax principles. As such it attracts indexation not taper relief (CGM 57295).

17.22 A gain can be apportioned under this provision to a UK company as well as to an individual (although it may then be exempted from UK tax under a

17.23 Anti-avoidance

double tax agreement). A gain can also be apportioned to a non-UK settlement – and then attributed to the settlor or beneficiaries under the settlement provisions.

No apportionment is made to a UK resident who is an individual if he is not domiciled in the UK (*TCGA 1992, s 13(2)*).

17.23 It should also be mentioned, although not strictly anti-avoidance, that although a non-resident is generally outside the scope of CGT (and corporation tax on chargeable gains) tax is charged on capital gains arising in a year in which the non-resident is carrying on a trade in the UK through a branch or agency if they relate to UK assets used (or formerly used) for the purpose of the trade (*TCGA 1992, ss 10A, 10B*). The disposal must occur at a time when the trade is still being carried on. Such gains are of course taken out of *s 13*.

If an asset within the scope of CGT is removed from the UK (but the owner remains with the scope of CGT) there is a deemed disposal and reacquisition of the asset at its market value at the time of its removal (*TCGA 1992, s 25(1)*). This does not apply if the asset is removed from the UK contemporaneously with the owner ceasing to carry on a trade in the UK through a branch or agency (*TCGA 1992, s 25(2)*). There is also a deemed disposal and reacquisition where a non-resident ceases to carry on a trade in the UK through a branch or agency (*TCGA 1992, s 25(3)*).

17.24 The tax charge on capital gains of non-UK settlements depends on whether or not the settlor has an interest in the settlement. Broadly speaking, he does so if any property which is or may at any time be comprised in the settlement is, or will or may become, applicable in any circumstances whatever for the benefit of any of the settlor, his spouse (or civil partner), a child of the settlor or his spouse, the spouse of such a child, a grandchild of the settlor or his spouse, the spouse of such a grandchild, a company controlled by any one or more of the above persons or a company associated with such a company (*TCGA 1992, Sch 5, para 2*). If the settlement was created before 17 March 1998, the reference to grandchildren and their spouses does not apply unless either:

- assets have been added to the settlement after that date (other than by way of a transaction entered into at arm's length);

- the settlement was previously UK resident and it has emigrated after that date;

- the terms of the settlement were altered after that date to bring in grandchildren or their spouses (or companies they control) as beneficiaries; or

- a grandchild, or his spouse (or a company controlled by such persons) actually receives a benefit after 16 March 1998 and could not have enjoyed the benefit under the terms of the settlement as they stood on that date.

(TCGA 1992, Sch 5, para 2A)

17.25 If the trustees are participators in a close company or a non-UK company that would be a close company if it were UK resident, any gains apportioned to them under *s 13* are treated as gains of the trustees (and nothing in any double tax agreement is to be read as preventing the charge to tax being imposed on the settlor) *(TCGA 1992, s 79B)*.

If a UK settlement becomes non-UK resident there is a deemed disposal and reacquisition of all of its assets at the time it ceases to be UK resident (other than any used for the purpose of a trade that continues to be carried on in the UK through a branch or agency) *(TCGA 1992, s 80)*. A non-resident settlement is also liable to CGT if it was UK resident at any time in the tax year in which the disposal takes place *(TCGA 1992, s 83A)*.

17.26 Where the settlor has an interest in the settlement and he is domiciled in the UK and resident or ordinarily resident in the UK for at least part of a tax year, the gains of the settlement (before taper relief) for that year are treated as realised by the settlor *(TCGA 1992, s 86)*. Losses arising to the settlement in the same year are set against the gains but brought forward losses cannot be deducted.

If the settlor does not have an interest in the settlement (or is not UK domiciled and resident or ordinarily resident) in a tax year, the gains of the settlement are attributed to any beneficiary who receives a benefit from the settlement (including the settlor if he is a beneficiary and is non-UK domiciled) *(TCGA 1992, s 87)*. If there are gains of earlier years that have not yet been attributed to a beneficiary, such gains must be attributed (on a first in first out basis) to beneficiaries first (except to the extent that such gains arose before 5 April 1981).

17.27 The amount of gains attributed to a beneficiary is of course limited to the amount of capital payments received by him. A capital payment is any payment which is not chargeable to income tax on the beneficiary (or if the beneficiary is not resident or ordinarily resident in the UK which is received otherwise than as income) *(TCGA 1992, s 97(1))*. It should be borne in mind that a capital distribution can trigger an income tax charge under *ICTA 1988, ss 739* or *740*, in which case the amount treated as income will not be treated as a capital gain as well. The conferring of any benefit on a beneficiary is also treated as giving rise to a capital payment equal to the value of that benefit. An interest free loan repayable on demand was held to create a benefit equal to the annual

17.28 *Anti-avoidance*

interest foregone in *Billingham v Cooper* [2001] STC 1177. Rent free accommodation of a property owned by the settlement would create a benefit equal to the rental value of the property.

17.28 Where more than one beneficiary receives a capital payment from the settlement in a tax year the unallocated gains (of both the current and earlier years) are allocated to them in proportions to the values received by each. Curiously, gains are apportioned to non-UK resident beneficiaries even though such an apportionment will take the gain out of the scope of UK tax. If a beneficiary received earlier capital payments that have not been allocated against gains they must be added to his payments for the tax year.

The amount of gains apportioned to a beneficiary is treated as a capital gain received by that beneficiary in the tax year concerned. It is not eligible for taper relief (*TCGA 1992, Sch 4C, para 11*). However, this does not mean that no taper relief is due. The gains apportioned are the gains after taper relief due to the settlement.

17.29 In calculating the tax payable by the beneficiary, a surcharge of 10% pa of the tax (for a minimum of six years) also applies. No surcharge is payable if the gain is distributed by 1 December following the tax year to which it relates. The 10% is calculated from that 1 December (that was the day that CGT was due prior to the introduction of self-assessment). The surcharge means that gains of overseas settlements that are taxed on the beneficiary attract an effective tax rate of up to 64%.

If gains are realised in an overseas settlement it may be worth considering making a capital payment to every beneficiary of the settlement each year equal to his capital gains tax annual exemption. The attribution of gains to the beneficiary will then not trigger a tax charge.

ITTOIA 2005, SS 619–648; TCGA 1992, SS 77–79 – SETTLEMENTS WHERE THE SETTLOR RETAINS AN INTEREST

17.30 Income and gains of a UK resident settlement are also treated as income or gains of the settlor if he has an interest in the settlement. The anti-avoidance rules are narrower than those which apply to overseas settlements.

Income which arises under a settlement is treated as income of the settlor (and not of the settlement) if the settlor has an interest in the settlement (*ITTOIA 2005, s 624*). A settlor has an interest in a settlement for this purpose if it is, or will or may become, payable to the settlor or his spouse or civil partner in any circumstances (other than only on specified contingencies).

Income of a settlement is also treated as income of the settlor (and not of the settlement) if it is paid to (or for the benefit of) (or otherwise treated as income of) a child of the settlor who is under 18 and unmarried (and does not have a civil partner (*ITTOIA 2005, s 629*).

17.31 Most people know these rules. Most people can also recognise a settlement where there is a formal trust deed. The problems mainly arise where there is not a trust deed. A settlement is defined to include 'any disposition, trust, covenant, agreement, arrangement or transfer of assets' (*ITTOIA 2005, s 620(1)*). This is a very wide definition. It has, however, been cut down by the courts which have consistently held that even under this wide definition a bona fide commercial transaction cannot constitute a settlement. There must be an element of bounty for a settlement to arise.

In *Thomas v Marshall (Inspector of Taxes)* (1953) 54 TC 178 the House of Lords confirmed that an outright gift is a settlement as it is a transfer of assets. Normally, this does not matter, as the settlor will not retain an interest in the income generated by a gift or by the investment of money gifted. However, a gift to infant children will constitute a settlement so as to tax the donor parent on any income that it generates.

17.32 An outright gift to the donor's spouse or civil partner is excluded from constituting a settlement in which the donor retains an interest provided that the gift carries a right to the whole of the income and that the property gifted is not wholly or substantially a right to income (*ITTOIA 2005, s 626*). A gift subject to conditions or one in which the property gifted, or any property derived from it, might become payable or applicable for the benefit of the donor is not an outright gift (*ITTOIA 2005, s 626(4)*).

17.33 There are a number of cases in which an arrangement has been held to constitute a settlement. The main ones are:

- The issue of preference shares, paid for out of their own money, to infant children of the controlling shareholder combined by the payment of a dividend on these shares (*Copeman (Inspector of Taxes) v Coleman* (1939) 22 TC 594.
- The issue of 76% of the shares in a shelf company to children of the other 24% shareholders combined with the payment of a dividend (*Butler (Inspector of Taxes) v Wildin* (1989) 61 TC 666. The two 12% shareholders introduced a property development opportunity to the company and organised the development without remuneration.
- The creation of a settlement for the benefit of the settlor's two sons with the trustees appointing shares on the sons contingently on their surviving for four days and the sons selling that contingent interest and entering into

17.34 *Anti-avoidance*

an agreement with the purchaser to buy from them the shares when the interest fell in (*Chinn v Collins* (1980) 54 TC 311). The House of Lords held that there was an overall 'arrangement' and that the bounty given by the father on creating the settlement was only completed by the distribution to the sons.

- Payments in trust for the taxpayer's children made under an order of the divorce court (*Yates v Starkey* (1950) 32 TC 38).
- The surrender of a mother's interest under a will so that the assets passed to her children (*IRC v Buchanan* (1957) 37 TC 365).
- An actor working for a company owned by his children at a salary far below the income which his services generated (*Crossland* (*Inspector of Taxes*) *v Hawkins* (1960) 39 TC 493).
- An interest-free loan to a settlement (created by someone else) for the benefit of the lender's children (*IRC v Leiner* (1964) 41 TC 589).
- The transfer of assets to a company in return for the issue of shares partly to the transferor and partly to his children (*IRC v Morton* (1941) 24 TC 259). The transferor was held taxable on the whole of the accumulated income of the company because he controlled the company and so could wind it up.
- The guarantee of an overdraft of a trust for the guarantor's children with the trust using its dividend income to repay the overdraft so that the bank would release the security of the guarantor (*IRC v Wachtel* (1970) 46 TC 543).

17.34 Mention also of course ought to be made of the case of *Jones v Garnett* [2006] STC 1667, where the House of Lords has held that there was a settlement but that the exception in the settlement legislation for an outright gift to a spouse applied. In that case Mr and Mrs Jones each subscribed for one share in a shelf company, Arctic Systems Ltd, for £1. The company provided consultancy by making available the services of Mr Jones. Both Mr and Mrs Jones were paid salaries but the bulk of the profits were distributed as dividend. The arrangement was held to be that Mr Jones provided bounty by agreeing to work for the company at a very low salary on the understanding that it would use the funds generated by his labour to pay dividends on the share held by Mrs Jones.

17.35 A further income tax anti-avoidance rule is contained in *ITTOIA 2005, s 633*. This provides that where a capital sum is paid, directly or indirectly, by a settlement to the settlor or his spouse it is to be treated as income of the settlor up to the amount of 'income available'. The problem is that a capital sum is defined as including a loan to the settlor and the repayment of a loan made by the settlor (*ITTOIA 2005, s 634(1)*).

The 'income available' is the undistributed income of the settlement less any part treated as income of the settlor under some other provision (*ITTOIA 2005, s 635(2)*). It is not only the undistributed income for the tax year in which the

Anti-avoidance **17.38**

capital payment is made. It includes undistributed income of earlier years. If the capital sum exceeds the income available the excess is carried forward against income of later years until the whole of the capital sum has triggered a tax charge.

17.36 Where the charge is triggered by a loan to the settlor income arising in a tax year after that in which the loan is repaid is excluded (*ITTOIA 2005, s 638(1)*). Where the charge is triggered by the repayment of a loan by the settlor and he subsequently makes a further loan (at least equal to the original one) no charge in respect of the original repayment arises for a tax year subsequent to that in which the new loan was made (*ITTOIA 2005, s 638(4)*).

This provision will not normally apply to an interest-in-possession settlement as such a settlement will have no undistributed income, as all of its income belongs to the beneficiaries as it arises.

The House of Lords have held that a payment to a third party in settlement of a liability of the settlor was not a payment to the settlor by way of loan (*Potts' Executors v IRC* (1950) 32 TC 211) but this decision has been overturned by what is now *ITTOIA 2005, s 634(5)* so it no longer provides a route to avoid the charge.

17.37 *ITTOIA 2005, s 641* extends *s 633* to a capital sum paid to the settlor by a body corporate connected with the settlement if an associated payment is made by the settlement to the body corporate. A body corporate is connected with a settlement for this purpose if it is a close company (or would be if it were UK resident) and the settlement is a participator in it, or if it is controlled by such a company (*ITTOIA 2005, s 637(8)*). An associated payment means any capital sum paid to the body corporate (and any other sum paid or assets transferred to it other than for full consideration in money or money's worth) in either the five years preceding the payment of the capital sum by the company or the five years following it (*ITTOIA 2005, s 643(3)*).

17.38 The corresponding capital gains tax provision is *TCGA 1992, s 77*. This taxes capital gains of a UK settlement on the settlor (and not the trustees) if at any time during the tax year concerned the settlor has an interest in the settlement. He does so if either:

- any property which is (or may at any time be) comprised in the settlement (or any derived property) is, or may or will become, payable to or applicable for the benefit of the settlor or his spouse (or civil partner) in any circumstances whatsoever;

- the settlor or his spouse or civil partner enjoys a benefit deriving directly or indirectly from any property which is comprised in the settlement (or from any derived property);

17.39 *Anti-avoidance*

- any such property may become payable or applicable for the benefit of a child of the settlor at a time when he is under 18 and unmarried (and does not have a civil partner); or

- such a child enjoys a benefit derived from the settled property.

(ITTOIA 2005, s 77(2), (2A))

Capital losses suffered by the settlement in the same or earlier tax years can be set against the gain *(ITTOIA 2005, s 77(1))*.

ICTA 1988, S 768 – CHANGE IN OWNERSHIP OF COMPANY-DISALLOWANCE OF LOSSES

17.39 Taxpayers are frequently tempted to seek to avoid corporation tax by the purchase of a company with substantial corporation tax losses that the purchaser anticipates being able to use to shelter future profits of his own company.

There are a number of anti-avoidance provisions designed to thwart such ambitions. That is not to say that purchased losses can never be successfully utilised, but the circumstances in which this can be done are limited. Anyone contemplating purchasing a loss company needs to be aware of the relevant provisions and form a view as to their impact. Any payment for losses ought to be conditional either on HMRC accepting that the losses are available to the purchaser or, preferably, on their actually having been utilised.

17.40 Before looking at *ICTA 1988, s 768* and the other anti-avoidance rules; it is worth remembering the basic criteria for the carry forward of losses. A trading loss can be carried forward only so long as the company continues to carry on the trade *(ICTA 1988, s 393(1))*. This is subject to the proviso that where a company ceases to carry on a trade and at any time within the following two years, the trade (or an interest in it of at least 75%) belongs to a company owned by the same person as owned the original trade at some time within a year prior to the cessation the successor company is entitled to relief for the brought forward losses of the original company *(ICTA 1988, s 343(3))*. Ownership of the trade in this context clearly means indirect ownership, ie is the ownership of the successor company the same, or nearly the same as that of the original one? The carry forward losses are restricted where all of the liabilities of the original company were not taken over by the successor company. An amount of losses equal to the liabilities not transferred (less any assets not transferred) is excluded from relief.

This provision is often used in insolvencies. A receiver will transfer the trade from an insolvent company to a newly formed subsidiary company and seek to sell the subsidiary with the benefit of the losses transferred.

17.41 *ICTA 1988, s 343* also applies where the successor company carries on the activities of the original company's trade (or part of those activities) as part of its trade. The brought forward losses can be used only against profits from that part though (and if only part of the trade is taken over, only the appropriate part of the losses can be used) (*ICTA 1988, s 343(8)*).

There are a couple of points to watch. In *Falmer Jeans v Rodin* (1990) 63 TC 55) one group company manufactured jeans and another marketed them. The two trades were merged into the marketing company. HMRC contended that manufacturing was a different trade to manufacturing and selling, but it was held that *s 343(8)* enabled the manufacturing losses to be used as manufacturing was part of the trade of manufacturing and selling. It is by no means clear that the same result would have applied if the marketing had been merged into the manufacturing company as selling is an adjunct to manufacturing so the separate marketing activity would have ceased to exist. If it is wished to merge two trades one of which is loss-making it is normally likely to be safer to merge the profitable one into the unprofitable so that there is no transfer of losses.

17.42 The second point is that it was held in *Wood Preservation Ltd v Prior* (1968) 45 TC 112 that a company ceased to be the beneficial owner of its trade when it entered into a contract to sell it. Accordingly, it is then too late to enter into a *s 343* reconstruction. The same applies in a liquidation. A company ceases to beneficially own its trade when a liquidator is appointed. (*Pritchard v M H Builders (Wilmslow) Ltd* (1968) 45 TC 360).

It also needs to be realised that once a trade ceases the losses die with it. Even if it subsequently restarts exactly the same trade the losses can no longer be utilised against future profits. However, this does not apply where the trade is suspended, as opposed to ceasing and being restarted. It is a question of fact whether a trade has ceased. If there are no activities for a period but the trade is merely in suspension it is wise to minute that fact and what steps are being taken to resume trading. For example, a property dealing company may be looking for a suitable new property so there are no activities to be shown in its accounts but if the directors are actively looking for a suitable property they ought to evidence that fact to minimise the risk of the company being held to have ceased trading.

17.43 Another risk is that a change in activities can amount to a cessation of one trade and the commencement of a different trade. For example, a brewing company ceased brewing and continued to sell beer manufactured to its specification by another brewer. It was held that it had ceased its trade of brewing and started a different trade of beer selling (*Gordon & Blair Ltd v IRC* (1962) 40 TC 358). A trade of IT consultancy was held to be a different trade to dealing in computers and computer software (*Kawthar Consulting Ltd v Revenue and Customs Comrs* [2005] SWTI 1237). In contrast the assembly of electric food mixers for retail sale was held not to be a new trade but an extension of the

17.44 *Anti-avoidance*

company's existing trade of manufacturing gas cookers for sale to other group companies (*Cannon Industries Ltd v Edwards* (*Inspector of Taxes*) (1965) 42 TC 625).

It is only once it has been ascertained that a loss is available for carry forward on general principles that *ICTA 1988, s 768* needs to be looked at to ascertain whether it might prevent the loss from being utilised.

17.44 The section applies where either:

- within a period of three years there is both a change in the ownership of a company and a major change in the nature or conduct of a trade carried on by the company; or
- at any time after the scale of activities in a trade carried on by a company has become small or negligible and before there is any considerable revival of the trade, there is a change in the ownership of the company.

Where one of these tests is met losses incurred before the change of ownership (including in the pre-change portion of the accounting period in which the change occurs) cannot be carried forward past the change in ownership (*ICTA 1988, s 768(1), (2)*).

17.45 Both of the above tests involve vague concepts, so it is often difficult to judge whether or not the provision applies. When does a change in the nature or conduct of a trade become a major one? What is meant by 'small' or by 'a considerable revival'?

The legislation gives some guidance on the first question, but it is not very helpful. A major change in the nature or conduct of a trade includes:

- a major change in the type of property dealt in, or services or facilities provided, in the trade; and
- a major change in customers, outlets or markets of the trade.

(*ICTA 1988, s 768(4)*)

17.46 HMRC have given some guidance (SP 10/91). They will not regard a major change as having occurred if the company has made changes:

(a) to increase its efficiency, such as moving its manufacturing operations from three obsolete factories into one;

(b) to keep pace with developing technology, such as replacing enamel by plastic or mechanical by electronic components;

(c) to keep pace with developing management techniques; or

(d) to rationalise its product range by withdrawing unprofitable items and, possibly, replacing them with new items of a kind related to those already produced.

They give as examples of a major change:

- a dealer in saloon cars switching to dealing in tractors (although switching to a different make of car would be acceptable);
- a public house changing to a discotheque – although this would be a matter of degree (at what stage does a pub with a DJ become a discotheque with a bar?); and
- a company that fattens pigs for their owners switching to buying pigs for fattening and resale – it is not clear why this is not simply a change to increase efficiency within (a) above!

17.47 The only case to have come before the courts under *ICTA 1988, s 768* is *Willis (Inspector of Taxes) v Peeters Picture Frames Ltd* (1983) 56 TC 436. Prior to the sale the company manufactured and sold picture frames to a large number of customers. After the sale it sold its picture frames only to its new parent company (but the parent took over supplying to many of Peeters' old customers). It was held that this was not a major change. The judgment of Gibson LJ in the Court of Appeal of Northern Ireland gives some useful guidance as to the factors to be taken into account in deciding whether or not there has been a major change.

17.48 There is a change of ownership of a company if either:

- a single person acquires more than half of its ordinary share capital;
- two or more persons each acquire a holding of 5% or more of the ordinary share capital and together their holdings amount to more than 50%; or
- two or more persons each acquire a holding of the ordinary share capital and the holdings together amount to over 50% disregarding any acquisition of under 5% unless it is an addition to an existing holding and the two together exceed 5%.

(*ICTA 1988, s 769(1)*)

It seems clear that 'acquires' in this context, means 'takes a transfer of', not comes to hold, ie if a person who owns 50% purchases another 5% (so that he now holds over 50%) he has only acquired 5%.

17.49 Where a loss is disallowed under this provision any capital allowances that become unrelievable (as they formed part of the disallowed loss) are not taken into account in calculating a subsequent balancing charge (*ICTA 1988, s 768(6)*).

17.50 *Anti-avoidance*

Similar provisions disallow a carry back of a trading loss to a time before the change of ownership *(ICTA 1988, s 768A)*; to the deduction of management expenses *(ICTA 1988, s 768B)*; to Schedule A losses *(ICTA 1988, s 768D)*; and to losses on intangible fixed assets *(ICTA 1988, s 768E)*. There is also a restriction on setting management expenses arising after the change in ownership against a capital gain on a disposal of an asset acquired intra-group after the change if that asset is sold within three years of the change *(ICTA 1988, s 768C)*.

17.50 There are further restrictions on the use of capital gains tax losses. *TCGA 1992, s 177A* contains complex rules in relation to 'pre-entry losses' and *s 177B* restricts the use of post entry losses against pre-entry gains.

TCGA 1992, s 177A limits the gains against which a 'pre-entry loss' can be set to those arising:

- on a disposal by the company before the date on which it became a member of its new group ('the entry date');
- on a disposal by the company after the entry date of an asset which it held immediately before that date;
- on a disposal of an asset acquired by the company after the entry date provided that that asset:
    - was not acquired intra-group; and
    - has been used or held solely for the purpose of a trade which the company carried on before the entry date and continued to carry on until the disposal of the asset.

(TCGA 1992, Sch 7A, para 7(1))

17.51 A pre-entry loss is an allowable loss that accrued to the company before it became a member of a group (or a different group) and the pre-entry proportion of an allowable loss accruing to the company on a pre-entry asset (ie one that it held at the time it joined the group) *(TCGA 1992, Sch 7A, para 1(2))*. The pre-entry proportion is determined on a time apportionment basis.

TCGA 1992, s 177B prevents a pre-entry gain being reduced by a post-entry loss. A pre-entry gain is one realised in an accounting period in which the company joins a group of companies, and a post-entry loss is a loss arising in that same accounting period but after the company has joined the group.

ITA 2007, SS 102–116 – LOSSES OF LIMITED PARTNERSHIPS, ETC

17.52 Where an individual is a limited partner in a limited partnership the aggregate loss relief that he can claim in respect of a loss (including capital

Anti-avoidance **17.55**

allowances) sustained in the partnership trade is limited to the individual's contribution to the firm. This is the amount of his contribution to the trade at the end of the year of assessment in which the loss arose (or at the time he ceased to be a partner if earlier) (*ITA 2007, s 104(4)*). The aggregate relief that can be claimed by a corporate partner is similarly limited to the contribution to the firm (*ICTA 1988, s 118*).

A person's contribution to a trade at any time is the aggregate of:

- the amount that he has contributed to the trade as capital (and has not directly, or indirectly, drawn out or received back); and

- the amount of any profits or gains from the trade to which he is entitled but has not received (in money or money's worth)

(*ITA 2007, s 105*)

17.53 A general partner is treated as a limited partner for the purpose of these provisions if he is not entitled to take part in the management of the trade and is entitled to have his partnership liabilities beyond a certain level discharged by some other person (*ITA 2007, s 106*).

This restriction also applies to members of an LLP (other than in respect of a loss in the first four years of assessment (*ITA 2007, s 107*). In the case of an LLP the member's contribution is the greater of the amount subscribed by him or the amount of his liability on a winding up. The amount subscribed by him for this purpose is the amount he has contributed to the LLP as capital less any part of that amount that he has directly or indirectly drawn out (or received back); he draws out during the next five years; he is entitled to draw out; or he is entitled to require another person to reimburse to him (*ITA 2007, s 108*).

17.54 The amount of loss relief that can be claimed by a 'non-active' partner in a general partnership is similarly restricted (but only in respect of losses incurred in the tax year in which the trade commences or the following three years) (*ITA 2007, s 110*). A non-active partner is one who spends on average less than ten hours a week personally engaged in activities carried on for the purposes of the trade (*ITA 2007, s 112*). The disallowed amount is not lost; it can be carried forward against future profits from the trade (*ITA 2007, s 110*).

VATA 1994, SCH 1, PARA 2 – AGGREGATION OF ACTIVITIES OF SEPARATE PERSONS

17.55 These provisions are aimed at preventing the avoidance of VAT by fragmenting a business into different mini-businesses in different ownerships,

17.56 *Anti-avoidance*

some or all of which are below the VAT registration threshold. It needs to be considered whenever a new business is spun off from an existing one.

HMRC have power to direct that two or more separate persons should be treated for VAT purposes as a single person carrying on the activities of a business described in the direction – which will of course embrace the combined businesses of those persons. To include a person in a direction HMRC must be satisfied that:

- he is making or has made taxable supplies;
- his business activities form part of wider activities carried on by him and one or more other persons and those combined activities should properly be regarded as a single business;
- the taxable supplies of that single business would exceed the VAT registration limit; and
- one of the main reasons for the person carrying on his activities in the way he does is the avoidance of a liability to be registered.

(VATA 1994, Sch 1, para 2(2))

17.56 Where a direction is made each of the constituent members is jointly and severally liable for the whole of the VAT payable by the combined business, the constituent members are treated for VAT purposes as a partnership carrying on the combined business and supplies by any of the individual members are treated as made by the combined business. The businesses have 14 days from the notice of the direction to decide who should be responsible for dealing with the VAT. If they do not decide within this period, HMRC will make the direction for them *(VATA 1994, Sch 1, para 2(6), (7))*. HMRC cannot include in a direction a person who makes wholly exempt supplies.

The direction cannot be made retrospectively, but once a direction has been made a new person can be added by HMRC to the deemed business with retrospective effect to the date he commenced business *(VATA 1994, Sch 1, para 2(4))*.

17.57 HMRC have successfully used this power to combine:

- a bakery business carried on by a husband with a café business operated by his wife *(TSD & Mrs M E Williams*, VTD 2445);
- four separate tax consultancy and financial advisory services operated by a husband, his wife, a partnership between him and his wife and a company controlled by the two *(Osmond v C & E Comrs* [1989] STC 596);

Anti-avoidance **17.58**

- two fish and chip shop businesses, one of the husband and one of his wife, both operated from the same shop at different times (*I & A J Lee*, VTD 2640);
- 26 associated companies each providing a launderette and dry cleaning service (*South West Launderettes Ltd*, VTD 2608);
- the businesses operated by a hairdressing salon owner and three self-employed hairdressers (*A S Lewis*, VTD 3329);
- a gymnasium and a health food shop that were together marketed as a health studio (*M J & P Summers*, VTD 3498);
- a service station and a video club (*Old Farm Service Station Ltd*, VTD 4261);
- a fitness club and beauty salon (*West End Health and Fitness Club*, VTD 4070);
- separate businesses for UK and overseas sales of model aircraft (*A D Head*, VTD 4828);
- separate taxi and wedding car hire businesses (*A & J Harris*, VTD 4882);
- a pub and bed and breakfast business carried on from the same premises (*W P & Mrs D K M Spence*, VTD 5698);
- holiday cottages and a nearby restaurant (*S & L Taylor*, VTD 9125);
- a restaurant and gift shop (*J Roy*, VTD 9384);
- a car wash and a car spares business (*Allerton Motors*, VTD 9427);
- fairground amusement operators (*EM, PG & CP Evans*, VTD 10532);
- pubs and catering businesses (*P & R Jarvis*, VTD 3920; *DJ & Mrs I R Coe*, VTD 10911; *Tracey J Holt*, VTD 10942; *A E & M E Fraser*, VTD 16761);
- a series of partnerships all set up by one person each with a different driving instructor, together with a series of companies each of which operated a launderette (*J O Chamberlain v C & E Comrs* [1989] STC 505);
- an individual and his three sons each carrying on a business as ice cream vendors (*D Gregario & Sons*, VTD 9105),
- an individual and three companies each operating a launderette (*I Lyons*, VTD 2451).

17.58 In determining whether a separation is artificial, regard must be given to the extent to which the different persons are closely bound to one another by financial, economic and organisational links (*VATA 1994, Sch 1, para 1A(2)*).

17.59 *Anti-avoidance*

These cases do not mean that everyone in one of the above situations is likely to be faced with an aggregation direction. It is very much a question of fact. There are a number of VAT tribunal decisions on similar facts that were decided in favour of the taxpayer. For example, in *S & A Trippitt* (VTD 17340) Mr Trippitt ran a pub and his wife operated a bed and breakfast business from the same premises just like Mr and Mrs Spence. However, the aggregation direction was set aside. The reason for this distinction was that the detailed facts were different. Mr and Mrs Trippitt had separate bank accounts, the bed and breakfast accommodation had its own entrance and access to that part of the premises was not available to pub customers. Mrs Trippitt employed her own staff, albeit that they used the pub kitchen and lounge to cook and serve breakfast. Mrs Trippitt paid her husband 35% of her turnover to cover the use of his premises, including telephone and utilities. This was held to be a realistic commercial and arm's-length arrangement. Mr and Mrs Spence may well have been unlucky. Their businesses were also completely separate but they were cheque signatories on each other's bank accounts, they helped one another out from time to time and the tribunal seem to have thought that sharing the property expenses was uncommercial. It is certainly hard to see how the tribunal could have felt that 'the arrangements for carrying out the details for the running of the hotel and restaurant side were inconsistent with their being run as separate commercial activities'.

VATA 1994, SS 43–44 – GROUP OF COMPANIES

17.59 Unlike for corporation tax, for VAT purposes group treatment is not automatic. Companies must elect to be taxed as a group and a *Companies Act* group of companies can pick and choose which companies to include in a group and which to leave as separate entities. This clearly gives scope for manipulation so it is perhaps not surprising that there is a lot of anti-avoidance legislation in relation to VAT groups.

Companies do not even have to be members of a *Companies Act* group to be included in a group registration. The basic test is that in order to group two companies they must each be established (ie incorporated) in the UK or have a fixed establishment in the UK and one must control the other or both must be controlled by either the same person or by two or more people carrying on business in partnership (*VATA 1994, s 43A(1)*).

17.60 In addition, in relation to large companies:

- not more than 50% of the benefits of the 'relevant business activity' must accrue, directly or indirectly, to one or more third parties; and

- if consolidated accounts were to be prepared for the person who controls the companies, GAAP would require them all to be treated as subsidiaries in those accounts (or would do but for the company being immaterial), and no third party would be required by GAAP to include any of the companies as a subsidiary.

(*VATA 1994, s 43AA*, and *VAT (Group Eligibility) Order 2004, SI 2004/1931*)

17.61 This restriction only applies to a company whose turnover exceeds (or is expected to exceed) £10 million a year and, even then, only if the company is not a 100% subsidiary, is managed (directly or indirectly) in respect of the business activity concerned by a third party in the course or furtherance of its business or is the sole general partner of a limited partnership.

In certain circumstances HMRC can direct, either in relation to a particular transaction or in relation to a particular company, that either the supply should not be treated as a group supply or the particular company should be treated as a member of a particular group if it is eligible to join that group (or should not be treated as a member of the group of which it is in fact a member) (*VATA 1994, Sch 9, para 3*). The direction can be made retrospectively. HMRC can also vary or withdraw the direction. A direction can be made if:

(a) a relevant event has occurred, ie a company joined a group, left a group or entered into any transaction;

(b) there has been (or will or may be) a taxable supply on which VAT is chargeable otherwise than by reference to the supply's full value, that supply is not wholly zero-rated, and charging VAT on the supply other than by reference to its full value gives rise to a tax advantage;

(c) head (b) would not have been satisfied (in relation to that or some other transaction) if its relevant supply had not taken place; and

(d) if the relevant event was entering into a transaction, it is not a one-off transaction.

(*VATA 1994, Sch 9A, para 1*)

For the purpose of (b) a tax advantage is deemed to arise only if someone has become entitled to claim relief for input tax (or a tax repayment) in relation to the supply (*VATA 1994, Sch 9A, para 1(4)*).

17.62 The purpose of this provision is to thwart schemes where a supplier acquires goods or services, recovers the input tax and then joins the customer's group, or a company receives an advance payment for a supply when a member of a group and then leaves the group before acquiring the goods to be sold so as to be able to reclaim the input tax without someone else accounting for VAT on the corresponding output.

17.63 Anti-avoidance

HMRC cannot make a direction under this provision if they are satisfied that the change in the group status of the company, or the transaction, had as its main purpose (or one of its main purposes) a genuine commercial purpose unconnected with the conditions that trigger HMRC's right to make a direction (*VATA 1994, Sch 9, para 2*). HMRC have said that in applying *Sch 9A*:

- They will interpret entering into a transaction as meaning entering into a contract or other disposition, eg entering into a lease will be a transaction but paying rent under it would not be.

- A supply at less than full value means only a supply which to some extent is treated as intra-group for VAT purposes; it does not include a supply at an undervalue.

- In deciding issues concerning the commercial purpose exemption, HMRC will be prepared to consider the term in its broadest sense where the context of any particular case allows.

- They will not make a direction with effect from an earlier date than is required to nullify the tax advantage derived from the relevant event.

- Once the tax advantage targeted has been corrected satisfactorily they will consider any subsequent application to join or leave the group subject to their normal discretion in such matters.

- If they believe that a tax avoidance scheme has been implemented they will discuss their concerns with the taxpayer (except where fraud is suspected) and give him a chance to explain whether the commercial purpose test applies, before making a direction

(Statement of Practice 24.6.1996)

17.63 In addition to this major anti-avoidance provision, HMRC have power to refuse a group registration or to refuse to allow an additional company to join a group registration, or to refuse to allow a company to leave a group registration, if they consider that the eligibility conditions are not met or if they consider that refusal of the application is necessary for the protection of the revenue (*VATA 1994, s 43B(5)*). This power must be exercised within 90 days of the application for the group registration, or the change, and can be exercised within that period even if they have already approved the registration or change.

The meaning of 'protection of the revenue' was considered by the VAT tribunal in *National Westminster Bank plc*, VTD 15514. The tribunal felt that the phrase can cover any loss of revenue which is not de minimis; it is not limited to tax avoidance schemes. It also felt that HMRC must weigh the effect on the taxpayer of refusing grouping against the loss of tax. Following this case HMRC said that if they have concerns that the revenue loss does go beyond the accepted consequences of VAT grouping they will ask the taxpayer to comment on the impact on his business of a refusal before refusing an application (Business Brief 15/99).

17.64 HMRC also have power by notice to terminate a company's membership of a VAT group, although they cannot do so retrospectively unless the reason for the termination is that they believed that the eligibility conditions are no longer met (when they can terminate group treatment from the date they ceased to be met) (*VATA 1994, s 43C*).

A company cannot be a member of more than one VAT group at the same time. Once it is a member of a VAT group it cannot join another (*VATA 1994, s 43D*). This prevents a company being a member of a VAT group and at the same time becoming a member of another – such as that of a partially exempt customer – by exploiting the different tests of control in the *Companies Act* definition of a subsidiary.

ICTA 1988, S 770A – PROVISIONS NOT AT ARM'S LENGTH

17.65 *ICTA 1988, s 770A* and *Sch 28AA* contain the UK's transfer pricing legislation. They provide that where:

- provision ('the actual provision') has been made between any two persons ('the affected persons') by means of a transaction or series of transactions;
- at the time of the making of the actual provision, one of the affected persons was directly or indirectly participating in the management, control or capital of the other (or the same person or persons was participating in both); and
- the actual provision differs from the provision which would have been made between independent enterprises and confers a potential advantage in relation to UK taxation on one (or both) of the affected persons,

the profits and losses of the potentially advantaged person must be computed for tax purposes as if the arm's-length provision had been made instead of the actual provision (*ICTA 1988, Sch 28AA, para 1*).

17.66 This is a somewhat unwieldy sentence because, of course, it seeks to cover a wide range of situations. Broadly, it provides that where a transaction is entered into between connected persons at a non-arm's-length price or on non-arm's-length terms the arm's-length price must be adopted for tax purposes if that would result in a greater profit or other taxable amount than the price actually used.

17.67 *Anti-avoidance*

17.67 The arm's-length price must be computed, as far as possible in accordance with the OECD guidelines (which are published in a substantial loose-leaf volume entitled 'Transfer Pricing Guidelines for Multinational Enterprises and Tax Administrations'). These lay down three tests, namely:

- The arm's-length price.

- Where that is inappropriate, the transitional profits method, ie what is a fair split of the overall profits on the transaction.

- Global formulary apportionment of the group profits (but this is rarely used).

In applying these provisions a 'transaction' includes an arrangement, understanding or mutual practice. A 'series of transactions' includes a number of transactions each entered into in pursuance of (or in relation to) the same arrangement. A series of transactions can be treated as one by means of which provision has been made between two persons even if there is no transaction in the series to which both are parties, the parties to the arrangement do not include one (or even both) of those persons or there are transactions in the series to which neither is a party (*ICTA 1988, Sch 28AA, para 3*).

17.68 A person directly participates in the management, control or capital of another at any time if, and only if, that other is a body corporate or a partnership, which is controlled by that person. A person indirectly participates if, and only if, he would be treated as directly participating if the rights and powers attributed to him included:

(a) those which he is entitled to acquire at a future date or which he will be entitled to acquire in the future;

(b) those of other persons which are (or may be) required to be exercised on behalf of the potential participant (or under his direction or for his benefit);

(c) those of the person's spouse; brother, sister or lineal descendant, spouse's brother, sister or lineal descendant; the spouse of any such person; a trustee of a settlement of which the potential participant is a settlor or is one of the above relatives of the settlor; or if the potential participant is a trustee of a settlement, the settlor or one of the above relatives of the settlor; and

(d) those which would be attributed to a person with whom the potential participant is connected (ie within (c) above) if that connected person were himself the potential participant (ie the rights and powers attributed to connected persons are also attributed to the potential participant).

(*ICTA 1988, Sch 28AA, para 4*)

17.69 A person also indirectly participates in the management, control or capital of another if he is one of a number of major participants in the other. This test is satisfied if the other (the subordinate) is a body corporate or a partnership and each of two persons, one of which is the potential participator, has at least 40% of the rights and powers over the subordinate and taken together control the subordinate. In applying the test, all the rights and powers that can be attributed to each of the two persons under (a)-(d) above must, of course, first be attributed to each person (*ICTA 1988, Sch 28AA, para 4(7)*). This applies the transfer pricing rules on a transaction between a company and a major shareholder if it has two major shareholders each of which (with its associates) owns at least 40% of the company.

17.70 A person can also be an indirect participant if the actual provision relates to financing arrangements for a company or partnership and the potential participator and other persons act together in relation to the financing arrangements (*ICTA 1988, Sch 28AA, para 4A*). However, this deemed rule applies only in relation to those financing arrangements. This provision has generated a great deal of criticism as it potentially applies to most venture capital investments, so putting an onus on the parties to demonstrate that the lenders are lending on arm's-length terms (which might be difficult as in most cases the loan will be linked to an equity investment).

17.71 There are a number of exemptions. The rules do not apply if the potentially advantaged person is a small company unless either the company irrevocably elects to apply the transfer pricing rules for the accounting period concerned, or the other party to the transaction (or a relevant transaction) is a resident of a non-qualifying territory, ie one with which the UK does not have a full double tax agreement (*ICTA 1988, Sch 28AA, para 5B*). Effectively, this requires a small company to make transfer-pricing adjustments only in relation to transactions with tax haven companies or other tax haven persons.

Nor is any adjustment required if the potentially disadvantaged company has been a dormant company at all times since 1 January 2004. A company that became dormant after that date and which has lent its funds interest-free to its parent or another group company will have to impute a market rate of interest to those funds and pay tax on such notional interest (*ICTA 1988, Sch 28AA, para 5*).

17.72 A medium-sized enterprise does not have to apply the provisions (except to the extent that it would have had to do so had it been small) unless HMRC serves a notice on it requiring it to do so (*ICTA 1988, Sch 28AA, para 5B*).

A company is small if it has fewer than 50 staff and its turnover and assets do not exceed €10 million (approx £7 million). It is medium-sized if it has fewer than 250 staff, its turnover does not exceed €50 million (approx £34 million) and its

17.73 *Anti-avoidance*

assets do not exceed €43 million (approx £30 million). Only two of these three tests need to be satisfied. A company that is neither small nor medium-sized has to self-assess the necessary adjustments.

17.73 If one person obtains a tax advantage and another party to the transaction who is within the scope of UK tax suffers a disadvantage, that disadvantaged person can elect to make a corresponding adjustment (*ICTA 1988, Sch 28AA, para 6*). For example, if A sells goods to B at an undervalue and both are UK resident companies A is a disadvantaged person (as its profits will be understated) and must increase its profit by substituting market value for the sale. B can then elect to also substitute market value for its purchase price so reducing its taxable profits by the same amount. This might seem a lot of work for nothing, but if one of the companies has losses, the adjustments will have a tax effect.

It should particularly be noted that transfer-pricing adjustments may need to be provided in relation to interest on loans. A special rule applies here. In determining the arm's-length provision, regard must be had to:

- whether the loan would have been made at all in the absence of the special relationship;
- what amount would have been lent in the absence of the special relationship; and
- the rate of interest and other terms that would have been agreed in the absence of the special relationship.

(*ICTA 1988, Sch 28AA, para 1A*)

17.74 Where a borrower has a deficit on its balance sheet, or takes a 100% mortgage to acquire a property, HMRC sometimes contend that no interest whatsoever is deductible as it would not have been able to borrow at all from an arm's-length vendor. That is not necessarily right. Indeed if one is prepared to pay a high enough interest rate it is almost always possible to borrow. In any event it should be realised that this is not an all or nothing test. For example, if a company borrows to buy a property, the value of the property itself will normally support a mortgage of 60–80% of the cost, so provided that the loan is secured on the property it is only the interest on the excess borrowing that is at risk of being disallowed.

If an arm's-length borrowing is initially taken and subsequently replaced by a borrowing from a connected person, it is difficult for HMRC to show that the company could not have borrowed at all at arm's length.

17.75 The test is applied at the time the loan is entered into, not when the interest is paid. Accordingly, if the initial borrowing can be readily justified it might be sensible to use a long-term loan with a series of break clauses. Conversely, if the borrower's financial position is poor, it might be preferable to use a series of one-year loans on the basis that the financial position might well be better in later years so it would become progressively easier to justify the borrowing.

If the actual provision involves a guarantee by another company, account also needs to be taken of whether the guarantee would have been given; or would have been for the same amount if the borrower and the guarantor were at arm's length (*ICTA 1988, Sch 28AA, para 18*). Curiously, this provision applies only to a guarantee by a company. It will not apply to one by an individual or a trust.

17.76 An actual provision confers a potential tax advantage in relation to UK tax if it creates a smaller amount of the person's profits for tax purposes (or a larger amount of losses) (*ICTA 1988, Sch 28AA, para 5*).

As profits include chargeable gains of a company it can apply to chargeable gains, but not to capital gains tax where the person is not within the charge to corporation tax.

However, there are a number of specific capital gains tax anti-avoidance rules that can apply to transactions at artificial values. A person's acquisition or disposal of an asset must be treated as taking place at market value (instead of the price actually paid) if he acquires (or disposes) of the assets otherwise than by way of a bargain at arm's length (*TCGA 1992, s 17(1)(a)*). Market value is not substituted though on the acquisition of an asset if there is no corresponding disposal and no consideration in money's worth (or the consideration is below market value) (*TCGA 1992, s 17(2)*). Transactions between connected persons are automatically deemed not to be under a bargain at arm's length – although again not if there is no corresponding disposal (*TCGA 1992, s 18(2)*).

A transaction at an artificial value could also trigger the value-shifting rules in *TCGA 1992, ss 29–34*, which create a part disposal of an asset where something is done to artificially reduce its value.

TCGA 1992, S 179 – COMPANY CEASING TO BE A MEMBER OF A GROUP

17.77 If a UK company acquires an asset intra-group and ceases to be a member of the group at some time within the following six years and while still owning the asset (or another asset or assets derived from it, or an asset onto which a gain on its disposal was rolled over) otherwise than a trading stock, there is a deemed disposal and reacquisition of the asset at market value (*TCGA 1992, s 179*). This disposal and reacquisition is deemed to take place at the time

17.78 *Anti-avoidance*

of the intra-group acquisition but the tax charge is treated as arising in the accounting period in which it leaves the group.

It should particularly be noted that the special tax rules that apply to company reconstructions do not refer to *s 179* gains, so a transfer of assets to a Newco to facilitate the reconstruction is likely to create a *s 179* charge when the company leaves the group as a result of the reconstruction.

17.78 The provision does not apply where two associated companies leave the group at the same time and the asset owned by the chargeable company was acquired from the other (*TCGA 1992, s 179(2)*). Two companies are associated for this purpose only if by themselves they form a group though, ie if one is owned by the other or both are owned by a third company (*TCGA 1992, s 179(10)*). It was held in *Johnston Publishing (North) Ltd v HMRC* [2006] STC (SCD) 779 that the two companies have to be associated both at the time that the asset is transferred and the time that they leave the group. In that case a company in sub-group 1 acquired an asset intra-group from a company in sub-group 2. Sub-group 1 was sold but immediately prior to the sale the vendor company was transferred from sub-group 2 to sub-group 1. The Special Commissioners held that the exemption did not apply.

17.79 There is a further exemption where a company leaves the group in consequence of another member ceasing to exist (*TCGA 1992, s 179(1)*). HMRC have said that, in their view, a UK company ceases to exist only when it is removed from the Companies Register. Accordingly, a disposal during the course of a company's liquidation will not attract the exemption. The exemption is probably intended only to make clear that if a dormant subsidiary is struck off the Register, leaving the parent company as a singleton company, that will not trigger the charge if the asset was previously acquired by the parent from the subsidiary.

It should, however, be realised that if a company sells its only subsidiary, both the subsidiary and the parent will cease to be members of the group as the group will cease to exist by virtue of the sale. Accordingly, a tax charge will arise in the parent company if it owns an asset acquired intra-group from the subsidiary within the six-year period.

THE TAARS

17.80 In addition to the specific anti-avoidance provisions, the legislation contains two 'TAARS' (Targeted Anti-Avoidance Rules aimed at only one aspect of a tax), one for capital gains tax and one for stamp duty land tax. At least the government call them TAARs. They are really general anti-avoidance rules aimed at only one aspect of a tax – often called mini-GAARs – as all anti-avoidance provisions are targeted at a specific device. The reality is that these TAARs are not targeted; they apply to any transactions that result in the effect at which they are aimed. Most anti-avoidance provisions are targeted at a specific scheme or device. They aim to block that scheme (and sometimes possible variants of it) but have no impact on other types of avoidance. A TAAR, in contrast, sets down a general principle of what is regarded as avoidance in the area to which it relates. It renders ineffective anything that breaches that principle. To achieve this, a TAAR has to be widely drawn because the draftsman cannot foresee what schemes might be developed in the future.

17.81 Because of this a TAAR creates uncertainty. A taxpayer who enters into what he perceives to be a bona fide commercial transaction is at risk that after it has been carried out HMRC might form the view that the transaction was carried out for tax avoidance purposes and require the taxpayer to prove that he had no such motive.

Uncertainty is a hallmark of a bad tax. Society cannot function effectively if when a person enters into a transaction he cannot reasonably foresee the tax consequences of doing so. Most people are reluctant to enter into transactions if they cannot gauge the tax consequences of doing so, as the tax burden is a crucial component of the profitability of the proposed transaction and the net return generated by the transaction is what makes a person decide whether or not it is worthwhile to enter into it.

Accordingly, a TAAR requires an advance clearance procedure to operate effectively. Unfortunately, the government seems to have set its face against clearance procedures so the UK's TAARs sadly lack that essential concomitant.

THE CGT TAAR (TCGA 1992, S 16A)

17.82 This was introduced in relation to corporation tax in respect of disposals after 5 December 2005. It was extended to capital gains of individuals and trusts for disposals after 5 December 2006. It provides that an allowable loss does not include a loss accruing to a person if:

- it accrues to the person directly or indirectly in consequence of, or otherwise in connection with any arrangements; and
- the main purpose, or one of the main purposes, of the arrangement is to secure a tax advantage.

(*TCGA 1992, s 16A(1)*)

17.83 It does not matter whether the loss accrues at a time when there are no chargeable gains from which it could otherwise have been deducted, or whether the tax advantage is secured for the person to whom the loss accrues or for any other person (*TCGA 1992, s 16A(3)*).

17.84 *Anti-avoidance*

'Arrangements' includes any agreement, understanding scheme, transaction or series of transactions (whether or not legally enforceable). A 'tax advantage' means a relief or increased relief from tax, a repayment or increased repayment of tax, the avoidance or reduction of a charge to tax or an assessment to tax, or the avoidance of a possible assessment to tax. Tax for this purpose means capital gains tax, corporation tax or income tax (*TCGA 1992, s 16A(2)*).

The SDLT TAAR (FA 2003, s 75A)

17.84 *FA 2003, s 75A* applies where:

(a) one person (V) disposes of a chargeable interest in land and another person (P) acquires either it or a chargeable interest deriving from it;

(b) a number of transactions (including the disposal and acquisition) are involved in connection with the disposal and acquisition ('the scheme transactions'); and

(c) the sum of the amounts of SDLT payable in respect of the scheme transactions is less than the amount that would be payable on a notional land transaction effecting the acquisition of V's chargeable interest by P on its disposal by V.

(*FA 2003, s 75A(1)*)

17.85 It requires SDLT to be paid on the notional transaction at (c) (and excludes from SDLT any of the scheme transactions that are land transactions) (*FA 2003, s 75A(4)*). The effective date of this notional transaction is the last date of completion for the scheme transactions (or if earlier the last date on which a contract in respect of the scheme transactions is substantially performed) (*FA 2003, s 75A(6)*). The chargeable consideration on this notional transaction is the largest amount (or aggregate amount)

- given by (or on behalf of) any person by way of consideration for the scheme transactions; or

- received by or on behalf of V (or a connected person of V (within *ICTA 1988, s 839*)) but excluding any consideration for a transaction which is exempt from SDLT by way of consideration for the scheme transactions.

(*FA 2003, s 75A(3)*)

17.86 In calculating the chargeable consideration on the notional transactions, consideration for a transaction is ignored if (or in so far as) the transaction is merely incidental to the transfer of the chargeable interest from V to P, such as if it is undertaken only for a purpose relating to:

- the construction of a building on property to which the chargeable interest relates;
- the sale or supply of something other than land; or
- a loan to P secured by a mortgage (or any other provision of finance) to enable P, or another person, to pay for part of a process, or series of transactions by which the chargeable interest transfers from V to P.

(FA 2003, s 75B(1), (3))

17.87 A transaction cannot, however, be treated as incidental if (or in so far as) it forms part of a process, or series of transactions by which the transfer is effected; the transfer is conditional on completion of the transaction; or it is of a kind specified in *s 75A(3)* (see below) *(FA 2003, s 75B(2))*. Any necessary apportionments need to be made on a just and reasonable basis *(FA 2003, s 75B(4))*.

Curiously, the legislation gives examples of some transactions that fall within the provision, namely:

- the acquisition by P of a lease deriving from a freehold owned (or formerly owned) by V;
- a sub-sale to a third person;
- the grant of a lease to a third person subject to a right to terminate;
- the exercise of a right to terminate a lease or to take some other action;
- an agreement not to exercise a right to terminate a lease or take some other action;
- the variation of a right to terminate a lease or to take some other action.

(FA 2003, s 75A(3)).

17.88 The provision does not apply if the reason why the SDLT is lower than on a straight sale is because of the special rules on alternative (ie Sharia compliant) finance arrangements, or those which relate to a right to buy or shared ownership leases *(FA 2003, s 75A(7))*. A transfer of shares or securities is ignored if it is the first of a series of scheme transactions *(FA 2003, s 75C(1))*.

For the purpose of this provision a 'transaction' includes a non-land transaction; an agreement, offer or undertaking not to take specified action; any kind of arrangement, whether or not it could otherwise be described as a transaction; and a transaction that takes place after the acquisition by P of the chargeable interest *(FA 2003, s 75A(2))*. The notional transaction attracts any relief, which it would attract if it were an actual transaction *(FA 2003, s 75C(2))*. It can

17.89 *Anti-avoidance*

qualify for SDLT reconstruction or acquisition relief if any of the scheme transactions is entered into in connection with the transfer of an undertaking (*FA 2003, s 75C(3)*).

The Ramsay principle

17.89 If a proposed transaction manages to circumvent a specific anti-avoidance rule it will not necessarily achieve its desired objective because of the *Ramsay* principle.

This principle was enunciated by Lord Wilberforce in the House of Lords in the 1981 case of *W T Ramsay Ltd v IRC, Eilbeck v Rawling* (1981) 54 TC 101, which were heard together. Lord Wilberforce first acknowledged the principle enunciated by Lord Tomlin in *IRC v Duke of Westminster* (1935) 19 TC 490 that 'every man is entitled, if he can, to order his affairs so that the tax attaching under the appropriate Acts is less than it otherwise would be'. He then went on to say:

> 'while obliging the courts to accept documents or transactions found to be genuine, as such, it does not compel the court to look at a document or a transaction in blinkers, isolated from any context to which it properly belongs. If it can be seen that a document or transaction was intended to have effect as part of a nexus or series of transactions, or as an ingredient of a wider transaction intended as a whole, there is nothing in the doctrine to prevent it being so regarded: to do so is not to prefer form to substance, or substance to form. It is the task of the court to ascertain the legal nature of any transaction ... and if that emerges from a series or combination of transactions, intended to operate as such, it is that series or combination which may be regarded.'

17.90 In subsequent cases the principle has been reformulated in a number of different ways and its ambit has been significantly cut down. In particular in *Furniss (Inspector of Taxes) v Dawson* (1984) 55 TC 324 Lord Brightman indicated that it requires two conditions, a pre-ordained series of transactions (in the sense of pre-planned, not necessarily specific transactions) and steps inserted into that series that have no commercial (business) purpose apart from the avoidance of a liability to tax.

In *MacNiven (Inspector of Taxes) v Westmoreland Investments Ltd* (2001) 73 TC 1 Lord Nicholls of Birkenhead said 'In *Ramsay* the House did not enunciate any new legal principle. What the House did was to highlight that, confronted with new and sophisticated tax avoidance devices, the court's duty is to determine the legal nature of the transactions in question and then relate them to the fiscal legislation'. He thought that this implied three elements:

Anti-avoidance **17.92**

- The court needs to ascertain the legal nature of the transaction – which may emerge from a series or combination of transactions intended to operate as such.

- What this does is to enable the court to look at a document or transaction in the context to which it properly belongs – but not to treat a transaction or step in a transaction as though it were a 'sham' or to go behind the transaction for some supposed underlying substance.

- Having identified the legal nature of the transaction, the courts must then relate this to the language of the statute. 'For example, if the scheme has the apparently magical result of creating a loss without the taxpayer suffering any financial detriment, is this artificial loss a loss within the meaning of the relevant statutory provision?'

17.91 The latest decision of the House of Lords in this line of cases is that given by Lord Nicholls of Birkenhead in *Barclays Mercantile Business Finance Ltd v Mawson (Inspector of Taxes)* (2004) 76 TC 446.

'The essence of the new approach was to give the statutory provision a purposive construction in order to determine the nature of the transaction to which it was intended to apply and then to decide whether the actual transaction (which might involve considering the overall effect of a number of elements intended to operate together) answered to the statutory description. Of course this does not mean that the courts have to put their reasoning into the straitjacket of first construing the statute in the abstract and then looking at the facts. It might be more convenient to analyse the facts and then ask whether they satisfy the requirements of the statute. But however one approaches the matter, the question is always whether the relevant provision of statute, upon its true construction, applies to the facts as found … the *Ramsay* case did not introduce a new doctrine operating within the special field of revenue statutes. On the contrary, as Lord Steyn observed in *McGuckian* [1997] 1 WLR 991, 999, it rescued tax law from being "some island of literal interpretation' and brought it within generally applicable principles".'

17.92 Lord Hoffmann in the *Westmoreland* case said:

'For present purposes, however, the point I wish to emphasise is that Lord Brightman's formulation in the *Furniss* case, like Lord Diplock's formulation in the *Burmah* case, is not a principle of construction. It is a statement of the consequences of giving a commercial construction to a fiscal concept. Before one can apply Lord Brightman's words, it is first necessary to construe the statutory language and decide that it refers to a concept which Parliament intended to be given a commercial meaning capable of transcending

17.93 *Anti-avoidance*

the juristic individuality of its component parts. But there are many terms in tax legislation which cannot be construed in this way. They refer to purely legal concepts which have no broader commercial meaning. In such cases, the *Ramsay* principle can have no application. It is necessary to make this point because, in the first flush of victory after the *Ramsay*, *Burmah* and *Furniss* cases, there was a tendency on the part of the Inland Revenue to treat Lord Brightman's words as if they were a broad spectrum antibiotic which killed off all tax avoidance schemes, whatever the tax and whatever the relevant statutory provisions ...

The limitations of the *Ramsay* principle therefore arise out of the paramount necessity of giving effect to the statutory language. One cannot elide the first and fundamental step in the process of construction, namely to identify the concept to which the statute refers. I readily accept that many expressions used in tax legislation (and not only in tax legislation) can be construed as referring to commercial concepts and that the courts are today readier to give them such a construction than they were before the *Ramsay* case. But that is not always the case. Taxing statutes often refer to purely legal concepts. They use expressions of which a commercial man, asked what they meant, would say "You had better ask a lawyer". For example, stamp duty is payable upon a "conveyance or transfer on sale": see *Sch 13, para 1(1)* to the *Finance Act 1999*. Although slightly expanded by a definition in *para 1(2)*, the statutory language defines the document subject to duty essentially by reference to external legal concepts such as "conveyance" and "sale". If a transaction falls within the legal description, it makes no difference that it has no business purpose. Having a business purpose is not part of the relevant concept. If the "disregarded" steps in *Furniss v Dawson* [1984] AC 474; 55 TC 324 had involved the use of documents of a legal description which attracted stamp duty, duty would have been payable.'

17.93 The *Westmoreland* case, like *Ramsay*, involved a circular transaction. The shareholder, a pension fund, was owed money by Westmoreland. It lent the company further funds to enable it to pay the interest on the debt. This crystallised the interest as deductible within Westmoreland. The pension fund then sold Westmoreland as a tax shelter. The interest was held to be deductible as the statute provided that interest should be deducted once it had been paid and that had undoubtedly happened.

The *Barclays Mercantile* case involved a finance lease of an oil pipeline where the purchase price for the pipeline had effectively circulated wholly within the Barclays group. HMRC contended that no expenditure had been incurred as the vendor had paid it back to Barclays. It was held that the legislation required expenditure to be incurred to acquire the machinery or plant for the purpose of leasing it in the course of the trade. Those statutory requirements were concerned wholly with the acts and purposes of the lessor. It said nothing about what the lessee should do with the purchase price, so the fact that it had paid it back to Barclays could not affect Barclays Mercantile's entitlement to the capital allowances.

THE MINISTERIAL STATEMENT OF 2 DECEMBER 2004

17.94 It is probably appropriate to end this chapter with a warning to those engaged in tax planning in relation to employment income. In a Parliamentary Statement on 2 December 2004, the Minister said that she was 'giving notice of our intention to deal with any arrangements that emerge in future designed to frustrate our intention that employers and employees should pay the proper amount of tax and NICs on the rewards of employment. Where we become aware of arrangements which attempt to frustrate the intention we will introduce legislation to close them down from today'.

Accordingly, those seeking to avoid such tax should be aware that even if they successfully circumvent the current anti-avoidance rules and the *Ramsay* principle there is a significant risk that the arrangements will be thwarted by future legislation introduced with retrospective effect!

Index

[*References are to paragraph number*]

A

Abroad, *see* Residence (country of)
Accommodation
   available in UK, relevance to residence   8.20, 8.21
   non-domiciled employee for, tax position   8.48
Accumulation and maintenance trust   14.8, 14.31
   pre-22 March 2006   14.74, 14.79–14.81
Administrator   13.5, 13.6, 13.8
Agricultural building, *see* Capital allowances
Agricultural property relief   2.84, 2.85, 11.57, 12.1 *et seq*
   broiler houses   12.45
   buy and sell agreements   12.62, 12.63
   CGT, interaction with   12.31
   clawback   12.4, 12.46
      limiting   12.5
   company, farming   12.24, 12.57
   concessionary reliefs   12.22
   contract farming   12.60
   cottages   12.1, 12.44–12.50
      valuation provision   12.44
   estate planning   12.23 *et seq*
      death, delaying gift until   12.35, 12.47
      deed of variation   12.37
      discretionary trust, use of   12.25–12.27, 12.30
      double relief, obtaining by 'recycling'   12.28, 12.29

Agricultural property relief – *contd*
   estate planning – *contd*
      examples of effective use   12.31, 12.32
      settlement with lifetime interest, use of   12.36
      will drafting   12.33, 12.34
   farmhouse   12.1, 12.2, 12.44–12.50
      'character appropriate'   12.46, 12.47, 12.49
      charge on, effect of   12.39, 12.40
      occupation ancillary to agricultural land   12.44, 12.48
      test to qualify for relief   12.48, 12.49
      unoccupied   12.46
   holiday letting   12.51, 12.52
   investments, BPR compared   12.6
   licence or let for grazing etc, effect of   12.50
   life assurance, use for   12.29
   lifetime gift, death within seven years   12.4, 1.25
   land   12.1, 12.50
      fallow   12.51
      habitat scheme, subject to   12.58
      non-agricultural use   12.54
      tenancy/surrender   12.50, 12.53, 12.55
   mortgage or charge on assets within   12.38–12.43
   borrowing on other assets to buy assets within relief   12.43
   tax planning issues   12.40–12.43
   ownership period   12.9–12.14

Index

Agricultural property relief – *contd*
  partnerships   12.7, 12.8, 12.24,
        12.55, 12.62, 12.63
  property within scope   12.1, 12.2
  rates of relief   12.3, 12.20–12.22
  sharing venture   12.59
  single farm payment scheme   12.61
  tenant farmer   12.56
  value, agricultural   12.15–12.19, 12.40
  woodlands, *see* Woodlands

Alternative investment market
  business property relief   9.4, 11.2, 11.3
  CGT taper relief   6.11
  EIS relief   9.5

Annuity   7.3, 7.4, 9.28–9.30,
  see also Pension

Anti-avoidance provisions   17.1 *et seq*
  background   17.1–17.5
  CGT   17.76, 17.82, 17.83
  company ceasing to be
      member of group   17.77–17.79
  company losses on change of
      ownership   17.39–17.51
  background, carry forward
      provisions   17.40–17.42
  change of ownership, when
      occurs   17.48
  major change in trade   17.45–17.47
  pre-entry loss   17.51
  restrictions on losses   17.49, 17.50
  dividend income spreading   1.123, 1.124, 1.128
  employment income,
    Ministerial Statement
      (2/12/04)   17.94
  group of companies   4.12, 4.13, 4.41
    VAT   17.59–17.63
  life assurance   9.24, 9.28–9.30
  personal service company   1.94–1.97, 1.130
  purchase of own shares   2.22
  Ramsay principle   17.89–17.93
  sale of owner-managed
      company   6.26

Anti-avoidance provisions – *contd*
  settlor retaining interest in
      settlement   17.30–17.38
  spouse exemption   13.62
  targeted anti-avoidance rules
      (TAARs)   17.80–17.88
    CGT   17.82, 17.83
    SDLT   17.84–17.88
  transaction in securities, *see*
      Transaction in securities
  transfer of assets abroad/to
      non-UK resident   17.11 *et seq*
    capital gains, non-resident
      company   17.20
    non-resident settlement,
      CGT   17.24–17.29
    property dealing through
      offshore company   17.13–17.20
    transaction held to fall
      within provisions   17.19
  transfer pricing   4.70, 17.65–17.76
    adjustments   17.73
    arm's length price,
      computing guidelines   17.67
    exemptions   17.71
    participation in
      management or
      control   17.65, 17.68–17.70
    'series of transactions'   17.67
    small company   17.71, 17.72
  VAT
    fragmentation of business   17.55–17.58
    group of companies   17.59–17.63

Arm's length, provision not at,
  see Transfer pricing

Assets, *see also* Capital
  allowances; Capital gains
  tax; Property
  business, inheritance tax
      relief, *see* Business
      property relief
  intangible   2.69–2.71
    see also Goodwill
  pension contribution in form
      of   10.28

Index

Assets – *contd*
  transfer abroad,
    anti-avoidance   17.11 *et seq*
Associate
  meaning   1.89–1.92
  purchase of own shares, and
    interests of   3.26, 3.28, 3.32, 3.72
Associated companies 1.85–1.92, 4.33, 4.34
Attendance allowance, person in receipt of 14.37, 14.49, 14.84

B

Beneficiary, *see* Trust
Benefits in kind   1.113, 1.143
Branch   8.56
  trustee having in UK   14.17
Building
  agricultural, *see* Agricultural property relief
  business property relief   11.2, 11.13
  historic, trust for maintenance   14.92
Business asset taper relief, *see* Capital gains tax
Business property relief   1.50, 1.109, 1.118, 1.119, 11.1 *et seq*
  'business'   11.4–11.8, 11.15, 11.54
    relevant business property   11.2, 11.14
    'wholly or mainly' test   11.7
  caravan park   11.5
  charge or mortgage on assets within   12.38–12.43
  claim required   11.1
  clawback   11.37–11.41
  conditions   11.2, 11.3
  contract for sale, effect of   11.33–11.35
    agreement types not caught   11.34
    binding contracts for sale   11.33
  death, on   11.45–11.50
    considerations   11.45
    discretionary trust, use of   11.49, 11.50
  double relief, obtaining by 'recycling'   11.50, 13.110

Business property relief – *contd*
  death, on – *contd*
    examples   11.46, 11.48
    rates   11.48
    rules applying   11.46
    will drafting and variation   11.46, 11.47
  excepted assets   11.14–11.22
    investment assets   11.15, 11.16
  groups of companies   11.23–11.27
    holding company, rules for   11.23, 11.24
    investment business, carrying on   11.25, 11.26
    'wholly or mainly' test   11.27
  hotel, etc   11.6, 15.19
  incorporation, on   2.78–2.83, 11.35
  investment 'business'   11.20–11.22, 11.54, 11.55
  land and buildings   11.2, 11.7, 11.13, 11.14, 11.19
    part exclusive business use   11.14
  lettings/rental returns   11.6, 11.16, 12.52, 15.18, 15.22
  lifetime gift   11.36 *et seq*
    CGT, interaction with   11.53
    clawback, avoiding   11.37–11.41
    gift with reservation   11.56
    order of gifts, relevance of   11.44
    protection against rate change, and risks of   11.51, 11.52
  liquidation or reorganisation of company   11.28
  loans   11.6
  milk quota   12.53
  ownership period   11.9, 11.56
    change in business   11.10
  partnership   11.29–11.32
  plant and machinery   11.2
  property construction   11.6
  rates   11.1, 11.51
  replacement property   11.41–11.43
    conditions for   11.41, 11.42
  scope of relief   11.1
  settlement with interest in possession   11.2, 11.11, 11.12
    beneficial entitlement   11.11

Index

Business property relief – *contd*
   shares   11.2, 11.3, 11.7, 11.14
      investment holding   9.4, 11.15, 11.20
      lifetime transfer followed
         by sale of company   11.36
      replacement property rule
         for   11.43
      winding up, effect of   11.28
      trading or hybrid company   11.2, 11.15
   funds applied for
      investment   11.20
   surplus cash held by   11.14, 11.17–11.19, 11.22
   'transferee'   11.39, 11.41
   value of business, 'net value'   11.13, 11.54

Business use of main residence 15.20–15.23

Business vehicle, *see* Trading vehicle

C

Capital allowances
   cessation of trade, plant and
      industrial buildings   7.7
   disincorporation, on   5.11, 5.14
   incorporation, on   2.17–2.28
      change in WDA   2.22
      industrial/agricultural
         building   2.23–2.28
      plant and machinery   2.17–2.21

Capital distribution   7.22 *et seq*
   business and non-business
      distinction   7.27, 7.31, 7.32
   CGT liability on receipt of   7.22
   dividend pre-dissolution
      contrasted   7.35–7.37
      example   7.37
      mixture of dividend and
         capital distribution   7.37
      post-6 April 2008 distribution   7.31–7.34, 7.36–7.38
   in specie distributions   7.34
   multiple distributions,
      timing issues   7.32
   small distributions   7.33

Capital distribution – *contd*
   taper relief (pre-6 April 2008)   7.23–7.30, 7.35
      calculation of gain   7.30
      cessation of trading, effect
         of   7.24, 7.25
      dilution of   7.38
      'inactive' periods   7.24, 7.25, 7.26
      minority shareholder
         position   7.23
      settlor-interested trust, use
         of   7.29
      time-apportionment   7.26, 7.27
      timing considerations   7.28, 7.29

Capital gains tax
   abroad, gains generated   8.33–8.35
   anti-avoidance provisions   17.76, 17.82, 17.83
   artificial value, transaction at   17.76
   BPR, and   11.53
   business asset, *see also* 'taper
      relief, business asset'
      below
      disposal into settlement   14.38
   changes to regime   2.34
   company, double charge   1.154, 1.155, 1.157–1.160
   death, CGT-free uplift on   11.36
   debt, irrecoverable   7.49
   disincorporation, no relief on   5.1, 5.2, 5.13
   divorce/separation, on   16.12–16.21
   EIS company relief, *see*
      Enterprise Investment
      Scheme
   gift relief   9.3
   group, within, *see* Group of
      companies
   hold-over relief   16.16, 16.17
      trustees, and   15.27–15.29
   incorporation, issues on   2.34–2.52
   indexation, withdrawal of   2.34, 2.97
   insolvent company,
      shareholder relief, *see*
      Insolvent winding up

Index

Capital gains tax – *contd*
  loan, irrecoverable, loss relief 7.49–7.53
    capitalisation of loan into new shares 7.54, 7.55
    conditions 7.50
    corporate lender, impairment loss claim 7.56, 7.57
    guarantee, for payment under 7.53
    'irrecoverable' 7.51
    waiver, effect of 7.52
  non-resident, position of, *see* Non-resident
  pension schemes 10.28, 10.36, 10 106
  'phoenix company' considerations 7.38–7.40
  principal private residence exemption 15.3–15.30
    absences 15.15–15.17
    business use/mixed use 15.20–15.23
    conditions 15.3–15.5, 15.15
    dependent relative relief 15.24, 15.25
    designation of home as 15.3
    divorce, and, *see* Divorce and separation
    election by taxpayer 15.9–15.12
    holiday home/second home, rules for 15.9–15.14
    job-related accommodation provision 15.14
    non-domicilary resident in UK 15.30
    occupation, quality of 15.8
    only or main residence 15.8–15.14
    'permitted area' 15.7
    personal representative relief 15.26
    renting out 15.18–15.19
    'residence' 15.6, 15.7
    separation of married couple 15.13

Capital gains tax – *contd*
  principal private residence exemption – *contd*
    three year exemption rule 15.8, 15.9
    'throughout the period of ownership' 15.15
    trustees, alternative relief 15.27–15.29
  purchase of own shares 3.1, 3.4, 3.5, 3.39, 3.42
  residence in UK 8.29
  settlements, *see* Trust
    non-UK resident, *see* Non-resident
  spouses, transfers between 13.29
  taper relief, business asset
    abolition of 2.34, 2.97, 5.16, 6.1
    capital distribution, on, *see* Capital distribution
    investor in unquoted trading company 9.2
    non-UK domiciled person 8.35
    owner-managed company sale, *see* Sale of owner-managed company
    purchase of own shares, and, *see* Purchase of own shares
  transfer of assets to a company by sole trader/partner, reliefs on 2.40–2.51, 2.93
    comparison of s 162 and s 165 2.52
    s 162 2.40–2.46, 2.94, 2.95
    s 165 2.47–2.51, 2.93
  VCT relief 9.15
  variation of will or intestacy, effect of 13.42, 13.43, 13.45, 13.51
  winding up family company, *see* Winding up

Caravan park 11.5
Charge scheme, IHT planning 15.71
Chargeable gains, see Capital gains tax

Index

Charitable incorporated organisation 1.75
Charitable trust 14.15, 14.90
Civil partners
  separation 16.1 *et seq*
    see also Divorce and separation
  Wills 13.25–13.29, 13.57, 13.65
Close company 1.90, 1.112
  ceasing to trade 7.12
Close investment holding company 1.93, 2.97, 7.12
Community interest company 1.78
Company 1.73–1.130
  associated companies 1.85–1.92
    'associate' 1.89–1.92
    'control' 1.88, 1.90, 1.91
  benefits in kind 1.113, 1.143
  benefits of being 1.80, 1.120 *et seq*
    profit level for tax benefit 1.138
  bonus 1.104–1.106, 1.120
  CIC 1.78
  capital/capital gains 1.153, 1.154, 1.157
  ceasing to be beneficial owner of its trade 17.42
  change in ownership, disallowance of losses 17.39–17.51
  choice as business vehicle,
    factors 1.4 *et seq*, 1.16, 1.17
    disclosure issues 1.19, 1.20
    decision-making 1.21
    exiting 1.28
    raising finance 1.23–1.25
  close 1.90, 1.112
  close investment holding company 1.93, 2.97
  corporation tax 1.83, 1.84
    CTAP 5.8, 7.5, 7.6
    CTSA 4.23
    rates 1.83, 2.2
  director
    address of 1.20
    exiting, *see* Management buy-out; Purchase of own shares

Company – *contd*
  director – *contd*
    loan to 1.115, 1.116
    pension provision prior to winding up, *see* Pension
    personal liability 1.25, 1.82
    remuneration/profit extraction 1.26, 1.104–1.106, 1.120, 1.140–1.14
    see also Dividends; Employment related securities
  dissolution 1.156, 5.5, 7.17–7.19
  dividends, *see* Dividends
  EIS company, *see* Enterprise Investment Scheme
  employees 1.27, 1.28, 1.104–1.106, 1.113–1.117, 1.120
    'employment-related securities' 1.144–1.148
    loan to 1.115, 1.116
  family, *see* Family company
  farming 12.57
  foreign 8.77–8.83
    case, CGT avoidance scheme 8.81–8.83
    decision on residence 8.77–8.80
  group relief, *see* Group of companies
  guarantee, limited by 1.75
  income spreading 1.120–1.130
  incorporation, *see* Incorporation
  insolvency 1.82
  interest on loan to 1.110–1.112
    advantages 1.111
  limited liability 1.80–1.82
    personal guarantees undercut 1.25, 1.81
  losses
    anti-avoidance on purchase of 17.39 *et seq*,
    see also Anti-avoidance
    carry forward 17.40–17.42
  managed service company 1.100, 1.101

566

Company – *contd*
  owner-managed, sale of, *see*
    Sale of owner-managed
    company
  pension   1.114, 1.120, 7.3, 7.4
  personal service company   1.94–1.99
    anti-avoidance rules   1.94–1.97, 1.130
    benefits retained   1.98
    issues for proprietors   1.98
  personally-held property used
    by company
    business property relief   1.119
    rent on   1.107–1.109, 1.60
  private limited   1.6, 1.22, 1.30, 1.74
  profits
    distribution/extraction   1.102–1.120, 1.139 *et seq*,
    see also Dividends
    retention   1.153, 1.154
  public limited   1.77
  purchase of own shares, *see*
    Purchase of own shares
  registration costs   1.8
  returns   1.9, 1.10, 1.19
  salaries   1.104–1.106, 1.120, 1.121
    dividends, interaction with   1.142, 1.150
    tax issues   1.138, 1.140–1.142
  service contract   1.121
  shareholder   1.28, 1.80, 1.81, 1.102, 1.103
    benefit to non-working   1.113, 1.151
    capital distributions to, on
      winding up   7.20–7.22
    capital gains   1.154, 1.157–1.159, 7.22
    controlling, BPR   1.119
    insolvent company, *see*
      Insolvent winding up
    loan to   1.115
    loan to company by   1.110–1.112
    see also Dividends;
      Purchase of own
      shares

Company – *contd*
  shares
    'employment-related
      securities'   1.144–1.148
    incentives related to   1.27
    small   1.10, 1.11
    divisions, separation of
      trade into   1.87
    rate of tax   1.83, 2.2
    transfer pricing exemption   17.71, 17.72
  spouses   1.120–1.130
  timing of tax payments   1.133
  trading
    business taper relief   6.11, 6.12
    see also Trade; Trading
      stock
  transfer of business to   1.129, 1.132
  unlimited   1.19, 1.76
Connected person   2.13, 2.38
  corporate lender, impairment
    loss claim   7.56, 7.57
  derivative contracts   4.73
  'no continuing connection'
    test, *see* Purchase of own
    shares
Corporation tax, *see* Company;
  Group of companies
**Corporation tax accounting
  period (CTAP)**   5.8
  winding up, effect on   7.5, 7.6, 7.10, 7.15
**Corporation tax
  self-assessment regime
  (CTSA)**   4.23
Creditor, *see* Winding up

D

Debt
  irrecoverable   7.49
  UK linked   8.38
Debt on a security   7.50, 7.55
Debt scheme, IHT planning   15.68–15.70
Derivative contract   4.73, 4.74
Director, *see* Company
Disabled person
  meaning   14.37, 14.49, 14.84

Index

Disabled person – *contd*
  trust for   14.14, 14.37
    IHT regime   14.74–14.78, 14.84
    vulnerable person   14.47–14.49
Discretionary trust   14.7, 14.9–14.14, 14.36
  APR, use for   12.25–12.27, 12.30
  accumulation and
    maintenance   14.8, 14.31
  BPR, use for   11.37, 11.38, 11.49, 11.50
  beneficiary, tax on payment
    to   14.24, 14.25
  IHT regime   14.38, 14.68–14.73
    entry charge   14.69
    exit charge   14.72, 14.73
    occasions for charge   14.68
    ten-yearly charge   14.70, 14.71
  Will, use in, *see* Will
Disincorporation   2.98–2.102, 5.1 *et seq*
  CGT position   5.1, 5.2
    asset transfer   5.13
    capital distribution,
      business taper relief   5.16, 5.18
    double tax charge   5.16, 5.18
    goodwill   5.6, 5.15
    property   5.14
  capital allowance cessation
    rules   5.11
  corporation tax accounting
    period, end to   5.8
  dissolution   5.3, 5.5
  example   5.6 *et seq*
  members' voluntary winding
    up   5.3, 5.4
  reasons for   5.1
  shareholder tax liabilities   5.16
  distribution prior to
    disincorporation, tax
    on   5.4, 5.5, 5.16
  'transaction in securities'
    aspects   5.17, 5.18, 7.40
  trading losses   5.9
  trading stock, value for
    transfer of   5.10
  VAT registered business   5.12

Dissolution   1.156, 5.5, 7.17–7.19
  restoration to Register   7.16, 7.19
Dividends   1.123–1.130
  disadvantages   1.149–1.155
    pension   1.149, 1.150
  employment-related
    securities, on   1.147, 1.148
  family company, use in   1.123 *et seq*
  formalities   1.152
  income spreading, use for   1.102, 1.103, 1.123–1.130
    anti-avoidance rules   1.123, 1.124, 1.128
    case on   1.124–1.127
  incorporation, advantage over
    salary   2.33, 2.62
  restrictions on payment   1.102
  salary, and   1.142, 1.150
  tax   1.103–1.105, 1.141
  tax free, paid by VCT   9.15
  waiver   1.150
  winding up/dissolution, prior
    to   7.35–7.37
Divorce and separation   16.1–16.48
  capital gains tax, disposals
    between spouses   16.12–16.21
    after decree absolute   16.15
    before end of year of
      separation   16.13
    between separation and
      decree absolute   16.14, 16.16
    court order, on   16.19
    hold-over relief   16.16, 16.17
    lump sum order   16.21
    time of   16.18–16.20
  capital gains tax and PPR
    exemption   16.29–16.41
  company or trust, funds
    extracted from   16.42–16.45
    offshore trust   16.43–16.45
  income tax   16.7–16.11
    maintenance   16.7, 16.8
    married couple tax
      reduction   16.9
    settlement rules   16.10, 16.11, 16.24, 16.25

Index

Divorce and separation – *contd*
  inheritance tax   16.22–16.26
    background   16.22
    maintenance of family   16.22
    spouse exemption   16.24
  life policy assignment   16.47, 16.48
  living together, when not treated as   16.12
  lump sum by court order   16.21
  matrimonial home and GCT exemption   16.29–16.41
    extra–statutory concession D6 and limitations of   16.33, 16.34
    identifying main residence   16.29, 16.31
    Mesher-type order   16.35, 16.37, 16.40
    one party retaining   16.34–16.41
    settlement   16.37, 16.38
    transfer, transferee's position   16.30
  non-UK domiciled spouse(s)   16.46
  outline of steps involved   16.2–16.6
    consent order   16.4, 16.17, 16.19
    court powers   16.5, 16.6
  pre-owned assets tax   16.28
  property adjustment order   16.6
  SDLT   16.26, 16.27

Domicile, *see also* Residence (country of)
  non-domicilary
    anti-avoidance provisions   17.11–17.29
    PPR relief   15.30
    spouse(s), on divorce   16.46
    transferor of assets   17.20

Double tax treaty, *see* Residence (country of)

Dwelling–house
  CGT principal private residence exemption, meaning for   15.6

E

Emigration
  CGT, cessation of trade on   8.61, 8.62
  date of disposal   8.64, 8.65

Employee
  anti-avoidance, Ministerial Statement (2/12/04)   17.94
  'employee benefit trust'   14.12, 14.13, 14.91
  job-related accommodation, and CGT private residence exemption   15.14
  life cover for   10.70, 10.71
  non-UK domiciled, employment income taxable on remittance basis   8.40–8.47
    assets paid, used or enjoyed in UK, etc   8.47
    dual contract, use of   8.42–8.46
    incidental duties performed in UK   8.40, 8.41, 8.43
    investments   8.47
    overseas duties   8.40, 8.43, 8.44
    resident in UK with foreign employer   8.40
    two or more employments with same employer   8.46
  non-UK domiciled, travelling expenses   8.48
  non-UK resident   8.51
  pension, *see* Pension
  working abroad under contract of employment, *see* Residence (country of)

'Employment-related securities'   1.144–1.148
  dividends   1.147, 1.148
  tax charges on acquisition   1.146

Endowment policy, *see* Investment products and schemes

Enterprise Investment Scheme
  approved EIS funds   9.17

Index

Enterprise Investment Scheme – *contd*
incorporation by individual
   trader, use on   2.53–2.58
subscription for shares in
   cash   2.54
qualifying companies   9.16
unquoted trading company
   shares, relief under   9.5–9.13
     AIM company shares   9.5
     CGT   9.7, 9.8, 9.10
     CGT deferral   9.9, 9.11
     income tax   9.6, 9.8, 9.10
     loss relief   9.8
     qualifying investors,
       conditions   9.10, 9.11
     receipt of value by investor,
       effect of   9.12
     withdrawal of relief   9.13
unapproved EIS funds   9.18
**Enterprise Management
Incentive**   1.27
Equity release schemes   15.58–15.60
European Economic Area
collective investment scheme
   operator/investment
   portfolio manager   10.8
group relief   4.21
   EEA tax loss condition   4.22
**European economic interest
grouping**   1.79
European Union
pension portability   10.115

F

Family company   1.120–1.130
see also Sale of
   owner-managed
   company
purchase of own shares   3.1 *et seq*
   see Purchase of own shares
winding up of, *see* Winding
   up
Farm land/house, *see also*
Agricultural property relief
agricultural property relief,
   included in   12.1, 12.2
   mortgage on, effect of   12.39

Farm land/house – *contd*
single farm payment scheme   12.61
Finance, raising   1.23–1.30
companies   1.23–1.25
Foreign company, *see*
   Non-resident
Forestry, *see* Woodlands
Funeral
executor arranging   13.7
expenses   10.76

G

Gift relief (CGT)   9.3
Gift schemes, *see also*
Investment products and
   schemes
discounted gift scheme, IHT
   Will planning   15.74
**Gift with reservation
provisions**   13.19, 13.81, 13.82,
   15.33–15.36
interaction with POAT   15.37,
   15.38, 15.45 *et seq*
Goodwill
business property relief,
   business value includes   11.13
definition   2.59, 2.60
   personal   2.60–2.63
disincorporation, transfer on   5.6,
   5.15
incorporation, CGT position   2.35,
   2.36, 2.56–2.68
   sale to company   2.56
   tax treatment   2.64
   valuation   2.61, 2.66–2.68
intangible fixed asset, tax
   treatment as   2.69–2.71
Group of companies   4.1 *et seq*
business property relief, *see*
   Business property relief
ceasing to be member,
   anti-avoidance   17.77–17.79
chargeable gains   4.25–4.37
   associated companies
     leaving group together   4.33,
     4.34
   depreciatory transaction,
     provisions for   4.51–4.58

Index

Group of companies – *contd*
  chargeable gains – *contd*
    dual resident investing
      company   4.30
    'exit charge'   4.25, 4.32
    joining group   4.48
    leaving group   4.32–4.37
    membership qualifications   4.26–4.28
    merger exemption   4.35
    non-resident member   4.29
    notional transfer election   4.37
    pre-entry gain   4.45, 4.50, 17.51
    pre-entry loss   4.46–4.49, 17.51
    reallocation of charge
      election   4.36
    residence qualifications   4.29
    same group, identification
      of   4.28
    share exchange
      intra–group   4.67
    substantial shareholdings
      exemption   4.1, 4.34, 4.51, 4.59–4.68
    trading or non-trading
      status   4.31, 4.64
    transfer of trade, *see below*
    transfer provisions   4.30, 4.31
  definitions   4.2–4.8
    equity holder   4.5, 4.6
    normal commercial loan   4.7
    ordinary share capital   4.3
    75% subsidiary   4.3
  derivative contract   4.73, 4.74
  dividends paid within, and
    subsequent sale of payer
    company   4.55
  group relief   4.9–4.24
    annual basis   4.10
    anti-avoidance   4.12, 4.13
    apportionment, time for   4.18
    claim   4.23
    dual resident investing
      company   4.19
    limits on   4.17–4.19
    losses which may be
      surrendered   4.15, 4.16

Group of companies – *contd*
  group relief – *contd*
    membership qualifications   4.11
    non-resident companies,
      conditions for   4.20–4.22
    payment for   4.24
    residence qualifications   4.14, 4.19
    time-limit for claim   4.23
  intangible asset   4.58, 4.74
  loan relationships   4.9, 4.10, 4.71
    effect of rules on groups   4.72
  ownership, tests for   4.4, 4.11
  overview of tax treatment   4.1
  payment of tax,
    'arrangements' permitted   4.75
  purchase of own shares,
    'substantial reduction'
    test   3.28, 3.29
  transfer of trade between
    members   4.38–4.44
    anti-avoidance   4.41
    capital allowances   4.38, 4.40, 4.41
    carry forward of losses   4.38, 4.40
    'common ownership' test   4.39, 4.40
    dual resident investing
      company   4.41
    part transfer, transferor's
      position   4.43
    trading stock   4.42
    transferee's position   4.44
  transfer pricing   4.70
  VAT
    anti-avoidance   17.59–17.62
    refusal of registration   17.63
Guarantee
  limited liability, undercutting   1.25, 1.81
  shareholder's personal, capital
    loss relief   7.53

H

Habitat scheme   12.58
Hancock annuity   7.3, 7.4, 10.77
  registered pension scheme, as   10.77

Index

Holiday home
CGT principal private
residence exemption, and   15.9
Holiday letting
business property relief   11.6
Home, family, *see also* Will
divorce, tax issues on, *see*
Divorce and separation
inheritance tax, *see*
Inheritance tax
principal private residence
exemption, *see* Capital
gains tax
sale at arm's length   15.57, 15.61
Home loan scheme   15.38, 15.50–15.52
guidance from HMRC   15.52
Home reversion scheme   15.59
Hotel
business property relief   11.6
private accommodation of
owner within   15.19

I

Income tax
beneficiary of a trust   14.24–14.26
divorce/separation, on   16.7–16.11
life policy, *see* Life assurance
policy
partnership   1.43–1.48
pre-owned assets tax   15.37–15.43
reliefs
EIS company, *see*
Enterprise Investment
Scheme
VCT   9.15
rents from property business   2.91
residence in UK   8.28
settlements, *see* Trust
shareholder
minority, pre-6 April 2008
taper relief   7.23
relief for capital loss on
winding up   7.44–7.48
see also Company
trust rate/dividend trust rate   14.21–14.24

Income tax – *contd*
Will variation, on   13.41, 13.49, 13.51
Incorporation   2.1 *et seq*
business property relief   2.78–2.83, 11.35
capital allowances   2.17–2.28
alternative relief   2.21, 2.47
changes   2.22
industrial/agricultural
building   2.23–2.28
plant and machinery   2.17–2.21
capital gains tax   2.34–2.52
assets chargeable   2.35
changes to   2.34
connected persons   2.38
considerations   2.35
EIS reinvestment relief, *see*
Enterprise Investment
Scheme
reliefs, and comparison of   2.37, 2.39–2.52
cashflow considerations'   2.12
corporation tax payment on,
timing   2.12
date, selecting   2.12, 2.20, 2.34
goodwill, *see* Goodwill
income tax at end of
individual trading   2.5–2.11
cessation computation   2.6, 2.7
overlap relief   2.8–2.10
inheritance tax   2.77
agricultural property relief   2.84, 2.85
BPR   2.78–2.83
intangible fixed assets   2.68–2.71
lease, grant of   2.76
legal formalities   2.3
national insurance
contributions   2.29–2.33
adjustments   2.31, 2.32
impact of   2.29, 2.30
stamp duty/stamp duty land
tax   2.72–2.76
stock, transfer of   2.13, 2.14
UK, in   8.84
VAT   2.86–2.90

Index

Incorporation – *contd*
  work in progress, transfer of   2.15, 2.16
Indexation allowance   6.6
Individual savings accounts (ISAs)   9.45
Industrial building, *see* Capital allowances
Inheritance tax
  agricultural property relief   2.84, 2.85
  business property relief, *see* Business property relief
  divorce/separation, on   16.22–16.25
  domicile in UK   8.30, 8.66
  gift with reservation provisions   13.19, 13.81, 13.82, 15.33–15.36
  home, family   15.31–15.74
    co–occupation   15.36, 15.59
    double charge provisions   15.55
    double trust or home loan   15.38, 15.50–15.52
    election for IHT by taxpayer   15.53–15.55
    equity release   15.58–15.60
    gift with reservation of benefit rules   15.33–15.36
    interest in possession trust, use of   15.47, 15.48
    lease carve out, use of   15.46
    lifetime mortgage   15.60
    nil-rate band   15.30, 15.63–15.67
    'occupation' by donee   15.34, 15.39
    pre-owned assets tax, and, *see* Pre-owned assets tax
    reversionary lease, use of   15.49
    tax planning schemes, effective end to   15.45–15.56
    tax planning schemes remaining possible, lifetime   15.57–15.61
    tax planning schemes remaining possible, Will   15.62–15.74
    undervalue, sale at   15.36

Inheritance tax – *contd*
  inter-spouse exemption, *see* Will
  location of assets in UK   8.66
  nil-rate band, *see* Will
  non-resident, *see* Non-resident
  partnership   1.50, 1.72, 1.118
  pension
    alternatively secured funds   13.99–13.101
    employer financed retirement benefit scheme   10.108
    lump sum death–in–service benefits   10.78, 10.79
  planning
    lifetime   15.56–15.61
    Will, in   15.63–15.74
  purchase of own shares to discharge liability on death   3.7, 3.8
  shareholder   1.118
  sole trader   1.118
  trusts, *see* Discretionary trust; Interest in possession trust
  wills, points for, *see* Will

Insolvent winding up   7.2, 7.14, 7.41
  shareholder relief   7.41–7.48
    claim procedure   7.48
    income tax relief offsetting capital loss   7.44–7.48
    irrecoverable loans, capital loss relief   7.49–7.53
    'negligible value' claim   7.41–7.43, 7.45, 7.48
    subscriber share requirement   7.46

Insurance company   9.21–9.36
  corporation tax rate   9.23
  life assurance, *see* Life assurance policy
  pension provider   10.8
  pension term assurance policy   10.72

Index

Insurance scheme
  IHT planning in Will   15.74
Intangible fixed assets   2.69–2.71
  see also Goodwill
  group, regime for   4.58, 4.74
  regime reform   2.69, 7.10
Interest in possession trust   14.8, 14.35, 14.36
  see also Will
  APR   12.36
  BPR   11.2, 11.11, 11.12
  beneficiary, tax on payment to   14.26
  death of life tenant   14.40
  GWR, use to avoid   15.47, 15.48
  IHT regime   14.74–14.85
    accumulation and maintenance trust   14.74, 14.79–14.81
    disabled person, trust for   14.84
    immediate post-death interest   14.82, 14.83
    pre-22 March 2006 IIP trust   14.75–14.78
    protective trust   14.85
Intestacy   13.5, 13.6, 13.8
  age of child for inheritance under   13.12, 13.13
  variation, deed of   13.35–13.43
Investment
  farming context   12.6
  unquoted trading company, in   9.1–9.4
  business asset taper relief for investor in   9.2
  business property relief   9.4, 11.2, 11.15
  CGT gift relief   9.3
  Enterprise Investment Scheme reliefs   9.5–9.13
    see also Enterprise Investment Scheme
  qualifying company   9.2
Investment business   1.58
  dual resident investing company   4.19, 4.30, 4.41

Investment business – *contd*
  incorporation of, considerations   2.91–2.97
  property lettings, and BPR   11.6
  trade contrasted   3.10
Investment products and schemes   9.35, 9.36
  carve out, varieties of   9.42–9.44
    beneficiaries   9.42
    IHT   9.43
    retention of reversionary interest by settlor, HMRC view on   9.43
  discounted gift   9.44
  endowment policy in trust, form of   9.35, 9.36
  gift and loan scheme for children   9.39–9.41
  ISAs   9.45
  PEPs, TESSAs and SAYE   9.46
  pension investment funds and schemes, *see* Pension
  spousal interest trust   9.37
    end to   9.38
  tax–free withdrawals   9.36

J

Joint venture arrangement   4.13

L

Land
  business property relief, *see* Business property relief
  farmland, *see* Agricultural property relief
Lease/letting, *see also* Business proeprty relief; Rents
  family home, and CGT
    exemption   15.17–15.19
    one room only   15.19
  gift with reservation issues
    co-occupation   15.36, 15.57
    lease carve out scheme   15.46
    reversionary lease scheme   15.49
  POAT, and rental payments   15.39

Index

Life assurance policy 9.21–9.26
agricultural property relief,
    use for 12.29
annuities 9.28–9.30
anti-avoidance 9.24, 9.28–9.30
assignment on separation or
    divorce 16.47, 16.48
expected group life policies 10.70, 10.71
group life policy for partners 9.32–9.34
legislation, rewriting of 9.31
life assurance company,
    corporation tax rate 9.23
non-qualifying 9.22, 9.25, 16.47
non-resident, for 9.25, 9.27
offshore 9.26
premium and proceeds,
    income tax 9.21, 9.22
'qualifying' 9.21, 16.47
trust, owned by 9.27

Life interest trust, *see* Will

Limited liability partnership 1.61–1.68
advantages 1.62–1.64, 1.69 *et seq*
agricultural property relief 12.7
choice as business vehicle 1.18
    disclosure drawback 1.19
    returns 1.9, 1.10
    small 1.10, 1.11
executor of will 13.4
formation 1.61
income tax 1.65
loss 17.52–17.54
members 1.62
    corporate 1.62, 1.65
use 1.64
VAT 1.66–1.68

Limited partnership 1.56–1.60
income tax and losses 1.59
nature of 1.56, 1.57
use 1.57, 1.58
VAT 1.60

Liquidation, *see also* Winding up
business property relief 11.28

Listed company, *see also*
Venture capital trust
business asset taper relief 6.15
business property relief 11.2

Loan
business property relief,
    whether 'business
    property' for 11.6
corporate lender, impairment
    loss claim 7.56, 7.57
relationship, *see* Loan
    relationship
settlor or spouse, to 14.33
shareholder, by
    conversion into new shares 7.54, 7.55
    irrecoverable, capital loss
    relief 7.49–7.53

Loan note 6.19, 7.55

Loan relationships 4.9, 4.10, 4.71, 4.72
capital loss relief not
    available 7.56, 7.57

Loan trust scheme 15.74

Losses
company, anti-avoidance
    provisions on change of
    ownership, *see*
    Anti-avoidance
disincorporation, trading
    losses on 5.9
EIS, relief under 9.8
groups 4.15, 4.16, 4.38, 4.40
    pre-entry loss 4.46–4.49, 17.51
irrecoverable loan, relief for,
    see Capital gains tax
limited partnership 17.52–17.54
targeted anti-avoidance rules
    for CGT 17.82, 17.83
winding up, shareholder relief 7.41–7.48

M

**Maintenance of historic
building, trust for** 14.92
Maintenance payments
tax relief 16.7, 16.8

Index

Married couple, *see also*
  Spouse
  tax reduction 16.9
Matrimonial home, *see* Home,
  family
Matrimonial proceedings, *see*
  Divorce and separation
**Members' voluntary winding
  up**, *see* Winding up
Mental disorder, person with,
  see Disabled person
Merger exemption 4.35
Mortgage
  agricultural/business assets,
    on, effect on reliefs 12.37–
    12.43
  matrimonial home
    gift of share in, consent of
      mortgagee 13.89
    IHT planning 15.57, 15.60, 15.74

N

Name, trading 1.13
National insurance 1.136, 1.137
  credit 1.120
  director/company employee 1.104–
    1.106, 1.142
  incorporation, on 2.29–2.33
  managed service company
    worker 1.100, 1.101
  partner 1.48
  personal service company
    worker 1.94, 1.96
  secondary contributions 1.136, 2.32
  self-employed and employee
    compared 1.136, 1.137, 2.29–
    2.31
  tax rates, combined effect 1.138
  trading vehicle decision, and 1.136–
    1.137
  winding up, liability on 7.13
National minimum wage 1.26
Nil-rate band, *see* Will
Non-resident 8.50–8.91
  anti-avoidance provisions 17.11–
    17.29

Non-resident – *contd*
  CGT 8.55–8.65, 17.23
    asset held for UK trade or
      profession removed
      from UK 8.60
    changes proposed 13.53
    cessation of trade or
      profession 8.61
    company 8.81–8.83, 17.20
    deemed disposals 8.60, 8.61
    emigration 8.61, 8.62
    exceptions to basic rule 8.56–
      8.59
    trustees 14.16, 14.17
    when individual chargeable 8.55
  company
    case, CGT avoidance
      scheme 8.81–8.83
    change of residence 8.87–8.89
    dual resident 8.90
    guidance on residence 8.80
    offshore, property dealing
      through 17.13–17.17
    trading in UK 8.85, 8.86, 17.23
    treatment as non-resident
      under double tax
      treaty 8.91
  employment income 8.51
  inheritance tax, non-UK
    domiciled individual 8.30,
      8.66–8.72
    Channel Islands/Isle of
      Man 8.67
    close company transfer of
      value 8.72
    domicile in UK for IHT 8.68
    double tax treaties 8.73–8.75
    excluded securities 8.67
    residence irrelevant 8.66
    settlement of non-UK
      property 8.71, 8.72
    spouse exemption limited 8.69,
      8.70
  investment income 8.50
  life assurance policy 9.25, 9.27
  pension schemes
    contributions 10.12

576

Index

Non-resident – *contd*
pension schemes – *contd*
    migrant member relief   10.112–10.114
    overseas schemes   10.109–10.116
  property income
    basic rule   8.53
    direct tax election   8.54
    non-UK company, held through   8.54
  settlement   14.50–14.66
    CGT   14.52–14.66, 17.24–17.29
    income tax   14.50, 14.51
    migrating from UK   14.60, 14.61
    migrating to UK   14.58
    protected settlement   14.54
    qualifying settlement   14.53
    settlor retaining interest   17.24
  spouse, IHT exemption   13.60
  trading income   8.52
  transfer of assets to, anti-avoidance provisions   17.11–17.29
  trustee   14.50–14.66
    CGT   14.52–14.66
    income tax   14.50, 14.51

O

Offshore company, *see* Non-resident
Offshore life policy   9.26
Offshore trust
  extraction of funds on divorce   16.43–16.45
  Will   13.53, 13.54
Open–ended investment company   10.8
Ordinary residence, *see* Residence (country of)
Overlap profits   1.37, 1.38, 1.45
  relief   2.8–2.10
Overseas bank account
  remittance basis of tax, avoiding   8.31–8.49, 15.30
Overseas company, *see* Non-resident

Overseas pension scheme, *see* Pension
Owner-managed company
  sale of company, *see* Sale of owner-managed company
  winding up, *see* Winding up

P

PAYE
  winding up, liability on   7.13
PEPs   9.46
Partnership, *see also* Limited partnership; Limited liability partnership
  agricultural property relief   12.7, 12.8, 12.24, 12.55, 12.62, 12.63
  benefits of being   1.69–1.72
    estate spreading   1.72
    income spreading   1.69–1.71
  business property relief   11.29–11.32
  capital gains tax   1.49
  choice as business vehicle   1.39–1.72
    sole trader contrasted   1.39
  company compared   1.20, 1.21, 1.24, 1.29, 1.132
    profit extraction   1.142
  conversion back to, *see* Disincorporation
  conversion of
    cessation computation on incorporation   2.6, 2.7
    company, to   2.5–2.16
      see also Incorporation
    LLP, to   1.62, 1.68
    sole trader, to   1.53
  family/spouses   1.68, 1.69
  formation   1.41
  general   1.40, 1.42, 1.51
  income tax   1.43–1.48
  inheritance tax   1.72, 1.118, 1.119
    business property relief   1.50
  joining/leaving   1.45, 1.52, 1.54
  life assurance   9.32–9.34
  loss, relief for   1.46, 1.47

Index

Partnership – *contd*
NICs 1.48
non-active partner 1.42, 1.47
number of partners, no
  restriction 1.4
profits 1.43–1.45
  overlap profits and relief 1.45, 2.8–2.10
  sharing 1.42
retirement of partner 11.32
Scotland 1.51, 1.57, 1.63
stamp duty land tax 1.54, 1.55
timing of tax payments 1.132, 1.135
VAT registration 1.51–1.53
Pension 10.1–10.116
A-Day, new regime from 10.2
allowances, tax-relievable 10.14–10.16
  annual 10.14, 10.17–10.22
  input period 10.23, 10.24
  lifetime 10.15, 10.16, 10.25–10.27, 10.98
approved scheme
  re–designated 10.103
benefits, restrictions on 10.39–10.42, 10.58–10.61
  amount of pension 10.42
  hazardous/sports
    occupations 10.39
  ill–health retirement 10.41
  minimum age 10.39
  retaining right to low
    retirement age 10.40
  trivial commutations 10.61
benefits in kind, tax charge on
  member's use 10.97
buy-out policies 10.62
capital gains tax 10.28, 10.36, 10 106
cash balance scheme 10.19
compensation payments to
  employers 10.58
compliance and
  sanctions 10.90 et seq
  appeals 10.102
  de-registration 10.94
  penalties 10.95–10.101

Pension – *contd*
compliance and sanctions – *contd*
  unauthorised payments
    rules 10.90–10.93
contributions, employer's 10.13
contributions, members' 10.10–10.12
  assets, in form of 10.28
  overseas members 10.12
  provisions as to 10.10
  refunds 10.58
  relief on 10.5, 10.6, 10.10–10.12
  tax relievable
    ceilings 10.14 *et seq*
death benefits 10.67–10.76
  funeral benefit 10.76
  lump sum 10.68, 10.69, 10.73–10.75
  permitted 10.68
  rules 10.67
defined benefits scheme 10.21, 10.42–10.45, 10.52, 10.75
dividends 1.149, 1.150
EFPOS 10.77
employer financed retirement
  benefit scheme
  (EFRBS) 10.13, 10.71, 10.85
  re-designation of FURBS
    as 10.106
  tax charges/exemptions 10.108
employer freedom as to
  scheme 10.3, 10.7
events report form 10.87
expected group life policies 10.70, 10.71
final salary scheme 10.21
form of payment 10.42–10.49
Hancock annuity 7.3, 7.4, 10.77
hybrid arrangements 10.22
ill–health 10.41, 10.60
inducement payment 10.85, 10.86
inheritance tax 10.78, 10.79
  discretionary trust, need for 10.78
investment funds, reliefs and
  restrictions 10.30–10.33
  employer loans 10.32

578

Pension – *contd*
  investment–regulated pension
      schemes   10.30, 10.34–10.38
    charges to tax   10.36, 10.37
    definition   10.35
    taxable property   10.37
    transitional exemptions   10.38
  lifetime annuity   10.42, 10.46
  lump sum
    commencement payment   10.10, 10.25, 10.50
    enhanced protection, transitional   10.75
    five–year guaranteed, transitional   10.73
    maximum to be taken   10.51–10.53
    payment on death   10.68, 10.69
    protected lump sums   10.54–10.57, 10.74
    repayment in of tax–free lump sum   10.29
    retained benefits, and   10.59
    stand-alone lump sum   10.57
    tax regime for   10.50–10.57, 10.69
  membership   10.2–10.6
  money purchase schemes   10.19, 10.20, 10.24, 10.51, 10.73
  NIC record for NIRP   2.33
  occupational pension scheme
    definition   10.5
    IRPS, as   10.35
  overseas employer   10.111
  overseas schemes   10.109–10.116
    migrant member relief   10.112–10.114
    portability of pension within EU   10 115
    qualifying recognised schemes (QROPS)   10 116
  penalties   10.95–10.101
  'pension scheme'   10.4
  pension sharing   10.80–10.84
    pension credit (post-A Day)   10.81–10.83

Pension – *contd*
  pension sharing – *contd*
    pension debit (post-A Day)   10.84–10.83
  personal pension scheme   10.2, 10.11, 10.39, 10.41
  protection of accrued rights   10.64–10.66
    enhanced   10.65, 10.99
    primary   10.66
  provider types   10.8
  Registered Pension Schemes Manual   10.1
  registered schemes   10.2, 10.8, 10.10
    de-registration sanction   10.94
    review of   10.103
  restrictions eased   10.3, 10.9, 10.14
  returns   10.87, 10.88
    accounting tax return   10.88
    Registered Pension Schemes Return   10.88
    reportable events   10.87
  scheme pension   10.43–10.45
  secured   10.42
    alternatively secured (ASP)   10. 25, 10.49, 10.79, 13.99–13.101
  surplus payments charge   10.96
  term assurance policy   10.72
  transfer of benefits   10.63
  transfer to appropriate person   10.101
  unapproved arrangements (FURBS/UURBS),
    review of   10.105
    benefits payments timing   10.107
    re-designation   10.106
    rules   10.106
  unauthorised payments   10.36, 10.87, 10.90–10.93, 10.104
    charge on   10.91
    scheme sanction charge   10.93, 10.104
    surcharge   10.92, 10.104
  unsecured   10.25–10.27, 10.42
    LA charge test   10.26, 10.27

Index

Pension – *contd*
  unsecured – *contd*
    maximum amount for
      pensions in payment 10.104
    winding up
      consideration prior to 7.3, 7.4
      penalty for deliberate 10.100
Personal representative
  CGT relief on sale of
    deceased's PPR 15.26
Personal service company 1.94–1.99
'Phoenix company' 7.38–7.40
  transaction in securities
    legislation, and 7.39, 7.40
Plant and machinery
  business property relief 11.2, 11.3
  capital allowances, *see*
    Capital allowances 11.2, 11.3
Pre-owned assets tax 15.37–15.43
  basic charge 15.43
  conditions for 15.38–15.40
  divorce/separation, on 16.28
  double charge provisions 15.55
  election for IHT by taxpayer 15.53–15.55
  example 15.43, 15.44
  exceptions 15.41
  GWR, interaction with 15.37, 15.38, 15.45 *et seq*
  'occupy' 15.39
  tax planning schemes 15.45–15.54
    effective 15.57–15.74
    home loan, guidance on 15.52
    home reversion scheme 15.59, 15.61
    ineffective, rules rendering 15.56
    reversionary lease,
      guidance on 15.49
  valuation 15.37, 15.42
Principal private residence
  exemption, *see* Capital gains tax
Private company, *see* Company
Profession or vocation 8.60, 8.61, 11.4
Property, *see also* Assets
  agricultural property relief 12.1, 12.44–12.50
  business property relief 11.2

Property – *contd*
  capital allowances, *see*
    Capital allowances
  non-resident holding UK
    property 8.53, 8.54
Protective trust 14.15
  IHT regime 14.74–14.78
Public company 1.77
Purchase of own shares 1.117, 3.1 *et seq*
  associates of vendor 3.32, 3.72
  disposal by, and substantial
    reduction test 3.34
  authority 3.66
  bonus issue by company prior
    to 3.37, 3.50
  CGT 3.1
  cancellation of purchased
    shares 3.64, 3.66
  capital treatment 3.55, 3.56
    advance clearance 3.59
    breach of rules 3.61
    eligibility 3.1, 3.4, 3.5, 3.39, 3.42
    mandatory if conditions
      satisfied 3.1, 3.56
  checklist 3.5
  clearance from HMRC 3.5, 3.6, 3.18
    application for 3.57–3.59
    joint clearance application 3.59
    'negative' 3.60, 3.62
    purchase in stages 3.35, 3.39
    single contract with
      multiple completion 3.41
  company law requirements 3.3, 3.63–3.67
    failure to comply 3.63
    HMRC require validity 3.63
    outline 3.66
  consideration 3.49
    payment conditions 3.15, 3.38, 3.66
  contract, inspection
    availability 3.67
  corporate vendor 3.68–3.71
  fees and costs 3.76

Index

Purchase of own shares – *contd*
  income distribution treatment 3.1, 3.43, 3.49–3.54
    exclusion of 3.2, 3.5
    potential traps 3.55
  inheritance tax payment
    purpose of 3.7, 3.8
  loan back by vendor 3.36, 3.37, 3.39
  multiple completion or separate tranches of shares 3.40, 3.41
  'no continuing connection' test 3.31, 3.32, 3.39
    anti-avoidance 3.33
    connection' 3.32
  ownership/retention period 3.24, 3.25, 3.67
    general rule and exceptions 3.24
    recently incorporated business 3.25
  payment 3.15, 3.38, 3.66
  phased purchase 3.39
  purpose of the payment 3.11–3.19
  residence in UK of vendor 3.20
    personal representative 3.23
    trustees, determination of residence rules 3.21, 3.22
  returns 3.73–3.74
  'scheme or arrangement' test 3.19, 3.33, 3.74
  stamp duty 3.75
  status as unquoted trading company 3.9, 3.10, 3.45
  'substantial reduction' in vendor's interest tests 3.26–3.30, 3.34
    anti-avoidance 3.33
    company profits, interest in, second test 3.27
    group of companies 3.28–3.30
    share capital threshold, first test 3.26
  taper relief 3.42–3.48
    business asset 3.44–3.46, 3.48
    dilution of 3.42, 3.44
    HMRC ruling on status, circumstances for 3.46

Purchase of own shares – *contd*
  taper relief – *contd*
    non-business asset 3.47, 3.48
    'qualifying company' for 3.44
    share ownership periods not counting for 3.44
    trading company status 3.45, 3.46
  tax treatment overview and guidance 3.1–3.4
  'trade benefit' test 3.12–3.18, 3.35
    case guidance on application of (*Allum v Marsh*) 3.16, 3.17
    guidance by HMRC 3.13
    interest in company retained by vendor 3.14, 3.26
    question of fact 3.15
  trustee vendor, *see* Trustee
  use of 3.1
  valuation of shares 3.77

Q

Quoted company, *see* Listed company

R

Ramsay principle 17.89–17.93
Real Estate Investment Trust 9.19, 9.20
Reconstruction or amalgamation
  business property relief 11.28, 11.35
Redundancy payments 7.6
Relative, *see also* Connected person
  business owner, of 1.68, 1.69, 1.120–1.130
  main residence used by dependent relative 15.24, 15.25
Remittance basis for tax, *see* Residence (country of)

Index

Rents, *see also* Investment
business
business comprising, whether
    qualifies for BPR   11.6, 11.16
non-resident receiving
    deduction of tax on   8.53
    election for direct tax   8.54
personally-held property, for
    company use of   1.107–1.109, 1.60

Reorganisation (company)
business property relief   11.28

**Reservation of benefit, gift
with**, *see* Inheritance tax

Residence (country of)   8.1 *et seq*
accommodation available in
    UK, relevance   8.20, 8.21
CGT
    individual intending to
        become non-resident,
        see Emigration
    non-resident, *see*
        Non-resident
    non-UK domiciled person
        resident in UK   8.63
ceasing to be resident   8.3, 8.6–8.20
company   8.77
    HMRC guidance   8.80
    question of fact   8.78, 8.79
deemed non-residence   8.15, 8.16
domicile   8.24–8.27, 8.30
    change to   8.24, 8.25
    concept   8.24
    inheritance tax, basis for   8.30
    non-UK domicile living in
        UK   8.26, 8.28, 8.31–8.49, 8.63
    origin, of   8.24, 8.27
    types   8.24
double tax treaties   8.4, 8.6, 8.15, 8.16
CGT for non-resident,
    interpretation issues   8.59
company treated as
    non-resident under   8.91
inheritance tax   8.73–8.75
tie-breaker clause   8.15

Residence (country of) – *contd*
emigration of UK resident   8.61, 8.62
employment contract, work
    abroad under   8.4, 8.7–8.10
aggregation of
    employments   8.8, 8.9
'full-time'   8.7
spouse, treatment of   8.10
HMRC guidance booklet   8.2, 8.4 *et seq*
leaving UK
    permanently/indefinitely   8.11, 8.12
meaning   8.2–8.4
mobile worker   8.5
'91-day test'   8.17–8.19, 8.23
    average, formula for   8.17
    arrival and departure days   8.19, 8.23
    days ignored   8.18
    HMRC concessions   8.23
no presence in UK during tax
    year   8.13, 8.14
non-resident, *see*
    Non-resident
ordinary residence   8.4, 8.21, 8.22
    meaning   8.21
    occasional residence
        contrasted   8.22
remittance to UK basis   8.28, 8.29, 8.31–8.49
    capital gains generated
        abroad   8.33–8.35
    deemed remittance   8.38, 8.39
    employment income from
        foreign employment,
        when taxable   8.40–8.47
    income and capital,
        separate accounts for   8.32
    mixed funds and taxpayer
        options   8.31, 8.36, 8.37
    presumption   8.31
    taper relief   8.35
    UK-linked debt, satisfying   8.38, 8.39
'reside'   8.14
self-employment income   8.10, 8.49

Residence (country of) – *contd*
  split–year concession 8.4
  student from abroad 8.21
  tax significance 8.1, 8.28–8.30
  travelling expenses and accommodation, non-UK domiciled employee 8.48
  trustees 14.16, 14.17
  vulnerable person 14.47
Residence (home)
  CGT principal private residence exemption, *see* Capital gains tax
  divorce, tax issues on, *see* Divorce and separation
  inheritance tax, *see* Inheritance tax
Reversionary lease scheme 15.49

S

SAYE scheme 9.46
Sale of owner-managed company 6.1 *et seq*
  anti-avoidance rules 6.26
  commercial reasons, advance clearance of 6.26
  consideration 6.2, 6.4, 6.16–6.20
    earn-out basis, sale on 6.21–6.25
    loan notes 6.18, 6.23–6.25
    new share issue 6.17, 6.23–6.25
    non-qualifying corporate bonds 6.20
    qualifying corporate bonds 6.19
  share sale, CGT 6.3–6.9
    calculation of capital gain 6.5
    cash consideration 6.4, 6.16
    date of disposal 6.4
    deferred consideration 6.4, 6.16–6.18, 6.21
    example 6.7
    indexation allowance 6.6
    post-6 April 2008 disposal 6.8
    pre-6 April 2008 disposal 6.3–6.7
  taper relief, *see below*
  structure of sale methods 6.3

Sale of owner-managed company – *contd*
  taper relief, business asset 6.7, 6.9–6.12, 6.19
    abolition of 6.1, 6.17, 6.19
    listed company 6.15
    ownership period 6.9, 6.10
    pre-6 April 2000 6.14
    principles 6.9
    sale before 6 April 2008 6.1, 6.2, 6.9
    spouse holding shares 6.14
    trading company or group, test for 6.12
    unlisted/AIM company 6.11
  taper relief, non-business asset 6.13, 6.22
  trade and asset sale, SDLT 6.3
  'transaction in securities' aspects 6.26
Second home 15.9–15.14, 15.36
Self-employment, *see* Partner; Sole trader
  abroad 8.10, 8.49
  NIC 1.136, 1.137
Service company
  managed 1.100, 1.101
  personal 1.94–1.99
Settlement, *see also* Settlor; Trust
  divorce or marriage breakdown, rules on 16.10, 16.11, 16.24, 16.25
  non-resident, *see* Non-resident
Settlor
  capital gains tax position 14.36, 14.41–14.49, 14.95
    derived property 14.45, 14.46
    disposal of property into settlement 14.38
    interest in settlement 14.41–14.44, 17.24, 17.30–17.38
    interest in settlement, non-resident settlement 14.55–14.57
    non-UK domicile 14.96

583

Index

Settlor – *contd*
  capital gains tax position – *contd*
    vulnerable person, trust
      for   14.47–14.49
  IHT
    beneficiary, settlor or
      spouse is   14.96
    discretionary trust regime   14.38, 14.68–14.73
    residence irrelevant for   14.67
    income treated as income of   14.27–14.35
    income paid to unmarried minor child   14.31
    interest in settlement retained   14.28–14.30
    loan or other capital sum received from settlement   14.32–14.35

Share incentive plan   1.27

Shareholder, *see* Company

Shares
  business property relief, see Business property relief
  farming company, in   12.24
  incorporation, CGT
    reliefs   2.40 *et seq*
    base cost   2.51
    consideration for asset transfer   2.40
    disposal within two years   2.46
    EIS reinvestment relief   2.53–2.58
  sale of, owner-managed company sale, *see* Sale of owner-managed company
  subscribing for, as 'transfer of assets'   17.18
  unquoted trading company, in, reliefs, *see* Business property relief; Enterprise Investment Scheme; Investment

Sole trader   1.31–1.38
  accounting and tax issues   1.32–1.37
    timing of tax payments   1.32, 1.33, 1.132, 1.134
  choosing as business vehicle   1.4, 1.12, 1.22, 1.31–1.38
  company compared   1.132
  conversion back to, *see* Disincorporation
  forming partnership, VAT notification   1.53
  incorporation as company   2.5–2.12
    cashflow considerations   2.12
    cessation computation   2.6, 2.7
    transfer of stock/work in progress   2.13–2.16
  inheritance tax   1.118, 1.119
  liability   1.31, 1.39
  overlap profits and relief   1.37, 1.38, 2.8–2.10
  partnership compared, example   1.69

Spouse   1.68, 1.69, 1.120–1.130
  see also Associate; Connected person
  CGT, and transfer to   13.29
  estate duty exemption   13.105
  IHT exemption, *see* Will
  non-resident, treated as   8.10
  non-UK domiciled individual, of   8.69, 8.70
  second wife, position of   13.23
  separation/divorce, *see* Divorce and separation
  settlor, of, capital sum to   14.33
  spousal interest trust   9.37, 9.38
    see also Will
  will provisions for, *see* Will

Stamp duty
  incorporation context   2.72
  matrimonial home, gift of   13.87
  purchase of own shares   3.75
  variation of Will   13.52

Stamp duty land tax
  disincorporation, on   5.14

Stamp duty land tax – *contd*
  divorce/separation, on   16.26, 16.27
  incorporation, on   2.73–2.76, 2.96
  matrimonial home, gift of   13.87
  partnership   1.54, 1.55
  targeted anti-avoidance rules
    (TAARs)   17.84–17.88
    non-application,
      circumstances for   17.88
    notional transaction,
      payment of tax on   17.85, 17.87
  trade and asset sale out of
    company   6.3
  variation of Will   13.52
Stock
  transfer on incorporation   2.13, 2.14
Subsidiary, *see* Group of companies

T

TESSAs   9.46
Takeover
  private company, by quoted company   6.17
  see also Sale of owner-managed company
Taper relief, *see* Capital gains tax
Targeted Anti-Avoidance Rules (TAARs)   17.80–17.88
Tax planning schemes (IHT)
  effective
    lifetime   15.56–15.61
    will, in   15.62–15.74
  ineffective since GWR and POAT rules   15.45–15.55
Trade
  company
    cessation of   17.43–17.47
    see also Winding up
    major change in   17.45–17.47
  non-resident carrying on, *see* Non-resident
  purchase of own shares, meaning for   3.10

Trade benefit
  purchase of own shares, meaning for   3.12–3.18
Trading stock
  asset acquired as, deemed capital asset for group CGT relief   4.31
  disposal on winding up   7.9
Trading vehicle
  choice   1.1 et seq
    administrative costs   1.7–1.13
    commercial aspects   1.16–1.22
    company, *see* Company
    control, retention of   1.21, 1.22
    differences between business sectors   1.3
    different products or projects   1.5
    exiting/ending business   1.28–1.30
    flexibility   1.5, 1.6
    hybrid   1.134, 1.135
    investment vehicle   1.58
    NI   1.136–1.137
    number of people involved   1.3
    personal liability   1.25, 1.31
    profit extraction   1.140 *et seq*
    tax costs and decisions   1.14, 1.15
Transaction in securities
  anti-avoidance rules   17.6–17.10
  advance clearance procedure   17.9
  disincorporation, application of provisions on   5.17, 5.18
  phoenix company, effect of legislation on   7.39, 7.40
  sale of owner-managed company   6.26, 7.39
Transfer of assets abroad/to non-UK resident
  anti-avoidance   17.11–17.29
Transfer of business as going concern
  CGT relief   2.40–2.46
    alternative relief compared   2.52

Index

Transfer of business as going concern
 – *contd*
VAT, incorporation of
  business 2.86–2.90
Transfer pricing 4.70, 17.65–17.76
see also Anti-avoidance
Trust 14.1 *et seq*
 background 14.1–14.7
 capital distributions, use for 7.29
 capital gains tax 14.36–14.49
  annual exemption 14.36, 14.37
  beneficiary becoming
   absolutely entitled to
   property 14.39
  disposal by beneficiary 14.40
  losses 14.40
  non-UK resident trust 14.52–14.66
  rate 14.36
  settlor 14.36, 14.38, 14.41–14.49
 charitable 14.15, 14.90
 child, for 14.9–14.11, 14.31
  see also Accumulation and
   maintenance trust
  aged 18–25 trust 14.11, 14.88, 1.489
  bereaved minor 14.10, 14.87
 disabled person, for 14.14, 14.37
 discretionary trust, *see*
   Discretionary trust
 double trust or home loan
   scheme 15.38, 15.50–15.52
 employee benefit trust 14.12, 14.91
  'newspaper trust' 14.13, 14.91
 endowment policy written in 9.35, 9.36
  carve out 9.42, 9.43
 gift and loan scheme for
  children 9.39–9.41
  spousal interest trust 9.37, 9.38
 income tax 14.21–14.35
  discretionary payment to
   beneficiary, grossing
   up 14.24, 14.25
  interest in possession trust 14.26
  settlor 14.27–14.35
  trust rate/dividend trust
   rate 14.21–14.24

Trust – *contd*
 inheritance tax 14.67–14.96
 interest in possession
  regime, *see* Interest in
  possession trust
  planning points 14.94–14.96
 standard or discretionary
  trust regime, *see*
  Discretionary trust
 transfer between
  settlements 14.93
 interest in possession, *see*
  Interest in possession
  trust
 life assurance policy, settlor
  benefiting from 9.27
 life interest under will, *see*
  Will
 non-resident settlement
  CGT 14.37, 14.52–14.66
  income tax 14.50, 14.51
  use in Will 13.53
 offshore, *see* Offshore trust
 pension scheme 10.78, 10.79, 10.88
 protective 14.15
  IHT regime 14.74–14.78
 Real Estate Investment Trust 9.19, 9.20
 settlement 14.18–14.20, 14.28
  ceasing to be UK resident 14.60
  meaning 14.19, 14.20
  non-UK resident 14.50–14.66
  'settled property' 14.18
  UK resident, taxation
   of 14.21 *et seq*
 settlor, *see* Settlor
 will trust 14.7, 14.10, 14.11
  see also Will

Trustee
 'associate', as 1.89–1.91
 family trust 14.5
 income tax 14.21
  non-UK resident 14.50, 14.51
 pension scheme
  death-in-service benefits,
   action on 10.78

586

Trustee – *contd*
  pension scheme – *contd*
    inducement payment,
      seeking advice
      recommended   10.86
    private principal residence
      relief, and   15.29–15.31
    property held by, whether
      'settled'   14.18
    purchase of own shares,
      vendor for   3.70, 3.71
    residence determination   3.21, 3.22
  residence   14.16, 14.17
    non-resident, income tax
      and CGT position   14.50–14.66
    non-resident, with UK
      resident beneficiary   14.62–14.66
    test for UK residence   14.16
  will, under, *see* Will

U

Undervalue
  relief for transfer of business
    assets on incorporation   2.47–2.51
    alternative CGT relief
      compared   2.52
  sale of home at   15.36
Unincorporated business, *see* Partnership; Sole trader
Unit trust
  scheme manager as pension
    provider   10.8
Unlimited company   1.19, 1.76
Unquoted trading company
  business property relief   11.2, 11.15
    surplus cash held by   11.14, 11.17–11.19
  investment in qualifying, tax
    reliefs, *see* Investment
  purchase of own shares,
    meaning for   3.9
  see also Purchase of own shares

V

Value/valuation, *see also* Undervalue
  agricultural property relief   12.15–12.19, 12.40
    agricultural cottage   12.44
  annual rental value for POAT   15.42
  business property relief, 'net
    value'   11.13, 11.54
  goodwill, on incorporation   2.61, 2.66–2.68
  shares   3.77
Value added tax
  anti-avoidance   17.55–17.58
    group of companies   17.59–17.63
  disincorporation   5.12
  incorporation by individual
    trader, issues on   2.86–2.90
  limited liability partnership   1.66–1.68
  limited partnership   1.60
  partnership   1.51–1.53
  transfer as going concern
    (TOGC)   2.86–2.90
Variation, instrument of, *see* Will
Venture capital trust   9.14–9.16
  listed company   9.14
  qualifying companies   9.16
  reliefs   9.15
Vulnerable person, trust for, *see* Disabled person

W

Will   13.1 *et seq*
  administrator   13.5, 13.6, 13.8
  age of child for inheritance   13.12, 13.13
    intestacy compared   13.12, 13.13
  agricultural property relief
    considerations   12.33, 12.34, 13.53, 13.56
  associated operations
    provisions   13.68–13.75
    independent advice, etc   13.71–13.75
    memorandum of lifetime
      gift   13.70

Index

Will – *contd*
associated operations provisions – *contd*
  settlement, gift into   13.69 *et seq*
business property relief
  considerations   11.46, 11.47, 13.53, 13.56
civil partners   13.25–13.29, 13.57, 13.65
disclaimer   13.46, 13.52
  no consideration   13.48
discretionary trust, use of   13.29, 13.31, 13.39, 13.41
  child beneficiary   13.26
  nil rate band, examples   13.107–13.109
  surviving spouse
    beneficiary   13.19, 13.26, 13.59
divorcee   13.31, 13.32
  gift to former spouse   13.63
executor   13.2, 13.4, 13.7
gift with reservation
  provisions   13.19, 13.81, 13.82
  disapplication   13.49
guardian of child   13.9
IHT clearance, qualified certificate   13.102
joint bank account   13.90–13.92
life interest   13.15–13.23, 13.27
  advantages   13.18–13.23
  alternatives   13.23
  capital assets retained   13.22
  drafting points   13.16, 13.17
  flexibility of   13.20
  gift with reservation provisions, and   13.19
  reversionary interests, creation of   13.21
maintenance of family, exemptions for   13.63 *et seq*
married couple, no children   13.25, 13.58, 13.63 *et seq*
married couple, with children   13.63 *et seq*
  larger estate   13.27–13.29, 13.58
  smallish estate   13.26

Will – *contd*
matrimonial home   13.76–13.89
  background   13.76–13.78
  cash gift later invested in   13.86
  charge scheme   15.73
  debt scheme   15.68–15.70
  discounted gift   15.73
  gift to non-spouse donee   13.81–13.84
  insurance scheme   15.72
  loan trust   15.74
  mortgage, considerations   13.89
  NRB scheme   15.63–15.66
  ownership   13.79, 13.80
  planning schemes for   15.62–15.74
  severance of joint tenancy   13.88
  share, gift of   13.85–13.87
  stamp duty/SDLT   13.87
need for   13.1
nil-rate band   13.65–13.68, 13.93 *et seq*, 15.32
  advising testator   13.107–13.110
  chattels   13.106
  claim for unused amount after death of survivor   13.95
  clawback   13.96–13.98
  legislative changes   13.94 *et seq*
  qualified clearance certificate   13.102
  records   13.103, 13.104
  second marriages   13.110
  tax planning using NRB scheme   15.63–15.65
offshore trust, use of   13.53, 13.54
  example   13.54, 13.55
pension funds (ASP), legislative modifications   13.99–13.101
  clawback adjustment   13.102
second wife, position of   13.23
single unmarried person   13.30
special directions in   13.11
spouse exemption   13.58–13.62
  anti-avoidance tracing section   13.62
  conditions   13.61

Index

Will – *contd*
  spouse exemption – *contd*
    non-UK domiciled spouse 13.60
    settlement in trust,
      availability on 13.59, 13.69
  stamp duty/SDLT 13.52
  survivorship 13.68
  trustee 13.3, 13.4
    extended powers 13.10
  types of 13.14
  variation, deed of 11.47, 12.37, 13.20, 13.35–13.56
    alternative uses 13.54
    beneficial interest
      re-directed 13.50
    CGT purposes 13.42, 13.43, 13.45, 13.51
    Checklist 13.56
    circumstances for 13.40
    disapplication of
      reservation with
      benefit rules 13.49
    election 13.44, 13.45
    income tax effect 13.41, 13.49, 13.51
    legislative provision for 13.36
    multiple 13.38, 13.39
    no consideration 13.48
    non-resident trust 13.53–13.55
    notification duty 13.37
    second death, after 13.47
    widow(er) 13.31, 13.32

Winding up
  business property relief 11.28
  creditors
    position after liquidation 7.16, 7.19
    preferential 7.13
    unsecured 7.14
  dissolution 7.17–7.19
    bona vacantia, avoiding 7.18
  dividends, pre-liquidation 7.37
  family/owner-managed
    company 7.1 *et seq*
    CIHC 7.12
    corporation tax accounting
      period (CTAP) 7.5, 7.6, 7.10, 7.15

Winding up – *contd*
  family/owner-managed company – *contd*
    disposal of property, CGT
      considerations 7.8
    expenses of closure 7.5, 7.6, 7.11, 7.15
    liquidator, appointment
      notification 7.14
    overpaid tax, interest on 7.15
    patent royalties 7.10
    pension considerations 7.3, 7.4
    plant and industrial
      buildings, capital
      allowances 7.7
    redundancy payments 7.6
    tax liabilities, post-winding
      up 7.15
    tax liabilities, pre-winding
      up 7.13, 7.14, 7.21
    trading losses, reliefs and
      set-offs 7.10, 7.11
    trading stock/work in
      progress 7.9
  insolvent, *see* Insolvent
    winding up
  loss, shareholder relief 7.41–7.48
  members' voluntary 5.4, 7.1, 7.16–7.19
    capital distributions to
      members and taper
      relief, *see* Capital
      distribution
    special resolution 7.16
  'phoenix company' issues 7.38–7.40
  solvent 7.16
  surplus funds, distribution of 7.20–7.22

Woodlands
  agricultural property relief 12.1, 12.64–12.68
    conditions 12.67
    death, on 12.65, 12.66, 12.68
    land excluded 12.64
    scope of 12.64–12.66
    transfer subject to deferred
      estate duty charge 12.68

Index

Woodlands – *contd*
  agricultural property relief – *contd*
    'woodland'   12.64
Work in progress
  sale on winding up   7.9

Work in progress – *contd*
  transfer on incorporation   2.15, 2.16
Writing down allowance   2.17
  see also Capital allowances
  reduction in   2.22